Population and Politics

CW00816312

Every country, every subnational government, and every district has a designated population, and this has a bearing on politics in ways most citizens and policymakers are barely aware of. *Population and Politics* provides a comprehensive evaluation of the political implications stemming from the size of a political unit – on social cohesion, the number of representatives, overall representativeness, particularism ("pork"), citizen engagement and participation, political trust, electoral contestation, leadership succession, professionalism in government, power concentration in the central apparatus of the state, government intervention, civil conflict, and overall political power. A multimethod approach combines field research in small states and islands with cross-country and within-country data analysis. *Population and Politics* will be of interest to academics, policymakers, and anyone concerned with decentralization and multilevel governance.

John Gerring is Professor of Government at University of Texas at Austin. He is co-editor of *Strategies for Social Inquiry*, a book series at Cambridge University Press, and serves as a principal investigator of *Varieties of Democracy* (*V-Dem*) and the *Global Leadership Project* (*GLP*).

Wouter Veenendaal is Assistant Professor of Political Science at Leiden University. He is the author of *Politics and Democracy in Microstates* (2014) and *Democracy in Small States* (2018).

Population and Politics

The Impact of Scale

John Gerring
University of Texas at Austin

Wouter Veenendaal
Leiden University

CAMBRIDGE
UNIVERSITY PRESS

University Printing House, Cambridge CB2 8BS, United Kingdom

One Liberty Plaza, 20th Floor, New York, NY 10006, USA

477 Williamstown Road, Port Melbourne, VIC 3207, Australia

314–321, 3rd Floor, Plot 3, Splendor Forum, Jasola District Centre,
New Delhi – 110025, India

79 Anson Road, #06–04/06, Singapore 079906

Cambridge University Press is part of the University of Cambridge.

It furthers the University's mission by disseminating knowledge in the pursuit of
education, learning, and research at the highest international levels of excellence.

www.cambridge.org
Information on this title: www.cambridge.org/9781108494137
DOI: 10.1017/9781108657099

© John Gerring and Wouter Veenendaal 2020

First published 2020

Printed in the United Kingdom by TJ International Ltd, Padstow Cornwall

A catalogue record for this publication is available from the British Library.

Library of Congress Cataloging-in-Publication Data
Names: Gerring, John, 1962– author. | Veenendaal, Wouter, 1986– author.
Title: Population and politics : the impact of scale / John Gerring, Wouter
Veenendaal.
Description: Cambridge, United Kingdom ; New York, NY : Cambridge
University Press, 2020. | Includes bibliographical references and index.
Identifiers: LCCN 2019051770 (print) | LCCN 2019051771 (ebook) | ISBN
9781108494137 (hardback) | ISBN 9781108657099 (ebook)
Subjects: LCSH: Political geography. | Population – Political aspects. | Scaling
(Social sciences)
Classification: LCC JC319 .G5247 2020 (print) | LCC JC319 (ebook) | DDC
320.1/2–dc23
LC record available at https://lccn.loc.gov/2019051770
LC ebook record available at https://lccn.loc.gov/2019051771

ISBN 978-1-108-49413-7 Hardback
ISBN 978-1-108-71396-2 Paperback

Contents

Detailed Contents

Figures

Tables

Preface

Tuvalu, one of the world's smallest countries, has a population of 10,000. China, currently the world's largest country, has 1 billion plus. The population ratio between these two sovereign countries is roughly 1 to 136,400. China, one might say, contains 136,400 Tuvalus.

Similar contrasts may be found among subnational units within countries. In the United States, New Amsterdam, Indiana, has a reported population of twenty-seven, while New York City has a population of roughly 8 million, a ratio of 1 to 300,000. Both have governments, whose appointed tasks and legal responsibilities are quite similar (though New Amsterdam probably relies on surrounding county or special district governments to provide many of its services).

Even greater variety appears across electoral districts. The largest district in a country with a directly elected chief executive is composed of the entire country. The smallest district is usually found in a local election within a small municipality. Accordingly, the size ratio of constituencies for (a) the office of mayor of New Amsterdam, Indiana, and (b) the president of the United States is roughly 1 to 12 million.

Large discrepancies may occur even across districts for the *same office*. California, the most populous state in the United States, is sixty-seven times as large as Wyoming, the smallest state. Senators from California represent a constituency that is sixty-seven times as large as that of their colleagues from Wyoming.

We take these facts for granted. They are part of the world we inhabit. Some political units are large and others are small. *So what?*

In the classical tradition of scholarship, extending back to the ancient Greeks, size is perceived as a barrier to good governance and popular rule.[1] Plato (1960: 737) states forthrightly that the ideal polity should contain 5,040 citizens. Preferably, all citizens could assemble in a single

---

[1] The intellectual history is reviewed in Alesina and La Ferrara (2000), Almond (1956), D. Anckar (2002, 2004), D. Anckar and C. Anckar (1995), Colomer (2007), Dahl and Tufte (1973: ch. 1), Diamond and Tsalik (1999), Hadenius (1992: 61–62, 122–27), Lijphart (1977: 65), Ott (2000), Stasavage (2010), and Veenendaal (2013).

location to debate the issues of the day. Aristotle (1996: 1326a) believes that "a very populous city can rarely, if ever, be well governed." Rousseau has little to say in favor of large states, aside from their ability to secure sovereignty vis-à-vis external threats.

Not only is the government less swift and vigorous in seeing that the laws are observed, in preventing exactions, redressing abuses, and forestalling the attempts at sedition that can arise in distant places, but the people have less affection for its leaders, whom it never sees, for its country, which it regards as the whole world, and for its fellow citizens, most of whom are strangers. The same laws cannot be appropriate for all the various provinces, which have different customs and are situated in different climates, while a diversity of law can only engender conflict and confusion among peoples who, having the same leaders and in continual communication, move from one area to another and marry there, never knowing, as they become subject to other customary laws, whether their heritage is really theirs. Talents are hidden, virtues are ignored, and vice goes unpunished among all the multitude of men, unknown to each other, who are gathered together in one place because it is the seat of the supreme administration. The rulers, overburdened by the amount of business, see nothing for themselves, and their clerks govern the state. Finally, the measures necessary in order to maintain the central authority, which so many of its distant representatives try to evade or deceive, absorb all the energies of the public officers; what remains for the welfare of the people is insufficient, and there is scarcely enough for defense in case of need; in this way, a body too large for its own constitution declines and perishes, collapsing under its own weight (Rousseau 1994[1762], Book II, ch. 9: 82–83).

In a similar manner, Montesquieu is discouraged about the implications of size for political affairs.

It is in the nature of a republic to have only a small territory; otherwise, it can scarcely continue to exist. In a large republic, there are large fortunes, and consequently little moderation in spirits: the depositories are too large to put in the hands of a citizen; interests become particularized; at first a man feels he can be happy, great, and glorious without his homeland; and soon, that he can be great only on the ruins of his homeland. In a large republic, the common good is sacrificed to a thousand considerations; it is subordinated to exceptions; it depends upon accidents. In a small one, the public good is better felt, better known, lies nearer to each citizen; abuses are less extensive there and consequently less protected (Montesquieu 1989 [1748]: Part I, Book VIII, ch. 16: 124).

The classical tradition of scholarship initiated by Plato, Aristotle, Rousseau, and Montesquieu remains dominant in popular and academic work today. From the ancient Greeks to the present, most commentators have regarded scale as an obstacle to democracy and good governance.[2] When it comes to the politics of size, there are many paeans to modesty,

---

[2] See C. Anckar (2008), D. Anckar (2002, 2004), D. Anckar and C. Anckar (1995, 2000), Bryan (2010), Bryan and McClaughry (1991), Diamond and Tsalik (1999), Hadenius

but hardly any champions of grandeur. City-states are beloved while empires are loathed. Large polities might be respected for their eminence, or accepted because of their presumed efficiency, but they are not loved for their size. A political unit of great scale seems to threaten everyone's liberties. This impulse is reflected in recent reforms to decentralize power, bringing politics closer to the people (Bardhan 2002; Falleti 2010; Oxhorn, Tulchin, & Selee 2004; Rodden & Wibbels 2019). The same perspective informs work in sociology and industrial organization that examines democracy within organizations. Work in this tradition suggests that larger organizations are liable to the "iron law of oligarchy" (Bryce 1924; Mayhew 1973; Michels 1962; Mosca 1939: 53; Prewitt 1969; Scarrow 2002; Tan 1998, 2000). Again, big is bad while small is beautiful (Bodley 2013; Schumacher 1973).

There is a countervailing tradition, which may be characterized as *Madisonian*. In this view, first articulated in the influential Federalist Paper #10 (authored by James Madison), there are advantages to increasing scale.

The smaller the society, the fewer probably will be the distinct parties and interests composing it. The fewer the distinct parties and interests, the more frequently will a majority be found of the same party, and the smaller the number of individuals composing a majority. The smaller the compass within which they are placed, the more easily will they concert and execute their plans of oppression. Extend the sphere and you take in a greater variety of parties and interests; you make it less probable that a majority of the whole will have a common motive to invade the rights of other citizens; or if such a common motive exists, it will be more difficult for all who feel it to discover their own strength and to act in unison with each other (Hamilton, Madison, & Jay 2008 [1787]: 54).

According to Madison, a larger body, with a greater diversity of interests, is compelled to recognize differences of opinion and is therefore less likely to impose a tyranny of the majority (because there is no majority, or only a weak and temporary one, cobbled together from diverging interests). This dynamic seems likely to foster a more democratic polity as well as one that is better governed.

In light of this enduring philosophical debate – between, broadly speaking, the classical and Madisonian perspectives – it is curious that contemporary social scientists have not widely studied the issue of population.

In empirical work, population is usually treated as a background factor. It may serve as a covariate in a regression model. Or it may serve to select

(1992), Katzenstein (1985), Kohr (1978), Lijphart (1977), Mumford (1961), Ott (2000), Sale (2017), Schumacher (1973), and Srebrnik (2004).

a sample of cases that is similar enough to be meaningfully compared. Implicit in these research designs is an assumption that demographic factors matter. If demography were trivial, it could be ignored. The fact that it is generally included as a background factor suggests that social scientists take population seriously.

Yet population size is rarely the center of attention. It plays a supporting role, but hardly ever a starring role in the work of anthropologists, economists, political scientists, and sociologists. Demographers, of course, are deeply invested, but they tend to focus on the short-term causes and effects of population dynamics.

Our Approach

In this book, we investigate the role of scale (aka size) in structuring political outcomes. Every country, every subnational government, and every district has a designated population. This has a bearing on politics in ways that most citizens and policymakers are scarcely aware of.

As an example, let us briefly consider the United States. American society is often described as heterogeneous (a mix of diverse religions, ethnicities, and races), disconnected (where citizens bond with their own kind rather than with those who are different from them), and individualistic (low on social cohesion). Political commentators often complain about problems of descriptive representation (e.g., the underrepresentation of minorities in elective offices), responsiveness (elected officials who do not appear to represent the views of their constituents), constituency connections (elected officials who do not maintain close ties to their district), trust in political institutions (currently at a historic low), and participation (e.g., low voter turnout and low levels of political engagement with respect to more costly forms of participation such as party and interest group membership). Everyone notes the fragmented nature of American political institutions. Liberals are disturbed by the weakness of the American welfare state, which taxes and spends at much lower levels than other advanced industrial countries and consequently does not achieve much wealth redistribution. All of these problems may be viewed, in part, as a consequence of size. The United States is one of the world's largest countries and is subject to scale effects common to large countries.

Now let us consider the tiny country of Malta, an island state in the Mediterranean with a population of roughly 420,000. Maltese society is homogeneous and densely networked, resulting in a hothouse political environment. Citizens and politicians are in direct contact with each other, generating high responsiveness among politicians and an intricate set of particularistic exchanges. Voter turnout commonly exceeds

95 percent (without compulsory voting laws), demonstrating a high level of political engagement. At the same time, power is concentrated in the hands of a ruling party, which faces few checks and balances in its attempts to penetrate society. These phenomena may also be viewed as scale effects.

Of course, it is difficult to reach a determination about the role of scale for particular countries, particular subnational governments, or particular districts. It would be difficult, for example, to distinguish the influence of scale on the development of the American welfare state from the influence of myriad other factors – the early timing of (white) male suffrage, the absence of socialism, the individualistic political culture, the constitutional structure, the electoral system, and the heterogeneous nature of American society.

Whatever narrative one might craft is susceptible to the fundamental problem of causal inference: one cannot replay history with alternate scenarios that vary only in the causal factor of theoretical interest (Holland 1986). We are at pains to imagine what trajectory the territory now occupied by the United States would have followed had the thirteen colonies not united into a single federation (developing, let us say, into fifty independent countries) or had the colonies never separated from Britain (remaining within an even larger, transatlantic political body) or united with Canada (creating a different but also much larger body). Unit-level counterfactuals are highly speculative, especially when dealing with distal causes such as demography, where mechanisms are varied and difficult to trace.

For this reason, we examine scale effects at a general level, with sidelong glances at particular cases. Arguably, we have a better chance of sorting out "universal" (population-level) causal effects than "particular" (unit-level) causal effects. We assume that if a scale effect is persistent across a large sample – of countries, subnational governments, or districts – there is a good chance it is operating in a particular setting. Accordingly, we may infer scale effects for the United States and Malta even if we cannot observe them directly.

Our goal is to conduct as thorough a survey of the subject as possible, integrating extant studies as well as our own ongoing work, the product of many years' labor. The empirical scope encompasses many types of political communities – nation-states, subnational governments, and electoral districts. Coverage varies by subject due to data limitations, but many analyses reach back a century or two (occasionally, three). On this empirical basis, we argue that scale effects in the modern era are pervasive. (We do not make explicit claims about the *pre*modern era.)

Some of these scale effects are clearly negative in import. For example, we argue that increases in scale are apt to attenuate representativeness and participation. Some scale effects appear in a more positive light. For example, increases in scale enhance electoral contestation, the regularity of leadership succession, and professionalism, while attenuating particularism (including clientelism and vote-buying). Other outcomes have no clear normative implications. In summary, scale effects are ambivalent.

While this may seem an unprovocative conclusion, it goes against the grain of the classical tradition of scholarship, which we reviewed briefly earlier and which remains dominant today. In particular, it is worth underlining our claim that larger communities are *less* likely to concentrate political power. Accordingly, a government that rules over a large population is more likely to establish multiple, independent centers of power and less likely to take an interventionist approach to taxing, spending, and regulating. This part of our argument may be characterized (broadly) as Madisonian.

However, this book does not align itself with either side of this long-standing philosophical debate. We draw inspiration and arguments from both sources, and from many others besides. In taking an eclectic approach our hope is to elucidate the influence of scale on politics in a comprehensive fashion while bearing in mind the many nuances of this relationship – which, as it happens, fit neither framework very neatly.

Our findings should help with practical decisions about scaling, indicating when it might make sense to scale up, or down. And they are essential when dealing with the side effects of scale. We note that most constitutional reforms have a scale effect; they increase or decrease the scale of governing units or they increase or decrease the power of units operating at different levels. In this respect, our topic touches on virtually every question of institutional design.

The Road Ahead

In Chapter 1, we explore differences of scale as manifested in political communities around the world, how scale affects our choice of subjects to study, and the relevance of scale to questions of institutional design. Finally, we present the main arguments of this book.

In Chapter 2, we review prior work on the subject and discuss obstacles to reaching inferences about the causal role of scale. This "methods" chapter will be of intense interest to some readers and perhaps of only peripheral interest to others, who may choose to skip it entirely. Readers should be aware, however, that methodological issues vetted here are not repeated in later chapters, which means that the empirical analyses that follow may not be entirely understandable to those who have not slogged through Chapter 2 (which is considerably longer than the other chapters).

The next section of this book focuses on outcomes that, we argue, are subject to scale effects: cohesion (Chapter 3), representatives (Chapter 4), representativeness (Chapter 5), particularism (Chapter 6), participation (Chapter 7), contestation (Chapter 8), institutionalized succession (Chapter 9), professionalism (Chapter 10), concentration (Chapter 11), intervention (Chapter 12), power (Chapter 13), and civil conflict (Chapter 14). Within each chapter, we set forth arguments for why scale might matter, followed by empirical sections in which the theory is tested – drawing on our own work and the work of others – and a final section that summarizes the findings.

Chapter 15 explores several additional outcomes in a more schematic fashion in order to offer a more complete picture of the possible impact of scale on politics. This includes (a) regime types (democracy/autocracy), (b) social inequality, (c) economic development, and (d) public services. For these outcomes, we find little evidence of scale effects.

The concluding chapter pulls together the material of this book into a more synoptic account. We begin by elucidating the somewhat unique features of this project, which consist of tracing all the possible outcomes influenced by the scale of political communities. Next, we summarize the findings presented in previous chapters and reflect on their truth-value. Following, we identify a series of recalcitrant trade-offs mandated by scale. Finally, we consider whether there is an optimal size for political communities.

Acknowledgments

This book progressed at a demographic pace – that is to say, slowly, over a very long period of time. In keeping with the demographic metaphor, we find that at the end of several decades we have accumulated a substantial store of research. Small effects, stretched over time, have a cumulative yield.

During that time, we worked on multiple projects that eventually found their way – sometimes, in altered form – into various sections of this book. This includes Chapter 8 (Gerring, Palmer, Teorell, & Zarecki 2015), Chapter 9 (Gerring & Knutsen 2019), and Chapter 11 (Gerring, Maguire, & Jaeger 2018). We are grateful to the publishers, and to our coauthors – Jillian Jaeger, Carl Henrik Knutsen, Matt Maguire, Max Palmer, Jan Teorell, and Dominic Zarecki – for permission to adapt material from these works.

We are grateful to those who shared data, helped to identify or collect data, or gave advice on the various analyses that found their way into this book. This includes Kym Anderson, Alejandro Avenburg, Taylor Boas, Lee Cojocaru, Jack Corbett, Brian Frederick, Ben Geys, Adam Glynn, Jillian Jaeger, Kyosuke Kikuta, Bethany Lacina, Ray La Raja, Jack Levy, Stelios Michalopoulos, Branko Milanovic, Vicente Royuela Mora, Erzen Oncel, Miguel Rueda, Susan Scarrow, Matt Shugart, Peverill Squire, Rein Taagepera, Rebecca Weitz-Shapiro, Chris Welzel, Ned Wingreen, and Chris Wlezien. Robert Boatright, Miriam Golden, and Glenn Robinson deserve special thanks for their efforts to collect or clean data used in specific analyses.

Brendan Apfeld and Daniel Weitzel helped prepare tables, figures, and replication files, and Rozemarijn van Dijk helped prepare the index.

We are grateful to interview respondents in small states and territories who were willing to share their knowledge and experiences in lengthy interviews conducted over the past several years. A complete list of respondents is included in Appendix A. Part of this field research was sponsored by a research grant from the Netherlands Organisation for Scientific Research (VENI 451–16–028).

We are grateful for advice and feedback on sections of the manuscript as it evolved. Comments were graciously offered by Bethany Albertson, Jack Corbett, Mike Findley, Michael Gibbs, Ken Greene, Alan Jacobs, Evan Lieberman, Johannes Lindvall, Amy Liu, Xiaobo Lu, Raul Madrid, Gary Marks, Rick Morgan, Christoph Nguyen, Max Palmer, Soren Serritzlew, Shane Soboroff, Zeynep Somer-Topcu, Bat Sparrow, Arun Swamy, Tore Wig, reviewers for Cambridge University Press, and participants at a colloquium held at the Population Research Center, University of Texas at Austin. We are thankful, finally, to our editor at Cambridge University Press, John Haslam.

Part I

Framework

1 Scaling the Political World

Everything occurs within a context, and that context is essential for making sense of social phenomena. For example, in explaining an election, a civil war, a killing, a marriage, or a bribe one would want to know something about the geography, culture, history, economy, and sociology of the place in which the event occurred.

Less often considered is the *demographic* context, which in this book refers to the number of people engaged in an event, either as direct participants or as bystanders. Whether people are negotiating, fighting, playing, praying, mating, exchanging goods, protesting, voting, or something else entirely, the number of participants and onlookers is likely to affect how the event plays out. Large communities behave differently than small communities. This is our premise.

We begin this chapter by taking stock of differences in scale across political communities. Next, we show that size affects our choice of subjects, with larger communities garnering the lion's share of attention from academics and (we assume) the popular press. In the final section, we introduce a series of hypotheses that guide the research that follows in Part II of this book.

Differences of Scale

Differences of scale across political communities are extreme. As a point of departure, consider the South Asian subcontinent. India, with more than 1 billion inhabitants, is roughly 3,000 times larger than the Maldives, a tiny island nation in the Indian Ocean. With a population of roughly 350,000, the Maldives is half the size of Sikkim, the smallest Indian state. While they are both countries, and both enjoy formal sovereignty, India and the Maldives are countries of a very different sort. And their differences derive, in part, from their vastly different scale.

The extraordinary demographic variation on display across nation-states may be visualized in a bar diagram in which categories are defined by decimal places (10,000, 100,000, . . .), as shown in Figure 1.1. Panel (a) demonstrates that most countries are small, many are tiny, several are large, and two are

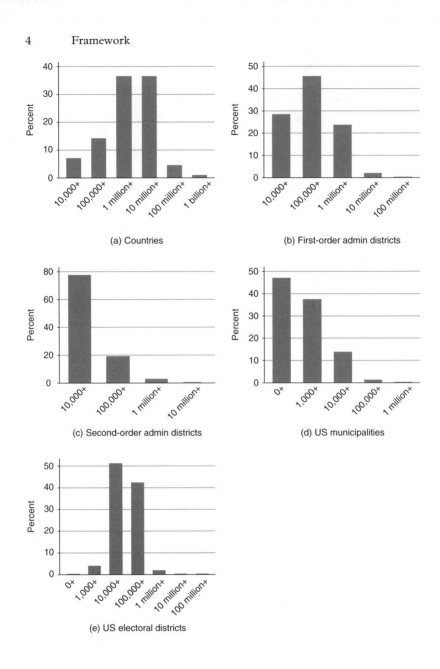

(a) Countries

(b) First-order admin districts

(c) Second-order admin districts

(d) US municipalities

(e) US electoral districts

Figure 1.1 The distribution of population across political communities

Units	N	Min.	Max.	Mean	SD	Year	Source
(a) Countries	197	10,000	1,358,000,000	36,000,000	136,000,000	2014	Faris et al. 2017
(b) 1st-order admin districts	4,135	0	200,000,000	1,612,263	7,118,583	1992–2014	Law 1999
(c) 2nd-order admin districts	38,571	0	21,800,000	155,553	614,364	1991–2014	Law 1999
(d) US municipalities	19,509	0	8,174,959	9,897	80,116	2010–14	US Census 2014
(e) US electoral districts	98,103	77	291,000,000	207,821	2,576,192	1960–2012	Gerring et al. 2015

Figure 1.1 (cont.)

humongous (China and India). Although the average population of the world's countries was 37 million in 2014, one half of the world's countries had fewer than 7.5 million citizens and one quarter had fewer than 1.8 million citizens. In size, the Maldives is much more typical than India.

To gauge variation across subnational administrative districts, we enlist data from an exhaustive dataset put together by Gwillim Law (1999). *First-order administrative districts* (e.g., US states, German *Länder*, Canadian provinces), of which Law counts more than 4,000 throughout the world, range widely in size, though just a few have more than 10 million people, as shown in panel (b). *Second-order administrative districts* are much more numerous ($N = 38,571$), and consequently are smaller in size. Most fall between 10,000 and 1 million in population, as shown in panel (c).

While we tend to associate vast differences across subnational units with large countries such as the United States, even the world's smallest countries may embody considerable variation. Consider the federally organized Republic of Palau, a Pacific island country with 20,000 inhabitants and sixteen federal states. With a population of 12,000, the largest Palauan state (Koror) houses more than half of the country's population, while the smallest state (Hatohobei) has a population of only 44 (250 times smaller). Despite its diminutive size, Hatohobei has the same institutions as other Palauan states, and maintains a nine-member legislature, a council of traditional leaders, a governor, a lieutenant governor, a legislative clerk, a treasurer, a Hatohobei projects supervisor, and two officials in charge of Hatohobei maintenance (Davis & Hart 2002: 202–04).

To get a better sense of *local-level* political units, we examine the distribution of population across US municipalities, shown in panel (d) of Figure 1.1. Of nearly 20,000 municipalities, one quarter have populations of less than 368 and one half fall below 1,145. These are miniscule political communities, much smaller than Plato's (1960: 771) projected ideal for a democratic republic, which he calculated to be 5,040 citizens – a number that excluded slaves, women, foreigners, and minors, and therefore represented only a fraction of the permanent residents in a polis.

Let us turn, finally, to *electoral districts*. Panel (e) displays the size of districts in the United States at national, state, and local levels. Here we find a distribution that extends from close to zero to 326 million, the population of the entire country, which serves as the presidential electorate.[1] Evidently, variability in US electoral districts is almost as great as that found across countries.

Skewness

If depicted on a *linear* scale, all of these population distributions – across countries, first- and second-order administrative districts, municipalities, and electoral districts – have a common shape. The great majority of data points cluster at the left end of the spectrum while a few form a long right tail.

To make this point visually, panel (a) in Figure 1.2 displays the distribution of country populations on a linear scale. The skewed distribution is apparent, with most of the data points (i.e., most of the countries) clustered on the left end of the scale.

Panel (b) in Figure 1.2 transforms these data by the natural logarithm, generating a distribution that is closer to the assumptions of a normal curve. The logged transformation of population is also closer to our intuitive sense of how population might affect various outcomes of interest, as explained in subsequent chapters. Consequently, causal analyses in this book generally use logged values of population. At present, however, our focus is on description rather than causation.

Positive (right) skewness is likely to characterize population distributions across any set of political communities that is not regularly redrawn (i.e., redistricted). It is partly an artifact of the statistic itself, which is bounded at zero but has no right bound. Thus, even if population growth/decline was entirely stochastic – a product of rolls of the dice – one would expect, over time, that the right tail would grow, generating a skewed distribution. (Large stochastically generated decreases cannot cross zero while large increases would be registered.)

Of course, demographic change is not entirely stochastic; in the modern era, populations have tended to grow if left to their own devices. (Only recently have a few human populations reverted to zero or negative

---

[1] For further examples of variations in electoral district size in the United States, see Bingle (2016: ch. 2).

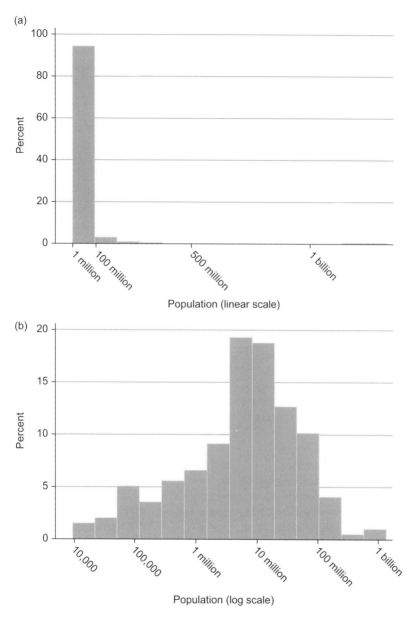

Figure 1.2 Country populations, linear and log

Countries and their populations displayed on (a) linear and (b) logged scales.

growth.) This dynamic enhances the skewness of populations across communities so long as the factors contributing to population growth are unevenly distributed across communities and persistent. If Factor A drives growth, and is found in Community 1 but not Community 2, the population disparity between the two communities will increase so long as Factor A persists.

As an empirical matter, the range (the difference between minimum and maximum values) of most population distributions has increased considerably over the past century. In 1900, the smallest sovereign countries (mostly European microstates) claimed a little over 10,000 citizens while the largest country (China) claimed 400 million. In 2010, the smallest country once again had about 10,000 citizens while the largest (again China) had 1.3 billion. The left tail is stable, in other words, while the right tail grows. By this reckoning, demographic differentials across nation-states are more marked today than they were a century ago, or at any previous point in history.[2]

The same pattern of increasing range is likely to be in evidence across subnational units – unless regularly reapportioned. Here, the positive skew is assisted by migration patterns that favor some areas over others. In particular, urbanization exerts an inexorable pull on the distribution of populations. Cities generally become larger while the rest of the country atrophies (in relative terms). Frequently, growth is centered on a few densely populated regions, while other regions fall behind. In the United States, for example, California and Texas continue to grow while many of the smallest states are stable, or grow only very slowly. In most countries, this pattern of uneven development is very old and shows no signs of reversal.

While the range (between minimum and maximum values) is likely to continue to increase over time, the entire *distribution* of values across all the units seems to be more stable. In Figure 1.3, we graph the Lorenz curve and compute the associated Gini index of inequality, for populations in countries throughout the world in 1800, 1900, and 2000. The line of perfect equality bisects the square. The area between this line and the actual distribution of population represents departures from equality. So, the more a curve bends outward – away from the line of perfect equality – the more unequal the distribution.

A quick look at the figure confirms that population is distributed very unequally across countries. Gini indexes hover around 0.80. By way of

---

[2] Matters are somewhat different if one counts empires as sovereign units (Lake & O'Mahony 2004).

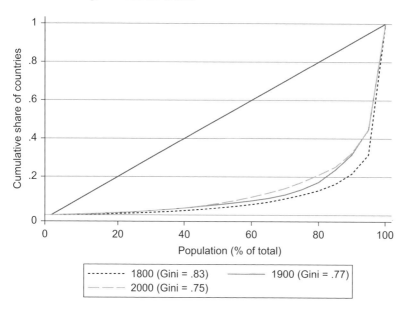

Figure 1.3 Distribution of population across countries through time

The distribution of population across countries in 1800 ($N = 53$), 1900 ($N = 94$), and 2000 ($N = 194$), as measured by the Lorenz curve and associated Gini index.

contrast, the Gini index for *income* across countries at the present time is about 0.65 (Hellebrandt & Mauro 2015). Population is much more unequally distributed across countries than per capita income.

One can see that the distribution of population has become slightly more equal over the past two centuries. However, the more remarkable historical feature is the stability of the distribution, with a few countries containing the lion's share of the people in the world in all periods (Russett 1968).[3] This is perhaps all the more remarkable given that our samples of sovereign countries have changed so much over this period – from 53 in 1800, to 94 in 1900, and to 194 in 2000.

Organizational Types

Having examined the scale of political communities, let us compare these scale differences with those found across other sorts of organizations. To do so, we return to the range (min.–max.) as a measure of dispersion.

---

[3] A higher Gini index indicates a higher level of inequality, with the scale bounded at 0 – perfect equality – and at 1 – where one unit contains all values.

Table 1.1 *Size contrasts across different organizational types*

	Small	Large	Ratio
Political communities			
Senatorial districts (United States)	Wyoming (546,000)	California (37 million)	1:67
States (India)	Sikkim (611,000)	Uttar Pradesh (200 million)	1:327
Nation-states	Tuvalu (10,000)	China (1.364 billion)	1:136,400
Cities (United States)	New Amsterdam, IN (27)	New York (8 million)	1:300,000
Different offices (United States)	Mayor, New Amsterdam, IN (27)	President (323 million)	1:12,000,000
Other communities			
Political science departments	Bryn Mawr (9)	Oxford (68)	1:8
Universities	Ecole Normale Superieure (1548)	Indira Gandhi National Open (4 million)	1:2,600
Firms (United States)	Wikimedia (57)	Walmart (2.1 million)	1:37,000
Interest groups (United States)	The Balloon Council (200?)	AARP (38 million)	1:190,000

The first organizations listed in Table 1.1 are political communities – US senatorial districts, Indian states, nation-states, US cities, and the constituencies of different elected offices in the United States. Next, we consider organizations that are neither polities nor electoral districts, and thus do not fit our definition of a political community. This includes political science departments (enumerated by the number of tenured and tenure-track professors), universities (size of student bodies), US firms (number of employees), and US interest groups (individual members). For each community, we include the (approximate) size of one very small exemplar and one very large exemplar, along with the ratio of their sizes (small:large).

Across these nine community types, the largest ratio (small:large) is found across offices within the United States, followed by cities within the United States and then countries across the world. The smallest dispersion is found across political science departments, which are presumably constrained at the high end. (There is a limit to how many people a university sees fit to employ to study politics.)

The stylized comparisons in Table 1.1 suggest that there may be greater dispersion across political communities than across other sorts of communities. This, in turn, may be a product of the lack of functional size constraints that political communities face. Note that other communities usually form in order to fulfill a particular function, e.g., to teach (departments and universities), to make money (firms), or to lobby (interest groups). Usually, there is a point at which an organization operates most efficiently. Beyond this point, further expansion is likely to be costly for the organization or its members. Taking on a new member of a university or firm is a decision that is taken seriously because of the cost of this decision for the organization. Likewise, joining an organization is taken seriously because of the cost of this decision (either in membership dues or other obligations) for the joiner.

By contrast, political communities do not face strong efficiency constraints (Chapter 12). To the extent that they exist, they are probably marginal compared with efficiency constraints faced by other sorts of organizations. New members of a political community receive benefits but also contribute (e.g., in taxes) to the community they join. The net cost:benefit ratio – for the community and for the individual joiner – is unclear. Political communities are thus free to expand or contract without losing their ability to perform basic functions – at least, up to a certain (rather difficult to identify) point.

This is reflected in the fact that membership in political communities is typically inadvertent, an unintentional by-product of place of birth or of economically or educationally motivated migration. People do not (typically) join political communities in the same way they would join a club, a church, or a firm – as the end product of an extensive search and with the express intention of becoming a member of that collectivity. We end up in political communities for other reasons.

Of course, neighborhood searches are intensive and exacting. However, the decision to live in Neighborhood A rather than Neighborhood B is likely to hinge on the availability of affordable and attractive housing, convenient transportation, good schools, and other logistical concerns. The *politics* of A and B are (usually) less important.

Whatever the reasons, it seems likely that scale differences are greater across political communities than across other organizations. As a consequence, scale may be a more important structuring feature of politics than of other activities. Greater variation in a causal factor usually results in stronger causal effects.

Empirical Regularities

To bring this section to a close, we offer the following tentative conclusions, understood as empirical regularities. First, the distribution of population across political communities is generally characterized by extreme skewness, with lots of small units clustered at the left end of the spectrum and a few very large units out on the right tail. Second, over time, the range (from minimum to maximum) tends to increase, as population continues to grow in some communities and stagnates or declines in others. However, the entire distribution of population across units – as measured, e.g., by the Gini coefficient – tends to remain more stable. Finally, the distribution of memberships across political communities (with the notable exception of regularly reapportioned single-member districts) tends to encompass a greater range of values than the distribution of memberships across other sorts of organizations.

A Scale-Biased View of the World

How does the skewed distribution of political communities affect our choice of topics to study?

As one examines the body of work produced by economists, historians, political scientists, sociologists, and scholars in other, related fields, it becomes apparent that most of the attention is garnered by the largest units. In Africa, scholars and journalists focus on the Congo (DRC), Egypt, Ethiopia, Kenya, Nigeria, South Africa, or Uganda. In East Asia, China and Japan are the most studied polities, while Indonesia rises in the ranks. In South Asia, the 200-pound gorilla is India. In the Americas, Brazil, Mexico, and the United States occupy center stage. In Western Europe, Germany, France, Italy, and the United Kingdom lead the pack. Big countries attract attention, small countries are less studied, and microstates are almost completely ignored (Veenendaal & Corbett 2015).

In similar fashion, the study of subnational regions is dominated by the largest regions. In the United States, for example, work on California, New York, and Texas is voluminous while work focused on smaller states is rare. Likewise, the study of municipal politics is generally dominated by a country's largest cities. In the United States, this would include New York, Los Angeles, Boston, and Chicago. In France, a more centralized polity, the city of Paris overshadows all others.

The same bias affects our study of public officials. According to one calculation, "among the approximately 490,000 elected positions at all levels of American government, about 475,000 are found in local government while fewer than 16,000 are present at the state and federal levels – a ratio of 30:1" (Sokolow 1989: 23). Yet an army of academics trains its sights on national executives (presidents, prime ministers, monarchs) and national parliaments. Few pay any attention to those further down the hierarchy.

In sum, scholarly attention, and (so far as we can tell) the attention of popular commentators, tends to focus on the right tail of the distribution, i.e., on a very small number of very large communities and their political leaders.

To gauge scale biases in a more systematic fashion, we conduct two analyses. For each analysis, we record the number of hits for a web search that incorporates a country's name and the word *politics*, e.g., "Belize" + "politics." The first analysis, shown in panel (a) of Figure 1.4, utilizes Google Scholar, a database of scholarly publications. The second analysis, shown in panel (b), utilizes Web of Science, a more restricted database focused primarily on journals. Scatterplots show country population on the X axis and hits from these two databases on the Y axis. (Both axes are transformed by the natural logarithm.)

Visual inspection of these scatterplots reveals an extraordinarily tight fit. The size of a country's population explains 56 percent (Google Scholar) and 67 percent (Web of Science) of the variation in scholarly attention paid to countries around the world, according to these two databases. Adding predictors such as per capita GDP (log) to this simple bivariate model increases the fit only marginally. It would appear that size is the overriding factor determining scholars' choice of topics to study.

From a certain perspective, this scale bias is entirely appropriate. After all, this is where the people are, and where the power is (these two features are closely related, as shown in Chapter 13). The United States has more impact on the world than Canada. California has more sway than Wyoming. New York has more influence than New Amsterdam, Indiana. And so forth. If larger units are more important, they are surely more worthy of study. Likewise, politicians with larger constituencies are generally more powerful, and for that reason more attractive as a focus of study.

The study of smaller communities is also often constrained by a lack of data. Microstates are rarely included in cross-national datasets. *Historical* data for small countries are even harder to obtain. And data for subnational units are severely limited, at least by comparison to what is available for national units. We know a lot about the United States, a little about American states, something about large cities, and virtually nothing about smaller communities. This means that the study of smaller communities is time-consuming, expensive, and in some cases simply impossible.

Nonetheless, the problem of knowledge bias is troublesome. Smaller units, considered collectively, contain a good many people. Whether one is considering countries, regions, cities, or electoral districts, many of the

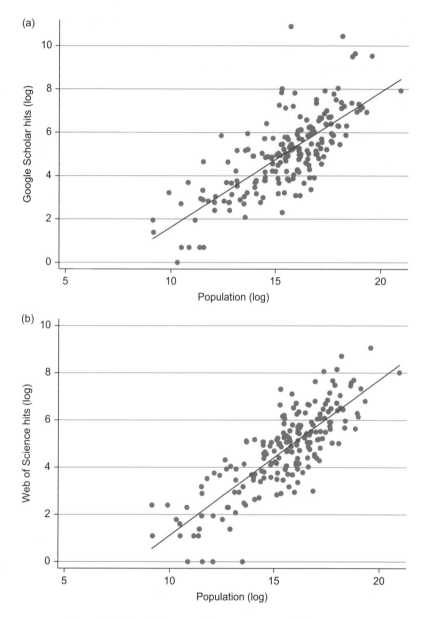

Figure 1.4 Topic frequency by country population

Scatterplot of country population (log) and number of publications (log) mentioning that country in 2016 within two databases: (a) Google Scholar ($N = 192$, $R^2 = 0.56$) and (b) Web of Science ($N = 192$, $R^2 = 0.66$). Fitted values overlaid.

world's citizens live in modest political communities. Likewise, most public officials serve in local or regional governments or at the bottom tier of the administrative hierarchy, as we have observed.

In addition, smaller communities provide important sources of information from which we may learn. Neglecting those cases limits our opportunities to understand the world and raises the possibility that what we know is not true, or true only for a subset of political communities – the mega-states, mega-regions, megacities, and mega-districts. Insofar as size matters to outcomes of concern to us, one must worry about the fact that our knowledge of the world is based on highly unrepresentative samples.

Of course, whether the scale bias in our study of the world matters to our knowledge of the world depends upon whether large political communities are fundamentally different from small communities. If they are not, no harm is caused by studying the former and inferring the latter. But if they are, we run the risk of major misperceptions of reality. Scale biases in our selection of topics matter insofar as there are scale *effects*.

Scale Effects

Causally oriented work in the social sciences may be categorized according to the number of causes (X_{1-n}) and effects (Y_{1-n}) that a study chooses to investigate. There are three principal options: *one-to-one*, *many-to-one*, and *one-to-many*, as illustrated in Figure 1.5. (No one undertakes to investigate many causes and many outcomes; that would be a truly unbounded enterprise.)

Most article-length work in the social sciences is focused on a single cause and a single outcome, sometimes described as "effects of causes" (Holland 1986), which we call *one-to-one*. A few articles, and many books, are more ambitious, seeking to identify all the causes – or at least all the

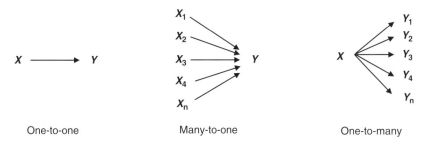

One-to-one   Many-to-one   One-to-many

Figure 1.5 A typology of causes and effects

principal causes – of an outcome, sometimes described as "causes of effects" (Holland 1986), which we label *many-to-one*.

This book assumes a third format that is less frequent in the annals of social science. We attempt to investigate all the possible outcomes stemming from a single cause, a *one-to-many* design. Of course, we cannot hope to be entirely comprehensive. But we can claim greater comprehensiveness than any prior study of the subject.

This ambition imposes considerable demands upon the authors, who cannot claim expertise in all of these highly diverse areas of research. Nonetheless, we believe that grappling with the one-to-many causal question offers advantages that could not have been achieved by a more targeted approach. First, we are able to impose a common (i.e., somewhat standardized) template on the analysis of each outcome. This means that scale effects can be compared in a meaningful way. Second, we are able to ponder possible interactions across various outcomes. Third, we can consider common mechanisms across the various relationships. And, finally, we have an opportunity to gauge the "net" effect of population increases (decreases) – some of which are undoubtedly positive, others negative, and still others of uncertain import.

In this section, we divide up the immense subject of "scale effects" into twelve outcomes for which we believe scale effects are plausible and pervasive: (a) cohesion, (b) the number of representatives and the representation ratio, (c) representativeness, (d) particularism, (e) participation, (f) contestation, (g) institutionalized succession, (h) professionalism, (i) concentration, (j) intervention, (k) power, and (l) civil conflict. For each outcome, we identify a hypothesis that will orient the substantive chapters of this book (Part II).

Cohesion, the topic of Chapter 3, refers to the "togetherness" of a community. This includes the degree of homogeneity (ethnic, linguistic, racial, religious, economic, or ideological), the density of interconnections (networks), and the prevalence and perception of deviance/conformity. We hypothesize that increases in scale diminish social cohesion. Larger communities should be less cohesive.

Representatives, the topic of Chapter 4, refers to the number of representatives in a polity. To operationalize this concept, we examine the size of legislatures and cabinets. We hypothesize that increases in scale increase the number of representatives, though in a sublinear fashion. Larger communities have more representatives, but not in a strictly proportional fashion. This, in turn, has repercussions for the *representation ratio*, the ratio of citizens to representatives, which also increases with the size of a community.

Representativeness, the topic of Chapter 5, refers to the faithfulness with which politicians reflect the interests, values, and characteristics of the citizens they are intended to represent. This may be measured by the degree of correspondence between citizens and their representatives – either demographically or programmatically. It might also be measured by the intimacy of constituent–representative connections. It may, finally, be measured by the degree of trust between citizens and their representatives – largely a product of the degree of representativeness that citizens perceive. We hypothesize that increases in scale depress representativeness. Larger political communities should be associated with leaders who are less representative and constituents who feel less connected to them.

Particularism, the topic of Chapter 6, refers to ad hoc, targeted efforts by politicians to cultivate the support of specific citizens or groups of citizens (or clients), and the allegiance of those citizens to their leader (or patron). To operationalize the concept we look at party strength/weakness, preferential voting, vote-buying, campaign spending, pork, and corruption (generally considered). We hypothesize that increases in scale depress particularism. Larger political communities should be associated with less particularism.

Participation, the topic of Chapter 7, refers to citizen activity whose goal is to influence political decisions, e.g., voting (in elections, initiatives, and referenda), party membership, donating to political parties or organizations, joining nongovernmental organizations, engaging in public debate, contacting elites or citizens, deliberating in citizen assemblies, and various forms of contentious politics. It also includes feelings of political efficacy, which are closely tied to acts of participation. We hypothesize that increases in scale depress participation. Larger political communities should have lower rates of participation.

Contestation, the topic of Chapter 8, refers to the degree of election-based contestation in a political community. Where contestation is minimal there is little organized opposition and the incumbent party captures most of the votes and seats. Where contestation flourishes there are more competitors than available seats, and a tight race for votes and seats. Empirical indicators include the vote share of the largest party, the difference between the top two vote-getters, overall party system fractionalization, legislative fractionalization, and turnover. We hypothesize that increases in scale enhance contestation. Larger political communities should experience higher contestation.

Institutionalized succession, the topic of Chapter 9, refers to the process by which changes in the top leadership post – typically the chief executive (president, prime minister, or monarch) – are effected. If this process occurs regularly, peaceably, under well-established rules, and in a meritocratic (or at least non-nepotistic) fashion, we regard it as institutionalized. This may be operationalized by the length of tenure of top leaders, by the presence of hereditary rule, or by a composite index that captures several dimensions of this process. We hypothesize that increases in scale help to institutionalize the process. Larger political communities should be associated with more institutionalized patterns of leadership succession.

Professionalism, the topic of Chapter 10, implies that important political tasks are delegated, through a well-defined division of labor, to individuals with extensive training and experience, who are recruited and promoted in a meritocratic fashion, who view their job as a full-time career, and whose positions are adequately staffed and remunerated. It also implies that professionals abide by a set of formal rules, and are not subject to ad hoc or special considerations. To operationalize the concept we examine legislative capacity, bureaucratic capacity, the educational attainment and salaries of political elites, and the number of voluntary associations. We hypothesize that increases in scale enhance professionalism. Larger political communities should attract public servants who embody "Weberian" ideals.

Concentration, the topic of Chapter 11, refers to the degree to which political power in a community is focused or diffused. A theoretical maximum is achieved when a single individual or ruling group makes all important policy decisions in a community. A theoretical minimum is attained in a setting where power is widely dispersed and where numerous actors hold effective vetoes. (This concept is not intended to capture the democraticness of a polity. We assume that popular rule is consistent with concentration, as in France, or with power dispersion, as in the United States. Likewise for autocratic rule.) Empirical indicators of (de)concentration include federalism, the number of regional authorities, the Regional Authority Index (Hooghe & Marks 2016), bicameralism, revenue decentralization, capital city size (as share of general population), and overall checks and balances (Beck et al. 2001). We hypothesize that increases in scale decrease the concentration of political power. Larger political communities should have more fragmented political institutions.

Intervention, the topic of Chapter 12, refers to the degree to which governments intervene in the economic and social affairs of citizens – sometimes framed as "statism" or "big government" in contrast to "laissez-faire" or "limited government." To operationalize this concept we explore aggregate measures of state size and strength (fiscal policy and government personnel), social policy expenditure (health and education), and moral policy (the regulation of alcohol and drugs, gambling, sexuality, reproduction, end of life, diet, dress and comportment, vagrancy, language, holidays, religion, and family). We hypothesize that increases in scale decrease the reach of government. Larger communities should have less intrusive governments.

Power, the topic of Chapter 13, refers to the internal autonomy and external influence of a political community vis-à-vis other communities. Indicators of relative power are political, military (size of armed forces), economic (GDP, iron and steel production, trade and aid dependence), and cultural (universities, patents, tourists). We hypothesize that increases in scale enhance a community's overall power. Larger communities should be more powerful.

Civil conflict, the topic of Chapter 14, refers to violent political conflict over territory or control of government (e.g., civil war). This is measured as battlefield casualties per capita. We hypothesize that scale effects on conflict are curvilinear. The probability of conflict increases with scale up to an inflection point, and then decreases. Medium-sized communities should experience the most civil conflict.

In Chapter 15 we explore several additional outcomes – *regime types* (democracy/autocracy), *social inequality, economic development*, and *public services* – in a more schematic fashion in order to give a more complete picture of the possible impact of scale on politics. For these outcomes, we find little evidence of scale effects.

In summary, as the size of a community grows we expect more representatives, a higher representation ratio, less representativeness, less particularism, less popular participation, more electoral contestation, more institutionalized patterns of succession, more professionalism, less power concentration, less interventionist policies, and greater overall power. For civil conflict, we expect that the impact of scale is curvilinear – first increasing and then decreasing. For other outcomes, including regime types, social inequality, economic development, and public services, we expect no scale effects. These relationships, along with the indicators we use to measure each outcome, are summarized in Table 1.2.

Clarifications and Caveats

Having laid out the main arguments, summarized in Table 1.2, we must now issue several important clarifications and caveats.

First, scale effects are presumed to be monotonic, with the notable exception of civil conflict. But they are not linear. Increases (decreases) at the lower end are more consequential than increases (decreases) at the higher end. Note that a community of 10,000 that gains an additional 10,000 members has doubled in size. By contrast, a community of

Table 1.2 *Hypothesized scale effects*

↓	**Cohesion:** togetherness, i.e., members identify and behave as members of a unitary group. *Indicators*: heterogeneity, connectedness, deviance (behavior), deviance (perceptions).	*Ch.* 3
↑	**Representatives:** number of leaders who purport to play a representative role. *Indicators*: size of legislature, size of cabinet.	4
↑	**Representation ratio:** number of citizens per representative. *Indicator*: citizens/legislator.	4
↓	**Representativeness:** representatives reflect the interests, values, preferences, and characteristics of constituents. *Indicators*: demographic representativeness, programmatic representativeness, constituency connections, political trust.	5
↓	**Particularism:** efforts by politicians to cultivate the support of specific individuals or groups. *Indicators*: independent candidacies, weak parties, preferential voting, vote-buying, campaign spending, pork, corruption.	6
↓	**Participation:** citizen activity whose purpose is to affect politics or policy. *Indicators*: citizen assemblies, party membership, voter turnout, other activities, political efficacy.	7
↑	**Contestation:** electoral competition for political office. *Indicators*: largest party, difference between top parties, party system fractionalization, legislative fractionalization, turnover.	8
↑	**Institutionalized succession:** turnover among top leaders is regular, governed by law, and nonhereditary. *Indicators:* nonhereditary rule, constitutional succession, regular succession.	9
↑	**Professionalism:** leaders and officials follow professional norms. *Indicators*: education, capacity and salary of public officials, meritocratic recruitment, number of voluntary associations.	10
↓	**Concentration:** decision-making power is monopolized by a small circle. *Indicators*: number of subnational regions, federalism, Regional Authority Index, bicameralism, separate powers, revenue decentralization, capital city/total population, checks and balances.	11
↓	**Intervention:** government involvement in citizen affairs, i.e., infrastructural power. *Indicators*: moral policy (regulation of behavior), fiscal policy (taxing, spending), personnel policy (number of government employees), social policy (redistribution).	12
↑	**Power:** autonomy from, and influence over, those outside a community. *Indicators*: political, military (armed forces), economic (GDP, iron and steel production, trade and aid dependence), cultural (universities, patents, tourists).	13

Table 1.2 *(cont.)*

∩	**Civil conflict:** violent political conflict within a community. *Indicators*: battlefield casualties per capita.	14
Ø	**Regimes:** democracy, understood as a holistic concept. *Indicators*: Lexical index (Skaaning), Political rights (FH), Polity2 (Polity IV), Polyarchy (V-Dem), BMR (Boix, Miller, Rosato).	15
Ø	**Inequality:** the distribution of valued goods including wealth, health care, education, and status. *Indicator*: Gini index of income inequality.	15
Ø	**Economic development:** the productive capacity of a community. *Indicators*: GDP per capita, GDP per capita growth.	15
Ø	**Public services:** quality of services provided by government. *Indicators*: various.	15

Hypothesized causal effect of a larger population: increase (↑), decrease (↓), curvilinear (∩), null/ambiguous (Ø).

100,000 that gains an additional 10,000 members has increased by only 10 percent. It stands to reason that politics in the smaller community will be more strongly affected. This idea is encapsulated in a logarithmic functional form, displayed in Figure 1.2. In this fashion, we can consider population increases (decreases) in percentage terms rather than in terms of absolute numbers.

Second, the outcomes presented in Table 1.2 are not entirely distinct and independent. They overlap in many respects and often reinforce each other. This sort of complexity is inevitable in a schema that attempts to integrate a wide range of intersecting phenomena – a *one-to-many* research design.

Third, these hypotheses express tendencies rather than hard-and-fast rules. There are bound to be exceptions, and we expect some degree of causal heterogeneity across varying contexts. We urge readers to weigh these arguments against the cases they know best. At the same time, we urge readers to consider the totality of the evidence – which may or may not line up with the cases they know best.

Fourth, all of the outcomes of theoretical interest in this study are subject to multiple causes. We are not claiming that scale is the only – or even the main – cause. Thus, when we assert that scale affects an outcome we assume that all else is equal. For example, the notion that larger districts lead to lower turnout presumes that other factors affecting turnout (e.g., district magnitude and the composition of the electorate) remain the same. This is known as the ceteris paribus assumption, and it underlies any causal argument about an outcome that is subject to multiple causes or contextual effects.

Finally, the causal mechanisms that generate these scale effects are many and various. To explore these pathways we present theoretical arguments at the beginning of each substantive chapter, summarized in a causal diagram.[4]

Scope-Conditions

We turn now to the ambit of the arguments, their scope-conditions.

The hypotheses summarized in Table 1.2 are intended to apply to political communities of all types and at any level of government – supranational, national, or subnational. A political community might serve as a *polity* (a body that enjoys some degree of policymaking power and a governmental apparatus to wield that power) or an electoral *district* (a geographic unit used to select representatives to a governing body). Note that while all scale effects apply to polities, only some scale effects apply to electoral districts (cohesion, representativeness, particularism, participation, and contestation).

A few of the outcomes of theoretical interest presume the existence of multiparty elections. However, most scale effects are general in purview; they extend to both democratic and nondemocratic contexts. Accordingly, when we use terms like "constituents" and "representatives" readers should not assume a democratic context. After all, political leaders in authoritarian states also regard themselves as representatives of the people and there is a sense in which they strive to play (or are constrained to play) a representative role, even in the absence of multiparty elections (Rehfeld 2006).

The historical scope of our framework stretches back to the turn of the twentieth century. Many of the arguments probably extend further back in time, and occasionally we examine evidence of that. However, we are hesitant to make general claims on this score. Transformations in technology, economics, and ideology, as well as the development of new political institutions, have altered scale

---

[4] Although theory precedes empirics in each chapter, we do not wish to imply that the formulation of the theory preceded the empirical analysis. In most cases, we had a good look at the data before we finalized the argument. In this respect, this book follows an *exploratory* research design, understood as one where theory and empirics inform each other and develop in tandem (Rueschemeyer 2009).

effects in fundamental ways. As such, the object of our study is quite different from that which confronted Plato, Aristotle, Rousseau, and Montesquieu.

These caveats notwithstanding, the arguments presented in this book are quite broad. They may even qualify as social science "laws," depending upon one's understanding of that vexed term (Kincaid 1990, 2004; S. Larsen 2005; Taagepera 2008).

Evidently, one loses detail by embracing a wide-angle theoretical lens. This may be frustrating to readers who would like a more specific narrative, explaining particular outcomes in particular places. Yet a theoretical framework that embraces a large population and a large set of outcomes also brings some advantages.

First, big arguments tell us more about the world. There is also an opportunity for linking together our knowledge of disparate subjects, part of an ongoing search for "consilience" in science (J. Wilson 1989).

A second advantage of theoretical breadth is falsifiability (Popper 1959). By virtue of a large scope, big arguments are given more opportunities to fail. And the more diverse are the contexts in which an argument is tested, the more unlikely success becomes. Note that some of these contexts are likely to include unpropitious cases for the hypothesis. If test results are nonetheless consistent we have stronger reason to believe that the relationships being tested are systematic rather than stochastic.

A final advantage to thinking big is that we have a better opportunity of identifying the limits of an argument. By pressing the bounds of theory outward we are likely to encounter resistance, i.e., areas where the theory doesn't work, or where additional background factors must be taken into account. Scope-conditions become clear when the envelope is pushed too far.

Our hope is that the quest for social science laws will help us move toward a more accurate and comprehensive portrayal of scale effects. Some of our claims will doubtless be disproven, or qualified by scope-conditions or moderators that we had not anticipated. Note that claims about causal mechanisms are not analyzed empirically, a large gap for future empirical work to explore.

By putting a large target on the wall we hope to stimulate discussion, critique, and revision. Advances in knowledge are achieved by integrating and refining extant theories. We trust that others will rework our framework, just as we have reworked theirs.

2   Approaches

In recent years, geography has been rediscovered as a distal cause lurking behind many outcomes (Diamond 1998). We suspect that demography, once a staple of social science theorizing (Malthus 1798), may also be ripe for rediscovery.

Like geography, demography operates silently, behind the scenes, and over many years. The impact of population is sometimes compared with the impact of a glacier. Both move slowly and imperceptibly while carrying enormous freight and altering everything in their path.

The surreptitious quality of demography means that we have to work hard to tease out its causal role. The payoff is that we shall learn about an ingredient of politics that is ubiquitous and underappreciated.

In Chapter 1, we made specific allegations, summarized in Table 1.2. In this chapter, we review the literature on the subject, the methodological challenges facing this research question, and the methods we have chosen to deal with them.

This is essential reading for those who wish to understand the details, and the rationale, for the analyses that follow. We purposefully package as much of the methodological discussion as possible in this chapter so as to allow for a more economical presentation of evidence in subsequent chapters. (Readers who are primarily interested in the substantive argument and findings of this book may skip this chapter entirely, or return to it later.)

Even so, readers should appreciate that the evidence and analysis contained in this book are diverse. A more focused discussion of methodological issues can be found in papers published elsewhere (authored by us and by others). Here, we enter the subject from a general vantage point.

We begin by surveying extant work on our subject and on related subjects. Next, we discuss the concept of a political community and its measurement. In the third section, we consider the difficulty of treating scale as a causal factor. The fourth section lays out the modeling strategies employed in quantitative analyses to follow. The fifth section discusses

24

various outcomes of theoretical interest. The final section introduces some of the data sources that we rely on to measure right and left side variables.

Extant Work

To clarify our subject it is important to distinguish it from several adjoining topics. In this section, we review (a) alternate meanings of scale, (b) scale as an outcome, (c) multilevel governance, (d) empirical regularities in scale, and (e) research on small groups. Finally, we offer a brief review of work focused on the size of political communities – our chosen topic.

Alternate Meanings of Scale

In this book, "scale" or "size" refers to the population of a community, understood as a relatively stable demographic feature of that community. This should be distinguished from a number of other topics.[1]

First, demography comprises other aspects such as *fertility, age distribution, density*, the *geographic distribution* of a population across a territory, and *migration*. These features lie outside the purview of this book (except insofar as they may serve as confounders).

Second, scale may refer to dramatic *changes* in population, i.e., growth or decline. Over the long sweep of human history population growth, and consequent increases in density, seem to have been a precondition of economic and technological progress (Boserup 1965; Kremer 1993). In the modern era, beginning with Thomas Malthus (1798), writers have linked short-term population growth to a variety of ills including dislocation, environmental degradation, repression, regime change, social revolution, and war (Ehrlich 1968; Goldstone 1991, 2002; Goldstone, Kaufmann, & Toft 2012; C. Henderson 1993; Hendershot 1973; McNeill 1990; Organski & Organski 1961; Urdal 2006; H. Weber 2013; Weiner 1971; Weiner & Teitelbaum 2001). A number of studies argue that demographic transitions foster democracy, or at least democratic stability (Cincotta 2008, 2008–09; Cincotta & Doces 2012; Dyson 2012). However, this relationship is difficult to distinguish empirically from the process of modernization, which may also affect regime transitions and which therefore serves as an intransigent confounder. Our focus, in any case, is on population size, rather than on episodes of dramatic population increase or decrease.

---

[1] For an even wider array of interpretations see Gibson, Ostrom, and Ahn (2000).

Sometimes, scale refers to the *context* of an event or an attitude, which may differ according to the perceptions of the actor (Enos 2017; Wong 2010). For example, Hankinson (2018) contrasts renters' support for new housing (a) in their immediate neighborhood and (b) in the larger metropolitan area. He finds that renters are more disposed to development when the latter is envisioned on a citywide scale than when it is envisioned on a neighborhood scale – presumably because in the latter case they would experience some of the negative externalities. This scale effect is not a product of size per se and thus falls outside our theoretical ambit.

Sometimes, scale refers to the size of an *economy*, as measured by GDP or per capita GDP (Crowards 2002; Downes 1988; Taylor 1969). Needless to say, economic size is not the same as demographic size, as some countries are a lot wealthier (per capita) than others.

Scale may also refer to the geographic *area* encompassed by a political community, e.g., an empire (Taagepera 1978) or a nation-state (Abramson 2017; Olsson & Hansson 2011). Territory and population are correlated in the obvious sense that if a territory is enlarged it will almost certainly encompass more people. However, the relationship between population and territory in the world of actually existing political communities is not very tight. Countries like Mongolia encompass large territories but few people, while countries like Bangladesh are modest in territory but immodest in population. Likewise, rural districts are often large in expanse while being small in population. Consequently, demographic and territorial size are weakly correlated. In this study, territory is understood as a *prior* cause – one factor, among several, that can increase or decrease the population of a community, as discussed in what follows.

Scale As an Outcome

For some writers, scale is an outcome to be explained. In this vein, scholars have examined why some countries are larger than others and why the size of states has varied over time (Alesina & Spolaore 1997, 2003, 2005; Bolton & Roland 1997; Bolton, Roland, & Spolaore 1996; Friedman 1977; E. Green 2012; Lake & O'Mahony 2004; Wittman 1991, 2000). Scholars have also examined why subnational units are created, amalgamated, and divided (Gomez-Reino & Martinez-Vazquez 2013; E. Green 2010; Grossman & Lewis 2014; Hassan 2016; Malesky 2009). This body of work lies in the background of our quest insofar as it bears on questions of causal identification (see later in this chapter).

Multilevel Governance

For other writers, scale is embedded in questions about levels and units of government and how to organize duties and responsibilities across them. This tradition of scholarship is known variously as multilevel governance (Hooghe & Marks 2016; Hooghe, Marks & Schakel 2010), constitutional federalism (Bednar 2008; Riker 1964; Watts 1998), fiscal federalism (Boadway & Shah 2009; Breton & Scott 1978; Filippov, Ordeshook, & Shvetsova 2004; Gadenne & Singhal 2014; Inman & Rubinfeld 1997; Konrad & Geys 2010; Musgrave 1959; Oates 1972, 1999, 2005; Rodden 2005; Tullock 1969), local governance (Bardhan & Mookherjee 2006; E. Ostrom 1972), public administration (Dubois & Fattore 2009), devolution (M. O'Neill 2000), delegation (Mookherjee 2006), fragmentation (Grossman, Pierskalla, & Dean 2017), polycentrism (E. Ostrom 2010), indirect rule (Gerring et al. 2011), and decentralization (Besley & Coate 2003; Kollman 2013; Rodden & Wibbels 2019; Rubinchik-Pessach 2005; Treisman 2007).

We use "multilevel governance" as a generic term of reference because it seems to be the most encompassing. But readers should bear in mind that there are many labels, and these terms are not perfect synonyms.

Granted, it is sometimes difficult to differentiate the impact of scale per se from the impact of multilevel governance. For example, an initiative to decentralize power within a political community – from a single superordinate unit to smaller subordinate units – is a change in multilevel governance as well as a change in the scale of governing units. Our theoretical interest is focused on the latter. We are concerned with the size of a community, not its place within a hierarchy of communities.

Empirical Regularities

Another tradition of work examines empirical regularities occasioned by scale. Linguist George Kingsley Zipf (1949) noted a relationship between the rank and frequency of words, $P_n = 1/n^a$, where P_n is the frequency of a word ranked nth and the exponent a is almost 1. Accordingly, the second item occurs approximately one-half as often as the first, and the third item one-third as often as the first, and so on. This apparent law has been applied to the rank and size of firms (Axtell 2001), cities (Gabaix 1999), and other phenomena.[2] Other regularities, usually in the form of power laws, have been noted in the relationship between body mass and metabolic rate, the size and complexity of civilizations (discussed briefly

[2] Batty (2006) questions the regularity of this law.

in Chapter 10), the number of employees and assets of companies, the size of cities and their attributes (Bettencourt & West 2010, 2011), and many other topics (Pumain 2006; West 2017).

Persistent relationships such as these are intriguing, not least because they offer the prospect of predicting outcomes and thereby informing public policy. However, one should bear in mind that the functional form of these relationships varies – some are superlinear, some are sublinear, and others may be non-monotonic. Likewise, the causal mechanisms at work in generating these power–law relationships are likely diverse. In some cases, it may be appropriate to view size as a cause, and in other cases probably not. Even so, we are inspired by this body of work to think broadly about our topic.

Small Groups

A causal role for scale is widely acknowledged in the study of small to medium-sized groups and organizations. At the turn of the twentieth century, Georg Simmel (1902a: 2) proposed that "the sociological structure of a group is essentially modified by the number of the individuals that are united in it." Subsequently, a research trajectory has evolved to test this intuition in various settings (Bales 1950; Blau 1970; Fine 2012; Gastil 2010; Hall, Johnson, & Haas 1967; Hamburger, Guyer, & Fox 1975; Harrington & Fine 2006; Homans 1950; Isaac, Walker, & Williams 1994; Kimberly 1976; Poole & Hollingshead 2005; Soboroff 2012; Thomas & Fink 1963; Verba 1961; see also the journal *Small Group Research*).

Groups of special interest include work teams (Aubé, Rousseau, & Tremblay 2011; Kameda et al. 1992), firms (Carroll & Hannan 2000; Ijiri & Simon 1977; Ingham 1970; Lucas 1978; Rainnie 2016; Stanley et al. 1996; Stein 1974), unions (Faunce 1962), interest groups (Esteban & Ray 2001; Olson 1965), juries (Saks 1977), prisons (Farrington & Nuttall 1980), government agencies (Jung 2013), utopian communities (Dunbar & Sosis 2017; Gastil 2014), crowds (Goffman 1963; Le Bon 1896; Levine & Crowther 2008), networks (Katz et al. 2004), and communities facing common-pool resource dilemmas (Agrawal & Goyal 2001; E. Ostrom 1990).

We draw on this literature wherever it seems relevant. Note that very small groups can often be studied through experiments, which vastly enhances prospects for causal inference. It is not always clear, however, the extent to which the dynamics of small-group interaction map onto large political communities. One can find politics in any group, but this is not quite the same thing as politics as it plays out in a self-governing community with sovereignty over a fixed territory. Polities are not only larger than the typical group; they also enjoy a more wide-ranging and open-ended mandate. Thus, we regard findings based on small-group research as suggestive but not conclusive.

Scale and Political Community

We come, finally, to the topic of interest in this book: scale – understood as population – as it pertains to political communities, i.e., polities or electoral districts.

Virtually any analysis focused on political communities is obliged to take account of the population of those communities as a background condition. One can hardly compare Community A to Community B without taking note of their relative sizes.

In experiments, posttreatment analyses using a matching estimator, and most-similar case studies the size of communities is generally held constant by design, as the researcher's theoretical interests lie elsewhere. Evidently, this sort of study is not informative about the possible causal role of scale.

In observational studies using a regression-based estimator it is common for population to vary across groups. In this setting, the coefficient for population might be regarded as an estimate of causal effects. However, the chosen model may – or may not – be well identified for this purpose. The problem is that the design of a study focused on some other causal factor of theoretical interest is often inappropriate for estimating the causal effect of background covariates. It might involve posttreatment bias (the inclusion of covariates that are affected by size), it may omit a crucial confounder, or the chosen estimator may be inappropriate. One should not regard studies focused on other subjects as tests of our theoretical question simply because they include a covariate measuring population.

Thus, although scale is ubiquitous in studies of political communities it is also severely undeveloped. Only a small number of studies focus squarely on the causal role of population in politics.

Of these, there is one acknowledged classic, a slender monograph by Robert Dahl and Edward Tufte, published in 1973, called *Size and Democracy*. It would be difficult to summarize the wealth of theories and hypotheses laid out in this prescient book, which sketched the contours of an entire field of study and is cited repeatedly in the pages that follow.

At the same time, it is important to recognize the limitations of this seminal volume. The theoretical scope is restricted to nation-states with a democratic form of government. The authors' arguments are also based on a narrow empirical foundation, as few studies of scale had been conducted at the time and little evidence was available upon which to test the authors' conjectures. Accordingly, the book is short – 140 pages – and filled mostly with speculative hypotheses, supported here and there by data drawn from the United States and Europe.

In an interview conducted near the end of his life, Dahl was asked whether there were any projects that, in hindsight, he wished he had been able to pursue. He responded,

In a lifetime we can only do so many things. I wish I had taken the subject of size and democracy further. The whole issue of scale has fascinated me from the beginning and continues to fascinate me. My book with Tufte ... opens up the problem of scale. But I regret that I have not had and won't have more time to think that through. If I were twenty years younger, I would mine the problem of scale (quoted in Munck & Snyder 2007: 130).

Dahl would be gratified to know that, in the decades since *Size and Democracy* appeared, a substantial body of academic work has accumulated on the subject. Most of these studies are focused on *local government* (e.g., Black 1974; Denters et al. 2014; Hansen 2015; Hoch 1976; Lago-Peñas & Martinez-Vazquez 2013; Lassen & Serritzlew 2011; Lewis 2011; Oliver, Ha, & Callen 2012) or on *small states* (e.g., C. Anckar 2000, 2008; D. Anckar 1997, 1999, 2002, 2004; Anckar & Anckar 1995, 2000; Clarke & Payne 1987; Corbett 2015a, 2015b; Dommen & Hein 1985; Farrugia 1993; Hintjens & Newitt 1992; Kisanga & Danchie 2007; Levine 2016; Ott 2000; Patapan, Wanna, & Weller 2005; Richards 1982; Srebrnik 2004; Wolf 2016).

We aim to integrate this evolving body of work along with our own contributions. The present volume thus represents an attempt to present new results as well as to synthesize extant work on a large subject. In this fashion, we hope to assist in the cumulation of knowledge, an oft-discussed problem in an era of social science when finely focused studies have tended to displace broadly scoped work.

Conceptualizing and Measuring Political Communities

In this study, we are concerned with the size (population) of political communities. A community may be of any size so long as it serves a political function. This is a little confusing, as we tend to think of communities being small and local. However, for our purposes it is essential to identify an umbrella term that describes political units of all sizes – villages with a dozen inhabitants, nation-states and empires of a billion plus, and even the whole world (which has a protean political organization in the United Nations). "Community" refers to all of these political groupings.

Political communities may serve two functions – as polities or as electoral districts.

A *polity* is a political community that enjoys some degree of policymaking power. Polities may be supranational (e.g., the European Union), national (e.g., France), or subnational (e.g., regions, departments, and municipalities within France). Always, there is an organizational apparatus – a *government*.

A *district* is a geographic territory (and the electorate encompassed by that territory) from which an official is elected. Districts may be national (as they are for presidential elections and for parliamentary elections in Israel and the Netherlands) or subnational.

Many communities function as both polities and districts. For example, the state of California is a polity as well as a district (for presidential, senatorial, and gubernatorial elections). Readers should bear in mind that some of our arguments pertain to polities and districts, while others refer only to polities (as noted in Chapter 1).

Whether they serve as polities and/or districts, political communities are almost always formally defined, i.e., by statute or treaty. They are also likely to be represented on maps and may be delimited by visible borders, e.g., a fence or guard post. National borders are generally more permanent and more tightly regulated than internal borders, and hence more apparent to citizens (Simmons 2019). Some internal borders follow topographic features of the natural landscape (rivers, oceans, mountains); others follow the distribution of population, with urban areas integrated into a municipality and outlying regions being part of a separate governing body; still others have no apparent logic. An extreme case of arbitrariness is provided by US congressional districts, which do not follow any natural or demographic features of the landscape and change with each decennial census.

It follows that some communities are likely to be well understood by citizens, forming an integral part of their identity. Others are likely to seem artificial or are unknown. (Many Americans do not know what congressional district they belong to.)

Perceptions of political community matter to some outcomes of concern in this book. For example, in Chapter 3 we investigate perceptions of deviance, which are partly a product of which community(ies) an individual believes herself to be a member of – an imagined community (Anderson 1983). The situation is complicated by the fact that citizens are members of multiple political communities nested within each other. Some are quite small (e.g., a city council district) and others quite large (e.g., a typical nation-state).

Wherever our theorizing rests upon citizen attitudes and behavior we need to keep the relative salience of communities in mind. However, from the perspective of measurement the boundaries of communities are usually fairly clear. In the modern era, we generally know where one jurisdiction ends and another begins, and approximately how many people reside within each. Moreover, for many outcomes of concern in this book citizens' perceptions – e.g., about which community(ies) they belong to – are not very relevant.

Demographic Scale

Demographic scale is usually measured by the number of *citizens* who officially reside in a political community. Generally, we abide by official definitions of who is, and is not, a citizen. Thus, we count as citizens of the United Arab Emirates only those that the state recognizes as citizens, even though a majority of permanent residents are noncitizens. In most modern settings, the distinction between citizens and permanent residents is fairly trivial. (The Gulf emirates are unusual in this respect.)

For outcomes that hinge upon elections, demographic scale may also be measured by the size of the *electorate*, i.e., those who are legally qualified to vote in an election. In the contemporary era, when elections usually recognize universal adult suffrage, the distinction between citizens and electors is minimal (the main difference is that children are excluded from the electorate). Because citizens are often easier to count than electors, we usually rely on the former to operationalize the concept of scale. But in some circumstances, e.g., in periods prior to universal suffrage, it is vital to disambiguate – at least for some outcomes.

In order to test the relationship of demographic scale to an outcome of theoretical interest we transform population from a linear measure to a *logarithmic* measure (using the natural logarithm). This captures the widely accepted notion that there are diminishing marginal effects to an increase in population size. An increase of 1,000 matters more to a polity of 10,000 than to a polity of 10 million. The logarithmic transformation allows us to gauge the impact of percentage changes (rather than absolute changes) in community size.

Granted, the true functional form might be something other than linear or logarithmic. It might even be non-monotonic, as we argue for civil conflict (Chapter 14). We explore these options wherever theory or data seem to justify it. Generally, we find that a logarithmic transformation outperforms the linear (untransformed) population index and that there is little empirical or theoretical justification for non-monotonic functional forms. We do not explore other options, as this opens the door to curve-fitting exercises of questionable generalizability. However, we acknowledge that other functional forms may provide a better fit for the data and *may* be generalizable – an issue we postpone for future research.

Scale As a Causal Factor

Measuring the population of political communities is fairly straightforward, with the caveats noted earlier. Understanding the *causal* role of scale is much more complicated. Note that the size (population) of a society is linked to every other aspect of that society. Under the circumstances, how can one imagine changing the scale of a community without changing anything else? What are the ceteris paribus conditions of such an argument?

To clarify foreground (scale) and background (everything else) we propose the following thought experiment. At a global level, imagine that people are chosen randomly to inhabit countries of varying sizes (large and small). At a country level, imagine that citizens of a country are chosen randomly to inhabit regions of varying sizes within that country. At a municipal level, imagine that citizens of a region are chosen randomly to inhabit cities of varying sizes. At an electoral district level, imagine that citizens of a country, region, or city are chosen randomly to inhabit districts of varying sizes.

In these thought experiments we must assure that all background conditions are the same (probabilistically). By randomizing the selection of people we assure that those chosen to inhabit small and large communities are similar to each other. We must also randomize the selection of territories so that each is roughly proportional to the number of people living within it. (If territories are the same size then those with lots of people will be more densely settled, which constitutes an important confounder since it may affect outcomes of interest.) Likewise, the topography, climate, natural resources, and other geographic features of these territories – countries, regions, or cities – must be randomized. And likewise for preexisting infrastructure (transport, communications, buildings, farms, et al.).

These are purely fanciful thought experiments. There is no way they could be implemented in the real world, for practical and ethical reasons. Nonetheless, we can imagine their implementation, and this helps to elucidate the causal meaning of scale, i.e., how one might manipulate scale while keeping all else equal in order to estimate the impact of scale on some outcome of theoretical interest.

A more realistic thought experiment involves merging or splitting neighboring political communities that already exist. This happens in the real world – with countries, regions, municipalities, and electoral districts – so it is something we can easily wrap our minds around. For our purposes, it is important to imagine that this merging and splitting be random, or as if random (not affected by factors that might also affect the outcomes of theoretical interest). This is the claim made by studies of scale focused on municipal amalgamation or redistricting (Blom-Hansen, Houlberg, & Serritzlew 2014; Ennser-Jedenastik & Veenendaal 2015; Gerring et al. 2015; Hansen 2013; Lassen & Serritzlew 2011).

A potential problem with such natural experiments is that they are unable to distinguish short- and long-term effects. Typically, a difference-in-difference analysis compares outcomes just prior to, and just after, the reassignment of boundaries. By restricting the temporal scope, potential confounders associated with the passage of time – including contamination across units – are minimized. However, short-term effects may not be very interesting theoretically. For example, when district or municipal boundaries are reassigned the process is often highly conflictual. There are winners and losers, and the losers are not happy with the outcome. Likewise, the impact of a government reorganization in the short run introduces a good deal of confusion and uncertainty. For both reasons, we can anticipate that it will take a while for equilibrium results to manifest themselves. This, in turn, suggests that the results of interest – for policymakers and for social scientists – are long-term rather than short-term. One might of course adjust the terms of the analysis to examine outcomes over the longer term, but this introduces new potential confounders as well as lots of background noise, and as a matter of practice is rarely done.

In any case, natural experiments of this sort are rare and occur mostly in very small political communities. Larger units such as regions and nation-states are almost never reassigned in an as-if random fashion. To be sure, some postcolonial boundaries appear to have been drawn in a highly arbitrary fashion, leading to the possibility of clean comparisons (Alesina, Easterly, & Matuszeski 2011). However, some difficult assumptions are associated with treating straight-line borders as natural experiments (McCauley & Posner 2015), and these cases are rare and highly unrepresentative, so it is difficult to generalize upon this sample.

Because of these difficulties, most of the evidence put forth in this study is "observational"; that is, it bears little resemblance to a scientific experiment. Although observational research is currently out of favor (Gerber, Green, & Kaplan 2014), it has several characteristic virtues that perhaps should be more widely appreciated.

The first virtue of observational research is realism. The data-generating process occurs naturally rather than in response to the researcher's manipulation or the rare (and presumably unusual) occurrence of a natural experiment. Consequently, the task of generalizing from sample to population is less fraught.

The second strength of observational data (at least in this context) is the ability to gather large samples that better represent the population of interest and are less prone to stochastic error. With respect to nation-states, we can conduct tests that integrate virtually the entire population of sovereign states. In the case of subnational polities and districts, we can incorporate large samples from a variety of countries around the world. Many of our tests extend across a century or more. Insofar as one wishes to elucidate general laws of social science, this is a decisive advantage.

Antecedent Causes

These virtues notwithstanding, observational data inevitably raise questions about causal identification. In our case, the problem is exacerbated by the ambiguity of the data-generating process.

Consider the factors that account for variation in scale across political communities. These prior causes may be classified as *membership, boundary*, or *demographic*. Membership involves changes to the civil or political rights of a class of people living within a political community. For example, when women, slaves, or eighteen-year-olds are granted suffrage the size of an electorate is enlarged. Boundary factors involve changes to the boundary of a political or electoral unit, as when a country enlarges (or contracts) or an electoral district is enlarged (or contracted). Demographic factors involve fertility, mortality, and (in- and out-) migration. These are the various possible causes of change in the size of a political community.

Changes in membership conditions or boundaries are directly manipulable (by policymakers) and thus are fairly easy to interpret in a causal fashion. We know, or can readily imagine, what the background conditions associated with a change in X might be. These treatments fit handily within the potential outcomes model of causality (Morgan & Winship 2015). Unfortunately, these sorts of changes occur rarely and may be associated with confounders. When a new class of citizens is enfranchised we are looking at a change in the *type* of voter, as well as the size of the electorate. Boundary changes are perturbations of the polity or district, which means we must reckon with any effects those perturbations might have on outcomes of interest.

In any case, most of the variation in size that we can observe across political units is a product of demographic forces that work slowly and silently over long periods of time. This differentiates our study from most contemporary social science studies, where both cause and effect generally have short time horizons (Guldi & Armitage 2014). Pierson (2004: 79) comments,

> Both in what we seek to explain and in our search for explanations, we focus on the immediate – we look for causes and outcomes that are both temporally contiguous and rapidly unfolding. In the process, we miss a lot. There are important things that we do not see at all, and what we do see we often misunderstand.

Our study falls in what Pierson would label the long-long quadrant, featuring a slow-moving cause and (mostly) slow-moving effects. As such, variation cannot be interpreted as the product of discrete treatments. Consequently, it is somewhat difficult to envision what a change in X means, holding all other factors constant. For this reason, some might regard the size of political units as a noncausal feature of the world (Holland 1986).

Our view is more forgiving. We look upon a factor as a potential cause if its *antecedents* are in principle manipulable. This fits within an instrumental-variable approach to causal inference. Note also that country boundaries – a manipulable (in principle) treatment – are the basis for one of our instruments in two-stage analyses discussed later in this volume. In this loose sense, we may regard size as a causal factor within the potential outcomes framework (Morgan & Winship 2015).

Mechanisms and Confounders

When we attribute causal properties to scale we mean to include factors that lie downstream (causally) from the size of a community while excluding factors that are not directly the product of scale. The first may be understood as *mechanisms* and the latter as potential *confounders*.

Insofar as community characteristics are the product of community size they lie within the purview of our explanation; they are "downstream" from scale. For example, we argue that larger communities are, by virtue of that fact, likely to be more heterogeneous than smaller communities (Chapter 3). As such, heterogeneity is downstream from scale. To be sure, if heterogeneity is caused mostly by selective migration (in-migration of people who are very different from those currently living in a community), this is unrelated to the treatment and therefore needs to be partialled out of the analysis. This is a tricky matter as it is not always obvious how much of the heterogeneity effect is a product of sheer size and how much is a product of other factors.

Most of the background characteristics associated with political communities – wealth, education, culture, age distribution, population density, and so forth – have nothing to do with scale per se and are thus rightly viewed as potential confounders. Fortunately, the population of communities is not strongly associated with most other demographic characteristics. (Across nation-states there is virtually no association between population size and the share of populations that are old or young, for example.) By the same token, small countries *are* often associated with isolation, island landmasses, English colonialism, and particular regions of the world. When comparing subnational communities (i.e., regions, municipalities, or districts), smallness is sometimes associated with a low level of modernization, e.g., diffuse, rural settlements, agricultural economies, little education, and poverty. These factors will need to be controlled wherever they are relevant to the outcome, either by conditioning in a regression framework or by focusing on subsets of units that are similar across these background characteristics.

Conclusions

Although these threats to inference are severe, it is important to appreciate that they are not at all unusual. Many factors of interest to social science are not directly manipulable, do not feature discrete treatments and proximal outcomes, and are subject to myriad confounders. This includes classic social science topics such as identity, ideology, democracy, and inequality (Gerring 2012: ch. 9).

When one claims that inequality affects some outcome (e.g., growth, populism, polarization, civil war, or democratic breakdown) one is imagining a counterfactual in which a country has the same values on everything relevant to an outcome except inequality (Acemoglu & Robinson 2006). Country *A* with high inequality is the same as Country *B* with low inequality. This is a very difficult scenario to wrap one's mind around. How could wealth be redistributed without other things – probably also fundamental to the outcome – also changing? What would Brazil be like if wealth was equally distributed? What would Sweden be like if its Gini index approximated Brazil's?

Scale (we are relieved to say) is more tractable than inequality. Yet, because changes in the scale of a community arise in different ways, it is important to clarify what sort of change in *X* we envision when we say that scale "causes" an outcome. What is the hypothetical counterfactual and what are the background conditions? That is why we have spent so much time on this question.

Analytic Strategies (Large-N)

The burden of this project is to show that population matters for a diverse array of outcomes. Where possible, we seek to test a hypothesis across different units of analysis, different parts of the world, and different time periods. For each analysis, we seek to obtain a sample that is broad and representative in coverage so as to enhance the generalizability of the finding. (The term "sample" does not imply that units are sampled randomly from a known population; it merely indicates the set of observations under study.)

In this section we review analytic strategies. This includes (a) estimators and specifications, (b) longitudinal and latitudinal comparisons, (c) subnational units, (d) national units, (e) instrumental variable analysis, (f) measurement of impact, (g) possible mechanisms, and (h) replicability.

Estimators and Specifications

Most of the analyses in subsequent chapters follow a similar template. The template is more uniform for cross-national analyses since these analyses share a lot in common. Where units of analysis are subnational there is more contextual variation and hence more variation in modeling strategies. Even so, it will be helpful to lay out the general approach to empirical analysis so this ground does not need to be covered repeatedly in subsequent chapters.

An estimator is chosen based on the distribution of the outcome: ordinary least squares (OLS) for continuous outcomes with more or less normal distributions, tobit for continuous outcomes with left-censored distributions, ordered logit for ordinal outcomes, logit for binary outcomes. Since OLS is easiest to interpret, and also easier to compare (since most of our outcomes are continuous), we employ OLS even when the distribution of the outcome seems to call for a more esoteric estimator if there is little difference in fit between the two estimators. (Here, the non-OLS estimator is relegated to a robustness test.)

Wherever multiple observations are taken from a single unit over time, standard errors are clustered by the treatment unit. Thus, in a cross-national panel analysis standard errors are clustered by country. In a panel analysis of US states standard errors are clustered by state. Where individuals form the units of analysis but the treatment is administered at group levels, standard errors are clustered at the group level. Thus, in an analysis of turnout in which the individual-level turnout is the unit of analysis but the size of a group is understood as the size of countries, standard errors are clustered by country. This should help to mitigate the problem of correlated errors.

In cross-country analyses right-side variables are usually lagged two decades behind the outcome. This serves to mitigate the possibility of endogeneity and to measure longer-term effects, which are of greater theoretical interest than short-term effects. We use a one-year lag, or no lag at all, when the relationship of population to an outcome does not seem susceptible to X/Y endogeneity or is deemed to be proximal rather than distal. Since population is sluggish, moving slowly and almost always in a monotonic (increasing) fashion through time, the choice of lags has minimal impact on estimations.

With this setup, a chosen outcome measure is regressed against population (log). The first model in each table is regarded as the benchmark model. It includes only those factors that are deemed essential in order to avoid confounding. Usually, we include annual dummies, an established strategy for controlling period effects.

The second model is often a fuller specification. This builds on the benchmark model, adding other covariates that may, or may not, influence the outcome but may also be influenced by population (raising the possibility of posttreatment bias).

If there are extreme outliers, we include a robustness test that excludes those outliers.

If the analysis is cross-national, the final model is usually an instrumental variable (IV) model, as discussed later. The specification for this IV model follows the benchmark, replacing year dummies with decade dummies in order to render the analysis tractable. To conserve space, we do not show results from the first stage of this two-stage model.

Further robustness tests are often conducted in work (our own, or others') published elsewhere.

The choice of covariates for each model is contingent upon the outcome under investigation, which determines what factors might be regarded as potential confounders. However, some national-level covariates are ubiquitous enough to be mentioned here. These include *GDP per capita*, transformed by the natural logarithm; *urbanization* (share of population living in urban areas); *years independent*, transformed by the natural logarithm; *state history* (a variable measuring a country's experience of statehood back to AD 0, constructed by Louis Putterman and collaborators [Bockstette, Chanda, & Putterman 2002]); *democracy*, measured by the Lexical index of electoral democracy (Skaaning, Gerring, & Bartusevičius 2015); and dummies for major geographic *regions* of the world (Eastern Europe and Central Asia, Latin America, Middle East and North Africa, Sub-Saharan Africa, Western Europe and North America, East Asia, Southeast Asia, South Asia, the Pacific, and the Caribbean).

A complete list of country-level variables – including full definitions, data sources, and descriptive statistics – is located in Appendix B. Descriptive statistics for analyses where countries are *not* the chosen unit of analysis may be found below the relevant data table.

Asterisks accompanying a coefficient indicate conventional thresholds of statistical significance: *** $p < 0.01$, ** $p < 0.05$, * $p < 0.10$ (two-tailed tests). We recognize that these thresholds are arbitrary and that p values represent only one form of uncertainty, and can be especially misleading when research designs are nonexperimental. We also recognize the problems that arise when measuring statistical significance against a null hypothesis, which may not be theoretically or practically meaningful. Still, p values and arbitrary thresholds are helpful for representing one sort of uncertainty (based on repeated sampling), and are especially useful when attempting to systematically compare results from a great many analyses focused on diverse outcomes, as we do in this book.

This raises a larger point. Standardization – of samples, units of analysis, predictors, variables, specifications, robustness tests, and other matters – is useful insofar as it allows for systematic comparisons. (This is a core element behind extreme bounds analysis [Leamer 1983] and meta-analysis [M. Hunt 1997], though specifications are often allowed to vary.) Otherwise, estimates suffer from an apples and oranges problem: we do not know whether one predictor is more robust than another and we cannot compare coefficients and t statistics. Standardization is also helpful insofar as it limits opportunities for "fishing" – choosing only those models that confirm the author's hypothesis, and ignoring others. If every outcome must undergo the same set of tests, failure is harder to dodge. A negative implication of standardization is that one may occasionally apply models that are inappropriate. This is why there is some flexibility – especially in specification – across the tests reported in subsequent tables. In this fashion, we hope to have found a reasonable accommodation between standardization and flexibility.

Longitudinal and Latitudinal Comparisons

Ideally, one would hope to enlist both *longitudinal* (time-series or through-time) and *latitudinal* (cross-sectional or cross-unit) evidence of the relationship between size and politics. Where the combination of these two forms of analysis is justified this is all to the good, and several chapters make use of it. Unfortunately, it is not always justified. In this section, we explain why latitudinal comparisons usually provide a better test of scale effects.

As a general matter of research design, longitudinal analysis, which may take the form of a panel analysis with fixed effects or a single time-series, is preferred whenever there is sufficient change over time in the variables of theoretical interest and wherever changes in X are unaccompanied by potential confounders. The unit under observation must remain substantially the same from t to $t + 1$, or changes among background factors must be easily identified and measured (and thereby controlled).

Unfortunately, this is generally not the situation when population is the causal factor of interest. Demographic changes through time are generally quite subtle and highly trended, making it difficult to distinguish signal from background noise. Where demographic changes depart from the highly trended norm, potential confounders often appear. Note that countries with the highest population growth rates in the twentieth century are usually countries that are doing poorly. When a country is unstable, when government services are poor, and when rates of urbanization are low, the result is likely to be high fertility, leading over time (once mortality rates have stabilized) to high population growth. A number of countries in Sub-Saharan Africa currently fit this description, including the Central African Republic, Niger, and South Sudan. Countries whose populations are growing quickly are very different from countries whose populations are growing slowly, or contracting (e.g., Japan, Italy, or Russia at the present time). For this reason, it is tricky to interpret short-term changes in population as a causal factor.

We can of course look at longer time periods, thereby enhancing variation in the causal factor of interest. For example, we may compare the United States in 1776 and 2018, a period of nearly two and a half centuries during which the population enlarged more than 100 fold. However, many fundamental transformations occurred during this period. Under the circumstances, it would be foolhardy to attribute changes in political practices or institutions from 1776 to 2018 to demographic change unless one could confidently measure and condition all the potential confounders – essentially, everything else of consequence that changed during two and a half centuries that was not a product of demography.

On rare occasions, the population of a community changes in dramatic fashion over a short period of time, offering a discrete "treatment." However, this sort of rupture is invariably the product of a highly unusual event – a war, famine, genocide, massive migration, major political reform, or fission/fusion of countries. For example, the population of China fell dramatically during the Great Leap Forward (1958–62).

Unusual events of this sort are difficult to measure and to account for in an analysis; consequently, they are likely to serve as confounders. China in 1962 was different from China in 1958 in ways that go well beyond the disappearance of 23–55 million people (estimates vary). One must also appreciate that even the most cataclysmic population drops represent only a small change in the total population of a country. While 40 million (near the middle of the range of estimates) is a lot of deaths, China was also the largest country in the world, and those deaths represented only 6 percent of its population, whose upward trajectory was interrupted for only a few years. Substantial changes in population, of the sort that are likely to impact the nature of political institutions, happen slowly over many decades or centuries.

In summary, neither short- nor long-term changes in population are easily interpretable as evidence of causal relationships. By contrast, cross-sectional variation has two benefits. It incorporates enormous variation in the factor of theoretical interest and it is interpretable in a causal fashion (with caveats noted). It is relevant that China is the largest country throughout the modern period, a fact evident in cross-sectional comparisons across nation-states. It is not relevant (for present purposes) that China had a high population growth rate in the early and mid-twentieth century, that this normal rate began to fall in the 1970s, or that it dropped precipitously for a brief period between 1958 and 1962.

To the extent that size influences politics in a generalizable ("law-like") fashion we must pay attention to variation in scale that is caused by common factors such as the area and carrying capacity of the land and regular demographic dynamics that operate over secular-historical time. For this reason, we privilege latitudinal evidence over longitudinal evidence in most of the analyses that follow. This, indeed, is the usual approach to size when scale is the variable of theoretical interest, as shown in studies reviewed at the end of each substantive chapter.

Subnational Units

Some of the arguments in this book can be explored across subnational units – e.g., cities, regions, or electoral districts (see Table 2.1). These micro-level units are often helpful in establishing internal validity. Note that while there are only 200 or so countries, subnational units are numerous – especially within large countries like the United States. The US Census reports 39,044 general purpose local governments, including 19,492 municipal governments, 16,519 township governments, and 3,033 county governments. In addition, there are 50,432 special purpose local governments, including 37,381 special districts, 13,726

Table 2.1 *Outcomes and measures*

Measure	N	S	Measure	N	S	Measure	N	S
Cohesion (Ch. 3)	✓	✓	**Contestation** (Ch. 8)	✓	✓	**Power** (Ch. 13)	✓	
Heterogeneity	✓	✓	100 – vote share of largest party	✓	✓	GDP	✓	
Connectedness	✓	✓	Dif. b/w top two vote-getters	✓	✓	Iron, steel production	✓	
Deviance – behavior		✓	Party system fractionalization	✓	✓	Trade dependence	✓	
Deviance – perceptions		✓	Legislative fractionalization	✓		Aid dependence	✓	
Representatives (Ch. 4)	✓	✓	Turnover	✓	✓	Military power	✓	
Legislature size	✓	✓	**Institutionalized succession** (Ch. 9)	✓		Personnel	✓	
Cabinet size	✓	✓	Tenure	✓		Expenditures	✓	
Representation ratio (Ch. 4)	✓	✓	Monarchy	✓		Naval tonnage	✓	
Constituents/representative	✓		Regular leadership succession	✓		Universities	✓	
Representativeness (Ch. 5)	✓		**Professionalism** (Ch. 10)	✓	✓	Patent applications		
Demographic	✓		Legislative professionalism	✓		Tourist arrivals	✓	
Programmatic	✓		Legislative capacity	✓		**Civil conflict** (Ch. 14)	✓	
Constituency connections	✓		Meritocratic recruitment	✓		Battlefield casualties per capita	✓	
Political trust	✓	✓	Statistical capacity	✓		**Regimes** (Ch. 15)	✓	
Particularism (Ch. 6)	✓		Education of public officials	✓		Lexical index	✓	
Independent candidacies	✓		Salary of public officials	✓	✓	Political rights (Freedom House)	✓	
Party strength	✓		Voluntary associations (N)	✓		Polity2 (Polity IV)	✓	
Preferential voting		✓	**Concentration** (Ch. 11)	✓		Polyarchy (V-Dem)	✓	
Vote-buying	✓	✓	Federalism	✓		BMR (Boix, Miller, Rosato)	✓	
Campaign spending	✓		Bicameralism	✓		**Social inequality** (Ch. 15)		
Pork		✓	Revenue decentralization	✓		Gini index of income inequality	✓	
Corruption, overall	✓		Capital city pop/country pop	✓		**Economic development** (Ch. 15)	✓	✓

Table 2.1 (cont.)

	N	S		N	S		N	S
Participation (Ch. 7)			Checks and balances	✓		GDP per capita	✓	
Citizen assemblies		✓	**Intervention** (Ch. 12)			GDP per capita growth	✓	
Party membership	✓	✓	Moral policy		✓	**Public services** (Ch. 15)		
Voter turnout	✓	✓	Fiscal policy		✓	Quality of public services		✓
Other activities		✓	Personnel policy	✓	✓	Gov't effectiveness (WGI)	✓	✓
Political efficacy	✓		Social policy	✓		Various	✓	✓

Outcomes and measures employed in the substantive chapters of this book. *N*: national-level tests. *S*: subnational-level tests.

independent school districts, and 1,452 dependent public school systems.[3] That is just one country, albeit a large and decentralized one.

Despite their abundance, subnational communities pose several serious obstacles to causal inference. First, data for these units are scarce, especially for countries in the developing world. Often, we know the population of a subnational unit but not much else.

Second, some outcomes of theoretical interest are prerogatives of national-level governments. Local and regional governments have no responsibility for monetary policy or foreign affairs, for example, and differences in political institutions are minimized by virtue of being part of the same national unit. Thus, many questions of interest in this book simply cannot be addressed at subnational levels.

Third, subnational units are often redefined – new states, municipalities, or districts are formed, or old ones are reconfigured. This can serve as an advantage in causal inference, but only if the reassignment of borders is random, or as-if random. Typically, the creation and re-creation of subnational units is a political process, responding to political incentives, and thus endogenous to factors that we wish to examine.

Fourth, subnational units are prone to diffusion and spillover. Conditions obtaining in one unit are likely to affect conditions in neighboring units, meaning that they are not truly independent. Of course, this is also true of national units. But it is less true, meaning that assumptions of unit independence are more plausible (especially if the model includes regional covariates).

Fifth, subnational units experience a great deal of mobility across units. This means that the population of any single unit is in flux, and may be affected by outcomes of theoretical concern. For example, if crime is high and jobs are scarce in one community, residents may flee to another community where conditions are better. This means that any attempt to ascertain the impact of scale on crime or jobs is vexed by X:Y endogeneity.

Finally, large subnational units are typically quite different from small subnational units. They are apt to be more urbanized, more networked, with more advanced economies and more skilled labor forces, more likely to be located near transport hubs, and more likely to be populated by immigrants from the countryside and from other countries. All of these contrasts constitute potential confounders unless they are correctly identified and conditioned in the analysis – a difficult trick to perform.

Thus, for a variety of reasons, the analyses found in subsequent chapters rest more often on countries than on subnational units. Of course, we

---

[3] www.nlc.org/number-of-municipal-governments-population-distribution.

do not mean to suggest that national units are exempt from the afore-mentioned problems. But, surely, they are less susceptible.

National Units

The preeminence of nation-states ("countries") in our analyses reflects the preeminence of the state in social science and in public life more generally. Nation-states are the dominant political units of our time. No apologies are needed for a state-centric research design. However, we are also obliged to consider the methodological entailments of this design.

We begin with a definition of the subject, which follows convention and therefore aligns with most existing datasets. A *country* is a polity that the international community recognizes as having de jure (though not neces-sarily de facto) sovereignty over a territory. Countries are parties to international treaties and are eligible (presuming other criteria are met) to serve as members of international bodies such as the League of Nations and its successor, the United Nations. Somalia is a country by this legalistic definition while Somaliland is not (at least, not yet). We count Taiwan and Palestine as countries, despite their ambiguous legal status in some international organizations.

The borders of a country, by our understanding, extend to areas that are formally integrated into the metropole (where the capital is located) on equal terms. Thus, Guadeloupe and Martinique are treated as part of present-day France. However, if some regions are governed under very different laws and procedures, those outside the metropole are regarded as outside the boundaries of the country. Empires (so-called) often have this characteristic. Note that governance within the British metropole was quite different from governance in its overseas possessions, e.g., in North America, India, and Africa. Even today, overseas territories such as Gibraltar and the Falkland Islands are subject to distinct governance regimes. Consequently, these territories are not considered part of the United Kingdom in our analyses.

With this understanding of the subject, let us consider some of the *dis*advantages of working with nation-states as units of analysis. First, countries are macro-level units, which means that there is apt to be a diffuse relationship between inputs (causes) and outputs (outcomes), with plenty of intervening factors lying in between. Mechanisms will be hard to observe or interpret. Second, there are a modest number of states – 200 or so at the present time, and many fewer in previous years (within the modern era). So the number of units in a cross-national study is limited, especially when one considers the problem of data availability. Since most of our leverage comes from cross-sectional comparisons, cross-national analyses are subject to the problem of small samples. Third, states are extremely heterogeneous. While variation in population is essential for present purposes, variation in other factors may confound the analysis unless properly measured and conditioned in a statistical model. For all these reasons, reaching causal inference from cross-national data is perilous (Kittel 2006; Seawright 2010; Summers 1991).

There are also some benefits to employing states as units of analysis – beyond their obvious relevance for the world we live in – which may be briefly reviewed. First, there is enormous variation in size across countries (Chapter 1), offering considerable leverage on the causal question of theoretical interest.

Second, countries are less susceptible than lower-level units to migration. In an era of well-defined boundaries and strict immigration controls, it is much easier to move to a nearby city within a single country than to emigrate to a foreign land. Thus, changes to a country's population generally occur slowly, through population growth rather than migration. While international migration gets a lot of attention, it accounts for a very small portion of the total population of most countries. This mitigates some concerns about causal identification.

Third, state boundaries are sticky. That is, once a state gains international recognition it tends to retain its original borders (more or less) over long stretches of time. In the modern era, interstate conflict rarely results in a dramatic and permanent realignment of borders (Zacher 2001). Even very weak states seem to survive (Diehl & Goertz 1992; Jackson & Rosberg 1982b). As such, state borders may be regarded as exogenous – or, at least, as more exogenous than subnational borders.

To be sure, there are instances of new states winning autonomy from older states. In recent years, East Timor has gained independence from Indonesia, Eritrea from Ethiopia, Montenegro from Serbia, Palau from the United States, and South Sudan from Sudan. However, secession usually leaves the larger state intact, retaining a majority of its former population and allowing us to treat that unit in a continuous fashion through time. Newly formed states enter our analysis once they have gained international recognition, at which point their borders are apt to remain fairly stable. The stickiness of borders is the general rule in the twentieth century, and these stable states dominate our samples.

Granted, we must be concerned with the problem of how borders are assigned, and why some states are large and others small. Possible causal factors include economies of scale, burdens of heterogeneity, the necessity of self-defense, the prominence of international trade, technological developments affecting transport, communications, warfare, and administration, and threats to sovereignty (Alesina & Spolaore 2003; Hiscox & Lake 2001; Wittman 1991, 2000). However, these factors affect all countries more or less equally. They do not explain why some countries are larger than others at a particular point in time (since they are all subject to the same technological and international system effects). As such, these factors are orthogonal to our (predominantly cross-sectional) analyses. To the extent that these factors change over time, leading to a change in the average or ideal size of states, their influence is captured by annual or decade dummies in our analyses.

To the extent that one can account for variation in the size of states at particular points in time, one might point to geography (Kitamura & Lagerlöf 2015) or to the distinctive historical trajectories of each region of the world. It is hoped that by controlling for relevant geographic features (e.g., with regional dummies), these factors can be conditioned and potential confounders blocked.

The assignment of borders nonetheless raises two intriguing questions of causal inference.

The *modifiable areal unit problem* suggests that the results of any analysis may be contingent upon the arbitrary placement of borders (Openshaw 1984: 3). This problem arises in an obvious way when borders serve merely as data containers. In an analysis of census tracts, for example, one would want to know whether a different assignment of borders for those tracts would lead to (substantially) different results. However, countries are not merely reporting units; they are objects of theoretical interest. If we reassign a country's borders, we are, in effect, creating a different country. This does not make the counterfactual experiment less interesting, but it suggests that the problem of causal inference is not correctly described as a modifiable areal unit problem.

A second issue with respect to borders is the stable unit treatment value assumption, aka *SUTVA* (Morgan & Winship 2015; Rubin 2005). Note that the boundaries of countries are mutually constituted. In the modern era, when all terra firma except the Antarctic is claimed by one state or another, the borders of one country determine the borders of another. France ends where Germany begins, so if France expands, then Germany contracts, and vice versa. This is true overseas as well; borders do not have to be neighboring in order to be mutually determined.

There is no obvious solution to this problem of causal inference, though it does not seem to trouble social scientists very much. Note that virtually any method of data collection that is spatial (i.e., it collects data in geographically defined units) incorporates contiguous spatial units, whether they are nation-states, regions, municipalities, electoral districts, school districts, or neighborhoods. Perhaps SUTVA is more problematic where the causal factor of theoretical interest is aggregate size, since a movement in the border separating two communities may have a large effect on the size of both communities. Helpfully, most of the outcomes of concern are measured on a per capita basis, so changes in borders would not have a huge impact.

Leaving aside the assignment of country borders, one may also worry about the exogeneity of population growth. In particular, one must be concerned if demographic changes respond to political cues. Insofar as governments are keen to grow their populations, or constrain their growth, we face a problem of X/Y endogeneity – with the outcome of interest (political institutions) affecting the cause (demography).

However, most studies suggest that population-level changes in fertility such as the well-known demographic transition play out in ways that governments are at pains to control. Even the most draconian laws, such as China's one-child policy undertaken in the 1970s, seem to have had a modest impact on that country's dramatic fertility decline, which demographers believe owes more to urbanization, education, rising income, and changing norms than to government policy – though there's no question that the Chinese government hastened its arrival (Hesketh, Lu, & Xing 2005). Likewise, China's recent attempt to reboot population growth does not seem very effective. Fertility rates continue to fall. Summarizing centuries of such attempts across the world, Howe and Jackson (2012: 43) comment that "leaders have been perpetually disappointed by their population policies – by how they fail so much more often than they succeed."

In summary, government policies usually affect aggregate population growth only at the margins (Childs et al. 2005; Van de Kaa 2006) – with the obvious exception of instances of genocide, policy-induced famine (e.g., the Great Leap Forward or the Soviet famine of 1932–33), or civil war. As such, we may regard the population of countries as exogenous – conditional on observed factors that might affect fertility rates such as per capita income and urbanization.

Instrumental Variable Analysis

One would like to be able to explain the population of countries in a fashion that is clearly exogenous to the outcomes of theoretical interest. Unfortunately, this is not possible. However, one can assuage some concerns about nonrandom assignment by enlisting instrumental variable (IV) designs.

Our chosen instruments are *territory* and *agricultural suitability*, both transformed to a logarithmic scale. Territorial expanse is measured by the land area of a polity (Weidmann, Kuse, & Gleditsch 2010). Agricultural suitability involves a variety of geographic endowments that are presumed to favor agricultural production, including climate, soil, and terrain. For this, we utilize a summary index drawn from the Agro-Ecological Zones system (GAEZ) developed by the Food and Agriculture Organization (FAO) of the United Nations.

Together, these two geographic factors predict roughly half of the variability in population (log) across countries. This fits with a commonsense story in which demography responds, over time, to the amount of land available and the carrying capacity of that land.

Of course, the model assumes that country borders are exogenous, an issue we have already broached. In this circumstance, the assumption bears special consideration since some of the outcomes of interest might conceivably affect the size and shape of nation-states, and thus violate the assumptions of an IV model.

Specifically, one might be concerned that successful states occupy more territory, and more productive territory (as measured by agricultural suitability). By contrast, less successful states may remain small, or start big and end up small (due to defeat, defection, or dissolution). This is a fairly good summary of political history in the *pre*modern era, when strong states expanded and weak states shrunk or disappeared. States that survived, and thrived, were generally the fittest, conforming to an evolutionary logic.

However, the most effective states in the premodern era – including all of the European powers – lost their overseas holdings and are thus reduced in the modern era to relatively modest holdings. By contrast, ramshackle polities in the nineteenth century such as Russia, China, Brazil, the Dutch East Indies, British Nigeria, and British India managed to become or remain independent, retaining control over most of their territory in the twentieth century, and thus developing into the world's largest states. It is not the case, therefore, that success in the early modern era presages population size in the modern era. If anything, the reverse may be closer to the truth. Britain is modest in size while its former colony, India, is huge, to take just one example. In any case, we control for state history, year of state formation, and length of independence – three factors that should proxy for historic state capacity – in our analyses wherever it seems warranted.

One might also be concerned that one of our instruments, agricultural suitability, influences modernization, which in turn may affect political institutions. However, our IV models usually condition on per capita

GDP, so this potential violation of the exclusion restriction is, in principle, blocked.

All things considered, we believe that IV analysis offers a plausible way to model the relationship between scale and politics where countries are the units of analysis. As with any analysis where the instrument is not randomized, causal inference depends upon assumptions about the data-generating process that cannot be definitively proven or disproven. The assumptions required for inference in this case are fairly strong and certainly do not qualify as a natural experiment. In this respect, and in others, IV analyses are problematic in many social science settings (Young 2017). Accordingly, we regard these analyses as robustness tests, not benchmark models.

Impact

Although we don't regard point estimates from regression models of observational data as terribly precise, it is important to show that they are nontrivial. Thus, for most benchmark models we present an accompanying figure showing predicted values of the outcome as scale increases, holding other covariates at their mean. This line is surrounded by a 95 percent confidence interval to give a sense of the varying precision of the estimate at different levels. To further clarify the practical meaning of changes in scale on various outcomes, we include descriptive statistics – mean, standard deviation, minimum, maximum – in Table B2 (for country-level variables) or in the notes section underneath each graph (for within-country analyses).

Readers should be aware of the implications of a logarithmic functional form. It means that an increase (decrease) in size at the bottom end of the population scale has a much greater impact on outcomes than a comparable increase (decrease) at the top. Adding 100,000 citizens to Tuvalu is likely to be transformative, while adding 100,000 citizens to India is trivial. The logarithmic format allows us to consider hypothetical changes in scale as a share of those already present in a community.

Readers should also be aware that arguments about scale are about *big* changes in scale. One should not imagine that small increases in population realized by a community over the course of a few years would have important ramifications for any of the outcomes investigated in this book. However, comparisons between "small," "medium," and "large" countries are warranted. If one wishes to understand why politics in the Federated States of Micronesia (pop. ~100,000) is different from politics in the Dominican Republic (pop. ~10 million) – or, for that matter, in China (pop. ~1.4 billion) – size is an essential element of that explanation. This also speaks to our choice of estimators, which privilege cross-sectional comparisons over longitudinal comparisons, as noted.

Mechanisms

Having discussed the problem of assessing causal effects, it is important to say a few words about the mechanisms that might explain relationships between scale and politics.

For each outcome, we surmise that there are multiple mechanisms, i.e., a number of pathways through which scale affects the shape of politics. These are laid out at the beginning of each chapter and summarized in a causal diagram.

Despite our interest in theory, the empirical analyses that follow are focused almost entirely on the main causal effect – the relationship of scale (X) to an outcome of theoretical interest (Y). We do *not* attempt to test putative causal mechanisms (M).

The primary reason for this omission is empirical intractability. We note that when attempting to estimate causal mechanisms all the problems of inference applicable to causal effects apply *plus* those specific to mediation models (Gerring 2010; Imai et al. 2011). This is not an easy task. In our case, pathways from X to Y tend to be multiple, overlapping, subject to contextual variability, and also difficult to measure.

For these reasons, and because of space constraints, we shy away from the challenge of demonstrating theoretical arguments about mechanisms. We note that in the work of social science it is rarely possible to test causal mechanisms that apply to macro-level outcomes in a rigorous fashion. In this respect, we are in good company – or perhaps we should say *bad* company. At any rate, we have a lot of company.

For this part of the argument we adopt the usual expedient: we rely on extant research and on what can be reasonably intuited about the world. Readers must judge whether or not our theorizing rests on strong microfoundations.

Replicability

For any study, readers are entitled to wonder whether its results are replicable. Could they be reproduced by another scholar following similar procedures? In recent years, the problem of replication has been recognized as a fundamental obstacle to knowledge cumulation (Freese & Peterson 2020). Bluntly stated, many published studies cannot be replicated either because the authors have not granted public access to their data or because they have not specified in sufficient detail the methods by

which they reached their conclusions. Of those studies that can be replicated in this narrow, technical sense, many show errors – for the most part
unintentional but nonetheless compromising. To facilitate future replication in this narrow, technical sense, we preserve all information pertaining
to data gathering, aggregation, and analysis in online files hosted on
Dataverse.

Replication in a broader sense refers to collecting new data – from the
same site or from a different site – and/or altering the procedures of the
original study in some fashion deemed to be in keeping with the theoretical aims of the original study. Here, successful replication is even more
difficult. Nonetheless, we have done what we can to maximize the generalizability of our arguments. Samples are large and effect sizes (in most
cases) substantial, reducing the possibility of stochastic error. We have
also implemented a variety of robustness tests. These involve variations
in: (a) outcome indicators, (b) samples, (c) functional form, (d) interactions among predictors, (e) specifications, and (f) estimators.

Of course, multiple analyses of a given hypothesis present a problem of
cherry-picking (aka fishing) – choosing to present those tests that support
the author's hypothesis and ignoring those that do not. However, in this
sort of study the incentive to cherry-pick is reduced. Note that our
theoretical claims are broad and probabilistic so we have little at stake
in any particular test. Indeed, readers will find that not all tests are passed
(at conventional thresholds of statistical significance).

At the end of each chapter, we produce a table that compiles the results
of all empirical studies – conducted by ourselves or by others – that are
relevant to a particular scale effect. This serves as a summary of the state
of current knowledge on a subject, i.e., how much work has been conducted, what sorts of research designs have been employed, what samples
have been tested, and what degree of consensus has been reached. Some
scale effects are strongly supported by the literature. Others have not been
widely studied, or are in dispute.

A tricky question remains of which extant studies deserve recognition
and which can be ignored. Little is served by repeating every comment on
scale and politics from Aristotle to the present. Where extant studies are
numerous, we try to include the most pertinent, influential, and comprehensive studies on a given topic, with special attention to more recent
work. We do not include unpublished work if it is not readily obtainable
on the World Wide Web. If our treatment of a topic includes no discussion of prior work, readers may assume it has not been researched – or we
are unaware of these studies.

In the final chapter, we assign subjective probabilities to each pur-
ported scale effect (see Table 16.1). This serves to summarize the findings

of this book and of a growing area of research devoted to scale and politics. It should also give readers a good idea of which scale effects are likely to replicate out-of-sample and which are more dubious.

Outcomes and Measures

Myriad outcomes are explored in this book, as explained in Chapter 1. Since these are broad concepts, they may be measured in a variety of ways. We select dependent variables from among available options so as to *maximize* (a) construct validity, (b) empirical coverage, (c) representativeness, and (d) sensitivity, and *minimize* (e) error.

Construct validity refers to the connection between a chosen indicator, or a set of indicators, and the concept it is intended to measure. There is little question about the construct validity of most indicators of participation. Voting is an indicator of participation, of this there is little doubt. However, citizens may participate in political affairs in multiple ways, and it is an open question which indicator, or which set of indicators, provides the best construct validity. Likewise for contestation. For more abstract outcomes (e.g., concentration), construct validity is even more difficult to assess. We reserve discussion of these issues for later chapters, but it is important to signal the difficulty at the outset.

Empirical *coverage* is important for several reasons. First, it enhances the size of the sample, increasing the power of the resulting analysis and reducing the possibility of stochastic error. Of particular concern are measures that are available for only a single point in time or over a short period during which the outcome is sticky (unchanging). The measurement industry has exploded in recent years, providing an enormous surfeit of indicators focused on various elements of democracy and governance (Christiane & Oman 2006; Coppedge et al. 2011; Williams & Siddique 2008). However, most of these data are available only for very recent years. Although we occasionally make use of these data, we are hesitant to rest conclusions on such a slender empirical basis. It is not clear whether the relationship of scale to politics today exemplifies long-term relationships or simply an isolated moment in time.

This segues into our next point: extensive coverage is usually important for ensuring the *representativeness* of a sample. This is true in a fairly obvious fashion as a sample approaches a census. Some of our cross-country samples include virtually all sovereign nation-states – though we face the usual obstacle of missing microstates.

Sensitivity deserves special attention. Some outcome measures are binary and sticky through time, offering little variation to exploit. Other indicators are more sensitive, offering a better gauge of how scale might affect an outcome. On this ground, we generally prefer interval indicators over ordinal indicators, and ordinal indicators over binary indicators.

Error, especially systematic error, is naturally a concern in choosing among potential indicators. For this reason, "objective" measures (that do not involve the judgments of coders or survey respondents) are preferred over "subjective" measures unless the goal is to capture attitudes or there is no way to adequately measure a concept objectively.

Of particular concern are biased perceptions of deviance (Chapter 3) and particularism (Chapter 6). Subjective measures based on polls of citizens, business people, or experts are likely to reflect violations of a norm rather than instances when a norm is followed, as violations are easier to track and more likely to be commented on in the press. "Bureaucrat caught cheating" is newsworthy; "Bureaucrat doing her job" is not. In a larger country, with a larger bureaucracy, biased perceptions of deviance may introduce systematic error into our analysis, as discussed in Chapters 3 and 5.

In striving for these five desiderata – construct validity, empirical coverage, representativeness, sensitivity, and accuracy – one often encounters trade-offs. An indicator may score high on one dimension but low on another. One also encounters considerable uncertainty with respect to construct validity, representativeness, and accuracy. Generally, there is no way to resolve this uncertainty.

Since there is rarely an obvious "best" choice among indicators for a concept, we resort to redundancy. That is, we choose several indicators in the hopes that, together, they will provide a balanced view of our subject. Our philosophy is that wherever measurement issues arise there is some comfort in multiple measures (unless, of course, all measures suffer the same defect).

To get a sense of the empirical material employed in subsequent chapters, Table 2.1 offers an overview of the main outcomes ($N = 17$) and their measures ($N = 70$). Some of the latter are measured only at national levels ($N = 39$) and others only at subnational levels ($N = 14$), while others can be measured at both levels ($N = 17$).

Evidently, we would like to test propositions at multiple levels. Unfortunately, some outcomes manifest themselves only at one level. For example, defense policy is quintessentially a national-level policy, so there is little we can do to explore this feature at subnational levels. In other cases, it may be theoretically possible to probe an indicator at multiple levels but we gain little leverage by doing so. Consequently, tests introduced in the following chapters often focus on a single level of analysis.

Data Sources

We make every effort to gather data widely. Cross-national samples usually extend to every region of the world. Frequently, 180–200 countries are included, which means that our sample is equivalent to a census of all countries in existence in the modern era. Historical coverage is more limited, though many analyses extend back to 1900 and a few extend further back in time.

Within-country analyses often enlist larger samples comprised of subnational units or individuals. However, they are also less representative of the world. Sometimes, they encompass only one or two countries.

The United States is especially prominent in our within-country analyses. It is a large country with a long and fairly stable history of which there are ample historical records, including data about elections and elective offices back to the colonial era. It features many subnational units of widely varying sizes – states, counties, municipalities. Importantly, the electoral system is constant across most governmental units, almost all of which employ single-member districts and first-past-the-post rules. This means that an important background condition (for outcomes of interest that are election-based) is held constant. For all these reasons, the United States offers tremendous leverage on the theoretical question of interest. It also happens to be a country where a great deal of scholarly research is focused, so our surveys of the literature are also, inevitably, US-centric. We trust that, over time, further studies will be conducted in different venues so that we gain a better sense of the generalizability of findings centered on the United States and other First World venues.

Data for our analyses are drawn from standard aggregators such as the World Development Indicators (World Bank 2016) and Quality of Government (Teorell et al. 2013), from the dataset of latent variables produced by Chris Fariss and associates (2017), as well as many additional sources introduced in the course of the chapters that follow. Appendix B describes all country-level variables – their definition, sources, and descriptive statistics. Variables used in subnational analyses are described in the text or in work published separately (cited in the text).

A few data sources are fairly new and therefore may not be well known to readers. This includes Varieties of Democracy (V-Dem), the Multilevel Election Archive (MLEA), and the Global Leadership Project (GLP). In this section, we offer a thumbnail sketch of these projects in order to give the reader a better sense of the evidentiary basis of the analyses that follow.

Next, we discuss qualitative data drawn from fieldwork conducted by Veenendaal in small states and territories around the world.

Varieties of Democracy (V-Dem)

Varieties of Democracy is an effort to code various features of democracy and governance on an annual basis for all countries and many semi-sovereign entities (e.g., colonies or dependencies) in the modern era. The first wave of data collection began in 1900 and a second wave, just completed, extends coding back to 1789 for most variables.

Of the 400 or so variables, roughly half are factual in nature – coded from a diverse set of sources by the project team. The rest are coded by multiple country experts, generally about five. Most experts do not possess the requisite expertise to code the entire V-Dem question-naire, which means that a single country will typically be coded by a dozen or more experts, each working on different facets of the questionnaire. To date, V-Dem has engaged more than 2,500 country experts – roughly 60 percent of whom are nationals or permanent residents of the country they code. (Exceptions are required for a few countries where it is difficult to find in-country coders who are both qualified and independent of the governing regime.) About 35 percent are women, and more than 80 percent have PhDs or MAs and are affiliated with research institutions, think tanks, or similar organiza-tions. To ensure the security and independence of coders, their iden-tity is confidential. Coding is carried out using a specially designed online survey tool.

To combine expert ratings for a particular country/indicator/year into a single "best estimate" for each question, V-Dem employs methods inspired by the psychometric and educational testing literature. The underpinnings of these measurement models are straightforward: they use patterns of cross-rater (dis)agreement to estimate variations in relia-bility and systematic bias. In turn, these techniques make use of the bias and reliability estimates to adjust estimates of the latent – that is, only indirectly observed – concept (e.g. executive respect for the constitution, judicial independence, or property rights) in question. These statistical tools allow one to leverage the multi-coder approach to both identify and correct for measurement error, and to quantify confidence in the relia-bility of the estimates. Variation in these confidence estimates reflects situations where experts disagree, or where little information is available because few raters have coded a case.

The majority of expert-coded questions are ordinal: they require raters to rank cases on a discrete scale, with five or so response categories. To achieve scale consistency, an ordinal IRT model is fit to each question, treating coders' ordinal ratings as imperfect reflections of continuous latent concepts. While an IRT model takes ordinal values as input, its output is an interval-level estimate of the given latent trait (e.g. election violence). The IRT models allow for the possibility that coders have different thresholds for their ratings, estimating those thresholds from patterns in the data and adjusting latent trait estimates accordingly. This is especially important for a multi-rater project like V-Dem, where coders from different geographic or cultural backgrounds may apply differing standards. Finally, IRT models assume that coder reliability varies, and thus produce estimates of rater precision. These estimates are used – in combination with the amount of available data and the extent to which coders agree – to arrive at a confidence interval for each estimate.

Project documents available on the V-Dem website provide further information about the dataset, the methodology, the measurement model, the codebook, and the coding units. A book-length monograph provides an overall introduction (Coppedge et al. 2020). Hereafter, references to the Varieties of Democracy project contain only the acronym (V-Dem).

Multilevel Elections Archive (MLEA)

The Multilevel Elections Archive (MLEA) collects data for most election types, classified as (a) lower or unicameral chamber of national legislature, (b) upper chamber of national legislature, (c) gubernatorial, (d) lower or unicameral chamber of regional legislature, (e) upper chamber of regional legislature, (f) mayoral (executive serving a municipality), or (g) council (assembly serving a municipality).

Election data are compiled from a wide range of sources, including the Constituency-Level Elections Archive (CLEA) (Kollman et al. 2011), Global Elections Database (Brancati 2007), Election Passport (Lublin 2013), and additional sources specific to the United Kingdom, Brazil, Sweden, the United States, Mexico, and Russia.

The resulting sample is the largest of its kind, including 88 countries, 2,344 elections, 79,658 districts, and more than 400,000 district-level contests. A *contest* refers to a district-level race for a particular seat(s). For example, a US national election might feature one presidential contest, 33 US Senate contests, 435 US House contests, and myriad state and local contests. An election for the Israeli Knesset or the Dutch Tweede Kamer (leaving aside other offices that may be on the ballot) features one contest because there is only one (nationwide) district.

It is important to bear in mind that some countries are represented in MLEA by contests drawn from a single election while other countries are represented by tens of thousands of district-level contests. The data are also distributed unevenly through time, with more data from the contemporary period. Only the United States, Canada, Australia, and several European countries provide electoral data back to the nineteenth century. Even so, MLEA offers considerably more coverage than all extant datasets of its sort. For further discussion and descriptive statistics see Gerring, Palmer, Teorell, and Zarecki (2015), and accompanying online appendices.

Global Leadership Project (GLP)

The Global Leadership Project (GLP) is the first dataset to offer biographical information on a wide range of political elites throughout the world. Leaders are classified into ten categories: (1) the apex, (2) the next ten, (3) the executive, (4) cabinet members, (5) executive staff, (6) party leaders, (7) assembly leaders, (8) supreme court justices, (9) members of parliament (MPs), and (10) unelected persons. Most of these categories are defined in formal terms (statutory or constitutional). A few are informal, resting on the judgment of coders.

Data on these elites are gathered primarily from a lengthy questionnaire. For each leader, country experts code age, sex, marital status, ethnicity, religion, native language, additional languages spoken, place of birth, previous job experience, previous political experience, highest level of education attainment, universities attended, principal course of study, party affiliation, current position, and tenure of service. Several other questions reflect country-level characteristics such as population, the names of political parties, the names of salient ethnocultural groups, the electoral system, salaries of MPs, and so forth. (These country-level characteristics are coded either by experts or by consultation of primary and secondary sources.)

Most of the individual-level questions are coded on the basis of publicly available information, often contained on government websites or CVs. Country experts chosen for this task are generally serving as academics, graduate students, or professionals involved in some aspect of politics (such as the civil service or a nongovernmental organization [NGO]). Since the questions of interest are mostly factual – and the nonfactual questions do not have a pronounced partisan or ideological slant – it was deemed sufficient to recruit only one coder per country.

The first round of data collection for the GLP encompasses 145 sovereign and semi-sovereign nation-states and 38,085 leaders (an average of

262 per country), each of whom is coded along 31 dimensions, producing approximately 1.1 million data points in a cross-sectional format centered on 2010–13. If all questions for all leaders in the chosen 145 countries were completed, the dataset would possess roughly 1.2 million data points. Because of missing data, the current dataset includes 838,501 data points (cells in a matrix dataset). (This means that, overall, about 32 percent of the data is missing.) With these data, one can compare the characteristics of leaders within countries, across countries, and across regions – though only for a single point in time. The second round of data collection, just completed, provides two time periods for each country, and will shortly become available on the GLP website. For further information, see Gerring, Oncel, Morrison, and Pemstein (2019) and the GLP website.

Fieldwork in Small States and Territories

Statistical analyses are complemented by qualitative data gathered from research on small states and territories. "Small" is of course a matter of degrees. Our use of the term refers to polities or jurisdictions with populations of less than 1 million, a handful of whom have fewer than 100,000 inhabitants.

Over the past decade, Veenendaal has conducted ethnographic field research in Europe (Liechtenstein, Malta, San Marino), the Caribbean (Aruba, Bonaire, Curaçao, Saba, St. Kitts and Nevis, St. Maarten, St. Eustatius, Suriname), Africa (Seychelles), and the Pacific (Palau, Vanuatu). In each polity or territory, Veenendaal interviewed politicians, journalists, academics, and representatives of civil society organizations. Interviews were conducted in Dutch (Suriname and Bonaire), German (Liechtenstein), Italian (San Marino), or English. (All translations to English that appear in quoted passages are by the author.)

Respondents were selected to ensure a diversity of political views, institutional backgrounds, and other factors that might affect their perspective on politics. Appendix A includes a complete list of interviews. (Specific sources are not identified in the text in order to preserve confidentiality.) In addition to these lengthy interviews, Veenendaal observed politics at work while in residence in these microstates and consulted government documents, press reports, and secondary sources.

Although small states are generally excluded from large-N comparative research by virtue of poor data coverage and apparent inconsequence (Veenendaal & Corbett 2015), they have a central bearing on our topic, defining one tail of the demographic spectrum. With respect to population, small states are "extreme cases" (Gerring 2017).

They are also amenable to an ethnographic style of research. Due to their small dimensions and general lack of attention, small states offer highly accessible political venues. With few exceptions, even the most high-ranking public officials were willing to participate in semi-structured interviews. Respondents were generally keen to share their political experiences and views during these lengthy exchanges. None of this would have been possible in a large state, where leaders are generally much too busy to pass time with itinerant academics.

Of course, this poses a problem of sample bias if conclusions are based *only* on knowledge of small states. Thankfully, an abundance of research on larger states makes it possible to compare and contrast across these venues with relative ease.

Qualitative data from these research sites are especially helpful in providing insight into causal mechanisms that may lead from X to Y. Note that a good deal of the action in our various theoretical arguments occurs outside the framework of formal institutions and is therefore difficult to measure in a systematic fashion – especially if illicit. By triangulating across the results of our quantitative and qualitative analyses, we hope to understand both formal institutions and informal practices.

Conclusions

A virtue of our key input variable is that it is relatively easy to measure. We can usually ascertain the population of a polity or district; small errors in measurement are unlikely to affect the results presented here, and may be regarded as stochastic.

Our arguments are fairly general, i.e., applicable to a wide range of settings. Consequently, it is often possible to conduct multilevel tests of the same hypothesis. We can examine polities and districts, as well as individuals, and we can do so at multiple levels – supranational, national, and subnational. We can compare political behavior horizontally (at the same level) and vertically (across levels within the same overall unit). For example, we can compare American cities with each other, and with states and federal offices. We can also enlist varied genres of evidence – latitudinal and longitudinal, quantitative and qualitative. Insofar as a consistent finding emerges from these varied approaches we may regard that finding with greater confidence. These are the benefits of multi-method research.

However, scale is also rather intractable in other respects. To begin with, the researcher cannot manipulate the treatment, meaning that experimental approaches are unavailable, for practical and ethical reasons. No country is likely to allow researchers to adjust its borders, or the borders of states, municipalities, or districts, for the sake of social science. We can sometimes extrapolate from experiments conducted with small groups. And natural experiments occasionally arise when districts are reassigned or local governments are merged or divided. However, most of the evidence introduced in subsequent chapters is neither experimental nor quasi-experimental. It is, broadly speaking, observational.

Because potential confounders are rampant, we must measure and condition on background factors in order to block these "backdoor" paths from X to Y. Potential confounders differ across analyses so they are difficult to discuss in the abstract; we defer this discussion to the substantive chapters that follow. Where possible, we make use of instruments in a two-stage analysis. However, because of the many assumptions required, instrumental-variable analyses are regarded as robustness tests rather than baseline models. Although some outcomes can be pursued at multiple levels – national and subnational – and over long periods of time, other outcomes can be examined only at national levels, and perhaps only for a very limited period of time.

It should be clear that theory drives our empirical endeavors. We have not shied away from difficult questions simply because they are less tractable. For each theoretically important question we have attempted to weigh the evidence and reach conclusions as best we can, knowing that the evidence is stronger in some cases than in others. We try to indicate this in the chapters that follow and also in a final table that summarizes results from this book and assigns an uncertainty score to each finding (see Table 16.1).

Before concluding, it is important to address a knotty logistical problem. Readers can appreciate the difficulty of presenting a great deal of evidence – all of it quite complex and open to varying interpretations – in a parsimonious fashion. On one hand, there is a risk of presenting results without proper explanation or sufficient empirical tests – leaving it to the reader to accept the authors' word that the findings are "robust." On the other hand, there is a risk of clogging up the text with endless data tables and figures accompanied by jargon-filled discussions of methodological issues.

We have striven to find a happy medium. For each outcome that is subjected to a formal empirical analysis several models are offered. Further robustness tests are relegated to work published elsewhere. With respect to methodological issues, we have endeavored to vet all major issues in this chapter so as to tread lightly on these subjects in subsequent chapters. Further details may be found in cited work.

Part II

Scale Effects

3   Cohesion

Cohesion, as the term is used here, refers to the togetherness – or "sticking-togetherness" (Gross & Martin 1952: 553) – of a community, i.e., the sense in which members identify and behave as members of a coherent, unitary group.[1] Rousseau expresses the core idea: "The further the social bond is stretched, the weaker it gets" (Rousseau 1994[1762] Book II, ch. 9: 81).

Features associated with cohesion include homogeneity, dense networks, conformity to social norms, and high social capital. Whether these are regarded as causes or effects, or as constitutive of the concept, need not concern us here. Where cohesion is high, these associated traits should also be high. Where cohesion is low, these associated traits should also be low.

Readers may be surprised that we have packaged all of these traits together as part of a single, omnibus concept. However, they are hard to disentangle – conceptually and empirically – and they are functionally interdependent. The degree of homogeneity/heterogeneity in a community is likely to affect the density of human interconnection in that community, just as the density of networks will affect the development (over time) of greater homogeneity/heterogeneity, to take one example. Cohesion is a holistic phenomenon and for that reason merits a holistic treatment.

We regard this as a first-order sociological effect of scale, with important repercussions for political outcomes. As such, it serves primarily as a mechanism in a larger story about outcomes of a more explicitly political nature, laid out in subsequent chapters. If this were a sociological treatise we would no doubt be interested in disentangling the various elements of cohesion, but since this is a political treatise it suits our purposes to lump them together.

In any case, our "lumpy" treatment has a distinguished lineage, echoing Ferdinand Tönnies' (2011[1887]) distinction between *Gemeinschaft*

---

[1] This is similar to the definition proposed by Festinger, Schachter, and Back (1950: 164): "the total field of forces which act on members to remain in the group."

Figure 3.1 Scale effects on cohesion

and *Gesellschaft* and Emile Durkheim's (1976) distinction between *mechanical* and *organic* solidarity. Variously framed, this core distinction has occupied anthropologists and sociologists for centuries and has inspired a large body of research, a small sample of which is cited in the pages that follow.

With this broad understanding of the concept, we argue that scale attenuates cohesion. Following Simmel (1902a: 5–6), small communities are subject to centripetal tendencies while large communities are subject to centrifugal tendencies. A raft of contemporary studies have made similar claims (D. Anckar 1999; Aubé, Rousseau, & Tremblay 2011; Bollen & Hoyle 1990; Denters et al. 2014: ch. 4; Moody & White 2003; Soboroff 2012; Wasserman 1982; Wilson & Baldassare 1996). Since we cannot explore all facets of cohesion in this short chapter, we focus on three elements with presumed relevance to politics: *heterogeneity*, *connectedness*, and *deviance*. The gist of our argument is summarized in Figure 3.1, though readers should bear in mind that these aspects of cohesion interact with each other.

Heterogeneity

Social heterogeneity, aka diversity, refers here to any set of beliefs, values, and identities of relevance to politics. They might be cultural, i.e., ethnic, religious, linguistic, or racial. They might be economic, i.e., diversification among sectors, products, occupations, and social classes. Or they might be ideological, i.e., variations in political preferences. In all likelihood, they will be some combination of these.

With this understanding, we argue that larger communities are apt to be more heterogeneous. Specifically, for any given attribute there is likely to be a greater *range of variation* in a large community than in a small community.

To make this point in a more explicit fashion let us imagine that a set of political communities is generated by drawing samples randomly from a population. These communities might be nation-states drawn from the population of the entire world or districts drawn from the population of a nation-state.

Let us further stipulate that some of the samples are small and others are large, generating small and large communities. Within the large communities we would expect to find more ethnicities, more languages, more religions, more ideologies, more economic sectors, and so forth.

Of course, if one is looking at a limited number of features that are present in every sample, their *distribution* will be similar across communities of various sizes. Each group in the population will register the same proportion in all samples, large or small (on average).

However, rare features in the general population are more likely to appear in a large sample than in a small sample. If we think of attributes as infinite ways of identifying discrete groups, there will be more groups (a larger set of social categories) in a large sample than in a small sample.

The point is bolstered when one considers the *viability* of social groups. Miniscule groups may not be large enough to sustain themselves demographically, and are likely to die out or diffuse over time. Miniscule groups are also at pains to influence political outcomes. Larger groups, by contrast, are likely to be more enduring and more viable – economically, politically, sociologically, and demographically. They can maintain organizations (e.g., clubs, fraternities, churches, trade associations, hobbyist groups, newspapers) and social practices (e.g., street festivals, holidays, protests, religious rituals). The larger the population pool, the more of these activities can be sustained. This reinforces our supposition that larger populations are able to create and sustain greater internal heterogeneity.

Large communities, by virtue of their size, may even *encourage* greater heterogeneity. In a community of millions, it is often hard to find one's place. This sort of community is necessarily diffuse, by virtue of being so encompassing. *Gemeinschaft* does not come naturally in a very large group. Indeed, a case can be made that humans' ability to maintain meaningful relationships is limited by the size of our neocortex; accordingly, core communities have an optimal size measured in the hundreds rather than the thousands or millions (Dunbar 1992; Dunbar & Sosis 2017). Whatever the reason, it appears that individuals within a very large community often look for smaller units that form a tighter fit to their interests and values and that provide a stronger sense of membership and belonging.[2]

---

[2] Typically, subgroups within a larger population form among people who live in proximity to each other. However, distinctive social identities sometimes persist across vast territories, as is the case with diaspora communities. In the modern era, advanced

Although our discussion has focused on social groups, the same relationship between scale and diversity should also exist among economic sectors. Kuznets (1963: 16) writes: "if we compared two nations, . . . one small and the other large, we would expect the range of economic activities to be wider in the latter than in the former." A larger society provides a larger base of workers, with a larger range of skills, a larger pool of capital to draw upon, and a larger group of consumers to sell products to. Together, this should encourage the development of a more diversified economy.

Evidence

A long tradition of sociological work examines the connection between community size and heterogeneity (Black 1974; Coser 1956: 144; Hwang & Murdock 1988; Milgram 1970; Sadalla 1978; Simmel 1950: 397; T. Wilson 1986; Wirth 1938). Of this voluminous work we touch on only a few studies, complemented by Veenendaal's small-state ethnography.

Religion is a common focus of community studies. Ogburn and Duncan (1964: 142) report that the size of American cities is monotonically related to the number of religious denominations located in those cities. In 1936, small cities (pop. 25,000–50,000) housed an average of 24 denominations while big cities (pop. 1 million+) housed more than 100.

Ideology is harder to define, but nonetheless essential to our topic. Levendusky and Pope (2010) exploit survey data from the Cooperative Congressional Survey Study (CCES) to estimate ideological diversity in states and congressional districts across the United States. The latter is measured (a) as the *variance* of responses within a community (state or district) and (b) as the distance between the two *primary groups* within a community. With these measures, the authors conduct a multivariate regression analysis to explore various demographic features that might explain heterogeneity across US communities. Among a set of twelve predictors, only population (log) is found to be a significant predictor of both measures of heterogeneity, validating our claim that scale and diversity are strongly associated.

The absence of strong ideological differences in small settings emerges as one of the most robust findings in our qualitative research. Interview respondents in all small states and territories acknowledged that programmatic differences between parties or individual candidates are scarce and

communication and transportation networks facilitate non-proximal networks. In these respects, population – rather than territory – may be the relevant measure of size.

difficult to identify; instead, politics revolves primarily around personalities and family/client groupings. When asked about differences between political parties in San Marino, a high-ranking public official answered,

Frankly? I see none. Formally, like in Italy, we can consider two blocs: one of Christian-democratic origin, the other one of socialist origin, and previously a third one of communist origin. But I see no difference. ... You asked me why you would vote for the one or the other. This is because I know you, or maybe I trust in you because we were in school together, [or] we worked together for a while. I consider you to be an honest person or maybe I consider you as a possible solution of one of my problems.

As a third measure, we turn to what is undoubtedly the most common empirical approach to heterogeneity, grounded in ethnic and/or linguistic identities. Sometimes, these concepts are distinguished; sometimes, they are considered together, with language being regarded as a sign of ethnic identity. We use the composite term "ethnolinguistic" to encompass both elements.

In Table 3.1, we regress various measures of ethnic and/or linguistic diversity on population (log). Our benchmark model includes a single geographic covariate: latitude, measured as the distance of a country from the equator (log). This is widely regarded as a factor in economic and political development, and also shows a strong relationship with our measures of heterogeneity. In a second specification, we add a vector of region dummies. Both specifications are intended to be minimal, including only factors that are geographic and therefore strictly exogenous. Since measures of ethnolinguistic identity are fairly stable over time, we focus our analyses on a single year – 2000.

The first set of regression tests focuses on a *distributional* measure of heterogeneity, the Herfindahl index of fractionalization, which measures the probability that two randomly chosen individuals from a population will be members of the same group. Measures of ethnic, linguistic, and ethnolinguistic fractionalization are drawn from work by Alesina et al. (2003) and Fearon (2003). It will be seen that there is scarcely any relationship between the size of countries and their heterogeneity by this measure, confirming our hunch that the distributional aspects of heterogeneity are unrelated to population size (see also D. Anckar 1999).

Next, we examine the *absolute number* of groups within each country, using data on linguistic groups compiled by Michalopoulos (2012) from the World Language Mapping System (2006). This is essential for our purposes as it counts all languages spoken by more than 1,000 inhabitants. Other sources, including Alesina et al. and Fearon, generally count only groups that are fairly large in proportion to the total population. This

Table 3.1 *Ethnolinguistic heterogeneity*

	Distributional measures						Absolute measures		
Outcome	Ethnic Fract.		Linguistic Fract.		Ethnolinguistic Fract.		Number of Groups (log)		
Source	(Alesina et al. 2003)		(Alesina et al. 2003)		(Fearon 2003)		(Michalopoulos 2012)		
Estimator	OLS	OLS	OLS	OLS	OLS	OLS	OLS	OLS	2SLS
Model	1	2	3	4	5	6	7	8	9
Population (log)	0.018*	0.008	0.017	0.012	−0.006	0.020*	0.506***	0.562***	0.810***
	(0.098)	(0.012)	(0.011)	(0.012)	(0.012)	(0.011)	(0.062)	(0.069)	(0.094)
Latitude (log)	✓		✓		✓		✓	✓	✓
Region dummies		✓		✓		✓		✓	✓
Countries	181	181	175	175	153	153	149	149	149
R^2	0.146	0.361	0.074	0.370	0.219	0.476	0.411	0.589	0.545

Units of analysis: countries. *Year:* 2000 (approximate). Constant omitted. *Estimators:* OLS (ordinary least squares), 2SLS (two-stage least squares, using land area and agricultural suitability as instruments), robust standard errors. *** $p < 0.01$, ** $p < 0.05$, * $p < 0.10$ (two-tailed tests)

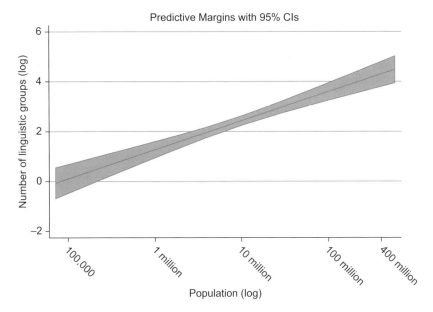

Figure 3.2 Number of ethnolinguistic groups, predicted values

Predicted values for number of linguistic groups, log (Y), as population (log) changes, surrounded by 95 percent confidence interval. Based on Model 8, Table 3.1, with covariates set to sample means.

truncates the available data in an arbitrary – and for our purposes, biased – fashion, as it means that small groups are more likely to be counted in a small country (where they comprise a sizeable proportion of the total population) than in a large country (where their proportion is negligible). Indeed, the number of languages per country counted by Michalopoulos far outstrips the number of languages counted by other sources.

To identify the relationship between heterogeneity and population we begin by replicating our previous specifications. Model 7 includes only latitude (log). Model 8 adds a vector of regional dummies, which we regard as our benchmark specification. In Model 9, we build on the benchmark to conduct an instrumental variable analysis, where territorial area and agricultural suitability serve as instruments for population. All three tests reveal a strong association between population and linguistic diversity.

To gain a sense for what this means, we graph predicted values for the outcome in Figure 3.2. Here, one can see that a change in population from 100,000 to 1 million is projected to increase the number of linguistic groups from one to four. A population increase from 1 million to

10 million is associated with an increase from four to thirteen. And so forth.

In additional robustness tests (available upon request) we include all other variables identified by Michalopoulos (2012) as potential causes of linguistic diversity in our benchmark model (seriatim). This includes (a) year of independence, (b) average temperature 1961–90, (c) average monthly precipitation 1961–90, (d) distance from coast, (e) average elevation across regions, (f) standard deviation of elevation across regions, (g) dispersion in elevation across regions, (h) standard deviation of agricultural suitability across regions, (i) migratory distance from Addis Ababa, (j) percent indigenous (people who can trace their ancestry back to AD 1500), (k) dispersion in agricultural suitability across regions of a country, (l) years since transition to sedentary agriculture, (m) population density (AD 1500), and (n) population density (present). None of these additional covariates disturbs the estimated relationship between population and linguistic diversity in our benchmark model, and most are not robustly correlated with the outcome.

Discussion

Stepping back from the empirics, let us consider how heterogeneity features in the broader argument of this book. For us, heterogeneity is a downstream effect of scale. But for some readers, heterogeneity may appear to be the real cause lurking behind our analyses. From this perspective, population is a proxy for diversity. This is an important objection, so we want to spend some time explaining and defending our treatment of the subject.

First, there is a question of causal priority in the data-generating process (in the real world). An increase (decrease) in the population of a political community should result in an increase (decrease) in heterogeneity. As a country grows, it should diversify, as discussed. The reverse, however, is not true. An increase (decrease) in heterogeneity has no apparent implications for the size of a political community. From this perspective, it is plausible to treat heterogeneity as a downstream effect of scale.

Second, there is a question of potential confounders. In Chapter 2 we discussed various obstacles to causal inference associated with population, concluding that the subject was difficult but not intractable. By contrast, heterogeneity is more susceptible to spurious associations. Note that heterogeneity refers to identities, values, and beliefs, which are affected by virtually everything under the sun – including politics, the outcome of interest. It is widely acknowledged that countries with modern economies and strong states are likely to be more homogeneous, for example. And there is very little sense in which preferences can be treated as exogenous. So it is difficult to analyze the causal impact of heterogeneity on politics without a great many strong – and generally unprovable – assumptions.

Finally, there are obstreperous problems of measurement. While population is fairly easy to operationalize, heterogeneity is subject to insuperable barriers. Scholars do not agree on how to conceptualize and measure social identity – e.g., language, ethnicity, race, social class (Abdelal et al. 2009). Other elements of heterogeneity such as those associated with ideology are even more difficult to measure – though, arguably more important for political outcomes. Typically, scholars treat variation in ascriptive characteristics as a proxy for ideological characteristics, but this is obviously not a very satisfactory solution. People of different languages, ethnicities, and races may agree, and people with the same ascriptive characteristics may disagree.

Related, there are problems of aggregation. To fully encompass all elements of heterogeneity one would have to identify which elements of identity and ideology matter for a question, develop indicators for each, measure them across relevant political communities, and then aggregate them into a single index (or several noncollinear indices). Any attempt to achieve this is bound to be ridden with assumptions, each of which may be questioned. This is not to say that it is invalid. It is to say, rather, that since there are so many ways to skin this cat, any result is subject to important caveats about the way the key concept is conceptualized and measured. There are equally serious problems of data availability and conceptual equivalence across diverse contexts, inhibiting the measurement of heterogeneity globally and historically.

Leaving these difficulties aside, let us consider the matter empirically using data that are currently available and widely used – namely, data on ethnic, linguistic, and religious fractionalization (a distributional measure of heterogeneity). Our concern here is with fractionalization as a potential confounder in the analyses that follow. Could population be a proxy for fractionalization? If heterogeneity is measured in the standard fashion – through a Herfindahl index of fractionalization – the cross-country correlation with population is slight, as shown in the first part of Table 3.1. Thus, adding a measure of ethnic, linguistic, or religious fractionalization to any of the models shown in subsequent pages of this book is unlikely to affect the relationship between scale and the outcome very much. And, in fact, it does not (see, e.g., Table 12.1), as these factors are virtually orthogonal to one another at country levels.

Recall that our argument for heterogeneity as a downstream effect of scale hinges on a nonstandard conceptualization of heterogeneity. Rather than distributional measures such as the Herfindahl index we treat heterogeneity as the *number of sizeable (nontrivial) groups*. Here, the empirical relationship to scale is quite strong, as shown in the second part of Table 3.1. And here, we would expect the inclusion of a heterogeneity covariate to substantially attenuate the estimated impact of scale on various political outcomes. Of course, we do not want to include downstream factors in our models, as it introduces posttreatment bias. And since the measurement of heterogeneity is fraught (for reasons discussed earlier), we hesitate to conduct a mediation analysis as it is bound to be misleading.

To recapitulate, we are not arguing against the importance of heterogeneity, however it might be conceptualized and measured. We are convinced that this factor has important implications for politics, as many studies indicate (e.g., Alesina et al. 2003; Alesina, Baqir, & Easterly 1999; Lieberman 2009). But we see no reason to conclude that scale effects are *reducible* to heterogeneity, and certainly not to distributional measures of heterogeneity (such as the Herfindahl index).

Connectedness

The scale of a political community plays an important role in structuring interpersonal contact among members of that community. Small communities tend to have denser social networks (Coser 1956; P. Fischer 1953; Mayhew & Levinger 1976b; Milgram 1970; Simmel 1950; Wirth 1938), and a wealth of "weak ties" (Granovetter 1973). Citizens are likely to meet face to face in social settings – weddings, funerals, holidays, sporting events, schools, and clubs, and in the street. They are likely to intermarry, and they are likely to have interlocking networks of friends, family, and colleagues. In a small society, "everybody knows everybody" – if not personally, then one or two degrees removed (Corbett 2015b; Laslett 1956). As a minister in the government of Liechtenstein remarked,

We are a population of only 37,000 people, most of them related by blood or by other relationships somehow. We know each other, most people know each other, so when you go out to the street you will always meet somebody who you personally know.

By contrast, larger communities are likely to be more anonymous, impersonal, and perhaps even atomized (Wirth 1938: 13). Or they may be separated into distinct groups that interact primarily with each other rather than with other groups (Fischer 1973; Wirth 1938: 11), generating "bonding" but not "bridging" social capital (Putnam 2007) and perhaps separated spatially (but see Hwang & Murdock 1988). While each group may have a high level of internal cohesion, the community as a whole is likely to be fragmented.

The interconnectedness fostered by small scale should, in turn, foster a common sense of identity, attachment, and social trust (Wheelan 2009; but see Kasarda & Janowitz 1974), and prevent the development of hardened social cleavages. It should also mitigate deviance and free-riding (Albanese & Van Fleet 1985; Freudenburg 1986; Latane 1981; Levine & Moreland 1990; Simmel 1902a, 1902b; Soboroff 2012: 3), as members can monitor one another easily and enforce social norms (Carpenter 2007). This issue is taken up at greater length later.

The enforcement of social norms may be viewed positively or negatively – as a pressure to conform to the group and to reject outsiders. "Strong in-group bonds sustain rigidity and bigotry," note Hibbing and Theiss-Morse (2002: 186; see also Baldacchino 2012; Blau 1974; Mutz 2002). Connectedness is not always a good thing. But it nonetheless has important ramifications.

A behavioral indicator of disconnectedness may be found in the tendency to factionalism and schism, which Madison suggested (in Federalist #10) was more likely to become manifest in larger communities. Supporting that hypothesis, a study of US churches over the past century finds that the most persistent predictor of schism is the size of the church body, with larger bodies being more prone to schism (Liebman, Sutton, & Wuthnow 1988). Likewise, a cursory review of parties, social movements, and other voluntary associations suggests that larger bodies are generally more prone to factionalism (Soboroff 2012: 3), though the issue has not been widely researched.

Deviance

Cohesion should reduce deviance, a point widely noted by scholars (Albanese & Van Fleet 1985; Freudenburg 1986; Latane 1981; Levine & Moreland 1990; Simmel 1908; Soboroff 2012: 3).

A good deal of attention has been devoted to this question with respect to criminal behavior, arguably the most damaging form of deviance. The expected positive relationship between scale and crime (Wirth 1938) appears in most cross-sectional analyses (Glaeser & Sacerdote 1999). However, the empirical relationship is equivocal in longitudinal analyses (Archer & Gartner 1984), an issue that has yet to be fully resolved (Rotolo

& Tittle 2006). It could be that here, as in other settings, increases and decreases in population are associated with potential confounders (see Chapter 2). For example, a municipality that experiences a growing population is likely to be well governed and have a dynamic economy, thus attracting ambitious, hard-working migrants, who are gainfully employed and less prone to criminal activity. Likewise, a municipality with a shrinking population is likely to have the opposite set of characteristics, and may lose its most ambitious, hard-working citizens through out-migration. These sorts of factors – most of which are resistant to measurement – may affect crime rates, biasing estimates for the regressor of interest (population).

Whatever the actual causal relationship between population and deviance might be, we argue that there is likely to be an even stronger relationship between scale and *perceptions* of deviance. This is important because perceptions of deviance feed into political trust and many other outcomes of concern to the quality of governance.

In making this argument, we assume that judgments about the quality of a society or government are strongly affected by pathologies, i.e., actions that deviate from widely shared social norms about what is acceptable. Crime, terrorism, and corruption are good examples. If citizens are aware of specific instances of these pathologies – an especially violent crime, an act of terrorism, or an incidence of grand corruption – this may change attitudes about the community where the event occurred.

Now, suppose that miscreants and malcontents (e.g., criminals, corrupt officials, and insurrectionists) are evenly distributed throughout the world. Small and large communities thus contain the same share of deviants and the same share of deviant activity. However, large communities will contain more deviants and more deviant activities than small communities (Ogburn & Duncan 1964). If deviance is equally distributed across populations, it describes the same *share* of people in both communities but a larger *number* of people in the large community. The key point is that raw numbers may matter more in coloring people's perceptions because of the difficulty of distinguishing between *incidents* and *incidence rates*.

Consider the topic of crime. Since there is more criminal activity in a large community there are more events – and more gruesome events – to discuss. It is no accident that "Son of Sam," the famous serial killer, appeared in New York rather than Hoboken, New Jersey. Statistically speaking, it was 150 times more likely, as New York is roughly that much larger than Hoboken. Inhabitants of large communities are likely to conclude that crime is a serious problem, while those in a small community may conclude that there is not much going on and not much danger to worry about. Similar ratios may be inferred across nation-states. On the assumption of "equal distribution of deviants," there are 136,400 times as many miscreants in China as in Tuvalu.

It is not hard to see why citizens of large communities might come to perceive their community as especially violent and their government as incapable or even complicit. Indeed, many studies have shown that perceptions of criminality are higher in larger urban areas than in smaller urban or rural areas – though, of course, this may be due to other factors (Baumer 1978; Boggs 1971; Braungart, Braungart, & Hoyer 1980; Christenson & Dillman 1974; Clemente & Kleiman, 1977; Franklin, Franklin, & Fearn 2008; Lebowitz 1975; Sacco 1985).

One might also consider the topic of civil conflict, which we take up in Chapter 14. Studies have shown that civil war is more common in large countries than in small countries. But this may be largely a product of the fact that there are more potential civil warriors – i.e., groups with a potential motive for revolt – in a large country.

Consider, finally, the topic of corruption, which we take up in Chapter 6. Most measures of this concept rely on respondents – ordinary citizens, businesspeople, or experts – to judge the level of corruption in a community. Because respondents don't know how prevalent corruption really is, they rely on reports of corruption that are filtered through the media or through word of mouth. Such reports generally focus attention on negative outliers – outrageous stories of sloth or sleaze. (Positive outliers, e.g., the super-diligent civil servant who works nights and weekends and refuses all bribe opportunities, are hard to identify and not very note-worthy.) In a large country there are more officials, and hence more corrupt officials (by the assumption of equal distribution of deviants). If the judiciary and the news media are doing their jobs, there will also be more incidents of corruption to report. And this, in turn, may lead respondents to believe there is more corruption overall, even though there may be no more corruption *per capita* than in a small country.

The mass media magnify this perceptual bias. Newspapers report crime rates occasionally, e.g., once a year when government bureaus issue their annual report. But they report specific crimes *every day*. The same may be said for casual conversation – in cafes, workplaces, and around kitchen tables. Few are interested in discussing aggregate trends; specific crimes, by contrast, are enthralling. So we do not view the media as the source of the problem. Media reports reflect a widespread bias in human perception that would exist even in the absence of a professional cadre of journalists.

One might suppose that this bias would be rectified by another human characteristic: the propensity to find novel and unusual things to talk about. In a small community, where "nothing happens," news may be constructed from the most trivial events. In this atmosphere, the smallest peccadillos seem to receive outsized attention, generating tempests in a teapot. Likewise, in a large community, where crime and other deviant activity seem ubiquitous, citizens may become inured. After a while, nothing shocks them.

However, there is no reason to assume that enhanced sensitivity – or habituation – to deviance changes norms of what is acceptable and unacceptable. Exposure to violent crime does not make crime morally acceptable. People living in high-crime areas may become inured to lurid reportage, but this does not mean that they will come to regard murder as an acceptable way of life. Likewise, people living in very corrupt political environments may be bored with the latest report of malfeasance, but this does not mean that they will come to regard corruption as justified. Even in Nigeria, where webs of corruption seem to implicate virtually everyone, there is considerable outrage (D. Smith 2010).

We assume, therefore, that understandings of what is and is not acceptable are more or less the same in small and large communities. However, these realities are differently viewed. Citizens of large communities are likely to reach more pessimistic conclusions with respect to the quality of their society and their political system by virtue of the constant drumbeat of alarming reportage. Citizens of small communities, where less is going on, are likely to have greater faith in their fellow citizens and their government. If so, size matters in a perceptual fashion, even if the causal effect of population on incidence *rates* of deviant behavior is hard to determine.

Summary

Table 3.2 summarizes extant studies, as well as our own analyses, on topics related to social cohesion. Readers will recall that this is a large topic and rather difficult to bound. Many additional studies – mostly from sociology and social psychology – might be added to this inventory. However, we doubt that they would change the overall picture, which points fairly strongly in one direction: size is inversely correlated with cohesion.

The first dimension, *heterogeneity*, is complicated, as the concept can be conceptualized and measured in many ways. Nonetheless, the results posted in Table 3.2 suggest a fairly strong consensus. Studies focused on subnational units – denominations, communities, high schools, states, and congressional districts – show a strong relationship between scale and heterogeneity. This, however, may be a product of selective membership

Table 3.2 *Scale and cohesion: Inventory of analyses*

Indicators	Countries	Treatment units	Years	Units of analysis	Research design	Effect	Study
Heterogeneity							
Social heterogeneity	United States	Local communities (100)	(1)	Individuals (1,468)	Cross-sectional	↑	Wilson 1986
Ideational heterogeneity	United States	States (50), districts (435)	(1)	States (50), districts (435)	Cross-sectional	↑	Levendusky & Pope 2010
Ethnic, religious fractionalization	(119)	Countries (119)	(1)	Countries (119)	Cross-sectional	∅	D. Anckar 1999
*Ethnic, linguistic fractionalization	(181)	Countries (181)	(1)	Countries (181)	Cross-sectional	∅	Table 3.1
*Linguistic groups (N)	(149)	Countries (149)	(1)	Countries (149)	Cross-sectional	↑	Table 3.1
*Not speaking official language (%)	(144)	Countries (144)	(1)	Countries (144)	Cross-sectional	↑	Table 3.1
Connectedness							
Cohesion perception	United States	College (1), city (1)	(1)	Individuals (102; 119)	Cross-sectional	↓	Bollen & Hoyle 1990
Social embeddedness	(4)	Municipalities (228)	(1)	Individuals (6,212)	Cross-sectional	↓	Denters et al. 2014
Trust, cohesion, commitment	United States	Individuals (50)	(1)	Individuals (50)	Experiment	↓	Soboroff 2012
Community attachment	United States	Sample points (74)	(1)	Individuals (2,164)	Cross-sectional	↓	Wasserman 1982
Sense of community	United States	County (1)	(1)	Individuals (1,017)	Cross-sectional	↓	Wilson & Baldassare 1996
Group intimacy	United States	University (1)	(1)	Students (75)	Cross-sectional	↓	Fischer 1953

Table 3.2 *(cont.)*

Indicators	Countries	Treatment units	Years	Units of analysis	Research design	Effect	Study
Group productivity	United States	Work groups (329)	(1)	Members (2,623)	Cross-sectional	→	Wheelan 2009
Community attachment	United Kingdom	Districts (100)	(1)	Individuals (2,199)	Cross-sectional	∅	Kasarda & Janowitz 1974
Density of acquaintanceship	United States	Communities (4)	(10)	Individuals (597)	Cross-sectional	→	Freudenburg 1986
Church schisms	United States	Denominations (175)	(90)	Individuals (559)	Cross sectional	↑	Liebman, Sutton, & Wuthnow 1988
Deviance – behavior							
Counterproductive behavior	United States	Work teams (97)	(1)	Individuals (341)	Cross-sectional	→	Aubé, Rousseau, & Tremblay 2011
Crime	United States	Cities (634)	(3)	Individuals (18,106)	Cross-sectional	↑	Glaeser & Sacerdote 1999
Homicide	United States	Cities (?)	(4)	Cities (?)	Cross-sectional	↑	Archer & Gartner 1984
Homicide	(34)	Countries (34), cities (34)	(74)	Country- & city-years (?)	Cross-sectional	↑	Archer & Gartner 1984
Crime	United States	Cities (348)	(30)	Cities (348)	Cross-sectional	∅	Rotolo & Tittle 2006
Deviance – perceptions							
Fear of crime	United States	Cities (?)	(3)	Individuals (1,499)	Cross-sectional	∅	Braungart, Braungart, & Hoyer 1980
Fear of crime	United States	Cities (?)	(1)	Individuals (842)	Cross-sectional	↑	Boggs 1971
Fear of crime	United States	Cities (?)	(2)	Individuals (2,700)	Cross-sectional	↑	Clemente & Kleiman 1977

Fear of crime	United States	Cities (21)	(1)	Individuals (2,599)	Cross-sectional	Ø	Franklin, Franklin, & Fearn 2008
Concern for law and order	United States	Cities (?)	(1)	Individuals (3,101)	Cross-sectional	↑	Christenson & Dillman 1974
Perception of crime	Canada	Cities (7)	(1)	Individuals (879)	Cross-sectional	↑	Sacco 1985

Treatment units: units exhibiting variation in scale. *Years*: number of years over which data are collected – not to be confused with the frequency of observations, as data may or may not be annual and may be averaged across years. *Research design*: the main, or benchmark, research design – classified as cross-sectional (where the analysis is driven primarily by variation across units) or panel (where the analysis is driven primarily by variation through time). *Effect*: scale effect is positive (↑), negative (↓), curvilinear (∩), or null/ambiguous (Ø). A scale effect is considered significant if it passes a modest bar of statistical significance, i.e., p < 0.10 (two-tailed test) in the benchmark model. Number of countries, treatment units, years, or observations in parentheses.

(sorting), and thus it is difficult to interpret as a causal effect of size. Studies focused on nation-states show no relationship if heterogeneity is measured with a distributional index (e.g., fractionalization) but a strong relationship if measured by the total number of social groups. Because recent migration patterns across countries account for a small share of the total population, and because this sorting process works against our hypothesis (since small countries are apt to have a larger share of migrants), we regard this as strong evidence for the argument that scale enhances heterogeneity (properly understood).

Evidence and theory are especially strong for the second dimension – *connectedness*. Only one study out of ten fails to reject the null.

The third dimension, *deviance*, is difficult to conceptualize and measure. Nonetheless, some tentative findings emerge. In small groups, size seems to enhance the probability of deviant behavior (Aubé et al. 2011). But it is not clear that these pathologies are realized in larger communities organized for political purposes. To measure deviance in this context scholars usually rely upon measures of criminal activity. Unfortunately, crimes are not always reported, and one must worry about systematic error. Moreover, it is difficult to separate the background characteristics of communities from their scale: urban areas, which tend to be large, are quite different from rural areas, which tend to be small. Even so, most cross-sectional studies suggest that larger communities have more crime. However, these results are not entirely stable and seem to depend upon model specification. Panel analyses are perhaps even more prone to confounding since factors that drive increases and decreases in population may also affect crime.

In any case, we have argued that the issue of deviance is quintessentially a matter of perception. Although there has been less focus on this aspect of deviance, there are good reasons to expect a robust (positive) relationship between perceptions of crime and other deviant behavior and the size of a community. This is, indeed, what studies seem to show, as tracked in the final section of Table 3.2.

4   Representatives

A representative, for present purposes, is a public official who purports to represent a group of citizens. We leave aside for the moment any judgments about whether, or to what extent, they actually achieve this goal – an issue taken up in the next chapter. All we are concerned with at present is the claim to represent and its acceptance by at least some of the people regarded as constituents (Rehfeld 2006).

Who does this broadly defined category include? It certainly includes those who are elected to public office, whether or not those elections are free and fair. Note that elected leaders in electoral authoritarian states, where there is no party competition, claim to represent their constituents, and we suspect that at least some of those constituents regard this claim as credible. In common parlance, members of a legislature are regarded as representatives, suggesting that they are expected to play a representational role, even if unelected. The category "representative" may also include unelected officials if they are expected to perform a representative function. For example, an advisory or lawmaking body such as a committee may be appointed in order to represent specific constituencies. Heads of state and heads of government, who perform important ceremonial or lawmaking functions, are supposed to represent state interests in foreign and domestic affairs. They too are representatives, in common parlance. However, we would probably not regard bureaucrats, military officials, and (unelected) judges as representatives since they owe their loyalty to those who appoint them and to the body of statutory and constitutional law from which their authority derives and do not have constituents in the usual sense of the term.

Our particular interest is in the *number* of representatives in a polity. Since heads of state and government are usually singular – at most a small handful, as in the Swiss collegial presidency or the Andorran co-princes – our question may be reduced with only slight loss of information to the size of the legislature or the size of the cabinet. We assume that all members of a legislature or a cabinet perform a representational function (in principle).

As it happens, there is considerable variance in the size of legislatures around the world, suggesting that this feature may structure political behavior in important ways. At the present time, the Micronesian Congress, with 14 members, is the smallest lower house, while China's National People's Congress, with 2,980 members, is the largest.[1] Less variance can be found among regional and local governments, though tenfold differences are not unusual. Cabinets vary in size from five (Liechtenstein) to forty-seven (Sri Lanka).

Why should we care about the number of representatives in a polity?

A larger legislature or cabinet offers greater scope for representing a diversity of groups and interests (Chapter 5), and a larger legislature may also enhance participation, if it means that constituencies are smaller (Chapter 7). Larger representative bodies may also encourage greater particularism (Chapter 6) and greater overall spending (Weingast, Shepsle, & Johnsen 1981; but see Pettersson-Lidbom 2012). A smaller legislature may encourage greater contestation if it means there are larger districts (Chapter 8). In a variety of ways, small legislatures seem to operate differently from large legislatures (Baldwin 2013). So the size of a representative body is not inconsequential.

In this chapter we explore why some representative bodies are larger than others, with particular focus on the role of scale. In the first section, we lay out a number of possible explanations for this relationship. In the second section, we test the theory as it applies to the size of legislatures. In the third section, we test the theory as it pertains to the size of cabinets. In the final section, we explore the ramifications of legislative size for the *representation ratio* – the number of citizens each representative represents.

Theory

Most writers who have addressed the issue assume that the number of representatives ought to grow with the size of the population they are intended to represent. But why, exactly, is this so? The reasoning has mostly to do with the capacity of a body to perform its designated function, i.e., to represent.

Representativeness, an issue taken up in the next chapter, involves representing the characteristics of a population in a body that thereby can "stand for" the people – their values, interests, and so forth (Pitkin 1967). Of course, the correspondence between citizens and their representatives is never perfect. The only way it could be perfect is if

---

[1] Inter-Parliamentary Union database: www.ipu.org/.

individuals represented themselves, e.g., in an assembly of citizens – the *absence* of representation. Anything short of that will probably involve some sacrifice of fealty between citizens and representatives.

The degree of sacrifice depends on the size of the representative body. The larger the body, the more opportunities it has to represent the variegated features of a population. This does not mean that large bodies are *necessarily* more representative. Size, by itself, does not assure representativeness. However, the size of a body imposes a hard constraint on the representative capacity of that body. The point becomes clear if one considers the limiting case – a representative body of one (e.g., a president or monarch). Evidently, it is impossible for a single individual to adequately represent the features of a population that is not entirely homogeneous. As the body expands, it becomes capable of representing greater diversity.

Consider the matter from the perspective of sampling theory. There is always some loss of information when one tries to capture the characteristics of a population in a sample. Rare characteristics are especially problematic. Imagine a body of n members intended to represent some characteristic (e.g., race, ethnicity, language, occupation) of Z individuals in a population of N citizens. If Z/N is less than $1/n$, then this characteristic cannot be accurately represented in the body. Of course, the feature can be *over*represented, but this creates another representational problem: namely, Z is granted greater weight in the body than they deserve.

Thus, we expect that the size of a representative body has a substantial impact on its ability to represent its intended constituency. Larger bodies have greater representative capacity, all things being equal.

It stands to reason, therefore, that if the size of a population grows – along with increasing diversity (Chapter 3) – demands to expand the size of existing representative bodies become likely. Likewise, in a situation where no representative bodies are currently in place (e.g., in the case of a state or local polity recently granted self-rule), the size of the population will affect the choice of how large to make that representative body. Larger populations are likely to demand larger legislatures and cabinets.

This is not simply a matter of "pressure from below," though one can imagine that smaller groups, and groups who feel excluded under the status quo or worry that they will be excluded in the future, will be especially vocal. One must also consider the ambitions of powerful elites, each of whom expects a seat at the table. If such leaders – and the groups they represent – are randomly distributed, we expect more of them in a larger population. Again, this should translate into pressure to expand the size of representative bodies.

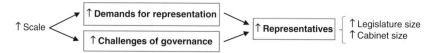

Figure 4.1 Scale effects on representatives

A second possible pathway concerns the challenges of governance. A larger population presumably introduces greater complexity into the process of making and implementing the laws of the land. If we take seriously the role of legislators as lawmakers we must acknowledge that the demands placed upon them will grow as a community grows. This means that they will need more people to staff committees, to write legislation, to perform administrative and oversight tasks, and to carry out other duties. Some of these tasks may be delegated to subordinates, but others require representatives who are duly invested with lawmaking power. Insofar as a larger legislature or cabinet brings more people, with wider fields of experience and broader networks, into the political process, it may enhance the quality of governance.

In summary, the interests of a variety of groups – some of them classifiable as citizens and others as political elites – coincide on the question of scale and the size of representative bodies. Our theory, featuring two principal pathways, is illustrated in Figure 4.1.

A Sublinear Relationship

We have set forth a simple argument for why there ought to be a monotonic relationship between scale and the number of representatives in a polity. Yet this is unlikely to be a linear relationship. Increases in the size of a population and the size of its legislature or cabinet are unlikely to match each other one for one. We do not expect China's legislature to be 136,400 times the size of Tuvalu's, for example. Rather, the impact of scale is likely to diminish as scale increases, generating a sublinear relationship.

This is what we project for all scale relationships, and it is incorporated into our logarithmic measurement of population (Chapter 2). Note that an increase of 10,000 represents a doubling of Tuvalu's population while it represents a tiny increase (proportionately) of China's billion-plus population.

In this instance, however, additional considerations lead us to expect attenuation. This is because the size of a legislature becomes unwieldy as it grows larger, imposing a constraint on its ability to perform its designated tasks, e.g., collective deliberation.

The appropriate or optimal size of a legislature is, accordingly, often conceptualized as a trade-off. In Federalist #10, Madison comments,

> However small the republic may be the representatives must be raised to a certain number in order to guard against the cabals of a few; and ... however large it may be they must be limited to a certain number in order to guard against the confusion of a multitude. (Hamilton, Madison, & Jay 2008 [1787]: 53)

For Madison, the size of a governing body induces a trade-off between the danger of tyranny ("cabals of the few") on one hand, and incapacity ("confusion of a multitude") on the other. Brooks, Phillips, and Sinitsyn (2011) interpret this as a trade-off between representing diversity (for which size is a virtue) and representing the median voter (for which a single representative is ideally suited). Auriol and Gary-Bobo (2012) propose a trade-off between representing citizen views (for which size is a virtue) and decision-making efficiency and expertise (for which size is an impediment).

We see no easy way to resolve exactly why the relationship between scale and legislative size is sublinear. In all likelihood, a variety of factors are at work. For our purposes, the important implication of a sublinear relationship is that increases in scale translate into increases in the ratio of constituents to representatives, which we refer to as the *representation ratio* – a concept elaborated in the third section of this chapter.

Evidence: Legislature Size

As a proxy for the total number of representatives in a polity we focus first on the size of the legislature. One has a choice whether to focus on the lower/unicameral chamber, the upper chamber, or both together. The latter takes account of all members and thus appears to offer a better approximation of the total number of representatives. However, historical data on upper chamber membership are scarce, and many upper chambers do not play important policymaking roles. Moreover, dual chambers with overlapping constituencies may not be the best way to assure representation, especially for very small groups. Arguably, a unicameral legislature with 100 members offers better representation than a bicameral legislature comprised of two 50-member chambers.

In any event, the three measures are fairly highly correlated across national legislatures at the present time, as shown in Table 4.1. Our approach is to rely on a combined measure when data for the upper chamber are available, to rely on the lower chamber where they are not, and to report results for all three measures wherever it is not too cumbersome to do so.

Table 4.1 *Intercorrelations among measures of legislature size*

	Lower	Upper
Upper	0.83 (79)	
Combined	0.98 (192)	0.89 (78)

Pearson's r correlations among three measures of legislature size: (a) lower or unicameral chamber, (b) upper chamber, and (c) both chambers combined. All measures are transformed by the natural logarithm. *Year:* 2018. *N* in parentheses.

A number of studies have shown a relationship between the size of a polity and the size of its legislature. Taagepera (1972) examines the size of lower-chamber (or unicameral) national legislatures in 1965. Auriol and Gary-Bobo (2012) replicate this exercise with more recent data and also examine US state legislatures. Taagepera and Recchia (2002) examine the size of upper chambers. Stigler (1976) examines national legislatures for noncommunist states and lower-chamber state legislatures in the United States. All of these studies point to a log–log relationship, which we adopt in our baseline models.[2]

Our goal is to extend the empirical ambit of the foregoing analyses so as to arrive at a more precise and generalizable estimate of the relationship between scale and legislature size. We gather a cross-national sample from a variety of sources that includes virtually all countries and extends back to the eighteenth century. Next, we collect data for US polities – national, state, and local, including state legislatures observed back to the founding of the first American colonies in the seventeenth century.

National Legislatures

As a first pass at the question of scale and legislative size, we draw recent data on the size of parliaments from the Inter-Parliamentary Union (IPU). This source includes 192 countries, virtually the entire universe of nation-states. Because the IPU keeps records on both upper and lower houses, we add their sizes together (wherever legislatures are bicameral), offering a combined count. The scatterplot in Figure 4.2 shows an extremely strong relationship between the size of a country and the size of its

---

[2] This simple functional form turns out to offer a better fit for the data than the cube root function proposed by Taagepera (1972) and is also consistent with the approach taken to other scale effects elsewhere in the book. Of course, we cannot rule out the possibility that the cube root offers the true causal relationship hidden in the data.

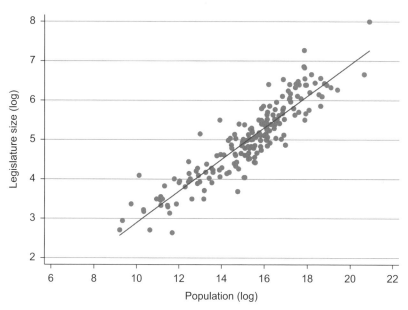

Figure 4.2 Legislature size

Y axis: legislature size (log) including both houses, where bicameral.
X axis: population (log). *Year*: 2018. Countries (*N*): 191. Best-fit
regression line overlaid. $R^2 = 0.82$.

legislature. Indeed, this simple bivariate model explains 82 percent of the
variance in legislature size.

The highest residuals in this model are associated with the United
Arab Emirates (UAE) and Micronesia, which have smaller legislatures
than the model predicts, and the United Kingdom and San Marino,
which have larger legislatures than the model predicts. However,
overall model fit is very tight and there are no extreme outliers, as
Figure 4.2 demonstrates.

By the same token, if we adjust the model to compare actual and
predicted values in their *linear* (unlogged) form, we find that the fit is
much looser and some countries with modest residuals lie quite far from
their predicted values. The US Congress, with a combined House of
Representatives and Senate membership of 535, is considerably smaller
than its predicted value of 740. This conforms with a common view that
the US Congress is too small (Frederick 2010; *New York Times* Editorial
Board 2018). (Bear in mind that this judgment involves a shift from
a descriptive model to a normative model.)

To gain a historical sense of this subject we focus on the lower or unicameral chamber of national legislatures, including all years for which suitable data for legislative size are available. Data for 2018 are drawn from the IPU, as noted. Data for previous years are drawn from V-Dem, which does not include appointed (nonelected) seats or non-partisan elections. One may regard this as a healthy correction or as a measurement error, depending upon one's theoretical perspective. (Unelected members or members elected in nonpartisan elections may perform a representative function, as noted.) In any case, our sample is affected only at the margins, as most legislatures are selected through elections that are formally partisan and most seats are elective.

A third data source is employed where data from the IPU and V-Dem are missing. The Comparative Constitutions Project (CCP) codes provisions pertaining to the size of legislatures wherever constitutions prescribe them (Elkins, Ginsburg, & Melton 2009). Occasionally, the provision states a minimum or maximum size. We record the maximum unless there is only a minimum. In some instances there is a constitutional formula based on national population, which we use to calculate the expected size of the legislature in each year.

Once values are obtained from these three sources, we fill in missing values within each country's time-series by projecting past values forward so as to generate a country-year time-series that is complete from the first observation to the present. We ignore interregnums, i.e., periods in which the legislature is displaced or dissolved. (Dropping these observations would have little impact on our findings, as our sample contains few interregnums.) The resulting index of lower/unicameral legislative size incorporates 200 countries observed – wherever possible – on an annual basis from 1780 (or year of independence) to the present, a total of roughly 17,000 country-year observations. Across this sample, the mean legislature size is 181, the minimum is 1 (the Gambia, prior to independence, when only one seat was elective), the maximum is 2,980 (China), and the standard deviation is 221. As with most measures of size (see discussion in Chapter 1), the distribution has a long right tail of which China is the extreme outlier. (The distribution is considerably more symmetrical when logged, as it is for the regression analyses that follow.)

Over time, annual increases in legislative size outnumber decreases – but not overwhelmingly (1,430 to 654). There is, in short, little evidence of a "ratchet" effect. This is consistent with the aggregate pattern across countries, which is plotted over time in Figure 4.3. (We omit the eighteenth and early nineteenth centuries as the country samples are too small to allow for generalization.) It will be seen that average legislature size

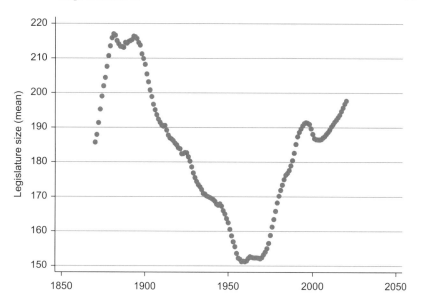

Figure 4.3 Legislature size over time

Mean size of the lower or unicameral chamber of natural legislatures in countries around the world, averaged for each year (1870–) and then smoothed over a ten-year period.

decreases through the mid-twentieth century, after which it begins to increase, rebounding almost to its previous peak in the late nineteenth century.

To explore the relationship of interest more fully a series of regression tests is presented in Table 4.2. Model 1 includes only the outcome and the predictor of interest, both of which are transformed by the natural logarithm, as discussed. Model 2 adds a variety of covariates. Model 3 is an instrumental variable model. Model 4 is a panel estimator with country fixed effects along with year dummies. (We rarely employ a longitudinal style of analysis in this book, for reasons explained in Chapter 2. However, in this instance the long time-series and apparent absence of time-varying confounders justifies a departure from our usual approach.)

The remaining tests in Table 4.2 focus on alternate measures of legislative size – the upper chamber only (Model 5) and a composite index combining the membership of both chambers (Model 6). For these analyses we are limited to a single cross-section, as the IPU does not provide time-series data. (Note that Model 6 matches the scatterplot in Figure 4.1.)

Table 4.2 *Legislature size*

Chamber	Lower/Unicameral				Upper	Combined
Estimator	OLS	OLS	2SLS	OLS	OLS	OLS
Right-side lag (years)	20	20	20	5	20	20
Model	1	2	3	4	5	6
Population (log)	0.410***	0.372***	0.442***	0.157***	0.307***	0.401***
	(0.023)	(0.021)	(0.036)	(0.036)	(0.030)	(0.015)
GDP per cap (log)		−0.063				
		(0.072)				
Protestant		0.000				
		(0.001)				
Years since independence (log)		0.029				
		(0.019)				
Democracy (Lexical index)		0.006				
		(0.013)				
English colony		−0.002				
		(0.104)				
Muslim		−0.001				
		(0.001)				
Country dummies				✓		
Region dummies	✓					
Year dummies	✓			✓		
Decade dummies			✓			
Countries	196	182	179	197	78	191
Years	241	197	241	240	1	1
Observations	14,899	10,952	14,060	15,709	78	191
R^2	0.625	0.757	0.631	0.349	0.564	0.825

Outcome: size (number of members) of national legislature (log). *Units of analysis*: country-years. Constant omitted. *Estimators*: OLS (ordinary least squares), 2SLS (two-stage least squares, using land area and agricultural suitability as instruments), standard errors clustered by country. *** $p < 0.01$, ** $p < 0.05$, * $p < 0.10$ (two-tailed tests)

All tests in Table 4.2 show a strong relationship between the size of a country and its legislature. Bivariate models explain 60–80 percent of the variance, and the coefficient for population declines only slightly when a vector of background covariates is added (Model 2). Moreover, none of these background factors seems to bear a strong relationship to the outcome judging by t statistics and the slight improvement in fit between Models 1 and 2. For the most part, the estimated coefficient for population (log) is stable. The only serious attenuation is in the fixed-effect specification (Model 4), presumably a result of the sluggish nature of the variables.

US Legislatures

Legislatures exist at every level of government, and it is not clear that patterns observable at national levels are repeated at subnational levels. To explore the latter, we examine the size of legislatures across polities in the United States, as reported in Table 4.3.

We begin, in Model 1, with a sample that incorporates data from every level of government – national (Senate and House), state (upper and lower chambers of each state), and local (city councils located in Alabama, California, and Georgia). Variables are measured in 2014 or adjacent years and are treated as a single cross-section. A total of 961 legislatures is included, the vast majority of which are at municipal levels and many of which are quite small.

The remaining tests in Table 4.3 focus exclusively on state and colonial legislatures. Data for the postindependence period (1776–) are drawn from Dubin (2007), which records the size of lower and upper chambers separately. Data are annual except in a few cases where legislatures were in continual flux – Massachusetts (House), New Hampshire (House), and Ohio (House and Senate) – where we record changes at decadal intervals (for the periods of flux).

For the colonial era, we draw on Greene (1981: 461) and Squire (2017: 22). Here, the size of legislatures is recorded for the legislature at large (lower and upper, if bicameral), and data are available for only four points in time: the founding, 1700, 1730, and 1770. We interpolate missing values so as to arrive at an annual time-series that is continuous with our data for the postindependence period. (We leave aside small colonies such as Plymouth and New Haven that composed a portion of a later colony or state.)

Over the postindependence period (1776–2018), changes to legislature size are considerably more common in lower chambers than upper chambers. Increases outnumber decreases overall, as one might expect (449 versus 132). Instability was much more common in the eighteenth and nineteenth centuries than in the twentieth century, when legislatures – perhaps following the example of the US House of Representatives – tended to "freeze" their memberships. In any case, there is considerable variation to explore, both cross-sectionally and through time. The largest legislature is Massachusetts, which in 1812 reached the astonishing size of 789 – 749 members of the House plus 40 members of the Senate. The

Table 4.3 *US legislature size*

Legislatures	National, State, Local	State: Upper chamber	State: Lower/ Unicameral chamber	State/col- ony: Both chambers	State/col- ony: Both chambers
Period	2014	1776–2018	1776–2018	1619–2018	1619–2018
Model	1	2	3	4	5
Population	0.237***	0.197***	0.234***	0.238***	0.246***
(log)	(0.054)	(0.034)	(0.067)	(0.055)	(0.042)
State dummies					✓
Year dummies		✓	✓	✓	✓
Legislatures	959	50	50	50	50
Years	1	243	243	400	400
Observations	959	9,049	9,126	10,477	10,477
R^2	0.495	0.506	0.233	0.632	0.825

Outcome: size (number of members) of legislature (log). *Units of analysis*: legislature-years. Constant omitted. *Estimators*: OLS (ordinary least squares), standard errors clustered by state. *** $p < 0.01$, ** $p < 0.05$, * $p < 0.10$ (two-tailed tests). Descriptive statistics below.

	Obs.	Mean	Std. Dev.	Min.	Max.
Model 1					
Legislature size, both chambers (log)	961	1.74	0.89	0	6.08
Population (log)	961	9.75	2.63	4.00	19.59
Models 2–5					
Legislature size, upper chamber (log)	9,055	3.46	0.42	1.95	4.20
Legislature size, upper chamber (log)	9,132	4.58	0.53	3.04	6.62
Legislature size, both chambers (log)	10,483	4.70	0.67	2.30	6.67
Population (log)	11,998	13.18	2.12	5.22	17.47

smallest legislature in the postindependence era, Delaware, had a combined membership for its upper and lower houses of only 30 members from 1776 to 1897. The smallest legislature in the colonial era – New Jersey, in 1668 – had a membership of 10.

Trends over time in mean legislature size (counting both upper and lower houses) are shown in Figure 4.4. We find a modest trend toward larger legislatures during most periods, with a sharp increase during the revolutionary era. Legislature size peaked in the mid-twentieth century – at about 150 members – after which there is a small attenuation (a reversal of historical patterns found among national legislatures, shown in Figure 4.3).

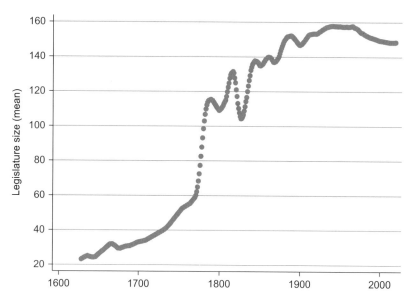

Figure 4.4 US state legislature size over time

Mean legislature size for US state legislatures (combined membership of lower and upper chambers), averaged for each year and then smoothed over a ten-year period.

To interrogate the relationship between scale and legislative size in the United States, we regress the former on the latter in a series of tests displayed in Table 4.3. Model 1 includes all manner of legislatures – national (House and Senate), state (house and senate), and local (city council) – a total of 959, most of which are city councils, observed in a single year. Model 2 includes state upper chambers, observed back to 1776. Model 3 includes state lower or unicameral chambers, also observed back to 1776. Model 4 includes both chambers of the state or colonial legislatures, observed back to 1619. Model 5 adds state fixed effects, shifting the burden of the analysis from cross-sectional variation to over-time variation.

The apparent relationship between scale and legislative size within the United States is attenuated relative to estimates of this relationship at national levels (Table 4.2). Coefficients hover around 0.2 (compared to 0.4 for cross-national models) and r^2s are also about half those found in our cross-national tests. This is perhaps because there is less variation in polity size and legislative size at subnational levels.

Nonetheless, the relationship between population and legislative size is persistent and strong, judging by t statistics and model-fit statistics. In the bivariate specification, Model 1, population explains nearly half of the variability in legislature size. Estimates are also remarkably stable across models that vary in time periods, legislature types, and estimators, offering strong support for our thesis.

Changes over Time

Thus far, we have examined the relationship between scale and legislative size in a transhistorical fashion, as a constant feature of political life. This is the big-picture story. But there are also reasons to suppose that the relationship may have changed over time. To gain a sense of the temporal components of this relationship we conduct rolling regressions in which the benchmark models from our national and subnational analyses are repeated on a moving window of forty years, beginning in the late eighteenth century and continuing to the present. This offers a moving snapshot of the relationship between scale and legislature size across two centuries.

The results of this exercise are displayed in side-by-side panels in Figure 4.5. A quick examination of the Y axes demonstrates a feature that we have already remarked upon. Demography has much greater impact on legislature size across countries than it does across US states. But the more salient feature of these graphs is the marked attenuation in our estimates over the course of two centuries. The estimated coefficient for population (log) drops by about one-half in both datasets.

A number of factors may be at work. First, legislature size seems to stabilize as polities mature. This may be a product of growing constitutional stability, which occurs over time in most polities (Elkins et al., 2009: 131). It could be that polities come to regard legislative size as a fixed element of the political firmament, something that defines their state or country. While continuing to tinker with other constitutional features – individual rights, electoral systems, and so forth – citizens and politicians may see no reason to adjust the number of representatives. Note that the latter may require reconstructing assembly halls and office buildings, not to mention electoral districts and constituencies. Another possibility is that the growing unpopularity of politics and politicians – and legislatures in particular – in the twentieth century has soured the public on the idea of adding to their ranks.

In any case, the repercussions of institutional rigidity are clear. If legislature size is fixed while populations continue to grow, then the relationship between the two is apt to attenuate over time. Consider Figure 4.6, where we plot changes in legislative size for national

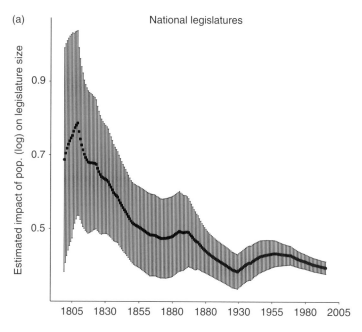

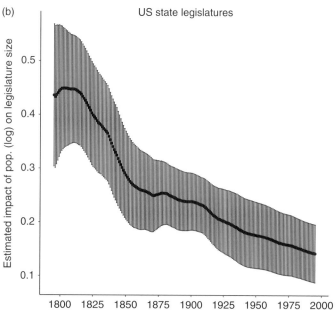

Figure 4.5 Rolling regressions

Estimated coefficients, surrounded by 95 percent confidence intervals, for
population (log) in benchmark models iterated at forty-year intervals
across two centuries. Panel (a): national legislatures (Model 1, Table 4.2).
Panel (b): state legislatures (Model 1, Table 4.3).

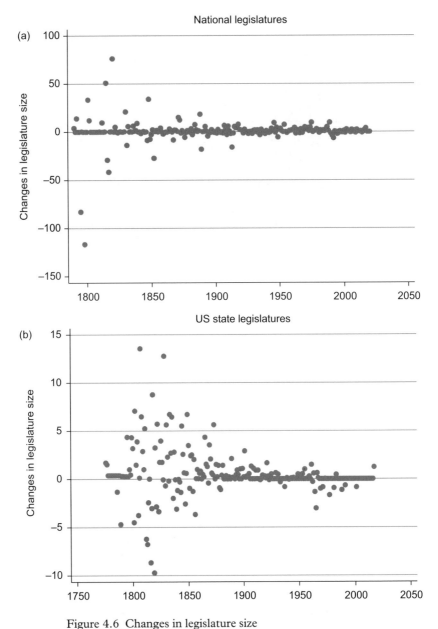

Figure 4.6 Changes in legislature size

Mean yearly changes in legislature size for (a) national legislatures
(lower or unicameral chamber) and (b) US state legislatures (upper and
lower chambers).

legislatures and US state legislatures over two centuries. It is apparent that reforms of this nature have become rarer and rarer as time goes by. Evidently, there is no opportunity to adjust institutions to suit demographic circumstances. In this light, it is understandable why the log–log relationship has become more tenuous.

Evidence: Cabinet Size

As a second measure of representative bodies we focus on the size of cabinets, as mandated by statute. For most countries, this is identical to the actual size of cabinets. Even where there is some slippage, the difference between de jure and de facto cabinet sizes is not more than a handful at the present time.

Data for 2018 are drawn from the GLP (second round). Data for 1950, 1960, and 1970 are drawn from Liu and Apfeld (2016). Data are missing between 1970 and 2018. However, the statutory sizes of cabinets are fairly stable so missing values are unlikely to have much impact on our analysis.

To test the relationship between population and cabinet size we adopt the format employed in our analysis of national legislatures (see Table 4.2, Models 1–3). The outcome, cabinet size, is transformed by the natural logarithm, setting up a log–log relationship.

In Table 4.4, Model 1 includes only the regressor of interest, population (log), along with year dummies. Model 2 includes a variety of additional covariates that might help explain variation in the size of representative bodies. Model 3 is an instrumental variable model.

Results across these three models are quite stable, with population showing itself to be a consistent predictor of cabinet size. However, the effect is marginal relative to our earlier analysis of legislature size. In the bivariate model, population explains only 15 percent of the variation in cabinet size. We presume that this flows from the smaller variability in cabinet size, relative to legislature size. After all, the functions of government do not vary enormously across countries. Every country has a foreign secretary, and few (if any) have more than one. And ministers without portfolio are often powerless. It could also be the case that cabinet size is less visible to the populace and thus less responsive to the causal mechanisms outlined in our theory. One might add that a cabinet office involves representative functions as well as bureaucratic functions. Insofar as members of a cabinet are viewed as agency chiefs, they fall outside our theory.

In any case, none of the other predictors tested in Model 2 show a strong relationship to the outcome. Against this backdrop, our demographic framework does a creditable job explaining the shape of institutions.

Table 4.4 *Cabinet size*

Estimator	OLS	OLS	2SLS
Model	1	2	3
Population (log)	0.087***	0.095***	0.079***
	(0.014)	(0.020)	(0.022)
GDP per capita (log)		−0.018	
		(0.031)	
Protestant		−0.001	
		(0.001)	
Years since independence (log)		−0.013	
		(0.017)	
Democracy (Lexical index)		−0.002	
		(0.010)	
English colony		0.039	
		(0.067)	
Muslim		−0.000	
		(0.001)	
Region dummies		✓	
Year dummies	✓	✓	✓
Countries	170	163	164
Decades	4	4	4
Observations	430	380	423
R^2	0.385	0.439	0.384

Outcome: size (number of members) of cabinet (log). *Units of analysis:* countries. Constant omitted. *Estimators:* OLS (ordinary least squares), 2SLS (two-stage least squares, using land area and agricultural suitability as instruments), robust standard errors. Right-side variables lagged ten years. *** $p < 0.01$, ** $p < 0.05$, * $p < 0.10$ (two-tailed tests)

Representation Ratio

Thus far, we have attempted to explain why some legislatures and cabinets are larger than others. We have shown that the relationship between population and the size of representative bodies assumes a log–log functional form, which we regard as strong evidence that demographics affects the shape of institutions.

Arguably, the more important political question is how the number of representatives structures the *representation ratio* of citizens (constituents) to representatives. For present purposes, we limit our discussion to leg-islatures – leaving aside cabinets and other representative bodies.

Let us define N as the number of citizens in a community and n as the number of representatives in that community. The representation ratio is, very simply, N/n.

At one extreme lie systems of direct democracy, where every citizen represents himself or herself. Here, $N = n$ and the representation ratio is therefore 1. In this case, there is no representation at all (in the usual sense of the term).

In all other cases, the representation ratio is greater than one. A limiting case is a polity with no legislature at all and where only one individual plays a representative role, e.g., a president or monarch. Here, $n = 1$ and the representation ratio is therefore $N/1$.

What is the "right" representation ratio? The US Constitution, one of the first constitutions to deal self-consciously with its representative func-tion, asserts that "The number of Representatives shall not exceed one for every thirty Thousand." Note the implicit concern that legislatures might be *too large* relative to the populations they represent. In hindsight, one might have the opposite concern, voiced originally by the Anti-Federalists: that legislatures would be too small for their growing populations.

Consider the US Houses of Representatives. In 1789, each member of the House represented roughly 30,000 people, as stipulated by the Constitution. (The true number was even fewer if one counts only those who enjoyed full citizenship rights.) Through the nineteenth century representatives were added each decade. Since 1911, House membership has been maintained at approximately 435, while the population con-tinues to grow. Today, each member of the House represents about 700,000 constituents. For present purposes, what is important is that the ratio of constituents to representatives has grown through all eras of US history, as illustrated in Figure 4.7. A similar trend is found across US colonial and state legislatures, as shown in Figure 4.8.

Now consider the relationship between scale and the representation ratio. To do so, we examine a large sample of US legislatures – national, state, and local (the sample employed in Model 1, Table 4.3). Figure 4.9 graphs the population of these constituencies on the X axis. On the Y axis, we show the representation ratio, i.e., number of citizens represented by a single legislator, N/n. There is an extraordinarily tight fit, as shown by the overlaid regression line. As the population increases, so does the represen-tation ratio. Indeed, about three-fourths of the variability in representation ratios is explained by the population size of their constituencies.

At national levels, we find a similar relationship and even greater variability in representation ratios. For Suriname, with a population of

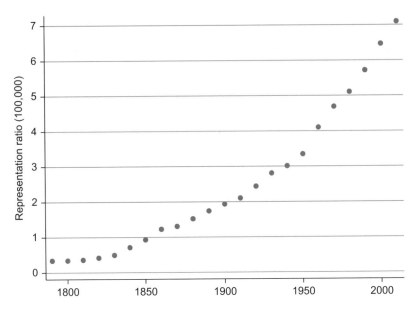

Figure 4.7 Representation ratio, US House districts over time

Representative ratio: mean population (100,000s) per representative for the US House of Representatives, 1790–2010.

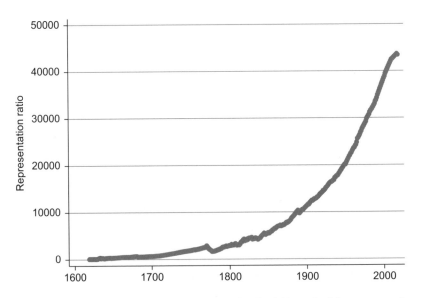

Figure 4.8 Representation ratio, US colonial/state legislatures over time

Representation ratio: mean population per representative for US colonial and state upper and lower houses (combined), 1619–2018.

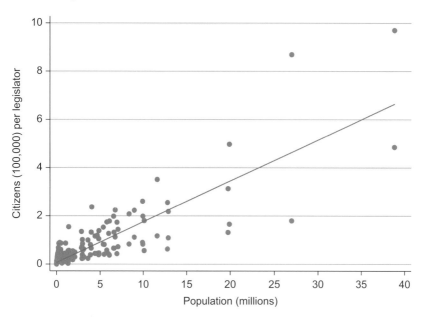

Figure 4.9 Representation ratio of US legislatures

Representation ratio for all US legislatures – national, state, local
($N = 959$) – in 2014. Regression line overlaid. $R^2 = 0.75$.

roughly half a million and a legislature of fifty-one, the representation
ratio is roughly 30,000/1. That is, for every leader there are 30,000
citizens. For the United States, the ratio is (roughly) 500,000/1.

To test the relationship in a comprehensive fashion we include data for
190 countries – excluding India and China, which comprise highly influential cases in this linear (non-logarithmic) analysis. The relationship is
graphed in Figure 4.10, along with a best-fit regression line. Here, population explains four-fifths of the variability. In other words, this one factor,
by itself, explains most of what we need to know about why some countries offer smaller constituencies than others.

This remarkably strong correlation is a direct implication of the log–log
relationship between population and legislature size, which we observed in
the previous section of this chapter. Although the leadership class expands
with community scale, the increase is sublinear. Increases in the size of the
leadership class do not keep pace with increases in population. This corroborates Mosca's (1939: 53) hypothesis that "the larger the political community the smaller will be the proportion of the governing minority to the
governed majority" (see also Bryce 1924; Mayhew 1973; Prewitt 1969).

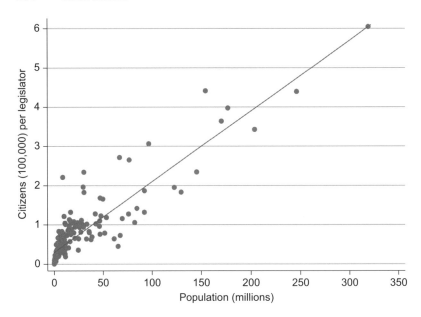

Figure 4.10 Representation ratio of legislatures

National legislatures (N) = 190 (China and India excluded). *Year:* 2018.
Y axis: citizens (100,000s) per legislator. *X axis:* population (millions).
Regression line overlaid. R^2 = 0.81.

Summary

Table 4.5 summarizes extant studies, as well as our own analyses, of
the relationship between scale and the number of representatives,
proxied by legislature size. The results are unanimous. Both extant
work and our own analyses show a positive relationship between population and legislature size (number of members). Moreover, there is
consensus among scholars that the relationship assumes a log–log
functional form.

Although previous studies were limited in scope, our analyses have
tracked national legislatures and US state legislatures back to the seventeenth century. We have also included local legislatures for the present
era. This more comprehensive examination of the matter bears out previous findings, though we have discovered some potentially important
nuances.

First, the relationship between scale and legislature size appears to be
weaker subnationally than it is cross-nationally, presumably because the
variance is diminished at subnational levels. Second, the relationship

Table 4.5 *Scale and representatives: Inventory of analyses*

Indicators	Countries	Treatment units	Years	Units of analysis	Research design	Effect	Study
National legislature size							
Lower/unicameral	(120)	Legislatures (120)	(1)	Legislatures (120)	Cross-sectional	↑	Taagepera 1972
Lower/unicameral	(37)	Legislatures (37)	(1)	Legislatures (37)	Cross-sectional	↑	Stigler 1976
Lower/unicameral	(111)	Legislatures (111)	(1)	Legislatures (111)	Cross-sectional	↑	Auriol & Gary-Bobo 2012
Upper	(58)	Legislatures (58)	(1)	Legislatures (58)	Cross-sectional	↑	Taagepera & Recchia 2002
*Lower/unicameral	(196)	Legislatures (196)	(241)	Legislatures (196)	Cross-sectional, panel	↑	Table 4.2
*Upper	(78)	Legislatures (78)	(1)	Legislatures (78)	Cross-sectional	↑	Table 4.2
*Lower and upper	(191)	Legislatures (191)	(1)	Legislatures (191)	Cross-sectional	↑	Table 4.2
Subnational legislature size							
State lower/unicameral	United States (1)	Legislatures (49)	(1)	State legislatures (49)	Cross-sectional	↑	Stigler 1976
State lower and upper	United States (1)	Legislatures (49)	(1)	State legislatures (49)	Cross-sectional	↑	Auriol & Gary-Bobo 2012
State upper	United States (1)	Legislatures (49)	(1)	State legislatures (49)	Cross-sectional	↑	Stigler 1976
*National, state, local	United States (1)	Legislatures (961)	(1)	Legislatures (961)	Cross-sectional	↑	Table 4.3
*State upper	United States (1)	Legislatures (49)	(243)	Legislature-years (9,049)	Cross-sectional	↑	Table 4.3
*State lower/unicameral	United States (1)	Legislatures (50)	(243)	Legislature-years (9,126)	Cross-sectional	↑	Table 4.3

Table 4.5 (cont.)

Indicators	Countries	Treatment units	Years	Units of analysis	Research design	Effect	Study
*State lower and upper	United States (1)	Legislatures (50)	(400)	Legislature-years (10,477)	Cross-sectional, panel	↑	Table 4.3
Cabinet size							
*Cabinets (national level)	(168)	Cabinets (168)	(1)	Cabinets (168)	Cross-sectional	↑	Table 4.4

Treatment units: units exhibiting variation in scale. *Years*: number of years over which data are collected – not to be confused with the frequency of observations, as data may or may not be annual and may be averaged across years. *Research design*: the main, or benchmark, research design – classified as cross-sectional (where the analysis is driven primarily by variation across units) or panel (where the analysis is driven primarily by variation through time). *Effect*: when the scale of a community increases, the designated outcome goes up (↑), down (↓), up and down (∩), or experiences no perceptible change (∅). A scale effect is considered significant if it passes a modest bar of statistical significance, i.e., p < 0.10 (two-tailed test) in the benchmark model. Number of countries, treatment units, years, or observations in parentheses.

attenuates over time, presumably because legislative size is "frozen" while populations keep growing.

But let us not lose sight of the forest in the midst of the trees. Over all samples, time periods, and estimators, population is a massive predictor of legislative size. Indeed, it is the *only* strong predictor we have been able to identify. This represents a departure from most of the findings of this book, where there are multiple causes and population explains a modest portion of the variance.

We have spent little time discussing potential confounders in this chapter because we cannot surmise what they might be. Certainly, legislative size does not affect population size. And we cannot conceive of any hidden – as yet unmeasured – factors that might drive both sides of this well-established causal model.

By way of conclusion, it is worth reiterating that the log–log functional form between demographic size and legislative size implies that the number of constituents per member *declines precipitously* as the scale of a polity grows. The legislature does not grow in tandem with population, so the representation ratio increases with each increase in population, as shown in the previous section.

5   Representativeness

In the previous chapter, we explored the relationship of scale to the number of elites playing representative roles in a polity, operationalized by the size of the legislature or cabinet. We found a strong log–log relationship between scale and representative size. As the size of a community grows so does its legislature, but in a sublinear fashion. This, in turn, drives the representation ratio – the ratio of citizens to each legislator – which grows larger as communities increase in size.

In this chapter, we explore the role of scale in structuring *representativeness*, the faithfulness with which politicians reflect the interests, values, and characteristics of the citizens they are intended to represent. This may be measured by the degree of correspondence between citizens and their representatives – either demographically or programmatically. It may also be measured by the vibrancy of constituent/representative connections. It may, finally, be measured by the degree of trust between citizens and their representatives, which we regard as an outcome measure of representativeness since it is partly a product of the degree of representativeness perceived by citizens.

Representativeness is presumed to have positive repercussions for society and fits with an intuitive understanding of democracy. If people rule, then political elites should be representative of the people. Demographic representativeness is usually assumed to foster greater programmatic representativeness. Where certain groups – e.g., women or minorities – are excluded, policies may be biased against their interests (Chattopadhyay & Duflo 2004; Mansbridge 1999; Preuhs 2007; Swers 1998, 2002, 2005). Moreover, the inclusion of women, minorities, and underprivileged socioeconomic classes in the councils of power may enhance the status of these groups in society more generally, as they serve as positive role models and as symbols of social acceptance (Phillips 1995). Likewise, where politicians are programmatically unresponsive, the result may be profligate rent-seeking and an underprovision of public goods. The benefits of political trust for a polity are perhaps self-evident (Braithwaite & Levi 1998).

Of course, demographic and programmatic representativeness do not always foster substantive representation, understood as legislating *in the interests* of constituents (Pitkin 1967). The "delegate" role should not be confused with the "trustee" role. Sometimes, descriptive representation leads to the choice of poorly educated or otherwise unprepared public servants. Sometimes, representativeness stands in the way of partisan contestation, an issue taken up in Chapter 8. Sometimes, responding to constituency pressures leads to bad – or at least short-sighted – public policy. Sometimes, public trust is not warranted.

In short, representativeness is good if all other things are equal. But it should not be assumed that all other things are equal.

With this as background, we sketch a theory about how scale affects representativeness. Next, we explore evidence for this relationship with respect to (a) demographic representativeness, (b) programmatic representativeness, (c) direct constituency connections, and (d) political trust. A brief conclusion summarizes our findings and findings contained in the extant literature.

Theory

We conceptualize the influence of scale on representativeness with a simple principal–agent model. Here, we assume that constituents – the principals – prefer leaders who are like them (in whatever ways seem politically relevant), who agree with them, and who stay in touch with them. In politics, closeness is a virtue. Accordingly, constituents generally prefer to keep their leaders on a short leash – as delegates rather than trustees. Leaders – the agents, in this model – may, or may not, share that perspective.

Now, let us consider the role of scale. At one theoretical limit, our argument is true by definition. In a community of one, the member is both principal and agent. Here, there is no possibility of deviation. As scale increases, we expect that cohesiveness decreases (Chapter 3) and the probability of deviation increases. The latter occurs because various factors attenuate the principal–agency relationship. These factors include: (a) the selection of the agent, (b) signals emanating from the principal, (c) information available to principal and agent, (d) connections between principal and agent, and (e) methods by which the principal might sanction the agent. As a secondary effect – of lower representativeness – we anticipate that political trust will also decline as the size of a community increases. We turn now to the various strands of this argument, encapsulated in Figure 5.1.

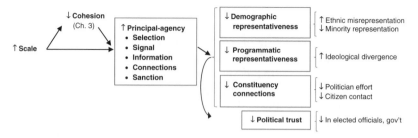

Figure 5.1 Scale effects on district representativeness

We begin with the process of *selection*. Most representatives hail from the community they represent. Sometimes, this is statutorily or constitutionally mandated; virtually everywhere, it is common practice. "Parachuting" is rare. Now, imagine that representatives are chosen randomly (by lot) from a community. If a community is homogeneous there is a greater probability that the chosen individual will be representative of the community than if the community is heterogeneous. Indeed, if a community is perfectly homogeneous it is impossible to select a *non*representative representative. Likewise, if the community is very heterogeneous it will be impossible to identify a perfectly representative representative (so to speak). No matter who that person is, her attributes are bound to deviate from those exhibited by a large section of the constituency. A single individual cannot speak more than one or two languages with perfect fluency; cannot worship at multiple altars; cannot claim descent from more than one or two ethnicities; cannot accrue occupational experiences in all sectors of the economy; and so forth. Since size fosters heterogeneity (Chapter 3), we can anticipate that size will foster departures from the ideal of closeness between constituents and their representatives if the selection process is purely stochastic, or includes some stochastic component.

Second, let us consider the *signal* (directive) by which the principal makes known her wishes to the agent. In a small, homogenous community there is likely to be a clear signal about what politicians should look like, what they should think, and how they should behave. By contrast, in a large community cultural and ideological characteristics are likely to be more heterogeneous. Both size and heterogeneity make it difficult to ascertain what the "majority" is and what it wants.

Third, there is a problem of *information*. In a small community citizens are likely to know a good deal about potential leaders and leaders currently occupying public office. If they do not, they can easily gather that information by inquiring of their neighbors. It should be fairly easy to monitor candidates and officials to discover whether, or to what degree, they are representing them. By contrast, in a large community information is harder to obtain because interpersonal networks are weaker and because of the greater anonymity conferred by large populations. Consequently, it is more difficult to monitor public officials.

Fourth, there is the problem of establishing and maintaining *connections* between citizens and leaders. Once chosen, the leader of a small community will find it easy to stay in close contact with her constituents – to visit them, solicit their views, attend their weddings and funerals, and so forth. Social media and telecommunications also facilitate contact on platforms like Facebook, Instagram, and WhatsApp. There is no excuse for ignoring the constituency, and doing so will not be taken lightly. By the same token, there is considerable payoff for cultivating the constituency. A hard-working politician can establish personal relationships with a sizeable share of her constituents if the constituency is small, and these relationships may pay off in the form of a personal vote (Cain, Ferejohn, & Fiorina 1987). However, as the constituency grows this form of interaction becomes less practicable. An indefatigable politician can meet only so many people face to face. Even if the hand-shaking extends to a large share of constituents, relationships are not ongoing and likely to be fairly superficial. It is simply not possible to maintain direct ties to constituents in a district numbering in the hundreds of thousands. Constituents understand this, and are not likely to blame the representative of a big state or country if she does not attend their son's wedding; clearly, she has other things to do. So the intimacy of constituent: representative connections is apt to weaken as the size of a community grows.

Finally, there is the problem of *sanction*. In order for principal–agent relationships to work the principal must have the capacity to punish the agent if she deviates from conformity to community norms and widely held positions on issues. Evidently, to sanction a wayward politician, citizens – or, at least, a large number of them – must act in concert, and this raises a difficult problem of coordination. However, in smaller and more interconnected communities it should be easier to solve collective action problems. This means that retribution is a more serious threat than it would be in a large, heterogeneous community.

A Stylized Depiction

To illustrate these points and contemplate their consequences we present a stylized depiction of two communities in Figure 5.2. Community (a) is small and homogeneous while Community (b) is large and heterogeneous.

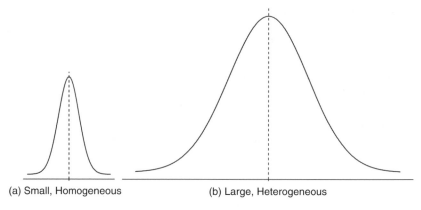

(a) Small, Homogeneous   (b) Large, Heterogeneous

Figure 5.2 Illustration of the principal-agency problem

Stylized depictions of the distribution of opinion or attributes in two communities: (a) small and homogeneous and (b) large and heterogeneous. *Vertical line*: the position taken by a representative aiming to please as many members as possible.

Homogeneity/heterogeneity is depicted along a single dimension, though readers can imagine multiple dimensions if they prefer. Each community is represented by a single politician who wishes to be as representative as possible, positioning herself at the midpoint of the distribution.

Note that although both representatives are occupying the center, the representative from community (b) will leave a lot of constituents unhappy, as their ideal-points lie far from the midpoint in our stylized portrayal of preferences. The diagram suggests that scale, and attendant heterogeneity, must attenuate representativeness if the latter is measured by the mean distance between the representative and *each constituent*.[1]

Moreover, because community (b) comprises greater numbers and greater dispersion of preferences, the programmatic "signal" emanating from the electorate is weaker. Under the circumstances, it may be difficult for anyone to determine where the midpoint lies, which provides cover for the representative to deviate ("shirk"), without being apprehended (Harden & Carsey 2012). Shirking is understood in this context as a representative occupying a position away from the central tendency, i.e., to the left or right of the vertical lines in Figure 5.2.[2] She may be either pro- or antiabortion if the district is split on these dimensions. Shirking is possible, indeed perhaps unavoidable, and retribution less likely. Perhaps

[1] Achen (1978) calls this "proximity."
[2] This is the approach Miller and Stokes (1963) take.

some votes will be lost but others may be gained. And accusations of elitism or "losing touch" will be difficult to prove. In a constituency of millions a clever politician can always find some influential constituency who supports her.

Caveats

Now, we must insert several caveats.

First, we have defined representativeness in a very broad fashion, including both ascriptive characteristics (sex, race, religion, and so forth) and ideology (values and positions on issues). Evidently, politicians can do little about the former, and much about the latter. So some of our principal-agency arguments apply only to ideology. That said, politicians can choose to emphasize certain ascriptive aspects and deemphasize others; they may even dissemble. So the distinction between what politicians *are* (in some essential sense) and what they do and say is not a strict dichotomy.

Second, our arguments may be generalized to a multi-seat district, where there is space for multiple parties and their issues, or to an entire country. However, scale effects are presumably mitigated. That is, the more representatives are available to represent a single district or country, the easier it is to represent the distribution of characteristics and preferences in that community, even if it is very heterogeneous. Thus, we expect increases and decreases in size to have a greater impact on representativeness in a single-member context than a multimember context.

Third, we should point out one piece of the puzzle that appears to run counter to our argument. In Chapter 8 we show that scale enhances political contestation, which means that sanctioning through a general election loss is less likely in a small community. This is an important counter-tendency. However, seat turnover due to a general election loss is a fairly blunt instrument, and an unusual one. It is unlikely to come into play – even in the most competitive district – unless the politician deviates in a major fashion on a very salient issue.

With these caveats, we conclude that there are good reasons to imagine that the size of a community affects the selection of politicians, the signals emanating from the electorate, information available to citizens, direct contact between citizens and their representatives, and ways citizens might sanction their representative. Nearly all arrows point in the same direction. Accordingly, we argue that in a small community leaders are likely to be closely aligned with the ascriptive and ideological features of the community they represent. A high degree of representativeness is possible. By contrast, in a large, heterogeneous community it is virtually impossible for leaders to achieve this feat and they have less incentive to try.

Trust

As a secondary effect, we expect that *political trust* will be lower in a large community, since trust takes its cues (in part) from the degree of representativeness achieved between constituency and representative. Subasic and Reynolds (2011: 176) note that "at the core of leader–follower relations is a sense of psychological connection in terms of shared social and psychological group memberships, where leaders are those group members who are seen to best embody 'our' shared goals, values, beliefs and aspirations" (see also Turner & Haslam 2001). In a similar vein, Bianco (1998: 258) writes: "Constituents will always trust their representative if they are sure that a common interest exists." The connection between leaders and constituents thus hinges upon a perception of shared membership. Since smaller groups are apt to be more homogeneous, we can anticipate stronger identification between citizens and elites in a smaller political community.

Ultimately, one might argue that the roots of group identity and corresponding suspicion of perceived outsiders is sociobiological insofar as evolutionary pressures favor cooperation among small groups that are geographically separated from one another (Hamilton 1964; Olsson et al. 2005). If so, the norm of self-rule is as old as group identity and follows logically from it. Note that local rule usually corresponds to rule by people who are perceived to be "like us," while distant rule corresponds to rule by people who are classified as "them." In any case, we regard political trust as an aspect, or outcome indicator, of representativeness.

Evidence

Representativeness, according to our understanding, involves three direct components – demographic representativeness, programmatic representativeness, and constituency connections – and one indirect component (trust), assumed to be a reflection of representativeness. We explore each of these components in the sections that follow.

Demographic Representativeness

Demographic representation refers to the degree to which a representative body mirrors the demographic characteristics of its constituency. This includes ethnicity, language, religion, race, age, socioeconomic background, and any other feature that might be regarded as politically relevant. Perfect representation means that a body provides an exact mirror of the community. Deviations from this ideal may be regarded as deficits, especially if the underrepresented group is also disadvantaged.

The usual term for this is "descriptive representation." However, this concept seems to imply a good deal more than can be easily measured or proven. So we adopt the more straightforward notion of demographic representativeness.

A number of extant studies focus on the *size of legislatures* (number of members). Schraufnagel and Bingle (2015) compare the characteristics of US state legislatures (upper and lower chambers) with the characteristics of states along two dimensions of socioeconomic status: the share who have not received a high school diploma and the share who qualify for Medicaid. They find that legislatures with a greater number of seats are more likely to represent these disadvantaged groups. Kjaer and Elklit (2014) examine the representation of women and youth in municipal councils in Denmark. Their simulation-based study suggests that council size (number of seats) is associated with greater representation of these groups.

It is unsurprising that the number of positions (seats) affects the representational capabilities of a body (e.g., a district or legislature). Our focus is, however, on the role of population, i.e., the number of constituents per representative, which we called the *representation ratio* in Chapter 4.

To test the question at country levels we utilize data from the Global Leadership Project (GLP). The GLP asks expert coders to identify the ethnolinguistic identity of national political elites – including members of parliament, the executive, and the supreme (or constitutional) court. It also assesses the share of these groups in the general population. To measure the representativeness of the elite class (R_B) we compare the representation of groups within the elite to their representation in the general population using a transformed version of the Rose Index of Proportionality:

$$R_B = \sum_{t-1}^{n} |G_{\text{Pi}} - G_{Bi}|$$

where G_P is group *i*'s share of the population, G_B is group *i*'s share of a political body, and *n* is the number of groups in the population. A value of zero describes a perfect correspondence between the body politic and a political body. Deviations from zero, i.e., misrepresentation, are potentially infinite, generating a long right tail. To mitigate this right skew, the index is transformed by the natural logarithm.

Table 5.1 *Ethnic misrepresentation*

Estimator	OLS	OLS	2SLS
Model	1	2	3
Population (log)	0.039**	0.040**	0.080**
	(0.019)	(0.019)	(0.039)
Elite positions (log)	−0.153***	−0.155***	−0.232***
	(0.047)	(0.047)	(0.082)
GDP per capita (log)		0.019	
		(0.029)	
Region dummies	✓	✓	✓
Countries	114	114	109
Years	1	1	1
Observations	114	114	109
R^2	0.369	0.373	0.376

Outcome: ethnic misrepresentation index (log). *Units of analysis*: country-years. Constant omitted. *Estimators*: OLS (ordinary least squares), 2SLS (two-stage least squares, using land area and agricultural suitability as instruments), standard errors clustered by country. Right-side variables lagged twenty years behind the outcome. *** $p < 0.01$, ** $p < 0.05$, * $p < 0.10$ (two-tailed tests)

The first set of tests in Table 5.1 regresses this measure against population. Bear in mind that this is a negative measure of representativeness – the higher the score, the greater the deviation from perfect demographic representation. Because we are interested in the impact of population on representation *net* the size of the representative body, we control for the total number of elites (log) on the right side of the model. Model 1 also includes a panel of regional dummies. Model 2 adds per capita GDP. Model 3 is an instrumental variable model.

Across all three models, population shows a positive and fairly stable relationship to the outcome. Political elites with larger constituencies are less representative of ethnocultural groups than political elites with smaller constituencies.

To gauge the magnitude of this effect, we graph the projected increase in ethnocultural misrepresentation as population increases. As illustrated in Figure 5.3, a shift in population from 100,000 to 1 million corresponds to an increase in misrepresentation of about 0.10, which is equivalent to half of a standard deviation on the logarithmic scale.

Granted, it is difficult to ascertain precise relationships between constituency size and representation when one is aggregating at such a high level. A better approach, arguably, focuses at the district level, although

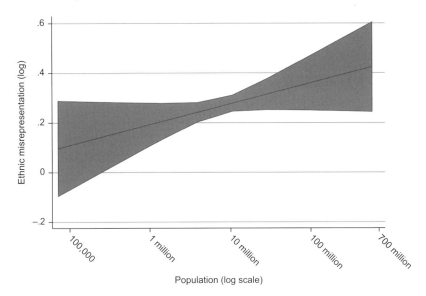

Figure 5.3 Ethnic misrepresentation, predicted values

Predicted values for ethnic misrepresentation, log (Y) as population (log) changes, surrounded by 95 percent confidence interval. Based on Model 1, Table 5.1, with covariates set to sample means. Descriptive statistics (Y): mean = 0.262, SD = 0.190, min = 0, max = 0.841.

doing so narrows the purview of the analysis and hence its generalizability. Our analysis scopes down to contests within electoral districts to upper and lower chambers of state legislatures in the United States.

To gain a sense of the data, consider the state of California. California has a bicameral legislature where the lower house, the California State Assembly, has eighty members elected for two-year terms and the upper house, the California State Senate, has forty members elected for staggered four-year terms. Elections are held every two years, at which point all Assembly members, and half of Senate members, are chosen. This means that every two years there are sixty contests, which form our primary units of analysis. Senate districts are twice as large as Assembly districts, which renders a controlled comparison, as all other aspects that might affect the choice of minority candidates are held constant.

California is a fairly typical state. In most states, the lower house is at least twice as large (in membership) as the upper house, meaning that upper-house districts are at least twice as large as lower-house districts. (One state, Nebraska, is unicameral, and therefore excluded from our analysis.) In our sample, the mean population of upper-house seats is 162,341 and the mean population of lower-house seats is 63,970.

The dependent variable of interest is the probability of a seat being won by a minority group, specifically a person of African-American, Asian, Latino, or Native American heritage. A higher probability will be regarded as enhancing descriptive representation. The independent variable of interest is the size (population, log) of the district. This is accompanied by state and year dummies in order to focus the comparison on contests held within the same state in the same election.

Results are posted in Table 5.2, where we find a strong negative association between district size and the probability of minority representation. Minorities are more likely to be elected in smaller districts, as expected. Specifically, they are more likely to be elected to the lower chamber of the state legislature than to the upper chamber.

To see why this might be so, let us return to our theory. We conjectured that voters generally prefer representatives who are like them (demographically). It follows that the higher the percentage of African-American voters in the district, the greater the likelihood of an African-American representative being elected in that district. Ditto for Asians, Latinos, and Native Americans. However, the relationship is probably not linear, but perhaps approximates an S-curve. That is, the chance of minority representation increases only marginally when the share of a minority increases from 0 percent to 20 percent, it increases at a much faster rate between 20 percent and 50 percent, and it slows down again at higher levels. If minority populations are geographically concentrated, it follows that the likelihood of a district containing a large minority population (say, greater than 30 percent) is greater in a smaller district. And this, in turn, should enhance minority representation.[3]

Indeed, further analysis (not shown) reveals that ethnic groups that are more geographically clustered such as African-Americans and Native Americans are more responsive to district size than ethnic groups that are more dispersed such as Latinos and Asians.

Another piece of corroborating evidence comes when we introduce a variable measuring the share of minorities in a district. This factor, by itself, explains half of the variation in minority representation, and swamps any effect from district size. So the impact of district size on minority representation is most likely registered through the social composition of a district.

---

[3] To be sure, clustering also means that there are more "wasted" minority votes – votes that exceed the number needed to elect a minority member, and thus may lower the total number of African-Americans that could be elected statewide. However, if voters (or at least some voters) base their choice on race, this is probably less of a problem for a minority candidate than the obverse – too few minority votes in a district.

To be sure, since minority representatives at the state level are still relatively rare in the United States, our findings are prone to the pitfalls of rare events. Scholars have not yet taken a look at this issue in other countries, especially those that employ multimember districts. So one must be careful about generalizing. Even so, the available evidence suggests that scale has an important impact on the probability of minority representation. If districts were smaller in the United States, there would be a higher share of minority representatives, all things equal.

Programmatic Representativeness

Representativeness may also be understood according to the degree of correspondence, or congruence, between the views of constituents and their representatives. Where correspondence is high we say that programmatic representativeness exists. (We avoid the term "responsiveness" because it is exceedingly difficult to test the degree to which the behavior of representatives is causally affected by the views of their constituents [Matsusaka 2015; Wlezien 2017; Wlezien & Soroka 2007].) We argue, following Dahl and Tufte (1973: 85) and – much earlier – the Anti-Federalists who opposed the US Constitution (Kenyon 1955), that increases in the size of a constituency attenuate representativeness.

Table 5.2 *Minority representation, district level (United States)*

Model	1
Population (log)	−0.523***
	(0.136)
State dummies	✓
Year dummies	✓
States	50
Districts	843
Years	5
Observations	7,456
R square (pseudo)	0.127

Outcome: 1 = minority (Black, Hispanic, Asian, or Native American) occupies a state legislative seat, 0 = seat occupied by someone else. *Units of analysis*: district-years. *Estimator*: logit, standard errors clustered by state. Constant omitted.
*** p < 0.01, ** p < 0.05, * p < 0.10 (two-tailed tests)

A good deal of political science work has been conducted on the relationship between diversity and programmatic representativeness. Summarizing this literature, P. Jones (2013: 482) writes,

Representatives of heterogeneous constituencies are less able to identify policy platforms that a majority of voters prefer (Bailey and Brady 1998; Ensley et al. 2009), are less responsive to the political preferences of their constituents (Bishin 2003; Bishin et al. 2006; Dennis et al. 2000; Fiorina 1974; Gerber and Lewis 2004; Gulati 2004; Kuklinski 1977), and are more likely to abstain from taking votes in Congress altogether.

If one assumes that larger districts are more heterogeneous, as argued in Chapter 3 (see also Levendusky & Pope 2010), it follows that larger districts are also likely to be less programmatically representative.

However, we have been able to identify just a few studies that focus explicitly on the relationship between *population* and programmatic representativeness.

Frederick (2010: ch. 5) compares (a) the voting behavior of members of the US House of Representatives with (b) the political views of their constituents, both arrayed on a left–right spectrum. To measure (a), he relies on DW-NOMINATE scores, a latent variable measure of ideology based on roll-call votes in the House. To measure (b), he uses the percentage of the two-party vote cast for the Democratic Party within each district. First, (b) is regressed against (a) to obtain an expected value of (a) for each member. Second, the absolute value of the difference between (a) and the expected value of (a) for each representative is calculated. This forms the dependent variable for a second regression model that includes a measure of population size of each district, along with a panel of controls. The sample covers four congresses (with dummies for each included in the regression model to account for time effects). Results support the thesis that size leads to greater divergence between constituency opinion and representative behavior.

A second study follows a similar methodology but focuses on the US Senate, where there is much greater variability in size and hence (one would presume) greater leverage on our theoretical question. Kenna (2016) uses DW-NOMINATE scores to measure the ideal-points of US senators. To measure the ideology of constituents at state levels he employs an index based on congressional election returns and interest group ratings of candidate ideology (Berry et al. 1998). The outcome of theoretical interest is again the distance between a senator's ideal-point and the state's ideal-point (the state's median point on the Berry et al. scale). This analysis also reveals that larger districts (states) are associated with greater distances, i.e., lower representativeness.

We do not undertake our own analysis of this question as we cannot envision substantial improvements in these studies, and we have no reason to quarrel with their findings.

Constituency Connections

To properly represent constituents, representatives must stay in close contact with them – seeking out their views, understanding their life situations, and soliciting their support. This may be achieved by visits to special events occurring in the constituency, "surgeries" (scheduled meetings with constituents, usually in a constituency office), personal communication (by letter, telephone, email, or the Web), allocation of staff to constituency service, surveys of constituents, and so forth. We theorize that constituency connections – aka "reciprocal communication" (Dahl & Tufte 1973: 88) – should be stronger and more intimate in smaller political communities.

A wealth of testimony from politicos and citizens confirms that personal connections between leaders and constituents are fostered by small scale (Corbett & Veenendaal 2018; Oliver, Shang, & Callen 2012; Rogowski 1987: 204; Veenendaal 2013). A minister in Liechtenstein argued,

We are not a political elite; a political group of people who are far away from reality, but we are involved in daily life, involved in relations with the citizens. And we know about their emotions, about their wishes, about their whereabouts. Or if we don't want to know, they will tell us anyway.

Indeed, politicians truly live cheek by jowl with their constituents. A journalist in Liechtenstein reports,

Here, you go out on an evening to the cinema and you might have the prime minister sitting beside you. And you can talk to him about the weather, but you can also talk about politics, and you can also talk about anything that bothers you. So the politicians are closer to the people, which basically means that the chances that they are making politics for the people is also higher.

In similar fashion, a prominent politician from the Pacific island state of Palau (population: 20,000) testifies:

I know maybe 95 percent of the people in the Republic. Now I may not know their name, but if I see that person I know their face, and probably 80 percent or 85 percent of the time I know where that person lives. Because you campaign a couple of times and you meet these guys, the same people. And so these are our constituents, you know their mandate; they talk to you, get your number and talk to you, so it's very, very close.

In smaller communities citizens also expect to meet their representatives on a regular basis, and may lose patience when this does not happen.
One former Maltese member of parliament, who had just been promoted
to minister, reports,

People are sometimes frustrated, because they are SMS-ing me, and I tell them
that we will set a meeting. And they come here thinking that they will meet the
minister, but they are meeting my customer care team. They are annoyed because
they say, "I voted for you, and I have to see you." They still think that they voted
[name], so they still want to meet [name].

In a similar vein, another Maltese official remarks,

I believe that when you have such a small population, basically whatever each and
every politician is not only doing, but also thinking about doing, is easily trans-
mitted and known to the rest of the population. And therefore, different from
what critics argue, probably we are the most scrutinized and accountable politicians on the continent.

By contrast, in a large district or polity it is more difficult to establish and
maintain person-to-person relationships.

In the United States, a raft of studies compare leader–constituency relationships in the Senate and the House, where the ratio of constituency sizes is
roughly 9:1 (Fenno 1982; Oppenheimer 1996; Parker 1986; Uslaner 1981).
Atlas, Hendershott, and Zupan (1997: 222) summarize this literature:

Compared to their House counterparts, members of the Senate: go home to their
constituencies less frequently; allocate less of their personal staff to home offices
than to Washington offices; and campaign and are evaluated more on the basis of
their policy stances than on their personal accessibility.

Other studies compare US senators to each other, capitalizing on variations
in state size (Hibbing & Alford 1990; Krasno 1994; Lee & Oppenheimer
1999; Oppenheimer 1996). Hibbing and Alford (1990: 594) write,

Compared to their counterparts in populous states, constituents in lightly populated states are much more likely to report having met personally with their
senator and/or with a member of the senator's staff, having received mail from
the senator, or knowing someone who has met the senator. They are somewhat
more likely to have seen the senator on television and to have heard the senator on
the radio. ... They are more likely to define the performance of their senator in
terms of pork-barrel politics rather than decisions on controversial national issues.
And they are much more likely to be able to recall the name of their incumbent
senator.

One study examines size differences across US House districts.
Although the differences are small, the effects seem substantial.
Frederick (2008: 375) reports,

Individuals are less likely to report having contact with and to attempt to contact their House incumbent as the population of the district escalates. They also have a higher probability of claiming their member is out of touch with the district and have a greater propensity to believe their House member would not be helpful if they need assistance. Constituents in larger House districts evaluate the performance of their representatives less favorably and feel less warmly toward them.[4]

Similar results are found when comparing state legislatures in small and large states (Squire 1993).

Across municipalities in the United States there are also enormous variations in size, which provide fodder for another level of analysis. Muzzio and Tompkins (1989: 91) write,

Smaller districts enhance the capacity of a council member to serve constituents and communities. Studies suggest that there is an increasing "case" orientation among American city council members, especially those based in districts or wards.[5]

Thus, across a range of venues scholars have found a consistent relationship between size and representative/constituent relations. Smaller is more intimate, and this enhances citizens' opportunities to scrutinize and exercise control over their representatives.

Political Trust

Political trust, in the words of one expert, "reflects evaluations of whether or not political authorities and institutions are performing in accordance with normative expectations held by the public . . . In brief, an expression of trust in government is a summary judgment that the system is responsive and will do what is right even in the absence of constant scrutiny" (Miller & Listhaug 1990: 358; see also Levi & Stoker 2000). We regard expressions of trust as convergent with – and as an empirical matter, virtually indistinguishable from – expressions of *confidence, support, satisfaction,* and *perceived responsiveness.*

With this understanding, we argue that scale has a negative impact on political trust. This is consistent with the concept of a *radius of trust,* where trust is strong among a core group of family and friends, and attenuates as connections to the individual become weaker (Hu 2017).[6] The evidence on this hypothesis may now be briefly reviewed.

Across municipalities with identical functions, a number of studies show that larger jurisdictions garner less trust than smaller jurisdictions (Baldassare 1985; Denters 2002; Denters et al. 2014: Part III; Rahn &

---

[4] See also Frederick (2010: ch. 4).   [5] See also Heilig and Mundt (1984: 83–91).
[6] Although the radius of trust is usually applied to generalized trust, it would seem to be equally applicable to political trust. (Politicians are people too.)

Rudolph 2005; but see Charron, Fernández-Albertos, & Lapuente 2013). Across legislative constituencies in the United States, trust in politicians and perceived responsiveness is higher in smaller constituencies (Bowen 2010: 119). Comparing US senators in differently sized states, Lee and Oppenheimer (1999: 47) find that "constituents in less populous states evaluate their senators more favorably than those in larger states."

In a quasi-experimental study of mergers across local governments in Denmark, trust declined in merged municipalities while it remained stable or declined only slightly in un-merged municipalities (Hansen 2013). (One might wonder whether this result is partly a product of a disruptive merger rather than of the size of the resulting jurisdictions. For contrasting results, see C. Larsen 2002.)

Political trust in large countries seems to be considerably lower than in small countries (Matsubayashi 2007). Likewise, when scholars compare units at different levels, those that are smaller elicit higher levels of trust. Local institutions are more trusted than regional institutions, regional institutions are more trusted than national institutions, and national institutions are more trusted than supranational institutions (Berezin & Diez-Medrano 2008; Nielsen 1981).[7]

Although the point seems virtually uncontested, we examine the matter ourselves. The Global Competitiveness Report, produced by the World Economic Forum (Schwab & Sala-i-Martin 2015), surveys businesspeople in countries around the world on a variety of questions, including public trust in the ethical standards of politicians. The survey has been conducted annually over the past decade, producing country-level estimates for a short panel. Country coverage is somewhat higher than other comparable surveys and on this account is more useful for our purposes.

In Model 1, Table 5.3, we regress this outcome against the population of countries along with annual dummies. Model 2 adds a set of covariates to the model. Model 3 is an instrumental variable analysis. Point estimates from these three models are very similar. Respondents in large countries are considerably less likely to report that politicians are trustworthy.

To gain a better sense of how country size may affect perceptions of politics, we graph the predicted values of political trust against population. Figure 5.4 shows that an increase in population from 100,000 to 1 million is associated with a half point decrease on this seven-point index of political trust (about half a standard deviation). It follows that when

---

[7] An exception to this last generalization can be found in China, where the national government is trusted more than local or regional governments (Li & O'Brien 1996).

Table 5.3 *Political trust*

Outcome	Trust in Politicians			Trust in Government	
Presumed treatment unit	*Countries*			*Municipalities*	
Units of analysis	*Countries*			*Individuals*	
Estimator	OLS	OLS	2SLS	OLS	OLS
Model	**1**	**2**	**3**	**4**	**5**
Population of country (log)	−0.230*** (0.045)	−0.306*** (0.061)	−0.297*** (0.084)		
Population of municipality (log)				−0.006*** (0.001)	−0.005*** (0.001)
GDP per capita (log)		0.013 (0.140)			
Urbanization		1.432** (0.651)			
GDP per capita growth		0.004 (0.014)			
Protestant		0.020*** (0.003)			
Years independent (log)		0.089 (0.092)			
State history		0.092 (0.348)			
Democracy (Lexical index)		−0.069 (0.042)			
English colony		0.248 (0.166)			
Muslim		0.005 (0.003)			
Country dummies					✓
Income dummies (for each bracket)					✓
Education dummies (highest level attained)					✓
Annual dummies	✓	✓			✓
Decade dummies			✓		
Countries	147	92	142	85	85
Time periods	9	9	9	4	4
Observations	1,190	765	1,156	199,668	168,078
R-squared	0.465	0.655	0.468	0.0006	0.158

Outcomes: trust in politicians (Models 1–3), trust in government (Models 4–5). Constant omitted. *Estimators*: OLS (ordinary least squares), 2SLS (two-stage least squares, using land area and agricultural suitability as instruments). (An ordered probit estimator, an option for Models 4–5, shows very similar results.) Standard errors clustered by country in Models 1–3. *** $p < 0.01$, ** $p < 0.05$, * $p < 0.10$ (two-tailed tests)

Vars. (Models 4–5)	Obs.	Mean	Std. Dev.	Min.	Max.
Trust in government	289,619	2.42	0.94	1.00	4.00
Municipal population (log)	224,923	9.10	4.09	0.00	13.12

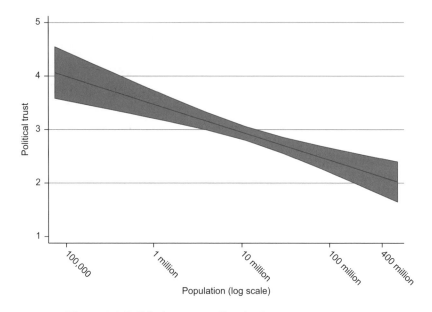

Figure 5.4 Political trust, predicted values

Predicted values for trust in politicians (*Y*) as population (log) changes, surrounded by 95 percent confidence interval. Based on Model 1, Table 5.3, with covariates set to sample means. Descriptive statistics (*Y*): mean = 2.99, SD = 1.18, min = 1.25, max = 6.48.

comparing communities of *very* different sizes – e.g., São Tomé and India – one can expect substantial differences in political trust.

The second portion of Table 5.3 examines a different measure of political trust. This measure is a product of the World Values Survey (WVS), a global survey administered in eighty-five countries across several waves, beginning in the 1980s (different countries are included in each wave of the survey so it is not a balanced panel). Among the many questions on the WVS is a question about confidence in government. Response categories include (1) none at all, (2) not very much, (3) quite a lot, and (4) a great deal. Country coverage for WVS is not nearly as extensive as for the Global Competitiveness Report, so the cross-country sample is limited. However, WVS also asks respondents about the size of the town in which they live. Answers are grouped into categories (0–2,000, 2,000–5,000, and so forth). We transpose these categories into a linear scale by recoding each category at the lower bound (0, 2000, 5000, and so forth). This scale is then transformed by the natural logarithm to match other analyses in this book. (Findings are robust when analyses are replicated with the original categories, considered as a vector of dummies.) Towns define locality for most people, and also function as a governmental unit in most countries. Consequently, the size of the town in which a citizen lives may affect their overall confidence in government.

In Model 4, we regress trust in government against the size of a respondent's local community, as described. In Model 5, we add several covariates that may serve a confounding role, including country dummies and some individual-level characteristics. Estimates for the impact of population on trust in government are negative in both models, as expected, and highly significant. Note that because WVS is an extraordinarily large, multi-wave survey, and because we treat individual respondents as the unit of analysis, the total number of observations is close to 200,000. In a sample of this size there is little threat from stochastic features of the data-generating process. Note also that in Model 5, due to the inclusion of country dummies, we are effectively comparing responses of citizens from the same country living within small and large communities. This eliminates problems of cross-country comparability, which vex many cross-country analyses. However, this analysis also means that we may be comparing different kinds of respondents since small towns and large cities tend to attract different sorts of people. It is possible that these subject-level differences – rather than size per se – are driving the results, even though we control for individual characteristics such as income and education.

No single analysis can hope to alleviate all doubt about the relationship between scale and political trust. However, the fact that similar results are obtained from country- and municipal-level definitions of community, coupled with the many prior studies reviewed earlier in this book, give us confidence in the general finding. Community scale seems to exert a negative effect on political trust.

Summary

Table 5.4 summarizes extant studies, along with our own analyses, of scale and representativeness.

Table 5.4 *Scale and representativeness: Inventory of analyses*

Indicators	Countries	Treatment units	Years	Units of analysis	Research design	Effect	Study
Demographic representation							
*Ethnic misrepresentation	(114)	Countries (114)	(1)	Countries (114)	Cross-sectional	←	Table 5.1
*Minority representation	United States	State legislative districts (843)	(4)	District contests (7,456)	Cross-sectional	→	Table 5.2
Programmatic representation							
Ideological divergence	United States	Congressional districts (435)	(8)	Congressional terms (1,750)	Cross-sectional	←	Frederick 2010
Ideological divergence	United States	States (50)	(29)	State-years (1,522)	Cross-sectional	←	Keena 2016
Constituency connections							
Politician effort allocation	United States	States (50)	(19)	State-years (958)	Cross-sectional	→	Atlas, Hendershott, & Zupan 1997
Various	United States	States (50)	(1)	States (50)	Cross-sectional	→	Hibbing & Alford 1990
Contact	United States	States (50)	(5)	Individuals (969)	Cross-sectional	→	Oppenheimer 1996
Trust in							
Elected officials	(4)	Municipalities (234)	(3)	Individuals (4,826)	Cross-sectional	→	Denters et al. 2014: ch. 8
Local government	United States	Cities (55)	(1)	Individuals (9,043)	Cross-sectional	→	Rahn & Rudolph 2005
Quality of institutions	(9)	Countries (9)	(6)	Regions (117)	Cross-sectional	→	Charron et al. 2013
State government	United States	States (48)	(5)	Individuals (27,430)	Cross-sectional	→	Bowen 2010

Local government	Denmark	Municipalities (60)	(2)	Individuals (900)	Cross-sectional	→	Hansen 2013
Local government	Denmark	Municipalities (38)	(3)	Individuals (50,765)	Cross-sectional	Ø	Larsen 2002
National government	(22)	Countries (22)	(1)	Individuals (18,198)	Cross-sectional	→	Matsubayashi 2007
Local government	Denmark	Communities (275)	(1)	Individuals (1,856)	Cross-sectional	→	Nielsen 1981
*Politicians	(147)	Countries (147)	(9)	Country-years (1,190)	Cross-sectional	→	Table 5.3
*Government	(85)	Municipalities (?)	(4)	Individuals (199,668)	Cross-sectional	→	Table 5.3

Treatment units: units exhibiting variation in scale. *Years*: number of years over which data are collected – not to be confused with the frequency of observations, as data may or may not be annual and may be averaged across years. *Research design*: the main, or benchmark, research design – classified as cross-sectional (where the analysis is driven primarily by variation across units) or panel (where the analysis is driven primarily by variation through time). *Effect*: when the scale of a community increases, the designated outcome goes up (↑), down (↓), up and down (∩), or experiences no perceptible change (Ø). A scale effect is considered significant if it passes a modest bar of statistical significance, i.e., p < 0.10 (two-tailed test) in the benchmark model. Number of countries, treatment units, years, or observations in parentheses.

Although the question of demographic and programmatic representation is of enormous interest to scholars, few systematic studies focus
explicitly on population – net district magnitude, electoral system,
and other background characteristics – as a predictor of representation. Our analysis of ethnic representation, presented in Table 5.1, is
the only study of the subject we are aware of. It shows an unambig-
uous negative association between the size of a country and its propensity to mirror the ethnic attributes of the population, once the size
of the legislature is controlled. We also find a negative association
between the likelihood of achieving minority representation in US
state legislatures and the size of those constituencies, as shown in
Table 5.2.

We were able to locate just a few studies of scale and programmatic
representation. Both indicate that the size of a constituency negatively
impacts the degree to which representatives adhere to the preferences of
the median voter. However, one must qualify these findings with the
caveat that the attitudes of the mass public, and the behavior of representatives, is very difficult to measure.

Constituency connections are a frequent subject of study. All studies
that we are aware of point in the same direction: smaller communities
foster closer relationships between representatives and constituents. One
must be slightly concerned that most of these studies are conducted in the
United States. Even so, there is no reason a priori to expect that this
relationship operates differently in other contexts. Indeed, our own fieldwork in small states and territories around the world strongly confirms the
hypothesized relationship.

Our final topic, trust, has also been extensively studied. Subnational
studies – focused on regional or municipal governmental units – show that
larger units almost invariably elicit a lower degree of trust. This result is
replicated in our own analyses, focused on countries and municipalities
across the world. Larger governmental units, and politicians representing
those units, are viewed by citizens as less trustworthy.

6 Particularism

Particularism refers to targeted efforts by politicians to cultivate the support of specific citizens or groups of citizens (aka clients), and the allegiance of those citizens to their leader (aka patron). By contrast, *universalism* refers to political strategies based on political parties and their encompassing ideologies, and the provision of public goods that benefit a wide array of constituents. While a universalist approach to politics adheres to uniform rules, impersonal bureaucratic routines, and programmatic policies, particularism is sensitive to personal relationships, local constituencies, and quid pro quo agreements.

It is not easy to summarize the ramifications of particularism/universalism. Even so, it may be helpful to survey the field in a schematic fashion before proceeding.

In a wide-ranging discussion of clientelism, Hicken (2011: 302) writes, "The starting point (stated or unstated) for most of the literature is that clientelism is inefficient at best and downright dangerous at worst." He goes on to qualify that view, pointing out that – although inefficient – clientelism may serve as a method of redistribution in poor societies that do not have well-developed welfare states (Kitschelt 2000). Even so, it seems clear that clientelism is never a first-best policy mechanism. The literature on corruption, which encompasses elements of clientelism, is even more pessimistic about the policy effects of this pathology (Mauro 1995; Shleifer & Vishny 1993).

Other forms of particularism – e.g., constituency service, targeted campaign spending, and pork – are more innocuous. Indeed, they may be viewed as signs of political responsiveness, and may serve justifiable policy goals. However, many observers are skeptical that highly targeted efforts serve the best interests of the larger community. Ad hoc, informal approaches to campaigning and policymaking are an invitation to abuse. Helping friends, neighbors, and associates usually means allocating resources in an inefficient manner. As such, particularism may be viewed as the flip side of representativeness, our topic in the previous chapter. Here, we highlight the largely *negative* repercussions of close constituent–representative ties.

With this understanding, we begin by sketching a theory of how scale might impact particularism. Next, we examine the question empirically using a variety of indicators including partisanship, targeted campaign expenditures, pork or earmarks, constituency service, vote-buying, clientelism, and corruption. A brief conclusion draws together the results of these analyses.

Theory

To understand the relationship between scale and particularism we take the perspective of political leaders, who must cultivate support among constituents in order to survive. We presume that all leaders require a certain level of support, even if they are not subject to multiparty elections and even if their support is limited to a small segment of the population. In this respect, our theory applies broadly – to democracies as well as autocracies.

Of course, the specific ways in which scale affects leaders' strategies vary across contexts. Where multiparty elections are in place, particularism is likely to be manifested through the electoral system. Where multiparty elections allow for preferential voting, this is a natural avenue for particularism. In poor societies where multiparty elections are in place, particularism is likely to appear in the form of vote-buying. Particularism has many manifestations, each of which is crafted to fit within a set of social and institutional incentives and to please a specific clientele. Our theory must be adjusted to fit the varied contexts in which leaders strive for power.

Whatever the context, leaders face a choice in their bid to build support among important constituencies. They may pursue a particularistic course of action, investing in policies that benefit a small section of the community in a targeted (and possibly illegal) fashion. Or, they may pursue a universalistic course of action, investing in policies that benefit a large share of the citizenry through some formal (and legal) rule that establishes eligibility. With respect to campaign strategies, one may distinguish between vote-buying or personal and solidaristic appeals, on one hand, and programmatic appeals (ideology) attached to a political party, on the other. With respect to public policies, one may distinguish between private or club goods, on one hand, and public goods, on the other.

We recognize that these contrasts are a matter of degrees. Accordingly, we regard these two options as ideal-types. In any case, for heuristic purposes it is helpful to draw the contrast sharply.

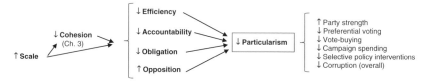

Figure 6.1 Scale effects on particularism

Scale affects the choice between particularism and universalism in a number of ways, as diagramed in Figure 6.1. Larger communities are less cohesive, as discussed in Chapter 3. This, along with scale itself, affects the viability of particularism through several secondary mechanisms: (a) efficiency, (b) accountability, (c) obligation, and (d) opposition.

Efficiency

The size of a political community (a polity or district) affects the relative efficiency of particularistic and universalistic strategies for cultivating support.

Let us first consider a scenario in which districts of varying size draw on the *same* pool of resources. For example, US senators – selected from large and small states – are equal in power and draw on the resources of the federal government. It makes sense that senators from small states should be more concerned with particularistic benefits because those benefits go further on a per capita basis (Atlas, Hendershott, & Zupan 1997: 221). A million dollars in Wyoming (pop. 546,000) translates into roughly two dollars per constituent, while a million dollars in California (pop. 37 million) translates into roughly three cents per constituent. Accordingly, particularistic benefits likely play a larger role in the election prospects of the senator from Wyoming than those of the senator from California.

Where politicians draw on *different* resource pools, presumably proportional to the population of their constituencies, this argument no longer holds. As an example, one might consider the situation facing the governors of Wyoming and California. In principle, both leaders could raise an equal amount of revenue per capita, to be distributed in any way they see fit. Here, dollars go just as far in California as in Wyoming.

Yet, even here, it may be less efficient for politicians representing a large district (e.g., California) to devote their energy and resources to particularized benefits. Consider the logistics of dispensing payments for votes – or pork – in a constituency numbering in the millions. It is not clear how to practice particularism on a massive scale without the routinization and bureaucratization that, in effect, transforms particularism into universalism. One needs rules, and dedicated bureaucrats, to get the job done. (The alternative is to involve a great many intermediaries, at great cost and consequent waste.)

While the efficiency of particularistic strategies attenuates with size, the efficiency of universalistic strategies does not. Indeed, they may become more efficient as the size of a constituency grows. Consider universalistic policies such as social security or defense. Here, one can anticipate economies of scale such that per capita costs decline as the size of a community grows (Chapter 12). Consider also universalistic electoral strategies that are grounded in political parties and programmatic positions on issues. Here, we can also anticipate economies of scale. The per capita cost of advertising one's party or ideology increases at a sublinear rate with the size of a constituency.

In summary, the relative cost of particularistic and universalistic strategies changes as political communities become larger. For reasons of efficiency, we predict that scale will condition the relative prominence of these tools for a rational politician, who wishes to maximize her political support.

Accountability

As a community grows, particularistic agreements between a politician and her constituents become harder to monitor and to enforce, raising problems of accountability on both sides (Medina & Stokes 2007: 76–77).

Consider the problem of reward. If a politician employs her political capital to obtain a particularized benefit for her community – e.g., a new road or school – she will naturally seek to take credit for that effort, hoping to be rewarded at the next election (or in some other manner, if the regime is not democratic). In a large district, however, contact between representatives and constituents is minimal and citizens are less likely to recall what their member has done for them. Claiming credit for particularized benefits is therefore more difficult (Abramowitz & Segal 1992; Binder, Maltzman, & Sigelman 1998; Crespin & Finocchiaro 2013; Hibbing & Alford 1990; Oppenheimer 1996). By contrast, claiming credit for generalized benefits – e.g., a new social security policy that a broad swath of the public will utilize – is no more difficult in a large district than in a small district.

Now let us consider the problem of punishment if a politician or citizen reneges on her end of the (implicit or explicit) agreement entailed by the provision of a particularized benefit. When a politician promises to bring new roads to a town in exchange for election, citizens must monitor that promise and hold the leader to account if s/he fails to deliver. In a small community, citizens may accost that politician directly, or talk to local leaders who will intercede on their behalf. A politician in Seychelles testifies,

Social relations might affect your work; friends and family members may put pressure on you. Sometimes, politicians and other officials do not have the capacity to resist these pressures. People sometimes want to dictate: "If you don't give me this favor, I will go to the president!"

Alternatively, or additionally, aggrieved citizens may spread the word that this politician is not to be trusted, leading to negative repercussions for that individual and her family. Local relationships may suffice to sanction broken contracts so that relationships can be preserved (e.g., by compensating losers) or new relationships established.

In a large community, however, where a town represents only a fraction of the leader's constituency, it will be difficult to ensure compliance. Bear in mind that a politician with a large constituency has many duties and responsibilities. If she shirks on one promise, her failure may be lost amidst all the other promises she has made. Even if a town's citizens notice, they have little recourse, for they are a small share of the electorate. In a community numbering in the millions, the only practical option may be to shift support to a different group, e.g., a different party or an organization that works outside the realm of party politics (if there are no elections or elections are not open to multiparty contestation).

By the same token, if the leader delivers on her promise to build a road in the town, she will have a hard time monitoring compliance on the part of town citizens, who may not hold up their end of the implicit agreement, i.e., they may support a different politician in the next election. In a large community, pork may be overwhelmed by other issues that inevitably flurry across a busy political stage. And a leader with millions of supporters will be at pains to keep track of the voting behavior of every town in her constituency.

The same accountability dilemma arises in the context of vote-buying. In a small community, politicians can organize poll-watchers to get out the vote and to oversee their voting, exerting pressure on "their" people to turn out and to vote correctly. A Maltese politician explained how this works in practice:

They [party officials] will phone you up, on the day of election, 12 o'clock, saying you haven't voted yet. They know, they have the list of the people who did not vote. They are inside, and they phone you up. At 3 o'clock in the afternoon again; at 6 o'clock they phone you up again.

If citizens renege on their commitment, this will thus be easier to assess in a small and homogeneous community like Malta, where everyone is expected to vote the same way, than in a large and diverse community, where expectations are mixed and vote tallies harder to interpret.

The larger the community, the harder it is for politicians to monitor compliance and to exact punishment. Targeted, quid pro quo agreements are therefore discouraged in favor of universalistic policies – which are much easier to monitor and enforce in a large community. In all these settings, mechanisms of accountability seem to favor particularistic policies in small communities and universalistic policies in large communities.

Obligation

Particularism is never (or hardly ever) a short-term transaction, for the problems of monitoring and compliance that bedevil accountability relationships (reviewed earlier in this chapter) can never be entirely solved through quid pro quo agreements. Because principals cannot ensure that agents will hold up their end of an (implicit or explicit) agreement, successful pork-barrel politics, vote-buying, or constituency service depend to a considerable degree upon mutual trust. And trust, in turn, depends upon establishing an ongoing feeling of connection and obligation between a leader and her constituents. To the extent that the bond is strong, a particularistic approach to campaigning and policymaking is reinforced. To the extent that the bond is weak, a universalistic approach to campaigning and policymaking is encouraged, *faute de mieux*.

Since feelings of obligation between citizens and their representative are fostered by close face-to-face relationships, we can expect them to be stronger, and more pervasive, in small communities. And this, in turn, should foster particularism. In the small Pacific island nation of Palau, a senator confesses,

We vote for people because of who they are, not for their performance. It's really because they came to a funeral, or they assisted your kids with some problem, or your relatives go for medical treatment, or you had a house party where they donated to you.

Long-term dyadic relationships of this sort are inherently particularistic. The politician knows what services to provide for a client, and the client knows what is expected of her. They are tied together by bonds of mutual obligation. This is especially true in parts of the world with many poor and uneducated citizens and vast differences of power and wealth separating elites and masses.

Opposition

Particularistic actions benefit some people while excluding others. Often, they contravene widely held norms, and sometimes they are illegal. In a small community, such actions are likely to be enmeshed in a dense network that is difficult for outsiders to penetrate. If the beneficiaries are located in a single area and encompass important local elites, opposition is unlikely to develop. Who will decry a policy that benefits family, friends, and neighbors?

In a large community, however, there are bound to be people who fall outside the closed network within which particularistic benefits are shared. Because the large community is also more heterogeneous, networks are looser and less constraining. It will be easier for non-beneficiaries to speak up in opposition to a program that excludes them. And outsiders are likely to have significant resources they can muster, e.g., rival networks, media organizations, nongovernmental organizations (NGOs), and professional associations.

For particularistic policies that are illegal, or at least unsavory, one must also consider the risk of discovery. In a small community, pork and bribes may fly under the radar. After all, just a few people are involved and the sums are not large. However, in a large community, where particularistic policies must be scaled up, the risk of discovery and attendant publicity increases. Note that vote-buying and other corrupt activities – if operated on a large scale – require the participation of many intermediaries. An army of precinct captains will be needed in order to distribute payouts to a constituency numbering in the millions. Since it takes only one snitch to expose an entire operation, the probability of snitching (either to the authorities or to the media) increases in a linear fashion with the number of personnel engaged in the operation. As an operation scales up it is also more likely to attract notice from police, watchdog agencies, the media, and outside observers. Low-level operations are not terribly newsworthy. But a high-level, far-reaching operation grabs headlines.

Thus, we expect that scale is likely to enhance the probability of scandal, or at least of negative publicity. The more people and money are involved, the greater the likelihood that someone will get caught and that a scandal will ensue. For a political leader this could be career-ending, and may even land her in jail or in exile. Even in authoritarian systems, scandal is risky – both for the individual involved and for the system in which she is enmeshed. A high-level scandal may serve as the spark that lights a fire of popular revolt. For this reason, as well, we anticipate that leaders of large communities will be less inclined to pursue a particularistic style of politicking.

Granted, small communities have greater social cohesion (Chapter 3), and this should depress deviance. Insofar as actions we have defined as "particularist" are viewed as deviant by members of a community, one might imagine that a small community would be in a better position to monitor behavior and enforce sanctions.

However, particularism in politics is not always viewed as deviant by members of a small community. Indeed, if everyone, or nearly everyone, is engaging in a practice it is deviant *not* to participate. Specifically, where vote-buying, pork, and political corruption are rampant, these activities are likely to be perceived as normal. Or, alternatively, they will be normalized for members of the community but not for outsiders. For example, special funds reserved for a district may be perceived by members of that district as deserved ("democracy at work"), while special funds reserved for other districts are perceived as an example of special interests ("pork").

Observation of small states suggests that citizens may be tolerant, perhaps even encouraging, of corruption when it is perceived to benefit them. According to a Maltese journalist,

What you have is shared *omertà*: a culture, a consensus, an agreement in the community that this [corruption] should be allowed and encouraged because we benefit all from it. So corruption becomes not a sin that people fall into and then you punish them when you can punish them, but actually becomes a policy.

The result of this culture of impunity is that corrupt officials are unlikely to face retribution for their behavior. Consequently, we do not view the suppression of deviance as working against our thesis about scale effects on particularism. It may even support our thesis.

Evidence

Studies have shown that material incentives are less likely to be employed in larger groups (Bueno de Mesquita, Morrow, & Siverson 2002; Weldon 2006; Whiteley & Seyd 2002). Other studies suggest that clientelism and pork-barrel politics are more common in small districts and small polities (Baldacchino 2012; Benedict 1967: 8; Bray 1991: 22; Farrugia 1993: 222–24; Lowenthal 1987: 38–39; Ott 2000: 37–42; Parsons 1951: 508; Peters 1992: 128–29; Srebrnik 2004: 334–35; Sutton 2007; Wettenhall 2001: 181; Wood 1967: 33–34).

In their study of small states, Corbett and Veenendaal (2018: 10) write,

Rather than embodying a legal rational order, politicians in small states typically experience considerable pressure from constituents to personally provide material largesse. Failure to do so often leads to electoral defeat. Patronage in the public sector is common in small states, and public sector appointments are often made on the basis of political loyalties.

Our interview material from small states and territories around the world confirms that patron–client linkages are ubiquitous.

To test the argument in a systematic fashion we explore several measures of particularism (understood as the polar contrast of universalism): (a) party strength/weakness, (b) preferential voting, (c) vote-buying, (d) campaign finance, (e) pork, and (f) corruption (generally considered).

Party Strength

Party strength, or institutionalization, may be understood organizationally, e.g., by the existence of parties and – where they exist – by the size of a party's permanent staff, coherence among the party's leadership, formal rules for leadership selection, and the establishment of an organizational presence in constituencies. It may also be understood in terms of voting behavior (the "party in the electorate"), i.e., the strength of party as a voting cue and, more generally, the strength of partisanship in structuring the relationship between candidates and voters. In a partisan setting, parties structure the electoral connection and voters choose based on the programmatic agendas posed by the parties. In a nonpartisan setting, we assume that voters are motivated by their views of the personal characteristics of candidates, by shifting, ad hoc issues that do not fit neatly into party ideologies, or by material incentives (vote-buying or pork).

Where parties are weak, particularism ought to thrive. Indeed, the strength of parties is often regarded as a negative indicator of particularism (Hicken & Kuhonta 2015; Levitsky 1998; Mainwaring & Scully 1995; Wellhofer & Hennessey 1974). This is true, we maintain, in democratic as well as autocratic contexts. We expect greater particularism in nonparty authoritarian regimes (e.g., Somoza's Nicaragua or Imperial China) than in party-centered authoritarian regimes (e.g., Sandinista Nicaragua or Communist China).

Our theoretical expectation is that parties thrive in larger communities, while smaller communities are more likely to be governed through personalistic, ad hoc arrangements by which politicians craft independent (nonpartisan) relationships with their constituents.

This expectation is borne out in studies of small states, where writers often note the weakness of political parties and the predominantly personalistic, non-programmatic nature of political contestation (Anckar &

Anckar 2000; Corbett & Veenendaal 2018; Rich, Hambly, & Morgan 2006; Sutton 2007; Veenendaal 2015). The smallest states in the Pacific have no political parties at all, belying Schattschneider's (1942: 1) famous thesis that "democracy is impossible save in terms of political parties." In Palau, where parties are completely absent, a politician notes that:

> Everybody has a platform and ideas, but they forget them when they come to office. ... They are not elected because of this, but because of family and clan relationships, and their personality.

Even when parties are present, they are often weakly institutionalized or lack programmatic coherence. A minister in Liechtenstein's government states,

> If you look at the parties, you cannot say that one party is left-wing and one party is right-wing. So you have all kinds of people as believers in one party, and if I meet the people of my party I can have a whole spectrum of people – from very liberal to almost socialist.

Interviews with political elites in small states reveal that party ideologies or programs play a minimal role in electioneering. According to one party leader in Suriname,

> If you were to speak with political leaders about their ideas, you would find that they tend to be very similar. So politics here is not about ideas, but it's about the persons running the political parties, and their mutual relationships. Look at their personal lives and connections, and you will know how they run the state.[1]

To assess the institutionalization of political parties in a systematic fashion we look, first, at the relative ubiquity of political parties. Although most national-level parliamentary elections are partisan, some are dominated by independent candidacies. Of course, this may be a product of government attempts to limit the influence of parties and/or the reluctance of politicians to band together in a single cohesive (and necessarily restricting) organization. But it may also be a product of the perceived irrelevance of political parties – to politicians and perhaps to voters. Both of these factors may be affected by the size of a polity. In a small polity, for example, it may be more defensible for leaders to erect barriers to the formation of political parties than in a large polity.

A useful approach to measuring the strength of political parties across countries and through time is to count the number of independents,

---

[1] Translated from the original Dutch: "Als je met politieke leiders over hun ideeën zou praten, zou je ontdekken dat die heel erg hetzelfde zijn. Dus politiek hier draait niet om ideeën, maar om de personen aan het hoofd van de politieke partijen, en hun onderlinge verhoudingen. Kijk naar hun persoonlijk leven en connecties, dan weet je hoe de staat gerund wordt."

i.e., members of the lower or unicameral chamber of the national legislature that are not declared members of a political party. This is transformed into a share (%) of seats in the legislature to produce an *independents* index that varies from 0 to 100. Peaks emerge at both extremes, as one might expect, but a good deal of variation also arises in between.

Table 6.1 begins with a series of tests in which this index is regressed against population. In Model 1, we include only regional dummies and annual dummies. In Model 2, we add a series of potential confounders to the specification. Model 3, our instrumental variable model, returns to the benchmark specification. Results of these tests, which are remarkably consistent across all three models, show that larger countries have fewer independents (as a share of seats in the national legislature), offering an important signal of the strength of political parties.

Our second measure of party strength is a national-level index of party institutionalization developed by Bizzaro, Hicken and Self (2017) as part of the V-Dem project. This index is composed of indicators measuring *party organization* (How many political parties for national-level office have permanent organizations?), *party branches* (How many parties have permanent local party branches?), *party linkages* (Among the major parties, what is the main or most common form of linkage to their constituents? [response categories range from clientelistic to programmatic]), *distinct party platforms* (How many political parties with representation in the national legislature or presidency have publicly available party platforms that are publicized and relatively distinct from one another?), and *legislative party cohesion* (Is it normal for members of the legislature to vote with other members of their party on important bills?). These five indicators are added together to form the Party Institutionalization Index. (Additional tests with the Party Strength Index developed by Bizzaro et al. 2018 yield similar results.)

This set of tests, displayed in the second section of Table 6.1, mirrors those in the first section. Model 4 is a minimal model with only regional dummies and annual dummies. Model 5 is a "full" model with a host of additional covariates that might affect party development. Model 6 is the instrumental-variable model, with our usual instruments. Results across these models are consistently positive – larger countries are associated with more institutionalized political parties.

To gauge the impact of scale on party institutionalization, we graph the predicted values from Model 4, Table 6.1, against population, as shown in Figure 6.2. Note that an increase in population from 10,000 to 100,000 is associated with an increase of a tenth of a point on the 0–1 scale.

Table 6.1 *Party strength*

Outcome	Independents			Party institutionalization		
Estimator	OLS	OLS	2SLS	OLS	OLS	2SLS
Model	1	2	3	4	5	6
Population (log)	-1.928***	-1.766**	-1.645**	0.047***	0.020**	0.049***
	(0.563)	(0.877)	(0.672)	(0.010)	(0.009)	(0.014)
GDP per		-0.847			0.044**	0.154***
capita (log)		(1.926)			(0.019)	(0.016)
Urbanization		0.254			0.172*	
		(6.846)			(0.087)	
Democracy		-1.153*			0.039***	
(Lexical index)		(0.595)			(0.006)	
Elections since		-2.923			0.033*	
1900 (log)		(1.770)			(0.018)	
Protestant		0.012			0.002***	
		(0.019)			(0.000)	
Muslim		-0.039			0.000	
		(0.072)			(0.001)	
Mineral wealth		-0.000			-0.000***	
per capita		(0.001)			(0.000)	
English colony		3.743			0.046	
		(2.635)			(0.033)	
Region dummies	✓	✓	✓		✓	
Annual dummies	✓	✓		✓	✓	
Decade dummies			✓	✓		✓
Countries	194	152	177	173	156	162
Years	114	106	112	115	107	115
Observations	2,861	1,831	2,614	11,893	8,582	11,209
R-squared	0.386	0.248	0.159	0.0917	0.657	0.394

Outcomes: number of independents as percentage of lower (or unicameral) chamber of the national legislature (Models 1–3), party institutionalization index (Models 4–6). *Units of analysis*: country-years. Constant omitted. *Estimators*: OLS (ordinary least squares), 2SLS (two-stage least squares, using territory and agricultural suitability as instruments). Country clustered standard errors in brackets. *** p < 0.01, ** p < 0.05, * p < 0.10 (two-tailed tests)

Preferential Voting

Measuring particularistic voting patterns at the individual level is difficult. It requires a survey instrument that can accurately perceive voters' intention when casting a ballot, distinguishing between partisan or

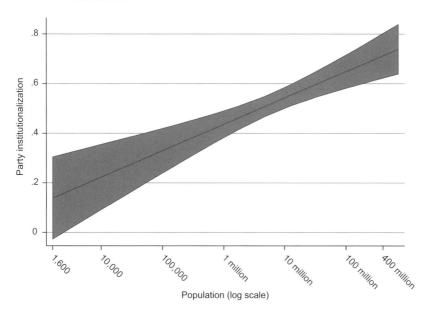

Figure 6.2 Party institutionalization, predicted values

Predicted values of party institutionalization index (Y) as population (log) changes, surrounded by 95 percent confidence interval. Based on Model 4, Table 6.1, with covariates set to sample means. Descriptive statistics (Y): mean = 0.50, SD = 0.29, min. = 0.00, max, = 1.00.

ideological motives and personal affiliations (Cain, Ferejohn, & Fiorina 1987).

Some electoral systems build this distinction into the voter's choice-set. Specifically, "open-list" systems give voters the option of voting for a party or for individual candidates (within the same party list or across lists). We interpret the latter choice as a signal of particularism, which may be motivated by personal connections (friends, family, "homestyle") and/or material incentives (e.g., patronage or vote-buying).

We note, in passing, that small states often employ electoral systems that facilitate preferential voting. In Europe, countries like Liechtenstein, Luxembourg, Malta, and Monaco employ an electoral procedure of panachage, in which voters can express multiple votes for candidates from different political parties, showing the primacy of personality over party. In similar fashion, Pacific island states employ electoral systems like the Borda Count (Kiribati and Nauru) or SNTV (Vanuatu) that facilitate preferential voting and are not widely used in other parts of the world (Reilly 2002).

District magnitude is negatively associated with preferential voting according to theory (Carey & Shugart 1995) and one empirical study (Samuels 1999). Since district magnitude might be viewed as a downstream property of constituency size (seats are usually assigned on the basis of population), these studies suggest that scale is an underlying cause of preferential voting. However, the direct relationship between population and preferential voting has not been systematically assessed.

To do so, we require a setting where open-list electoral rules obtain and where district population and district magnitude are not perfectly collinear. Such a setting is provided by municipal elections in Brazil, where the size of councils and the size of municipalities covary in a less than perfect fashion (Pearson's r = 0.82). Although this degree of collinearity poses problems in small samples, the large number of municipalities in Brazil allows us to distinguish the direct and indirect (via district magnitude) effects of population.

Brazilian municipalities are useful in another respect: they provide tremendous variation in the factor of theoretical interest. Across 5,540 municipalities for which population is available, the smallest municipality has 805 citizens and the largest 11,300,000, with a mean of 33,870 and a standard deviation of 200,673. Of course, municipalities vary in many respects, some of which may be regarded as confounders. The following analyses offer a number of specifications in order to test the scale–preferential voting relationship under different assumptions.

The outcome in Table 6.2 is the share of votes in a municipal election that are cast for specific candidates (as preferential votes) as opposed to political parties (as party-list votes). Model 1 is a spare model including only the variable of theoretical interest, with errors clustered by state. Model 2 adds a series of covariates including district magnitude (the number of council seats, log) and dummies for each state. The estimated coefficient for population is negatively associated with preferential voting – and remarkably stable – across these varied specifications.

Of particular interest is the result for district magnitude, which appears to show a positive relationship to preferential voting (contrary to previous research). If population is removed from Model 3, the "correct" (i.e., negative) sign on district magnitude is restored. However, this suggests that the previous finding (Samuels 1999) may have been misinterpreted: district magnitude is negatively associated with preferential voting because it is proxying for population.

In Figure 6.3, we show the impact of a change in district size on preferential voting, using the estimates from Model 1, Table 6.2. Accordingly, a shift in district size from 1,000 to 10,000 is associated with a decline in preferential voting of roughly one standard deviation,

Table 6.2 *Preferential voting in Brazilian municipalities*

Model	1	2
Population (log)	−0.006***	−0.008***
	(0.001)	(0.000)
Urbanization		0.000
		(0.000)
Household income per capita		0.000***
		(0.000)
District magnitude (log)		0.007***
		(0.002)
State dummies		✓
States	26	26
Observations (municipalities)	5,540	5,524
R-squared	0.159	0.401

Outcome: preferential votes in council elections. *Units of analysis*: Brazilian municipalities. Constant omitted. *Estimator*: ordinary least squares regression. Standard errors clustered by state in brackets. *** p < 0.01, ** p < 0.05, * p < 0.10 (two-tailed tests). Descriptive statistics below.

Variable	Obs.	Mean	Std. Dev.	Min.	Max.
Preferential voting	5,568	0.93	0.02	0.59	0.98
Population (log)	5,540	9.42	1.15	6.69	16.24
Urbanization	5,542	63.83	22.04	4.18	100.00
Household income per capita	5,542	436.90	197.85	116.00	1700.00
District magnitude (log)	5,552	2.31	0.20	2.08	4.01

a substantial change. (Bear in mind that most of the values among our sample of Brazilian municipalities cluster near the mean, i.e., 0.93.)

Vote-Buying

Perhaps the most pervasive form of particularism in poor countries with multiparty contestation is vote-buying, where parties or candidates offer money to citizens in exchange for a change in vote or a decision not to vote (F. Schaffer 2007). In this setting, the size of a district is thought to play a particularly important role, with larger districts being less prone to vote-buying (Remmer 2010a). Historical studies of "rotten boroughs" generally note a higher rate of treating (gifting), patronage, and outright vote-buying in small districts (Cox 1987: 57; O'Gorman 2001: 67; O'Leary 1962: 231).

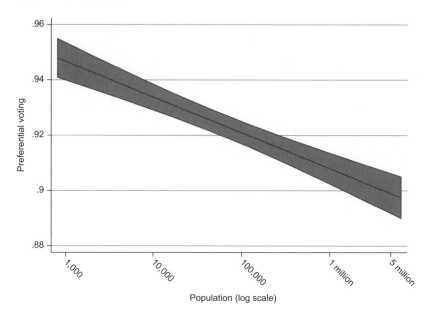

Figure 6.3 Preferential voting, predicted values

Predicted values of preferential voting (Y) as population (log) changes, surrounded by 95 percent confidence interval. Based on Model 1, Table 6.2, with covariates set to sample means. (For descriptive statistics see Table 6.2.)

Likewise, contemporary studies of vote-buying generally find a negative relationship between the size of a district and the prevalence of purchased votes (Brusco, Nazareno, & Stokes 2004; Gingerich & Medina 2013; Medina & Stokes 2007; Rueda 2017; Stokes et al. 2013).

Our observation of small states confirms that vote-buying is a commonly used tactic to obtain the support of poorer voters. In Suriname, for example, the interior districts are very sparsely populated but overrepresented in parliamentary seats. As a journalist indicates, vote-buying is a common strategy to acquire the support of the impoverished indigenous voters in these districts.

The president recently went to the interior – Amerindian territory – where he distributed chicken bolts and some other things. The whole village received packages; well that means that these people are inclined to vote for you. And it's not coming out of his own pockets; this is state money.

In a study of Argentina, Stokes (2005: 321) surveys 1,920 randomly chosen adults across three provinces and myriad municipalities.

Respondents were asked whether they had received any goods from a political party during a recent election campaign, whether receiving goods influenced their vote, whether they had turned to a locally important political actor for help during the past year, and whether, if the head of their household lost his or her job, the family would turn to a party operative for assistance. Across most of these outcomes, the size of the respondents' municipality bears a negative relationship to the probability of a positive answer.

In a recent study focused on Colombia, Rueda (2017) examines an even smaller unit of analysis – the polling station. To measure vote-buying, he looks at survey responses (like Stokes) as well as several statistical models that are intended to predict vote-buying. He finds that polling stations with fewer voters experience more vote-buying.

Campaign Finance

In many settings, vote-buying is rare or nonexistent. Nonetheless, money plays an important role in electoral campaigns through the mechanism of campaign finance (Casas-Zamora 2005; La Raja 2008; Norris & Abel van Es 2016; Scarrow 2007). Here, too, we expect higher levels of investment (per capita) in smaller districts or polities. Money for campaigns should matter more (on a per capita basis) where there are fewer voters. And money should take a more particularistic form in smaller political communities.

To address this question, Lee and Oppenheimer (1999: 99–115) examine funding sources for US House and Senate campaigns. Specifically, they look at funding obtained from political action committees (PACs) as a share of total funding raised by candidates for US Congress. Political action committees are viewed as a narrow form of political engagement, in which an investment is often intended to benefit a particular sector, union, or business (Snyder 1993). Lee and Oppenheimer find that House candidates raise a larger share of their campaign finances from PACs than Senate candidates, and that small-state Senate candidates raise more from PACs (proportionately) than large-state Senate candidates. Both patterns fit the thesis that population is inversely related to particularistic patterns of campaign finance.

Lee and Oppenheimer (1999: ch. 3) examine patterns of access to US senators. Interviews with lobbyists and other elite-level participants reveal that senators from small states are more accessible to special-interest lobbying, and perhaps more likely to be swayed, than senators from big states. The authors note that the latter face so many demands on their time that lobbyists have trouble getting a hearing, and they have so many funding sources that any single source is unlikely to hold much sway. Senators from small states are more available, and more needy. It follows – though it is virtually impossible to prove – that they may also be more likely to trade votes for money.

Our tests expand upon those conducted by Lee and Oppenheimer, utilizing a much larger database of US elections collected in the Congressional Primary Elections dataset (Boatright, Moscardelli, & Vickrey 2017). We focus on spending and not on the more difficult question of quid pro quo arrangements. The dataset measures primary and general election spending for each election cycle beginning in the 1970s, and covers a variety of offices including the presidency, House of Representatives, Senate, and governorships. Spending is disaggregated by district, i.e., House district (for congressional elections), and state (for senatorial, gubernatorial, and presidential elections). Thus, there is considerable variation in the size of districts (a) between congressional districts and states and (b) across states.

The first set of analyses in Table 6.3 focuses on total campaign spending per capita (log). In Model 1, this outcome is regressed against population (log) along with a panel of year dummies representing each election cycle. In Model 2, we add a vector of dummy variables representing each region of the country and another vector of dummies representing each office (presidency, House of Representatives, Senate, governorships). In Model 3, we replace office dummies with dummies for each state, while restricting the sample to House and Senate elections. In this fashion, we directly compare spending for elections to the upper and lower chambers of the US legislature for the same state in the same year. This is perhaps the strongest analysis, since it parses out potential confounders associated with each state (e.g., wealth, education, urbanization, and political culture). The estimated coefficient for population is negatively signed, and fairly stable, across all three models.

To gain a sense of the magnitude of the effect we plot predicted values for campaign spending per person within a district as the size of a district changes, based on estimates in Model 1, Table 6.3. The graph in Figure 6.4 indicates that an increase in population from a - half million to 1 million is accompanied by a decrease in per capita spending of about one dollar – a sizeable effect. Of course, increases at the high end of the scale have less impact due to the logarithmic shape of the relationship. But since most districts are modest in size – and many are far smaller than a half million – our exemplar is well chosen.

In a second set of analyses we look at a category of campaign donations that originate from PACs. Political action committees are disaggregated

Table 6.3 *Campaign spending*

Outcome	Spending				PAC Donations		Spending
Units of analysis	*Districts*				*Districts*		*Countries*
Elections	All	All	House and Senate	All	All	House and Senate	All
Model	1	2	3	4	5	6	7
Population (log)	-0.998***	-1.150***	-0.987***	-0.105***	-0.208***	-0.103***	-0.263*
	(0.030)	(0.069)	(0.032)	(0.006)	(0.027)	(0.005)	(0.147)
GDP per capita (log)							1.661***
							(0.386)
Tax revenue (% GDP)							-0.057**
							(0.027)
Region dummies		✓			✓		
State dummies			✓			✓	
Office dummies		✓	✓	✓	✓	✓	
Year dummies	✓	✓	✓	✓	✓	✓	
Countries	1	1	1	1	1	1	19
Districts	534	534	533	519	519	519	
Years	27	27	18	16	16	16	1
Observations	8,081	8,081	7,273	6,028	6,028	6,028	19
R-squared	0.325	0.342	0.293	0.114	0.141	0.163	0.5823

Outcomes: campaign spending per capita (log), PAC donations per capita (log). *Units of analysis*: district-years (Models 1–6), countries (Model 7). *Constant omitted. *Estimator*: ordinary least squares. Standard errors (clustered by district in Models 1–6) in brackets.
*** p < 0.01, ** p < 0.05, * p < 0.10 (two-tailed tests)

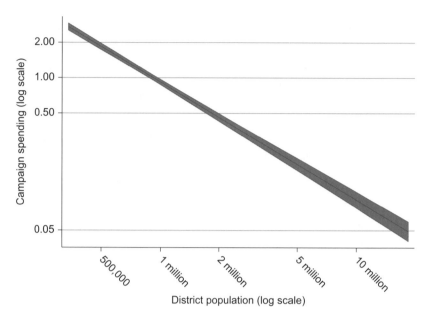

Figure 6.4 Campaign spending, predicted values

Predicted values of campaign spending, log (Y), as population (log) changes, surrounded by 95 percent confidence interval. Based on Model 1, Table 6.3, with covariates set to sample means. Descriptive statistics (Y, unlogged): mean = 20.64, SD = 156.95, min. = 0, max. = 2637.96.

by source – corporate (the largest subcategory), labor union, political party, lobby organization, and unaffiliated. Since results are robust across these different categories we present only the total, aggregated statistic – all PAC receipts calculated on a per capita basis and transformed by the natural logarithm. This variable is regressed against district population in a series of tests that parallel those in Models 1–3. Results shown in Models 4–6 also show a strong (negative) relationship to district size.

In the third section of Table 6.3 we move up a level of analysis to look at variation in campaign spending across countries. Here, very little data has been collected and so our ability to parse the relationship between scale and campaign finance spending is limited. The only cross-national dataset that we are aware of covers spending by major parties in nineteen democracies, generating a cross-sectional dataset centered on 2011 (Poguntke, Scarrow, & Webb 2016). The sample is extremely small and exclusively European, and there is limited variation in population across the chosen countries, so we must approach the following analysis with caution. To measure campaign spending, we utilize a statistic created by the authors that measures total party income per registered voter – which is virtually identical to per citizen except that citizens ineligible to vote by reason of age are excluded (Poguntke et al. 2016: 664). Our model regresses this per capita spending statistic (log) against country population (log) along with several covariates. Results are weak, but nonetheless suggest a negative relationship between population and campaign spending (significant at the 90 percent threshold).

Pork

Thus far, we have focused on electoral connections between politicians and constituents. In this section, we turn to the policy components of a particularistic regime. Accordingly, we look for instances where politicians can exercise discretion in the application of public policy so as to reward narrowly defined categories of constituents, aka "pork" (Olken & Singhal 2011).

In the developing world, selective interventions often take the form of welfare payouts. Focusing on a popular food security program in Argentina, the Programa Nacional de Seguridad Alimentaria (PNSA), Weitz-Shapiro (2012, 2014) attempts to determine whether mayors intervene personally in decisions about who is entitled to receive food support. Extensive fieldwork suggests that "it is not uncommon for mayors in such municipalities to devote significant time to receiving and acting on individual requests for social assistance" (Weitz-Shapiro 2014: 82). This involvement seems geared to reward supporters and punish opponents, and thus serves as the linchpin of a highly clientelistic system. To explore variation, Weitz-Shapiro administers a survey of elite respondents in 126 Argentinian municipalities. For our purposes, the salient result is the persistent negative effect of population (log) on the probability of mayoral intervention. Larger municipalities are apparently less subject to this form of clientelism.

Research on legislatures – across nations and across US states – shows a strong connection between membership size and government expenditures. Larger legislatures spend more, a relationship often attributed to the incentives of members in smaller districts to generate particularized benefits (Bradbury & Crain 2001; Buchanan & Tullock 1962; Shepsle & Weingast 1981; Weingast 1994). Scoping down – from legislatures to districts – research on the US Senate shows that smaller states receive a larger share of benefits from legislation packaged in a particularistic fashion (Lee 1998, 2000).

To explore this issue in a more precise fashion we need a suitable measure of pork, one that can be calibrated across districts of varying sizes within a country. To that end, Golden and Picci (2008) count national expenditures on public works projects as a proxy for pork in Italy through the postwar period (1953–94).[2] The first measure includes all capital improvements including construction of roads, airports, ports, and public buildings (but not maintenance). The second measure focuses on expenditures for roads and airports, under the assumption that the latter may be more susceptible to politicization. Both measure annual average infrastructure investments in millions of lire at constant 1990 prices. We reconfigure these statistics as per capita measures, which are then transformed by the natural logarithm to provide a more reasonable fit to the right-skew of the data. (Results are not dependent upon logging.) Spending is measured at the provincial level, providing ninety-two units observed across a four-decade period.[3]

Table 6.4 shows the results of four tests in which public works expenditures are regressed against population (the size of provinces). The first set focuses on total expenditures and the second set on roads and airports. For each outcome, two specifications are explored. The first includes only the regressor of interest along with a vector of year dummies. The second adds a series of covariates that might serve as confounders. The estimated coefficient for population is negative, statistically significant, and nearly identical across the twin specifications for each outcome, suggesting a robust relationship. Larger provinces attract less pork per capita, by these measures.

To gauge the impact of district size on expenditures we graph the predicted values for public works expenditures against population based on the results of Model 1 in Table 6.4. Each axis in Figure 6.5 represents a logged scale, in accordance with our regression model. However, the tick marks show unlogged values so that the nonlinear relationship can be understood in everyday terms. Accordingly, we see that an increase in population from 100 to 500 predicts a drop from 85 to 55 million lire annually, a 35 percent decline in per capita spending.

---

[2] This is a common interpretation of public works programs (Ferejohn 1974), though it may be disputed (Cadot, Röller, & Stephan 2006).

[3] The addition of several provinces in later years is dealt with by aggregating up to the original ninety-two units, thus preserving constant units throughout the period of observation (Golden & Picci 2008: 274).

Table 6.4 *Pork (Italy)*

Outcome	Total		Roads, Airports	
Model	1	2	3	4
Population (log)	−0.237***	−0.263***	−0.385***	−0.354***
	(0.044)	(0.080)	(0.060)	(0.054)
GDP		3.22e-06*		3.79e-06**
		(1.73e-06)		(1.81e-06)
Area		5.07e-07**		5.78e-07***
		(2.20e-07)		(1.73e-07)
District magnitude		−0.004		−0.014***
		(0.006)		(0.003)
Year dummies	✓	✓	✓	✓
Provinces	92	92	92	92
Years	40	40	40	40
Observations	4,833	4,368	4,833	4,368
R-squared	0.863	0.857	0.678	0.686

Outcomes: (a) total expenditures per capita (log) for public works projects and (b) expenditures per capita (log) for roads and airports in Italy, calculated as annual investments in millions of lire at constant 1990 prices. *Units of analysis*: province-years. Constant omitted. *Estimator*: ordinary least squares. Standard errors (clustered by province) in brackets. *** $p < 0.01$, ** $p < 0.05$, * $p < 0.10$ (two-tailed tests). *Data source*: Golden and Picci (2008). Descriptive statistics below.

Variable	Obs.	Mean	Std. Dev.	Min.	Max.
Public works exp. per capita (log)	4,833	4.04	1.42	0.00	7.65
Roads, airports exp. per capita (log)	4,833	2.656285	1.160778	0.00	6.667309
Population (log)	5,207	6.22	0.74	4.55	8.30
GDP	5,207	7332.81	17330.72	28.40	199782.00
Area	5,207	332129.10	189179.70	21168.00	967452.00
District magnitude	4,739	23.10	11.69	1.00	54.00

Corruption (Overall)

Corruption is usually defined as the abuse of public power for private gain. Typically, there is a dyadic relationship between a public servant, who offers information or services, and a citizen, who pays for them or offers some service in return. This dyadic relationship fits neatly with our conceptualization of particularism. Indeed, many of the practices explored in previous sections are widely viewed as corrupt. However,

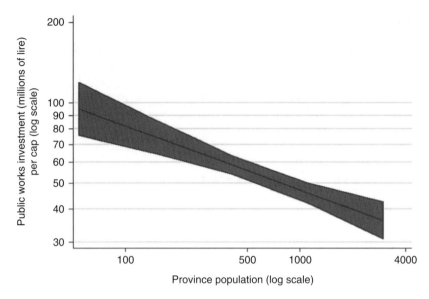

Figure 6.5 Pork, predicted values

Predicted values of public works expenditures, log (*Y*), as population of Italian provinces (log) changes, surrounded by 95 percent confidence interval. Based on Model 1, Table 6.4, with covariates set to sample means. For descriptive statistics see Table 6.4.

when corruption is the key term one usually has in mind a wide range of corrupt activities – vote-buying, bribery, fraud, theft, and so forth. It is a broad and diffuse concept.

To measure corruption at large at country levels, one is forced to rely on survey-based indices such as those produced by Transparency International (Lambsdorff 1999), the Worldwide Governance Indicators (Kaufmann, Kraay, & Mastruzzi 2011), and V-Dem (McMann et al. 2016). Most measures draw on mass surveys or surveys of businesspeople, while V-Dem draws on country experts. Some try to distinguish the specific type and location of corruption, but all are likely to reflect a general *gestalt* – a perception of overall levels of corruption in a country.

For some purposes, cross-national indicators of corruption are perfectly serviceable. However, for our purposes there are reasons to worry that they might be subject to systematic bias. Knack and Azfar (2003) note that among the subset of small countries in the world those with better governance are more likely to be included in extant corruption indices. Cross-country correlations are subject to this sample bias.

A second issue concerns the measurement of corruption. Cross-national indices rely on mass or expert perceptions of corruption, as noted. This is likely to reflect the salience of corruption in the popular press. And this, in turn, may be a product of the size of the public sector. Where there are many public servants, there are many individuals who are in a position to abuse their power. If corruption-prone public servants are randomly distributed, we would expect more reports of corruption to surface in larger countries simply as a product of greater numbers. This, in turn, may influence perceptions of deviance, as discussed in Chapter 3.

To overcome the problem of subjective judgment, some measures of corruption have chosen to frame their questions narrowly so as to measure only events that are actually experienced by the respondent or the respondent's family or firm (rather than vague ideas of what is going on "out there"). For example, the World Bank Enterprise Surveys include a question on bribe incidence, understood as "the percentage of firms experiencing at least one bribe payment request across 6 public transactions dealing with utilities access, permits, licenses, and taxes."[4] This is surely a step in the right direction. However, it is poorly suited for our purposes. Note that large countries are likely to have large firms, and these firms – by virtue of their size – are likely to have more dealings with government. This means that they are more likely to surpass a threshold-based measurement instrument.

Empirical research on scale and corruption using these sorts of indicators is not definitive. Fisman and Gatti (2002) and Xin and Rudel (2004) find a positive correlation between country size and political corruption. Elbahnasawy and Revier (2012) find no such relationship. Our own cross-national analysis (not shown) corroborates the null result. Our ethnographic observation of small states suggests that corruption is rife, though we cannot compare behavior systematically to similarly situated large states.

By virtue of mixed findings, and potential problems of sample bias and measurement, we must conclude on an equivocal note. There are no empirical grounds for concluding that scale is positively or negatively related to corruption, considered as a composite concept.

Summary

The topic of particularism is a large one, and therefore difficult to bound. We are sure that our brief survey has not identified all studies that test the relationship of size to various outcomes that might be classified as

---

[4] World Bank, Enterprise Surveys (www.enterprisesurveys.org/).

particularistic/universalistic. Nonetheless, those studies that we have surveyed in this chapter, summarized in Table 6.5, gesture toward a growing consensus. Smaller polities, and smaller districts, are especially prone to the development of particularistic ties between leaders and their constituents.

Political parties are antithetical to particularism, so their condition in different polities is especially revealing. We find that legislatures in larger countries have fewer independents (representatives unaligned with any major party). We also find that a composite measure of party institutionalization shows a pattern of higher scores in larger countries. Both signal a strong relationship between the size of a country and the strength of political parties in that polity.

Preferential voting is a signal that voters have a strong connection to a candidate, separate and apart from their connection to a party or ideology. As such, it is a good indicator of particularistic voting behavior. We find a strong negative relationship between the size of a district and the likelihood of voters exercising a preferential vote option in municipalities across Brazil. To be sure, this finding has not been replicated across other countries or by other studies, so it should be treated as preliminary.

Vote-buying may be regarded as the quintessential act of electoral particularism, as a direct exchange of goods displaces a potentially programmatic relationship between constituent and representative. Multiple studies indicate that vote-buying is more common in larger districts (polling stations, provinces, or municipalities). Of course, vote-buying is not common everywhere and is rarely encountered in advanced industrial countries, so this indicator is limited in reach.

Another way of measuring particularism in electoral politics is through records of campaign finance. We reason that higher than average spending in a constituency indicates that candidates are trying hard to forge a special bond with voters, one that is likely to be particularistic in nature – about personality or pork rather than party or ideology. Echoing earlier studies, we find that spending per capita is higher in smaller districts and smaller countries.

Pork – where a policymaker delivers a targeted good for a constituent or constituency in return for their support – may be regarded as a direct measure of particularism. Because policy actions of this sort are usually hard to observe, and hard to differentiate from interventions that are intended to serve a larger purpose, this is not a widely studied phenomenon. Nonetheless, extant findings confirm our theoretical expectations, and our own analyses – based on data gathered by Golden and Picci (2008) – show a negative relationship between the amount of money

Table 6.5 *Scale and particularism: Inventory of analyses*

Indicators	Countries	Treatment Units	Years	Units of Analysis	Research Design	Effect	Study
Political parties							
*Independents	(194)	Countries (194)	(114)	Country-years (2,861)	Cross-sectional	→	Table 6.1
*Party institutionalization	(173)	Countries (173)	(117)	Country-years (11,893)	Cross-sectional	←	Table 6.1
Preferential voting							
*Preferential voting	Brazil	Municipalities (5,540)	(1)	Municipalities (5,540)	Cross-sectional	→	Table 6.2
Vote buying							
Vote buying	Colombia	Polling stations (632)	(7)	Individuals (4,473)	Cross-sectional	→	Rueda 2017
Vote buying	Argentina	Provinces (3)	(1)	Individuals (1,920)	Cross-sectional	→	Brusco, Nazareno, & Stokes 2004
Vote brokerage	Brazil	Municipalities (721)	(1)	Municipalities (721)	Cross-sectional	→	Gingerich & Medina 2013
Campaign finance							
Money from PACs	United States	States (50)	(4)	Incumbent senate races (71)	Cross-sectional	→	Lee & Oppenheimer 1999: ch. 4
*Spending	United States	Districts (534)	(27)	District-years (8,081)	Cross-sectional	→	Table 6.3
*PAC donations	United States	Districts (519)	(16)	District-years (6,028)	Cross-sectional	→	Table 6.3
*Spending	(19)	Countries (19)	(1)	Countries (19)	Cross-sectional	→	Table 6.3

Table 6.5 (cont.)

Indicators	Countries	Treatment Units	Years	Units of Analysis	Research Design	Effect	Study
Pork							
Distributive programs	United States	States (50)	(7)	Distributive programs (2,324)	Cross-sectional	→	Lee 1998
Transportation plans	United States	States (50)	(6)	Transportation plans by state (350)	Cross-sectional	→	Lee 2004
Food provision	Argentina	Cities (126)	(1)	Informants (2,660)	Cross-sectional	→	Weitz-Shapiro 2012, 2014
*Public works spending	Italy	Provinces (92)	(40)	Province-years (4,833)	Cross-sectional	→	Table 6.4
Corruption							
ICRG	(59)	Countries (59)	(15)	Country means (59)	Cross-sectional	←	Fisman & Gatti 2002
CPI	(95)	Countries (95)	(3)	Country-years (179)	Cross-sectional	←	Xin & Rudel 2004
CPI and CC	(150)	Countries (150)	(7)	Country-years (628)	Cross-sectional	Ø	Elbahnasawy & Revier 2012

Treatment units: units exhibiting variation in scale. *Years*: number of years over which data are collected – not to be confused with the frequency of observations, as data may or may not be annual and may be averaged across years. *Research design*: the main, or benchmark, research design – classified as cross-sectional (where the analysis is driven primarily by variation across units) or panel (where the analysis is driven primarily by variation through time). *Effect*: when the scale of a community increases, the designated outcome goes up (↑), down (↓), up and down (∩), or experiences no perceptible change (Ø). A scale effect is considered significant if it passes a modest bar of statistical significance, i.e., p < 0.10 (two-tailed test) in the benchmark model. Number of countries, treatment units, years, or observations in parentheses. *ICRG*: International Country Risk Guide (PRS Group). *CPI*: Corruption Perceptions Index (Transparency International). *CC*: Corruption Control (World Bank Governance Indicators).

(per capita) spent on public works projects (a widely used measure of pork) in Italy and the size of constituencies.

Our final measure of particularism is corruption, broadly conceived. Unfortunately, because of the perceptual nature of this topic it is especially prone to bias. Specifically, observers in larger communities – where there are likely to be more acts of political corruption (by virtue of larger populations of civil servants and politicians) – are apt to confuse the raw number of acts with the frequency of such acts. The raw number of corrupt actions are thus impossible to distinguish from the corruption rate (the number of corrupt actions per civil servant). Thus, we do not regard extant studies of size and corruption as dispositive. Nor are they unanimous in their reported results.

7   Participation

Political participation refers here to any activity by citizens (non-elites) whose goal is to affect politics or policy.[1] Participatory activities include voting (in an election, initiative, or referendum); donating to political causes; working for a party or a nongovernmental organization (NGO); contacting other citizens or elites; signing a petition; taking part in a boycott, demonstration, or strike, along with other varieties of "contentious politics" (Tarrow & Tilly 2015); attending a citizens' assembly; and engaging in public debate. Note that participation overlaps with larger, more abstract concepts such as civil society, social capital, and civic engagement – though we try to retain a tight focus on the act of participation.

The ramifications of participation are the subject of an extensive and long-running debate among lay commentators and political scientists. Many view popular participation as essential to democracy (Barber 2003; Dalton & Wattenberg 2000; Fung & Wright 2003; Mansbridge 1983; Pateman 1970; Pitkin & Shumer 2001). Others are more skeptical, arguing that the ability to participate – and the threat that heretofore quiescent citizens might enter the fray – is more important than the actual rate of participation at any given point in time (Rosanvallon 2008; Schudson 1998). A third perspective points to the fact that participation is a response to different sorts of motivations. If the motivation is public-spirited, we may anticipate positive repercussions from popular participation. If the motivation is private-spirited or xenophobic, the repercussions are less beneficent. There is good participation and bad participation (Chambers & Kopstein 2001).

A related debate concerns the degree to which participation rates affect the nature of public policies. Early studies, focused mostly on the United States, discovered that the issue-positions and party affiliations of voters and nonvoters are fairly similar (Bennett & Resnick 1990; Schaffer 1982;

---

[1] For discussion of various meanings of this term see Teorell (2006).

Wolfinger & Rosenstone 1980). From this perspective, it matters little that many citizens do not participate. More recent evidence suggests that voters and nonvoters are not identical, and that there might be important partisan effects from increasing (or decreasing) turnout rates (A. Fowler 2015; Fraga 2018).

In any case, it is not clear that opinion polls comparing participants and nonparticipants adequately represent the counterfactual of theoretical interest. If nonparticipants became participants, the process of participation might change their perspectives on politics. Casting a ballot – not to mention more active forms of engagement – can be a transformative experience. Likewise, if excluded segments of the electorate were to become regular voters, it is likely that politicians and parties would adjust their messages to appeal to these new constituencies. The question of participation thus carries a very specific implication: if participation rates – at the very least, voter turnout rates – were higher, involving most of the adult population in a community, policy outcomes might be different because the electorate would more closely resemble the total (adult) population. Cross-national empirical studies seem to corroborate this notion. Specifically, higher turnout among the poor across electorates in countries around the world is associated with higher welfare benefits, suggesting that participation might be playing a causal role (Hicks & Swank 1992; Hill & Leighley 1992; Lijphart 1997; cited in Leighley 1995). In short, there are good reasons to imagine that varying turnout levels have policy repercussions, even if we cannot test the counterfactual in a very satisfactory fashion.

With this as preface, we turn to the question of interest. Why do some political communities elicit higher levels of participation than others? We argue, following a long tradition of work (e.g., Dahl & Tufte 1973), that the size of a community has important, and markedly negative, effects on political participation. We begin by presenting the theory. Next, we explore the subject empirically. A short conclusion summarizes the results.

Theory

A citizen's choice to participate is affected by many factors, some of them individual characteristics such as education and income, and some of them group characteristics (for overviews see Barnes et al. 1979; Blais 2006; D. Campbell 2013; M. Franklin 2004; Leighley 1995; Verba, Schlozman, & Brady 1995). Here, we focus on a single contextual factor – the size of a community.

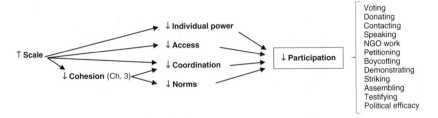

Figure 7.1 Scale effects on participation

As scale increases, we surmise, participation declines. We argue that four mechanisms come into play – *individual power, access, coordination,* and *norms* – as diagramed in Figure 7.1.

Individual Power

We begin by considering the capacity of individual citizens to affect community-level outcomes. It should be clear that this power is inversely proportional to the size of the community. Thus, if participation is purposeful – i.e., designed to affect election outcomes, public opinion, and policy outcomes – we can expect participation to decline as the size of a community grows. Individual citizens matter less, their power is reduced, and hence the probability of their participating in politics.

For participation in most political activities, individual power declines in a linear fashion as numbers increase. The value of a single vote, or of a single person at a demonstration, is directly proportional to the size of the group engaging in these activities. This means that Anthony Downs's (1957) well-known "paradox of voting" (why do people vote if their chance of influencing the result is miniscule?) applies to a lesser extent to smaller communities, where the value (or potential decisiveness) of a single vote is higher (cf. Blais 2000: 24–29; Hansen, Palfrey, & Rosenthal 1987).

If one takes a broad view of participation, this relationship may be said to hold for any regime type. In an autocracy, citizens may exert influence on leaders by withholding support, by protesting, by threatening to leave, or by taking up arms. It follows that an individual citizen in a small autocracy should have greater power than an individual citizen in a large autocracy, even though the difference may be less apparent and more difficult to measure than it is across democratic regimes.

Access

When participation is focused on influencing elite decision makers – executives, legislators, judges, bureaucrats – we must consider the availability of access points. This, in turn, is a product of the representation ratio, the ratio of citizens to representatives. We have shown that this ratio increases as scale increases (Chapter 4), meaning that citizens will have fewer access points.

Interviews with citizens and elites in microstates offer direct testimony of the extraordinary access citizens enjoy. A journalist in St. Kitts and Nevis revealed that many citizens have the cell phone number of their representatives and can reach them directly. A government minister in the Seychelles stated,

It [smallness] puts government very close to the people. The public has very good access to the highest-ranking officials in the government, and here I am talking about the president, [the] vice president, and the ministers. We are in contact with our people and are connected very closely with the people.

In San Marino, the country with the most favorable (smallest) citizen: member of parliament ratio in the world, a parliamentarian remarked:

Everyone, even the most insignificant individual, can influence politics. Every citizen has access to political leaders because they are friends, because they are related, or because they love each other. See, this closeness means that even the last citizen, the least important citizen, has the possibility to exert influence.[2]

In large states, by contrast, citizens are at pains to contact their representatives. They may write letters, send emails, or protest in the streets, but their individual voices are unlikely to be heard. They enjoy very little access to this tiny, cloistered elite.

Coordination

As the size of a community grows, coordination problems multiply. The most obvious problem concerns forms of participation that demand physical presence. In order to vote, protest, or otherwise engage, participants must travel to a designated location. In a large community we can presume that at least some segments of the population will be dispersed, making it more difficult to participate (Brady & McNulty 2011; Dyck & Gimpel 2005) and requiring effective transport networks to bring people together. This is especially difficult if they must congregate at one time in

---

[2] San Marino has a population of 30,000, and a parliament (the Consiglio Grande e Generale) with sixty members. This means that each member represents 500 citizens.

one place, placing strains on even the most advanced systems of transport. In a small community we can presume that citizens live closer together, perhaps within walking distance. Here, no special transportation infrastructure is required in order for citizens to mobilize.

An additional logistical barrier is encountered if everyone must congregate in one location. Note that only so many people can pack into an auditorium, stadium, or public square. Even if everyone in the community wishes to participate, opportunities may be limited or made more arduous by the coordination challenge of getting all participants into the same physical location and finding a way for them to communicate with one another once they arrive.

Coordination barriers are perhaps even more important with respect to organization. Note that virtually any type of participation, in order to be effective, requires a good deal of background work. Even an election, where the day is stipulated by law, requires a lot of preparation if participation is to be maximized. For non-electoral modes of participation – e.g., petitioning, boycotting, demonstrating, striking – organizational problems are much more imposing. Citizens must be educated, persuaded, and disciplined so that they can act in a concerted fashion. Free-riding must be discouraged.

Coordination problems are directly affected by scale, but they are not simply a matter of numbers. As the size of a community grows, cohesion attenuates, as discussed in Chapter 3. This too complicates the task of coordination. Larger, more diverse communities are less tightly interconnected, and the weakness of these social networks is likely to depress participation (Klofstad 2011; Knoke 1990; Lake & Huckfeldt 1998; Leighley 1990; McClurg 2003). By contrast, strong networks should make it easier for citizens living in small, homogeneous communities to mobilize each other, or for a small number of elites (members of parties and organizations) to trigger a mobilizational cascade (J. Fowler 2005). Indeed, Oliver (2000: 369) finds that citizens in large cities are less likely to be contacted by a fellow citizen or a member of a party or campaign than citizens in small cities.

Norms

Participation, finally, is responsive to social norms, i.e., widely held ideas about what is appropriate or inappropriate. Here too the heterogeneity of large communities may affect the propensity of citizens to participate. Bear in mind that our definition of heterogeneity refers to any politically relevant identity – whether based in ascriptive identities, material circumstances, or ideas (Chapter 3).

In the present context, ideological diversity may be the most relevant. When members of an (ideologically) heterogeneous community speak to one another about politics, they are likely to disagree. This introduces cross-pressures, which may weaken a citizen's sense of conviction about what is appropriate and inappropriate. And this, in turn, may depress participation. If one is unsure about what is right, or afraid that the consequences might introduce conflict into a relationship or cognitive dissonance into one's own life, the prospect of participating is less pleasant and consequently participation is less likely to occur (Alesina & Ferrara 2000; D. Campbell 2013: 41–43; Costa & Kahn 2003; Mutz 2002; Putnam 2007).[3]

Granted, if social networks are homogeneous *within* a broader community that is heterogeneous, the depressive effects of diversity on participation may be muted (D. Campbell 2013: 42). But this requires a level of segregation that is unusual in modern settings. Some political actions are inherently public, e.g., placing a poster in one's front yard or a bumper sticker on one's car, attending a rally, or signing a public petition. Others in the community will find out, and this is likely to lead to conflict if there is disagreement about the goal.

For those living in a homogeneous community, political participation is a venue for affirming group identity. It is what "we" do to affirm our ideals and our way of life, and to defend those ideals against potential threats from "them" (those outside the community). Participation thus helps to establish one's membership in the community, reinforcing social ties among family, friends, neighbors, and associates. It resonates with deeply held feelings of personal identity. On the small Caribbean island of Saba (pop. 2,000), a politician reports:

I think you feel obligated to vote, or they make you feel obligated. If you don't, they make you feel guilty. My family in particular always supported the WIPM party; from when I was a child we just supported this party. ... Because your parents tell you, "elections are coming up and we have to vote, and everybody has to vote for the WIPM party."

Political participation is engaging insofar as one is playing as part of a team, a form of community engagement that has much in common with sporting events – including both the festive aspect (e.g., hats, jerseys, signs, and other paraphernalia) and the violent aspect (e.g., hooliganism).

[3] A few studies contradict this finding. However, some of these studies seem liable to problems of causal inference. For example, Quintelier, Stolle, and Harell (2012: 868) report that "young people who have more diverse social networks are in fact more likely to participate in a variety of social and political activities." But it is not clear that their diverse networks caused them to participate at higher levels. Indeed, it could be the reverse, as the authors point out.

Finally, in a small, homogeneous community with strong network ties political participation is more visible. People know whether you have turned out to vote, to sign a petition, to protest, or to attend a community meeting. This awareness, and the public shame (or approbation) that accompanies it, is a potent factor in stimulating participation. In societies like Iceland or Malta, where turnout commonly exceeds 90 percent, *not* voting can result in social sanctions (Hirczy 1995). Experiments have shown that informing citizens about the behavior of their neighbors (e.g., whether they have voted) enhances turnout (Gerber, Green, & Larimore 2008).

Other Possible Pathways

There may be additional pathways from population to participation. In this section, we note two of these and state why we believe they are fairly minor, or at any rate difficult to interpret.

First, let us consider the possible impact of *particularism*, introduced in the previous chapter. *Particularism* refers to targeted efforts by politicians to cultivate the support of specific citizens or groups of citizens (aka clients) and the allegiance of those citizens to their leader (aka patron). It includes vote-buying, campaign spending, and targeted policy interventions ("pork"), as well as long-term dyadic relationships of a clientelistic nature.

Particularism may boost participation through the mechanism of campaign spending (Holbrook & Weinschenk 2014). It may also affect participation by offering citizens direct material incentives to get involved in politics (F. Schaffer 2008: 6). There is some evidence to suggest that vote-buying is largely focused on supporters, with the intention of enhancing their likelihood of turning out to vote, and that these efforts are successful (Nichter 2008; Vicente 2014). Consistent with this, it is sometimes alleged that high turnout rates in nineteenth-century America were partly a product of material incentives (Cox & Kousser 1981).

On the other hand, vote-buying is sometimes intended to suppress the vote (by discouraging opponents from participating). Likewise, transitions from "dirty" to "clean" electoral processes are often hard to interpret because vote tabulations during the pre-reform era were probably inflated (Simpser 2012). Most important from a theoretical view, electoral manipulations may have a discouraging effect on voters, lending the impression that the system is crooked and their votes don't count. Particularistic activities may also depress electoral competition and the development of strong parties, which in turn is likely to depress turnout.

In summary, it is difficult to reach strong conclusions about the long-term impact of particularism on participation. It may be minimal or null, due to countervailing factors. More work is needed in order to sort things out.

A second factor to consider is *electoral contestation*. In Chapter 8 we argue that contestation (often measured by the closeness of the vote by the top parties or candidates) increases in larger polities and districts. Considerable research (as well as intuition) suggests that contestation enhances turnout (Blais 2000). So, for this measure of political participation (but perhaps not for others), a larger size has some positive effects. However, the contestation effect on turnout does not appear to be especially strong (Blais 2006) and, consequently, is probably overwhelmed by the depressing effects of scale on turnout, as sketched in the previous sections.

Caveats

Now we must issue several caveats and clarifications.

First, there is a question about the appropriate definition of *community*. Most of the causal mechanisms that we have cited depend upon a citizen's perceptions of her community. Yet whether a citizen considers herself a member of a small or large community is subjective. For example, a citizen voting in a presidential election might consider her community to be the nation (the constituency of the president, as defined by the constitution), or the locality. A citizen voting in a big-city mayoral election may consider their community to be their municipality (as defined by its official jurisdictional boundaries) or the larger metropolitan area within which the municipality is situated. So far as we can tell from the studies cited in what follows, scale effects are present regardless of which definition of community is chosen. But we cannot say for sure which definitions of community are most salient when citizens make up their minds to engage in some form of political participation.

Second, the impact of scale on participation is likely to vary across different forms of participation. We presume that scale effects are generally greater where participation is more burdensome. Thus, we would expect a greater scale effect on demanding forms of participation such as attending a meeting or a protest than on less demanding forms of participation such as voting.

Third, scale effects are likely to be affected by background conditions, e.g., political culture, electoral law, and communication technology. We anticipate that these interaction effects impact the magnitude – but not the direction – of the causal relationship. As such, they are ancillary to the theory (ceteris paribus conditions).

One background condition, *power*, is especially nettlesome because it is often correlated with the causal factor of theoretical interest. Where the size of a polity or district is larger, the power of the officeholder is likely to be greater. For example, the president of a country has a much larger constituency than a backbench legislator and is also much more powerful. The power of the office increases the salience of an election and the stakes of that election. Both are likely to enhance turnout, as well as other forms of participation intended to influence the election or the behavior of the official holding that office. Thus, in considering – and testing – the relationship of scale to participation it is essential to compare units that have equal power (in formal, constitutional terms). Note that the direction of anticipated bias runs against our hypothesis, so any failures to control for power will attenuate (rather than inflate) estimates of the true impact of scale on participation.

Evidence: Extant Studies

Participation may be measured across several dimensions. First, there is a *participation rate*, i.e., the number of citizens who engage in an activity understood as a share of the community. This is usually the easiest feature to measure, and dominates our empirical indicators. Second, there is the *quality* of engagement, i.e., frequency and intensity, awareness, independence, and deliberateness. Finally, there is the *range of activities* in which citizens participate, which may be limited to voting (usually the easiest form of participation) or extended to other, more costly, activities. When we use the term *participation* we mean to encompass all three dimensions, even though we may be able to measure only one or two. Because feelings of *efficacy* tend to accompany participation (Clarke & Acock 1989), we treat efficacy as part of the same general outcome.

A large body of work has accumulated on the question of scale and participation, which we hope to integrate into the following discussion. To render the discussion tractable, we distinguish the following topics: (a) citizen assemblies, (b) political parties, (c) voting and related activities, and (d) efficacy. In the final section, we discuss the results of a recent meta-analysis.

Citizen Assemblies

If participation means actual decision-making by citizens, then the vehicle for that process is likely to be an assembly of citizens such as appeared in

Athens and other ancient polities in the Mediterranean region (Hansen & Nielsen 2004; Sinclair 1991). Present-day exemplars include Swiss municipalities and cantons (Ladner 2002; Linder 2010), New England town meetings (Bryan 2010), workplaces (Pateman 1970), and other arenas where citizens meet to discuss problems pertaining to their community (Fung & Wright 2003). All might be considered instances of the classical democratic idea, which has come to be known as *direct democracy*, where each citizen has equal power and plays an equal role in decision-making (Barber 2003; Pateman 1970; Pitkin & Shumer 2001).

When participation means physical attendance at a single location the coordination problem posed by community size is acutely manifest. One can fit large numbers of people into a stadium, but one may question whether the result is truly participatory. Plato estimated the ideal polity to be 5,040 citizens. Mansbridge (1983: 286) concludes, "It is unlikely that any face-to-face democracy has ever encompassed more than 15,000 citizens. In ancient Athens, 4,000 to 6,000 of the 40,000 eligible citizens usually gathered in the assembly; and the Swiss cantons of Uri and Nidwalden each made room once, in the fields outside their capitals, for as many as 4,000 citizens in their annual Landesgemeinde." In contemporary microstates, direct democracy is rare (D. Anckar 2004). Some insist that true equality of participation can only be achieved in much smaller groups, perhaps numbering in the double digits (Gastil 2014).

The association between scale and participation is addressed in a recent study of governmental forms across municipalities in Switzerland. Across 2,900 municipalities, Ladner (2002: 820) finds that the prevalence of local assemblies varies inversely with municipality size, and no assemblies exist in municipalities with populations of more than 20,000.

One may debate the threshold at which participation in an assembly becomes impractical, or grossly unequal (insofar as some will participate more than others). The Swiss evidence suggests that the impact of scale is severe. Among municipalities with local assemblies, citizen attendance ("turnout") varies inversely by municipality size, and the slope is steep. For the smallest municipalities (< 249), participation is about 30 percent. For the largest municipalities (10,000–20,000), participation is less than 5 percent (Ladner 2002: 823). Note that even in the smallest units, participation in direct democracy is extremely low relative to the rates that are typical for less demanding forms of participation. Ladner (2002: 826) comments:

Assemblies with more than 400 participants may lead to the very essence of direct participation being lost. Participation in such meetings diminishes rapidly with increasing size, if only for the simple reason that the capacity of meeting halls is limited and because larger municipal size implies most people having to travel further to the meeting place. Furthermore, larger municipalities tend to limit the competence of the communal assembly to very few matters (budgetary decisions) and transfer other decisions to the ballot voting procedure.

It would seem that citizen assemblies are practical expedients only in the smallest communities, or in situations where differential participation is unproblematic (e.g., because one prefers those with the highest stakes in a policy to attend).

Virtual assemblies, assembled in online communities, are more capable of dealing with large numbers. From a purely technical standpoint, there is no limit to an online community. Even so, the scale of a community seems to affect the viability of the format. In Liechtenstein, for example, many citizens are members of the popular Facebook group *Stammtisch Liechtenstein*, which refers to a table at a pub (*stammtisch*) where people gather to socialize. In this online group, the latest political developments and rumors in Liechtenstein are shared and discussed. No equivalent online community exists for large political communities, presumably because the viability of interpersonal communication declines as scale increases. It is not clear what a "Stammtisch Deutschland" would look like or how it would function.

Political Parties

Citizen assemblies (real or virtual) probably qualify as the most demanding form of participation, so it is not surprising that they are subject to strong scale effects. With other forms of participation one might anticipate that scale effects would be less stringent.

Political parties are key elements of virtually any representative democracy, and thus provide an important window through which to examine the influence of scale on politics. Van Biezen, Mair, and Poguntke (2012) examine party membership rates (party members as a share of the general electorate) across twenty-seven European democracies. Weldon (2006) enlists a similar research design, again focused mostly on Europe. Both studies find that small countries have considerably higher rates of party membership than large countries.

Weldon (2006) also examines membership activism *within* parties, i.e., the share of party members who report devoting some time to party activities in the past year. Activism is measured through a survey instrument across twenty-nine parties in five democracies. Activism turns out to be a function of party size. Larger parties have a smaller share of active members, seeming to confirm Robert Michels's (1962) gloomy assessment of the inevitable rise of oligarchy (see also Scarrow 2002; Tan 1998, 2000).

Voting et al.

A final category of participation focuses on voting and other participatory activities that occur at the level of districts or polities. Most studies explore variation across municipalities – towns, cities, or counties – and occasionally electoral districts for higher-level offices.

Larson (2002) examines various forms of political participation across thirty-eight Danish municipalities through survey evidence. He finds that voter turnout as well as most forms of influencing correlate inversely with the size of municipalities.

Frandsen (2002) examines turnout rates in local elections over four decades across five European countries. Turnout is found to be consistently higher in small municipalities in all the countries reviewed, although the strength of the relationship varies across countries.

Oliver (2000) compares municipalities and metropolitan areas of varying sizes across the United States in order to determine levels of citizen activity in contacting locally elected officials, attending community board meetings, attending meetings of voluntary organizations, and voting in local elections. Scale effects are found across three of the four outcomes, even while controlling for a wide range of community- and individual-level covariates. (The estimated effect of size on voting turnout, the least demanding form of participation, is negative but insignificant.)

Keena (2016: ch. 2) examines (a) turnout across a range of US elections – Senate, governor, and state legislature – and (b) donations across Senate elections, finding a strong negative association between district size and propensity to participate. In similar fashion, Trounstine (2012) examines turnout across more than 4,000 US cities, finding a strong negative relationship between size and participation. Across US constituencies of various sorts, Bowen (2010: 120) finds that face-to-face meetings with representatives (though not contacts in general) are more common in smaller constituencies.

Remmer (2010a) examines turnout across districts of varying sizes in Costa Rica in both mayoral and presidential elections. Larger districts manifest lower turnout rates, even when controlling for demographic and political features of those districts. Individual-level data corroborate these findings for mayoral elections but not for presidential elections, perhaps because the latter are less parochial. (It is, technically, a much larger district, as discussed earlier.) In a similar study, focused on cross-regional variation in Argentina, Remmer (2010b) finds that larger regions experience lower turnout rates.

Denters et al. (2014: Part IV) examine a variety of political activities in four countries – Denmark, Netherlands, Norway, and Switzerland. They find that participation rates are generally lower in larger municipalities, a trend that is consistent across most (though not all) of the selected activities.

Across metropolitan areas in eleven (mostly European) countries, a large collaborative project headed by Jefferey Sellers, Daniel Kübler, Melanie Walter-Rogg, and R. Alan Walks (2013: 431) finds turnout to be systematically lower in larger constituencies.

Not all studies find a statistically significant relationship between scale and declining participation. Several municipal-level studies suggest a null finding (e.g., Carr & Tavares 2014; Kelleher & Lowery 2004; Stein & Dillingham 2004; Tavares & Carr 2013). Another study shows a positive but very weak effect (Caren 2007).

We are aware of only one study published in recent years that reports a positive and highly statistically significant association between municipal or constituency size and participation. Kelleher and Lowery (2008) examine survey responses from nearly 7,500 respondents located in twenty-six small to mid-sized cities in the United States, finding that size predicts higher levels of (self-reported) voter registration and organizational membership. Several factors may explain this unusual result. First, the authors focus on voter registration rather than turnout. One may surmise that registration in a city is affected by statewide regulation and by citywide initiatives – led by a campaign, a party, or a civil society group – or by some other idiosyncratic feature that has little to do with size per se but nonetheless affects the outcome. Second, the sample – comprised of twenty-six treatment groups – is small. Third, it is a convenience sample, and quite possibly unrepresentative. Fourth, among the chosen cities only one – Philadelphia – is large, and therefore may serve as an influential case. Fifth, size is measured in a linear, rather than log-linear fashion – departing from conventional practice and also granting greater weight to the lone outlier. Pending further research, we must regard this study as highly tentative.

Arguably, the strongest research designs involve municipal amalgamations or splits. Here, one is able to compare participation rates prior to, and after, a municipal reorganization, holding most background factors constant. Sometimes, there is also a pure control group, provided by a set of municipalities whose status does not change. Unfortunately, most studies involve amalgamation rather than division, and amalgamation – the joining of two previously independent municipalities – may be especially disruptive. If subsequent participation declines because communities are upset about the consolidation – which may have been imposed from above by a higher level of government – this is not really a product of scale, per se. Even so, this confounder is probably small and presumably attenuates over time.

Kraaykamp, Van Dam, and Toonen (2001) focus on municipal amalgamations in the Netherlands over a two-decade period. They find amalgamations are accompanied by a modest decline in turnout, which moderates further through time. This result suggests a much smaller scale effect than most purely cross-sectional analyses report.

Ennser-Jedenastik and Veenendaal (2015) examine the effects of municipal mergers on levels of political participation in the Austrian province of Styria from 2010 to 2015. They find that turnout declined more rapidly in merged municipalities than in those unaffected by mergers. However, they point out that the observed effects might be explained by accompanying factors such as opposition to the municipal merger or a lack of identification with the newly merged municipality – in line with our concerns about confounders.

National-level analyses are less common, presumably because of the many potential confounders that cross-national data impose. Even so, results are generally consonant with municipal- or district-level analyses. Most studies find that larger countries experience lower turnout in both parliamentary and presidential elections (Blais & Carty 1990; Blais & Dobrzynska 1998; Endersby & Krieckhaus 2008; Franklin 2004; Kostelka 2017).

Efficacy

As the size of a community grows, we surmise that feelings of political efficacy attenuate. Efficacy is understood here as the perceived ability to affect a political outcome, e.g., an election result or policy decision in a community.

Older studies of this question are equivocal (Finifter & Abramson 1975). But more recent studies lend fodder to the thesis that citizens in larger communities have less confidence in their ability to impact politics than citizens in smaller communities (Bowen 2010; Weldon 2006).

Lassen and Serritzlew (2011) exploit a natural experiment in order to test this question. In the first decade of the twenty-first century, Denmark undertook a far-reaching reform to merge smaller municipalities across the country. Using individual-level survey data from before and after the merger, the authors compare responses to questions about political efficacy by citizens living in amalgamated municipalities to the responses by citizens living in municipalities unaffected by the reform. A difference-in-difference design makes use of the arbitrary nature of the reform (which was outside the ability of most municipalities to affect), while utilizing both longitudinal and latitudinal evidence. The existence of a set of unaffected municipalities allows the authors to control for temporal confounders. They find that feelings of efficacy declined markedly for citizens living in amalgamated municipalities relative to citizens in unaffected municipalities.

There is, again, a small problem of interpretation. This stems from the fact that the treatment bundles together a number of features that are difficult to disentangle. Municipal amalgamation increases the size of city districts – the treatment of theoretical interest. But the reform also disturbs existing political communities and governance structures, and in Denmark it was (for the most part) forced upon citizens, some of whom were probably not enthusiastic about the prospect. The treatment effect may be a product of any of these factors, or some combination of them.

Noting this problem, the authors point out that the size of the effect is correlated with the size of the treatment, not merely with the fact of being treated. Where municipalities grow the most, feelings of efficacy decline the most. This seems to indicate that size, and not other features associated with the intervention, are driving the treatment effect. Of course, the dislocating effects of amalgamation are also correlated with the size of the treatment, so this does not entirely resolve the question. Even so, the most plausible interpretation of this exemplary study is that increases in size are accountable for decreases in political efficacy.

Meta-analysis

To better gauge the state of research on the causes of participation we turn to a recent meta-analysis conducted by Cancela and Geys (2016). The authors canvass a large number of local- and national-level studies published over the past several decades, and a wide range of potential causal factors. Their meta-analysis shows that scale has a negative impact on participation in 57 percent of the studies ($N = 79$) and 53 percent of the tests ($N = 366$) that examine this question (Cancela & Geys 2016: 267). Studies focused on subnational variation (across districts within a country) show a somewhat stronger relationship. Here, population predicts lower turnout in 69 percent of all studies ($N = 36$) and 70 percent of all tests ($N = 121$) (Cancela & Geys 2016: 270).

This is not an outstandingly high percentage, though it is higher than most other causal factors considered in the meta-analysis. We suspect that some of the studies where population failed to clear the bar of statistical significance were under-powered or were characterized by questionable specifications (e.g., the inclusion of covariates that are endogenous to district size, and hence posttreatment).

Meta-analysis is useful for bringing together a large number of studies of the same subject. The cost of this aggregation is that the details of the various studies are lost. We do not know what covariates were included in the models, how turnout was measured in each analysis, and whether population was measured in a linear or log-linear fashion. Consequently, it is difficult to judge questions of causal identification. (For this reason, we do not record estimated effect sizes.) Nonetheless, the standard result is confirmed: population (usually) predicts lower turnout.

Evidence: New Analyses

Although extant studies have strong claims to internal validity they are limited in range, and hence in external validity. Most studies focus on a single country; a few encompass several countries. But virtually all studies center on the Organisation for Economic Co-operation and Development (OECD). A rare exception is Kostelka (2017), but even this extensive analysis incorporates only a fraction of the cross-country data available.

Our focus, in common with other wide-ranging studies, is on turnout – the easiest, and hence most common, form of popular participation in modern polities. To provide a more encompassing test of scale effects on participation we conduct two analyses, the first focused on districts and the second concentrated on countries.

District Analysis

Turnout data are available for a subsample of the Multilevel Election Archive (MLEA) database (described in Chapter 2). This includes elections held in fifty-four countries across more than 35,000 districts over two centuries, producing more than 180,000 district-level election observations. Presidential elections are not included in the global sample because of the very limited data that are currently available and their potential to skew the analysis by virtue of extreme values on the predicator of theoretical interest.

Analyses, displayed in Table 7.1, are conducted with errors clustered by district. Model 1 is a bivariate model, including only the regressor of theoretical interest along with country and year dummies. Model 2 adds several additional covariates that might be expected to affect turnout. Model 3 adds a set of dummy variables measuring various electoral laws governing the allocation of votes at district levels, which replace district magnitude (thereby allowing a larger sample, since data for district magnitude are limited).

Table 7.1 *District-level turnout*

Model	1	2	3
Population (log)	−2.392***	−3.611***	−3.032***
	(0.113)	(0.103)	(0.095)
Secret ballot (dummy)		−4.535***	0.333
		(1.406)	(1.248)
Electoral system dummies			✓
Independents dummy			✓
District magnitude (log)		✓	
Election type dummies		✓	✓
Country dummies	✓	✓	✓
Year dummies	✓	✓	✓
Countries	54	43	54
Districts	35,171	32,909	35,171
Years	205	205	205
Observations (contests)	180,711	166,635	180,711
R-squared	0.629	0.594	0.647

Outcome: district-level voter turnout (MLEA). *Units of analysis*: contests.
Constant omitted. *Estimator*: ordinary least squares. Standard errors, clustered by
district, in brackets. *** p < 0.01, ** p < 0.05, * p < 0.10 (two-tailed tests).
Descriptive statistics below.

Variable	Obs.	Mean	Std. Dev.	Min.	Max.
Turnout	180,740	52.55	19.81	0.05	100.00
Population (log)	180,711	9.46	1.80	4.01	17.15
Secret ballot	180,740	0.99	0.12	0.00	1.00

Results are robust across all three models. Population (essentially, the size of the electorate within each district) is strongly and consistently associated with lower turnout. To gauge how large this effect is, we graph predicted values from the benchmark model (Model 1, Table 7.1) in Figure 7.2. This shows that an increase in district size from 1,000 to 10,000 is associated with a decrease in voter turnout of roughly 5 percent – a considerable depression in citizen engagement.

Cross-Country Analysis

To get a more complete picture of how participation varies across countries we examine turnout in national elections as a share of voting-age

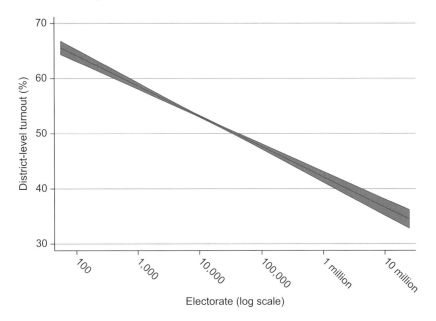

Figure 7.2 District-level turnout, predicted values

Predicted values for district-level voter turnout (Y) as population (log) changes, surrounded by 95 percent confidence interval. Based on Model 1, Table 7.1, with covariates set to sample means. Descriptive statistics (Y): mean = 52.55, SD = 19.81, min. = 0.04, max. = 100.

population. These data originate with IDEA (2002; see also Solijonov 2016), and is included in the V-Dem dataset. The resulting analysis (for the unrestricted sample) includes 154 countries and more than 1,300 elections, with data extending back to the mid-twentieth century (and somewhat further for a few countries).

In analyses shown in Table 7.2, turnout is regressed against population (log) in a variety of specifications, treating (national-level) elections – presidential and/or legislative – as units of analysis. This means that countries with a greater number of elections have greater influence on the model. To mitigate this issue, and to mitigate temporal autocorrelation, standard errors are clustered by country.

Most analyses are restricted to elections that are moderately democratic, under the presumption that population will impact turnout only where elections matter. As a threshold, we employ Level 4 of the Lexical index of electoral democracy, which marks the existence of minimally competitive elections for both the executive and the legislature.

Table 7.2 *Turnout*

Estimator	OLS	OLS	OLS	2SLS
Sample	Lexical ≥ 4	Unrestricted	Lexical ≥ 4	Lexical ≥ 4
Model	1	2	3	4
Population (log)	−2.603***	−1.912**	−2.420***	−1.710*
	(0.829)	(0.831)	(0.903)	(1.027)
Urbanization	21.105***	5.914	11.970	19.735***
	(7.084)	(8.430)	(7.870)	(6.845)
GDP per capita (log)			−2.254	
			(2.239)	
Educational attainment			−0.238	
			(0.838)	
Cumulative number of elections (log)			2.264	
			(2.055)	
Suffrage (% adult citizens qualifying)			0.429***	
			(0.162)	
Minimum voting age			−1.736*	
			(0.878)	
Vote-buying			1.380	
			(1.216)	
Election boycott			2.803*	
			(1.495)	
Subnational government layers			−4.650	
			(2.913)	
Multiparty election			0.399	
			(2.373)	
Free and fair election			−0.211	
			(1.878)	
Electoral system dummies	✓	✓	✓	✓
Compulsory voting dummies	✓	✓	✓	✓
Election type dummies			✓	
Region dummies	✓	✓	✓	✓
Year dummies	✓	✓	✓	
Decade dummies				✓
Countries	113	154	113	108
Years	78	78	78	78
Observations	983	1,333	943	963
R-squared	0.427	0.309	0.505	0.402

Outcome: turnout, i.e., the share of adult voting-age population that cast a vote according to official results (V-Dem). *Units of analysis*: country-years. Constant omitted.
Estimators: OLS (ordinary least squares), 2SLS (two-stage least squares, using territory and agricultural suitability as instruments). Country clustered standard errors in brackets. *** $p < 0.01$, ** $p < 0.05$, * $p < 0.10$ (two-tailed tests)

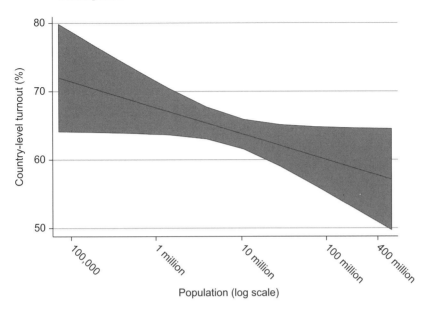

Figure 7.3 Turnout, predicted values

Predicted values for country-level voter turnout (Y) as population (log) changes, surrounded by 95 percent confidence interval. Based on Model 1, Table 7.2, with covariates set to sample means. Descriptive statistics (Y): mean = 63.99, SD = 19.76, min. = 2.14, max. = 223.70. (Ten observations surpass 100 but they do not serve as high-leverage points in the analysis.)

Model 1 includes population, urbanization, a vector of electoral system dummies (registering difficult electoral laws), compulsory voting (disaggregated into a series of dummies that measure different sorts of sanctions), a vector of regional dummies, and annual dummies. Model 2 maintains the same specification but removes the sample restriction, allowing any election in our database (democratic or quasi-democratic) to enter the analysis. Model 3 returns to the restricted sample, this time with additional covariates. Model 4 is an instrumental-variable model.

Results posted in Table 7.2 show a negative relationship between population and turnout across all four models, though the relationship is somewhat attenuated in Model 2 (including polities that hold elections under markedly undemocratic conditions) and Model 4 (the instrumental variable design).

To gain a sense of the impact of this relationship, Figure 7.3 plots predicted values for turnout as population changes, based on estimates from Model 1, Table 7.2. One can see that an increase in a country's population at the lower end of the spectrum, e.g., from 100,000 to 1 million, translates into a modest (but nontrivial) reduction in turnout of about 6 percent.

Summary

In contrast to some of the other topics in this book, the relationship of scale to participation is well studied, as demonstrated in the discussion of this chapter and Table 7.3, which summarizes many of these studies along with our own analyses.

Note that a preponderance of work on this topic shows a negative association between scale and political participation. Indeed, there is a long-standing consensus that participation – including subjective feelings of efficacy – is lower in larger communities, all other things being equal.

Some studies have found that the relationship of population to turnout is more robust at district levels (within countries) than at national levels (across countries). This is apparent in the meta-analysis conducted by Cancela and Geys (2016). Our analyses do not support this interpretation. Note that the estimated coefficient for population in our district-level analysis – 2.4 (Model 1, Table 7.1) – is almost identical to the estimated coefficient for population in our country-level analysis – 2.6 (Model 1, Table 7.2). This is a remarkable fact, and testament to what is – at least, according to our analyses – a highly stable relationship. Of course, the standard errors are much smaller in the district-level analysis due to vast differences in sample size: $N \sim 180,000$ in our district-level analysis while $N \sim 1,000$ in our cross-national analysis. This may account for the greater inconsistency of results in national-level analyses conducted by other scholars, where samples are generally much smaller.

Before concluding we must address the implications of *multilevel governance* for participation. If the evidence presented in this chapter is correct, the size of a large country discourages participation at national levels. At the same time, a large country is likely to feature multiple levels of government (Chapter 11), allowing more opportunities for citizens to engage in politics. One might wonder if the multiple opportunities for participation in a multitiered government compensate for the restricted opportunities available at the national level. All things considered, perhaps being a citizen in the United States and Malta is similar in terms of the opportunities each polity offers for citizen participation. The American citizen has less access to national politics than the citizen of Malta, but there are a range of additional levels (not available to the citizen of Malta) at which the American may engage.

Table 7.3 *Scale and participation: Inventory of analyses*

Indicators	Countries	Treatment units	Years	Units of analysis	Research design	Effect	Study
Assembly attendance	Switzerland	Municipalities (2,900)	(1)	Municipalities (2,900)	Cross-sectional	→	Ladner 2002
Party membership	(5)	Countries (5)	(1)	Parties (29)	Cross-sectional	→	Weldon 2006
Party membership	(20)	Countries (20)	(1)	Countries (20)	Cross-sectional	→	Mair & Van Biezen 2001
Party membership	(27)	Countries (27)	(1)	Countries (27)	Cross-sectional	→	Van Biezen, Mair, & Poguntke 2012
Turnout	United States	Municipalities (108)	(1)	Municipalities (108)	Cross-sectional	Ø	Verba & Nie 1972
Turnout	(24)	Countries (24)	(138)	Elections (509)	Cross-sectional	→	Blais & Carty 1990
Turnout	(91)	Countries (91)	(23)	Elections (324)	Cross-sectional	→	Blais & Dobrzynska 1998
Turnout	Netherlands	Municipalities (?)	(3)	Individuals (5,483)	Cross-sectional	→	Van Houwelingen 2017
Turnout	Netherlands	Municipalities (1,015)	(20)	Municipalities (?)	Panel: amalgamations	→	Kraaykamp, Van Dam, & Toonen 2001
Turnout	(5)	Municipalities (unclear)	(40)	Municipalities (?)	Cross-sectional	→	Frandsen 2002
Turnout	Costa Rica	Districts (453)	(1)	Districts (453)	Cross-sectional	→	Remmer 2010a
Turnout	Austria	Municipalities (542)	(5)	Municipality means (542)	Cross-sectional	→	Ennser-Jedenastik & Veenendaal 2015
Turnout	(65)	Countries (65)	(76)	Elections (453)	Cross-sectional	→	Kostelka 2017
*Turnout	(54)	Districts (35,171)	(205)	Contests (180,711)	Cross-sectional	→	Table 7.1
*Turnout	(162)	Countries (162)	(83)	Elections (1,546)	Cross-sectional	→	Table 7.2
Turnout	United States	Cities (38)	25	Mayoral elections (332)	Cross-sectional	Ø	Caren 2007

Table 7.3 (cont.)

Indicators	Countries	Treatment units	Years	Units of analysis	Research design	Effect	Study
Efficacy	(5)	Countries (5)	(2)	Individuals (1,333)	Cross-sectional	Ø	Finifter & Abramson 1975
Efficacy	United States	States (50)	(8)	Individuals (8,705)	Cross-sectional	→	Bowen 2010
Efficacy	Denmark	Municipalities (271)	(6)	Individuals (2,028)	Panel: amalgamations	→	Lassen & Serritzlew 2011
Various	United States	Cities (2,194)	(1)	Individuals (2,038)	Cross-sectional	→	Oliver 2000
Various	Denmark	Municipalities (38)	(1)	Individuals (50,765)	Cross-sectional	→	Larson 2002
Various	(4)	Municipalities (4,143)	(1)	Municipalities (4,143)	Cross-sectional	→	Denters et al. 2014
Various	United States	Municipalities (100)	(1)	Individuals (750)	Cross-sectional	→	Carr & Tavares 2014
Various	United States	Communities (26)	(1)	Individuals (7,418)	Cross-sectional	+	Kelleher & Lowery 2008
Various	Portugal	Municipalities (278)	(1)	Municipalities (278)	Cross-sectional	→	Tavares & Carr 2013

Treatment units: units exhibiting variation in scale. *Years*: number of years over which data are collected – not to be confused with the frequency of observations, as data may or may not be annual and may be averaged across years. *Research design*: the main, or benchmark, research design – classified as cross-sectional (where the analysis is driven primarily by variation across units) or panel (where the analysis is driven primarily by variation through time). *Effect*: when the scale of a community increases, the designated outcome goes up (↑), down (↓), up and down (∩), or experiences no perceptible change (Ø). A scale effect is considered significant if it passes a modest bar of statistical significance, i.e., p < 0.10 (two-tailed test) in the benchmark model. Number of countries, treatment units, years, or observations in parentheses.

It is certainly the case that larger countries offer more avenues of participation – more levels of government, more elective offices, and hence more ways of engaging in politics. But the multitude of opportunities does not make participation easier. In fact, it makes it harder, and probably less efficacious overall.

First off, we must consider the preeminence of national elections in most countries, as national governments generally hold the lion's share of political power. If participation in national elections is lower in the United States than in Malta, this is probably *not* compensated by opportunities for participation at subnational levels. Second, in a large country participation at lower levels of government is *also* likely to be lower because these low-level bodies will have less policymaking power and less salience in the public eye, and also because the multiplication of offices raises barriers to participation by making it more difficult to follow political affairs and by complicating the task of voting. It is easier to cast one ballot for one office, which is responsible for all (or nearly all) public policies (as in Malta) than to cast multiple ballots for multiple offices, each of which is responsible for somewhat different – but perhaps overlapping – functions (as in the United States). The problem is compounded if elections for different bodies are held in a staggered fashion (on different dates). Thus, we conclude that deconcentrated power in a large polity does not compensate for the disempowering effects of scale.

8   Contestation

Contestation, as we use the term, refers to the degree of electoral competition in a political community. Where there are no elections, there is no contestation. Where elections occur but there is little organized opposition, the incumbent party or person captures most of the votes and seats, and turnover is rare; contestation is low.[1] Where opposition is robust and turnover frequent, contestation is high.

Contestation is a critical element of electoral democracy. Indeed, the terms are often used interchangeably. Note that the latter is commonly understood as contestation among leadership groups vying for the electorate's approval during periodic elections (Becker 1958; Dahl 1956, 1971; Sartori 1976: 217; Schattschneider 1942; Schumpeter 1950 [1942]; Strøm 1992). Indices of contestation thus offer an important signal of the health of an electoral democracy. In this vein, some scholars regard turnover as a sine qua non test of democracy (Alvarez, Cheibub, Limongi, & Przeworski 1996).

Electoral contestation is also a linchpin of accountability – a crucial element in the electoral model of democracy. If incumbents face no effective challenge they have no incentive to serve the electorate, and whatever misdeeds they commit are likely to go unpunished. Indeed, studies show that contestation is associated with greater activity on the part of representatives (Konisky & Ueda 2011) and greater responsiveness or accountability (Ansolabehere, Snyder, & Stewart 2001; Beer & Mitchell 2004; Gordon & Huber 2007; Griffin 2006; P. Jones 2013; Powell 2000; but see Brunell 2008; Cleary 2007; Fiorina 1973). Studies also suggest that contestation fosters higher turnout (Blais & Lago 2009). Lachat (2011) finds that competitive elections lead to more programmatic voting decisions, affecting the character of campaigns. Contestation, finally, is associated with strong

---

[1] These features of the concept are widely agreed upon, though there are other more peripheral aspects of contestation that fall outside our minimal definition (e.g., Bartolini 1999, 2000; Strøm 1989).

parties, a topic discussed in Chapter 6 and also a key element of the electoral model of democracy.

Indicators of contestation based on votes and seats offer a reflection of the larger, more diffuse concept of electoral democracy. If there are no elections at all, then there is neither contestation nor electoral democracy. Here, the two concepts are perfectly in synch. If there are elections, the quality of those elections – the degree to which they are free and fair – are likely to be reflected in the dispersion of votes, and hence in indices of contestation. If the incumbent party buys votes on a massive scale, imprisons opposition leaders, monopolizes sources of campaign finance and access to the media, or simply prevents other parties from appearing on the ballot, little contestation will be registered.

However, contestation does not offer a *perfect* reflection of the quality of electoral democracy. Sometimes, incumbents win big even though the rules of the game are fair (e.g., Lyndon Johnson in the US presidential election of 1964). Sometimes, incumbents lose even though the rules of the game are unfair (e.g., Malaysia or Maldives in 2018). Likewise, vote- or seat-based measures take no notice of suffrage. They do not reflect non-electoral dimensions of democracy such as judicial independence, rule of law, civil liberty, horizontal accountability, the strength of civil society, etc. Thus, contestation is rightly viewed as an element of electoral democracy but should not be conflated with that larger topic (which we take up in Chapter 15).

Leaving democracy aside, electoral contestation may also improve the quality of *governance*, promoting greater efficiency and fewer political rents (Barro 1973; Stigler 1972; Wittman 1989). Several studies argue that contestation enhances prospects for political reform and good governance (Borges 2008; Geddes 1994; Grzymala-Busse 2007; Heller, Kyriacou, & Roca-Sagalés 2011; Ting et al. 2013), including lower levels of corruption (Weitz-Shapiro 2012), and political protest (Arce & Mangonnet 2013). Murillo and Martinez-Gallardo (2007), however, find no statistically significant relationship between a measure of party contestation (based on seats in the legislature) and propensity to institute market reforms in Latin America. Trounstine (2008) finds that US municipalities dominated for a long period by a single group resulted in lower spending and a narrower distribution of benefits. A raft of studies also suggests that interparty contestation leads to stronger growth performance (Berkowitz & Clay 2012; Besley, Persson, & Sturm 2010; Padovano & Ricciuti 2009).

Of course, extreme contestation can have deleterious effects, especially if parties utilize paramilitary groups to round up supporters and intimidate opponents as occurred in Weimar Germany and contemporary

Jamaica (Co. Clarke 2006). One should also bear in mind that in winner-take-all elections, contestation usually entails a decline in responsiveness and trust (Brunell 2008; Brunell & Buchler 2009; Buchler 2005, 2011). Since only one candidate or party can win, all those supporting the losing candidate or party are not likely to be well represented and are likely to be less trusting of the candidate who wins. In a highly competitive district, this is nearly half of the voters. The same dynamic does not apply in an electoral system in which votes are allocated proportionally to candidates and there are multiple seats in a district (proportional representation).

These flaws notwithstanding, contestation seems to be associated with more good things than bad. (For a wide-ranging discussion, see Bardhan & Yang 2004.) With this as background we turn to the causes of contestation. Why do some communities experience higher contestation than others?

Many factors assuredly contribute to electoral contestation (Somit et al. 1994). In this chapter, we focus on a distal feature – demography – that we believe to be sizeable and persistent, perhaps more so than any other single causal factor. We argue that the size of a community affects the level of contestation at a structural level, operating beneath the surface and conditioning many of the proximal factors that have received attention from other scholars.

We begin by offering a theoretical account of the impact of scale on contestation. This account operates a little differently at polity levels and at district levels, prompting us to construct separate theoretical accounts. Next, we introduce our data and a variety of empirical tests. A short conclusion summarizes the results.

Theory: Polity Level

We assume that politics is a method of solving coordination problems and resolving conflict (which we regard as essentially the same function). As the size of a community grows, so does its heterogeneity (Chapter 3). Both size and heterogeneity complicate the task of coordination and the number of potential conflicts. Informal mechanisms of consultation and deliberation are unlikely to work very well on a large scale. A community of millions cannot sit down together and

Figure 8.1 Scale effects on contestation at polity levels

talk. Thus, the need for an institutionalized mechanism of resolving conflicts grows with size.

Of course, coercion offers another option, and this may be the first recourse of leaders loath to sacrifice their power. However, coercion is not always viable. And it is less likely to be successful in a large, diverse society that is ridden with conflicts. Unless normative consensus can be gained, that society is likely to fragment. In practical terms, this means that the leader is faced with a decision to rule autocratically over a smaller community or to cede some of her power under an institutionalized system of rule. We assume that some leaders will choose the latter, or will be forced to choose the latter. The key point, in any case, is that size alters incentives for leaders and masses, both of whom have greater need for an institutionalized mechanism of resolving conflict.

The most common institutional mechanism for resolving conflict in the modern era is elections. We anticipate, therefore, that the larger the political community, the more likely it is that a community will adopt elections and allow for some degree of multiparty competition. We can also anticipate that those elections will be hotly contested, for a heterogeneous society is likely to generate a fragmented field, where no single candidate or party is able to monopolize the vote.

This simple theoretical schema is illustrated in Figure 8.1.

Theory: District Level

Having examined the sources of contestation in a general fashion at polity levels, we turn to the district level. Assuming multiparty competition is allowed, a number of more subtle factors come into play. These may be articulated as *mechanical* or *strategic*, as summarized in Figure 8.2.

Mechanical Effects

Contestation is fostered by an effect that is "mechanical" insofar as it rests on the composition of a district rather than on changes in the behavior of voters or elites within that district.

Figure 8.2 Scale effects on contestation at district levels

Table 8.1 *The mechanical effect, an illustration*

	Voters	Party A	Party B	Contestation
District 1	50,000	75%	25%	Low
District 2	50,000	25%	75%	Low
Districts 1 & 2	100,000	50%	50%	High

An illustration of the mechanical effect, i.e., how larger districts – in this example, formed by combining two smaller districts – can achieve higher contestation without any change in voter behavior.

As a stylized example, consider two equal-sized single-member electoral districts, illustrated in Table 8.1. Each district has two candidates on the ballot, one from Party *A* and the other from Party *B*. In District 1, 75 percent of the voters favor Party *A* while 25 percent favor Party *B*. In District 2, these numbers are reversed: 25 percent of the voters favor Party *A* while 75 percent favor Party *B*. So constituted, both districts will be uncompetitive so long as voting behavior follows party identification.

Now consider the effect if these two districts are combined into one larger (single-member) district and voters' preferences hold constant. In this larger district, both parties command exactly the same level of voter support and contestation reaches its theoretical maximum (in the context of two-party contestation and first-past-the-post rules).

Importantly, this mechanical effect is not realized when the same party is ahead in both districts. In this situation, the hypothetical aggregation of two districts into one results in a simple averaging of voting behavior across the lower-level districts. It follows that the mechanical effect generates either (a) an increase or (b) no change in party contestation. This result is generalizable to multiparty contestation as well as multimember districts where seats are allocated by party lists so long as ceteris paribus conditions obtain.

Evidently, we cannot assume that voting behavior will remain constant when the size of a district changes. Neither can we expect decisions by political elites to remain constant when faced with a dramatically different political environment. Thus, we expect that mechanical effects are reinforced by *strategic* effects, to which we now turn.

Challengers

Incumbents typically enjoy many advantages over challengers. This includes experience, name recognition, campaign finance, access to media, a staff of professional advisors, the ability to set the agenda, and other perquisites of office (e.g., the ability to dispense jobs and pork). Although it is no easy trick to win reelection, it is fair to say that incumbents (whether understood as individuals or parties) enjoy an institutionalized advantage. As such, the quality of the challenger serves as a key predictor of contestation within a district (Jacobson & Kernell 1983; Mann & Wolfinger 1980; Van Dunk 1997). This prompts us to consider how the size of a district may impact challenger quality.

Let us suppose that the supply of high-quality politicians and parties – those with the requisite background, skills, networks, funds, and ambition to mount a viable campaign – is equally distributed across a country (or across the world). It follows that a larger district (or country) will contain a larger pool of strong challengers, and a very small district may contain *no* persons or parties with the requisite skill set and ambition (Dometrius & Ozymy 2006).

Of course, it is not simply the distribution of talent that we might want to consider but also motivation. Ceteris paribus, we imagine that a larger political community offers a larger stage for the ambitious to strut. It may also offer higher compensation (Chapter 10). For those interested in fame and fortune, which we assume includes the most ambitious and qualified challengers, the prospect of entering politics in a large district may be more attractive than the prospect of entering politics in a small district.[2]

Thus, the size of a district, by conditioning the supply of strong challengers and their motivation to seek public office, should impact the overall level of contestation in a district.

Cohesion

As size grows, social cohesion is diminished (Chapter 3), and this has important ramifications for the ability of an incumbent to maintain electoral control of a district.

Typically, small communities have dominant cultural codes to which all members of society are expected to adhere, mitigating efforts to mobilize political opposition (Baldacchino 2012). Dahl and Tufte (1973: ch. 6) refer to this as the "costs of dissent." Likewise, when people relocate they often sort themselves according to shared sociological, cultural, and political characteristics. Both of these factors should enhance local-level

---

[2] Sokolow (1989) finds that local officials in small jurisdictions are not very ambitious, which is to say they do not necessarily see their work as a stepping-stone for higher office. This fits with our argument that small communities do not engage the most ambitious individuals.

homogeneity. In the smallest districts, politics may be dominated by a single family or clan. A politician from Palau remarks,

It is very much those who have big families and clans, you know that they will win for sure. . . . A social network normally runs through the family and the clan, and so if you don't have that as your base to run, it's very slim to none for you to win.

By contrast, a large community provides many potential cleavages for an opposition candidate or party to exploit. Social diversity thus serves as an important causal pathway from size to enhanced electoral contestation (Aistrup 2004; Gronke 2000; Koetzle 1998; Sullivan 1973; Trounstine 2008; but see Ensley, Tofias, & De Marchi 2009).

By the same logic, in a large polity or district there are likely to be a greater number and variety of organizations. This includes businesses, labor unions, professional associations, religious and ethnic associations, universities, media outlets, and other organizations situated within civil society. Insofar as social and economic organizations provide a base for political organization, the richness and diversity of this organizational field should provide fodder for political opposition. A small district, by contrast, may encompass only one or two important organizations, which are likely to be closely linked to the incumbent – either because they launched his/her career or because s/he has managed to coopt them. For present purposes, it hardly matters whether the incumbent controls the organizations, the organizations control the incumbent, or they have a synergistic relationship. The key point is that there is likely to be a strong connection between the holders of political and socioeconomic power (Sutton 2007). By contrast, in a large community characterized by numerous organizations with varying interests and perspectives, it will be more difficult to establish and maintain an exclusive power elite (Mills 1967).

In a larger community, greater diversity should also make it more difficult for a single officeholder or party to adequately represent the views of constituents, as discussed in Chapter 5. Where constituent views are conflicted, there is no way that a representative can be responsive to everyone. Whatever s/he does, someone will be disappointed, perhaps even outraged. Likewise, media reporting in a large community may be more critical of elected representatives than media reporting in a small community, where everyone is perceived to be on the same team (Hess 1991: 57). Accordingly, Binder, Maltzman, and Sigelman (1998) find that the popularity of US senators is inversely related to the size and diversity of their state. Studies focused on the US House of Representatives (Frederick 2010), governors (King & Cohen 2005), and state legislatures (Squire 1993) report similar findings.

Evidence: Country Level

Contestation has rarely been studied at national levels. The only index with broad coverage, developed many years ago by Tatu Vanhanen (2000), has not been updated and includes some ad hoc coding decisions that make it closer to a measure of democracy than a measure of contestation per se (for further discussion see Gerring, Hicken, et al. 2018).

We focus here on the *largest-party* formula: 100 minus the share of votes won by the largest vote-getter. This formula produces an index of contestation that is highly correlated with indices based on other formulas such as the *top-two* (100−the difference between the two top vote-getters) or *incumbent-challenger* (100−the difference between the incumbent and the nearest challenger) formulas.

Electoral data is drawn from a variety of sources as described in Gerring, Hicken, and colleagues (2018). Both parliamentary and presidential elections are included. Where these elections are held in the same year, we take the average value across the two elections. Where multiple elections for a single office (president or parliament) occur in a single year, we record the *last* of these elections as the value for that year. We code all years *prior* to the first election or during an *electoral interregnum* (when elections are interrupted or the elective body is prorogued) as zero (0), signaling an absence of electoral contestation. Years *in between* elections are filled in with results from the previous election unless there is an electoral interregnum. The assumption is that results from the last election characterize the state of electoral contestation until the next election.

The resulting variable is left-bounded, with many observations bumping up against zero. Accordingly, we adopt a tobit regression model for the following tests, displayed in Table 8.2, where contestation is regressed against population (log). In Model 1, we include two covariates – per capita GDP (log) and English colony (a dummy variable recording whether a country was at any point an English colony) – along with decade dummies. (Annual dummies are not tractable in a tobit model.) Model 2, a spare model, restricts the specification to the variable of theoretical interest and decade dummies. Model 3 is a full specification including all variables in the benchmark along with additional factors that could serve as confounders but might also be downstream from population. Model 4 is an instrumental variable model.

Results posted in Table 8.2 show a strong and fairly stable relationship between country population and contestation across all models. To gauge the impact of this relationship, Figure 8.3 graphs predicted values for the outcome against population based on estimates from the benchmark model. Note that values below zero refer to the values that (according to the tobit

Table 8.2 *Contestation*

Estimator	Tobit	Tobit	Tobit	IV tobit
Models	1	2	3	4
Population (log)	3.973***	2.655**	3.194***	3.934**
	(0.941)	(1.303)	(0.812)	(1.983)
GDP per capita (log)	13.93***		1.013	14.48***
	(1.559)		(1.999)	(1.652)
English colony	9.973**		5.308*	6.479
	(4.313)		(3.113)	(4.751)
Urbanization			12.28	
			(7.973)	
Latitude (log)			−3.267**	
			(1.608)	
Island			2.658	
			(3.590)	
Mineral wealth			−0.00191*	
			(0.00107)	
Years since			−0.497	
independence (log)			(0.822)	
Protestants (%)			0.109**	
			(0.0437)	
Muslims (%)			0.0385	
			(0.0530)	
Ethnic fractionalization			−16.67**	
			(7.429)	
Religious fractionalization			2.344	
			(6.552)	
Linguistic fractionalization			8.676	
			(7.340)	
Democracy (Lexical index)			8.442***	
			(0.494)	
Electoral system (dummies)			✓	
Regions (dummies)	✓	✓	✓	✓
Countries	197	197	143	164
Years	227	227	107	215
Observations	21,424	21,424	8,149	18,871
Pseudo likelihood	−56,129	−57,468	−27,920	−80,738

Outcome: contestation (100-share of votes garnered by largest vote-getter in presidential and/or parliamentary election). *Units of analysis*: country-years. *Lag structure*: right-side variables measured at t−1. Constant omitted. *Estimators*: tobit, IV tobit (instrumental variable analysis using territory and agricultural suitability as instruments). Country clustered standard errors in brackets. *** p < 0.01, ** p < 0.05, * p < 0.10 (two-tailed tests)

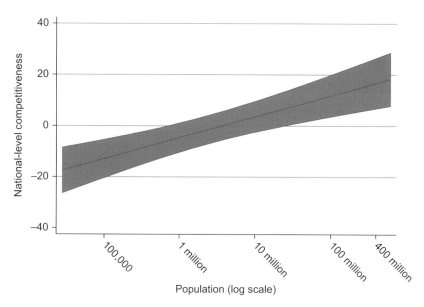

Figure 8.3 Contestation, predicted values
Predicted values for country-level contestation (*Y*) as population (log) changes, surrounded by 95 percent confidence interval. Based on Model 1, Table 8.2, with covariates set to sample means.

estimator) would have been realized if the scale were not truncated. Note also that because of the logged scale, the impact of population on contestation is much greater at lower levels of population than at higher levels. For example, an increase in population from 100,000 to 1 million is associated with a (roughly) ten-point increase in contestation. This is equivalent to an increase from 10,000 to 100,000 (on the low end) or 10 million to 100 million (on the high end). In any case, the effect is nontrivial. Larger polities generate considerably higher levels of party-based contestation.

Evidence: District Level

While country-level analyses focus on contestation writ large, district-level analyses focus on variation across districts. There is no meaningful variation to explore in countries that do not hold elections or do not allow multiple parties to compete in elections. So, our district-level analysis is restricted to countries and periods where multiparty competition exists. One can think of this as measuring the *degree* of contestation rather than the existence/non-existence of contestation. To distinguish these topics we refer to contestation across districts as *competitiveness*.

As our main indicator we continue to use the largest-party index (100−vote share of the largest party). This is a highly sensitive indicator, offering meaningful variation for every district and every election that is open to multiparty contestation. Importantly, other measures of competitiveness are highly correlated and render very similar results (Gerring et al. 2015). *Turnover* is explored in the final set of analyses.

The causal factor of theoretical interest is the size of the electorate (the number of eligible voters in a district). This is proxied by the population of a district in our analyses. Note that in the modern era of universal suffrage these statistics are highly correlated. Consequently, tests that are restricted to constituencies where we can measure the actual size of the electorate are nearly identical to those that use population as a proxy.

A handful of academic studies examine the connection between size and competitiveness at district levels in the United States. These studies use indices based on the performance of the largest party or the two largest parties; occasionally, they examine turnover. Patterson and Caldeira (1984) look at competitiveness across states (aggregating across a variety of state-level elections). Aistrup (2004) examines state house elections aggregated by county. Lascher (2005) looks at county board of supervisor elections in California. Hajnal, Lewis, and Louch (2002) tally local elections of all sorts across California. Hogan (2003) examines primary elections for state legislative races in twenty-five states. Hibbing and Brandes (1983) examine variation across Senate elections. Trounstine (2008) looks at large cities using a specially constructed indicator of monopoly control. Most of these studies support our argument that larger districts encourage greater competitiveness. However, the hypothesis has scarcely been studied outside the United States.

Global Analysis

The first set of tests displayed in Table 8.3 utilize all data available from the Multilevel Elections Archive (MLEA) introduced in Chapter 2. This includes eighty-eight countries, some of which offer time-series data extending back to the eighteenth century.

In Model 1, competitiveness is regressed against population along with country and year dummies. Model 2 adds a covariate measuring district magnitude (log), a feature that is likely to affect competitiveness but that is also likely to be highly correlated with the size of a district. Model 3 replaces district magnitude (for which data coverage is limited) with a set of dummy variables representing different sorts of electoral system laws as well as different office types.

Estimates from models in Table 8.3 show a positive relationship between the size of a constituency and the level of competitiveness

Table 8.3 *District-level competitiveness*

Model	1	2	3
Population (log)	2.914***	2.133***	2.014***
	(0.050)	(0.045)	(0.054)
District magnitude (log)		7.806***	
		(0.071)	
Electoral system dummies			✓
Office type dummies			✓
Country dummies	✓	✓	✓
Year dummies	✓	✓	✓
Countries	88	70	88
Districts	79,928	77,198	79,928
Years	225	225	225
Observations (contests)	387,448	368,413	387,448
R-squared	0.288	0.313	0.356

Outcome: competitiveness (100−share of largest vote-getter). *Electoral system dummies*: (a) single-member district (SMD); (b) majoritarian, block ballot; (c) proportional representation (PR), average magnitude < 9; (d) PR, average magnitude > 9, closed list; (e) PR, average magnitude > 9, open list; (f) mixed (SMD and MMD); (g) secret ballot. *Office type dummies*: (a) upper chamber, (b) lower chamber, (c) governor, (d) upper chamber of state legislature, (e) lower chamber of state legislature, (f) mayor, (g) council. *Units of analysis*: district-level contests. Constant omitted. *Estimator*: ordinary least squares, standard errors clustered by district. *** $p < 0.01$, ** $p < 0.05$, * $p < 0.10$ (two-tailed tests). Descriptive statistics below.

Variable	Obs.	Mean	Std. Dev.	Min.	*Max.*
Competitiveness	418,213	38.84	18.27	0.00	96.13
Population (log)	388,860	10.01	1.75	3.71	19.49
District magnitude (log)	423,793	0.20	0.67	0.00	5.01

within a district. Coefficients across the three models are also fairly stable, suggesting that the relationship is not subject to specification choices.

Before continuing, let us consider this estimate in a more practical fashion by constructing a plot of predicted competitiveness as the size of a constituency changes. Figure 8.4 shows a fairly steep curve with a tight 95 percent confidence interval. The logarithmic format of the independent variable suggests a causal relationship with decreasing returns. Specifically, each nonlinear increment shown on the X axis – 100;

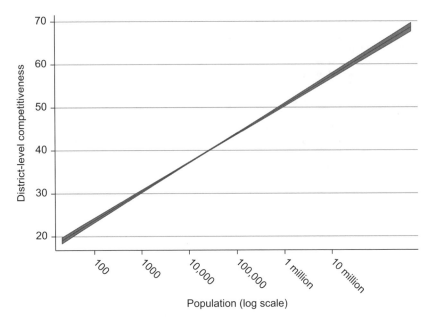

Figure 8.4 District-level competitiveness, predicted values

Predicted values for district-level competitiveness (Y) as population (log) changes, surrounded by 95 percent confidence interval. Based on Model 1, Table 8.3, with covariates set to sample means. (For descriptive statistics see Table 8.3.)

1,000; 10,000; 100,000; 1 million; 10 million – translates into an increase of just under 10 percent in anticipated levels of competitiveness.

Additional tests explore the relationship between scale and competitiveness in a longitudinal fashion, employing a variety of fixed-effect estimators (Gerring et al. 2015). Of course, global analyses must contend with an extraordinary degree of heterogeneity, both in the measured treatments and in background factors that may serve as confounders. No matter how many robustness tests one performs, some potential confounders may remain at large because they are impossible to measure and test across such a large sample. The following sections focus on smaller settings where causal inference is probably more tractable.

Precincts

In the second section of this chapter we introduced the idea of a mechanical effect – that increased contestation in larger electorates is partly the product of aggregating populations with opposing partisan preferences. A simple hypothetical example was explored. However, we also argued that the impact of electorate size on competitiveness is not solely the product of this mechanical effect but also of strategic factors stemming from challenger supply and social cohesion.

In order to demonstrate this point we must find a way to isolate the mechanical effect from the data-generating process. This is achieved with data from the ROAD (1984–90) and HEDA (2000–12) archives, which record American election results by *precinct* – a unit smaller than the smallest electoral district under examination (see Appendix B in Gerring et al. 2015). We then compare voting behavior at the precinct level when voters are subjected to varying treatments, i.e., exposure (via an election ballot) to a vote choice for a particular office in a particular election (a *contest*). For example, in a single precinct on a given election day, a voter may be exposed to contests for the state legislature, state senate, US House of Representatives, US Senate, governorship, and presidency. Most of these contests take place in differently sized districts, which therefore define the magnitude of the treatment, as measured by population. In this manner, we can explore how the same group of voters – members of a single precinct – responds to partisan vote choices occurring simultaneously in differently sized districts. Because we calculate competitiveness at the precinct level rather than at the treatment level, we are able to eliminate mechanical effects that arise solely from aggregating and disaggregating voting units (districts). Any changes in contestation registered in these analyses must arise from changes in vote choice, i.e., split-ticket voting. (If all voters in a precinct vote straight party tickets, there will be no alteration in competitiveness across contests.) Such changes in vote choice must be the product of other (non-mechanical) factors, classified as "strategic" in our theoretical discussion.

The analysis in Table 8.4 estimates the effect of population on competitiveness within a precinct across varied contests – state house, state senate, US House, US Senate, governorship, and presidency. We employ precinct-year fixed effects and cluster standard errors at the contest level, reflecting the fact that the competitiveness of a given contest across multiple precincts is not independent. Observations are weighted by the total number of ballots cast in a precinct-year so that smaller precincts do not dominate the results. The coefficient on population thus measures the average change in competitiveness within a precinct across simultaneous elections as the size of the district (for each election) changes.

We find a positive and statistically significant relationship between the size of the electorate for a particular contest and precinct-level competitiveness. Specifically, within the same precinct, a state senate race is, on average, 1.3 percent more competitive than a state house race, a US House race is 1.9 percent more competitive than a state senate race,

Table 8.4 *Precinct-level analysis*

Model	1
Population (log)	0.013***
	(0.001)
Precinct dummies	✓
Year dummies	✓
Years	1984–2012
Contests	31,410
Precinct-years	1,512,577
Observations (N)	5,157,710
Adj. R2	0.468

Outcome: Competitiveness (100−share of largest party) using two-party vote. *Units of analysis*: precinct-level election returns for US elections for all states and years where data are available (see Appendix B in Gerring et al. 2015). Constant omitted. *Offices*: presidency, Senate, House, governorship, state senate, state house. Observations weighted by total ballots cast in each precinct-year. *Estimator*: ordinary least squares regression with precinct-year fixed effects, standard errors clustered by electoral contest. *** p < 0.01, ** p < 0.05, * p < 0.10 (two-tailed tests)

a US Senate or gubernatorial race is 2.8 percent more competitive than a US House race, and a presidential election is 5.0 percent more competitive than a state-level election. While many of these differences are relatively small, they are statistically significant and establish that the mechanical effect does not explain the entire observed increase in contestation as the size of the electorate increases.

In addition to isolating the mechanical effect of district size on competitiveness, the analyses contained in Table 8.4 provide an especially strong test of our main hypothesis. Note that we are comparing the effect of varying treatment conditions on the same voters – a within-subjects design (Judd, Kenny, & McLelland 2001). The treatments – voting for various offices on the same ballot – are administered sequentially. The only potential problem of causal inference is posed by interference across treatments. It is virtually inevitable that top-of-the-ballot choices influence down-ballot choices, or the reverse. However, "coattails" are not a principal concern in the present setting. First, this sort of interference mimics the real world, so our estimated causal effect has greater generalizability than one induced in an artificial laboratory setting where subjects might be asked to vote for only a single office. Second, this sort of interference presumably diminishes the treatment effect that one would anticipate if ballot choices were artificially segregated, exerting a downward bias on our estimates.

For these reasons, we regard precinct-level analyses as providing the most demanding test of our hypothesis. At the same time, note that by eliminating the mechanical effect we are also underestimating the total impact of population on competitiveness. The research design pursued in this section, while appropriate for isolating the mechanical effect, is not appropriate for measuring the total impact of population on competitiveness. By measuring competitiveness at the precinct level, we are able to hold constant the identity of the subjects (voters). Yet by holding constant the identity of the subjects, we are also holding constant a feature – constituent diversity – that, according to our theory, is likely to influence competitiveness. Specifically, if through population growth, socialization of new voters, and sorting citizens aggregate in districts that are homogeneous – and if this homogenization effect is strongest at the smallest level – then the full impact of size on competitiveness can be estimated only when district membership is allowed to vary over time. For these reasons, other research designs – presented earlier and later in this volume – offer a more accurate overall assessment of the theorized relationship.

Council Elections

Elections to local councils offer a special window into the size–contestation relationship, one that is, at least in certain respects, less prone to confounders. We focus on three countries that provide good coverage of district-level data for local elections in the contemporary era: the United Kingdom, Brazil, and Sweden. Results from benchmark models are contained in Table 8.5. Descriptive statistics, and complete results, including multiple robustness tests, can be found in online Appendices *C* (United Kingdom), *D* (Brazil), and *E* (Sweden) of Gerring and colleagues (2015).

British council elections at the ward (district) level may be observed over the past century, thanks to data compiled by Rallings, Thrasher, and Ware (2006). During this time, and especially over the past four decades, numerous changes in ward size occurred as a result of mergers and splits in local governing units, i.e., parishes, boroughs, and councils. So far as can be discerned, these dramatic increases and decreases in electorate size are not accompanied by other changes that might have affected ward-level competitiveness. Most elections were conducted in single-member districts and with first-past-the-post rules, and those that did not are excluded from our sample. Changes in powers and duties delegated to local offices occurred occasionally and were sometimes coincident with a reorganization of offices.

Table 8.5 *Council elections*

Country	United Kingdom	Brazil	Sweden
Estimator	RE	RE	OLS
Model	1	2	3
Population (log)	2.843***	2.063***	2.212***
	(0.125)	(0.143)	(0.787)
Urban		0.039***	
		(0.007)	
Income		−1.199**	
		(0.529)	
Literacy		0.142***	
		(0.023)	
District magnitude (log)		9.126***	−4.050
		(0.697)	(2.745)
County/borough dummies	✓		
State dummies		✓	
District dummies			✓
Year dummies	✓	✓	✓
Years	1912–2003	1996–2010	1966–73
Districts	24,823	5,510	278
Contests (N)	121,378	20,219	834
R2 (within)	0.124	0.269	(0.118)

Outcome: Competitiveness (100−share of largest party). *Units of analysis*: district-level contests. Constant omitted. *Estimators*: RE (random effects), OLS (ordinary least squares), standard errors clustered by district (ward/municipality). *** $p < 0.01$, ** $p < 0.05$, * $p < 0.10$ (two-tailed tests)

However, accounts of this process do not suggest patterns that are likely to correlate in a consistent fashion with changes in ward size (Alexander 1982; Game & Wilson 2011; Rallings & Thrasher 1997; Rao & Young 1997).

In Model 1, Table 8.5, competitiveness is regressed against population along with county/borough and year fixed effects. Standard errors are clustered by ward, which in this setting serves as the lowest-level district. Note that merged (or divided) wards are generally contained within a larger unit – referred to variously as a County Borough Council, County Council, District Council, Greater London Council, London Borough Council, Metropolitan Borough Council, Metropolitan County Council, or Unitary Authority. We label this larger unit a *county/borough*, and assign unique dummies to each one. Because the boundaries of a county/borough generally remain constant through time (during its period of existence), the inclusion of dummies for each county/borough in our model has the effect of comparing levels of competitiveness across local districts (wards) within a county/borough in a given year. Arguably, the main feature distinguishing these districts is population.

In Model 2, we explore Brazilian council elections for four elections held between 1996 and 2010 across 5,510 districts, generating 20,000+ contests. Council elections employ open-list PR rules, with the municipality as the multimember election district. While occasional mergers and divisions across municipalities occurred during this period, data are not available on the pretreated units. Consequently, there is no pattern in the data-generating process that might be interpreted as a natural experiment. Likewise, the time series is too short (and the variable of theoretical interest too sluggish) to justify the use of district fixed effects. Fortunately, we can measure some background covariates at the district level including urbanization, income, literacy, and district magnitude, and we can also control for state-level features with a vector of dummies.

In Model 3, we examine local elections in Sweden. Here, we focus on a single intervention observed across a narrow slice of time. In order to accommodate falling population in rural municipalities and the perceived need for more efficient local government units in a period of rapid welfare state expansion, Swedish municipalities were merged from 1965 to 1974. A bill introduced by the Social Democratic government led to the aggregation of 1,031 municipalities into 282 "blocs" with a predicted population size of at least 8,000 people in 1975. For the most part, these new blocs aligned with geographical circumstances related to industry and the economy and clustered around a central town or village (*centralort*). Mergers of municipalities were originally expected to occur voluntarily, but by 1969, less than 10 percent of the required mergers had occurred. The government then decided to force the remaining mergers, most of which occurred in 1971 and 1974 (Brantgärde 1974: 14–44; Wallin 1973: 18–31; Wångmar 2006: 71–72). As a consequence, increases in electorate size in Swedish municipalities were driven by forces largely exogenous to local political actors. We observe three elections: 1966, under the pre-reform system (900 municipalities, mean electorate: 5,934); 1970, with a few reformed districts in place (464 municipalities, mean electorate: 12,164); and 1973, with the reform completed (278 municipalities, mean electorate: 20,455). All elections were held with closed-list PR rules and no statutory threshold for representation. We treat the final post-reform districts ($N = 278$) as our units of analysis. This means that results for the 1966 and 1970 elections are aggregated up, weighting results for smaller districts by size.[3] Model 3 includes district and year fixed effects along with a measure of district magnitude (i.e., local assembly size), which expanded with each district merge.

Results from all three tests, summarized in Table 8.5, show a positive relationship between district size and competitiveness. Estimated coefficients are also remarkably similar, despite the different contexts and varied estimators.

Suffrage Reforms

Suffrage reforms focused on specific classes of voters offer yet another opportunity to test our hypothesis. Drawing on the PIPE dataset (Przeworski 2013), we construct binary variables to measure major suffrage reforms focused on women and youth. *Female suffrage* is coded 0 prior to universal female (adult) suffrage, and 1 after suffrage is granted to that group (separately from males). *Youth suffrage* is coded 0 prior to the extension of suffrage to younger voters, and 1 thereafter. (Only one youth suffrage extension is coded for each country.)

Our dummy-variable coding represents the final reform – when universal suffrage within the specified demographic category was achieved, regardless of prior reforms. It does not specify *how much* of an increase in eligible voters that final reform represented. We exclude male suffrage, and instances where male and female suffrage were inaugurated together, because such reforms usually occurred in a piecemeal fashion over a long period of time and are associated with a host of potential confounders (World War I, the formation of mass parties, the crystallization of party cleavages, the inauguration of new electoral laws, and other perturbations of the late nineteenth and early twentieth centuries).

In order to analyze the impact of suffrage reforms on competitiveness it is necessary to observe a country pre- and posttreatment. This means that reforms must occur after the inauguration of multiparty contestation and district-level data must be available for before and after the reform. Eight female suffrage reforms and twenty youth suffrage reforms meet this criterion, as listed in Table 8.6.

Analyses displayed in Table 8.6 focus on the immediate effects of suffrage reform, as revealed by first-difference regression models. We assume that longer-range causal effects are subject to a variety of

---

[3] Results for the 1966 and 1970 elections were coded from Sveriges Officiella Statistik: Allmänna Val, and for the 1973 elections they were downloaded from www.scb.se. Matching across units is based on Ivarsson (1992).

Table 8.6 *Suffrage extensions*

Model	1
ΔFemale suffrage	2.221***
	(0.593)
ΔYouth suffrage	1.305***
	(0.212)
Electoral system dummies	✓
Year dummies	✓
Years	1788–2013
Countries	63
Districts	75,769
Contests (N)	323,424
R^2	0.014

Outcome: ΔCompetitiveness (100−vote share of largest party) from one election to the next. *Units of analysis*: district-level contests. Constant omitted. *Estimator*: ordinary least squares "first-difference" regressions, standard errors clustered by district. *** $p < 0.01$, ** $p < 0.05$, * $p < 0.10$ (two-tailed tests)
Female suffrage extensions: Belgium (1919), Greece (1956), Ireland (1923), Liechtenstein (1984), Norway (1909), Switzerland (1971), United Kingdom (1928), United States (1920). *Youth suffrage extensions*: Australia (1974), Austria (1970), Belgium (1981), Brazil (1990), Finland (1972), France (1978), Greece (1985), Iceland (1934), India (1989), Ireland (1973), Jamaica (1976), Korea (2000), Luxembourg (1974), New Zealand (1975), Norway (1921), Portugal (1976), Sweden (1948), Turkey (1995), United Kingdom (1970), United States (1971).

confounders and thus not very informative. In Model 1, the change in competitiveness from one election to the next is regressed against the change in suffrage status for our two suffrage variables, along with dummies representing each year and each electoral system type. Coefficients for both variables of theoretical interest are positive and statistically significant. The advent of female suffrage seems to have had a larger estimated effect on competitiveness than youth suffrage, as one might expect.

We interpret these causal effects as the product of increasing diversity (declining cohesion) within the electorate, as laid out earlier. By admitting new voters with distinctive interests and values, electoral contestation is enhanced. Although the admission of women and youth did not upset established party systems in any country, our analysis suggests that it attenuated the hold of dominant parties at the constituency level. Indeed, studies of female suffrage suggest that newly admitted voters were not carbon copies of the existing electorate: women voted differently (sometimes more conservatively) than men (Harvey 1998: 146–51; Inglehart & Norris 2000). Although youth vote choice subsequent to franchise extension has not been extensively studied, our analysis suggests that 18–21-year-olds behaved somewhat differently in the voting booth than adults.

Turnover

Another approach to contestation at district levels examines *turnover*, understood as a change in party control for a particular office – executive (presidential, gubernatorial, mayoral) or legislative, at any level of government (national, regional, local). Turnover has a very distinct – and presumably consequential – meaning in single-member district (SMD) elections. It is harder to define and presumably less consequential in a multimember district, where control is a matter of degrees. Thus, we restrict the following analyses to SMD contests.

Table 8.7 shows several tests in which turnover is regressed on population. Model 1 is a global analysis, incorporating all (SMD) lower house elections for which data are available, spanning twenty-four countries, 12,755 districts observed over varying periods (maximum: 220 years), and generating data for 74,328 contests. We include country and year dummies in this analysis to control for country-specific effects and for effects that may vary over time. Across this massive sample, district size is correlated with the enhanced probability of party turnover.

Granted, lower house (single-member) districts are fairly evenly distributed within most countries in the modern era, so there is not a great deal of (within-country) variation in population to exploit. (Country dummies are included in Model 1.) To find better contrasts, the remaining tests in Table 8.7 focus on the United States, a country with a great many elective offices, serving constituencies of different sizes, most of which are SMDs.

In Model 2, we focus on US Senate elections, capitalizing on the fact that senators enjoy equal power but hail from districts of greatly varying sizes. (A senator from California represents sixty-seven times as many constituents as a senator from Wyoming, we noted in Chapter 1.) Here, we control for sociological factors that may affect competitiveness, including urbanization and income per capita. We find that the impact of scale on turnover in this model is considerably enhanced relative to the benchmark model.

In Model 3, we cultivate a more fine-grained analysis – comparing elections to the US Senate and House of Representatives. This model includes state dummies, along with our usual year dummies. This means

Table 8.7 *Turnover*

Scope	Global	United States	United States	United States
Level	National	National	National	State
Offices	Lower house	Senate	Senate, House	Upper, Lower house
Model	**1**	**2**	**3**	**4**
Population (log)	0.029★★★	0.045★★★	0.059★★★	0.020★★★
	(0.005)	(0.016)	(0.007)	(0.004)
Year dummies	✓	✓	✓	✓
Country dummies	✓			
State dummies			✓	✓
Urbanization		✓		
Income per capita (log)		✓		
Countries	24	1	1	1
Districts	12,755	50	7,270	19,106
Years	220	69	218	36
Observations (contests)	74,328	1,215	34,541	60,501
R2 overall	0.2376	0.1030	0.2596	0.0889

Outcome: turnover (change in party control) in single-member district elections. *Units of analysis*: district-level contests. Constant omitted. *Estimator*: ordinary least squares, standard errors clustered by district. *Source*: MLEA. (All results robust with a logit estimator. Results in Models 3–4, which can be constructed as a binary treatment – upper/lower house – are robust with a matching estimator.) Descriptive statistics below.

Variable	Obs.	Mean	Std. Dev.	Min.	Max.
Model 1					
Turnover	74,400	0.29	0.45	0.00	1.00
Population (log)	112,048	11.12	1.86	3.71	17.15
Model 2					
Turnover	1,400	0.24	0.43	0.00	1.00
Population (log)	1,490	14.57	1.09	10.82	17.34
Model 3					
Turnover	34,613	0.22	0.41	0.00	1.00
Population (log)	35,219	12.52	0.85	10.12	17.34
Model 4					
Turnover	100,782	0.15	0.36	0.00	1.00
Population (log)	80,800	10.84	0.92	8.89	13.95

that we are effectively comparing Senate and House elections in the same state and the same election to each other. In a few states, like Wyoming, only one member is elected to the House and this representative competes in a statewide district, just like the two senators from that state. But in most states, House members have smaller districts than their Senate counterparts, generating a basis for comparison. California currently has fifty-three House districts, meaning that the average House district is 1/53 the size of the (statewide) Senate district. This analysis shows an even stronger scale effect on turnover.

In Model 4, we conduct a similar analysis at the state level, comparing elections to the upper and lower chambers of state legislatures across the country. Note that all states except Nebraska have two chambers, and the upper chamber is generally quite a bit smaller, generating a difference in district size. This difference is not as great as the average difference between Senate and House seats (nearly 5:1), but it is large enough (roughly 2:1) to warrant comparison. This analysis maintains state and year dummies – so, again, we are able to compare outcomes for different offices in the same state and the same election. Since there are a great many state legislative seats, observed over several decades, we are able to assemble a substantial sample – more than 19,000 districts and more than 60,000 district-level contests. This analysis shows a similar scale effect, though not quite as large as in previous analyses. Across all these comparisons, districts with larger scales are more likely to produce turnover in party control of a seat.

Evidence: Nongovernmental Organizations

Research on contestation has focused mostly on elections to governmental bodies, as reviewed in the previous sections. However, there is also an extensive literature on contestation within *non*governmental organizations, e.g., labor unions, political parties, interest groups, and firms. Building on Robert Michels's notion of an iron law of oligarchy, the general assumption is that larger organizations are likely to experience less contestation.

Empirical studies of union democracy, following in the wake of Lipset, Trow, and Coleman's (1956) landmark study, generally treat individual unions as units of analysis. Studies that we have run across report mixed findings (e.g., Edelstein & Warner 1975: 97–98). However, sample sizes tend to be fairly small and highly heterogeneous, inhibiting the author's ability to generalize about the possible role of union size. (Big unions are apt to be different from small unions in many ways other than membership size.)

One exception is an early study by Faunce (1962), which focuses on union *locals* within the United Auto Workers (UAW). A survey of

delegates at a union convention in 1959 yields 1,815 responses, representing 753 UAW locals. Respondents were asked a series of questions
intended to elicit the quality of participation and contestation; we focus
exclusively on the latter. Leadership turnover seems to be higher in
smaller locals, running against our argument. However, this could be
because the job itself is not highly valued and leaders voluntarily retire.
This interpretation is bolstered by the finding that elections are much
more likely to be uncontested in smaller locals. In addition to greater
contestation, large locals are also more likely to exhibit the organizational
features expected in contested elections, e.g., rival slates of candidates,
issue differences between the slates, and a semblance of permanent party
organization. "Whatever factionalism exists in small locals is less likely to
be institutionalized" (Faunce 1962: 297).

Contestation within *political parties* has also received some attention.[4]
Kenig, Rahat, and Tuttnauer (2015) examine parties in fourteen
European democracies from 1965 to 2012. They find that the size of
party is generally associated with more competitive races for party leadership, as judged by (a) the number of races that are uncontested, (b) the
number of declared candidates, (c) the margin of victory between the
winner and the runner-up, and (d) the rate of incumbent victory. For our
theoretical purposes, however, the authors' choices in data analysis are
not ideal.[5]

To adapt the data to current purposes, and to make the analysis more
consistent with other analyses in this chapter, we focus on the *margin of
victory* in party leadership races. This variable is very close (theoretically
and empirically) to the "largest vote-getter" variable employed in previous analyses. It is transformed to take a positive score when there is
greater contestation using the traditional formula: 100−(share of vote
obtained by highest vote-getter−share of vote obtained by next highest
vote-getter). Cases of no contestation, where the margin of victory is 100,

---

[4] Schumacher and Giger (2017) develop an index of the relative power of activists and
leaders within parties, which bears ambivalently on our topic.

[5] First, the main regression table treats size in interaction with party status – in or out of
government (a binary variable). The listed coefficients and standard errors refer, therefore, to outcomes for parties when out of government. Second, not all of these relationships pass the conventional bar of statistical significance. This may be due to the small
sample or to model specifications that include posttreatment (relative to party size)
variables. Third, parties are measured by their vote share rather than their vote size.
(Our theoretical argument suggests that the absolute size of parties, not their relative
size, should affect organizational behavior.) Fourth, parties are grouped into three sizes –
small, medium, and large – which involves a loss of information, and also treats the
relationship as linear (whereas our theory assumes a log-linear transformation). Finally,
instances of no competition (where there is no challenger to the incumbent) are excluded
from most analyses. (These instances are integral to our theory.)

render a score of zero on this contestation index. To measure the "population" of each party we calculate the share of each party's vote multiplied by the size of the country – a reasonable proxy for the size of the electorate given that turnout is fairly high in these countries. This gives us a rough measure of the size of each party in each election. This statistic is transformed by the natural logarithm, paralleling other analyses.

Results of these analyses are shown in Table 8.8. Model 1 is a minimal model, including only the variable of interest (party votes) and annual dummies. Model 2 is a fuller specification, including several background variables that may affect contestation – whether a party is currently in the ruling coalition (a government party), and a tripartite coding of party ideology (Left, Center, and Right, with Center as the excluded category). Note that party size is robustly associated with greater contestation, measured by the distance between the two highest vote-getters in leadership contests. Results are robust with a tobit estimator, which may be important in light of the left-bounded nature of our sample (in some leadership contests there is no opposition, rendering a score of zero).

Importantly, these analyses do not measure the number of participants or eligible participants but rather the size of the party itself. This is plausible if we think of party size conditioning the rules of leadership selection, which may restrict participation to party leaders or extend suffrage to rank-and-file party members. This is analogous to the logic employed in country-level analyses shown in Table 8.2.

It would also be helpful to know the actual number of participants in each contest or – even better – the number *eligible to participate* under party rules. The latter would be analogous to the size of a country or district electorate. Unfortunately, neither of these pieces of information is available.

However, Kenig and colleagues (2015) provide a typology of party rules, coded as (1) party members and voters, (2) delegates to convention and party councils, and (3) the parliamentary party group. We combine (2) and (3) into a single category, generating a dummy variable in which contests where rank-and-file party members are allowed to participate are coded 1, and all other contests are coded 0. This allows us to compare the most inclusive sort of participation rule with two considerably less inclusive rules. The resulting variable forms the basis for Model 3 in Table 8.8.

All three analyses in Table 8.8 support our general hypothesis – that larger constituencies lead to more contested leadership contests. We hope that as better data become available we will be able to provide a more precise estimate of this effect within political parties – and for that matter, across other organizations with elective leaders.

Table 8.8 *Intraparty contestation*

Model	1	2	3
Party size (log)	5.705*	6.294*	
	(3.082)	(2.919)	
Selectorate = members/ voters (dummy)			22.739**
			(7.570)
Government coalition		−7.915	−7.098
		(5.279)	(4.195)
Left party		−4.135	1.495
		(5.119)	(4.669)
Right party		2.323	4.314
		(4.910)	(5.223)
Year dummies	✓	✓	✓
Countries	14	14	14
Parties	100+	100+	100+
Years	47	47	47
Observations (contests)	503	503	520
R2	0.0987	0.111	0.118

Outcome: contestation, i.e., 100 minus the vote differential between top-two vote-getters. *Units of analysis*: party leadership contests. Constant omitted. *Estimator*: ordinary least squares, standard errors clustered by country. *Source*: Kenig, Rahat, and Tuttnauer (2015), adapted by the authors. (All results robust with a tobit estimator.) Descriptive statistics below.

Variable	Obs.	Mean	Std. Dev.	Min.	Max.
Contestation	520	35.52	38.62	0.00	99.90
Party votes (log)	511	14.70	1.38	10.78	17.34
Selectorate = members/ voters	528	0.22	0.41	0.00	1.00
Government coalition	528	0.35	0.48	0.00	1.00
Left party	528	0.35	0.48	0.00	1.00
Right party	528	0.32	0.47	0.00	1.00

Summary

Although the topic has not been extensively researched, most studies that examine the question find a positive association between the size of communities and their level of electoral contestation. These studies, along with our own, are summarized in Table 8.9.

There appears to be an extremely stable relationship between size and political contestation across different governmental bodies. It is remarkable that estimates of the impact of population on contestation in our

Table 8.9 *Scale and contestation: Inventory of analyses*

Indicators	Countries	Treatment units	Years	Units of analysis	Research design	Effect	Study
Country-level							
Top-two	(197)	Countries (197)	(226)	Country-years (21,068)	Cross-sectional	↑	Gerring, Hicken, et al. 2018
Incumbent-challenger	(197)	Countries (197)	(226)	Country-years (21,068)	Cross-sectional, panel	↑	Gerring, Hicken, et al. 2018
*Largest party	(197)	Countries (197)	(227)	Country-years (21,424)	Cross-sectional	↑	Table 8.2
District-level							
Top-two	United States	States (50)	(10)	State means (50)	Cross-sectional	↑	Patterson & Caldeira 1984
Top-two	United States	Counties (2,929)	(3)	County-years (8,707)	Cross-sectional	↑	Aistrup 2004
Top-two	United States	Municipal elections (350)	(1)	Municipal elections (350)	Cross-sectional	↑	Hajnal, Lewis, & Louch 2002
*Largest party	(88)	Districts (79,928)	(225)	Contests (387,448)	Cross-sectional	↑	Table 8.3, Gerring et al. 2015
Fractionalization	United States	States (25)	(2)	State legislative elections (50)	Cross-sectional	∅	Hogan 2003
Turnover	United States	States (48)	(34)	Senate elections (48)	Cross-sectional	↑	Hibbing & Brandes 1983
Turnover	United States	Counties (35)	(6)	County board elections (385)	Cross-sectional	↑	Lascher 2005

	United States	Cities (244)	(69)	City council elections (700+)	Cross-sectional	↑	Trounstine 2008
Turnover							
*Turnover	(24)	Districts (12,755)	(220)	Contests (74,328)	Cross-sectional	↑	Table 8.7
Intraparty							
*Top-two	(14)	Parties (100+)	(47)	Leadership contests (503)	Cross-sectional	↑	Table 8.8

Treatment units: units exhibiting variation in scale. *Years*: number of years over which data are collected – not to be confused with the frequency of observations, as data may or may not be annual and may be averaged across years. *Research design*: the main, or benchmark, research design – classified as cross-sectional (where the analysis is driven primarily by variation across units) or panel (where the analysis is driven primarily by variation through time). *Effect*: when the scale of a community increases, the designated outcome goes up (↑), down (↓), up and down (↑↓), or experiences no perceptible change (∅). A scale effect is considered significant if it passes a modest bar of statistical significance, i.e., $p < 0.10$ (two-tailed test) in the benchmark model. Number of countries, treatment units, years, or observations in parentheses.

benchmark country-level analysis (Model 1, Table 8.2) are very close to estimates obtained from our benchmark district-level analysis (Model 1, Table 8.3).

Work on *non*governmental bodies is much rarer. Faunce's (1962) study of UAW locals is not subjected to a standard statistical test, and therefore is not included in Table 8.9. Adapting data from Kenig and colleagues (2015), we provide a rough test of contestation within political parties (Table 8.8). Results offer tentative support for our theory. But it is important to note that the sample does not include parties outside of Europe and does not include precise estimates of the factor of greatest theoretical interest – the number of party members who are qualified to participate in each leadership contest. For a stronger test we await further data.

In the next chapter, we examine turnover in the highest office, for which we reserve a special name – succession – and for which we conjecture that somewhat different causal mechanisms apply.

9   Institutionalized Succession

Polities are vulnerable during periods of leadership transition (Kokkonen & Sundell 2014; Treisman 2015). This is especially true wherever transitions occur in an ad hoc, disorderly, or nepotistic fashion. This often inaugurates a period of extreme uncertainty and – sometimes – of instability. At the extreme, succession provides the occasion for violent conflict, aka "wars of succession" (Jones & Olken 2009; Miller 2012; Wolford 2016). Calvert (1987: 27) points out that "the history of state formation in Western Europe is a history of succession struggles" – among them, the Thirty Years' War (1618–48), the War of the Spanish Succession (1701–14), the War of the Polish Succession (1733–38), and the War of the Austrian Succession (1740–48). Ezrow and Frantz (2011: 6) report that "of the 340 leadership transitions that occurred in dictatorships from 1946 to 2009, 160 brought the regime down." It is no wonder that leadership succession is a politically sensitive issue.

In some polities, however, leadership succession occurs regularly, under well-established rules, and in a meritocratic (or at least non-nepotistic) fashion. Here, we can say that political power at the apex has been institutionalized. Note that most leaders would probably prefer to prolong their tenure in office indefinitely and, when the time is right (perhaps at their demise), pass on their position and prerogatives to a family heir. Thus, if political succession occurs regularly, in an orderly and lawful manner, and is not restricted to family heirs, it must be because leaders are constrained to follow the rules.

The point at which rules of succession are regularized may be regarded as the point at which a new organization – e.g., a party, polity, or regime – becomes institutionalized (Bunce 1981; Calvert 1987; McCauley & Carter 1986; 't Hart & Uhr 2011). Typically, the institutionalization of charisma occurs sometime after the death of the founder. For example, the leadership transition in China from Jiang Zemin to Hu Jintao from 2002 to 2005 signaled, in the words of one writer, that,

Formal rules and compliant procedures have prevailed over factional politics based on informal personal relations among the political elites of the Chinese Communist Party (CCP). The smoothness of the Jiang–Hu transition is the result of the growing institutionalization of the political process, which explains why Jiang's political clout has substantially eroded since his retirement.[1]

Likewise, the recent abrogation of the two-term rule by President Xi Jinping has prompted Sinologists to conclude that the leader's power is no longer constrained and that the system is becoming deinstitutionalized (Shirk 2018). Regular and orderly leadership succession is, one might say, the sine qua non of political institutionalization.

With this as background, we turn to the question of theoretical interest. Why have some polities institutionalized the process of leadership succession while others have not?

Though the topic of political succession has attracted scholarly attention, most of this work is descriptive in nature or focused on the causal impact of succession and succession regimes (Burling 1974; Frantz & Stein 2017; Goody 1966; Kokkonen & Sundell 2014; Kurrild-Klitgaard 2000). There is no general theory that might explain why succession occurs in a more institutionalized fashion in some settings than in others. Evidently, democracy plays an important role, but even across countries that share the same regime type there is enormous variation.

We argue in this chapter that leadership succession is conditioned (among other things) by the size of a polity, with larger communities experiencing more frequent, and more regular, succession. In the first section, we lay out our theory. In the following section, we examine the question empirically using three measures of succession to the top political office: tenure in office, monarchy, and a composite index of institutionalized leadership succession. A brief conclusion summarizes the findings.

Theory

Larger polities, we contend, are apt to develop more institutionalized systems of leadership succession – governed by rules rather than rulers, administered by merit rather than ascriptive characteristics or personal connections, and characterized by a process that is regular and orderly. This is because larger polities are less cohesive (Chapter 3), which generates more veto holders (an issue discussed in Chapter 11), and with more veto holders the ruler will find it more difficult to hold on to power

---

[1] Huang (2008: 80–81). For a longer-term view of leadership succession in China see Ebrey (2006).

Figure 9.1 Scale effects on institutionalized succession

indefinitely and to pass on power to his/her heirs. The outline of this argument is summarized in Figure 9.1.

To explain this dynamic we must reconstruct the interests of political elites and their interaction. Every national community has a number of powerful actors, aka *elites*. We assume that each elite actor is linked to a set of followers whom the actor represents, albeit perhaps in a less-than-perfect fashion. This support base might be found in the military, a sector of the economy, a religious organization, an ethnic group, a clan or (extended) family, or some other body.

Elites and their supporters have a strong stake in how power is organized within a polity. Because they represent powerful social bases, different elites may be in a position to hamper a smooth leadership transition. If unhappy with the process or the choice, they may refuse to recognize the successor, remove their support from the regime, or even take action to mobilize their supporters against the regime. Because their consent is essential for a smooth transition, elites may be regarded loosely as veto holders (Tsebelis 2002). Bear in mind that successions are moments fraught with peril for many regimes. This is why departing leaders and their successors look eagerly – sometimes desperately – to elites to validate each change of power.

We assume that all elites would prefer to monopolize power and to exercise it in an unconstrained fashion in perpetuity. This is their ideal-point. If they are unable to do so, we presume that they would prefer to impose limits on the exercise of power by others. Whether elites support an institutionalized system of leadership succession depends, therefore, upon where they sit.

Following this logic, elite preference-orderings may be summarized as the intersection of two dimensions: (1) who holds power (understood as control over the executive office) and (2) whether that power is limited. Within this matrix, illustrated in Table 9.1, all actors have the same overall preference orderings: A (to hold power without constraints) > B (to hold power with constraints) > C (to be out of power in a system with constraints) > D (to be out of power in a system without constraints).

The most consequential distinction among different elites is between the incumbent (the current officeholder) and nonincumbents. All else

Table 9.1 *Power and preferences*

		Limit Power	
		No	Yes
Hold power	Yes	A	B
	No	D	C

Hold power: an elite or his/her ally occupies the top leadership position. *Limit power*: power exercised by the top leader is constrained; in particular, the process of succession is institutionalized. *Preference-ordering*: $A > B > C > D$.

being equal, incumbents prefer a noninstitutionalized system based on the current power configuration, which they control ($A > B$). This means that they can rule without interference until their demise or until their chosen retirement, in either case passing on power to someone who will carry on their legacy – presumably a close family member or ally. *Non*incumbents prefer to institutionalize power ($C > D$), and in particular the process of leadership succession – offering hope that they, or their allies, may occupy the top position at some point in the not-too-distant future.

We presume that the size of a community is related to the number of elite actors in that community. A larger community, with more social groups (greater heterogeneity, as discussed in Chapter 3), will produce more elite actors.[2] Since only one can occupy the top office in this simplified schema, the ratio of nonincumbents to incumbents increases monotonically with community size.

This fact, we argue, makes it more difficult for any single actor to obtain and to secure (for her lifetime) untrammeled exercise of power. The current leader, although she might rule in an absolute fashion, must be concerned about threats to this power as many plot her demise.

Granted, a larger number of nonincumbent elites also enhances coordination challenges among the aspirants. One might expect this to play into the hands of the incumbent, who could divide the opposition and thereby resist calls for institutionalization. However, this coordination problem is mitigated by a consensus over shared goals: limiting the power of the incumbent. Only in this way can they hope to hold office themselves one day, or at least constrain the depredations of current and future rulers. Because their incentives align on this crucial point, coordination challenges may be surmounted.

---

[2] This is reflected in the relationship between population and the number of representatives, discussed in Chapter 4. However, in this case we do not want to equate elite actors with representatives.

This argument may be viewed as an extension of the idea of power-balancing, which plays a crucial role in theorizing about relations among states (Jervis 1997: 131; Levy & Thompson 2005; Waltz 1979: 117). Note that in the international arena, where national cultures and ideologies are extremely heterogeneous, small states frequently band together to limit the ambitions of a hegemon. Our argument may also be viewed as a special instance of power-sharing, which sometimes paves the way for democratic transitions or at least for institutions of power-sharing that constrain the ruler (Bratton & Van de Walle 1997; Chenoweth & Stephan 2011; Collier 1999).

Admittedly, nonincumbents do not always coalesce. However, they still pose a danger to the incumbent. Elites may passively resist, withdrawing their support from the regime, refusing to pay taxes or to enforce the law of the land over territory under their control. They may also sponsor violent reprisals. Assassinations and coups are often carried out by dissident elites. Some elites may have the capacity to wage costly civil insurrections, which can compromise the security of the regime vis-à-vis international actors and provide an opening for other parties to make claims for autonomy or independence. In short, aggrieved elites can do a great deal of damage, lowering the value and power of the top office and reducing the expected longevity of the current leader.

We surmise that these structural features of large communities alter the incentives of all elites – the incumbent as well as nonincumbents, who must consider the prospects of ruling if they should ever succeed to the top leadership position. While everyone's ideal-point remains focused on A, elites may acclimate themselves to the prospect of B or C if A seems unattainable over the long term. In large polities with many contending elite groups the shadow of the future presents leaders with the bleak prospect of option D, being out of power in a noninstitutionalized system. This is presumably the worst of all possible outcomes since one's possessions and one's very life are likely to be in jeopardy. In this context, non-myopic leaders may prefer to institutionalize leadership succession today, trading off current losses ($A \rightarrow B$) for future gains ($D \rightarrow C$). One way to mitigate the risk of bargaining failures is through institutions that reduce information asymmetries and mitigate commitment problems (Boix & Svolik 2013; Svolik 2012; Walter 2009).

In this stylized narrative we have treated elites as unitary actors, leaving aside the possibility of *alliances*. One might imagine that a single actor could assure his longevity, and the longevity of his family or clan, by forming strategic alliances with other actors. However, a voluntary alliance of this nature would presumably involve an exchange. The ruling actor would forfeit some prerogatives in order to obtain the consent of various allies. In this fashion, power would be effectively constrained. We imagine that such an agreement would lead eventually to an institutiona- lized system of leadership succession – for if practices of succession are unconstrained, it will be difficult for allies to exert any control over the future. The prospect of alliances among rival elites thus illustrates pre- cisely the expectations of our theory. It is, in fact, an important mechan- ism by which power is likely to become institutionalized in a setting with many rival elites.

In summary, we argue that an institutionalized system of succession is more likely to be achieved as the size of a community increases. A larger community has more elite actors striving for power. The greater the number of actors, the harder it will be for any single leader to establish power and maintain it indefinitely, passing it on to family members when s/he retires or dies. Thus, elites are likely to agree to limit the tenure of the ruler and establish a regularized and at least somewhat meritocratic system for ensuring the circulation of elites in the top office, thereby sharing power over the long haul. In this respect, practices of leadership succession instantiate the principle of shared rule (Przeworski 1991).

Evidence

To test our theory about the impact of scale on succession we examine two specific measures – tenure in office and monarchy – along with a composite index of institutionalized leadership succession.

Tenure

In a study of small states, Sutton (1987: 16) argues that ministers and heads of government remain in office longer in small states than in larger countries. Many small states in Africa, the Caribbean, or the Pacific have prime ministers or presidents who remain in office for decades on end, and their leadership style tends to become more autocratic over time, making succession a charged issue. According to an informant in St. Kitts and Nevis, where at the time of the interview the prime minister had been in office for nearly twenty years:

He is now going to be twenty years our prime minister. And I have seen in this last election that the prime minister's party got more and more desperate in terms of the things they would do, in terms of the things they would say just to stay in power.

In this section, we follow up this observation by taking a more compre- hensive look at the issue of leadership tenure.

The Archigos dataset (Goemans, Gleditsch, & Chiozza 2016) records the identity of the principal ruler – generally a monarch, president, or prime minister – in countries around the world, which we analyze from 1900 to the present. From these raw data, we calculate the tenure of each leader. This calculation is unaffected by the mechanisms by which an individual might attain and maintain office. A spell ends only when a ruler leaves office – whether by voluntary resignation, death in office, assassination, coup, loss of an election, or some other exigency. Intervening events – e.g., reelection, failed reelection, revolution, or other – have no bearing on the coding. If a ruler gains, loses, and later regains office, each spell is coded separately. Units of analysis are country-years, so multiple leadership transitions in the same year are coded in the same fashion as a single leadership transition. The resulting statistic is transformed by the natural logarithm to account for the expected diminishing effects of scale on tenure and to mitigate the problem of especially long-serving leaders (who may serve as influential cases).

Model 1 in Table 9.2 regresses this outcome, tenure in office (log), against population (log) and democracy, along with annual dummies. Democracy is included in the benchmark specification because of its strong impact on leadership tenure and because we wish to differentiate its impact from that of scale. Model 2 adds several additional covariates to the benchmark model. Model 3 returns to the benchmark specification, which forms the basis for an instrumental variable analysis. In all three models, scale is negatively correlated with leadership tenure – though the relationship is slightly weaker in the full model (possibly a by-product of the reduced sample).

Working from estimates in the benchmark model of Table 9.2, we calculate predicted values for leader tenure as population changes. These are displayed for varying population levels in Figure 9.2. Note that an increase in population from 100,000 to 1 million translates into an expected reduction in tenure of roughly five years. We regard this as a substantial effect, with the usual caveat that – due to the logarithmic nature of the relationship – it is greatest at the left end of the population spectrum.

Monarchy

Hereditary patterns of succession are institutionalized insofar as a successor is clearly designated; as a result, leadership transitions are more likely to occur in a peaceful and orderly fashion (Kokkonen & Sundell 2014). However, the principle of hereditary rule is also a sign of a lack of

Table 9.2 *Tenure of top leaders*

Estimator	OLS	OLS	2SLS
Model	1	2	3
Population (log)	−0.478***	−0.379*	−0.489*
	(0.176)	(0.225)	(0.259)
Democracy (Lexical index)	−1.074***	−0.527***	−1.073***
	(0.119)	(0.148)	(0.119)
GDP per capita (log)		−1.082	
		(0.809)	
Urbanization		1.223	
		(2.541)	
Years independent (log)		−0.086	
		(0.192)	
State history		−1.884*	
		(1.082)	
Annual dummies	✓	✓	
Decade dummies			✓
Countries	169	104	164
Years	93	93	93
Observations	7,954	5,972	7,878
R-squared	0.144	0.206	0.135

Outcome: tenure (continuous years in office) of top leaders (Archigos). *Units of analysis*: country-years. *Lag structure*: right-side variables measured at t−20. Constant omitted. *Estimators*: OLS (ordinary least squares), 2SLS (two-stage least squares, using territory and agricultural suitability as instruments). Country clustered standard errors in brackets. *** p < 0.01, ** p < 0.05, * p < 0.10 (two-tailed tests)

institutionalization insofar as (a) successors are chosen in a blatantly un-meritocratic, explicitly nepotistic fashion, and (b) the designated successor holds office for life. Thus, in the modern context, monarchy appears as a less institutionalized system of rule (though in premodern times it may be regarded as providing a more institutionalized system of rule).

Previous studies have indicated an elective affinity between smallness and monarchy (Corbett, Veenendaal, & Ugyel 2017). Interestingly, voters in Liechtenstein recently approved a significant increase in the power of the unelected prince at the expense of the democratically elected parliament and government. Although the king is no longer the sole ruler of Bhutan, his democratic initiative was met with widespread popular opposition (Turner, Chuki, & Tshering 2011). In many small states, monarchy is equated with the very existence of the state. Liechtenstein, for example, bears the name of its royal family. One informant declares,

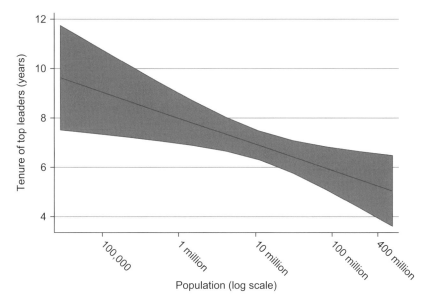

Figure 9.2 Tenure of top leaders, predicted values

Predicted tenure (years) of top leaders (Y) as population (log) changes, surrounded by 95 percent confidence interval. Based on Model 1, Table 9.2, with covariates set to sample means. Descriptive statistics (Y): mean = 7.19, SD = 8.13, min. = 1.00, max. = 68.00

For many people it is at the heart of our identity. Liechtenstein is a monarchy and as a Liechtensteiner you identify with the prince, and if you don't, you're not really a Liechtensteiner. It's as easy as that.

A *monarchy* is defined here as a polity with an executive office that is (a) hereditary, (b) monopolized by a single individual or (occasionally) jointly by several members of the same family, (c) endowed with life tenure, and (d) of nontrivial importance. Hereditary succession may be either de jure (a clear statement of principle by someone in authority) or de facto (a well-established practice, as evidenced by family trees showing relationships among successive rulers). Life tenure is assumed if there is no constitutional method of removing a sitting ruler and if rulers typically die in office. Where a hereditary executive has no share in policymaking and is displaced by a fully democratic body, we surmise that the monarch neither reigns nor rules; his or her power is trivial. Accordingly, we do not regard present-day United Kingdom or Sweden as monarchical regimes.

We employ this definition to code polities as monarchic or republican over the past century. This provides a dependent variable for a series of

Table 9.3 *Monarchy*

Estimator	Logit	Logit	IV Probit
Model	1	2	3
Population (log)	−0.279**	−0.513**	−0.264***.
	(0.113)	(0.201)	(0.077)
GDP per capita (log)		1.153**	
		(0.462)	
Urbanization		−4.136*	
		(2.340)	
Years independent (log)		0.407**	
		(0.175)	
Democracy (Lexical index)		−0.426***	
		(0.0983)	
Region dummies		✓	
Annual dummies	✓	✓	
Decade dummies			✓
Countries	196	149	179
Years	97	97	97
Observations	12,250	6,836	11,741
R-squared (pseudo)	0.0790	0.5406	
Wald chi2			51.29

Outcome: monarchy (Gerring, Wig, et al. 2019). *Units of analysis*: country-years. *Lag structure*: right-side variables measured at t−20. Constant omitted. *Estimators*: logit (logistic regression), IV Probit (probit model with continuous endogenous covariates, using territory and agricultural suitability as instruments). Country clustered standard errors in brackets. *** p < 0.01, ** p < 0.05, * p < 0.10 (two-tailed tests)

tests shown in Table 9.3. Model 1 is a benchmark specification, including only population and a vector of annual dummies. Model 2 is a fuller specification, adding several covariates to the benchmark. Model 3 is an instrumental variable model, following the benchmark specification.

Results for the variable of theoretical interest are consistent across all three models. To be sure, the estimated coefficient is somewhat stronger in the full specification, though standard errors are also inflated due to the greatly reduced sample. In any case, larger polities are more likely to adopt a republican form of rule in the modern era.

Composite Index

Our final measure is a composite index, embracing a variety of criteria that are presumed to mark the institutionalization of leadership succession. First, the previous executive leaves office in a regular fashion. That is, the process follows established principles and precedents as set out in a constitution or basic law. This excludes circumstances such as coups, seizure of power by another body, or forced withdrawal (in contravention of constitutional rules or norms). Second, the former executive is at liberty, i.e., does not face imprisonment, harassment, exile, or death because of actions taken while in office. (Note that prosecution for actions taken while occupying executive office indicates either that the executive violated the law or that s/he is being persecuted for political reasons. Both constitute a breach of constitutional protocol, and thus qualify as a lack of institutionalization.) Third, the current executive is chosen through regular procedures, as laid out in a constitution or basic law. Fourth, the current executive has no family connection to any previously serving executive – a connection that we regard as prima facie evidence of nepotism, including special advantages available to members of a well-connected family (Querubin 2016), and hence of personal rule. Finally, the current executive has been in office for a decade or less. We regard a longer term of office, even if constitutionally sanctioned, as prima facie evidence that power has been personalized and that the executive is not bound by institutions (Svolik 2012).

Important, these indicators focus on actual practices rather than written rules. Formal rules are irrelevant, from our perspective, unless they are followed. To be sure, de facto practices are generally harder to determine than de jure rules, imposing a more difficult task for coders who must make judgments about how to classify individual cases. Coding rules are laid out in the Archigos codebook, accompanied by extensive case descriptions (Goemans et al., 2016). In most instances the circumstances of a case seem fairly clear. In others we can imagine that knowledgeable observers might have different interpretations for how to code some of the criteria. While acknowledging the inevitability of error, we do not anticipate any systematic biases in measurement that might affect questions at issue in this analysis.

All five criteria are understood in a binary fashion, coded 1 if a criterion is satisfied and 0 otherwise. Coding is constant in between leadership transitions, which means that there is no missing data. The assumption is that important changes in a polity's level of institutionalization often occur, or become apparent, at the point of leadership turnover.

We aggregate these indicators into a single index by addition. The rationale behind this simple approach is that all five elements of leadership succession matter, they are partly substitutable, and one is at pains to determine which matter more. Under the circumstances, equal weighting provides a convenient and plausible method of

Table 9.4 *Institutionalized leadership succession*

Estimator	OLS	OLS	2SLS
Model	1	2	3
Population (log)	0.103***	0.135***	0.127**
	(0.038)	(0.043)	(0.057)
GDP per capita (log)	0.459***	0.231**	0.454***
	(0.065)	(0.103)	(0.065)
Urbanization		0.551	
		(0.359)	
Years independent (log)		0.017	
		(0.036)	
State history		0.104	
		(0.293)	
Protestant		0.002	
		(0.003)	
GDP per capita growth		0.004	
		(0.003)	
Mineral wealth per capita		−0.000	
		(0.000)	
Democracy (Lexical index)		0.051**	
		(0.020)	
English colony		0.433**	
		(0.167)	
Region dummies		✓	
Annual dummies	✓	✓	
Decade dummies			✓
Countries	174	97	167
Years	93	93	93
Observations	10,176	5,093	10,023
R-squared	0.149	0.393	0.172

Outcome: leadership succession institutionalization index. *Units of analysis:* country-years. *Lag structure:* right-side variables measured at t−20. Constant omitted. *Estimators*: OLS (ordinary least squares), 2SLS (two-stage least squares, using territory and agricultural suitability as instruments). Country clustered standard errors in brackets. *** $p < 0.01$, ** $p < 0.05$, * $p < 0.10$ (two-tailed tests)

aggregation that is also easy to interpret. Data for the resulting index stretch from 1840 to 2012, covering the sovereign history of 175 countries. Scores vary from 0 to 5, with a mean of 3.3, standard deviation of 1.5, and mode at 5.

In the analyses that follow, contained in Table 9.4, this index of leadership institutionalization is regressed against population along with suitable controls. Model 1, the benchmark, includes only per capita GDP (log)

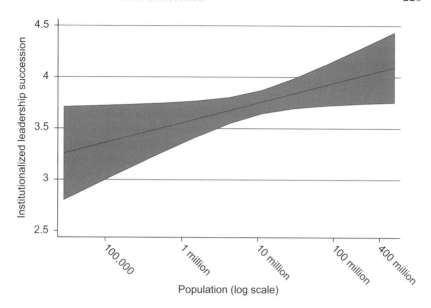

Figure 9.3 Institutionalized leadership succession, predicted values

Predicted values for institutionalized leadership succession index (Y) as population (log) changes, surrounded by 95 percent confidence interval. Based on Model 1, Table 9.4, with covariates set to sample means. Descriptive statistics (Y): mean = 3.65, SD = 1.27, min. = 0.00, max. = 5.00

and a vector of annual dummies. Model 2 adds further covariates. Note that by including *years independent* as a covariate we are attempting to model the learning that occurs as a state accrues experience in the task of governing. And, by including a widely used measure of state history – a country's history of "state-ness" extending back to year 0 – we are attempting to control for possible endogeneity between right- and left-side factors. Model 3 is an instrumental variable model, which builds on the benchmark specification. Estimates across these three models are strikingly consistent, demonstrating that greater population is associated with more institutionalized patterns of leadership succession.

Figure 9.3 displays how predicted values for the index of leadership succession institutionalization vary with population, following esti-mates from the benchmark model. This exercise shows that a shift in population from 100,000 to 1 million is associated with a half-point increase on our five-point scale (slightly less than one-half of a standard deviation).

Summary

Sociologists have examined the relationship between size and succession within organizations. Although we have not surveyed this field in a comprehensive fashion, most studies seem to find a positive relationship between size (judged by number of members) and turnover rates of top managerial personnel. This pattern is reported, for example, across corporations (Grusky 1961; Harrison, Torres, & Kukalis 1988), academic departments (Pfeffer & Moore 1980), and public health and mental health programs (Kriesberg 1962). Although one may doubt that the same mechanisms are at work within sovereign polities and independent organizations, it is nonetheless noteworthy that a congruent empirical pattern exists.

Unfortunately, there is no extant work – at least, none that we are aware of – devoted to the influence of scale on leadership succession in a polity's top office. Thus, we close by reviewing the findings of our own analyses, presented in Tables 9.2–9.4 and in accompanying figures.

Our first analysis examines the tenure of top officials, i.e., those who exercise executive power (in a real, and not merely formal, sense). We find that tenure is shorter among leaders of larger countries, all else being equal.

The second analysis examines the prevalence of monarchy, where the top leader serves for life and his/her replacement is chosen by hereditary rules of succession. We find that in the modern world monarchs are much more likely to rule over smaller countries.

The final analysis focuses on a composite index of institutionalized leadership succession, where the highest score is reserved for a polity in which the previous executive leaves office in a regular fashion; in which the former executive is at liberty, i.e., does not face imprisonment, harassment, exile, or death because of actions taken while in office; in which the current executive is chosen through regular procedures, as laid out in a constitution or basic law; in which the current executive has no family connection to any previously serving executive; and in which the current executive has been in office for a decade or less. Consistent with the previous analyses, we find that institutionalized leadership succession is correlated with the size of a country.

All in all, we regard this evidence as providing a strong case for the argument. However, the lack of previous work on this topic, and the number of potential confounders, suggests caution. Future research will be needed before we can conclude with confidence that scale encourages a more institutionalized pattern of leadership succession.

10   Professionalism

A century ago, Max Weber noted a transformation in Western political life. Formerly, public officials were composed largely of local notables who "lived for politics," i.e., they were motivated by purposive goals. Now, it seemed, those who entered politics "lived off politics," i.e., they were motivated by the material gains that politics provided. The essay, first published in 1917 and subsequently translated as "Politics As a Vocation" (M. Weber 1961), has become one of the most widely read works of political science, and marks the inauguration of the study of professionalism in political science and sociology (Borchert & Zeiss 2003; Schlesinger 1966). For Weber, and for many American progressives at the turn of the twentieth century, the idea of politics as a profession was linked to the rise of party machines, which seemed to derogate both good government and idea-driven politics.

From our perspective, the important contrast is not materialist v. idealist but rather *professional* v. *amateur*. Contra Weber, professionals may be guided by purposive goals beyond adherence to professional norms. To say that a politician is a professional does not imply that she has no ideological moorings. And it certainly does not imply that she is interested only in material gain. Indeed, professional training should serve as a ballast against a narrowly self-interested approach to politics.

Professionalism (in our reading) means that important tasks are delegated through a rational division of labor to individuals with extensive training and experience, who are recruited and promoted in a meritocratic fashion, who view their job as a full-time career, and whose positions are amply staffed and remunerated. It also implies that professionals abide by a set of formal rules, and are not subject to ad hoc or special considerations. (As such, it dovetails with our discussion of institutionalized succession in the previous chapter.) Professionalism is the hallmark of *legal-bureaucratic* rationality, to invoke another Weberian concept.

Work on professionalism usually focuses on "the professions," e.g., law, medicine, and academics (Abbott 2014; Freidson 2001). Our interest is in politics. Specifically, we wish to understand the degree of professionalism evinced by elected and appointed public officials as well as members of political organizations in civil society such as political parties, interest groups, and voluntary associations.

Professionalism is a key element of *state capacity* but should not be confused with the latter. State capacity is a more expansive concept (Hanson & Sigman 2013; Hendrix 2010), including additional factors such as revenue extraction, which are inversely correlated with scale (Chapter 11).

In any case, professionalism is generally viewed favorably by policy-makers and academics. It is amateurs, not professionals, who are blamed for the ideological polarization and organizational weakness of contemporary American parties (Miller & Schofield 2003; Polsby 1983; J. Wilson 1962). Granted, within a system of fragmented parties profes-sional politicians intent upon reelection may wreak a certain amount of havoc (Ehrenhalt 1992). However, it is not clear that politicians responding to reelection incentives can be blamed for the present stalemate in American politics. In parliamentary democracies, the appearance of highly professional members of parliament (MPs) has been associated with the formation of "cartel" parties immune to pop-ular pressures (Katz & Mair 1995) and with the development of a political class whose interests may diverge from those of their consti-tuents (Borchert & Zeiss 2003). Even so, amidst the many complexities of modern politics it is hard to see how the services of professionals can be dispensed with. The case for professionalism seems especially strong when one considers the bureaucracy, an arena where professionalism is – or at any rate, should be – the guiding creed. Again, our argument takes its cues from Weber (1961).

Leaving aside the ramifications of professionalism, we turn to its causes, which have attracted much less attention. We begin by laying out a theory for how scale fosters professionalism. Next, we test this proposition in several venues. A short conclusion summarizes the evidence.

Theory

There is no general theory, or even a well-defined body of work, devoted to professionalism in politics. At best, there are a series of studies on specific subjects (cited in the next section of this chapter).

Our interest is focused on the role of scale in fostering professionalism. We argue that three mechanisms are critical: (a) capital, (b) human capital, and (c) complexity. The latter is affected by social cohesion,

Figure 10.1 Scale effects on professionalism

a topic introduced in Chapter 3. The interrelationship between these various causes and the outcome of interest is diagramed in Figure 10.1.

Capital

Professionalism depends, in the first place, on material resources. After all, politics is expensive. Recall that we are not talking solely about government officials but also about supporting institutions that help make government work such as political parties, trade associations, non-governmental organizations (NGOs), and the media.

The size of a political community is the main source available to satisfy this demand. An exception would be a situation where a polity benefits from "free money" – obtained from higher-level political bodies, foreign governments, or international organizations, or from the extraction and taxation of natural resources. However, these sources do not usually bode well for professionalism; indeed, they may undermine that goal (Moore 2004).

In any case, a larger community affords more resources. Resources might come in the form of mandatory taxes (for governmental bodies) or voluntary contributions (for associations).

Human Capital

Resources provided by a community might also be *in-kind*, and the resulting labor might be contractual, volunteer, or conscript. It is difficult to overstate the human capital side of the story. One is at pains to recruit qualified people into politics if only a small pool of educated citizens is available (Chittoo 2011; Farrugia 1993). A larger community offers a larger labor pool, which should improve the quantity and quality of talent for all political positions, those that are elective as well as appointive, those in government as well as those in supporting organizations.

Furthermore, larger communities usually have one or more high-quality educational institutions, amplifying the importance of scale. Qualified individuals from a small community may be forced to move abroad to receive advanced training in their chosen profession; once they leave, there is no guarantee that they will return, suggesting that brain drain may be a larger problem in small communities than in large communities (Beine, Docquier, & Schiff 2008).

Arguably, the size of a community has greater relevance for the quality of governance in poor countries, where human capital is scarce, than in rich countries, where human capital is more plentiful. If a small share of people in a community possess the requisite education and skills to serve as a member of parliament, civil servant, or journalist, then the number of such "eligibles" will depend upon the size of the population. Larger populations will have more eligibles, even if they comprise a small proportion of the population.

Complexity

Scale entails more people, and those people embody greater heterogeneity and less overall cohesion (Chapter 3). This enhances the complexity of governance. However, the challenges of complexity can be overcome if politics is sufficiently institutionalized. In this sense, complexity serves as a gateway to professionalism.

There seems to be a persistent relationship between scale and *complexity*, aka formalization, differentiation, specialization, or division of labor. This line of thinking can be found in work by Aristotle (1996: 1326a), Adam Smith (1776), Emile Durkheim (1964[1893]), Georg Simmel (1902a, 1902b), Herbert Spencer (1898: 525–28), and Lewis Wirth (1938).[1] More recently, studies have noted this pattern in premodern societies (Berreman 1978; Carneiro 1967; Ember 1963; Feinman 2011; Johnson 1982; Kosse 1990, 1994, 2000; MacSweeney 2004; Naroll 1956), in firms (Chandler 1962; Chaney & Ossa 2013; Penrose 1959), in professional associations (Campbell & Akers 1970), in political parties (Michels 1962; Panebianco 1988; Tan 1998), and across a wide array of organizations and communities (Blau 1970; Caplow 1957; Grusky 1961; Kasarda 1974; Mayhew et al. 1972; Meyer 1972a, 1972b; Noell 1974; Nolan 1979b; Ogburn & Duncan 1964; but see Hall, Johnson, & Haas 1967).

Animal populations also exhibit a relationship between size and complexity (Jeanson et al. 2007). And so do individual species. As Darwin theorized, organisms – understood as biological systems – demonstrate

[1] See thumbnail intellectual history in Sadalla (1978).

a relationship between size and structure through the process of evolution (Bonner 1988, 2004).[2] Bigger units demand more complex forms of organization.

It seems plausible that the same general dynamic might hold true for political communities, where the size of a community enhances the complexity of governance tasks. Leaders must gather information on more citizens and on citizens who are more diverse, and they must synthesize that information into the decision-making process, implementing appropriate policies. With a larger population there are more people to monitor, to comprehend, and to rule, and a greater number of demands to process. All of these features augur for professionalization.

Specifically, officials will need to develop rules and procedures by which to handle recurrent issues; they cannot make decisions on an ad hoc, case-by-case basis. A premium will be placed on the technical capacity of officials; informal or general knowledge is unlikely to suffice. Over time, institutions are likely to develop highly specialized functions and highly specialized knowledge. Written rules will replace rules of thumb. And these rules are likely to gain normative sanction, or to be protected through institutional sanctions, such that leaders are obliged to follow them. The result is heightened professionalism.

Evidence

It is not obvious how to operationalize an abstract concept like professionalism. Here, we explore five general topics: legislatures, bureaucracies, the education of public officials, the salary of public officials, and voluntary associations. Since legislatures are easier to identify, and hence to study, we are able to enlist a variety of measures and a broad compass of countries. Data for bureaucracies are more limited, and for voluntary associations we can do no more than measure their number. Even so, we hope that the sum of our efforts is sufficient to test the thesis that scale enhances professionalism in politics across a wide range of venues.

Legislatures

For present purposes, a legislature will be understood simply as a large policymaking body composed of representatives that meets regularly and passes laws. Representatives may be elected or appointed.

---

[2] In citing this literature we do not mean to suggest that there is complete consensus on the positive relationship between size and institutionalization across these disciplines. However, there is a considerable body of work supportive of that thesis.

Because legislatures are usually at the center of politics and policymaking, and because they register enormous variation in professionalism (through time and across legislatures), they have come to be regarded as a bellwether. Where politics is professionalized, we expect to find a professional legislature (Canon 1989; King 2000; Palanza, Scartascini, & Tommasi 2016; Polsby 1968; Squire 1992).

Several federal countries offer significant variation in legislative institutions at the subnational level. In Switzerland, cantons enjoy considerable autonomy and may choose to establish a legislature or not. Of 2,900 municipalities, 405 (17.5 percent) have legislatures. Other cantons are run by popular assemblies of amateur politicians, aka citizen-legislators. Legislatures are found almost exclusively in larger municipalities. Thus, there is a very tight relationship between the size of a municipality and the probability of adopting a legislature-centered governance structure (Ladner 2002: 820). We regard the latter as an important signal of political professionalization.

In the United States, all states have legislatures; however, there is considerable variation in the degree of professionalism they exhibit. King (2000) examines state legislatures over four decades, measuring professionalism by (a) compensation (salary and living expenses), (b) days in session, and (c) expenditures for services and operations (minus legislator compensation) per legislator. With this tripartite index, he finds that increases in population are strongly correlated with increases in professionalism. This result replicates earlier studies of the US states employing similar methodologies (Mooney 1995).

At national levels, although all countries possess legislative bodies of some sort, their function and composition differ. In microstates, Corbett and Veenendaal (2018: 116) note that "politics is rarely a full time occupation . . .; typically, parliament only sits a few weeks of each year." Accordingly, politicians are apt to pursue a second career, fulfilling the ideal of the citizen-politician. Observers complain that "politicians do not take their job seriously, that legislating is hampered by the ineffectiveness of members and parliamentary support staff, and that the blurring between public and private activities offers considerable scope for corruption" (Corbett & Veenendaal 2018: 117; see also Corbett 2013). In Palau, for example, most politicians combine their job with a business. "It's a bad thing," comments one informant.

It's one of those situations where the resource constraint gives them [politicians] opportunities they would not normally have. The bad side to it is that politicians are in constant conflict between their private businesses and the good of the country. It drives me crazy. Because consistently bad decisions are made; both business decisions and political decisions; just really bad, because they are trying to protect their own interests.

A similar observation can be made for Malta:

This is a huge issue, because you are going to have a lawyer who is also a member of parliament, who might one day be in government. So you get all these conflicts of interest swirling around.

The oft-noted ineffectiveness of legislatures in very small countries offers fodder for the argument that size promotes professionalism.

To test the matter globally we rely on the V-Dem project, which offers several indicators of legislative professionalism including *control of resources* (In practice, does the legislature control the resources that finance its own internal operations and the perquisites of its members?), *committees* (Does the lower or unicameral chamber of the legislature have a functioning committee system?), and *staff* (Does each member of the lower or unicameral chamber of the legislature have at least one staff member with policy expertise?). These are combined by addition into a composite index.

Table 10.1 displays a number of tests in which this index of legislative professionalism is regressed against population. Model 1 includes only the regressor of interest along with annual dummies. Model 2 adds further covariates to the specification. Model 3, the instrumental variable analysis, builds on the benchmark specification. All three models show a strong relationship between country size and legislative professionalism, and estimates for the variable of theoretical interest are fairly stable.

To illustrate the magnitude of this relationship, predicted values from the benchmark model are graphed against population in Figure 10.2. Here, we can see that an increase in population from 100,000 to 1 million is associated with an increase of about one point in our legislative profession-alism scale (about one-third of a standard deviation). This is not a huge effect, but, like many scale effects, it becomes substantial if one compares communities at either end of the spectrum (very small and very large).

Bureaucracies

Studies of small states often note the shortage of qualified personnel needed to fill civil service positions. A report by the Caribbean Centre for Development Administration (CARICAD) finds that:

There is a scarcity of manpower and technical personnel in these governments to perform new, complex functions of national development because of the small size of the population, the difficulties of recruiting and maintaining qualified personnel in

Table 10.1 *Legislative professionalism*

Estimator	OLS	OLS	2SLS
Model	1	2	3
Population (log)	0.424***	0.600***	0.555***
	(0.151)	(0.141)	(0.205)
GDP per capita (log)		1.175***	
		(0.318)	
Urbanization		2.879**	
		(1.188)	
Democracy (Lexical index)		0.242***	
		(0.065)	
Protestant		0.007	
		(0.008)	
Muslim		−0.001	
		(0.007)	
GDP per capita growth		−0.002	
		(0.006)	
Mineral wealth		−0.000***	
		(0.000)	
English colony		−0.547	
		(0.443)	
Regional dummies		✓	
Annual dummies	✓	✓	
Decade dummies			✓
Countries	172	147	162
Years	117	97	117
Observations	11,024	6,264	10,762
R-squared	0.119	0.466	0.113

Outcome: professionalism index (authors). *Units of analysis*: country-years. *Lag structure*: right-side variables measured at t−20. Constant omitted. *Estimators*: OLS (ordinary least squares), 2SLS (two-stage least squares, using territory and agricultural suitability as instruments). Country clustered standard errors in brackets. *** $p < 0.01$, ** $p < 0.05$, * $p < 0.10$ (two-tailed tests)

view of the scarce financial resources of the public sector and the consequent low levels of the salaries; the difficulties of educating [the] officials to perform tasks requiring scientific and technical knowledge in view of the lack of opportunities for higher education, and the problem of retaining them when educated or trained externally. They tend to migrate to the larger, developed countries in which they have wider professional horizons, better remuneration for their work and better amenities for them and their families. (quoted in Baker 1992: 17)

All developing countries face common difficulties. But it seems likely that the usual obstacles to attracting and retaining human capital are

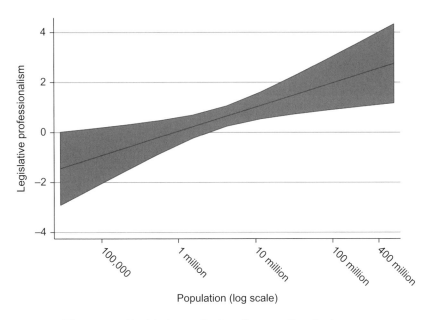

Figure 10.2 Legislative professionalism, predicted values

Predicted values of legislative professionalism (Y) as population (log) changes, surrounded by 95 percent confidence interval. Based on Model 1, Table 10.1, with covariates set to sample means. Descriptive statistics (Y): mean = 0.33, SD = 3.10, min. = −6.68, max. = 8.70.

heightened by small labor pools, especially at the top of the labor market (e.g., administrative heads and managers). We assume that similar shortages exist in subnational units, where the effective labor pool may be even smaller.

The problem, however, is not just the size of the labor pool. Another review of public administration in small states concludes with a litany of complaints:

Overextended personnel, small spare/reserve capacity, few specialists attracted or retained, inadequate compensation level, inappropriate and infrequent training, low turnover rate, small establishment, limited promotion and mobility, limited alternative employment, low morale and motivation, low job satisfaction, low productivity, low adaptability to changing conditions, shortage of management skills, low problem solving capacity, high level of fear and frustration, absenteeism, timid decision-making, continued systemic uncertainty, low level of innovativeness and entrepreneurship, excessive routine dependence … small size inhibiting the realization of rational-legal management systems. (quoted in Chittoo 2011)

These problems are aggravated by clientelism and patronage (Chapter 6), which frequently result in the appointment of party loyalists who are incapable of administering their agencies. An interest group representative in St. Kitts and Nevis complains:

The civil service has really become an extension of whichever party is there. It is routine that people are transferred and humiliated; it is customary that the government would take people who are supporters and fit them into positions for which they don't qualify. It's all patronage, it's all an attempt to farm out and say, "well you supported me, so here is a job," which means a few thousand dollars every month even though you don't have anything to do.

Paradoxically, despite the limited pool of skillful bureaucrats, the civil service of small states tends to be oversized, bulging with patronage appointments. In San Marino, a business leader contends,

Everybody wants to go into the public administration, because you will have money and certain work for the rest of your life. So everybody will do everything to get into the public administration; even giving their votes in exchange for work. And this thing happens everywhere, but in a small country you feel it stronger.

In Suriname, the administration has become so oversized as a result of patronage that many civil servants have nothing to do, and therefore do not even show up at work:

If you know how many of them are what we call ghost officers – it is unimaginable. And of course it is related to political parties; people have received these positions. ... So they are sitting at home, just hanging around, but receiving a government salary.

In short, there is considerable anecdotal evidence to suggest that public officials in small communities are not performing at the level of public officials in large communities. However, few attempts have been made to measure the professionalization of public officials on a global scale.

One effort in this direction is provided by Peter Evans and James Rauch, who gather information from expert surveys on bureaucratic recruitment practices (Evans & Rauch 1999; Rauch & Evans 2000). Questions on this topic ask experts to estimate what proportion of higher officials in the civil service enter via a formal examination system and, for those who enter through some other route, what proportion have university or postgraduate degrees. These are combined into an equal-weight index (assembled as part of the Quality of Government Dataset), intended to measure the extent of meritocratic recruitment in the civil service.[3]

[3] The survey includes several other questions relating to career opportunities in the civil service and to bureaucratic compensation. The first seems less relevant to our theoretical

The sample for this survey is limited to a set of thirty-five developing countries located in various regions around the world: Argentina, Brazil, Chile, Colombia, Costa Rica, Cote d'Ivoire, Dominican Republic, Ecuador, Egypt, Greece, Guatemala, Haiti, Hong Kong, India, Israel, Kenya, Korea, Malaysia, Mexico, Morocco, Nigeria, Pakistan, Peru, Philippines, Portugal, Singapore, Spain, Sri Lanka, Syria, Taiwan, Thailand, Tunisia, Turkey, Uruguay, and Zaire. Data were collected over a period of several years (1993–96) and are intended to register the state of affairs at that time, though the authors assert (with some justification) that these institutional rules are likely to remain constant over a much longer period of time. In any case, our analyses focus on the first year of the survey, 1993. (Results are virtually identical regardless of the chosen year – 1994, 1995, or 1996.)

Cross-sectional tests, summarized in the first section of Table 10.2, regress the Evans–Rauch measure of meritocratic recruitment against population (log) and an assortment of controls. Model 1 is a spare model. Model 2 adds several covariates. Model 3 is an instrumental variable model. All three models show a strong relationship between population and meritocratic recruitment practices. Of course, the sample upon which estimates are drawn is small and observed at a single point in time, so these results must be viewed with extreme caution.

To gain a broader picture of bureaucratic capacity we consider the extent to which government officials are able to gather and analyze data on their citizens. While the practice of gathering data has some unpleasant connotations – e.g., "legibility" (Scott 1998) or "surveillance" (Giddens 1985) – one can appreciate that the provision of public goods of any sort depends centrally on a government's capacity to monitor its citizens. With this in mind, researchers affiliated with the World Bank have developed an indicator of Statistical Capacity,

a diagnostic framework assessing the following areas: methodology; data sources; and periodicity and timeliness. Countries are scored against 25 criteria in these areas, using publicly available information and/or country input. The overall Statistical Capacity score is then calculated as a simple average of all three area scores on a scale of 0–100.[4]

This index, incorporated in the 2016 World Development Indicators (World Bank 2016), is regressed against population and other covariates in the second section of Table 10.2. Model 1 is a bivariate specification,

concerns and the second is superseded by our own data on salaries, which are much more encompassing.

[4] World Bank, Bulletin Board on Statistical Capacity (http://bbsc.worldbank.org).

Table 10.2 *Bureaucratic professionalism*

Outcome	Meritocratic recruitment			Statistical capacity		
Right side lag (years)	0	0	0	20	20	20
Estimator	OLS	OLS	2SLS	OLS	OLS	2SLS
Model	**1**	**2**	**3**	**4**	**5**	**6**
Population (log)	0.077***	0.069***	0.061**	3.643***	3.415***	2.304***
	(0.026)	(0.025)	(0.030)	(0.446)	(0.682)	(0.644)
GDP per capita (log)	0.177***	0.247***	0.170***		7.394***	
	(0.031)	(0.049)	(0.031)		(1.674)	
GDP per capita growth	0.004	0.002			0.039	
	(0.006)	(0.007)			(0.051)	
Mineral wealth	−0.000***	−0.000*			−0.007***	
per capita	(0.000)	(0.000)			(0.001)	
English colony	0.207***	0.140**			1.114	
	(0.055)	(0.055)			(3.746)	
State history		0.083				
		(0.113)				
Years independent (log)		−0.065*				
		(0.034)				
Urbanization		−0.347**			−10.308	
		(0.170)			(7.059)	
Protestant		−0.008			−0.045	
		(0.007)			(0.135)	
Muslim		0.000			−0.027	
		(0.001)			(0.044)	
Democracy					0.979**	
					(0.403)	
Regional dummies					✓	
Annual dummies				✓	✓	
Decade dummies						✓
Countries	34	33	34	144	111	130
Years	1	1	1	13	13	13
Observations	34	33	34	1,820	1,297	1,666
R-squared	0.618	0.704	0.613	0.194	0.568	0.138

Units of analysis: country-years. Constant omitted. *Estimators*: OLS (ordinary least squares), 2SLS (two-stage least squares, using territory and agricultural suitability as instruments). Country clustered standard errors in brackets. *** $p < 0.01$, ** $p < 0.05$, * $p < 0.10$ (two-tailed tests)

including only the regressor of theoretical interest along with year dummies. Model 2 adds many additional predictors. Model 3, an instrumental variable model, builds on the benchmark specification. All three

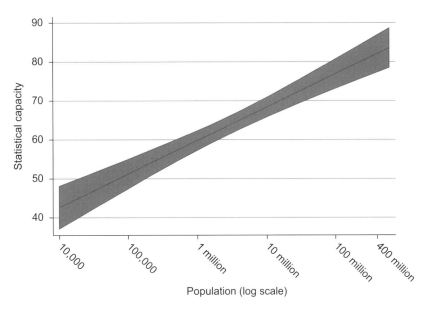

Figure 10.3 Statistical capacity, predicted values

Predicted values of statistical capacity (Y) as population (log) changes, surrounded by 95 percent confidence interval. Based on Model 4, Table 10.2, with covariates set to sample means. Descriptive statistics (Y): mean = 65.49, SD = 16.83, min. = 16.67, max. = 98.89.

models show a strong relationship between population and statistical capacity, and the estimates are also fairly consistent.

To gauge the impact of this relationship, we graph the predicted values for statistical capacity against population, building on the estimates contained in Model 4, Table 10.2. Figure 10.3 shows that an increase from 10,000 to 100,000 in the population of a country is associated with an increase in statistical capacity of about ten points on the World Bank scale (which ranges from 17 to 99, with a standard deviation of 17).

Education

The educational attainment of public officials is another important indicator of professionalism. Where elites are well educated, we expect that they will be more capable of fulfilling their duties, and perhaps less prone to corruption.

Other datasets have measured the educational credentials of top leaders (e.g., Besley & Reynal-Querol 2011; Goemans, Gleditsch, &
Chiozza 2009). However, the status of a chief executive may not be
indicative of the status of lower-level officials. To gain a more complete
picture of elite-level qualifications we employ data measuring the educational attainment of leaders – executives, members of parliament (lower
or unicameral chamber), and the supreme (or constitutional) court from
the Global Leadership Project (GLP). This is measured along a six-level
ordinal scale registering (for each individual) the highest level of education completed: (a) primary, (b) secondary, (c) higher non-university
education, (d) college or university, (e) postgraduate (anything except
PhD degree), or (f) PhD.

Across 145 countries, the GLP records educational attainment for
29,175 leaders. Aggregating up from individuals to countries, we obtain
a cross-country mean of 4.3, with a standard deviation of 0.4 and a range
of 3.1 (min.) to 5.3 (max.). There is, in short, considerable cross-national
variation in the level of education obtained by political elites throughout
the world.

The analysis is cross-sectional as each country is observed at a single
point in time. However, we anticipate that the educational attainment of
elites is a fairly "sticky" phenomenon – unlikely to fluctuate greatly
from year to year. Note that each country is represented by several
hundred individuals (all members of the lower or unicameral house, the
supreme court, and the executive), and turnover in these positions is apt
to be gradual.

Our analysis, presented in Table 10.3, regresses country-level
values against country-level characteristics, including population.
Model 1, the benchmark, includes per capita GDP. Model 2 offers
a fuller specification. Model 3, an instrumental variable model,
builds on the benchmark specification. These analyses indicate
a positive relationship between country size and the educational
attainment of political elites, though not in the IV model. Perhaps
with larger samples the relationship might be stronger and more
consistent; as it is, we are limited to the cross-sectional analysis of
a single year.

To get a better sense of what this might mean (if the relationship
is truly causal), we graph predicted values for the education of
public officials against population in Figure 10.4, using the estimates from the benchmark model. This shows that an increase
from 1 to 10 million translates into an increase of one quarter
point in our educational attainment index (about one-fourth of
a standard deviation). This is not a large effect. So, even if it is

Table 10.3 *Education of public officials*

Estimator	OLS	OLS	2SLS
Model	1	2	3
Population (log)	0.095*	0.116**	−0.027
	(0.049)	(0.050)	(0.072)
GDP per capita (log)	0.360***	−0.305	0.356***
	(0.073)	(0.186)	(0.077)
Urbanization		0.446	
		(0.635)	
Educational attainment		0.240***	
(general population)		(0.059)	
Democracy (Lexical index)		0.099**	
		(0.048)	
Countries	157	142	152
Years	1	1	1
Observations	157	142	152
R-squared	0.124	0.291	0.101

Outcome: educational attainment of political elites (GLP). *Units of analysis*: country-years. *Lag structure*: right-side variables measured at t−20. Constant omitted. *Estimators*: OLS (ordinary least squares), 2SLS (two-stage least squares, using territory and agricultural suitability as instruments). Country clustered standard errors in brackets. *** $p < 0.01$, ** $p < 0.05$, * $p < 0.10$ (two-tailed tests)

causal (which our IV analysis calls into doubt), we should not imagine that scale has a substantial impact on the education of political elites.

Salary

An important element of a professional identity is remuneration. Generally speaking, we expect public officials who are well paid to be more inclined to identify themselves with their chosen occupation and to take their professional responsibilities seriously. By contrast, where public officials are poorly remunerated, or work on a purely voluntary basis, one may assume that they view themselves as amateurs rather than professionals and that their public responsibilities may not be their highest priority. After all, they must earn a living somewhere, and if the job does not pay well, they may need to pursue a second line of work in order to make ends meet, or they may need to have an independent source of wealth. Salary, along with education and training, is thus an important measure of professionalism.

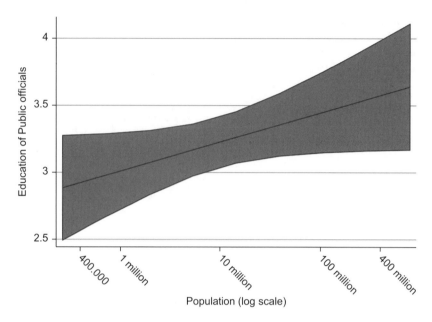

Figure 10.4 Education of public officials, predicted values

Predicted values of the education of public officials (Y) as population (log) changes, surrounded by 95 percent confidence interval. Based on Model 1, Table 10.3, with covariates set to sample means. Descriptive statistics (Y): mean = 3.18, SD = 1.27, min. = 0.00, max. = 5.00.

It is difficult to measure the wages of bureaucrats cross-nationally because this category is defined differently across the world and, even within a single country, is fairly malleable. Any cross-country comparison would necessarily hinge on who is defined "in" and who is defined "out," raising a problem of nonequivalence across cases. An even more fundamental problem is the availability of data, as this sort of information is not freely distributed by many governments and, where it is, may not be very credible.

In our cross-national analysis we focus, therefore, on a category of public officials – members of parliament (MPs) – who are highly visible, easily defined, and for whom official salaries are generally on display. We expect that the wages of other government officials (e.g., top civil servants) observe a similar relationship to scale, though we cannot verify this assumption. Salaries of MPs are collected for countries around the world as part of the GLP. Data are drawn primarily from parliamentary websites, though a variety of other sources are also employed. Salaries are converted to US dollars (USD) using current purchasing power parity.

This measure of compensation provides our dependent variable in the first section of Table 10.4, where we regress MP salaries against population. Model 1 includes two additional covariates with a strong impact on salaries – per capita GDP and urbanization. Model 2 adds a measure of democracy (which turns out to bear no relationship to salaries) as well as a vector of regional dummies. Model 3 is an instrumental variable model, building on the benchmark specification. All three tests show a strong relationship between country size and MP remuneration.

Figure 10.5 shows the predicted values generated by our benchmark model. One can see that an increase in population from 100,000 to 1 million is associated with an increase in salary of about $10,000 – a sizeable chunk of change. Big-country legislators are paid more than small-country legislators. And when one compares really big countries with really small countries – i.e., the two ends of the population scale – the contrast is dramatic.

In the second and third portions of Table 10.4 we examine within-country variation in the salaries of public officials. In the United States, we compare the offices of president, US Senate, US House of Representatives, governor, state senate and house, mayor, city manager, and city council – including all obtainable local offices. In the United Kingdom, we compare the offices of House of Commons, leader of local council, city council, and mayor – again, capitalizing on all available local offices.

For each country, we include two specifications. The first specification is a bivariate model with only population (log) on the right side. The second specification includes a variety of additional covariates that may serve as confounders – income per capita or median household income (whichever shows a stronger relationship to salary), dummies for each type of office (listed at the top of the table), and dummies for state (United States) or region (United Kingdom).

All within-country tests (Models 4–7) show a strong positive association between the size of a constituency and the official salary of the position. Note also that these subnational tests are less susceptible to confounders than the cross-national data analyzed in Models 1–3.

Of course, one must be cautious about potential measurement error. Public officials receive *non*-salary benefits, including generous pensions and health insurance benefits, reimbursements for travel, office, and other business expenses, and other perks – not to mention the opportunity to hold other offices and to sell their services in other ways, building on their position and their connections. One might also consider career

Table 10.4 *Salary of public officials*

	Global			United States		United Kingdom	
Sample	Lower or unicameral chamber of national legislature			President, US Senate & House, governor, state senate & house, mayor, city manager, city council		House of Commons, leader of local council, city council, mayor	
Offices							
Estimator	OLS	OLS	2SLS	OLS	OLS	OLS	OLS
Lag (years)	20	20	20	0	0	0	0
Model	1	2	3	4	5	6	7
Population (log)	4,800.73**	6,874.80**	4,916.00*	2,935.98***	10,043.18***	10,924.38***	8,116.40***
	(2,358.32)	(2,771.33)	(2,981.82)	(618.72)	(624.19)	(403.47)	(1,212.06)
GDP per capita (log)	15,257.98***	21,016.24***	15,757.65***				
	(4,477.09)	(5,208.85)	(4,435.08)				
Income per capita					0.073**		
					(0.04)		
Median income							0.06*
							(0.04)
Urbanization	61,332.90***	72,865.53***	61,428.03***				
	(21,418.36)	(25,786.55)	(21,028.32)				
Democracy (Lexical index)		−2,438.83					
		(1,895.14)					
Dummies . . .							
World region		✓					
Office				✓	✓		✓
State or region				✓	✓		✓
Countries	138	137	136	1	1	1	1
Years	1	1	1	1	1	1	1
Observations	138	137	136	4,397	4,358	1,286	1,056
R-squared	0.442	0.579	0.447	0.007	0.579	0.280	0.986

Outcome: salaries of public officials in US dollars (Models 1–5) or British pounds (Models 6–7). Constant omitted. *Estimators*: OLS (ordinary least squares), 2SLS (two-stage least squares, using territory and agricultural suitability as instruments). Country clustered standard errors in brackets.

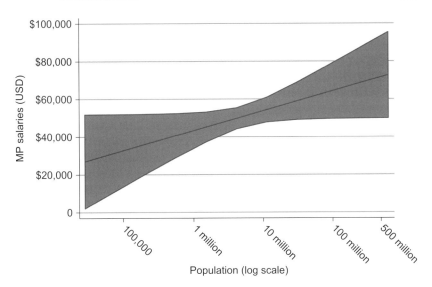

Figure 10.5 MP salaries, predicted values

Predicted values of MP salaries in US dollars (Y) as population (log) changes, surrounded by 95 percent confidence interval. Based on Model 1, Table 10.4, with covariates set to sample means. Descriptive statistics (Y): mean = $52,958, SD = $46,895, min. = 0, max. = $187,339.

opportunities after leaving public service, which in many countries is worth a great deal more than the job itself. It would be a mistake to regard official salaries as anything more than a lower bound on the total remuneration that public officials can expect to receive, over time, from their positions.

Nonetheless, it is reasonable to view official salaries as an indication of the professional status of a position. If a job is poorly paid – or purely voluntary (as in several communist countries) – it is apparent that the community does not regard it as a professional position. It also suggests that the loyalty of the officeholder may lie elsewhere. To the extent that these public servants make a living, it is for tasks other than their official work for the government, e.g., as party officials or as workers or consultants for a private sector firm. By the same token, where public officials are well remunerated we assume that their official salary composes a substantial share of their actual salary. As such, it is an indication that the government holds their services in high esteem, and they are likely to as well. And, as such, it may be appropriate to regard official salaries as a measure of professionalism, even if it is not the sum total of an elected politician's earnings.

Voluntary Associations

Where a voluntary association exists to represent an interest or value we expect that political activity on that issue will be channeled (in part or in total) through the association. Associations thus serve a crucial mediating function between the citizenry and government. We take this to be a vital indicator of the extent to which politics is professionalized. To be sure, voluntary associations may have nonprofessional help – volunteers motivated by their devotion to an issue. However, they will also have a permanent leader and staff, who are likely to be fairly well trained and experienced (at least, relative to amateur activists).

All things being equal, we expect that a larger community will support a larger number and variety of voluntary associations (Dahl & Tufte 1973: 35–39). To test this hypothesis we turn to a recent study by Schofer and Longhofer (2011), who employ an encyclopedia of associations published by Gale (2010) to measure the number of associations in 170 countries across the world from 1970 to 2006. Several categories of associations are included in this directory: (a) economic, trade, and industry associations; (b) social, political, and welfare-based associations (e.g., the Environment and Development Association of Ghana, the Brazilian Interdisciplinary AIDS Association, and the British Institute of Human Rights); (c) professional, educational, and scientific associations; and (d) recreational and cultural associations (Schofer & Longhofer 2011: 556). While many of these associations are not explicitly political in their goals we expect that they represent the views and interests of their members on selective topics, serving as highly focused lobbies.

Schofer and Longhofer construct indices with these data that aggregate all types of voluntary associations, as well as distinguishing among them (using the foregoing categories). In a variety of analyses – both pooled and fixed effect – they find a strong association between population (log) and associational richness. Large countries have more associations than smaller countries, even when controlling for a variety of background factors that might be expected to influence associational growth, e.g., per capita GDP, education, instability, democracy, the size of the state, global linkages, and foreign aid.

We must be careful not to interpret this result as an indication that larger countries have stronger civil societies. Participation rates in voluntary associations are likely to be lower as scale increases, as discussed in Chapter 7. That is why we treat the number of associations in a community as an indicator of professionalism rather than of popular engagement.

Table 10.5 *Scale and professionalism: Inventory of analyses*

Indicators	Countries	Treatment units	Years	Units of analysis	Research design	Effect	Study
Legislative professionalism	United States	State legislatures (50)	(31)	State legislatures (200)	Panel	↑	King 2000
Legislative professionalism	United States	State legislatures (50)	(10)	State legislatures (50)	Cross-sectional, panel	↑	Mooney 1995
*Legislative professionalism	(172)	Countries (172)	(117)	Country-years (11,024)	Cross-sectional	↑	Table 10.1
*Meritocratic recruitment	(34)	Countries (34)	(1)	Countries (34)	Cross-sectional	↑	Table 10.2
*Statistical capacity	(144)	Countries (144)	(13)	Country-years (1,820)	Cross-sectional	↑	Table 10.2
*Education	(157)	Countries (157)	(1)	Countries (157)	Cross-sectional	↑	Table 10.3
*Salary	(138)	Countries (138)	(1)	Countries (138)	Cross-sectional	↑	Table 10.4
Voluntary associations	(140)	Countries (170)	(36)	Country-years (4,849)	Panel	↑	Schofer & Longhofer 2011

Treatment units: units exhibiting variation in scale. *Years*: number of years over which data are collected – not to be confused with the frequency of observations, as data may or may not be annual and may be averaged across years. *Research design*: the main, or benchmark, research design – classified as cross-sectional (where the analysis is driven primarily by variation across units) or panel (where the analysis is driven primarily by variation through time). *Effect*: when the scale of a community increases, the designated outcome goes up (↑), down (↓), up and down (∩), or experiences no perceptible change (∅). A scale effect is considered significant if it passes a modest bar of statistical significance, i.e., p < 0.10 (two-tailed test) in the benchmark model. Number of countries, treatment units, years, or observations in parentheses. ?: unclear from text or unrecoverable from data.

Summary

Professionalism may be measured in many ways, and we have no pretensions of having covered the ground comprehensively. It is, after all, a large and abstract concept and scholars do not have a standard set of measures. Nonetheless, extant studies as well as our own analyses – both of which are summarized in Table 10.5 – suggest that scale is positively correlated with professionalism.

A number of studies focused on US states show a relationship between the size of a state and the professionalism of its legislature. In addition, we find one study of national-level voluntary associations that demonstrates a relationship between scale and number of NGOs in a country.

Since other topics are not widely studied we rely on our own analyses. These focus on national legislatures, bureaucracies, and the education and salary of public officials. All – except education – show a fairly strong relationship between the size of a country and the professionalism of its political class, supporting our thesis.

11   Concentration

In some polities, the exercise of political power is highly concentrated and in others it is widely dispersed. At one extreme stands North Korea, where a small cadre micromanages the personal lives of citizens with virtually no constraints (so far as we can tell). At another extreme lie polities like India, Switzerland, and the United States – along with confederations and international organizations such as the European Union, the United Nations, and the World Trade Organization – where decision-making power is diffused across many independent actors.

A theoretical *maximum* of concentration is achieved when a single individual or ruling group makes all important policy decisions in a polity. A theoretical *minimum* cannot be defined in a precise fashion but would be characterized by a wide dispersal of power and numerous veto holders. More specifically, where power is deconcentrated, governance is multilevel rather than single-level, rule is indirect rather than direct, the constitution is federal rather than unitary, and power is divided among independent institutions.

Note that power may be concentrated *horizontally* (at a single level of government) or *vertically* (between center and the periphery, for which the term *centralization* is sometimes reserved). Although independent, these dimensions are interwoven insofar as horizontal fragmentation usually enhances vertical fragmentation, and vice versa.

Although the concept of concentration is fairly encompassing, it should be differentiated from the adjacent concept of *regime type*. Democracy may be achieved in highly concentrated polities (e.g., France or Malta) or highly deconcentrated polities (e.g., the United States or India). Likewise, undemocratic polities may concentrate power (e.g., the French and Spanish empires and contemporary North Korea) or deconcentrate power (e.g., the British and Ottoman Empires and contemporary China). Of course, we recognize that the nature of a regime may affect the degree to which power can be concentrated or deconcentrated at any given point in time. There are also important interactions between institutions that structure regimes and institutions that structure concentration. These difficulties notwithstanding, regime type serves as a background condition – not a constitutive element – of concentration in our theoretical framework.

So defined, we may briefly consider the ramifications of concentration.

First, where power is deconcentrated the status quo is more difficult to change. A greater number of veto points is thus likely to translate into greater policy stability (Tsebelis 2000). One might counter that a fragmented system also gives greater opportunity for new ideas and for policy entrepreneurs who champion those ideas, which may enhance the probability of policy change. In this sense, a fragmented system is more pluralist and more open to adaptation (Kollman 2013; Truman 1951). Yet when power is fragmented, consensus is generally more difficult to construct, as each veto holder is likely to have a different view or interest; in the absence of consensus, change is impossible. Second, where power is deconcentrated, there will be less redistribution, as the government is less capable of extracting resources from society, and society – to the extent that it takes its cues from politics – may be less willing to sacrifice their resources for the commonweal.

When it comes to questions about the quality of governance and the provision of public goods it is difficult to say whether concentrated or deconcentrated systems are preferable. Many believe that only when power is diffused across many levels and many institutions are conditions optimal for constraining the abuse of power, achieving stability and credible commitment, ensuring property rights, and maximizing the utility of citizens with diverse values and interests (Breton 1996; Buchanan 1995; Elazar 1987; Gordon 1999; Inman & Rubinfeld 1997; Kollman 2013; North & Weingast 1989; Oates 1972; V. Ostrom 1971; Tiebout 1956; Weingast 1995). Others view power dispersion more skeptically – as an invitation to special interest politics, weak government, and coordination dilemmas (Bagehot 1963 [1867]; Bardhan & Mookherjee 2000; Gerring & Thacker 2008; Keefer, Narayan, & Vishwanath 2006; Prud'homme 1995; Schattschneider 1942). According to a third perspective, the success of dispersion is contingent (i.e., dependent on contextual factors and on the type of decentralization being considered) or mixed, setting in motion offsetting virtues and vices with no straightforward implications for the overall quality of governance (Bardhan 2002; Enikolopov & Zhuravskaya 2007; Oxhorn, Tulchin, & Selee 2004; Treisman 2007). We return to this question briefly in Chapter 16.

Everyone will agree that the question of concentration is consequential, even if they do not agree on what, precisely, those consequences are. With this as background, we proceed to the presentation of our theory. We then turn to cross-national empirical work on the subject, followed by a set of empirical tests. In the third section, we briefly review studies focused on the United

States and then conduct our own tests. A brief conclusion summarizes the results.

Theory

Extant research on the causes of power concentration focuses mostly on the vertical dimension of power, especially constitutional federalism and fiscal federalism, and on its proximal causes, e.g., the dynamics of party contestation, the interplay between national and subnational elites, and economic crisis (e.g., Benz & Broschek 2013; Crémer & Palfrey 1999; Dickovick 2011; Eaton & Dickovick 2004; Falleti 2005, 2010; Grossman & Lewis 2014; Manor 1999; Montero & Samuels 2004; O'Neill 2005; Strøm & Graham 2014; Wibbels 2006). A few scholars examine distal factors operating beneath the surface, e.g., geography, technology (communications, transport, military), economic development, urbanization, inequality, globalization, external threats (including outright war), colonial heritage, ethnocultural diversity, and democracy (Arzaghi & Henderson 2005; Dickovick 2011; Eaton & Dickovick 2004; Garrett & Rodden 2003; Gibler 2010; Hooghe, Marks, & Schakel 2010; Letelier 2005; Manor 1999; Strøm & Graham 2014; Veliz 1980; Wibbels 2005).

We suspect that most of these factors are limited in purview: they may affect some aspects of concentration but not others. In any case, it is not our goal to comprehensively assess all possible influences on concentration. Our goal is to home in on one distal cause that is fairly universal, namely, the size of a polity. We argue that the degree of concentration in a polity is affected by the number of people residing within that polity. The larger the polity, the more fragmented its institutional design (Dahl & Tufte 1973: 37–39; Hooghe & Marks 2016: ch. 3).

By way of entrée, let us consider an example of a nested hierarchy of political communities, moving from big to small:

- *United Nations* (global)
  - *European Union* (supranational)
    - *France* (national)
      - *Occitanie* (regional)
        - *Haute-Garonne* (departmental)
          - *Toulouse Métropole* (metropolitan)
            - *Toulouse* (commune)

Because these governing units are nested within each other we can compare political organization across levels, holding constant some of the historical and cultural factors that might be expected to influence constitutional choices. Note that we are concerned with the organization of power internally, not externally. (The extent to which each government is constrained by a higher-level government is not relevant here.) A glance at our exemplars suggests that power at higher levels is generally more diffuse, with numerous limitations on the exercise of executive power and many consequential decisions reserved for lower levels. Power at lower levels is more concentrated, with fewer horizontal or vertical constraints (Cole 2010: 307; Loughlin 2001, 2007).

Of course, in a nested relationship among polities it is true *by construction* that a higher-level polity has more subordinate polities than a lower-level polity. This does not mean, however, that power must be delegated. Lower-level units might be empty offices on an organizational chart, with no real independence or responsibility. So it is not a tautology to say that higher-level bodies tend to have less concentrated structures of power.

At the same time, one must appreciate that comparisons across different levels of government are fraught with potential confounders. The most important of these is that each level carries a different constitutional mandate, and many of their institutional features may derive from those differing mandates. That is why most of the analyses to follow in the empirical section of this study focus on comparisons across the *same type* of polity. We compare national governments to each other, regional governments to each other, and local governments to each other.

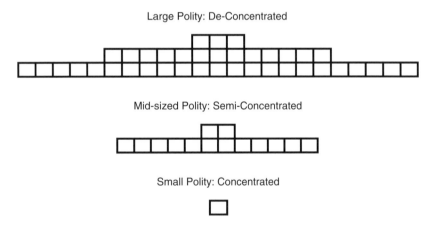

Figure 11.1 Schematic rendering of polity size and concentration
Subdivisions within a polity (squares), out of which three different polities are constructed.

A schematic illustration of the theorized relationship between size and concentration is provided in Figure 11.1. Here, we visualize three exemplars, where the size of each shape indicates the size of its total population and where each constituent unit (represented as a square) is roughly the same size. The large polity has thirty-nine population units, the mid-sized polity has fourteen, and the small polity only one. One must imagine that each unit contains the same number of people, e.g., 10,000, 100,000, or 1 million. (The precise number does not matter, but for the purposes of our model it must be constant across the three exemplars.)

Vertical divisions within these polities are represented in Figure 11.1 by tiers. The large polity has three tiers (e.g., national, regional, and local), the mid-sized polity has two, and the small polity has only one. *Horizontal* divisions within each tier are represented by boxes, which denote independent power centers – groups or organizations that influence (or perhaps even possess a veto over) policymaking at that level, e.g., a branch or agency of government or a political party or interest group that holds a share of power within government. The large polity features many independent power centers – three at the top tier, thirteen at the second tier, and twenty-three at the lowest tier. The mid-sized polity has a smaller number of independent power centers, and the small polity only one.

Size thus corresponds to power deconcentration, with the largest polity having the most dispersed political institutions and the smallest polity having the most concentrated institutions (indeed, no divisions at all, either vertical or horizontal). The modular quality of these diagrams corresponds to our theory, though it must be stressed that this is a highly stylized representation.

To explain the apparent connection between demography and institutions we identify two causal mechanisms – *heterogeneity* and *trust* –

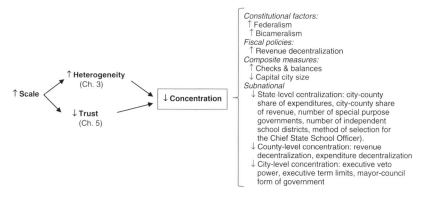

Figure 11.2 Scale effects on concentration

diagrammed in Figure 11.2. In sketching out these mechanisms we consider the dynamic that obtains when the population of a polity grows while other conditions remain the same. In this setting, we surmise that leaders face pressure to place limits on the exercise of power, either by fragmenting power at the center (horizontal deconcentration) and/or devolving power from center to periphery (vertical deconcentration). Sometimes these institutional reforms are undertaken in an explicit and intentional fashion, e.g., by statute or constitutional reform. At other times they occur slowly and unobtrusively.

Heterogeneity

Larger communities are more heterogeneous, as discussed in Chapter 3. Because of their heterogeneity, they may be difficult to govern in a concentrated fashion. Informational inputs are a lot more complicated, and will be hard to track if the center attempts to centralize all policy decisions. Informational asymmetries abound (Hooghe & Marks 2016: 9), and one-size-fits all solutions are unlikely to work.

To accommodate this diversity, power is likely to be deconcentrated. This serves as an efficient solution for leaders and citizens alike. Horizontal deconcentration involves the development of different institutions to serve different functions or different constituencies – e.g., native courts and colonial courts in the classic modality of indirect rule (Lange 2009; Morris 1972), or laws that apply differentially to citizens of diverse faiths (Waldron 2002).

Vertical deconcentration is efficient if preferences are geographically segregated and if externalities across regions are limited (Alesina et al. 1995: 754; Besley & Coate 2003; Bolton & Roland 1997: 1057–58; Oates 1972). Here too size also makes a contribution, as a larger polity is more likely to have subnational regions that can successfully internalize costs and benefits (Hooghe & Marks 2012: 181; Oates 2005: 357). It is therefore easier to decentralize power without introducing negative externalities in a large polity than in a small polity.

Trust

The dynamic between scale and deconcentration is not simply an efficiency-driven response to heterogeneous preferences, in our view. Following Hooghe and Marks (2016: 8), "one must go beyond the utilitarian benefits of governance to consider how individuals perceive themselves in relation to others." Here, we engage the delicate and inevitably subjective matter of political *trust*.

Through most of human evolution communities were small (Glassman 2017). It stands to reason that norms of trust developed within the confines of these closely knit communities, where bonds of interdependence and norms of reciprocity were strong, and where the distinction between insiders and outsiders was well defined and consequential. (We discussed these phenomena in connection with social cohesion in Chapter 3.) Not surprising, larger communities inspire less political trust, as discussed in Chapter 5.

The problem of trust cannot be solved simply by adjusting policy outputs, and often runs contrary to considerations of efficiency. Trust engages nontangible matters of security and respect. Trust is also forward looking; it concerns actions that may (or may not) be taken in the future. When a group distrusts government it means that its members are anxious about what that government might do next.

Concentrated bodies, by their very nature, are incapable of achieving credible commitment to policies that they might pursue in the future (North & Weingast 1989). As such, the problem of trust augurs for institutional solutions, i.e., constraints on the center that cannot be easily overcome, regardless of who happens to control the executive. We surmise, therefore, that large polities experience greater pressure to deconcentrate political power.

Important, a polity need not be democratic in order for considerations of trust to come into play. Even when state elites are not inclined to implement citizen demands, they must be cognizant of the costs of maintaining a form of political organization that is not perceived as legitimate. Illegitimacy may result in lax observance of the laws, tax avoidance, refusal of military service, and at the limit, secession or revolution – costs that even the most authoritarian ruler is obliged to reckon with.

By way of illustration, let us consider an oft-noted dynamic in the founding or reform of polities. Here, fissiparous groups may be granted a share of power, a guarantee of rights, or a constitutional settlement that assures their rights, as a condition of their agreement to join (or remain within) a larger polity (Lijphart 1977; Riker 1964). In this manner, vertical or horizontal deconcentration serves as a precondition for the birth or survival of a polity.

Of course, changes to the structure of a polity are not always based on threats of dissolution. Many changes, especially those that do not involve constitutional features of a polity, occur in an incremental fashion and are scarcely perceptible except over long periods of time. This would include levels of revenue and expenditure and other more nuanced measures of relative power. Insofar as demography functions as a cause of anything at a macro level, it is often a subtle relationship, more apparent in spread-sheets than in newspaper headlines or history texts. Even so, the highly visible, macro-level negotiations noted earlier may be indicative of a pervasive political dynamic, one that affects power negotiations at every level.

Evidence

Although our primary theoretical concern is focused on the modern era it is worth reflecting briefly upon the history of empires, the dominant mode of premodern political organization. Empires were large (by the demo-graphic standards of the day), and also rather loosely governed. In order to maintain a semblance of control over vast numbers of people, who generally spoke different languages and worshipped different gods, it was necessary for rulers to delegate power to local potentates. As an empire spread, power emanating from the center tended to attenuate. Moreover, the most long-lived empires were often those that governed indirectly, through intermediaries who enjoyed considerable autonomy – so long as they acknowledged the formal sovereignty of the metropole. The Holy Roman, Austro-Hungarian, British, Ottoman, and Mughal empires were object lessons in decentralized structures of rule (Burbank & Cooper 2010; Kautsky 1982; Newbury 2003; R. Robinson 1972). Ancient Egypt was an exception to this pattern, benefiting from a compact design and a central communication artery (the Nile) through which power could be projected. China was another exception, which also has a geographic interpretation – a relatively flat, unobstructed basin tra-versed by two navigable rivers (Diamond 1998).

The persistence of China as the world's largest polity in the modern era deserves some discussion. While it is true that power in contemporary China is more concentrated than our argument would suggest, it does not approach the level of concentration found in other (smaller) Asian dicta-torships, e.g., Brunei, Cambodia, Laos, North Korea, Singapore, or Vietnam. After Mao's death, power was decentralized as part of a series of reforms Deng and his successors undertook. A recent synthesis suggests,

The most useful way to think about the overall Chinese system at this point is to see it as a nested system of territorial administrations, with substantial policy initiative at each territorial level: the township, county, city, province, and Center. Officials at each level give much attention to garnering resources and striking deals that will benefit the locality governed by that level of state administration. Each is willing to allow lower levels to do what they wish so long as this does not upset their own plans. In the absence of formal institutional mechanisms and a legitimate constitutional framework to give this system regularity and predictability, much is sorted out in practice through consensus building and negotiation. (Lieberthal 2004: 317–18; see also Chung 2000; Xu 2011)

Indeed, it is sometimes argued that China embodies the ideal of federalism under authoritarian auspices (Montinola, Qian, & Weingast 1995).

In most other megastates, power appears to be strongly deconcentrated in the modern era. Many are constitutionally federalist (e.g., Brazil, Germany, India, Indonesia, Mexico, Nigeria, Pakistan, the Philippines, Russia, and the United States). Most have large party systems and fragmented political institutions. Thus, in a variety of ways large states appear to be ruled in a deconcentrated fashion.

By contrast, the literature on small states suggests a very different pattern. The vast majority of small states are governed by unitary constitutions, and the few exceptions (Comoros, the Federated States of Micronesia, Palau, and St. Kitts and Nevis) are archipelagic countries that seek to recognize distinct island identities. While most small states do have local or municipal governments, these are usually overshadowed by a much more powerful national government, in which power is concentrated.

In addition to a lack of vertical decentralization, studies frequently note the dominant position of the executive vis-à-vis the legislature and other potentially countervailing institutions in small societies (Baldacchino 2012; Benedict 1967: 53–54; Corbett & Veenendaal 2018; Eisenstadt 1977: 76; Richards 1982: 158; Sutton 2007: 203; Veenendaal 2014; Waschkuhn 1990: 143). The government, considered as a whole, often overshadows other institutions including the media, the judiciary, and civil society organizations, whose functioning is hampered by their lack of resources and financial dependence on government. As a spokesperson of a Maltese human rights NGO comments:

Our major concern is the influence government has on deciding bodies everywhere; on boards, on every aspect of a citizen's life, you know. I mean … you would need to apply for a planning permit, but the people deciding are people the government put on the board. … So it's just like a vicious circle, where people sometimes feel they can't get out of [it]. And you get to a point where you look around and you say, "okay, the government controls everything."

In addition to the intensity of the government's presence, individual leaders in small states often attain a centrality, or even an omnipresence, in political affairs. Examples of individual leaders who (by all appearances) dominated their respective political arenas include Lynden Pindling in the Bahamas (reg. 1967–92), Vere Bird in Antigua and Barbuda (1960–94), Makarios III in Cyprus (1950–77), France-Albert

René in Seychelles (1977–2004), and Lee Kuan Yew in Singapore (1959–90). Even in parliamentary systems in which the prime minister is supposed to be *primus inter pares*, power within the government is often concentrated in the head of government, with other ministries functioning as empty vessels. A former minister in the government of St. Kitts and Nevis argues:

> In our electoral process, a number of people get elected to office who are not people of independent means. So that when they get elected or nominated to office, they are also dependent on the prime minister who already has so much constitutional power. . . . And he has these people almost in a state of subservience to him.

Although plenty of testimony can be found to the truth of these propositions, they have not been tested in a comprehensive fashion. Large-*N* cross-national analyses generally center on democracies, the Organization for Economic Co-operation and Development (OECD), and the postwar era (e.g., Arzaghi & Henderson 2005; Garrett & Rodden 2003; Gibler 2010; Hooghe & Marks 2012; Hooghe et al. 2010; Letelier 2005; Wibbels 2005) – a sample across which variation in concentration is limited (relative to the whole population of nation-states). Many studies are limited to an even smaller set of countries, especially those that are highly decentralized or have recently centralized or decentralized (e.g., Benz & Broschek 2013; Dickovick 2011; Eaton 2004; Eaton & Dickovick 2004; Falleti 2005, 2010; Garman, Haggard, & Willis 2001; Grossman & Lewis 2014; Manor 1999; Montero & Samuels 2004; O'Neill 2005; Wibbels 2005; Willis, Garman, & Haggard 1999; Ziblatt 2006).

To tackle this vast subject we adopt a variety of country-level indicators of power concentration including subnational regions, federalism, bicameralism, revenue decentralization, capital city size, and checks and balances. We also probe a variety of subnational indicators focused on variation across states and localities within the United States. (Additional measures are tested in Gerring, Maguire, & Jaeger 2018.)

Constitutional and Fiscal Measures

Constitutional measures of power concentration include those that are defined by a country's basic law or that are sufficiently entrenched to be regarded as constitutional.

As a first pass we examine the *number of subnational regional authorities* in a country. Granted, the sheer number of regional authorities in a country is a very crude measure of their power vis-à-vis the center. Nonetheless, one may surmise that in a country with only one or several regions the center is likely to have a more secure hold on politics and policymaking than in a country with dozens of regions. In the latter, the center faces a formidable principal–agency problem: a great many subnational entities must be directed, overseen, coordinated, and (if necessary) reprimanded. Moreover, the smaller the unit (relative to the center), the greater its informational advantages are likely to be.

We recognize that the creation of very small subnational units some-times serves as a tool of centralization, as it was for the Napoleonic reforms under which *arrondissements* replaced *regions* as functional units of subnational governance in France (Hooghe & Marks 2016: ch. 4). However, the use of administrative units to recentralize power seems to be more common with second- and third-order administrative units (Green 2010; Malesky 2009) than with first-order administrative units. With the latter, the usual pattern is that new units are created in response to popular demands for self-rule, as in India, Spain, the United Kingdom, and the United States. Thus, it seems fair to regard the number of regional units in a country as a prima facie measure of vertical deconcentration.

A previous study of the sources of subnational regional authorities by Auffhammer and Carson (2009) finds a positive – though not especially robust – relationship between population and the number of first-order administrative districts in a country. However, the study is focused on ethnic heterogeneity, which we have argued is probably better regarded as downstream of population size (Chapter 3). Accordingly, estimates for population from this model are probably downward biased. Additionally, population is measured in a linear (rather than log-linear) fashion, whereas theory and well-established practice would suggest a declining marginal effect. For these reasons, we do not regard this study as a strong test of the hypothesis.

In our effort, we draw on the dataset produced by Gwillim Law (1999), which measures first-order administrative districts across nearly 250 sovereign and semi-sovereign countries in the contemporary era. Countries are observed at a single point of time within the 1992–2014 period; we presume that there is no significant time trend during this short period. We graph the relationship on a scatterplot with regional units (log) on the Y axis and population (log) on the X axis, as shown in Figure 11.3. Visual inspection reveals an extraordinarily tight fit. Indeed, a bivariate regression model (overlaid on the scatterplot) explains 80 percent of the variability on this outcome. Insofar as the number of regional authorities offers a proxy measure of deconcentration, this may be regarded as strong evidence for the thesis of scale effects. But we must also consult other measures.

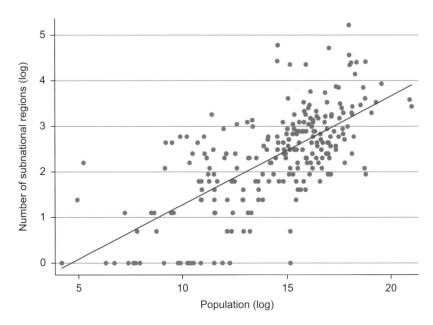

Figure 11.3 Regional authorities

Number of subnational regions (Law 1999) as a function of national population – both variables transformed by the natural log. Countries $(N) = 248$. $R^2 = 0.80$.

Foremost among these is *federalism*. This is understood as an institutionalized division or sharing of responsibilities between a national authority and semiautonomous regional units. Following Gerring and Thacker (2008: 88), polities are coded 0 if they are nonfederal (regional governments, if they exist, are granted minimal policymaking power), 1 if they are semi-federal (there are elective governments at the regional level but constitutional sovereignty is reserved to the national government), or 2 if they are fully federal (elective regional governments plus constitutional recognition of subnational authority).

Important, federalism is subject to a potential problem of endogeneity. It could be that large countries are federal because this constitutional arrangement made possible the birth and survival of a large, diverse country. This is the coming-together story of federalism (Riker 1964). If so, federalism generates scale rather than the reverse. There is no easy way to resolve this issue. Fortunately, other measures of concentration are less susceptible to this problem.

A second constitutional measure rests on the structure of the legislature. *Bicameralism* refers to the existence of two chambers and – if they exist – how closely matched their powers are, based on the coding of country experts enlisted by the V-Dem project. If one chamber overshadows the other we regard this as an example of weak bicameralism.

Another approach to measuring power concentration centers on the location of revenue authority – centralized (in the hands of a national state) or decentralized (to regional or local authorities). This is the approach taken by four recent cross-national studies (Arzaghi & Henderson 2005; Garrett & Rodden 2003; Panizza 1999; Treisman 2006). Results of these studies are equivocal. Three report that population has no effect on fiscal decentralization while one (Arzaghi & Henderson 2005) finds a positive association. However, one must bear in mind that the chosen samples are relatively small ($N \sim 42$ to 66) and centered on the OECD. Temporal coverage is also fairly thin, varying from ten to twenty-eight years.

To provide a more comprehensive test, we draw on a measure of revenue decentralization compiled by Enikolopov and Zhuravskaya (2007) from the Government Financial Statistics database (IMF). This index of subnational revenue, understood as share of total public revenue, provides the largest dataset of revenue decentralization that we are aware of.

Tests for federalism, bicameralism, and revenue decentralization are included in Table 11.1. (We do not bother with subnational regions as the bivariate patterns, shown in Figure 11.3, are overwhelming.) These tests follow similar formats, with the exception of the estimators (ordered logit for federalism, an ordinal outcome, and ordinary least squares for the others, which are interval scales). Analyses of federalism and bicameralism are restricted to country-years where multiparty elections are allowed, under the assumption that these concepts have little meaning in thoroughly autocratic contexts (Stepan 2001: 318).

Models 1, 4, and 7, the benchmark specifications, include only annual dummies. Models 2, 5, and 8 add several covariates to the benchmark. Models 3, 6, and 9 are instrumental-variable analyses, building on the benchmark specification. Results from these tests are strong in all specifications. The size of a country seems to enhance the likelihood of a federal constitution, a bicameral legislature, and decentralized revenue sources.

To visualize the impact of scale on revenue decentralization – the most common cross-national indicator of decentralization – we graph

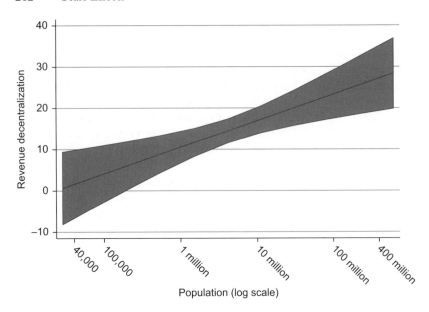

Figure 11.4 Revenue decentralization, predicted values

Predicted values of revenue decentralization (Y) as population (log) changes, surrounded by 95 percent confidence interval. Based on Model 7, Table 11.1, with covariates set to sample means. Descriptive statistics (Y): mean = 15.97, SD = 13.55, min. = 0.13, max. = 56.25.

its relationship to population in Figure 11.5, based on estimates from Model 7, Table 11.1. Note that an increase in population from 40,000 to 1 million is associated with a 10 percent increase in revenue decentralization, a sizeable effect (nearly one standard deviation).

Composite Measures

In the next set of tests, we examine composite measures that reflect a great many aspects of concentration. The most detailed effort of this nature is the Regional Authority Index (RAI) developed by Hooghe and Marks (2016: ch. 2). To measure the varying power held by regional governments in countries around the world the authors code ten dimensions of regional authority: institutional depth, policy scope, fiscal autonomy, borrowing autonomy, representation, lawmaking, executive control, fiscal control, borrowing control, and constitutional reform. These are combined into a single index through principal components

Table 11.1 *Constitutional and fiscal measures of power deconcentration*

Outcome	Federalism			Bicameralism			Revenue decentralization		
Sample	Lexical index > 2			Lexical index > 2			Unrestricted		
Estimator	Ordered logit	Ordered Logit	IV Probit	OLS	OLS	2SLS	OLS	OLS	2SLS
Model	1	2	3	4	5	6	7	8	9
Population (log)	0.591***	0.952***	0.480***	0.209***	0.323***	0.265***	2.712***	3.716***	3.722***
	(0.143)	(0.310)	(0.116)	(0.055)	(0.064)	(0.082)	(0.833)	(0.730)	(1.077)
Urbanization		-3.365			0.830			-4.040	
		(3.295)			(0.833)			(14.240)	
GDP per capita (log)		2.258**			0.296			4.088	
		(1.090)			(0.219)			(5.254)	
English colony		1.162			0.065			5.052	
		(1.327)			(0.281)			(4.761)	
Latitude (log)		-0.346			-0.010			0.032	
		(0.524)			(0.154)			(1.694)	
Muslim		0.010			0.002			0.083	
		(0.013)			(0.002)			(0.053)	
OPEC		2.802*			-0.257			-11.772***	
		(1.592)			(0.386)			(3.940)	
Protestant		-0.009			0.001			0.209***	
		(0.011)			(0.005)			(0.038)	
Democracy		-0.004			-0.024			-0.059	
		(0.196)			(0.059)			(0.502)	

Table 11.1 *(cont.)*

Outcome	Federalism			Bicameralism			Revenue decentralization		
Sample	*Lexical index > 2*			*Lexical index > 2*			*Unrestricted*		
Estimator	Ordered logit	Ordered Logit	IV Probit	OLS	OLS	2SLS	OLS	OLS	2SLS
Model	1	2	3	4	5	6	7	8	9
Region dummies	✓	✓			✓		✓	✓	
Annual dummies		✓		✓	✓		✓	✓	
Decade dummies			✓			✓			✓
Countries	131	87	121	171	138	171	101	71	100
Years	103	83	103	115	95	115	29	29	29
Observations	4,554	2,744	4,420	8,469	4,265	8,275	1,380	1,080	1,356
R2 *(pseudo)*	(0.132)	(0.318)		0.0926	0.275	0.0792	0.144	0.505	0.106

Outcomes: federalism, understood as an institutionalized division of responsibilities between a national government and semiautonomous regional governments (Models 1–3), bicameralism, i.e., the existence and asymmetry of two chambers in a national legislature (Models 4–6), revenue decentralization, i.e., subnational revenue as share of total public revenue (Models 7–9). *Units of analysis*: country-years. *Lag structure*: Right-side variables measured at t–20. Constant omitted. *Samples*: restricted to country-years where multiparty elections are on course (Lexical index > 2), unrestricted (except by data availability). *Estimators*: ordered logit, IV Probit (probit model with continuous endogenous covariates), OLS (ordinary least squares), 2SLS (two-stage least squares). Instrumental variable analyses employ territory and agricultural suitability as instruments. Country clustered standard errors in brackets. *** p < 0.01, ** p < 0.05, * p < 0.10 (two-tailed tests) analysis. Eighty-one countries are included in the index in a panel format extending from 1950 to 2010 (though many countries are not observed over the whole period). Population is found to be a strong predictor of variation in the RAI, with larger countries characterized by a higher score on this index of regional decentralization (Hooghe & Marks 2016: 44–45, 137).

Analyses based on the detailed and meticulous RAI overcome problems of conceptualization and measurement faced by earlier studies of regional authority (e.g., Arzaghi & Henderson 2005; Brancati 2008; Lijphart 1999). However, the sample of eighty-one countries is far from exhaustive and by no means representative of the global population of nation-states (being centered on democracies and the OECD). Neither does it extend very far back in time. To provide a more comprehensive examination of this question we draw on two indices that may be regarded as proxy measures of deconcentration.

Checks and balances refers to "the number of veto players in a political system, adjusting for whether these veto players are independent of each other, as determined by the level of electoral competitiveness in a system, their respective party affiliations, and the electoral rules" (Beck et al. 2001). This measure, drawn from the Database of Political Institutions (DPI), is transformed by the natural logarithm to reflect the right-skewed nature of the scale.

Capital city measures the population of the capital city in a polity as a share of that polity's total population, transformed by the natural logarithm. This is regarded as a summary measure of concentration, following the assumption that in polities where power is concentrated material and human resources will be concentrated at the center (Ades & Glaeser 1995; V. Henderson 2003). Galiani and Kim (2011: 128) comment:

First, government agencies and workers are concentrated in capital cities. Second, since governments make laws and redistribute income, capital cities may attract significant lobbying activity. To the extent that political corruption or rent-seeking behavior contributes to primacy, their impact is likely to be manifested in the growth of capital cities. Finally, capital cities may attract a disproportionate share of government resources for local infrastructure and amenities.

Note that one of the tests that follow includes a covariate measuring overall urbanization, so as not to confuse the status of the capital city with demographic conditions obtaining in the country at large.

Tests of these outcomes are presented in Table 11.2. Models 1 and 3 are regarded as benchmark specifications. For capital city, the benchmark includes only the regressor of interest and a vector of annual dummies. For

Table 11.2 *Composite measures*

Outcome	Checks and Balances			Capital City/Pop.		
Estimator	OLS	OLS	2SLS	OLS	OLS	2SLS
Model	1	2	3	4	5	6
Population (log)	0.064***	0.074***	0.074**	−0.439***	−0.411***	−0.551***
	(0.022)	(0.017)	(0.034)	(0.036)	(0.056)	(0.052)
GDP per capita	0.197***	0.024	0.201***		0.076	
(log)	(0.035)	(0.042)	(0.034)		(0.130)	
English colony	0.263***	0.125**	0.276***		−0.683***	
	(0.078)	(0.063)	(0.080)		(0.223)	
Urbanization		0.200			1.939***	
		(0.162)			(0.505)	
Latitude (log)		−0.030			0.083	
		(0.034)			(0.093)	
Muslim		−0.001			−0.002	
		(0.001)			(0.003)	
OPEC		−0.164*			−0.095	
		(0.084)			(0.223)	
Protestant		0.001			−0.003	
		(0.001)			(0.003)	
Democracy		0.074***			−0.003	
		(0.013)			(0.022)	
Regional dummies		✓			✓	
Annual dummies	✓	✓		✓	✓	
Decade dummies			✓			✓
Countries	170	163	170	184	159	172
Years	38	38	38	210	91	210
Observations	5,533	4,690	5,430	20,281	7,468	19,086
R-squared	0.248	0.501	0.243	0.442	0.527	0.385

Lag structure: right-side variables measured at t−20. *Units of analysis*: country-years. Constant omitted. *Estimators*: OLS (ordinary least squares), 2SLS (two-stage least squares using territory and agricultural suitability as instruments). Country clustered standard errors in brackets. *** $p < 0.01$, ** $p < 0.05$, * $p < 0.10$ (two-tailed tests)

checks and balances, the benchmark also includes GDP per capita (log) and English colony. Models 2 and 5 add a series of additional covariates. Models 3 and 6 are instrumental-variable models that build on the benchmark specifications.

Results from this set of tests reveal a strong and robust association between country size and these composite measures of power decentralization. Coefficients for the variable of theoretical interest are consistent, despite

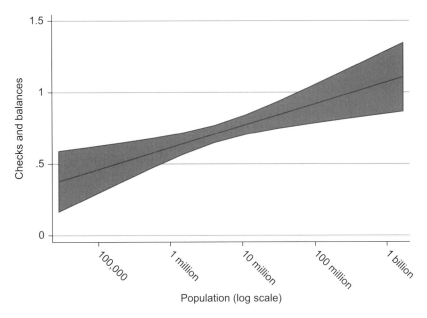

Figure 11.5 Checks and balances, predicted values

Predicted values of checks and balances index, log (Y), as population (log) changes, surrounded by 95 percent confidence interval. Based on Model 1, Table 11.2, with covariates set to sample means. Descriptive statistics (Y): mean = 0.71, SD = 0.66, min. = 0.00, max. = 2.89.

dramatic changes in specification, and all are statistically significant at a high threshold.

To visualize the impact of size on checks and balances, we utilize estimates from Model 1 to generate predicted values of the outcome, which are then graphed against population. Figure 11.5 shows that an increase in population from 100,000 to 1 million is associated with an increase of about 0.1 on our logarithmic index of checks and balances (which ranges from 0 to 2.89). This is not a large change, though it may be sufficient to alter many policy outcomes since a modest change in the threshold for legislative passage may have dramatic effects in the sort of legislation that can make it through the process and the sort of compromises that are necessary in order to clear that hurdle.

Within-Country Evidence: The United States

Problems of causal inference often arise when extremely large, heterogeneous units such as nation-states form the primary units of analysis. For a different identification strategy we turn to within-country evidence drawn from the United States.

While many studies have exploited subnational variation in the United States to understand the impact of (de)centralization on the quality of governance (e.g., Zax 1989), few have studied the sources of concentration and only two studies explore its connection to size. Wallis and Oates (1988) examine revenue decentralization across the fifty states and Clark (1968: 585) briefly reports on community structures across fifty-one localities. Results from these studies provide some support for our thesis, despite limitations in sample size and in the purview of outcomes surveyed.

In the analyses that follow, reported in Table 11.3, we explore institutional variation at the state, county, and city levels. Detailed variable definitions are provided in Table C1 and descriptive statistics in Table C2 of Gerring, Maguire, et al. (2018).

At the *state* level, we employ five measures of concentration: city-county share of expenditures (Model 1), city-county share of revenue (Model 2), the number of special purpose governments (Model 3), the number of independent school districts (Model 4), and the method of selection for the Chief State School Officer (CSSO), which may be either appointive or elective (Model 5). Measures of fiscal decentralization are widely used in cross-national studies as well as in studies focused on the United States (Wallis & Oates 1988; Xie, Zhou, & Davoodi 1999; Zax 1989). The number of special purpose governments and independent school districts is viewed as a key measure of political concentration in federalist systems (Foster 1993; Hammond et al. 2011; Nelson & Foster 1999). An elective CSSO presumably signals the independence of this official relative to other elected officials. All model specifications include a range of covariates that may affect concentration, and may (plausibly) serve to block confounders.

County-level analyses focus on revenue decentralization (Model 6) and expenditure decentralization (Model 7), i.e., fiscal instruments controlled by cities as a share of total city–county revenue or expenditures. These specifications involve a variety of covariates including state dummies.

At the *city* level, we can test three measures of concentration. In Model 8 we examine executive veto power – the ability of the top official (usually a mayor) to veto council legislation. In Model 9 we look at executive term limits, i.e., the imposition of any sort of term limit on the chief executive (usually a mayor). In Model 10 we focus on the choice of a mayor–council form of government – as opposed to a council–manager or commission format. Note that because very small cities often cannot afford to hire a city manager they may be constrained to adopt a mayor–council form of government where the mayor serves pro bono or for a nominal salary. This cost constraint, which hinges on the willingness of elected officials to

Table 11.3 *Within-country tests of power deconcentration*

Polities	State					County		City		
Outcome	City-county/total expenditures	City-county/total revenue	Special purpose governments	Independent school districts	CSSO selection	City/total expenditure	City/total revenue	Executive veto	Executive term limit	Mayor-council
Hypothesis	↑	↑	↑	↑	↑	↑	↑	↑	↑	↑
Estimator	OLS	OLS	OLS	OLS	Logit	OLS	OLS	Logit	Logit	Logit
Sample	Full	Full	Full	Full	Full	Full	Full	Full	Full	pop. > 50 k
Model	1	2	3	4	5	6	7	8	9	10
Population (log)	0.104***	0.124***	0.124***	0.028***	1.713**	0.044***	0.043***	0.212***	0.460***	0.380**
	(0.018)	(0.019)	(0.030)	(0.006)	(0.626)	(0.003)	(0.003)	(0.030)	(0.042)	(0.193)
Polities	51	51	51	51	51	3,153	3,153	7,503	7,503	2,225
Years	1942–2012	1942–2012	1942–2012	1942–2012	1942–2012	2000	2000	1986–2011	1986–2011	1986–2011
Observations	250	250	252	253	200	2,642	2,641	16,955	16,439	1,903
R2	0.612	0.610	0.419	0.475	0.196	0.757	0.787	0.079	0.100	0.237

Covariates for state-level analyses: Income per capita, Urbanization, Democratic Vote Share, College, Unemployment, Minority (%), Region (dummies). *Covariates for county-level analyses*: Urbanization, Minority (%), Income per capita, Democratic Vote Share, State (dummies). *Covariates for city-level analyses*: Urbanization, Black (%), Asian (%), Latino (%), Income per capita, County (dummies). County analyses are cross-sectional. State and city analyses represent a short panel, with standard errors clustered at the state and city level, respectively. Constant omitted. Estimators: OLS (ordinary least squares), Logit (logistic regression). *** $p < 0.01$, ** $p < 0.05$, * $p < 0.10$ (two-tailed tests) For variable definitions, sources, and descriptive statistics see Gerring, Maguire, and Jaeger (2018).

accept lower remuneration than appointed officials, lies outside the scope of our theory and has no plausible applicability to larger polities such as nation-states. Consequently, we limit the analysis in Model 10 to cities of at least 50,000 citizens. Specifications include a variety of background factors along with county dummies.

Analyses at all three levels support our contention that the size of a polity influences the way its institutions are structured, with larger polities adopting less concentrated systems of rule. Judging by the estimated coefficients, the effects are sizeable. For example, moving from a state with a population in the twenty-fifth percentile to a state with a population in the seventy-fifth percentile increases the probability of a directly elected CSSO by nearly 47 percent. Moreover, the impact of population on concentration is consistent across all measured outcomes, as shown in Table 11.3.

For a variety of reasons, which may now be summarized, we are fairly confident that the relationships depicted in Table 11.3 are causal. First, analyses below the state level enlist very large samples. Instead of 100+ nation-states, we can draw upon 3,000+ counties and 7,000+ cities. This diminishes the possibility of stochastic error as well as problems of collinearity among right-side variables. Second, the possibility of $X{:}Y$ endogeneity seems remote. Even if Tiebout sorting occurs, it is unlikely that varying levels of concentration across units have systematic effects on the quality of governance sufficient to stimulate widespread patterns of migration. Third, the borders of subnational units, while by no means random, are unlikely to be affected by the outcome of interest. Fourth, subnational units within a single country share many background characteristics, limiting the number of potential confounders. Ceteris paribus conditions are especially strong when comparing counties within a single state (using state fixed effects) or cities within a single county (using county fixed effects). Indeed, county- and city-level analyses are remarkably stable in the face of changes in specification, reflecting the large sample and the fact that covariates are not highly correlated with the variable of theoretical interest (population). Finally, the possibility of omitted confounders seems remote given that we have been able to measure and condition on many factors that might influence – or that might be correlated with factors that influence – institutional choices.

Summary

Political power is notoriously difficult to operationalize, so it would not be surprising if scholars disagreed on how to measure the degree to which power is concentrated or deconcentrated in a polity. Prior studies focus

Table 11.4 *Scale and deconcentration: Inventory of analyses*

Indicators	Countries	Treatment units	Years	Units of analysis	Research design	Effect	Study
Constitutional							
*Subnational regions	(248)	Countries (248)	(1)	Country-years (248)	Cross-sectional	↑	Figure 11.3
*Federalism	(131)	Countries (131)	(103)	Country-years (4,554)	Cross-sectional	↑	Table 11.1
*Bicameralism	(171)	Countries (171)	(115)	Country-years (8,469)	Cross-sectional	↑	Table 11.1
Fiscal							
Decentralization	(60)	Countries (60)	(10)	Country-years (180)	Cross-sectional	Ø	Panizza 1999
Decentralization	(42)	Countries (42)	(15)	Country-years (84)	Cross-sectional	Ø	Garrett & Rodden 2003
Decentralization	(52)	Countries (48)	(20)	Country-years (134)	Panel	↑	Arzaghi & Henderson 2005
Decentralization	(66)	Countries (66)	(28)	Countries (66)	Cross-sectional	Ø	Treisman 2006
*Decentralization	(101)	Countries (101)	(29)	Country-years (1,380)	Cross-sectional	↑	Table 11.1
*Decentralization	United States	States (50)	(70)	State-years (250)	Cross-sectional	↑	Table 11.3
*Decentralization	United States	Counties (3,153)	(1)	Counties (3,153)	Cross-sectional	↑	Table 11.3
Composite							
Regional Authority Index	(81)	Countries (81)	(60)	Country-years (3,775)	Cross-sectional	↑	Hooghe & Marks 2016
*Checks and balances	(170)	Countries (170)	(38)	Country-years (5,533)	Cross-sectional	↑	Table 11.2
*Capital city/country	(184)	Countries (184)	(210)	Country-years (20,281)	Cross-sectional	↓	Table 11.2
*Separate powers	United States	Municipalities (7,503)	(25)	Municipality-years (16,955)	Cross-sectional	↑	Table 11.3

Treatment units: units exhibiting variation in scale. *Years:* number of years over which data are collected – not to be confused with the frequency of observations, as data may or may not be annual and may be averaged across years. *Research design:* the main, or benchmark, research design – classified as cross-sectional (where the analysis is driven primarily by variation across units) or panel (where the analysis is driven primarily by variation through time). *Effect:* when the scale of a community increases, the designated outcome goes up (↑), down (↓), up and down (↕), or experiences no perceptible change (Ø). A scale effect is considered significant if it passes a modest bar of statistical significance, i.e., p < 0.10 (two-tailed test) in the benchmark model. Number of countries, treatment units, years, or observations in parentheses. Further discussion and empirical tests accompanying Tables 11.1–11.3 can be found in Gerring, Maguire, and Jaeger (2018).

primarily on fiscal decentralization, as shown in Table 11.4. Our own analyses tackle this outcome, as well as many others, in order to better encompass the variegated manifestations of political power.

Most of these analyses support the contention that scale is associated with deconcentrated power. Those that do not find a significant association between scale and deconcentration are characterized by relatively small and unrepresentative samples, which may explain their non-robust results. (Important, the coefficient for population is usually in the expected direction, even if it does not reach statistical significance at traditional thresholds.)

However, an important caveat should be noted before concluding our discussion of this massive and confusing topic. Power concentration may be affected by both the demographic and the geographic size of a polity. In this study, we make a theoretical choice to treat territory as a prior cause, and hence as an instrument in instrumental-variable analyses (Chapter 2). However, it could be that territory has direct effects on institutions (rather than operating indirectly through population). If so, it deserves to be included as a covariate on the right side of our causal models. Doing so attenuates – but does not eliminate – the influence of population on outcomes tested in this chapter. Even so, for most outcomes examined in this chapter, population has a much stronger empirical relationship to power concentration than territory, which is consistent with our decision to treat the latter as a prior cause (an instrument). With this caveat, we regard the results displayed in Table 11.4 as dispositive.

This result mirrors the pattern found in most organizations – firms, agencies, associations, unions, interest groups, and the like. In this literature ("org theory"), what we call *power concentration* is usually referred to as *centralization*, i.e., centralization of decision-making in the hands of an organization president or board. A recent textbook concludes that, "in general, research suggests that increasing size is associated with a decline in centralization" (Tolbert & Hall 2009: 63). Note that the mechanisms at work within an organization are likely to be somewhat different from the dynamics at work in a polity. Still, an interesting, broad pattern of congruence occurs across these very different species of social organization.

12 Intervention

Previous chapters dealt primarily with political attitudes, behaviors, and institutions. In this chapter, we undertake to explain the course of public policy – specifically, the degree to which governments intervene in the social and economic affairs of citizens. This includes "infrastructural power" (Mann 1986), the "welfare state" (Wilensky 1975), the regulation of moral behavior (Devlin 1959; Donzelot 1979; A. Hunt 1996, 1999; Steinmetz 1993), and all manner of other domestic policies.

One end of the imagined spectrum may be labeled "statist," "activist," or "Big Government," while the other end of the spectrum might be labeled "laissez-faire," "limited government," or "Small Government" – with the caveat that these terms express ideal types that no actual polity fully embodies.

Intervention is a contentious subject. While all may agree that the existence of a state is necessary for preserving order and providing basic public goods like security and property rights, there is visceral disagreement over how extensive the state's role should be. Scholars debate the extent to which the state is effective in redistributing income from rich to poor and in providing public goods such as physical infrastructure (communications, transportation, electricity), education, health care, unemployment insurance, and old age pensions (Castles et al. 2012; Shleifer 1998). Scholars also debate the extent to which fiscal and regulatory policies encourage growth, as the developmental state model suggests (Kohli 2004; Woo-Cumings 1986), or distort the market and discourage investment, as the neoliberal model suggests (Alesina & Perotti 1997; Buchanan & Tullock 1962; Shleifer & Vishny 2002).[1] These ostensibly empirical questions are intertwined with questions of justice that bear on the state's right (Hayek 1944; Nozick 1974) – or, alternatively, its responsibility (Rawls 1971) – to intervene in society.

We do not need to settle these questions in order to appreciate the importance of our topic, which addresses the prior question. Why are

---

[1] For further discussion see Bates (2008) and Wren (2008).

some governments big and others small? We begin by setting out our argument. In the empirical section, we turn to a variety of empirical terrains including the growth of the American state, the experience of small states (everywhere), and four policy realms – moral policy, fiscal policy, personnel policy, and social policy. A short concluding section summarizes the evidence.

Theory

Explanations of state intervention are many and various (Tanzi & Schuknecht 2000). Socioeconomic factors include modernization (Peacock & Scott 2000) and trade/globalization (Cameron 1978; Iversen & Cusack 2000; Katzenstein 1985; Rodrik 1998; Rudra 2002). Political-sociological factors include social heterogeneity (Alesina & Glaeser 2004), the organization of labor unions, and the strength of leftist parties (Cameron 1978; Esping-Andersen 1990). Among political institutions, scholars have identified regime type and a variety of democratic institutions – e.g., proportional representation, the size of parliaments, and unitary constitutions – as causes of government growth (Alesina & Glaeser 2004; Castles et al. 2012).

In this chapter, we highlight the role of polity size, which lies prior to many of the foregoing factors. For Rousseau, large scale signals intrusiveness and oppression.

[A]dministration is more difficult over large distances, just as a weight becomes heavier at the end of a longer bar, and it also becomes more onerous as the hierarchy of divisions increases; each town, to start with, has its administration, paid for by the inhabitants; each district too has its own, also paid for by the inhabitants; then each province; then the greater administrative areas, satrapies or vice-royalties, the cost of which increases from one level to the next, but still at the expense of the unhappy inhabitants; finally comes the supreme administration that crushes everything underneath. (Rousseau 1994[1762] Book II, ch. 9: 82)

Contra Rousseau, we argue that larger polities are *less* interventionist. The distance accorded citizens may be regarded positively, as a source of liberty, or negatively, as a source of neglect. Our focus, in any case, is on demography as a distal cause. Specifically, we argue that scale exerts a negative effect on intervention via decreased social cohesion, decreased vulnerability, decreased need for boundary maintenance, decreased representativeness and trust, decreased particularism, decreased concentration, and increased economies of scale, as diagramed in Figure 12.1. Many of these factors are introduced in other chapters, so our treatment here is brief and focuses on connections to public policy.

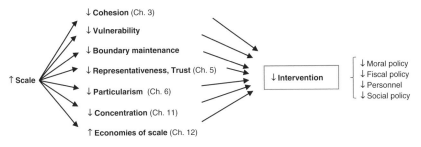

Figure 12.1 Scale effects on intervention

Cohesion

As a product of size, larger societies are less cohesive – more heterogeneous and more likely to experience lower levels of generalized trust and social responsibility (Chapter 3). Note that social welfare is a community good insofar as one identifies as part of that community. But if the community is heterogeneous, social identities may function in an exclusive rather than inclusive fashion. Citizens may not be inclined to sacrifice their tax dollars to support people different from themselves. This, in turn, may impede the development of expansive social policies (Alesina & Glaeser 2004).

By contrast, in small and homogeneous societies citizens are more likely to have the impression that beneficiaries of expensive social programs are people just like themselves – the *deserving* poor, in other words. The principle of reciprocity suggests that we should help others who are like ourselves, for someday we may find ourselves in their position. Small, homogeneous societies may therefore generate greater support for redistributive policies and public goods – the heart of the welfare state.

Relatedly, in a small society there is likely to be greater consensus on norms and values. In this environment there should be little objection to government actions that enforce those norms. Indeed, it may be expected. This is the communitarian ideal (Sandel 1982; Walzer 1983). By contrast, in a large society, where dissensus is the rule rather than the exception, there are fewer areas in which government can play a fiscal or regulatory role without upsetting important constituencies. The latter are likely to protest in defense of (what they see as) their individual rights and liberties. The absence of cohesion thus serves as a brake on government intervention even if the policy is focused on regulating moral behavior and requires little in the way of funding.

Vulnerability

Intervention is also fostered by the vulnerability of small communities (Chapter 13). Economic vulnerability means that capital and labor may be more inclined to see their fates as entwined, rather than antagonistic. Katzenstein (1985: 34; see also Rodrik 1998) writes,

> Economic openness and dependence established a compelling need for consensus, which through complex and delicate political arrangements has transformed conflict among the main social forces in small European states. Truces between business community and labor movement were expressed in Norway's "Basic Agreement" of 1935, Switzerland's "Peace Agreement" of 1937, Sweden's "Saltsjobaden Agreement" of 1938, the Netherland's fifth corporatist chapter of the new Constitution of 1938, and Belgium's "Social Solidarity Pact" of 1945.

Corporatism, in turn, led to an enhanced regulatory and fiscal apparatus, serving as the political backbone of welfare states in many small European states (Cameron 1978).

For similar reasons, consociational agreements are more likely to be struck and to stick in small states than in large states (Lijphart 1977; Lorwin 1971). Daalder (1974: 610) declares consociationalism to be "the privilege of small states." Here, heterogeneity is overcome by small size, which facilitates elite bargaining across ethnic or religious cleavages. This sort of institutionally mediated policy process is also likely to foster the growth of encompassing welfare states.

Before quitting this subject we must consider one possible counter-argument. The dependence of small communities on trade (including investment) may also constrain government intervention. In particular, policies that interfere with free trade will bear heavily on export-oriented producers and consumers. Since investors presumably prefer business environments with low taxes and few regulatory burdens, small communities – who must be especially sensitive to their preferences – may be constrained to limit the growth of the welfare state. Large communities, by contrast, enjoy greater freedom to set fiscal and regulatory policies as they see fit.

The forces of globalization thus appear to work against our argument. Note that although discussion of these topics often focuses on nation-states, the same dynamic ought to obtain among subnational units, i.e., states and localities, which also compete for scarce capital and across which capital is even more mobile. This is why we prefer the generic term *community* – capturing both national and subnational political units. Likewise, *trade* should be understood here to refer to economic exchanges (of goods, services, and investment capital) that extend beyond the borders of a community, whether that community is national or subnational.

Although plausible, arguments based on trade dependence are open to a number of objections. First, in considering the preferences of capitalists (i.e., investors) we must count not only low taxes and regulatory burdens but also other factors that investors prize when deciding where to place their bets. This includes infrastructure, human capital, security, and a well-developed legal system such that property rights, broadly construed, are clearly defined and enforced (Globerman & Shapiro 2002). These factors evidently require extensive government intervention – i.e., taxing, spending, and regulation.

Second, trade dependence means that communities are more vulnerable to international market fluctuations, over which they have no control. These vulnerabilities apply to both producers and consumers, and may prompt calls for greater government involvement – e.g., in social insurance, unemployment insurance, and other welfare initiatives – as a way to insulate citizens from market instability. In this respect, trade dependence may lead to more expansive state intervention (Cameron 1978; Iversen & Cusack 2000; Katzenstein 1985; Rodrik 1998; Rudra 2002).

Finally, one must consider the specific mechanisms by which fiscal and regulatory policies are crafted. While these mechanisms are typically conceptualized in a unidimensional fashion – from low intervention to high intervention – a good deal of nuance must be accounted for. Specifically, it is possible for governments to tax and spend at very high levels, and to regulate many aspects of social and economic affairs, without antagonizing the interests of businesses. They can do so by keeping business taxes low while raising revenue through a variety of tax instruments that have benefits, especially consumption taxes, and by pursuing regulatory goals in a cooperative manner with the businesses they seek to regulate. Nordic countries, as well as Switzerland, provide exemplars of this business-friendly approach to the welfare state, while the United States is often cited as an example of an antibusiness approach to taxing, spending, and regulation (Jasper 1990; Kagan 2001; Kelman 1981; Pontusson 2005; Steinmo 1996; Swenson 2002; Wilensky 2002; J. Wilson 1989).

Arguably, success in crafting welfare state initiatives that harmonize business interests with labor and consumer interests is partly the product of diminutive size. In addition, power concentration and the absence of veto players mean that small units can be much more flexible in crafting or adjusting their economic policies. It is easier to solve coordination problems when there are fewer actors and where social cohesion is high. This may explain why smaller societies are more likely to develop corporatist forms of economic representation and bargaining. Indeed, all of the states classified as possessing corporatist forms of labor and business intermediation are quite small (Katzenstein 1985; Western 1991).

For all these reasons, we surmise that trade dependence does not contradict the previous arguments for why scale should be inversely related to government intervention. It may even enhance them.

Boundary Maintenance

Public policy is not simply a mechanism for maximizing material objectives – income, education, health care, and so forth. It also serves as a mechanism for boundary maintenance, delineating what is unique and special about one community relative to other communities (Barth 1969; Douglas & Wildavsky 1983; Erikson 1966).

Our sense is that smaller communities may be more concerned with boundary maintenance than larger communities, and hence more absorbed with regulating moral policy. Nathanael Hawthorne's evocative story *The Scarlet Letter* is situated in a town, not in a large city or state. Indeed, it is difficult to imagine such a drama playing out on a large scale. (Examples of genocide and ethnic cleansing come to mind, but they are relatively rare.) Larger communities tend to adopt a more inclusive approach to membership and are less intent on retaining purity, establishing specific criteria for membership, and policing behavior.

Everyday language reinforces the impression that small is exclusive and large is inclusive. Compare "narrow sect" with "broad church," or "ideological party" with "catch-all party." We expect that the first of these paired comparisons will be small and restrictive, and the second large and encompassing. One might also consider different sorts of groups. It is presumably difficult to gain entry into a family or a club but not so difficult to gain entry into a party or social movement. Not coincidentally, the former is small and the latter is large.

Of course, these tendencies are reinforcing: a group with tight boundaries is probably less likely to expand, while a group with loose boundaries can more easily admit new members. However, attitudes toward boundaries may also be affected by size. The larger – and by extension, the more heterogeneous – the group, the harder it is to define who is "in" and who is "out." And, perhaps, the less important this issue becomes in light of other goals. These factors should affect the likelihood that governments will adopt an interventionist stance.

Representativeness, Trust

We demonstrated that larger communities are at pains to satisfy demands for representativeness, and experience lower levels of political trust (Chapter 5). Trust in public officials is essential if government is to intervene in society – collecting taxes, reallocating money, and regulating the market and private affairs. Where trust is lacking, we can anticipate that citizens will be loath to delegate power to the state. Even if they agree with a policy they may not trust the government to implement it fairly, now and in the future. In the absence of trust, campaign promises are only words and do not convey a mandate to rule – at least not in an expansive fashion (Braithwaite & Levi 1998).

Particularism

We argued that smaller communities foster intimate ties between politicians and citizens, leading to a particularistic style of policymaking (Chapter 7). As a result, we expect to find higher levels of specialized payoffs to specific constituencies.

A bit of patronage, pork, and vote-buying is insignificant in the grand budgets of modern public sectors. However, targeted spending sometimes translates into enduring fiscal commitments that grow in an inexorable fashion over time. An example of this is public pensions, which focus on a small cadre of public officials but consume an increasing share of many government budgets (Clark, Munnell, & Orszag 2006), and which have been linked to the power of public sector unions (Anzia & Moe 2014). Likewise, patronage appointments, a common response to particularistic political pressures (Golden 2003), can enhance the size of government if it means that civil servants are overpaid, oversupplied, and underproductive (Angelopoulos, Philippopoulos, & Vassilatos 2009).

Another area of particularism concerns the regulation of the market. Commonly, regulations evolve in response to demands from business sectors and labor unions. If regulations are constructed in a particularistic fashion they will serve to entrench special interests rather than to preserve contestation and provide public goods. For example, governments may establish licensing rules that limit entry into professions, allowing practitioners to maintain above-market prices (Svorny 2000). Over time, a particularistic style of policymaking can generate a large fiscal and regulatory load.

Deconcentrated Power

Now let us consider the role of political institutions. We argued in the previous chapter that larger communities foster more fragmented political institutions. Where power is deconcentrated, there are more veto points, and therefore fewer policy initiatives will clear the bar. It follows that these communities will also face greater difficulty in altering the status quo. Insofar as most legislation involves *increasing* the scope of governmental intervention, setting a low bar to governmental activity should translate into a more interventionist policy regime.

In principle, a concentrated political structure could also lead to the easy dismantling of interventionist policies if an anti-statist party gains control of government. However, once enacted, expansionist policies often generate constituencies among the beneficiaries of those policies. These constituencies become obstacles to overturning the policy, as passionate beneficiaries – who have something concrete to lose if a policy is overturned – typically outweigh the less passionate opposition of citizens who do not benefit from the policy but must pay for its costs. Concentrated benefits trump diffuse costs. In this fashion, government policy may experience a "ratchet effect" (Higgs 1989), expanding more easily than it contracts by virtue of positive feedback loops (Barnes & Burke 2015: 23–26; A. Campbell 2011, 2012).

Economies of Scale

A final factor to consider is the efficiency that comes from returns to scale. Larger firms usually can produce the same outputs with fewer inputs (Chandler 1990; Sawyer 1991; Stigler 1958). It stands to reason that similar economies of scale might be realized by governments (E. Robinson 1963).

Several reasons may be adduced. First, a larger government enjoys greater bargaining power when purchasing goods and services, so it may be in a position to negotiate a lower price. Second, managerial tasks may be conducted more efficiently over a larger number of units. In particular, administrative duplication may be avoided. Third, when producing its own goods and services, a larger government may benefit from a more advanced division of labor, allowing that government to take full advantage of specialized expertise that would not be supportable in a small government.

Finally, the costs of public infrastructure probably do not increase in a linear fashion with population. Once a transportation system is in place, additional people can use that road, railroad, harbor, or airport with minimal cost for upkeep and improvement – likewise for sanitation systems, electrical grids, and the administration of licenses and other regulatory apparatuses. Population growth places some strain on environmental policies, but any benefits from those policies are shared equally by all citizens, regardless of their number. The expense associated with defending a country likewise does not increase with population growth (indeed, it may decline insofar as a larger population makes a country more powerful). Public goods are non-rival.

Economists suspect that economies of scale tap out at a certain point, e.g., when the size of a firm begins to exacerbate problems of governance (communication, decision-making, oversight). If a curvilinear – U-shaped – relationship between scale and efficiency exists in firms, it is possible that it also exists in polities, for similar reasons. Thus, one might expect economies of scale to be non-monotonic after a certain (difficult to determine) point. (Empirically, we see no sign of this, however.) In summary, if there are economies of scale, and if the relationship is monotonic, larger communities should have smaller, less intrusive governments.

Evidence

To probe the thesis that size is related to levels of intervention we begin with a historical sketch of a single country – the United States. Next, we turn to an ethnographic analysis of small states. And finally, we explore specific policy areas – moral, fiscal, personnel, and social.

American Political Development

The United States is not a typical country in most respects, which may prompt skepticism that general lessons can be learned by examining its history. Yet every country exhibits "exceptional" features, and all of these features may impact their history of government intervention. Note also that the United States has always occupied a special position in debates over the development of the state and of social welfare policies. In scholarly terms, it is an especially prominent case. For our current theoretical preoccupation it is also well positioned, having undergone enormous changes in scale over its short history. Finally, the United States affords the prospect of comparing policymaking at different levels – national and subnational. Thus, for a variety of reasons, it is fruitful to dwell on the policy history of the United States prior to engaging cross-national comparisons.

Readers should appreciate that this is an outline of an argument that would demand a good deal of space if one were to offer suitable historical detail and appropriate footnotes to the voluminous literature on American political development. We regard this short sketch as an illustration of what that much longer study might look like. We do not expect readers to be entirely convinced, but we do hope they will glimpse the outlines of how demography could be integrated into the well-trodden narrative of American history.

In the eighteenth and nineteenth centuries, the dominant political units in the United States were state and local. A wealth of historical work testifies to the fact that these governmental units were intimately involved in the regulation of business, labor, property, morality, public health and safety, and in the establishment of public schools, canals, railroads, police, poor relief, and other early social welfare initiatives (Benson 1955; Bourgin 1989; Brock 1984; Bryce 1908: 53–48; Gerstle 2009; Go & Lindert 2010; Goodrich 1960; Handlin & Handlin 1969; Hartz 1948; Hurst 1956; Novak 1996; Scheiber 1969, 1972; Teaford 2002). At subnational levels, American governments were at least as interventionist as European national states – a little ahead in education and a little behind in poor relief and social insurance (Garfinkel, Rainwater, & Smeeding 2010: ch. 5; Lindert 2004: ch. 3).

Granted, the US federal government was also engaged, sponsoring the rise of a national postal service (John 2009), soldiers' pensions (Skocpol 1992), a railway system (Dunlavy 1994), and land grant colleges (Geiger 2014). However, relative to European national governments its involvement in social and regulatory policy was episodic and ad hoc, e.g., a response to wars and recessions or partisan demands for government patronage, often implemented through tariffs, one-time legislative packages, or giveaways of federal land. In the United States, domestic policies remained the province of state and municipal governments.

In the twentieth century, as the industrial revolution proceeded, it became difficult to legislate locally for problems that were clearly national in scope. During the Progressive and New Deal eras, the nexus of policy-making shifted accordingly from subnational to national levels (Graebner 1977), spurring an immense centralization of power (Skowronek 1982). Even so, that shift did not match the centralization of power occurring in governments elsewhere in the world. Only briefly and episodically – e.g., in response to the exigencies of the Great Depression – did the US federal government attain the taxing and spending authority of national states in other industrial economies. Where American social policy remained strong, it was in areas like education, where the primary initiative remained with states and localities or with private entities (Garfinkel et al. 2010; Goldin & Katz 1997; Lindert 2004: chs. 5–6), or in regulatory policy, including rights-based regulations, where direct costs to government were minimal and where judicial activity substituted for legislative activity (Keller 1981, 1990; Skrentny 2006).[2] In various respects, the

---

[2] Garfinkel et al. (2010) argue that the United States is less of a welfare state laggard than is traditionally thought. However, their measurement of welfare state engagement counts things like tax credits, subsidies, and employer contributions. While this might make sense for some purposes, our goal is to measure the degree of intervention exercised by the

United States is aptly described as a modern society imprisoned in a "Tudor" polity (Huntington 1968).

One might blame this pattern of policymaking on the deconcentrated institutions inherited from the federal US Constitution, where power was constitutionally divided between national and state authorities and, at each level, split among independent branches. From our perspective, however, constitutional features are endogenous to demography (Chapter 11). This seems especially clear in the present case, where the constricting nature of the US Constitution was a precondition of the federal compact that united thirteen separate, diverse, and jealous colonies into a single national state. Federation was possible so long as the national power was fettered – by a federal constitution, the Bill of Rights, and countervailing institutions ("checks and balances") at the national level (Rakove 1997).

In any case, it was not simply an institutional failing. New Yorkers were willing and able to solve coordination problems among themselves, and likewise for Virginians and Wisconsinites. But when it came to tackling these questions in a larger, national context – with Americans who were very different and distant from themselves – they were less successful. To make policy at the federal level, Americans had to come together across deep cultural and regional cleavages – Protestant versus Catholic, agrarian versus industrial, black versus white, not to mention the enduring scar of the Civil War, which pitted Northerners against Southerners (Bensel 1984).

Thus, even though the capacity of the American state continued to grow in the twentieth century, this growth did not compare with the growth of state power in other advanced industrial countries. It was at this point that America became a "welfare laggard."

Some argue that this failure had deep cultural roots in an anti-statist, libertarian political culture inherited from Britain (Hartz 1955; Lipset 1996). However, one must also consider ways in which demography conditioned the liberal myth. American liberalism was scarcely a well-defined ideology prior to the American Revolution. During the Revolution, the ire of libertarians was focused on George III and on the English Parliament, which oppressed the colonists (or so it seemed) with

government. Forbearing to collect a tax or compelling companies to contribute to an employee's benefits counts as a rather weak form of intervention. Note that tax credits can balloon the apparent size of the welfare state simply by raising the amount of money statutorily owed by citizens and then allowing them to hold onto it. In this respect, tax credits perform for the government the same function that consumer rebates and differential pricing (where there is a difference between the sticker price and the actual price) perform for companies and universities.

taxes. After the Revolution, Southerners, agrarians, and the Democratic Party that represented them adopted the mantle of liberty and anti-statism – motivated, in part, by the desire to protect the "peculiar institution" and, in the aftermath of the Civil War, ongoing racial segregation and oppression. In the twentieth century, the mantle passed to business interests, motivated to preserve low taxes and free markets, and the Republican Party that represented them (Gerring 1998).

Thus, throughout the life of the republic the intervention of big government has been feared for specific reasons by specific constituencies. While this might seem to corroborate the Hartzian story, one must bear in mind the components from which this tradition was built and sustained. Arguably, Americans regarded their government as an enemy because the community that government served was so large and so diverse. They had little faith that a government apparently removed from local control would do their bidding. Instead, it seemed more likely to be captured by special interests, who would use their power in selfish ways, undermining liberties and impugning property rights. Alternatively phrased, Americans feared that the American government would not do what they wanted because what they wanted (individually) was (collectively) quite diverse. Southerners did not want to lose their property (read: slaves). Northerners did not want to lose theirs (read: corporate capital). Protestants did not want to be ruled by Papists. Catholics preferred that the authority of the Protestant-dominated national government be kept to a minimum. (Prohibition was just one instance of the oppressions that Catholics rightly feared.)

Arguably, the hostility many Americans feel toward the state has never been a principled objection to state power or a principled defense of individual liberty. Instead, it has been a pragmatic defense of interests and values that are local in character. "States' rights" did not mean that government should be limited; it meant that the powers of the *national* government should be limited. It was a question of local control. Gerstle (2015: 4) points out that anti-statists "are surprisingly comfortable taking a libertarian stand with regard to federal government policies while supporting initiatives in their states that are plainly coercive in intent and effect." Majority rule is a comfortable adage with respect to local power – but not with respect to national power.

Massachusetts, Virginia, and Pennsylvania are "commonwealths." The United States, by contrast, is a multifarious society of warring tribes who gather together for common defense but have never been keen on sharing their wealth with one another or delegating power to a government that could rule over them in an authoritative fashion. The same factors that impeded the development of the welfare state also impeded the development of a unified labor movement and a political party representing the interests of the working class. Ironically, a large, diverse society was *not* ripe for universalistic, socialistic politics (Kraditor 1981).

By contrast, in little (and homogeneous) Sweden a strong labor movement, a social democratic party, and a solidaristic public philosophy developed in the early twentieth century. There, the state is viewed as the "people's home," echoing a myth with deep roots in Swedish history (Childs 1936; Heclo & Madsen 1987). The secret underpinning of the so-called *Swedish way* is a small and homogeneous society that views itself as having common interests and values. Smallness fosters a communitarian ethic and "socialist" (from an American perspective) public policies.

What could be accomplished in a state the size of Sweden was more difficult to achieve in a state that was, in the twentieth century, nearly the size of Western Europe. From this perspective, the growth of the American state was stunted by the difficulty of scaling up from subnational to national levels. Americans were not separated from their European forbears by constitutional or cultural barriers. Indeed, they came from Europe, and it is a "stretcher" (as Mark Twain might say) to imagine that those who left for the New World were so different from those who stayed behind. The vast majority emigrated for economic reasons, not because they held philosophical objections to their native political culture.

But there were more transplanted Europeans in the newly founded United States than in the countries they had left behind, a lot more (by the twentieth century). And migrants from Africa, Europe, and Mexico, along with the few surviving Native Americans, were collectively *much* more diverse than the societies they left behind. This complicated the task of state-building, meaning that the national government would have a smaller purview and taxing and spending programs would not be as extensive.

This argument is consonant with others that have attributed the weakness of American social policy to the extraordinary heterogeneity of the country (e.g., Alesina & Glaeser 2004; Lipset 1996) – an argument that may be generalized to explain taxation and social policies in other countries (Lieberman 2009). Where people are different from one another they are less inclined to identify as members of a single community and to support solidaristic policies.

However, we have more faith in population as an exogenous causal factor than in measures of heterogeneity, for a variety of reasons (articulated more fully in Chapter 3). First, the latter are likely to be endogenous to the former. That is, a larger population is likely to foster diversity while a small population will foster cohesion. Second, diversity is affected by so many factors – possibly including the outcomes of interest – that it is hard to interpret in a causal fashion. Finally, it is devilishly tricky to measure diversity since there are so many dimensions upon which people may differ. In their work on American exceptionalism Alesina and Glaeser (2004: 139) construct a bespoke index of "racial fractionalization" on which the United States scores high and the comparison cases – Austria, Belgium, Denmark, France, Germany, Italy, Netherlands, Norway, Portugal, Spain, Sweden, Switzerland, and United Kingdom – score low. This is certainly plausible – or was, at any rate, at the time of publication. But it seems to reduce the entire analysis to a single feature of American society that has little resonance in other societies, with the possible exception of South Africa. (The authors do not present a global index of racial fractionalization along the lines of fractionalization indices based on ethnicity, language, and religion [Alesina et al. 2003].) In Table 12.1 we interrogate this issue in a cross-national context, showing that various global indices of fractionalization bear only a weak relationship to government intervention as measured by fiscal policy.

Of course, we do not mean to imply that scale is the *sole* cause of American exceptionalism, the prime mover of everything that happened after 1776. We acknowledge that it is difficult to separate the influence of scale from all the other factors that may have affected the trajectory of American political development – the frontier, early democratization, social heterogeneity, weak parties, a weak and fragmented labor movement, a weak and evanescent socialist party, a liberal political culture, a majoritarian electoral system, constitutional fragmentation, and so forth (Garfinkel et al. 2010: ch. 5; Lipset 1996; Lipset & Marks 2001; Skocpol & Ikenberry 1983). The same problem inhibits our ability to reach unit-level causal inferences for most large-scale questions, as suggested in the Preface. This does not make case-level evidence irrelevant. However, such evidence must be complemented by other sorts of evidence, to which we now turn.

Small States

For a second empirical terrain we turn to small states. Baldacchino and Veenendaal (2018) find that in small polities the state is "ubiquitous and omnipresent," involved in all sorts of social interactions that would escape notice in a large polity. Not only is the state more active but it also has a more dominant position vis-à-vis other institutions, which are often weakened through political appointments, lack of funding, or political pressure. In small states, the central government typically controls –

directly or indirectly – a majority of public service jobs and a good many private sector jobs, meaning that many citizens are for all intents and purposes economically dependent on the state. Randall Baker (1992: 10) reports that in the British crown colony of St. Helena two-thirds of the active population are members of the civil service. Although this is admittedly an extreme example, it is fair to say that in a microstate little can be accomplished outside the purview of the state, which has a hand in many economic activities. There is, accordingly, very little separation between state and society.

The combination of power concentration (Chapter 11) and high levels of politicization amplifies the penetration of government and politics into citizens' private lives. In St. Kitts and Nevis, one informant remarks,

The government has become very big and intrusive. . . . At a certain point the government bought the sugar estate lands. Now if the government owns most of the productive land in a small society like this, and if the government controls most of the jobs apart from the private sector, then it gives the government a great deal of clout in terms of who will live and will die.

A similar situation exists in Suriname, as a member of parliament (MP) remarked during an interview:

The point is that we have politicized everything, this is the problem. As the Parliamentary Speaker once told me: "[E]ven the smallest grain of sand in this country has to do with politics." It is intertwined with everything; the trade unions have been encapsulated, the business sector as well, even churches have been penetrated by politics. And I think this is a very unhealthy situation.

In Chapter 6, we argued that small polities are prone to particularistic styles of policymaking and to patronage. Because jobs in the public sector are likely to be assigned on the basis of personal connections or party service, public employees risk losing their jobs whenever there is a change in government. The inescapability of government in small societies also limits the ability of citizens to freely express themselves, as this might harm them or their family members. An academic in St. Kitts argues,

You find that the long tentacles of government tend to permeate the entire society, so you get entangled in it. If anyone of us would wish . . . to build a house, you go to a government bank to get a loan, and it would be very unwise of you to go and oppose a government policy, knowing that they can fire you any time. And then you might have two or three children in school, or you might have a brother or sister also working for government, or government related. . . . So therefore, this sense of entanglement in government, it muzzles people's willingness to express themselves.

When asked to explain the extremely high turnout levels in Malta, a Maltese politician pointed out:

Because it's Russian roulette, it's do or die. If my party is in, I am going to get the favors. It is easier for me to get whatever I need. If my party is not in, I am finished. So we have to vote, because if not, you know, you risk 10–15 years being in opposition.

In summary, governments in small states appear to play an extraordinarily prominent role in the private lives of citizens in small polities, resulting in a general perception that politics are inescapable. In large polities, by contrast, the literature suggests – and our own experience confirms – that government is more distant, perhaps even aloof. We turn now to different sorts of public policies.

Moral Policy

Policies that are grounded in the perceived appropriateness – or deviance – of behavior we refer to as *moral*. This includes the regulation of recreational drugs (e.g., tobacco, alcohol, marijuana, and all variety of pharmaceuticals), gambling, sexuality and family (e.g., homosexuality, prostitution, incest, age of consent, marriage, miscegenation, venereal disease, rape, divorce, adultery, bastardy, abortion, childrearing), diet (e.g., fasts or prohibitions on certain foods), hygiene, dress, music, comportment (e.g., lewd behavior, decency, vagrancy), language (e.g., official and proscribed languages and censorship), religion, workdays and holidays, out-groups (e.g., immigrants, minorities, slaves, women), indigence and delinquency, and death (end of life, euthanasia). With respect to categories of legislation, moral policy relates most closely to criminal law, religious law, family law, and sumptuary law (Burke 1978; De Swaan 1990; Devlin 1959; Donzelot 1979; Gusfield 1963; Hunt 1996, 1999; Steinmetz 1993).

Our theory suggests that regulation of these sorts of policies is more common in smaller communities, where there is apt to be greater homogeneity and hence more consensus on contentious matters relating to morality. Note also that since these policies are usually understood as deontological moral absolutes, i.e., things that are categorically right or wrong regardless of their effects, there is less scope for compromise than there might be in other policy areas.

Unfortunately, intervention in moral policy is not an easy matter to measure and hence to test in a systematic fashion, and we are unaware of any wide-ranging work on the subject. However, some anecdotal evidence may be gathered for the proposition that smaller communities are more likely to regulate the moral affairs of their citizens.

Our research on small states suggests that they are more likely to regulate moral issues than their larger neighbors. At present, for example, microstates such as Andorra, Liechtenstein, Malta, Monaco, and San Marino are the only Western European countries in which abortion is prohibited.

In large countries, it appears that the regulation of morality is often regarded as appropriate for subnational regulation but not national-level regulation. In India, for example, alcohol is regulated – and sometimes prohibited – at state levels, but not at national levels (Luca, Owens, & Sharma 2015). Likewise, for other federal countries such as Canada and Nigeria (World Health Organization 2004). In the United States, the list of moral policies regulated at state levels – but not national levels – is long.

From the 1780s to 1860s, southern states stripped Africans and their descendants of legal and human rights; from the 1890s to 1950s, these same states denied African American citizens access to residential areas, jobs, parks, restaurants, water fountains, and toilets marked as white. In the early twentieth century, western states denied East Asian immigrants the right to own land. Various states denied people of all colors the opportunity to drink [alcohol]. Countless state laws regulated sexual behavior, forbade homosexual sex and many forms of contraception, and outlawed literature judged to be obscene. ... As many as half the states forbade marriage across the color line. So-called blue laws ordered the closing of stores and the shutting down of commerce on the Sabbath. As late as 1928, Massachusetts was using a 1640 blasphemy statute to prosecute individuals who had allegedly taken the name of Jesus Christ in vain. (Gerstle 2015: 2)

The American states, Gerstle (2015: 2) concludes, were "miniature Leviathans" that appropriated the constitutional doctrine of *police power* from a monarchist state (England) in order to justify their intrusive policies.

Of course, one might regard federalism as a constitutional constraint on what national governments can do – though our analysis suggests that institutions may be endogenous to demographics (Chapter 11). In any case, the same pattern is also evident when one compares state and local policies, which are not subject to constitutional constraints. Revealing, *local option* – a common lawmaking term in the United States – refers to "the ability of local political jurisdictions, typically counties or municipalities, to allow decisions on certain controversial issues based on popular vote within their borders. In practice, it usually relates to the issue of alcoholic beverage and marijuana sales."[3] Note that prohibition was a national law in the United States for only thirteen years, but it was a local law long before the passage of the Eighteenth Amendment to the

---

[3] Wikipedia entry for "Local option."

US Constitution and it remains a local ordinance in "dry" counties across the South (Clark 1976; Pegram 1998). It appears that the further down one goes – the smaller the governmental unit – the more likely it is that the unit will regulate moral policies.

Fiscal Policy

We turn now to features of government intervention that are easier to measure. The most common approach focuses on fiscal policy – namely, aggregate taxing and spending. *Revenue* may be regarded as a measure of the extractive capacity of government while *expenditure* is a measure of government's implementation capacity. (In practice, they are highly correlated.)

If one measures revenue and expenditure without adjusting to the size of the economy, populous polities will generate bigger governments, as they provide a larger tax base. This is not really a measure of intervention, however. To measure intervention we need to measure fiscal capacity relative to the size of the economy (as a share of GDP) or the size of the population (per capita).

An excellent opportunity to observe the influence of scale on fiscal policy is provided by amalgamations and splits of municipalities. Typically, researchers compare expenditures before and after boundary changes, with a control group provided by municipalities that remain constant (experiencing no change in boundaries). In this sort of natural experiment, larger municipalities have been found to have smaller governments in Brazil (Lima & Silveira Neto 2017), Israel (Reingewertz 2012), the German state of Brandenburg (Blesse & Baskaran 2016), and Sweden (Hanes 2015). However, the opposite finding, or null results, have appeared in studies of municipalities in Finland (Moisio & Uusitalo 2013), the Netherlands (Allers & Geertsema 2016), and Switzerland (Luchinger & Stutzer 2002). Several studies of municipal amalgamations in Denmark have been conducted, with mixed results (Blom-Hansen, Houlberg, & Serritzlew 2014; Blom-Hansen et al. 2016).

Studies using conventional cross-sectional designs also report mixed findings (e.g., Andrews & Boyne 2009; Avellaneda & Gomes 2015; Bel 2013; Drew, Kortt, & Dollery 2012; Holcombe & Williams 2009). In summary, when one looks at the relationship between population and the size of governments at municipal levels there is no consistent finding. This conclusion is supported by several recent surveys of the literature (Avellaneda & Gomes 2015; Blom-Hansen et al. 2014; Blom-Hansen et al. 2016; Holzer et al. 2009).[4]

---

[4] For helpful discussion of this question see Svorny (2003).

At national levels, by contrast, there is a fairly strong consensus that larger units generate lower levels of taxing and spending (Alesina & Spolaore 1997; Alesina & Wacziarg 1998; Rodrik 1998).[5] We follow these studies by looking at two measures of aggregate fiscal policy.

Tax revenue refers to compulsory transfers to the central government for public purposes, considered as a share of GDP (World Bank 2016). Analyses are presented in Table 12.1. Model 1 is a benchmark specification, including only the regressor of theoretical interest along with annual dummies. Model 2 adds a host of covariates. Model 3 is an instrumental variable analysis.

All three models show a strong negative association between population and revenue, considered as a share of GDP. It is true that some of the effect may be a product of the structure of political institutions in small and large societies. If larger countries have more decentralized systems of revenue collection (as argued in Chapter 11), then a measure of revenue that focuses only on revenue collected by central governments will reflect that fact. One may conclude that our estimates are biased upward as a product of government structure, which is to say that the negative association between size and revenue would be attenuated if one were able to measure *total* revenue – across all governments.

Our second measure of fiscal policy does just that. *Government consumption* encompasses spending by central, regional, and local governments. It includes current expenditures for purchases of goods and services, including compensation of employees and most expenditures on national defense and security (but not government military expenditures that are part of government capital formation), expressed as a share of GDP (World Bank 2016). Tests shown in Table 12.1 mirror those for government revenue. All three tests are again highly robust. The governments of larger countries spend less than their counterparts in smaller countries, confirming previous studies.

To gauge the magnitude of this effect, we graph the predicted values for government consumption against population based on estimates from the benchmark model. Figure 12.2 shows that a change in population from 100,000 to 1 million is associated with a decrease in government consumption (per GDP) of about 3 percent – a sizeable, though not spectacular effect. Note, however, that if we follow the trend line all the way to

---

[5] Shelton (2007) does not find robust results. However, the samples in that study are smaller than those employed in our analyses and several variables that probably should be considered endogenous to population (e.g., trade openness) are included in the models, which presumably attenuate the direct effect of population on government size.

Table 12.1 *Aggregate fiscal policy*

Outcome	Tax revenue				Government consumption			
Estimator	OLS	OLS	2SLS	OLS	OLS	2SLS	OLS	OLS
Model	1	2	3	4	5	6	7	8
Population (log)	-0.966***	-0.862**	-0.983**	-0.842***	-0.585***	-0.454**	-0.867***	-0.483**
	(0.273)	(0.346)	(0.439)	(0.204)	(0.213)	(0.221)	(0.178)	(0.223)
GDP per capita (log)		-2.445**			1.479**			1.645**
		(1.187)			(0.695)			(0.678)
Urbanization		2.251			1.077			0.575
		(4.183)			(2.510)			(2.389)
English colony		1.613			0.194			-0.103
		(1.456)			(0.917)			(0.926)
Latitude (log)		1.259*			0.445			0.230
		(0.698)			(0.480)			(0.505)
Muslim		-0.031			-0.012			-0.017
		(0.024)			(0.015)			(0.017)
OPEC		-0.848			-0.758			-0.578
		(4.046)			(1.314)			(1.345)
Protestant		0.012			0.019			0.017
		(0.023)			(0.014)			(0.013)
Age dependency ratio		0.565***			0.283*			0.145
		(0.162)			(0.145)			(0.105)
Democracy (Lexical index)		0.520**			-0.199			-0.063
		(0.214)			(0.200)			(0.139)

Religious fragmentation						0.962	−0.880
(Alesina et al. 2003)						(1.364)	(1.763)
Linguistic fragmentation						0.239	−2.039
(Alesina et al. 2003)						(1.554)	(2.373)
Ethnic fragmentation						−4.569**	−0.386
(Alesina et al. 2003)						(1.785)	(2.316)
Regional dummies	✓	✓			✓	✓	✓
Annual dummies	✓	✓		✓	✓	✓	✓
Decade dummies			✓				
Countries	157	147	149	180	165	171	167	158
Years	45	37	45	57	37	57	57	37
Observations	3,764	2,910	3,649	7,404	4,623	7,224	7,012	4,451
R-squared	0.0540	0.330	0.0530	0.0738	0.299	0.0637	0.132	0.331

Outcomes: tax revenue (share of GDP), government consumption (general government expenditures for goods and services as a share of GDP). *Units of analysis*: country-years. *Lag structure*: right-side variables measured at t−20. Constant omitted. *Estimators*: OLS (ordinary least squares), 2SLS (two-stage least squares using territory and agricultural suitability as instruments). Country clustered standard errors in brackets.
*** $p < 0.01$, ** $p < 0.05$, * $p < 0.10$ (two-tailed tests)

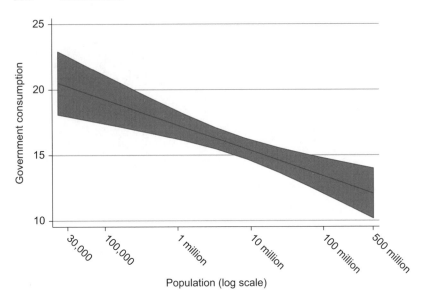

Figure 12.2 Government consumption, predicted values

Predicted values of government consumption as share of GDP (Y), as population (log) changes, surrounded by 95 percent confidence interval. Based on Model 4, Table 12.1, with covariates set to sample means.

the highest population levels we can see a cumulative shift of 15 percent – a very sizeable effect, and one that goes a long way toward explaining the greater fiscal intervention of small states relative to large states.

The final tests in Table 12.1 focus on measures of religious, ethnic, and linguistic fractionalization – all drawn from Alesina et al. (2003). Fractionalization indices, introduced in Chapter 3, use the Herfindahl formula to measure the probability that two randomly chosen individuals belong to the same group. We introduce them here because prior work suggests that heterogeneity, measured in this conventional fashion, may impact the size of government (Alesina & Glaeser 2004). Model 7 follows the benchmark specification and Model 8 follows the full specification. These tests suggest that there is only a weak relationship, at best, between fractionalization indices and aggregate fiscal policy. (Variations in these specifications, e.g., testing each fractionalization on its own, to reduce possible collinearity, has little impact on the results reported in Table 12.1.) They also confirm that the inclusion of these covariates has little impact on the regressor of theoretical interest, population.

Personnel Policy

A second measure of intervention focuses on personnel, i.e., government employees. This is a common benchmark when measuring the size and strength of states, and certainly an important factor in determining what a state can accomplish.

We measure government personnel in two ways – the total compensation expenditure for all government employees as a share of GDP and the total number of public sector employees as a share of population. Empirical tests follow those in Table 12.1. Results posted in Table 12.2 show that larger countries spend less on compensation (Models 1–3) and have fewer government employees (Models 4–6) than smaller countries.

Note that we previously showed that elected officials in larger countries are paid more (individually) than elected officials in smaller countries (Table 10.4), which suggests that it is the smaller number of officials – rather than their compensation – that is driving differences in overall compensation. This is supported by the results of Models 4–6 in Table 12.2.

Figure 12.3, a graph of predicted values based on the benchmark model, shows that a change in population from 100,000 to 1 million is associated with a reduction in employees as a share of the general population from 12 percent to 10 percent. This is roughly one-half of a standard deviation on this measure of government size, a modest but nontrivial decrease. If one follows the projected regression estimates out to the largest countries, at about half a billion, a country is projected to experience a reduction in public sector employment of roughly 7 percent – nearly two standard deviations. So again, we find that large differences in scale matter quite a lot for the style of governance.

Social Policy

In the final set of tests we examine two categories of government expenditure commonly associated with the welfare state and with the redistributive functions of government more generally. The first focuses on public health expenditures and the second on public education expenditures (both considered as a share of GDP). Our specifications follow those in previous tables, with one exception. In Model 4, we run a second instrumental variable model that excludes several cases with extremely high (probably erroneous) values for public health spending.

Results from these seven tests, depicted in Table 12.3, show a negative relationship between population and these two categories of social spending, confirming the general pattern that we observed with aggregate measures of fiscal policy.

Table 12.2 *Government employees*

Outcome	Compensation			Number		
Sample	Full	Full	Full	Full	Full	Full
Estimator	OLS	OLS	2SLS	OLS	OLS	2SLS
Model	1	2	3	4	5	6
Population (log)	−0.011***	−0.011***	−0.013***	−0.732***	−0.674***	−0.558*
	(0.002)	(0.002)	(0.002)	(0.267)	(0.205)	(0.323)
GDP per capita (log)	−0.003	−0.009	−0.002	0.192	1.271	0.033
	(0.004)	(0.008)	(0.004)	(1.238)	(1.163)	(1.224)
Urbanization	−0.002	−0.003	−0.008	6.736	−2.794	6.939
	(0.021)	(0.028)	(0.020)	(5.441)	(2.982)	(5.240)
English colony		0.002			−1.377	
		(0.008)			(1.012)	
Latitude (log)		0.003			−0.974	
		(0.004)			(0.820)	
Muslim		−0.000			−0.042*	
		(0.000)			(0.024)	
OPEC		0.004			1.106	
		(0.011)			(1.052)	
Protestant		−0.000***			0.061***	
		(0.000)			(0.015)	
Age dependency ratio		−0.001			0.215*	
		(0.001)			(0.123)	
Democracy		0.001			−0.182	
		(0.001)			(0.182)	
Regional dummies		✓			✓	
Annual dummies	✓	✓		✓	✓	
Decade dummies			✓			✓
Countries	151	144	143	83	66	80
Years	45	37	45	11	11	11
Observations	3,442	2,732	3,327	674	531	649
R-squared	0.202	0.300	0.191	0.191	0.712	0.159

Outcomes: Employee compensation expenditure (share of GDP), total number of public sector employees (share of population). *Units of analysis*: country-years. *Lag structure*: right-side variables measured at t−20. Constant omitted. *Estimators*: OLS (ordinary least squares), 2SLS (two-stage least squares using territory and agricultural suitability as instruments). Country clustered standard errors in brackets. *** $p < 0.01$, ** $p < 0.05$, * $p < 0.10$ (two-tailed tests)

To visualize the meaning of this relationship we graph the predicted values from our benchmark test of public health expenditure (Model 1, Table 12.3) against population. Figure 12.4 reveals that a change in population from 100,000 to 1 million is associated with a half-point

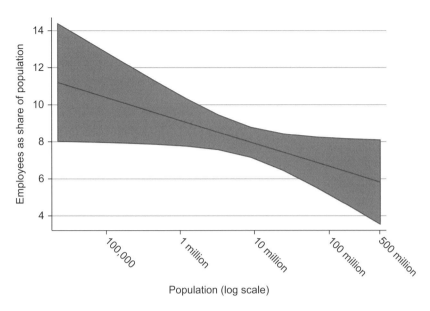

Figure 12.3 Government employees, predicted values

Predicted values of government employees as share of population (Y), as population (log) changes, surrounded by 95 percent confidence interval. Based on Model 1, Table 12.2, with covariates set to sample means.

increase in public health expenditures. Because this is measured as a share (percent) of GDP, this is quite a lot of money.

However, the relationship is neither as strong nor as robust as what we observed in previous analyses focused on aggregate fiscal measures (Table 12.1) and personnel (Table 12.2). Two factors may explain this attenuation. First, countries may define these health and education budget categories differently, generating measurement error in our cross-sectionally dominated analysis. Second, fewer economies of scale may be associated with health and education relative to other budget categories. Consider that the provision of health and education is labor-intensive, and providing services through larger units may not offer any cost advantage to governments in contracting with highly trained (and well-organized) teachers, doctors, and other professionals.

Summary

Extant work and our own analyses of the question of scale and government intervention are summarized in Table 12.4.

Table 12.3 *Public health and education spending*

Outcome	Public Health				Public Education		
Sample	Full	Full	Full	~~Outliers~~	Full	Full	Full
Estimator	OLS	OLS	2SLS	2SLS	OLS	OLS	2SLS
Model	1	2	3	4	5	6	7
Population	−0.194**	−0.161**	−0.122	−0.152**	−0.140**	−0.132**	−0.035
(log)	(0.083)	(0.063)	(0.075)	(0.070)	(0.062)	(0.063)	(0.092)
Urbanization		0.118				−0.454	
		(0.679)				(0.898)	
GDP per		0.075				0.206	
capita (log)		(0.197)				(0.192)	
English colony		0.323				0.814**	
		(0.240)				(0.324)	
Latitude (log)		0.027				0.050	
		(0.170)				(0.194)	
Muslim		−0.001				−0.004	
		(0.004)				(0.006)	
OPEC		−0.404				0.106	
		(0.274)				(0.442)	
Protestant		0.008*				0.017***	
		(0.005)				(0.004)	
Age dependency		0.169***				0.081*	
ratio		(0.031)				(0.044)	
Democracy		0.027				0.025	
		(0.046)				(0.063)	
Regional dummies		✓				✓	
Annual dummies	✓	✓			✓	✓	
Decade dummies			✓	✓			✓
Countries	187	150	174	174	185	163	173
Years	16	16	16	16	47	37	47
Observations	2,944	2,303	2,754	2,692	3,388	2,486	3,280
R-squared	0.0452	0.638	0.0120	0.0167	0.0410	0.241	0.0166

Outcomes: public health expenditure (share of GDP), public education expenditure (share of GDP). *Units of analysis*: country-years. *Lag structure*: right-side variables measured at t−20. Constant omitted. *Estimators*: OLS (ordinary least squares), 2SLS (two-stage least squares using territory and agricultural suitability as instruments). Country clustered standard errors in brackets. *** $p < 0.01$, ** $p < 0.05$, * $p < 0.10$ (two-tailed tests)

Here, one sees a stark contrast between subnational and national-level analyses. The former are mixed in outcome. Some show the expected negative relationship between the scale of political communities and the

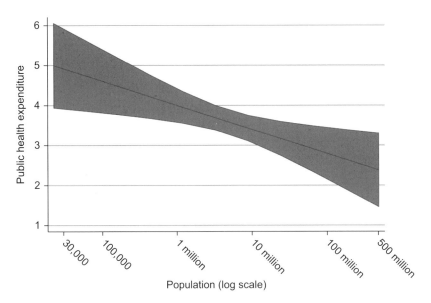

Figure 12.4 Public health expenditure, predicted values

Predicted values of public health expenditure as share of GDP (Y), as population (log) changes, surrounded by 95 percent confidence interval. Based on Model 1, Table 12.3, with covariates set to sample means.

scale of government (judged on a per capita basis and usually by some measure of taxing or spending). Others show no relationship, and one even shows a positive relationship. By contrast, *national*-level analyses show a strong (negative) relationship between the size of communities and the size of government – measured by fiscal policy, personnel policy, and social policy. (We have not been able to systematically test the incidence of moral policy.)

A number of explanations might be offered for this apparent paradox.

First, note that the subnational studies listed in Table 12.4 have fairly strong claims to internal validity. All employ large samples and many employ quasi-experimental designs that capitalize on the amalgamation (occasionally, the division) of municipalities. However, they may be hard to generalize precisely because they are so tightly focused. In particular, they generally examine short-term causal effects, which may or may not be illustrative of long-term effects. Note that lots of things may be stimulated by a municipal amalgamation, including administrative and policy reforms. There may even be agreements with public service unions to

Table 12.4 *Scale and intervention: Inventory of analyses*

Indicators	Countries	Treatment units	Years	Units of analysis	Research design	Effect	Study
Subnational							
Property tax	Brazil	Municipalities (787)	(1)	Municipalities (787)	Cross-sectional	↑	Avellaneda & Gomes 2015
Administrative costs	United Kingdom	Councils (384)	(1)	Councils (384)	Cross-sectional	→	Andrews & Boyne 2009
Expenditures	Australia	Councils (152)	(1)	Councils (152)	Cross-sectional	∅	Drew, Kortt, & Dollery 2012
Expenditures	United States	Municipalities (487)	(1)	Municipalities (487)	Cross-sectional	∅	Holcombe & Williams 2009
Expenditures	Brazil	Municipalities (5,561)	(1)	Municipalities (5,561)	Panel	→	Lima & Silveira Neto 2017
Expenditures	Israel	Municipalities (264)	(8)	Municipality-years (2,144)	Panel	→	Reingewertz 2012
Expenditures	Germany	Municipalities (1,319)	(15)	Municipality-years (6,249)	Panel	→	Blesse & Baskaran 2013
Expenditures	Sweden	Municipalities (2,498)	(3)	Municipality-years (4,508)	Panel	→	Hanes 2015
Expenditures	Finland	Municipalities (539)	(11)	Municipality-years (1,391)	Panel	↑	Moisio & Uusitalo 2013
Expenditures	Netherlands	Municipalities (418)	(14)	Municipality-years (4,433)	Panel	∅	Allers & Geertsema 2016
Expenditures	Switzerland	Municipalities (4)	(9)	Municipality-years (24)	Panel	∅	Luchinger & Stutzer 2002
Administrative costs	Denmark	Municipalities (239)	(1)	Municipalities (239)	Panel	→	Blom-Hansen et al. 2014
Expenditures	Denmark	Municipalities (239)	(1)	Municipalities (239)	Panel	∅	Blom-Hansen et al. 2016

National							
Public consumption	(134)	Countries (134)	(5)	Country-years (616)	Cross-sectional	→	Alesina & Wacziarg 1998
Expenditures	(23)	Countries (23)	(12)	Country-years (125)	Cross-sectional	→	Rodrik 1998
*Tax revenue	(154)	Countries (154)	(45)	Country-years (3,689)	Cross-sectional	→	Table 12.1
*Government consumption	(180)	Countries (180)	(57)	Country-years (7,347)	Cross-sectional	→	Table 12.1
*Personnel compensation	(151)	Countries (151)	(45)	Country-years (3,442)	Cross-sectional	→	Table 12.2
*Personnel, number of	(83)	Countries (83)	(11)	Country-years (674)	Cross-sectional	→	Table 12.2
*Health expenditure	(187)	Countries (187)	(16)	Country-years (2,944)	Cross-sectional	→	Table 12.3
*Education expenditure	(185)	Countries (185)	(47)	Country-years (3,388)	Cross-sectional	→	Table 12.3

Treatment units: units exhibiting variation in scale. *Years*: number of years over which data are collected – not to be confused with the frequency of observations, as data may or may not be annual and may be averaged across years. *Research design*: the main, or benchmark, research design – classified as cross-sectional (where the analysis is driven primarily by variation across units) or panel (where the analysis is driven primarily by variation through time). *Effect*: when the scale of a community increases, the designated outcome goes up ($\uparrow$), down ($\downarrow$), up and down ($\downarrow$), or experiences no perceptible change (∅). A scale effect is considered significant if it passes a modest bar of statistical significance, i.e., $p < 0.10$ (two-tailed test) in the benchmark model. Number of countries, treatment units, years, or observations in parentheses.

protect jobs, which would undercut efficiencies that might otherwise be gained by amalgamation. However, these short-term effects may or may not last into the longer term. Job protections presumably apply only to those currently employed, so downsizing may occur over time as employees resign or retire. Likewise, the instance of a municipal amalgamation may or may not exemplify political processes at work when the population of a municipality changes through normal demographic dynamics (population growth and migration). For these reasons we must be careful in attempting to generalize from municipal amalgamations – a highly unusual event – to the more general question of how municipal size affects government intervention.

Second, it could be that economies of scale exist for some governmental functions but not others, and that those with the greatest scale effects are located at the national level rather than at municipal levels. Baker (1992: 15) points out that "all truly sovereign small states have to uphold the extremely expensive trappings of sovereignty such as UN membership, the diplomatic corps, some defense posture, and so on." All of these functions (and many more) should benefit from economies of scale. Since they have no (or only a very faint) analog at local levels, this might help explain the local/national paradox.

Third, it could be that local governments subcontract many of their services, and the firms that they contract with may operate nationally and thus are large enough to realize economies of scale. If the prices paid by governments are set by a competitive market, then larger governments do not enjoy lower prices than smaller governments (for further discussion see Blom-Hansen et al. 2016). National governments, by contrast, may be constrained to buy goods produced domestically, which means that larger countries – with larger, more competitive markets – would presumably benefit from lower prices. In this fashion, economies of scale might be realized at national levels but not at local levels.

Fourth, it could be that the divergent results are an artifact of variability in the inputs and outputs. There is much less variation at local levels than at national levels. Consider differences in scale, the right-side variable of theoretical interest. Studies of municipal amalgamations are typically focused on instances where two smaller municipalities are merged into a single unit, a doubling in scale. While this might seem substantial, variation across countries is an order of magnitude greater. Cross-national datasets include small states like Luxembourg with populations of half a million or less, along with megastates like India and China, with populations of well over a billion. On the outcome, as well, one finds greater variation cross-nationally than subnationally. Some of this is constitutional or statutory. Note that national governments have greater freedom to set rates of taxing and spending than local governments, and a much wider range of taxing instruments and spending opportunities at their disposal. This means dispersion on both sides of the causal model is greater in cross-national studies than in local-level studies.

Finally, it could be that differences across countries are driven (at least in part) by other scale-based mechanisms, e.g., social cohesion, vulnerability, boundary maintenance, representativeness and trust, particularism, and power concentration, as summarized in Figure 12.1. Arguably, these mechanisms are more likely to manifest themselves at national levels than at subnational levels, accounting for the divergent patterns in national and subnational studies.

In summary, our paradox has many possible answers. We leave it for future research to tease apart which factor(s) might be responsible.

Another interesting feature of the relationship between scale and intervention is not apparent from results posted in this chapter or in other studies but deserves mention nonetheless. The cross-country relationship between scale and intervention is much stronger for the developing world than for the developed world. Specifically, when benchmark models in Tables 12.1–12.3 are replicated with split samples – dividing the world into "rich" and "poor" subsamples – the coefficient estimates for population are much stronger in the latter. That is, the demographic scale of countries appears to have a bigger impact on the scale of their governments in poor economies than in rich economies.

At first, we suspected that this might be a product of foreign aid, which contributes a nontrivial portion of government budgets in the developing world, and is tilted toward small countries. However, the inclusion of covariates measuring foreign aid has no impact on the relationships of theoretical interest.

Next, we considered variability in the outcome. While advanced industrial countries seem to be converging toward high levels of taxing and spending, in the developing world there is still immense variation. The standard deviation of government consumption across the poorer half of countries in our sample is almost twice the standard deviation of the richer half of the sample. If advanced industrial economies are converging, it could be because they are bumping up against some sort of ceiling effect with respect to the size of the state, or it could be that there are especially strong diffusion effects across the OECD community. In any case, the convergence of welfare states at high levels of GDP seems to account for why scale effects are stronger in the developing world than in the developed world. There is more room for Brazil and Uruguay to differentiate themselves than there is for Germany and Luxembourg. This also explains why cross-national analyses of fiscal policy that are centered on the OECD generally show weaker scale effects than analyses that encompass a global sample.

Other nuances could be explored. But these should not divert attention from the main result. Population is inversely related to most measures of government intervention. Larger governments intervene less in the lives of their citizens.

13   Power

Power is a notoriously difficult concept to define and to measure (Bell, Edwards, & Wagner 1969; Lukes 1986; Moriss 1987), so it is with some trepidation that we introduce this fraught topic. Nonetheless, demography appears to have immense ramifications for the power of communities, so it is not a topic that can be side-stepped.

As a working definition (adapted with some modifications from Dahl 1957), we say that one community, A, has power vis-à-vis another, B, insofar as A can get B (or members of B) to think or do things that B would not otherwise think or do. Implied in this definition is that if A has power over B, B does not have power over A. Power is asymmetric. Alternately stated, A is autonomous vis-à-vis B while B is not autonomous vis-à-vis A.

To exercise power is to serve as a causal agent. A notable difference between power and causality is that statements about power are vague about the outcomes that A can achieve. If A is powerful, it is assumed that A can get B to think/do a variety of things – though certainly not all things – that A desires. Another difference between power and causality is that power is a potentiality – the *capacity* to influence B. As such, studies of power usually focus on capabilities that are presumed to have causal force if they were implemented, even if (in the event) they were never implemented.

Power is an abiding concern for sovereign states, who must protect their sovereignty and defend their interests, and often aim to extend influence beyond their geographic borders. Accordingly, the impact of demography on state power is a recognized topic in the study of international relations and international political economy (Alonso 1987; Goetschel 2013; Hey 2003; Keohane 1969; Leroy 1978; McNicoll 1999; Salvatore, Svetlicic, & Damijan 2001; Sciubba 2010; Weiner & Russell 2001).

The idea that population might be important for national power is widely recognized among scholars. Hans Morgenthau, a leading figure in the realist tradition, declared that "no country can remain or become a first rate power which does not belong to the more populous nations of the earth" (Morgenthau 1993[1948]: 140–41; quoted in Krebs & Levy 2001: 64). In succeeding years, numerous scholars have echoed this sentiment (Bull 1987; Davis 1954; Hendershot 1973; Mearsheimer 2001; Organski 1958; Organski & Organski 1961). The assumption is also incorporated into the construction of the widely used Composite Index of National Capability (Singer, Bremer, & Stuckey 1972), which includes population as one of its component parts.

By the same logic, small states are often viewed as vulnerable (Baldersheim & Keating 2015; Benedict 1967; Clarke & Payne 1987; Duursma 1996; Harden 1985; Hintjens & Newitt 1992; Ingebritsen et al. 2012; Katzenstein 1985; Kisanga & Danchie 2007; Maass 2017; Vital 1967). Shridath Ramphal, secretary-general of the British Commonwealth (whose members include many microstates), suggested a poignant metaphor:

[I]t seems as if small states were like small boats, pushed out into a turbulent sea, free in one sense to traverse it; but, without oars or provisions, without compass or sails, free also to perish. Or, perhaps, to be rescued and taken on board a larger vessel. (quoted in Harden 1985: 5)

As a consequence of their vulnerability, small states are often dependent upon a major power to provide security, either through a formal treaty arrangement or informal understandings. Small states are also likely to be more sensitive to external obligations and constraints, including those imposed by international bodies (e.g., the International Monetary Fund, the World Trade Organization, and the World Bank), trading partners, multinationals, and key donors (Lake 2009). Small states, finally, are often vulnerable to non-state actors, e.g., pirates, mercenaries, smugglers, drug cartels, revolutionaries, and putschists. For these reasons, many small jurisdictions around the globe prefer retaining constitutional or military links with a larger metropolitan power in a semi-dependent fashion rather than declaring full and complete independence.

The idea that size brings power is solidly ensconced, as this brief perusal of the literature suggests. However, the thesis is rarely explored in a systematic fashion. In this chapter we begin by laying out a theoretical rationale. Next, we explore the thesis empirically across different dimensions of power – economic, military, and cultural.

Theory

Consider the various facets of power, which we classify as economic, military, and cultural. Each is the product (in part) of human beings. It follows that enhanced numbers of people should bring greater returns (ceteris paribus). *People* translate into *power*.

The point can be illustrated by examining limiting cases. The smallest possible community, consisting of one individual, wields almost no power because everything that individual needs to survive depends upon others, who by definition live outside the community. By contrast, the largest possible community, including the entire population of the world, must contain all the power in the world, as there is no other source of power.

If we assume that all persons are equally powerful, that their power can be combined in an additive fashion, and that power is relative, then the power of a single community can be represented as a ratio of n/N, where n is the population of the community and N is world population. In the foregoing example, the smallest possible community has a power of $1/N$ while the largest possible community (encompassing the entire world) has a power of $n/N = 1$.

Of course, things are not quite so simple. To begin with, the relationship between people and power is attenuated by technology, which vastly enhances the power of those individuals who possess it and can competently wield it. One man with a horse can defeat dozens of men on foot. One man with a machine gun can defeat hundreds of men with rifles. Likewise, the social and cultural impact of a single influential individual is magnified by modern media. Thus, we would expect the relationship between people and power to become weaker over time as technologies advance.

Second, as the size of a community grows so do problems of coordination. This suggests that people power is not a strictly linear function of the number of people. As elsewhere in this book, we treat population as a logarithmic function, which seems like a reasonable approximation of the notion that each additional person in a community matters somewhat less than previous persons in that community. Despite additional coordination problems, we expect the relationship to be monotonic. (There is no reason to suppose that increases in population lead to decreases in collective power, if all else is equal.)

At this point we must inquire what it is, exactly, that people do to generate power. Three mechanisms seem widely applicable.

First, people provide *economic resources*. They can be taxed, which is essential if the end product (that carries or exerts power) is produced by or facilitated by government. And they can serve as consumers, which is essential if the end product is sold in a market.

Second, people provide *human capital*. That human capital may be highly advanced (i.e., highly trained workers with expertise in a particular area) or it may be proletarian (manual labor). Both are essential.

Third, people provide *innovation*. They are inventors, entrepreneurs, and creators. This might be bundled together with human capital, but we prefer to emphasize it as a separate facet of people power.

To be sure, these three mechanisms – capital, human capital, and innovation – interact with one another. Innovations are more likely to be implemented (to become a product of some sort) if there is a large resource base. And they are more likely to lead to other innovations, in a cumulative fashion, if lots of innovators are present in the same society. Nonetheless, they are not equivalent, as each plays an independent role in generating power. The presumed relationships between scale and power are summarized in Figure 13.1.

Clarifications

Together, the capital, human capital, and innovation that a large population affords allows a large society to produce more of the things that a society wants and needs. This should promote greater self-sufficiency. This sort of power is *defensive* insofar as the society is free from outside pressures and influences. At the same time, having more of everything means that a larger society can project its power *outward* into the world. This might be attractive ("soft power") or coercive ("hard power"). It might involve the use of force or peaceful bargaining. In the latter case, a larger society is likely to have the upper hand by virtue of its larger market, larger military, larger government, and greater capacity overall. A large society can throw its weight around, where weight is understood as a manifestation of people power.

Although the question of power is raised in its starkest form in relationships among states, subnational units also engage in a struggle for power. They strive to defend their prerogatives (a limited form of sovereignty), to expand sources of revenue, and to influence national (and sometimes international) policy debates. In this endeavor, size

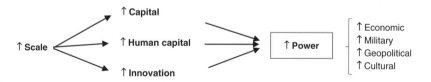

Figure 13.1 Scale effects on power

presumably counts. California is more powerful than Oregon just as the United States is more powerful than Canada. Thus, our theory pertains to all sorts of communities even though – by virtue of data availability and overall prominence – our examples and empirical analysis focus primarily on sovereign states.

A final caveat concerns the external environment. The impact of community size on community power is moderated by the character of the system within which communities operate. If there is no "system" at all – every community pursues its interests without institutional or normative constraints – we can anticipate that the population of each community will have enormous impact on its power. This is the model of anarchy assumed by the realist paradigm of international relations in its simplest form (Morgenthau 1993[1948]; Waltz 1979). By contrast, if there is a higher power, e.g., a system of agreements and international organizations, that governs relations among units, scale may matter less, at least in day-to-day affairs. Larger communities will still have more latent power, but they may be unable to exercise that power if constrained by international institutions and norms.

This raises fundamental questions about the source of that "higher power." We may presume (with realists) that it serves the interests of the more powerful communities; otherwise, it would be unlikely to persist, or would not have been instituted in the first place. If their power is, in part, demographic, then we can assume that the power of scale informs even the most highly institutionalized system – albeit in subtle ways.

We do not intend to sort out eternal questions in the subdiscipline of international relations but merely to point out their applicability to the present circumstance. The bottom line is that those who subscribe to a realist vision of the world are likely to see scale effects on power as fundamental, while those who subscribe to an idealist or institutionalist vision of the world may view scale effects as more latent than manifest.

Evidence

The argument vetted earlier in this chapter is largely commonsensical and is certainly not original. Nonetheless, it is worth exploring the question empirically in a variety of realms. To what extent does demography contribute to power?

We examine three arenas in which power seems likely to be manifested: *economic*, *military*, and *cultural*. Evidently, these spheres are intimately interconnected, with important synergies across all three arenas. Economic power usually translates into military power and military power often translates into economic power, for example. Even so, our tripartite classificatory scheme offers a helpful way to divide up an unwieldy subject.

We do not attempt to weigh the relative importance of these different arenas of power or the indicators that operationalize each of them. For example, we do not attempt to determine whether guns are more important than butter, whether an army is more important than a navy, and how, exactly, to count up the capabilities of an army or navy. We leave these (perhaps irresolvable) questions to others. Instead, we look for common patterns between (a) demography and (b) factors that experts regard as elements or signals of power, each understood with a ceteris paribus caveat.

Since power is a relative concept, judgments about population and power must be also understood as relative. Community A is "large" or "powerful" only by reference to other communities existing at that time. Our empirical cross-sectionally dominated analyses, which include annual (or decade) dummies, are well suited for this sort of synchronic comparison.

Economic Power

By virtue of their size, large states ought to produce more goods and services and ought to be more independent of international economic forces ("globalization") such as trade, investment, and aid. To test these propositions, we employ four measures of economic power: the total output of an economy (GDP, transformed by the natural logarithm), iron and steel production (a key ingredient of industrialization and of defense industries in particular), import dependence (imports of goods and services as a share of GDP), and aid dependence (development assistance as a share of GDP).

Each outcome is subjected to a standard battery of tests, displayed in Table 13.1. We begin with a benchmark specification including only population and year dummies. We proceed to a full specification including a variety of factors that may serve as confounders. And we conclude with an instrumental-variable analysis. Panels extend back as far as the data allow (which in the case of GDP is several centuries).

Results offer strong confirmation of the argument. Larger countries possess greater economic power measured along these four dimensions. Moreover, estimates for population are strong and generally fairly stable across specifications (the exception being foreign aid, which is inconsistent, though always statistically significant). This set of results is corroborated by earlier studies of trade dependence (Alesina & Wacziarg 1998;

Table 13.1 *Economic power*

Outcome	GDP (log)			Iron and steel (log)			Imports/GDP			Foreign aid/GDP		
Estimator	OLS	OLS	2SLS	OLS	OLS	2SLS	OLS	OLS	2SLS	OLS	OLS	2SLS
Model	1	2	3	4	5	6	7	8	9	10	11	12
Population (log)	0.839***	0.997***	0.753***	1.371***	1.442***	1.070***	−7.157***	−8.616***	−9.968***	−20.629***	−13.053***	−7.202**
	(0.037)	(0.002)	(0.061)	(0.134)	(0.085)	(0.225)	(0.522)	(0.995)	(1.801)	(5.260)	(1.891)	(2.959)
GDP per capita (log)		0.998***			1.407***			2.816			−36.207***	
		(0.004)			(0.185)			(2.070)			(3.836)	
Urbanization		0.007			2.650***			17.496			36.615**	
		(0.012)			(0.857)			(15.753)			(17.593)	
Latitude (log)		−0.006***			0.206			−2.476			1.465	
		(0.002)			(0.134)			(2.902)			(2.577)	
Mineral wealth		−0.000			−0.000			−0.002***			−0.000	
		(0.000)			(0.000)			(0.000)			(0.000)	
Regional dummies	✓	✓		✓	✓		✓	✓			✓	
Annual dummies	✓	✓		✓	✓		✓	✓		✓	✓	
Decade dummies			✓			✓			✓			✓
Countries	217	158	179	185	157	165	181	155	172	164	137	151
Years	515	107	220	197	107	197	51	47	60	50	47	50
Observations	40,668	10,049	24,311	14,288	9,476	13,666	6,939	5,534	6,702	6,188	4,959	5,808
R-squared	0.749	0.997	0.736	0.392	0.776	0.369	0.388	0.477	0.306	0.182	0.459	0.0966

Outcome: measures of economic power. *Units of analysis*: country-years. *Lag structure*: right-side variables measured at t−1. Constant omitted. *Estimators*: OLS (ordinary least squares), 2SLS (two-stage least squares using territory and agricultural suitability as instruments). Country clustered standard errors in brackets.
*** p < 0.01, ** p < 0.05, * p < 0.10 (two-tailed tests)

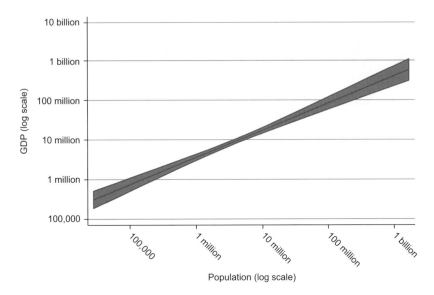

Figure 13.2 GDP, predicted values

Predicted values of GDP (log), as population (log) changes, surrounded by 95 percent confidence interval. Based on Model 1, Table 13.1, with covariates set to sample means.

Dahl & Tufte 1973; Easterly & Kraay 2000; Katzenstein 1985; Kuznets 1963; Perkins & Syrquin 1989) and aid dependence (Burnside & Dollar 2000; Hansen & Headey 2010; Isenman 1976).

To get a better sense of what these results mean we graph predicted values for GDP as population changes, as shown in Figure 13.2. Apparently, population is a major component of GDP, as the estimated values of the latter move up swiftly with increases in population. This is consistent with our model, where population and annual dummies together account for 75 percent of the variability in GDP.

Military Power

The ultimate test of a state's military power is its ability to win wars, or at least to defend its borders.

"If the history of war teaches any obvious lessons," write Howe and Jackson (2012: 44), "one is that victory usually goes to the larger state or alliance – particularly when victory is of critical importance to both sides."

Unfortunately, there are not enough wars in the modern era to make war a tractable outcome measure. Moreover, wars are not randomly assigned and the assignment process is likely to contain a great many confounders, which might bias any conclusions reached about the relationship between size and success.

Fortunately, foreign policy specialists have spent a good deal of time pondering the ingredients of military power. We focus on three variables that offer an overall picture of a state's military capabilities and are amenable to cross-national and cross-temporal measurement: (a) military personnel, (b) military expenditures, and (c) naval tonnage. The first two are drawn from the Correlates of War dataset (Singer et al. 1972) and the third is drawn from a new dataset compiled by Crisher and Souva (2014). All variables are transformed by the natural logarithm to offset their skewed distributions.

Regression models shown in Table 13.2 mirror those introduced in the previous section. For each outcome, three tests are imposed, as described earlier in this chapter. Remarkably, the coefficients for the key variable of interest (population) are fairly stable across all three specifications. The t statistics are also extremely high, suggesting the likelihood of a robust relationship.

To estimate the impact of a change in population on military power we show predicted values for military personnel as the size of a population changes, based on estimates from Model 1, Table 13.2. The graph, reproduced in Figure 13.3, shows a fairly dramatic increase, suggesting that the size of militaries is proportional to the size of countries.

Cultural Power

In addition to economic and military power, we must also consider the cultural aspects of power, which presumably affect the ability of a society to set the global agenda (what people are thinking about) and to project its vision and ideals with respect to that agenda.

Cultural power is similar to "soft power" (Nye 2005). However, the latter is widely viewed as a matter of popularity, i.e., how positively or negatively a country is viewed by the rest of the world (e.g., the IfG-Monocle Soft Power Index). Popularity, in turn, may be largely a product of what one does and what one appears to stand for, and hence not a product of power in the usual sense of the term. A country that is popular around the world (according to global surveys) such as Germany may not have the capacity to *change* attitudes around the world. The latter is what we have in mind by cultural power.

Measuring cultural power is not easy. However, we assume that countries that produce more cultural products have more cultural influence.

Table 13.2 *Military power*

Outcome	Military personnel			Military expenditures			Naval tonnage		
Estimator	OLS	OLS	2SLS	OLS	OLS	2SLS	OLS	OLS	2SLS
Model	1	2	3	4	5	6	7	8	9
Population (log)	0.669***	0.844***	0.567***	1.305***	1.501***	1.178***	1.303***	2.030***	1.121***
	(0.055)	(0.037)	(0.064)	(0.129)	(0.077)	(0.139)	(0.148)	(0.156)	(0.179)
GDP per capita (log)		−0.046			0.943***			0.863**	
		(0.083)			(0.174)			(0.345)	
Urbanization		1.039***			1.431**			3.273	
		(0.350)			(0.683)			(2.250)	
Latitude (log)		0.053			−0.033			−0.075	
		(0.058)			(0.111)			(0.324)	
Mineral resources		0.000			0.000			−0.000	
		(0.000)			(0.000)			(0.000)	
Regional dummies	✓	✓		✓	✓		✓	✓	
Annual dummies	✓	✓		✓	✓		✓	✓	
Decade dummies			✓			✓			✓
Countries	217	158	179	217	157	179	211	158	179
Years	197	107	197	197	107	217	147	107	147
Observations	25,204	10,049	23,341	24,625	9,964	22,928	19,992	10,046	18,807
R-squared	0.510	0.752	0.502	0.562	0.658	0.574	0.307	0.583	0.302

Outcome: measures of military power. *Units of analysis*: country-years. *Lag structure*: right-side variables measured at t−1. Constant omitted. *Estimators*: OLS (ordinary least squares), 2SLS (two-stage least squares) using territory and agricultural suitability as instruments). Country clustered standard errors in brackets. *** p < 0.01, ** p < 0.05, * p < 0.10 (two-tailed tests)

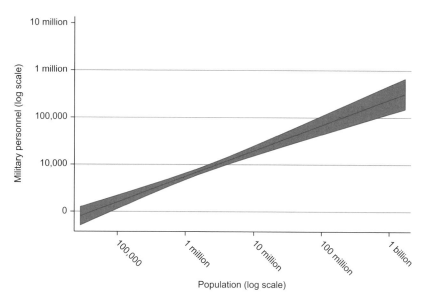

Figure 13.3 Military personnel, predicted values

Predicted values of military personnel (log), as population (log) changes, surrounded by 95 percent confidence interval. Based on Model 1, Table 13.2, with covariates set to sample means.

A cultural product might be a book, movie, website, college degree, event, or prize (acknowledging an accomplishment or contribution of some sort). We also assume that people are carriers of cultural power. Thus, membership in organizations that have some sort of cultural prominence should allow people hailing from different countries a venue to promote their views and values. Likewise, visitors to and from a country offer an opportunity for that country to showcase its values and perspectives.

Because cultural power might be projected through innumerable mechanisms, it is impossible to measure this phenomenon in a comprehensive fashion. Even so, one may suppose that most of the dimensions of cultural power are highly correlated. If so, a small number of proxies may be sufficient. We focus on (a) universities, (b) patents, and (c) tourists. All three measures are transformed by the natural logarithm as a partial cure for their long right tails.

Universities provide graduates who may go on to occupy positions of power and influence or make important contributions to some aspect of society or the economy. Knowledge is power. And the ability to educate people suggests a form of cultural power. Where students hail from and where they end up is probably less important than the fact that they graduate from a university located in a particular country. By virtue of educating a student, that country has an opportunity to influence how she views the world, a *bildung* that is likely to persist throughout her life.

Patents are widely viewed as a measure of scientific prowess, and a key ingredient in improving economic productivity. In the present context patents offer a measure of intellectual creativity and innovation. A country that produces a great many patents is probably influencing the world along other dimensions as well. Our measure, drawn from the World Development Indicators (WDI), focuses on patent *applications*. Although many will not succeed (perhaps for legal or political reasons that are particular to a country), the number of patent applications serves as an indicator of scientific creativity and productivity in a country.

Tourist arrivals, also drawn from the WDI, indicate the number of travelers from abroad who visit a country. (An alternate measure, *tourist departures*, is highly correlated and yields the same general finding.) This may signal that country's attractiveness as a destination or its inevitability, due to some constellation of economic or sociological advantages or its centrality in global networks. In any case, when people visit a country we presume that the host has an opportunity to woo them – to showcase its way of living and its view of the world.

For these three outcomes, we perform the same benchmark tests described previously. (The only difference between this set of specifications and the previous tables is that mineral resources – which we assume to be irrelevant for these outcomes – is removed. Maintaining it in these models has little effect on the variable of theoretical interest.) Results displayed in Table 13.3 are, again, remarkably stable across the three specifications. It would appear that population is a strong predictor of cultural power.

To gain a sense for what this means, we graph predicted values for the number of universities as population changes, based on the benchmark model. The resulting line (based on a log–log relationship) suggests that population has a substantial effect on the growth of universities, especially at the low end of the scale. For example, a hypothetical increase in population from 100,000 to 1 million corresponds to an increase in universities from zero to three – a quantum leap. As population expands to 10 million we expect the number of universities to roughly double (to seven or so).

Table 13.3 *Cultural power*

Outcome	Universities (log)			Patent applications (log)			Tourist arrivals (log)		
Estimator	OLS	OLS	2SLS	OLS	OLS	2SLS	OLS	OLS	2SLS
Model	1	2	3	4	5	6	7	8	9
Population (log)	0.412***	0.635***	0.462***	0.826***	1.125***	0.767***	0.565***	0.673***	0.416***
	(0.059)	(0.038)	(0.062)	(0.127)	(0.042)	(0.146)	(0.054)	(0.053)	(0.078)
GDP per capita (log)		0.301***			1.251***			1.186***	
		(0.067)			(0.168)			(0.130)	
Urbanization		0.415			1.691**			−0.405	
		(0.274)			(0.667)			(0.659)	
Latitude (log)		−0.061			0.348***			0.248**	
		(0.069)			(0.105)			(0.101)	
Regional dummies		✓			✓			✓	
Annual dummies	✓	✓		✓	✓		✓	✓	
Decade dummies			✓			✓			✓
Countries	177	167	170	149	137	146	186	175	173
Years	515	111	220	56	52	56	21	17	21
Observations	38,694	14,337	23,798	4,177	3,648	3,932	3,683	2,831	3,112
R-squared	0.487	0.788	0.515	0.276	0.847	0.257	0.375	0.777	0.274

Outcome: measures of cultural power. *Units of analysis*: country-years. *Lag structure*: right-side variables measured at t−1. Constant omitted. *Estimators*: OLS (ordinary least squares), 2SLS (two-stage least squares using territory and agricultural suitability as instruments). Country clustered standard errors in brackets. *** p < 0.01, ** p < 0.05, * p < 0.10 (two-tailed tests)

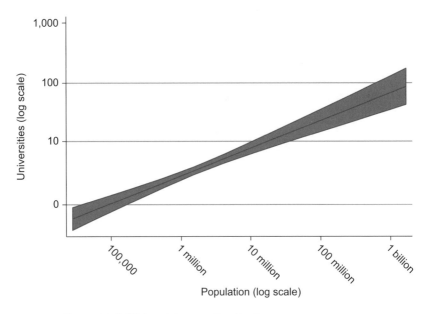

Figure 13.4 Universities, predicted values

Predicted number of universities as population changes, surrounded by 95 percent confidence interval. Based on Model 1, Table 13.3, with covariates set to sample means.

Summary

In contrast to many of the subjects undertaken in this book, the causal role of demography in enhancing the power of communities is fairly straightforward. More people means more power. There is not really any dispute over this thesis, though researchers will debate the value of population relative to other causal factors – a matter that lies outside the scope of this inquiry. All we are trying to establish is that, ceteris paribus, people bring power, and that they do so across multiple dimensions of power – economic, military, and cultural.

Our empirical analyses, coupled with analyses conducted by other scholars, are unanimous, as shown in the inventory of analyses displayed in Table 13.4. A large array of studies all corroborate the same basic pattern. The strength of this general relationship seems robust to any conceivable rejiggering of estimators, samples, and specifications.

Even so, one must bear in mind that the data-generating process is by no means as-if random and some outcomes have not been explored prior

Table 13.4 *Scale and power: Inventory of analyses*

Indicators	Countries	Treatment units	Years	Units of analysis	Research design	Effect	Study
Economic power							
*GDP	(217)	Countries (217)	(515)	Country-years (40,688)	Cross-sectional	↑	Table 13.1
*Iron, steel production	(185)	Countries (185)	(197)	Country-years (14,288)	Cross-sectional	↑	Table 13.1
Trade dependence	(137)	Countries (137)	(30)	Countries (137)	Cross-sectional	→	Alesina & Wacziarg 1998
Trade dependence	(124)	Countries (124)	(1)	Countries (124)	Cross-sectional	→	Dahl & Tufte 1973
Trade dependence	(158)	Countries (158)	(35)	Countries (158)	Cross-sectional	→	Easterly & Kraay 1999
*Trade dependence	(181)	Countries (181)	(51)	Country-years (6,939)	Cross-sectional	→	Table 13.1
Aid dependence	(40)	Countries (40)	(23)	Country-periods (191)	Panel	→	Burnside & Dollar 2000
*Aid dependence	(164)	Countries (164)	(50)	Country-years (6,188)	Cross-sectional	→	Table 13.1
Military power							
Military power	(83)	Countries (83)	(1)	Countries (83)	Cross-sectional	↑	Hendershot 1973
*Personnel	(217)	Countries (217)	(197)	Country-years (24,133)	Cross-sectional	↑	Table 13.2
*Expenditures	(217)	Countries (217)	(197)	Country-years (24,625)	Cross-sectional	↑	Table 13.2
*Naval tonnage	(211)	Countries (211)	(147)	Country-years (19,992)	Cross-sectional	↑	Table 13.2
Cultural power							
*Universities	(177)	Countries (177)	(515)	Country-years (38,694)	Cross-sectional	↑	Table 13.3
*Patent applications	(149)	Countries (149)	(56)	Country-years (4,177)	Cross-sectional	↑	Table 13.3
*Tourist arrivals	(186)	Countries (186)	(21)	Country-years (3,683)	Cross-sectional	↑	Table 13.3

Treatment units: units exhibiting variation in scale. *Years:* number of years over which data are collected – not to be confused with the frequency of observations, as data may or may not be annual and may be averaged across years. *Research design:* the main, or benchmark, research design. – classified as cross-sectional (where the analysis is driven primarily by variation across units) or panel (where the analysis is driven primarily by variation through time). *Effect:* when the scale of a community increases, the designated outcome goes up (↑), down (↓), up and down (∩), or experiences no perceptible change (∅). A scale effect is considered significant if it passes a modest bar of statistical significance, i.e., p < 0.10 ₍two-tailed test) in the benchmark model. Number of countries, treatment units, years, or observations in parentheses.

to the present study. Neither, for that matter, have we examined more than a small handful of the possible indicators of power – an ambient concept, if ever there was one. It is quite possible that some dimensions of power do not respond to demographic forces in quite the same way as those we have examined here.

14   Civil Conflict

We turn now to civil conflict, understood as a violent conflict in which the main protagonists are located within a political community (i.e., a country). In contrast to some of the other outcomes explored in this book, there is little dispute over the immediate ramifications of conflict. The impact of violence on virtually all policies and policy outcomes is negative (Collier 1999; World Bank 2011). One may dispute the size of this effect, and of course long-term effects may be ameliorating. But civil conflict – including civil war – is pretty much the worst outcome imaginable, so if scale has any impact on this result it is important to come to terms with what this impact might be.

Over the past half-century, intrastate conflict has displaced interstate conflict as the primary form of political violence across the world. Not surprising, the topic has received a good deal of academic attention, and a variety of arguments about the causes of conflict have been explored. Theoretical frameworks focus variously on ethnicity, inequality, topography, natural resources, economic development, famine, political institutions, and the motivations of combatants (Blattman & Miguel 2010; Cederman, Gleditsch, & Buhaug 2013; Lacina 2006).

Occasionally, demographic factors are included in a statistical model of civil conflict. However, population is usually a background condition of no substantive interest, and there has been little effort to theorize its impact on conflict.

This brings us to a problem of conceptualization and measurement. Conflict is usually measured as the number of conflict events occurring in a given period (e.g., one year). Since conflict is usually defined as an episode with a specified number of deaths, larger countries are sure to have more conflicts. They have more people to fight and to die. A scale relationship is inscribed in the definition. But this does not tell us very much about the causal influence of demography on conflict. To get at the latter our measure of conflict must be calculated a *per capita* basis and it must employ a fairly low fatality threshold for what constitutes a conflict event. This is how we frame the issue in the following discussion.

We begin by presenting a theory of why scale might have a curvilinear effect on civil conflict. Next, the theory is tested with a new measure of battlefield casualties that adopts a very low threshold of deaths in order for an event to qualify as a conflict and is thus less biased against small states than conventional measures. In the final section, we summarize the empirical findings.

Theory

To explain the relationship between scale and civil conflict we begin with three scale effects introduced in previous chapters.

First, social *heterogeneity* increases monotonically with scale, as discussed in Chapter 3. The reader will recall that heterogeneity is defined as the number of social groups, not their distribution (e.g., fractionalization). Social groups may be generated along ethnic, racial, religious, linguistic, regional, and/or economic lines; typically, several of these features coincide to define a group. As a population increases it is not only the number of groups that increases but also their differentiation. A large population is likely to feature groups that are very different from each other, while a small population will feature groups that share many things in common. (Heterogeneity is the flip side of cohesion.) This is important because social groups usually form the building blocks of sustained civil conflict. Conflicts begin or become conflicts across groups. (This does not presume an essentialist understanding of ethnicity, but it does presume that identities are not entirely free-floating. There is some essence to the construction of an ethnicity.)

Second, power *concentration* is reduced as scale increases, as discussed in Chapter 11. This means that leaders at the center of a large polity are likely to wield less power, and be subject to more veto points, than leaders of a small polity. This diffusion of power has important ramifications for civil conflict. In our reading of the evidence, power diffusion may encourage the formation and consolidation of ethnic identities (often regionally based) and perhaps even of protest movements of various sorts as these groups militate for their rights or jostle for position. This dynamic is centrifugal. However, they also provide incentives for elites and their followers to participate in constitutionally sanctioned politics, i.e., to play by the rules of the game. In this respect, power deconcentration – including specific institutions such as federalism, bicameralism, non-majoritarian electoral rules, and consociational bodies – may mitigate the probability of rebellions and other violent conflicts (Cohen 1997; Horowitz 1985; Lijphart 1977; Saideman et al. 2002).

Third, the *power* of a community – understood economically, militarily, and culturally – increases monotonically with an increase in population, as discussed in the previous chapter. We assume that the central state can appropriate most of this power, especially the military portion. This is important because most civil conflicts involve the state. Even where the state is not directly involved it may serve the role of policeman (suppressing group conflict) or referee (brokering and enforcing agreements). A powerful state is also capable of deterring other states or allied groups outside the community from interfering in a potential civil conflict, which is apt to reduce the scope and endurance of that conflict (Linebarger & Enterline 2016).

To visualize the interaction of these variables we depict three stylized communities in Figure 14.1. The first is small and homogeneous, supporting a small state with a high degree of power concentration. The third community is large and heterogeneous, supporting a megastate with a low degree of power concentration. The second lies somewhere in between.

In a small, homogeneous community, there is little to fight about. There may be conflict, but it is not of the visceral sort that might induce people to risk their lives for a cause. Likewise, information about citizens living within the community – and about the government – is readily available, limiting the prospect of misunderstandings and misinformation that might precipitate conflict. Networks are encompassing, so cleavages should be bridgeable before war breaks out.

A mid-sized community comprises more social groups, and they are more differentiated, so there is more to fight about. Moreover, each social group is sizeable relative to the general population and relative to the resources controlled by the state. This means they have the wherewithal to carry out a violent conflict that may endure for decades, costing many lives.

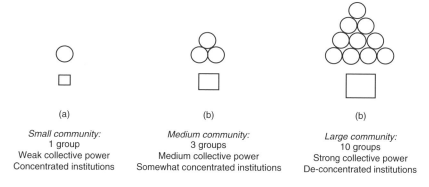

Figure 14.1 Schematic portrayal of three communities

In a large community, heterogeneity is even greater and hence potential flashpoints for conflict are innumerable. However, the state is extremely powerful, and this serves as a deterrent. Likewise, no single social group is likely to be large enough to mount a successful challenge on its own, for each group is marginal relative to the general population and resources of the state. Of course, groups can fight with each other. However, the sovereign power of the state may be sufficient to suppress that conflict (militarily) or to broker a peace.

In a large community, smaller conflicts may fester on the periphery for many years (Buhaug 2010) but are unlikely to claim many lives (as a share of the total population). Deep conflicts – ones that involve a large portion of the population – can arise only if social groups form alliances with each other, generating a polarized society in which two large coalitions fight each other or the state. This is a difficult coordination challenge because of the sheer number of groups, their differences from each other, and the problem of achieving trust across groups when the stakes are so high. (It is orders of magnitude more difficult than the sort of coordination we envisioned leading to an institutionalization of leadership succession [Chapter 9].) Additionally, a large community is likely to feature institutions that deconcentrate political power, offering space for subcommunities to govern themselves and room in the political apparatus for elites of all description to find a place. Accordingly, in a large community violent conflict is unlikely and, if initiated, is unlikely to claim many lives (as a proportion of the total population).

We conclude that the relationship of scale to violent civil conflict is curvilinear – increasing up to a certain point, and then decreasing, or at least flattening out. Medium-sized communities should experience the deepest and deadliest conflicts, for reasons summarized in Figure 14.2.

Pathway Cases and Thought Experiments

In addition to our stylized diagram (Figure 14.1) it may be helpful to consider several exemplary real-world cases. We draw on the region of South Asia as it provides extreme variation in scale while holding constant

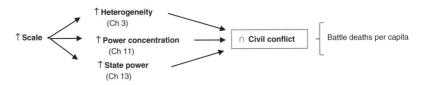

Figure 14.2 Scale effects on civil conflict

some background factors (e.g., of culture and history) that might serve as confounders. The three cases of special interest are the Maldives, a microstate with about 300,000 inhabitants; Sri Lanka, a mid-sized state of roughly 20 million; and India, a megastate with a population of about 1.3 billion.

The Maldives has lots of political conflict but virtually no violent conflict. Dissenters have been jailed and even tortured, but so far there have been hardly any fatalities (Musthaq 2014; Shaheed & Upton 2008). It fits our theory to a T.

Sri Lanka has endured a good deal of violent conflict over the past several decades between the Tamil Tigers (LTTE), agitating for separation, and the Sinhalese-dominated state, which adopted a policy of Buddhist nationalism in the late twentieth century (Tambiah 1986, 1992). During the course of the resulting war, the LTTE received ongoing support from Tamil communities in India and beyond, helping to sustain a bloody and protracted conflict. In the end, the Sinhalese majority was able to reassert control, but not before the loss of several hundred thousand lives (Bavinck & Rajeshkumar 2011). In 2018 a new wave of communal violence swept across the country, this time between Sinhala and Muslim groups. Clearly, Sri Lanka is a conflict-prone country.

India is a megastate with lots of violent conflicts, some of them lasting virtually the entire life of the republic. At the present time, there are two ongoing (on and off) insurrections, one in Kashmir (Malik 2002) and the other stretching across tribal areas of several northeastern states (Chakrabarthy & Kujur 2010). However, neither has claimed very many lives (as a share of the gargantuan population) and neither threatens to spread out of control. The many and various factions that might prefer an independent existence (outside the purview of India) are unable or unwilling to coordinate their efforts. Perhaps they are enticed to work within the system, whose federal structure offers plenty of scope for state-level autonomy (Adeney 2007).

In the event, with the notable exception of the Indo-Pakistani war that accompanied independence, the Indian state has been able to contain its conflicts, which remain regionally focused. Although neighboring Pakistan has tried at various points to fuel the flames of Hindu–Muslim conflict, it is unable to intervene in a meaningful way, given India's overwhelming demographic (and hence military) superiority. And although the Indian government has initiated a series of Hindu nationalist policies (directly parallel to Buddhist nationalist policies in neighboring Sri Lanka) calculated to rile the Muslim minority, clashes have – so far – been localized and contained. Frankly, there is not much that the geographically fragmented Muslim community can do when it comes to combating the Indian army.

For the sake of our argument, it is worth pointing out that the Indian state is not known for ruthless efficiency and its army is not in the first ranks of military powers. Thus far, India has not shown an interest in becoming a major player on the world stage. So we cannot attribute its success to Weberian or Clausewitzian accomplishments. What India does have is people and a deconcentrated political structure. This, in our view, is what distinguishes it from mid-sized polities such as Sri Lanka.

These points may be reinforced with a number of counterfactual thought experiments. One counterfactual is that the largest state, India, splits into many independent nation-states, along the lines of existing states (subnational regions). The first-order effect would be the creation of twenty-nine countries. If present trends continue, twenty or so would likely remain at peace while nine or so would likely experience moderate to high levels of conflict (Kashmir, Nagaland, Assam, Manipur, and several states where the Naxalites are active). Second-order effects would likely increase this level of violence. Groups heretofore deterred from violent combat might choose to mobilize under the assumption that their new adversary – a mid-sized state – is a less formidable opponent. Likewise, the relative balance of demographic power would have shifted in their favor, as their supporters now constitute a much larger share of the newly configured (much smaller) state. The new state would be at pains to limit outside involvement, which could provide additional resources for the insurrection. Thus, we anticipate that violence (operationalized as per capita casualties) would increase if India were to fission.

A second counterfactual imagines that India becomes even larger, swallowing up the Maldives and Sri Lanka. To make this counterfactual a little more realistic let us suppose that the British incorporated Sri Lanka into India and it remained part of the megastate from independence in 1947 to the present. Under this scenario, the relevant question is whether the LTTE would have formed in the first place and, if formed, whether it would have been capable of waging a bloody war for many decades. We believe this is an unlikely prospect, for the simple reason that its chances of victory would have been even less probable, and its ability to muster support – financial or materiel – from Tamils outside of Sri Lanka even less practicable. Note that their support base in Tamil Nadu is in India and hence under the control of state authorities, under our hypothetical thought experiment.

It is noteworthy that Tamils in India, located almost exclusively in the state of Tamil Nadu, have never organized a violent insurrection against the Indian federal government. Despite a nationalist ("Dravidian") movement of considerable power, and some considerable antipathy to the central state, conflicts have been contained within a constitutional frame (Swamy 1996, 1998).

A final thought experiment is perhaps even more revealing. Consider the possibility of a government that embraces the entire world, generating a single global state. This is a difficult counterfactual to wrap our minds around at the present moment. Even so, one can imagine that in such an instance the causal factors we have stipulated would come into play with even greater force. The prospect of resistance to a world government would seem extremely remote – remote enough, one imagines, to discourage all but the most determined (and irrational?) rebellions. And the prospect of coordination across multiple disaffected groups – e.g., Kurds in Southwest Asia, Naxalites in South Asia, Muslims in Mindanao – seems even more remote.

Evidence

Early studies of the relationship between scale and conflict are equivocal. Dahl and Tufte (1973: 112–13) find no consistent pattern among European democracies. On the basis of a larger sample of countries contained in Taylor and Hudson (1972), Hibbs (1973: 171, 232–38) finds a positive association between size and collective protest, but not armed attacks or number of deaths. Powell (1982: ch. 3) confirms these results, for the most part. Consulting a somewhat larger sample of countries (but still nowhere near the entire population of sovereign states), Ott (2000: 240) finds the reverse.

Recent cross-national work enlists comprehensive datasets such as the Uppsala Conflict Data Program (UCDP) non-state conflict database (Sundberg, Eck, & Kreutz 2012), which encompasses nearly all countries in the postwar era. Within this framework, Raleigh and Hegre (2009: 224) report, "the most robust empirical finding in country-level studies of civil war is that large countries have more civil wars than small countries. A country with a population of 10 million inhabitants has an estimated risk that is twice as high as one of 1 million inhabitants." Likewise, many micro- and macro-level studies have shown that concentrations of people are correlated with violence (Brückner 2010; Goldstone, Kaufmann, & Toft 2012; Raleigh & Hegre 2009; Urdal 2006; H. Weber 2013; Weiner 1971; Weiner & Teitelbaum 2001).

Raleigh and Hegre (2009) also point out that the conventional relationship between size and conflict could be compositional: there are more people to fight with in larger communities. If so, the size of a community affects the total number of conflicts but not conflicts per capita – which, presumably, is the outcome of practical and theoretical significance.

Consider that the absolute number of murders across countries or cities is of little interest. If someone tells us that there are more murders in India than in the United States we shrug our shoulders. Our interest is in the crime *rate*, the number of murders per capita. The same logic applies, or at any rate ought to apply, to civil conflict.

Measuring Conflict

Ascertaining the true relationship between scale and conflict is difficult because the latter is typically operationalized as an event that surpasses a – necessarily arbitrary – threshold of fatalities. If the threshold is high, e.g., the 1,000 death threshold used for civil wars in the Correlates of War dataset, it is more difficult to achieve in smaller communities, generating systematic bias. Note that 1,000 is one-tenth the population of Tuvalu and less than one-millionth of the population of China. So it is 1,000 times more likely that a conflict (as defined by Correlates of War) will occur in China than in Tuvalu, simply as a product of their populations.

An ideal index, for our purposes, would count the number of fatalities in a given year with no lower bound, or a very low lower bound. Fortuitously, such an index has recently appeared, thanks to the efforts of Bethany Lacina, the principal author of the Battle Deaths dataset, which tracks the number of battle deaths in countries around the world from 1946 to 2009 (Lacina 2009). In this dataset, and in the UCDP data upon which it draws, fatalities are counted if they surpass a threshold of twenty-five. Being a good deal lower than the Correlates of War index, this imposes less size bias upon the resulting index.

A concern remains about reporting bias. Domestic and international reporting – the first level of fact-gathering – is apt to be more extensive in larger countries, as is subsequent work by historians and social scientists. Big countries attract most of our attention, as shown in Chapter 1. And microstates are virtually off the map. Thus, one must worry about the possibility that fatalities are more likely to enter the dataset if they occur in a larger country, a pattern of error that would introduce systematic bias into our analysis.

Nonetheless, the Battle Deaths dataset is clearly the best source available, and a gigantic step forward from extant datasets. Thus, we are in a position to examine a time-honored subject in a more fine-grained manner than has hitherto been possible.

We ignore international conflict (i.e., conflict with another state or with nationals located in another state), which may have more to do with geopolitics than with domestic politics. Following coding categories devised by the UCDP and Peace Research Institute Oslo (PRIO) teams (Gleditsch et al. 2002), we focus on fatalities arising from civil (domestic) conflict, e.g., insurrections, violent protests, and civil wars. Data are aggregated by year, i.e., where multiple conflicts arise in the same country in a given year fatalities from those conflicts are combined.

For each conflict event, the Battle Deaths dataset offers three esti-mates – "low," "high," and "best." Unfortunately, it was apparently not possible to provide a best estimate for many events. In these cases, we derive a best estimate by averaging low and high estimates. (Results reported in what follows are robust if "low" or "high" estimates are used instead of "best" estimates.)

Of roughly 8,800 annual observations provided by sovereign coun-tries during the postwar period, roughly 1,000 register fatalities. As one would expect, most country-years are coded as zero – fewer than twenty-five conflict-related fatalities. Of 190 countries in our global sample, 97 exhibit no incidents of conflict, and 36 exhibit ten or more years in which conflicts occurred, as shown in Table 14.1. (Excluding these outliers has little impact on the stability of the estimates, as we see later.)

Tests

To gauge fatalities per 1,000 we divide fatalities by the total population (in thousands) of a country. A scatterplot of population (log) graphed against this variable, displayed in Figure 14.3, suggests a strong curvi-linear relationship. Indeed, the *only* instances of significant conflict occur in mid-sized countries.

To examine the relationship in a multivariate fashion, we regress fatalities per 1,000 against population (log) + population (log) squared, as shown in Table 14.2. Our analysis thus replicates the format of Lacina (2006), except that we model population with a quadratic.

Model 1 includes only the variables of theoretical interest along with annual dummies.

Model 2 replicates this benchmark specification, this time with a restricted sample consisting only of countries in the developing world – defined as those with a per capita GDP that surpasses the (approximate) mean in our total sample. The assumption behind this sample restriction is that richer countries are less susceptible to violent civil conflict (Blattman & Miguel 2010) and thus less likely to register the outcome of theoretical interest.

Table 14.1 *Incidence of civil conflict by country*

Albania	0	Lithuania	0	Kenya	1	Congo, DRC	11
Andorra	0	Luxembourg	0	Macedonia	1	Nicaragua	11
Antigua	0	Malawi	0	Madagascar	1	Angola	12
Armenia	0	Maldives	0	Moldova	1	Cambodia	12
Australia	0	Malta	0	Panama	1	Liberia	12
Austria	0	Marshall Is	0	Romania	1	Pakistan	13
Bahamas	0	Mauritius	0	Saudi Arabia	1	Afghanistan	14
Bahrain	0	Micronesia	0	Trinidad	1	El Salvador	14
Barbados	0	Monaco	0	Tunisia	1	Nepal	14
Belarus	0	Mongolia	0	Uruguay	1	Morocco	15
Belgium	0	Namibia	0	Cameroon	2	Thailand	16
Belize	0	Nauru	0	Comoros	2	Algeria	17
Benin	0	Netherlands	0	Congo, Rep	2	Burundi	17
Bhutan	0	New Zealand	0	France	2	Somalia	17
Botswana	0	Norway	0	Guinea	2	Bangladesh	18
Brazil	0	Oman	0	Mexico	2	Peru	21
Brunei	0	Palau	0	Serbia	2	Russia	21
Bulgaria	0	Poland	0	Tajikistan	2	UK	22
Canada	0	Portugal	0	Togo	2	Chad	23
Cape Verde	0	Qatar	0	Uzbekistan	2	South Africa	23
Cyprus	0	Saint Kitts	0	Azerbaijan	3	Sri Lanka	24
Czech Rep	0	Saint Lucia	0	Bolivia	3	Turkey	25
Denmark	0	Saint Vincent	0	Eritrea	3	Iran	26
Dominica	0	Samoa	0	Ghana	3	Uganda	28
Ecuador	0	San Marino	0	Haiti	3	Guatemala	33
Estonia	0	Sao Tome	0	Ivory Coast	3	Iraq	36
Fiji	0	Seychelles	0	Laos	3	Sudan	36
Finland	0	Singapore	0	Mauritania	3	Indonesia	37
Gabon	0	Slovakia	0	Paraguay	3	Ethiopia	44
Gambia	0	Slovenia	0	Suriname	3	Colombia	45
Germany	0	Solomon Is	0	Venezuela	3	Philippines	49
Grenada	0	Swaziland	0	Cuba	4	India	50
Guinea-Bissau	0	Sweden	0	Georgia	4	Burma	60
Guyana	0	Switzerland	0	Greece	4	Israel	60
Honduras	0	Taiwan	0	Mali	4		
Hungary	0	Tanzania	0	Djibouti	5		
Iceland	0	Tonga	0	Spain	5		
Ireland	0	Turkmenistan	0	Syria	5		
Italy	0	Tuvalu	0	Yemen	5		
Jamaica	0	Ukraine	0	Argentina	6		
Japan	0	UAE	0	Egypt	6		
Jordan	0	United States	0	Lebanon	6		
Kazakhstan	0	Vanuatu	0	Nigeria	6		
Kiribati	0	Vietnam	0	China	7		
Korea, North	0	Zambia	0	Malaysia	7		
Korea, South	0	Burkina-Faso	1	Niger	7		
Kuwait	0	CAR	1	PNG	7		

Table 14.1 *(cont.)*

Kyrgyzstan	0	Chile	1	Zimbabwe	7
Latvia	0	Costa Rica	1	Senegal	9
Lesotho	0	Croatia	1	Sierra Leone	9
Libya	0	DR	1	Mozambique	10
Liechtenstein	0	Eq Guinea	1	Rwanda	10

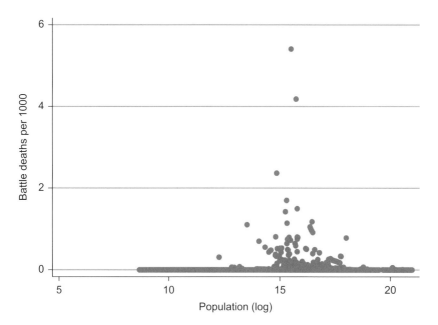

Figure 14.3 Scatterplot of population and civil conflict

Battlefield fatalities from domestic conflicts per 1,000 as a function of population (log), 1946–2009

Model 3 returns to the full sample, this time with the addition of several geographic, economic, and cultural covariates that may affect a state's ability to suppress insurgencies and maintain order.

Model 4 returns to the benchmark specification (again with the full sample), substituting a tobit estimator for the usual OLS estimator. (Tobit estimators are commonly employed for analyses with truncated or censored variables such as battle deaths, which are truncated at 0.)

Table 14.2 *Civil conflict*

Sample	Full	Developing countries	Full	Full	No outliers	Full
Estimator	OLS	OLS	OLS	Tobit	OLS	2SLS
Model	1	2	3	4	5	6
Population (log)	0.012***	0.031***	0.036**	0.533**	0.004**	0.015**
	(0.004)	(0.010)	(0.018)	(0.226)	(0.002)	(0.007)
Population (log)^2	-0.0004***	-0.001***	-0.001**	-0.0137**	-0.0001**	-0.0005**
	(0.0001)	(0.000)	(0.001)	(0.00666)	(0.00006)	(0.0002)
Temperature			0.000			
			(0.000)			
Elevation			0.000			
			(0.000)			
Desert			-0.000			
			(0.000)			
GDP per capita (log)			-0.009			
			(0.006)			
GDP per capita growth			-0.000			
			(0.000)			
Urbanization			-0.019*			
			(0.011)			
Mineral wealth			-0.000			
			(0.000)			
Protestant			-0.000			
			(0.000)			

	(1)	(2)	(3)	(4)	(5)	(6)
Muslim			-0.000			
			(0.000)			
English colony			0.005			
			(0.006)			
State history			-0.008			
			(0.011)			
Years independent (log)			-0.002			
			(0.001)			
Democracy (Lexical index)			0.000			
			(0.001)			
Regional dummies	✓	✓	✓	✓		
Annual dummies	✓	✓	✓	✓	✓	
Decade dummies		✓				✓
Countries	192	118	95	192	156	179
Years	63	63	62	63	63	63
Observations	11,221	4,129	5,057	11,221	9,009	10,567
R-squared	0.00753	0.0174	0.0404		0.00818	0.00359
Pseudo likelihood				5452		

Outcome: battle deaths per 1,000, derived from the Battle Deaths dataset (Lacina 2009). Units of analysis: country-years. Lag structure: right-side variables measured at t−1. Constant omitted. Estimators: OLS (ordinary least squares), 2SLS (two-stage least squares using territory and agricultural suitability as instruments). Country clustered standard errors in brackets. *** p < 0.01, ** p < 0.05, * p < 0.10 (two-tailed tests)

Model 5 excludes countries that have accumulated more than ten years of civil conflict (of any magnitude), so as to preclude the possibility that results are swayed by a small number of outliers.

Model 6 applies an instrumental variable approach to estimation in which population (log) and its quadratic are instrumented with land area (log), agricultural suitability, their quadratics, and an interaction term (land area * agricultural suitability). This approach mirrors earlier IV analyses with the notable complication that there are two instrumented variables and a larger panel of instruments (formed by transformation of the core instruments used in other analyses).

All tests show a highly significant and curvilinear relationship between scale and (per capita) conflict, though estimates vary across specifications. Important, the curvilinear relationship is accentuated in the smaller sample, focused on countries in the developing world (Model 2), as well as in the full specification (Model 3).

Naturally, one might choose other covariates to include in these models. We exclude measures of heterogeneity, for reasons discussed in Chapter 3. Nonetheless, it is worth noting that the inclusion of indices of ethnic, religious, and linguistic fractionalization (drawn from Alesina et al. 2003) in Model 3 has virtually no impact on estimates for the variables of theoretical interest; neither do these measures of fractionalization predict civil conflict. This is consistent with our theoretical framework, in which the number – rather than the distribution – of groups is related to political and social outcomes (Chapter 3).

To visualize the relationship between scale and civil conflict we graph predicted battle deaths from the benchmark model across the range of the observed values for population. Figure 14.4 reveals the expected inverted-U relationship. An increase in population is associated with an increase in conflict up to about 10 million. After that, the relationship reverses and further increases in population are associated with a decline in conflict. The curvilinear nature of this relationship is even more visible when developed countries are excluded, as shown in Figure 14.5 (based on Model 2 in Table 14.2).

It bears emphasis that the upward slope of these predicted values – from roughly 10,000 to 5 million along the logged scale of the X axis – is a lot steeper, and encompasses more of the data points, than the downward slope (after 10 million). Moreover, imprecise estimates along the right tail mean that the confidence interval of the final predicted value overlaps the apex of the curve (at 10 million). Accordingly, we cannot say for sure that there is

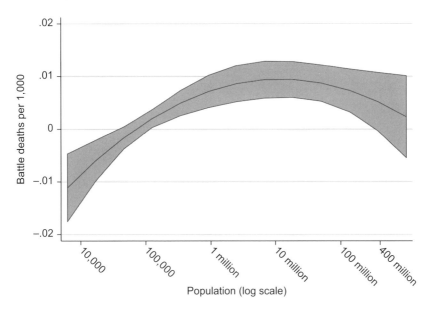

Figure 14.4 Scale and conflict, predicted values (full sample)

Predicted values of battle deaths per 1,000 (Y) as population (log) changes, surrounded by 95 percent confidence interval. Based on Model 1, Table 14.2, with covariates set to sample means. Descriptive statistics (Y): mean = 6.75E-06, SD = 8.37E-05, min. = 0.00, max. = 0.01.

a downward trend in battlefield casualties among the largest countries. There simply aren't enough of them to provide a precise estimate. However, these curves sure don't look very monotonic, and we can say for sure that the positive impact of scale on conflict deaths attenuates in a serious way once a country reaches the population mark of 10 million or so.

In other tests (not shown), we employ data drawn from the UCDP georeferenced event dataset (GED) (Croicu & Sundberg 2015), aggregated by country, in order to test the robustness of the relationship. Although coding procedures differ somewhat across the two sources, we find the same curvilinear relationship. Results are not significant at standard statistical thresholds – due, we believe, to the short time period encompassed by the UCDP GED, which begins in 1989 and therefore covers only two decades. (The same would be true if we limited our tests, using the Battlefield Casualties dataset, to a two-decade period.) Consequently, we regard this robustness tests as corroborating.

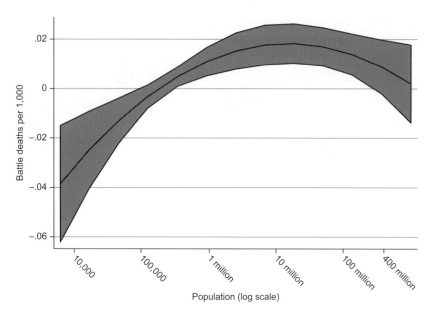

Figure 14.5 Scale and conflict, predicted values (developing countries)

Predicted values of battle deaths per 1,000 (Y) as population (log) changes, surrounded by 95 percent confidence interval. Based on Model 2, Table 14.2, with covariates set to sample means. Sample limited to developing countries.

Summary

Many studies of conflict employ population on the right side of a causal model. Typically, this variable is a strong predictor of conflict – both external and internal – leading scholars to assume that scale causes conflict in a monotonic fashion. This consensus result is evident in the first studies listed in Table 14.3.

However, most of these studies are not focused on scale but rather on other causal factors. Scale is regarded as a background factor, so these authors are not making claims about the role of size in fostering conflict.

We have shown that when employing a per capita measure of conflict that has a very low threshold for what qualifies as a conflict (and hence does not bias the measurement instrument in favor of smaller units), a curvilinear relationship is visible. Increases in scale enhance conflict (as the conventional finding suggests), but only up to a certain point. After this inflection point, increases in population are associated with

Table 14.3 *Scale and conflict: Inventory of analyses*

Indicator	Countries	Treatment units	Years	Units of analysis	Research design	Effect	Study
Internal armed conflict	(193)	Countries (193)	(50)	Country-years (7,640)	Cross-sectional	↑	Urdal 2006
Internal armed conflict	(14)	Grid-cells (sampled)	(44)	Grid-cells (sampled)	Panel	↑	Raleigh & Hegre 2009
Internal armed conflict	(37)	Countries (37)	(23)	Country-years (888)	Panel	↑	Brückner 2010
*Battlefield casualties	(192)	Countries (192)	(63)	Country-years (11,221)	Cross-sectional	∩	Table 14.2

Treatment units: units exhibiting variation in scale. *Years*: number of years over which data are collected – not to be confused with the frequency of observations, as data may or may not be annual and may be averaged across years. *Research design*: the main, or benchmark, research design – classified as cross-sectional (where the analysis is driven primarily by variation across units) or panel (where the analysis is driven primarily by variation through time). *Effect*: when the scale of a community increases, the designated outcome goes up (↑), down (↓), up and down (∩), or experiences no perceptible change (∅). A scale effect is considered significant if it passes a modest bar of statistical significance, i.e., p < 0.10 (two-tailed test) in the benchmark model. Number of countries, treatment units, years, or observations in parentheses.

a leveling off of conflict and then by decreases in conflict – though it should be stressed that the downward slope is less steep and less precisely defined than the upward slope.

A non-monotonic relationship would not be expected if conflict was the product of particular cultures or geographies that are conducive to conflict. In that instance, a monotonic relationship would presumably exist. This puts to rest a large set of potential confounders (unless they interact with each other so as to produce a non-monotonic relationship).

Even so, because our finding rests on a single indicator – and a fairly new indicator, at that – and has not been replicated elsewhere, we regard it with caution. It is possible that the result presented in Table 14.2 is spurious, i.e., the product of some unforeseen measurement error or specification problem.

A particular concern is that large countries might be different in some respect than mid-sized countries, e.g., more successful in generating consensus, more capable, or more patriotic. Perhaps this feature, rather than size per se, accounts for the downward slope of the trend line in Figure 14.4. Although our analyses include controls for state history and years independent, there may be other – less easily measured – factors that we have neglected.

A perusal of cases is not easy to interpret. China has an extremely long history, fairly high state capacity, and a population that is now dominated by a single ethnic group. Its success in forestalling civil conflict might be chalked up to these factors rather than to size. Likewise, the United States has forged a successful nation-state and the world's premier military power. Its success (ignoring for a moment the cataclysm of the Civil War) could also be explained by other factors. However, other megastates such as Brazil, Egypt, Indonesia, Nigeria, and Russia do not seem so different from mid-sized states in their regions. Here, the influence of scale on conflict is more plausible.

15   Other Outcomes

The main arguments of this book are explored at length in previous chapters. In this chapter, we consider several additional outcomes that have attracted attention from scholars and are of immense practical importance. This gives us a more comprehensive picture of our subject and also serves to bring potential confounders into view (i.e., factors that might affect conclusions reached in preceding chapters).

In the following sections we consider the possible effects of scale on *regimes*, *social inequality*, *economic development*, and *public services*. We offer an extended discussion and analysis of the first two topics and only brief reviews – based largely on the secondary literature – of the latter topics.

We conclude that the causal relationship of scale to these outcomes is unclear. Perhaps there is no relationship at all. Perhaps the relationship is marginal and therefore imperceptible with the flawed measurement instruments, small samples, and weak research designs at our disposal. Perhaps an important relationship is hidden in the data that we have not been able to detect. In any case, the evidence at hand does not allow us to reject the null hypothesis (no effect).

Regimes

In previous chapters we explored various facets of democracy – participation, representativeness, contestation, succession, and so forth. Here, we examine democracy as a holistic concept, including a wide variety of factors that (according to various theories) facilitate popular rule in the context of a sovereign state. We refer to the resulting classification as a *regime type* – which may be democratic, autocratic, or somewhere in between.

Examples of the autocratic dangers of scale were abundant in the premodern era. City-states were always small and sometimes democratic (at least by the standards of the day), while empires were large and made little pretense of representing popular opinion. A case in point is the transition of Rome from republic to empire, which was accompanied by an enlargement of territory and peoples and loss of popular control over the apparatus of government. These examples seem to confirm that when it comes to democracy, small is beautiful. Of course, communications and transport infrastructure were primitive in premodern eras and the principle of representation undeveloped. Under the circumstances it is not surprising that writers like Plato, Aristotle, Montesquieu, and Rousseau expressed reservations about the impact of size on politics.

Contemporary researchers are also skeptical about the capacity of communities to cope with the challenges of scale within a democratic framework (C. Anckar 2008; D. Anckar 2002, 2004; Anckar & Anckar 1995, 2000; Diamond & Tsalik 1999; Hadenius 1992; Ott 2000; Srebrnik 2004). As an empirical point of departure, writers note the many microstates throughout the world that now qualify as democracies. A short list includes Andorra, Antigua and Barbuda, the Bahamas, Barbados, Belize, Dominica, Grenada, Kiribati, Liechtenstein, Marshall Islands, Micronesia, Monaco, Nauru, Palau, St. Kitts and Nevis, St. Lucia, St. Vincent and Grenadines, Samoa, San Marino, São Tomé and Príncipe, Tuvalu, and Vanuatu. Regression tests, as well as informal comparisons, seem to confirm a negative association between size and democracy (Clague, Gleason, & Knack 2001; Colomer 2007; Diamond & Tsalik 1999; Hadenius 1992; Ott 2000; Srebrnik 2004; Stepan & Skach 1993).

However, these analyses rely mostly on bivariate models or very limited specification tests, and are usually focused on a narrow slice of time in the contemporary era. Anecdotally, one may counter lists of microstates with lists of macrostates, which are also predominantly democratic. A casual glance at the world's ten largest countries – China, India, the United States, Indonesia, Brazil, Pakistan, Bangladesh, Russia, Nigeria, and Mexico – reveals that all but one feature multiparty contestation, even if they are not perfectly democratic in other respects.

Note also that while many microstates do indeed achieve free and fair elections, a close look at their domestic politics suggests that smallness does not always lead to increased cooperation, harmony, or consensual politics – which extant studies often suggest are key mechanisms by which smallness leads to democratic institutions. Instead, many microstates experience sharply polarized and personalistic politics, coupled with pervasive patronage, clientelism, and nepotism (Richards 1982; Sutton 2007; Veenendaal 2013). These dynamics, which (arguably) stem from the diminutive size of microstates, may undermine prospects for free and fair elections. Accordingly, the survival of electoral politics in microstates may be a by-product of colonial history, geographical location, or international politics rather than size per se (Masala 2004; Veenendaal 2014).

We argue that no consistent relationship exists between size and regime type if the latter is understood as a system of governance centered on multiparty elections with broad suffrage – the hallmark of most regime indices. Small states are about as likely to develop and maintain democracy as large states. Whatever negative impact a large population might have on prospects for democracy are countered by positive effects, generating a null result.

Evidence

To measure regimes in the modern era we rely on a variety of widely used composite indices: the Lexical index of electoral democracy (Skaaning, Gerring, & Bartusevičius 2015),[1] the Polyarchy index from V-Dem (Teorell et al. 2019), the Polity2 index from Polity IV (Marshall, Gurr, & Jaggers 2013), the binary "BMR" index (Boix, Miller, & Rosato 2013), and the Political Rights index from Freedom House (freedomhouse.org). All outcomes are coded so that a higher score indicates greater democracy (this involves a reversal of the original scale for the Political Rights index).

Regression tests are displayed in Table 15.1. For each outcome, two specifications are chosen. The first is a spare model including the regressor of theoretical interest along with annual dummies and one additional covariate. This covariate is a dummy variable measuring the status of the country as an island (unconnected to a major continent). The second specification adds a variety of covariates that are commonly regarded as causes of democracy. (We do not include instrumental variable models, as the foregoing analyses do not seem to justify it.)

We employ a logit estimator for the binary BMR index and ordinary least squares (OLS) for all other outcomes. Since some of these outcomes might more properly be regarded as ordinal we also conducted robustness tests using an ordered logit estimator. Results (not shown) mirror those obtained with OLS.

The final tests in Table 15.1 employ a different measure of scale. Instead of measuring size in a logarithmic fashion we distinguish small states from all others. This accords with a threshold view of causal effects: size matters, but only up to a point. Typically, this threshold is set at a fairly low level, e.g., a half million or 1 million. We test both options, but show only the latter. (There is little difference in results.)

Tests shown in Table 15.1 do not show a consistent relationship between scale and regime type. To be sure, the coefficient for population

---

[1] This is the same measure of democracy that we occasionally employ as a covariate or filter variable in analyses in other chapters.

Table 15.1 Democracy

Outcome	Lexical		Polyarchy		Polity2		BMR		Political rights		Political rights	
Estimator	OLS		OLS		OLS		Logit		OLS		OLS	
Model	1	2	3	4	5	6	7	8	9	10	11	12
Population (log)	0.102 (0.083)	0.103 (0.079)	0.018* (0.011)	0.007 (0.009)	0.628* (0.340)	0.423 (0.270)	0.120 (0.0807)	0.158 (0.129)	0.020 (0.074)	0.089 (0.072)		
Small state (< 1 million)											0.459 (0.358)	−0.220 (0.360)
Island	1.380*** (0.334)	0.515 (0.372)	0.117** (0.053)	0.067* (0.040)	3.712*** (1.364)	1.593 (1.121)	1.058*** (0.352)	0.628 (0.473)	1.503*** (0.322)	0.382 (0.376)	1.288*** (0.356)	0.301 (0.343)
Urbanization		0.956 (0.717)		0.218** (0.092)		2.460 (2.705)		0.336 (1.283)		0.448 (0.685)		−0.383 (0.620)
GDP per capita (log)		0.294 (0.180)		0.059*** (0.021)		1.160* (0.668)		0.783** (0.319)		0.438** (0.194)		0.839*** (0.179)
English colony		0.365 (0.243)		0.038 (0.026)		1.455** (0.708)		1.058** (0.446)		0.601** (0.253)		0.483** (0.224)
Muslim		−0.006 (0.005)		−0.000 (0.001)		−0.016 (0.017)		−0.00443 (0.00856)		−0.006 (0.005)		−0.007 (0.004)
Mineral wealth		−0.000*** (0.000)		−0.000*** (0.000)		−0.000*** (0.000)		−0.000684** (0.000268)		−0.000*** (0.000)		−0.000*** (0.000)
Protestant		0.014*** (0.004)		0.002*** (0.000)		0.049*** (0.011)		0.0355*** (0.0101)		0.004 (0.003)		0.004 (0.003)
Region dummies		✓		✓		✓		✓		✓		✓

Annual dummies	✓	✓	✓	✓	✓	✓	✓	✓	✓	✓	✓	✓
Countries	191	159	166	156	163	156	189	137	191	157	191	159
Years	95	95	117	97	93	93	87	87	40	40	40	35
Observations	11,057	8,103	12,831	8,324	9,948	7,796	9,751	7,070	6,809	4,830	6,926	5,022
R-squared (pseudo)	0.153	0.469	0.201	0.644	0.124	0.527	(0.064)	(0.475)	0.120	0.550	0.125	0.562

Outcome: democracy, variously measured. *Units of analysis*: country-years. *Lag structure*: right-side variables measured at t−20 except in Models 11–12, where they are measured at t−1. Constant omitted. *Estimators*: OLS (ordinary least squares), logit (logistic regression). Country clustered standard errors in brackets. *** p < 0.01, ** p < 0.05, * p < 0.10 (two-tailed tests) is positive in most models. If a relationship exists between scale and democracy, it seems probable that scale *enhances* democracy, contrary to the classical argument. However, this relationship surpasses statistical significance (at a low threshold of 90 percent) in only one model, and is in any case diminutive. Thus, we cannot reject the null hypothesis of no effect.

Islands

Islands play an important role in our analysis as the only covariate maintained in all models.[2] If we remove the island dummy from specifications in Table 15.1, some of the tests reveal a negative correlation between size and democracy, vindicating the Lilliputian theory. However, there are good reasons to regard island status as an independent factor in democratization (C. Anckar 2008; Baldacchino 2012; Congdon Fors 2014; Dommen 1980; Doumenge 1985; Masala 2004; Srebrnik 2004; Sutton & Payne 1993; Veenendaal 2013, 2018).

First, islands are a geographic feature of the landscape. As such, they are clearly exogenous. By contrast, population may be endogenous; indeed, islands are usually quite small in population, presumably because there is little room to grow.

Second, island states are exposed to oceans and this, for a variety of reasons, may influence the propensity of a country to democratize. Indeed, a variable measuring distance to the nearest natural harbor turns out to be a much stronger (negative) predictor of democracy than island status, as shown elsewhere (Gerring, Tollefsen, et al. 2019). (Including harbor distance as a covariate in these models has the same effect as the island dummy, eradicating any relationship between population and democracy.)

Third, many island states are Christian – and more specifically Protestant – in religious orientation (C. Anckar 2008; Hadenius 1993: 126–27). Protestantism is thought to be an important predictor of democracy (Woodberry 2012; but see Anckar & Anckar 1995).

---

[2] States coded as islands in our regression tests include Antigua and Barbuda, Australia, Bahamas, Bahrain, Barbados, Cape Verde, Comoros, Cuba, Cyprus, Dominica, Dominican Republic, Fiji, Grenada, Haiti, Iceland, Indonesia, Ireland, Jamaica, Japan, Kiribati, Madagascar, Maldives, Malta, Marshall Islands, Mauritius, Micronesia, Nauru, New Zealand, Palau, Papua New Guinea, Philippines, St. Kitts and Nevis, St. Lucia, St. Vincent and the Grenadines, Samoa, São Tomé and Príncipe, Seychelles, Singapore, Solomon Islands, Sri Lanka, Taiwan, Tonga, Trinidad and Tobago, Tuvalu, the United Kingdom, and Vanuatu. Evidently, the concept of an island is somewhat ambiguous so this list could be coded somewhat differently – but not too differently.

Fourth, many islands have an extensive tutelary relationship with a European power, culminating in many years' experience with electoral politics and semiautonomous governance prior to independence. Because islands are generally small, their populations were overshadowed by European colonists to a greater extent than continental polities. Indeed, some island states like Mauritius and Seychelles had no native populations prior to the arrival of Europeans; others, like many Caribbean islands, experienced a dramatic fall in indigenous population due to a combination of disease, expropriation, and explicit genocide during the colonial period. The contemporary population of these islands consists primarily of the descendants of enslaved Africans who were imported to the islands, meaning that colonialism actually created many of these societies. For these reasons, one may suppose that the colonial experience was more transformative for island states than for other states (Baldacchino 1993; Caldwell, Harrison, & Quiggin 1980; Srebrnik 2004; Sutton 1999). To the extent that colonialism served as a force for democracy (Olsson 2009), this factor presumably acted with special force among island states. Moreover, few small island nations struggled for independence, and in most cases the transfer of sovereignty occurred more at the behest of the colonial power than on the initiative of the island nation itself. When independence was obtained, the political institutions inherited from colonial powers often remained intact. This may have helped set these microstates on a course to democratic rule.

Fifth, many island states are located in close proximity to a hegemon that exerts democratic influence on the region, e.g., the United States in the Caribbean and Australia in the South Pacific. Others are client states of their former colonial masters, who exert a similar pressure on these states to conform to democratic norms (Masala 2004; Veenendaal 2017).

Sixth, many island states have few natural resources, and thus do not suffer from the "resource curse" (Ross 2001). Seventh, most islands depend upon international trade or tourism for a large share of their national income. Eighth, living on an island may foster a greater sense of national community than one finds in land-based states (Anckar & Anckar 1995: 213, 220–22; Congdon Fors 2014; Royle 2001). Ninth, being geographically isolated, island states may be less militarist because their sovereignty is more secure than land-based states and because expansionist policies are more difficult to pursue (Clague et al. 2001: 22–23; Faris 1999).

Thus, quite a number of factors having little or nothing to do with size might explain the oft-noted association between islands and democracy. Note also that if island status affected democracy through the mediator of population, we should find that Population outperforms Island in our regression tests. In fact, we find the reverse. Island has a robust association with democracy in every benchmark (minimal) model. Its effect attenuates when other covariates are added, but these could be regarded as endogenous to geography. Thus, we conclude that no aggregate relationship exists between scale and regime type once geographic factors are accounted for.

Social Inequality

Social inequality, as the term is used here, refers to the distribution of valued goods such as wealth, health care, education, and status. With this understanding, large scale is often associated with greater social inequality. This attribution can be found in classical works of sociology and political theory (Millar 1806: 57–59, 67–68, 220–22, 236–37; Montesquieu 1748: 151–52; Pareto 1909: 416; Rousseau 1762: 97; Spencer 1882: 401), as well as in many contemporary accounts (Bodley 1999; Homans 1974: 361–63; Kuznets 1963: 30; Lenski 1966: 85; Mayhew & Schollaert 1980).

Is the traditional association of scale with inequality warranted? To address this question, we discuss issues of measurement, potential causal mechanisms, and possible confounders. Finally, we introduce some evidence, though the reader will see that it is not overwhelming.

Measurement

Scale is associated with inequality in an anodyne sense if inequality is measured by the *range between extremes*, i.e., the distance between the worst-off individual or group and the best-off individual or group in a community. In Chapter 3 we argued that larger communities are more heterogeneous across any conceivable dimension, including wealth, health, and education. It follows that a larger community is liable to contain individuals (or social groups) who are further apart along these dimensions. The larger the community, the more likely it is to include individuals who are extremely poor and extremely rich, for example. Since the high end of the income scale is unbounded, the richest person or group of people will drive inequality statistics based on the range between the minimum and the maximum.

However, this is probably not the best way to measure the concept. More commonly, inequality is measured across the *entire distribution* of a population, e.g., with a Gini index or Theil index (Cowell 2011). With this approach to measurement there is no reason to suppose, a priori, that larger communities will be more unequal. Note that if individuals within a larger society are chosen randomly to live in small or large communities, the distribution of wealth will be the same across both sorts of communities, big and small. Just as distributional measures of heterogeneity (e.g., the Herfindahl index) show no relationship to size (Chapter 3), distributional measures of inequality (e.g., the Gini index) should bear no relationship to size.

Of course, this does not exhaust the issue, for one might expect to find an association between scale and inequality for many other reasons.

Causal Mechanisms

In discussing potential causal mechanisms between scale and inequality we begin with those that are primarily *sociological* in nature.

In Chapter 3, we noted the role of small scale in fostering social cohesion. Insofar as social cohesion is a characteristic of small communities, one might conjecture that gross inequalities would violate the sense of unanimity and equality that underlies group identity. Likewise, in a small circle of friends and neighbors mutual obligations are apt to be strong and social sanctions potent. Accordingly, one would expect small-scale societies to redistribute wealth through informal mechanisms in order to preserve unity and protect the vulnerable. The most visible examples of this are found in societies where ritual prestation is practiced (Mauss 1954). But gift giving is by no means limited to primitive societies (Kranton 1996). Arguably, it expresses a universal norm of mutuality found among friends, family, and in small-scale societies. If so, one would expect scale to vary inversely with equality.

Yet social cohesion may also have negative implications for equality. Following a lifelong study of caste in India, Berreman (1978: 232–33) conjectures that scale impedes the perpetuation of ranked social inequality.

It is possible to disappear, to escape, to get lost, intentionally or not, in a large-scale society in ways and to an extent that are difficult or impossible in small-scale ones. That is, the anonymity, impersonality, fragmentation, diversity, complexity, and sheer magnitude of urban society make it possible for a person to go unrecognized and unidentified and thereby escape some of the consequences of his identity or status. Social mobility, identity manipulation, and passing are possible even when ascription is the rule. One can attempt to dissimulate his identity permanently (e.g., by moving to a strange city or neighborhood and altering his speech, name, dress, occupation, life-style, etc.), or situationally (e.g., by similarly concealing from his colleagues at work his family background, ethnic identity, or place of residence), or temporarily (e.g., by putting on Western clothing in order to spend a night on the town incognito). The fleeting, fragmented interactions which characterize large-scale, urban life facilitate such avoidance of the implications of ascribed status. . . .

In small-scale societies – villages, tribes, and bands – strangers are few and are regarded warily. The individual cannot legitimately escape his status. He is known in his totality to his fellows, is held accountable to them, and is responded to accordingly. His interactions with others are continuous and total; his statuses are well known, involute, inseparable from one another, and inseparable from his personal biography. He may escape some of their implications by experiencing a drastic, public change in his social role, but this is quite different from the private, publicly unremarked, and sometimes clandestine changes which occur in urban settings.

In short, the anonymity of large-scale societies may undermine the perpetuation of ascriptive categories, thereby tending toward greater equality. From this perspective, scale reinforces a shift from ascription to achievement.

Next, let us consider *political* dynamics. In the premodern era, democracy existed – to the extent that it existed at all – only in small polities, i.e., in bands, tribes, and some city-states. Even there, citizenship and holding office was generally limited to a narrow elite. In larger units, i.e., nation-states and empires, power was usually monopolized by a single person, family, or social class (Finer 1997). A case can be made that large scale precluded the possibility of democratic rule in the premodern era (Stasavage 2010). Insofar as political institutions serve to reinforce social conditions, deepening inequality (S. Clark 1995; Reinhard 1996; Richards & Van Buren 2001; Zmora 2000), we may conclude that scale fostered social inequalities. However, this argument seems to be limited to the premodern era, as we find no relationship between scale and regime type in the twentieth century (see earlier in this chapter).

In the modern era, we have shown that governments of smaller communities are more likely to adopt interventionist policies (Chapter 12), including redistributionist policies that should, over time, ameliorate inequality. This suggests that, over time, a relationship between scale and inequality may appear. We have also shown that participation rates decline in larger communities (Chapter 7). Since participation is generally skewed toward citizens who are better off, a lower participation rate usually entails a more class-skewed electorate, which may have consequences with respect for redistributionist policies (an issue discussed at the outset of Chapter 7). This also suggests that scale might engender greater inequality (Borck 2002).

In summary, sociological factors are ambivalent – they may augur for a positive or negative relationship between scale and inequality. Political factors seem to point toward a positive relationship: larger communities redistribute less and scale effects on participation should reinforce that effect.

Confounders

Before considering the evidence we must consider the potential confounders that may inhibit our ability to derive clear conclusions about the relationship between scale and inequality.

First, one might expect to find less inequality among people who live close together because they experience similar geographic conditions, historical forces, economic forces, and governance regimes. All of this should serve to create greater similarity in smaller groups than one would find among larger groups, where external factors are more heterogeneous. But it does not follow that scale *causes* inequality. It could be serving as a proxy for propinquity.

Second, and related, the equalizing or un-equalizing effects that follow from increases and decreases in scale may be a product of changing units of governance rather than of scale per se. For example, when two communities are joined together this is likely to equalize welfare among those brought under the rubric of a single government. East Germany and West Germany are closer in wealth today than they were before the reunification of the two states. By a similar logic, the fission of a large political community is likely to lead to greater inequality across the smaller territories that result. The dissolution of the Soviet Union offers a recent example, with the Baltic states increasing rapidly in wealth and the Central Asian republics stagnating (for the most part). These effects arise from who is included and excluded in a political community, not from the size of that community. It is a question of membership, not of scale.

Third, scale may arise as a product of wealth, meaning that those living in larger communities will have more surplus and hence greater opportunities for inequality. In premodern societies, small communities composed of bands or tribes were highly egalitarian, while larger communities composed of empires were grossly inegalitarian, with ranks defined according to ascriptive (hereditary) characteristics (Johnson & Earle 2000). Note, however, that in a Malthusian world, communities expand in size with available resources. Where there are few resources, communities are small. These communities must be fairly egalitarian as there is little to go around; everyone is living close to subsistence. By contrast, where resources are plentiful, communities will be comparatively large, and the surplus is sufficient to generate considerable inequality. Here, scale proxies for wealth.

Fourth, and related, communities with expanding economies are likely to attract migrants. If those migrants are predominantly rich or poor (or both), this will enhance inequality. Here too scale serves a proxy role, but is not causally responsible for inequality.[3]

Evidence

Our theoretical discussion has revealed some reasons to expect a positive empirical association between scale and inequality. However, there are also many reasons to expect this association to be spurious – a product of background factors rather than of scale per se. We turn now to the evidence.

Across *municipalities*, the issue of size and inequality has received a great deal of attention, especially in the United States. Older studies show conflicting findings – sometimes positive (Farbman 1995; Long, Rasmussen, & Haworth 1977), sometimes negative (Frech & Burns 1971; Murray 1969), and sometimes curvilinear (Nord 1980a, 1980b). More recent studies show a strong positive association between city size and inequality (Baum-Snow, Freedman, & Pavan 2018; Schwartzman 2017), though it seems that this may be a fairly new development and hence not a permanent feature of urban life in the United States.

The issue confronting us is whether this relationship should be interpreted as a causal effect of size, or a spurious correlation due to other factors. In the present era, there is considerable evidence to suggest that highly skilled workers, as well as less skilled foreign-born immigrants, seek employment in large cities (Combes, Duranton, & Gobillon 2008), with the result that municipal inequality rises, generating an association between scale and inequality (Schwartzman 2017). Looking deeper, one might cite features of certain urban areas that cause them to prosper, creating well-paying jobs that attract human capital. This could be the unmeasured confounder that causes the contemporary association between size and inequality at municipal levels in the United States.

Alternatively, one might regard income inequality in large cities as a product of agglomeration, which drives the demand for skills, and which, in turn, drives patterns of skilled migration (Baum-Snow et al. 2018). In this scenario, population causes migration causes inequality.

---

[3] Granted, one might also regard the aggregation of human population as a causal factor in economic development, generating a surplus that allows for inequality (Boserup 1965). In this indirect fashion, scale might be considered a cause of inequality. In any case, it is unlikely that this population-based dynamic of growth continues in the modern era, when communities are interconnected, innovations can diffuse, and goods can be exchanged across community boundaries. In this environment, there is little economic advantage to scale, as discussed in the next section.

However, note that gains from agglomeration depend more upon population density than upon population per se. That is presumably why it is realized at municipal levels but not at country levels, where populations tend to be more dispersed. Neither is it clear that agglomeration, by itself, would lead to prosperity, and hence to an asymmetric pattern of mobility. If a city is isolated from major transportation networks, if it has a low level of human capital to begin with, or if it is not viewed (for other reasons) as a desirable place to live and work, one would not anticipate gains from agglomeration to accrue. For these reasons, we do not view the association between city size and inequality as causal.

Moving to larger units, some corroboration can be found for the association between scale and inequality. In recent times, cross-country inequality has outstripped within-country inequality (Bourguignon & Morrisson 2002). Within countries, it seems probable that cross-regional inequality outstrips within-region inequality (Williamson 1965) and urban–rural inequality probably outstrips inequality found within cities or across the countryside (Young 2013). Each of these findings suggests that when one scopes down inequality is reduced, though the question has not been explicitly addressed and its causal properties are unclear.

To test the hypothesis in a more systematic fashion we examine the Gini index of income inequality across subnational regions and countries. To measure inequality at regional levels we draw on a recent study by Royuela, Veneri, and Ramos (2018) which traces patterns in 202 subnational regions located within Belgium, Canada, Chile, Czech Republic, Estonia, Finland, France, Greece, Italy, Luxembourg, Mexico, South Korea, Spain, the United Kingdom, and the United States. To measure inequality at national levels we draw on the World Development Indicators (World Bank 2017).

Although temporal coverage for income inequality is spotty, this statistic is famously sticky over time, so missing data may not be very consequential. Variability over short periods is primarily cross-sectional rather than longitudinal.

Table 15.2 shows a series of tests in which income inequality is regressed against population (log), with a variety of units and specifications. Model 1 focuses on subnational regions, with no additional covariates in the model. Model 2 adds per capita GDP (log) along with country and year dummies. Model 3 includes data for both regions and countries (for the fifteen countries in the Royuela et al. dataset). Model 4 adds per capita GDP (log) along with country and year dummies.

The remaining tests focus on national-level data, allowing us to incorporate more than 150 countries and a somewhat longer time period.

Table 15.2 *Social inequality*

Units	Subnational regions		Subnational regions, countries		Countries		
Model	1	2	3	4	5	6	7
Population (log)	1.066	0.327	0.850	0.564*	−0.973	−0.121	0.691
	(1.160)	(0.383)	(0.715)	(0.283)	(0.783)	(0.550)	(0.607)
GDP per capita (log)		−0.162		−0.421			−0.743
		(1.127)		(1.121)			(1.090)
Urbanization							−3.805
							(4.958)
English legal origin							5.064***
							(1.781)
Muslim							−0.032
							(0.023)
Mineral resources							0.000
							(0.001)
Protestant							−0.029
							(0.046)
Country dummies				✓			
Regional dummies (e.g., Africa)		✓		✓		✓	✓
Annual dummies		✓		✓	✓	✓	✓
Regions (subnational)	202	202	202	202			
Countries	15	15	15	15	153	153	120
Years	10	10	10	10	34	34	34
Observations	1,871	1,871	2,021	2,021	809	809	633
R-squared	0.0223	0.827	0.0202	0.822	0.0484	0.656	0.680

Outcome: social inequality, measured by the Gini index of income inequality. Constant omitted. *Estimator*: OLS (ordinary least squares), country clustered standard errors in brackets. *** p < 0.01, ** p < 0.05, * p < 0.10 (two-tailed tests). *Sources*: subnational data (Royuela, Veneri, Ramos 2018), national data (see Table B1).

Model 5 includes only the causal factor of theoretical interest along with year dummies. Model 6 adds regional dummies – especially important in this instance as inequality varies greatly across different world regions (note the jump in model-fit for this model relative to the benchmark). Model 7 adds a potpourri of additional factors that might plausibly affect inequality.

As the reader can see, the coefficient of interest shows different signs in different samples and specifications. Although the relationship is usually positive, it reaches statistical significance (at $p < 0.10$) in only one analysis. There is, in short, not much evidence of a causal relationship.[4]

Economic Development

We turn now to the question of economic development, aka growth. In premodern societies, positive scale effects on economic development seem plausible (Boserup 1965; Kremer 1993). Human settlements were largely isolated from one another so that the capacity of a civilization rested on people living in proximity to each other. Larger populations presumably provided an advantage in economic development, e.g., an economic base from which surplus could be extracted, a more advanced division of labor, and more innovation. Note that where production depends upon human labor power, more humans generally translate into more production.

In the modern world, where populations around the world are linked by transport and communications infrastructure and where machines provide the main source of power for economic production, the role of population is less clear.

Some macroeconomists theorize that insofar as innovation contributes to growth, larger societies should enjoy faster growth insofar as "(a) they have more resources to devote to knowledge creation and (b) the larger scale to which knowledge can be applied raises the returns to innovation" (Peretto & Smulders 2002: 603). There is some evidence to suggest that larger countries have enhanced capacity to innovate. The Global Competitiveness Report, produced by the World Economic Forum (Schwab & Sala-i-Martin 2015), surveys businesses on their access to technology. Responses show that businesses in smaller countries are more likely to license or to imitate technology from foreign companies while businesses in larger countries are more likely to conduct their own research and development.[5] However, other economists call into the

---

[1] This confirms the findings of earlier studies (e.g., Perkins & Syrquin 1989: 1743).
[5] See the *wef_ci* variable in QoG 2017 (Teorell et al. 2013).

question the adage that a larger population fosters larger investments in research and development, raising innovation and productivity (Dinopoulos & Thompson 1998; C. Jones 1999; Young 1998).

Leaving aside the question of innovation, some economists are nervous about the prospects of very small economies in a globalizing world. As more and more countries became independent in the postwar era – many of them extremely small – their fate in an increasingly interdependent world economy seemed uncertain. Summarizing this literature, Srinivasan (1986: 210) identifies five potential obstacles:[6]

- inability to exploit economies of scale in the production of goods and services
- vulnerability to . . . external economic shocks and natural disasters
- difficulties in obtaining private foreign capital
- limited independence in setting macroeconomic policies
- the tendency of . . . exchange-rate conversions to overstate the real incomes.

However, empirical studies have shown no relationship – or at least no strong relationship – between country size and economic growth in the postwar era (Alesina 2003; Alesina, Spolaore, & Wacziarg 2000; Armstrong et al. 1998; Easterly & Kraay 2000; Firebaugh 1983; Perkins & Syrquin 1989; Spolaore & Wacziarg 2005).[7]

This does not mean that small states are invulnerable. Indeed, their ability to compete successfully with large states is presumably contingent upon the existence of a liberal international order, one that protects the economic rights of all states and preserves the free movement of capital and goods (Alesina et al. 2000, 2004). Note that a larger country, by definition, provides a larger internal market. Thus, if there were no trade between countries, larger countries would surely outperform smaller countries. However, if foreign trade is available smaller countries' greater exposure to the international market may turn into an advantage, encouraging export-led development (Katzenstein 1985) and perhaps a more market-friendly regulatory environment. While small states suffer greater volatility – because they are more subject to international markets and currencies – they may enjoy rates of long-term growth that equal or surpass larger states. Of course, this depends upon the maintenance of a liberal international order; if this order should fail, we can anticipate that small states would be its first victims.

---

[6] We leave aside one factor – remoteness – that seems orthogonal to size.

[7] For further discussion see Benedict (1967), Briguglio (1995), Jalan (1982), Kaminarides, Briguglio, & Hoogendonk (1989), Khalaf (1976, 1979), Lockhart, Drakakis-Smith, & Schembri (1993), Milner & Westaway (1993), E. Robinson (1963), Rose (2006), and Streeten (1993).

To explore the mediating role of international conditions on scale effects one may examine the long-term relationship between population and economic performance. Our expectation is that size is positively correlated with growth during periods of protectionism, and negatively correlated (or uncorrelated) with growth during periods of liberalism. To test the proposition, we regress the first-difference of per capita GDP (log) on population (log), the first-difference of population (log), and per capita GDP (log), along with country and year fixed effects across fifty-year periods from 1800 to the present. Coefficients and 95 percent confidence intervals from these rolling regressions are plotted in Figure 15.1.

The results of these tests fit expectations fairly closely. At the beginning of the nineteenth century, when trade was impeded by high tariff barriers, larger countries perform somewhat better than smaller countries. Toward the end of the nineteenth century, as tariff barriers recede and world trade grows, smaller countries grow slightly faster. This pattern continues through the 1930s, when trade barriers are reimposed and world trade

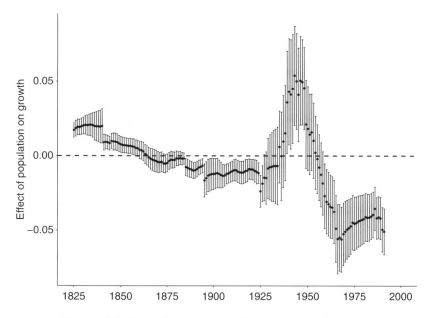

Figure 15.1 Size and economic performance through time

Results from a rolling regression of growth on population, 1800 to the present. For each fifty-year period, growth (the first difference of per capita GDP, log) is regressed on population (log), per capita GDP (log), year dummies, and country dummies. The estimated coefficient for population is plotted in the middle year of each period, surrounded by a 95 percent confidence interval (using clustered standard errors).

contracts, at which point large countries outperform small countries. In the postwar era as protectionism gives way to free markets and global trade expands (facilitated by the General Agreement on Tariffs and Trade [GATT] and its successor, the World Trade Organization [WTO]), the relationship reverses once again and small countries outperform large countries, this time by a considerable margin.[8]

Patterns shown in Figure 15.1 are fairly similar if we measure growth as the percentage change in per capita GDP, rather than the first-difference of per capita GDP (log). Patterns are also robust if we remove the first-difference of population (intended to purge the model of short-term population changes) from the right side of the model. Note, however, that the sample of countries changes somewhat from period to period, so some of the effects registered in this analysis may be compositional. Moreover, these changes may be endogenous to changes in the international order, as suggested by work on the size of nations (Alesina & Spolaore 1997, 2003). To offset this problem (partially), and to maintain a larger and more consistent sample, we include proto-countries prior to their formal independence so long as they had (in previous eras) a degree of geographic and economic coherence and so long as estimates for population and per capita GDP are available. For example, India is treated as a country prior to 1947 with the notion that it functioned as an economic unit even prior to independence.

In any case, we do not wish to make a strong claim for the causal role of size. Our claim, rather, focuses on the interaction between population size and the international economic order, which we have viewed as a time-bound relationship, fluctuating with changes in the latter. This result seems fairly robust and is strongly supported by economic theory.

Public Services

As a final topic we approach the question of public services, understood broadly to include all policies whose goal is to enhance the welfare of citizens, e.g., infrastructure, health care, education, and so forth. In Chapter 12 we explored the degree of government intervention, one component of which is fiscal policy, including the quantity of taxing and spending. Here, we are concerned with the *quality* of public services. Do they deliver? And do they deliver efficiently?

Work on multilevel governance (referenced in Chapter 2) addresses the impact of centralization/decentralization – or specific rules governing the

---

[8] For overviews of globalization over the past two centuries see Chase-Dunn, Kawano, and Brewer (2000), Frieden (2007), and O'Rourke and Williamson (2002).

relationship among units – on public services. Our question is different. We want to know whether size *per se* has an effect on public services.

A few studies directly address this question, comparing polities of different sizes or polities that have merged or split with their previous units. A research team at the Centre for Local & Regional Government Research, Cardiff University, utilizes surveys of citizen satisfaction (along various dimensions) and objective measures of performance for municipalities in the United Kingdom. Areas of interest include leisure and culture, processing benefits claims, housing, environment, social services, and education. Most tests do not yield statistically significant results, and of those that do pass conventional thresholds the relationships are sometimes positive, sometimes negative, and sometimes non-monotonic (Andrews et al. 2006).

Hansen, Houlberg, and Pedersen (2014) examine how various aspects of fiscal management respond to mergers of municipalities in Denmark, which are compared to a baseline set of municipalities that were not merged. They find that the merged municipalities show evidence of improved fiscal balance (between revenue and expenditure), greater liquid assets, and lower debt after several years. It seems possible that this results from increases in size, though it is also possible that the reorganization that resulted from amalgamation prompted these improvements in fiscal management.

Charron, Fernández-Albertos, and Lapuente (2013) report on a multicountry survey of the quality of public services, with primary focus on education, health, and policing. The survey was administered to respondents located in 116 localities across nine European Union countries. Results show that larger governmental units are perceived to have lower-quality services. The trouble is that we cannot determine whether these results reflect an underlying reality or simply a perception that things are not well run in large, heterogeneous communities – a persistent measurement problem that one encounters in any survey instrument that rests on subjective perceptions.

Jugl (2018) approaches the question at country levels using the index of Government Effectiveness as the primary outcome measure. This widely used index is based on a variety of national surveys compiled by the World Bank (Kaufmann, Kraay, & Mastruzzi 2011). She finds an upside-down U relationship, with optimal government effectiveness achieved in medium-sized countries (somewhere between 15 million and 94 million, depending upon the model). The finding is plausible, though also open to question.

A substantial literature questions the validity of the World Bank governance indicators (e.g., Langbein & Knack 2010). A particular issue of concern in this context is that perception-driven indices might be subject to systematic bias. Specifically, larger countries may project an image of worse performance simply because of their size, as discussed in Chapter 3. Jugl finds that alternate measures of governance are sometimes robust and sometimes not. Econometrically, Jugl is forced to deal with an extremely short time series (six years) and a very stable outcome, meaning that virtually all the variability in the outcome is cross-sectional and the resulting sample is quite small. This, in turn, means that results are likely to be subject to specification choices. In this case, the curvilinear finding is contingent upon the inclusion of a measure of democracy. A final issue of concern is that the downturn in government effectiveness that occurs after the inflection point is not very marked and is imprecisely measured, presumably because there are relatively few very large countries. In summary, Jugl presents a plausible hypothesis and a plausible set of empirical tests, but they are far from conclusive.

Rose (2006) examines a very large number of country-level outcomes, many of which could be regarded as proxies for public services. This includes economics (per capita GDP, human development index, inflation, trade openness, military spending, cars per capita, televisions per capita, telephones per capita, computers per capita), finance (Economic Freedom index, Institutional Investor Credit rating, ICRG Country Risk, IMD Competitiveness, World Economic Form Competitiveness, Economic Security Index, Domestic Bank Credit as share of GDP, Quasi-Liquid Liabilities as share of GDP, M3 as a share of GDP), health and education (life expectancy, infant mortality, DPT immunization, improved water, sanitation, literacy, primary school completion, gross secondary school enrollment, net secondary school enrollment), and institutions (democracy, political stability, government effectiveness, regulatory quality, rule of law, corruption, social infrastructure). These outcomes are regressed against population (log) along with selected controls in three formats: cross-sectional, fixed effects (in cases where outcomes are time-varying and observed over a longer panel), and instrumental variable (using area as an instrument). He finds only one very robust relationship – between country size and reduced trade openness (corroborating results presented in Chapter 13).

We conclude that the role of scale in the provision of public services is impossible to ascertain on the basis of extant studies.

Summary

We have argued that scale has no demonstrable effect – or at least no large effect – on democracy, social inequality, economic development, and public services. To reach these conclusions we have conducted a few original analyses while relying heavily on extant work. Although we have cited just a portion of the work that treats these vast subjects it may be helpful to pull together these findings by way of summarizing the evidence of this chapter. We do so in Table 15.3.

The first section of the table focuses on studies of democracy, variously measured. Most extant studies find a negative relationship between scale and democracy. Smaller countries are more apt to be democratic. This is true in some cross-sectional samples (i.e., in some chosen years with some chosen indicators of democracy). But it ceases to be true if the geographic features of countries are considered. In particular, we find that including a dummy for island obliterates any relationship between population and regime type. (This is also true for other measures of ocean exposure.) Granted, islands are generally small so there is a problem of collinearity to consider. However, geographic features are causally prior to population. São Tomé is small because it is a (small) island. So if island status (or other measures of ocean exposure) has any direct effect on regime type – and we have demonstrated quite a number of reasons to suppose that this is indeed plausible – then it must be taken into account, i.e., controlled in a regression analysis. At this point, the scale effect tails off into nothing, or virtually nothing (it is barely significant in several of the robustness tests shown in Table 15.1). We conclude that scale has little or no impact on democracy, considered as a composite concept.

No extant studies that we are aware of seek to probe the relationship between scale and social inequality at country levels. Our own analysis, displayed in Table 15.2, shows no relationship. (Indeed, the coefficient for population switches signs in various specifications and nowhere reaches statistical significance.) While there are many studies of scale and inequality at municipal levels, we are reluctant to regard these as providing strong evidence of causality, for reasons discussed. Thus, we do not include them in Table 15.3.

Extant studies of scale and economic performance are not numerous. Those that exist, however, almost invariably conclude that there is no such relationship – or that the relationship is vanishingly small. To be sure, we can expect that large countries would enjoy significant advantages in a different international trade regime, so if the liberal order fades in the future, this issue will need to be revisited. But for the moment, there is no cause to believe that size affects growth over the long term. This does

Table 15.3 *Scale and other outcomes: Inventory of analyses*

Outcomes and indicators	Countries	Treatment units	Years	Units of analysis	Research design	Effect	Study
Democracy							
Political rights (Freedom House)	(192)	Countries (192)	(33)	Country-years (192)	Cross-sectional	∅	Anckar 2008
Polity2 (Polity IV)	(237)	Countries (237)	(22)	Countries (237?)	Cross-sectional	→	Ott 2000
Political rights (Freedom House)	(132)	Countries (191)	(1)	Countries (191)	Cross-sectional	→	Diamond & Tsalik 1999
Bespoke index	(132)	Countries (132)	(1)	Countries (132)	Cross-sectional	→	Hadenius 1992
Political rights (Freedom House)	(168)	Countries (168)	(34)	Countries (168)	Cross-sectional	→	Clague et al. 2001
Political rights (Freedom House)	(168)	Countries (168)	(10)	Countries (168)	Cross-sectional	→	Stepan & Skach 1993
*Various	(191)	Countries (191)	(95)	Country-years (11,057)	Cross-sectional	∅	Table 15.1
Social inequality							
*Gini index of income inequality	(15)	Subnational regions (202)	(10)	Region-years (1,871)	Cross-sectional	∅	Table 15.2
*Gini index of income inequality	(153)	Countries and regions (217)	(10)	Country/region-years (2,021)	Cross-sectional	∅	Table 15.2
*Gini index of income inequality	(153)	Countries (153)	(34)	Country-years (809)	Cross-sectional	∅	Table 15.2

Economic development							
Various	(104)	Countries (104)	(40)	Countries (104)	Cross-sectional	∅	Alesina, Spolaore, & Wacziarg 2000
Various	(204)	Countries (204)	(3)	Countries (204)	Cross-sectional	∅	Armstrong et al. 1998
GDP per cap	(157)	Countries (157)	(10)	Countries (157)	Cross-sectional	→	Easterly & Kraay 2000
GDP per cap	(105)	Countries (105)	(27)	Countries (105)	Cross-sectional	∅	Firebaugh 1983
GDP per cap	(169)	Countries (92)	(38)	Country-years (92)	Panel	∅	Spolaore & Wacziarg 2005
Public services							
Various	United Kingdom	Municipalities (237)	(2)	Municipalities (237)	Cross-sectional	∅	Andrews et al. 2006
Fiscal management	Denmark	Municipalities (93)	(9)	Municipality-years (835)	Panel	↑	Hansen, Houlberg, & Pedersen 2014
Various	(9)	Countries (9)	(2)	Localities (116)	Cross-sectional	→	Charron, Fernández-Albertos, & Lapuente 2013
Government effectiveness (WB)	(176)	Countries (176)	(6)	Country-years (2669)	Cross-sectional	∩	Jugl 2018
Various	(200)	Countries (200)	(40)	Country-years (8000)	Cross-sectional	∅	Rose 2006

Treatment units: units exhibiting variation in scale. *Years*: number of years over which data are collected – not to be confused with the frequency of observations, as data may or may not be annual and may be averaged across years. *Research design*: the main, or benchmark, research design – classified as cross-sectional (where the analysis is driven primarily by variation across units) or panel (where the analysis is driven primarily by variation through time). *Effect*: when the scale of a community increases, the designated outcome goes up (↑), down (↓), up and down (∩), or experiences no perceptible change (∅). A scale effect is considered significant if it passes a modest bar of statistical significance, i.e., $p < 0.10$ (two-tailed test) in the benchmark model. Number of countries, treatment units, years, or observations in parentheses.

not mean that size is irrelevant, but it suggests that positive and negative effects balance each other out.

Public services is a harder topic to study, primarily because we lack a consensus indicator of this wide-ranging concept. In any case, the several studies that have undertaken to look at this macro-level relationship – summarized in Table 15.3 – report inconsistent findings. Again, we find no rationale for discarding the null hypothesis. But this conclusion must be tempered with the caveat that further research on this subject may unearth important patterns that have hitherto remained obscure.

This caveat should be extended to all the subjects investigated in this chapter. Some topics are relatively unexplored. Others are thoroughly studied but our empirical leverage is weak, due to the nature of the data. It seems quite likely that some of the null results registered in Table 15.3 will be revised if these evidentiary barriers can be overcome.

Part III

Conclusions

16   How Scale Matters

In this final chapter, we pull together the pieces of this large project into a more synoptic account.

We begin by discussing the relevance of scale for questions of public policy and institutional reform. Although the population of a political unit seems structural, it is not beyond our capacity to change, and even when change is impossible we must understand the nature of scale effects if we are to make good public policy.

In the second section, we summarize the findings presented in previous chapters. What scale effects appear to exist and how likely are they to be causal? How great is their impact, collectively?

In the third section, we offer a tentative – and very partial – theoretical synthesis, one that ties together many of the themes introduced in previous chapters. This synthesis centers on the role of population in generating coordination dilemmas and the way in which political institutions and policies respond to those dilemmas.

In the fourth section, we address trade-offs introduced by scale effects. This section veers into highly abstract territory, stepping back from the details to observe larger patterns. We argue that scale induces a series of trade-offs with respect to *efficiency* (preferences versus policies), *political relationships* (informal/personal versus formal/institutional), *systems of rule* (intensive versus extensive), *models of popular rule* (participatory versus competitive), *power* (individual versus collective), and *freedom* (where trade-offs are conditional on structural features of the landscape).

In the final section, we take on the question of whether large or small communities are preferable, overall. This issue may be understood as a question of providing better governance (*quality of governance*), as a matter of resolving functions to different levels of government (*multilevel governance*), or as a matter of what people want (*citizen preferences*).

The Relevance of Scale

Most political communities grow over time, while a few shrink. In either case, change is slow and it comes as a product of seemingly inexorable demographic trends. Even the most determined government can affect population growth and decline only at the margins. So from a policy perspective demographic scale does not seem to be a very useful lever.

Yet the size of a political community is also a product of its boundaries. Here, scale is directly manipulable and hence subject to intervention by policymakers, who have the authority to assign borders and to change them if they see fit.

Consider *national* communities. Although country borders seem highly stable, they have not always been so, and may not always remain so. The number of countries in the world has changed continually through the modern era – from about 40 in 1800 (depending upon how one defines sovereignty) to about 200 at the present time. Some border changes are the product of new countries formed from non-sovereign or semi-sovereign territories (e.g., former colonies). Other border changes are the product of fusion (e.g., German and Italian unification in the nineteenth century or the recent annexation of Crimea into Russia) or fission (as in Sudan, Czechoslovakia, Yugoslavia, and the Union of Soviet Socialist Republics). Secession movements have been increasingly active in recent years (Pavkovic & Radan 2013), and may lead to new statelets in the future.

Another sort of change is the creation of *supranational* political communities like the European Union, which extend across nation-states. Bear in mind that the European Union began as a trade regime, and regional trading unions have now sprung up in most parts of the world. Whether they will metamorphose into political units claiming a degree of sovereignty remains to be seen, but is certainly within the realm of possibility.

Changes in *regional* boundaries are more common. Although US states have generally retained their boundaries, India periodically subdivides extant states to create new states (Mawdsley 2002). France, in contrast, recently went the other direction and in 2016 reduced its number of metropolitan regions from twenty-two to thirteen, creating much larger communities. Reform of subnational boundaries is common in many countries around the world (Law 1999).

Municipal governments and administrative units are even more fluid, and often engineered for partisan purposes (Green 2010; Grossman & Lewis 2014; Hassan 2016). Some cities in the United States such as New York have annexed outlying suburbs, forming a municipal (or county) government that is more or less coterminous with the metropolitan area. Other cities such as Detroit have not grown with suburban sprawl, remaining centered on downtown areas (Rusk 2013; Teaford 1984; Weiher 1991). In Europe, some countries (e.g., the Netherlands) have been active in merging municipalities, while in others (e.g., Switzerland) municipal boundaries have remained stable over long periods of time.

Electoral districts are the most fluid of all. Redistricting is a continual challenge in countries with single-member districts, where in order to maintain parity across districts, border changes must accompany demographic changes. In some countries such as the United States, the issue is highly contentious and open to partisan or incumbent gerrymandering (Bullock 2010).

In addition to the changing shape of districts we must also consider their overall number. Legislatures may be formed or reformed so as to be large or small (Chapter 4). The US House of Representatives continued to grow in size until 1911, at which point it was fixed at 435. But it could be changed again by statute if lawmakers wished to do so. A larger legislature will produce smaller districts so long as district magnitude (the number of seats per district) remains constant. The president of France, Emmanuel Macron, recently proposed to cut the size of the National Assembly by a third, from 577 to roughly 385. If implemented, this reform would dramatically increase the size of electoral districts (Serhan 2017).

Changes in *electoral law* are also likely to affect the size of resulting districts. For example, a change from single-member to multimember districts – while holding constant the number of representatives – generates larger districts. Likewise, the combination of single-member and multimember seats means that some districts are likely to be large and others small. This form of electoral system, known as "mixed" or "mixed-member," is increasingly common (Shugart & Wattenberg 2003).

A similar logic applies to fundamental constitutional features of a polity such as the *structure of the executive*. Note that presidents, governors, and mayors draw on constituencies equal in size to the accompanying legislature. Therefore, unless the legislature is drawn from a single district (a la Israel and the Netherlands at national levels and Brazil at state levels), legislators are elected from districts that are considerably smaller than the corresponding executive. So a constitutional change in the selection of the executive – from presidential to parliamentary or vice versa – also entails a change in constituency size.

Consider, as well, *levels of government* in a polity. Higher-level political bodies, almost without exception, are larger. A presidential constituency is larger than a gubernatorial or mayoral constituency; likewise, the constituency for a national legislature is larger than a constituency for a state legislature or municipal council.[1] Since countries tend to retain institutional isomorphism across levels, the main difference between national, regional, and local governmental structures is often the size of the corresponding communities (polities and districts). It follows that any move to centralize or decentralize political authority has the effect of resituating decision-making to a larger or smaller venue.

While these constitutional reforms are highly visible, other changes in a polity are more subtle. Over time, relative power may shift from one body to another. If these bodies have varying sizes, then the influence of demography on politics will also shift. For example, power may shift from a small upper chamber to a larger lower chamber within a legislature, or vice versa. Presidents (elected by the whole country) may gain preeminence over legislatures (usually responsive to specific districts), or vice versa. Regions may gain preeminence over cities, or vice versa. Each of these changes entails a change in political scale.

Consider, finally, laws pertaining to *suffrage*. In an election, the relevant political community, one might argue, consists of those who can vote – the electorate. In the contemporary world, where universal suffrage is the usual rule, electorates are more or less equivalent to the adult population of citizens. However, this was not always so. And this means that extensions (and occasionally restrictions) of suffrage constitute an important change in political scale. In the 1989 South African election, under the apartheid regime, only 3 million people voted; in the 1994 election, 20 million people voted. Extensions of suffrage – to non-property holders, to excluded social groups, to women, and to youth – constitute important changes in political scale, relevant to many electoral outcomes.

Thus, although we are accustomed to view the size of political communities as static, there is considerable volatility in the demographics, boundaries, and relative political units through time. Many of these changes are subject to statutory or constitutional revision. Indeed, few issues of institutional design do *not* have a scale component, as all institutions have constituencies and all constituencies have a designated size. It follows that when policymakers consider institutional reform they ought to consider the scale effects of these reforms.

---

[1] Monaco, which has only one municipality, is an exception to this rule.

Of course, scale is not always amenable to change. National boundaries are sticky; it is difficult to increase or decrease the size of a nation-state in the modern era. Subnational boundaries are somewhat more fluid; however, shifting borders imposes costs on some set of actors and it is usually difficult to gain consensus for such reforms among citizens and policy-makers. Thus, as a practical matter, scale is often a fixed quantity – changing very slowly as a product of long-term patterns of migration, fertility, and mortality.

The structural quality of scale does not eliminate its policy importance, however. Even where scale is not subject to manipulation it is vitally important to understand what scale effects are at work in a given situation. If participation rates are low in a community, it is important to know to what extent this failure is a product of scale. Likewise for other outcomes explored in this book. Only when scale effects are properly understood can appropriate remedies be identified.

In summary, scale is important for policymakers not just as a treatment to manipulate but also as a background condition to take into account. Virtually every political problem has a scalar dimension. Figuring out that dimension should help to solve the problem, or at least to better understand its recalcitrance. With this as prologue, we turn to scale effects.

Scale Effects Revisited

Previous chapters have introduced a large range of outcomes – cohesion, representatives, the representation ratio, representativeness, particularism, participation, contestation, institutionalized succession, professionalism, concentration, intervention, power, civil conflict, regimes, social inequality, economic development, and public services. For each outcome we presented an argument and some evidence about the causal role of scale.

At this point in the narrative, readers may be wondering how likely it is that these hypotheses are true. This is not the place to rehearse the evidence or to revisit the lengthy methodological discussion presented in Chapter 2. What we *can* do is summarize our own – inevitably subjective – sense of the truth-value of these multifarious claims.

Table 16.1 displays all of the outcomes explored in this book along with measures chosen to operationalize them. For each measure, we indicate whether the evidence suggests a positive (↑), negative (↓), curvilinear (∩), or null (∅) scale effect.

Table 16.1 *Apparent scale effects*

As scale increases . . .	P	As scale increases . . .	P
↓ **Cohesion** (Ch. 3)		↓ **Concentration** (Ch. 11)	
↑ Heterogeneity	95	↑ Federalism	90
↓ Connectedness	95	↑ Bicameralism	90
↑ Deviance – behavior	70	↑ Revenue decentralization	95
↑ Deviance – perceptions	95	↓ Capital city pop/country pop	95
↑ **Representatives** (Ch. 4)		↑ Checks & balances	90
↑ Legislature size	95	↓ **Intervention** (Ch. 12)	
↑ Cabinet size	95	↓ Moral policy	70
↑ **Representation ratio** (Ch. 4)		↓ Fiscal policy	90
↑ Constituents/representative	95	↓ Personnel policy	95
↓ **Representativeness** (Ch. 5)		↓ Social policy	85
↓ Demographic	85	↑ **Power** (Ch. 13)	
↓ Programmatic	85	↑ GDP	95
↓ Constituency connections	95	↑ Iron, steel production	95
↓ Political trust	95	↓ Trade dependence	95
↓ **Particularism** (Ch. 6)		↓ Aid dependence	95
↓ Independent candidacies	90	↑ Military power	95
↑ Party strength	90	↑ Personnel	95
↓ Preferential voting	90	↑ Expenditures	95
↓ Vote-buying	90	↑ Naval tonnage	95
↓ Campaign spending	90	↑ Universities	95
↓ Pork	90	↑ Patent applications	95
Ø Corruption, overall	50	↑ Tourist arrivals	95
↓ **Participation** (Ch. 7)		∩ **Civil conflict** (Ch. 14)	
↓ Citizen assemblies	95	∩ Battlefield casualties per capita	70
↓ Party membership	95	Ø **Regimes** (Ch. 15)	
↓ Voter turnout	95	Ø Lexical index	70
↓ Other activities	90	Ø Political rights (Freedom House)	70
↓ Political efficacy	95	Ø Polity2 (Polity IV)	70
↑ **Contestation** (Ch. 8)		Ø Polyarchy (V-Dem)	70
↑ 100–vote share of largest party	95	Ø BMR (Boix, Miller, Rosato)	70
↑ Dif. b/w top-two vote-getters	95	Ø **Social inequality** (Ch. 15)	
↑ Party system fractionalization	95	Ø Gini index of income inequality	70
↑ Legislative fractionalization	95	Ø **Economic development** (Ch. 15)	
↑ Turnover	85	Ø GDP per capita	80
↑ **Institutionalized succession** (Ch. 9)		Ø GDP per capita growth	80
↓ Tenure	80	Ø **Public services** (Ch. 15)	
↓ Monarchy	80	Ø Quality of public services	60
↑ Regular leadership succession	80	Ø Gov't effectiveness (WGI)	60
↑ **Professionalism** (Ch. 10)		Ø Various	60
↑ Legislative professionalism	95		
↑ Legislative capacity	95		
↑ Meritocratic recruitment	80		
↑ Statistical capacity	95		
↑ Education of public officials	70		
↑ Salary of public officials	95		
↑ Voluntary associations (N)	95		

Hypothesized scale effect: positive (↑), negative (↓), curvilinear (∩), null or ambiguous (Ø). *P*: probability that the hypothesized scale effect is true (in the authors' judgment) on a 0–100 scale, where 50 means it is equally likely to be true or false.

Readers can appreciate that knowledge of the social world is a probabilistic affair. Accordingly, some of the conclusions posted in Table 16.1 are more likely to be true than others. One indication of this is provided by the quantitative empirical tests presented in previous chapters, as registered in coefficients, standard errors, and associated p values. These statistics offer important clues into causal inference. But they are not dispositive, especially when dealing with observational data. Note that statistics from a regression model are mute with respect to problems of systematic measurement error and or basic problems of research design. And they offer few hints about the likelihood of replicating a finding in a different setting (external validity).

Thus, it seems essential to offer a summary judgment of the probable truth-value of the various arguments vetted in previous chapters. This summary judgment should take into account *all* relevant clues, not just those that can be captured in a statistic. This includes our presumptive knowledge of the world and the deductive logic implicit in our theorizing. It includes previous scholarly attention to the question, i.e., the number of independent studies that have been conducted, the relative strength of these studies, and the pattern of findings. And it includes the empirical tractability of the hypothesis, i.e., whether there are potential problems of measurement and causal identification, and whether the proposition has been tested at multiple levels (e.g., national and subnational).

A summary judgment that includes so many different dimensions, most of which cannot be quantified, is necessarily subjective and obviously imprecise. However, it is a much better guide than p values and serves to put us on record in a transparent fashion so that strong claims can be distinguished from weaker claims.

Accordingly, P in Table 16.1 summarizes our subjective assessment of the probability that a hypothesized scale effect – or non-effect – is true. P varies in principle from 0 (definitely not true) to 100 (definitely true), with 50 indicating a 50 percent chance of being true.

All of our probability estimates except for corruption are larger than 50. However, most are not as large as common social science thresholds for statistical significance (95 percent or 99 percent). Some readers may view this as indicating a lack of confidence. However, as we have pointed out, confidence intervals and p values do not indicate overall uncertainty. Once additional elements are introduced it is natural that uncertainty would rise. Evidently, we don't want to attribute greater certainty than the data warrant. Recall that the evidence for arguments in this book is not definitive, for reasons discussed at length in Chapter 2.

One further issue demands consideration. Readers will appreciate that "truth" is a slippery concept. It is often difficult to say when a given argument has been verified or falsified by a piece of evidence. So it is important to specify the sort of tests that might confirm or disconfirm the foregoing arguments.

In the best of all possible (scientific) worlds, experimental tests would be devised in which the causal factor of interest – population – is randomly assigned to treatment and control groups, comprised of differently sized polities or districts. This is difficult, if not impossible, in the present context, as discussed.

Under the circumstances, the best that can be reasonably hoped for are replications of the sort of tests we have enlisted in the preceding chapters. With that in mind, let us suppose that a given research design outlined in one of the chapters in Part II is replicated with new samples drawn (in a random fashion) from the same population – perhaps with some (justifiable) alterations in measurement strategy or research design.

Granted, drawing a new sample from the global population of countries is difficult if the existing sample comprises most countries in the world, as many of our analyses do. However, one can resample from the same population of countries in a new period, e.g., sometime in the next decade.

$P = 90$ means that we think that the result of this hypothetical out-of-sample, in-population replication will give the hypothesized result (understood broadly as positive, negative, or curvilinear) in 90 percent of the replications. (If the samples are small, more replications will be required before an equilibrium result is attained.)

These are the sorts of replication studies that, we trust, will allow researchers to refine the hypotheses and findings laid out in this book so that true assertions are strengthened (P increases) and false assertions weakened (P decreases). In Bayesian terms, priors are updated. This is also a way to conceptualize the complex process of knowledge cumulation in the social sciences (Elman, Gerring, & Mahoney 2020).

Impact

Table 16.1 summarizes the scale effects investigated in this book, categorized broadly as positive (↑), negative (↓), curvilinear (∩), or null (∅). We have not attempted to summarize the strength of these relationships. For a sense of *how much* an increase or decrease in population may affect a given outcome the reader may examine figures showing predicted values based on benchmark regression models, sprinkled throughout this book.

For most outcomes, the impact of small population changes is modest. It takes a sizeable change in the size of a country, region, or district to bring an appreciable impact on outcomes that are (usually) responsive to myriad causes.

Even so, one must bear in mind that political units in the real world exemplify *enormous* differences of scale, as demonstrated in Chapter 1. Thus, an imagined change from 1,000 to 100,000, or from 1 million to 100 million, is in keeping with the actual distribution of population across political communities. If we want to understand scale effects – how politics in small and large communities differs – we must entertain "wild" thought experiments, for this is the wild and crazy nature of the real world.

A second point to note is the near ubiquity of scale effects. Of the seventeen outcomes listed in Table 16.1, scale appears to have a measurable impact on all but four. Of the seventy indicators listed in Table 16.1, scale has a measurable impact on all but twelve. We do not pretend that these outcomes were randomly chosen; neither is it clear how the population of policies and policy outcomes ought to be defined. But this sort of sampling is not necessary to reach a commonsense conclusion: scale matters for many things that we care about.

In this respect, demography is like other structural factors such as geography or constitutional-level political institutions. For any given policy or policy outcome these structural features may have only a marginal effect. But since they affect a great many outcomes, their *cumulative* impact is enormous.

A Common Theoretical Framework?

For most outcomes surveyed in this book scale is a distal cause. This means that scale makes its influence felt through many intervening factors. We have endeavored to lay out these causal paths in theoretical sections and causal diagrams located at the beginning of each chapter.[2] But we have not proposed a general theoretical framework.

---

[2] We have not attempted to prove these arguments. Doing so would be challenging given that so many of the posited mechanisms are difficult to measure, non-manipulable, and overlapping – rendering a mediation model impossible or uninformative (Gerring 2010; Imai et al. 2011). There is also the practical problem of length; we hesitate to add further to a narrative that is already protracted. We hope that future studies will rise to this challenge.

In this section, we contemplate what such a framework might look like.

To wrap our minds around the question let us consider the political settings afforded by a small and large community, illustrated schematically in Figure 16.1. Two features of this diagram are essential – size and heterogeneity. (For further discussion of heterogeneity see Chapter 3.) Each circle is intended to represent an identically sized social group with discrete interests, values, identities, and preferences. The small community (a) consists of one group with relatively homogeneous attitudes. The large community (b) encompasses sixty-two groups, each with somewhat different attitudes.

Now let us consider how a change in the size of a community – understood as an increase or decrease in the number of social groups – might affect its politics. The latter is understood as a series of *coordination challenges* – among citizens, between citizens and leaders, and across communities.

First, as a community grows there is less social cohesion (Chapter 3). This means that the community is less capable of solving coordination problems on its own, which places greater demands on government.

Second, as a community grows so do coordination challenges between citizens and their government. There are likely to be fewer representatives per citizen, weaker connections between citizens and their representatives, greater divergence of opinion between leaders

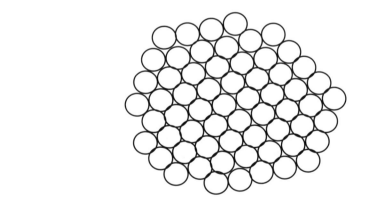

(a) Small community,   (b) Large community, composed
composed of one group   of multiple groups

Figure 16.1 Schematic portrayal of two communities

and citizens, and less trust of political institutions and political leaders (Chapters 4–5).

Third, as a community grows, the effectiveness of different methods of solving mass–elite coordination challenges shifts. Informal norms and sanctions for regulating political behavior and interpersonal mechanisms of political action (e.g., citizen participation, contact between citizens and representatives, particularistic agreements) become less effective. Formal rules (e.g., statutes, constitutional provisions) and specialized, functionally defined organizations (elections, political parties, interest groups, bureaucracies, and other professional bodies) become more effective. Politics is thereby institutionalized (Chapters 6–10).

Fourth, as a community grows, achieving optimal coordination among a large and diverse citizenry entails loosening the bonds between government and citizens. Consequently, the government of a larger community is less likely to concentrate political power at the center, to impose high tax rates, or to intervene in the lives of citizens (Chapters 11–12).

Fifth, as a community grows relative to other communities in its neighborhood (or in the world at large), coordination challenges across those communities attenuate. This is a product of the greater resources and power available to a large community. Rival communities are fewer (if incorporated into the large community) or weaker in a relative sense (if they remain independent) (Chapter 13).

In these respects, scale effects may be understood through the prism of a series of coordination games. To be sure, coordination challenges are not always solved in an optimal fashion. One has only to look at the many examples of failed states in the present era (Rotberg 2010; Scott 1998) and through human history (Diamond 2005; Kennedy 2010), and at the even greater number of armed conflicts (Gat 2008). At the same time, coordination failures are costly, so communities have an incentive to solve coordination problems. Also, competition between communities (i.e., across states in the international system and across subnational communities within a state) probably exerts pressure on actors to avoid suboptimal outcomes. Thus, although we do not want to presume a Panglossian world in which efficient outcomes are always attained, it seems reasonable to presume that efficient solutions – where coordination challenges are resolved – enjoy an advantage over inefficient solutions over the long run.

Evidently, this is not a very tight theoretical framework and there is much that it omits, so it is not terribly satisfactory as a general theory. Even so, it elucidates some common features in the arguments set forth in the foregoing chapters. Insofar as scale effects can be understood through a unified theoretical framework we believe that framework ought to center on coordination dilemmas and the ways in which political institutions respond to them.

Trade-Offs

If the hypotheses summarized in Table 16.1 are correct, large communities are quite different from small communities. In this section, we step back from the details to observe larger patterns, understood as a series of trade-offs. These concern *efficiency* (preferences versus policies), *political relationships* (informal/personal versus formal/institutional), *systems of rule* (intensive versus extensive), *models of popular rule* (participatory versus competitive), *power* (individual versus collective), and *freedom* (where trade-offs are conditional on structural features of the landscape).

Efficiency: Preferences vs. Policies

Efficiency may be defined in a very general fashion as maximizing outputs with a fixed set of inputs. In the present context, we distinguish between *preference* efficiency (matching preferences to policy) and *policy* efficiency (achieving desired policy outcomes).[3]

A small community is more capable of embodying the preferences of its citizens, all other things being equal. This follows from the greater homogeneity (Chapter 3) and representativeness (Chapter 5) of small communities. Scale detracts from preference efficiency.

It follows that the greater the heterogeneity of preferences across a larger society, the greater will be the efficiency benefits of scaling down. One gains little by scaling down if preferences are uniform. But if preferences vary, scaling down may yield a more efficient result (understood as one in which preferences match policies). Of course, those who share the same preferences must live together and the borders of political communities must be aligned with these shared preferences. Those who prefer high levels of redistribution must live together in a territorially contiguous space, separate from those who prefer low levels of redistribution, for example. Since people of like minds tend to live together, it is a reasonable assumption that scaling

---

[3] This section builds on a tradition of work on the size of states and fiscal federalism, e.g., Alesina and Spolaore (1997, 2003), Bolton and Roland (1997), Ellingsen (1998), and Oates (1972).

down will enhance preference efficiency and scaling up will compromise this goal.

At the same time, scaling up enhances *policy* efficiency. By this, we mean the ability to internalize the costs and benefits of a policy, avoiding positive or negative externalities. It should be clear that either type of externality is problematic. In the case of positive externalities, the community that implements a policy does not reap all of its benefits, which means that the good is likely to be under-provided. In the case of negative externalities, the community that adopts a policy is not subject to all of its negative consequences, which means it is likely to be over-provided.

Because of its tendency to spill across jurisdictions, environmental policy provides an especially good example of externalities, both positive and negative. A positive externality might result from a community's investment in a wastewater treatment plant or tighter regulation on auto emissions. A negative externality might arise from a community's embrace of a dirty fuel like coal or oil. The point is, the costs and benefits of these policies are not contained within the community if pollution travels across borders.

Readers will perceive that the problem of spillover is not simply a matter of population size but also of geography. A country that is larger or surrounded by natural boundaries (mountains, oceans) is less susceptible. From this perspective, the problem of policy efficiency is more a function of territory than of population.

However, not all spillover problems are solved by a well-circumscribed geography. Consider the problem of migration across communities. So long as some migration is allowed or cannot be prevented, migration may serve as a mechanism for policy spillover. Let us say that Community A has high taxes and generous social policies while Community B has low taxes and punitive social policies. It is logical to suppose that rich people will relocate from A to B and poor people will move from B to A.

Scale affects this dynamic because migrants generally compose a smaller share of the total population in a large community than in a small community and are thus less of a burden (or blessing). Imagine in our hypothetical example that one community is very small (e.g., 1,000) and the other very large (e.g., 100 million). It is easy to see that the former would be overwhelmed (or decimated) by very small population movements, while the latter would be scarcely affected. This suggests that population size affects the sensitivity of communities to policy externalities, at least insofar as the latter impact the decision to migrate across polities.

Wherever the costs and benefits of a policy are not internalized within a community there is a strong possibility of policy inefficiency because the interests of that community are not aligned with the interests of neighboring communities. Until a single world government exists, there will always be some allocative inefficiencies. But it is nonetheless the case that the larger the scale of a community, the less problematic this sort of inefficiency is likely to be.

Returning to the main trade-off – between preference and policy efficiency – let us consider the evidence. There is plenty of evidence for the impact of scale on preference efficiency, as discussed in Chapter 5. Policy efficiency, however, is harder to demonstrate. We know that externalities exist, and it stands to reason that they vary inversely with the size of the community. The harder question to resolve is the impact of these externalities on the course of public policy. Are smaller communities more likely to pursue policies with negative externalities and less likely to pursue policies with positive externalities? For example, are small countries less likely to adopt costly environmental policies than large countries (because they cannot internalize all the benefits)? We do not know enough about how scale affects the shape of public policies – and whether, in particular, incentive-based theories founded on potential externalities are correct. But the hypothesis is highly plausible.

Political Relationships: Informal/Personal vs. Formal/Institutional

Broadly speaking, political relationships may be characterized as *informal/personal* or *formal/institutional*.

In the former, it is who you are and whom you know that matters. These relationships tend to be ad hoc, flexible, and adaptable to particular contexts. Informality is not widely studied by political scientists, presumably because these patterns of behavior are often rather idiosyncratic and therefore resistant to generalization. Arguably, informality is a residual category, describing the absence of institutions. Consider the following political phenomena: anarchism, clientelism, factionalism, grassroots politics, neopatrimonialism, populism, and personalism. They don't share much in common aside from an emphasis on personal relationships that are not constrained by formal rules.

By contrast, when relationships are formal and institutional, the position that people occupy – their professional roles – is what matters. An institutionalized political community is one where institutions matter. There are rules and people follow them, which means that politics is depersonalized and rules prevail over the whims of leaders, ad hoc agreements, and personal or clientelistic arrangements, "a government of laws not of men," in the oft-quoted words of John Adams.[4]

In a *fully* institutionalized polity, important decisions are reached through regular procedures. These procedures are public and generally codified (in a constitution, statutes, or legal precedents). Procedures endure and are infused with value (normative force). Constitutions are more than "parchment" (Carey 2000). Additionally, tasks are differentiated by function and each agency or institution enjoys substantial autonomy within its recognized purview, establishing a division of labor with regular procedures for handling different activities. Positions are filled and careers advanced by adherence to a set of impersonal criteria, privileging considerations of merit rather than patronage. Finally, organizations are run by professionals who are highly trained, well staffed, and well remunerated, who pursue lifelong careers in public service, and who are committed to professional norms. As a consequence of all of these features, the outputs of a fully institutionalized domain ought to be stable and predictable. Political conflict is channeled through institutions – elected bodies, political parties, interest groups, nongovernmental organizations (NGOs), and bureaucratic agencies – rather than through clientelistic channels, violence, or other irregular avenues.[5]

The findings of this book suggest that scale encourages the institutionalization of political power, moving society away from informal, personal relationships and toward rational-legal authority (M. Weber 1961). Where communities are large, particularistic appeals – targeted on specific constituents – are less availing. As scale increases, the efficiency of "homestyle" campaigning, preferential voting, vote-buying, campaign spending, and pork decreases relative to alternative approaches of cultivating constituency support, i.e., party organization and programmatic appeals (Chapter 6). Where communities are large, electoral contestation tends to be more vigorous (Chapter 8) and succession to the top office

---

[4] *Massachusetts Constitution*, art. XXX (1780).

[5] The definition in this paragraph may be regarded as an ideal type ("maximal" definition), derived by aggregating attributes that are conceptually coherent and commonly associated with the concept of institutionalization. It draws on Ben-Dor (1975), Blondel (2006), Colyvas and Jonsson (2011), Huntington (1968), Lawrence, Winn, and Jennings (2001), Levitsky (1998), Olsen (2009), and Polsby (1968). We exclude the sometimes-invoked criterion of *adaptability* (Huntington 1968), since this does not follow logically from the core idea of rule-bound behavior. A well-institutionalized organization may be rigid (Olson 1982).

more regular (Chapter 9). Finally, in a large community power is apt to be deconcentrated – across several levels of government and (at each level) between multiple agencies of government (Chapter 11). As a consequence, many organizations interact when a policy is considered and there are many potential veto holders. This fosters an institutionalized policymaking sphere, as veto holders must negotiate with one another to reach decisions on matters of public policy.

Social scientists generally regard institutions favorably. This is apparent from the language that we use to describe the contrast between informal/personal and formal/institutional styles of governance. Accordingly, one might regard the institutionalization of politics that accompanies increasing scale as a positive development.

At the same time, one should bear in mind that scale-induced institutionalization is a response to necessity. The larger the group, the harder it will be to govern that group without a set of formal rules and highly structured organizations. Failure to institutionalize is likely to result in political breakdown and the possible dissolution of the polity. In some basic sense, institutionalization is a necessary condition of governance on a large scale. But this does not mean that very small communities ought to be governed in a highly institutionalized manner. There is no need for party politics in a small firm or department. Indeed, when highly institutionalized modes of governance are imposed on small communities they generally do not work as intended. The sham democracy of professional associations, where elections are held with no opposition and where votes are taken among "those present" (typically, a tiny and highly unrepresentative minority) is an example of this. Informality tends to trump formality when small numbers allow for less structured interactions.

Neither is it clear that this is entirely a bad thing. Informal transactions are probably more efficient when scale is small, even though they are also prone to favoritism. That is why we regard the contrast between these modes of politics – informal and formal, personal and institutional – as a trade-off. Some things are lost, and others gained, when the scale of a community increases.

Systems of Rule: Intensive vs. Extensive

In Chapter 11, we set forth a contrast between institutions that *concentrate* or *deconcentrate* political power. A theoretical maximum of concentration is achieved when a single individual or clique makes all important policy decisions in a polity. A theoretical minimum, though harder to define, is attained in a setting where power is widely dispersed and numerous actors hold effective vetoes. We argued that increases in the size of a polity are likely to lead to a dispersal of political power, e.g., a separation of legislative and executive functions, bicameralism, autonomous government agencies, distinct and semiautonomous levels of government, and divided party control.

In Chapter 12, we contrasted public policies that are *interventionist* ("statist," "activist," "Big Government") with those that are *limited* ("laissez-faire," "Small Government"). We argued that increasing the size of a polity is likely to decrease the level of intervention, as measured by moral policy, fiscal policy, personnel policy, and social policy.

Generalizing further, one might say that scale imposes a trade-off between intensive and extensive rule. Polities may be organized to rule *intensively* over a small populace or *extensively* over a large populace. Insofar as this trade-off exists it has many practical implications, which may be explored through historical counterfactuals.

Had the thirteen colonies of New England evolved into independent states rather than joining together in a confederation, we conjecture that each state would have developed a more concentrated system of rule – including more interventionist public policies – than that which currently exists at the national level in the United States. By the same token, if the colonies had extended their purview across the West as well as into Mexico and Canada, generating a larger polity, we conjecture that the United States would have developed into an even more fragmented nation-state, with an even less developed welfare state, than currently exists.

In a similar manner, we conjecture that if the European Union continues to admit new members, its governance structure is likely to become more fissiparous. If, on the other hand, "Brexit" succeeds and other members also withdraw from the union, the governance structure and policy interventionism of the rump European Union is likely to tighten.

With respect to global governance, we expect that such attempts will continue to be marked by highly decentralized governance structures and light policy intervention. It is no accident that international organizations such as the International Monetary Fund, the World Bank, the World Trade Organization, and the United Nations have much less concentrated power structures and weaker revenue-extracting instruments than the nation-states they represent.

Arguably, an *equilibrating* feature is inherent in political organization. Large polities reproduce the features of small polities by diffusing power internally (vertically and horizontally). Big states have many subnational units, each of which may enjoy a substantial degree of self-governance. Small polities reproduce the features of large polities by delegating power externally – joining trade associations and security associations, and forming confederations.

This has important implications for problems of coordination. Where states are small (and unified), problems of coordination arise primarily *between* polities. Where states are large (and fragmented), problems of coordination arise *within* polities while coordination problems between states are mitigated by their smaller numbers.

From this perspective, the size question appears less consequential. Although India is much bigger than the Maldives, this power is mitigated by a considerable delegation of power from the national government to state and local governments, giving citizens a good degree of local control. Needless to say, formidable coordination problems inhibit collective action across the 29 states, 7 union territories, 3,255 urban local bodies, and billion-plus citizens of that mega-nation.

The Maldives is smaller than India, and thus suffers fewer of these coordination problems within its small, unified government. At the same time, the Maldives is vitally affected by international markets, by international treaties and organizations, and by the looming shadow of India. So it faces a daunting coordination problem in its external relations – just as a local government within India faces a daunting coordination problem in dealing with the many other political bodies that lie above and beside it. Size affects structure, but in ways that might be viewed as self-regulating.[6]

Of course, we do not mean to suggest that things are truly equal and that size is therefore irrelevant. Being a citizen of a small state in India is not the same as being a citizen of the Maldives. The argument for functional equivalence – large and extensive vs. small and intensive – is true only to a degree.

Popular Rule: Participatory vs. Competitive

Over the millennia, two models of popular rule have predominated.

According to the first, people rule by deliberating and making decisions themselves, usually in citizen assemblies (Bryan 2010; Hansen & Nielsen 2004; Ladner 2002; Linder 2010; Sinclair 1991). This approach has come to be known as participatory democracy, direct democracy, or deliberative democracy (Barber 2003; Fung & Wright 2003;

[6] Diamond and Tsalik (1999: 120) note, "If institutional arrangements such as federalism and decentralization can mimic in some important respects the conditions of small states, then perhaps larger states may benefit from some of the same favourable conditions for democracy that are intrinsic to very small states."

Mansbridge 1983; Nelson & Wright 1995; Oldfield 1990; Pateman 1970; Pitkin & Shumer 2001; Zittel & Fuchs 2006).[7]

According to the second model, people rule indirectly by choosing representatives to govern them. These representatives stand for election at regular intervals, competing for citizen votes. The teams (i.e., parties) preferred by the voters are selected to hold the reins of government for a limited period of time, after which they may be replaced by a different team, setting in motion a system of accountability through successive elections. This mechanism of popular rule has come to be known as contestation, representative democracy, electoral democracy, or elite democracy (Becker 1958; Dahl 1956, 1971; Sartori 1976: 217; Schattschneider 1942; Schumpeter 1950[1942]; Strøm 1992).

Neither model is a pure type. Even the most citizen-centered polity has some shades of representation. After all, there are always leaders of some sort, even if their leadership positions are informal (Freeman 1972–73). And whatever mechanism was employed to identify those leaders may be used to identify alternative leaders, who presumably compete with the current leader(s) for the affections of the citizenry – making the process look a bit like representative democracy. Likewise, even the most elite-centered democracy has some shades of citizen participation. After all, citizens vote, and this vote is decisive in selecting leaders. Citizens also debate, deliberate, and pressure their leaders in between elections, using all the techniques at their disposal (which may include initiatives and referenda) – making the process look a bit like direct democracy. Thus, we regard participation and competition models as ideal types, which actually existing polities approach in varying degrees.

For present purposes, what is important is that scale affects the feasibility of each ideal type. In a very small polity, assemblies such as those used in New England town hall meetings or Swiss cantons can make all consequential decisions on local matters. Of course, institutions of direct democracy are rare in the contemporary world; but the point remains that their success is contingent upon small scale. If representatives exist, they are close to the people ("embedded"), and likely to reflect their views and interests (Chapter 5). Citizens, being few in number, can interact in an informal fashion with their representatives. If a leader transgresses, she can be brought to task in a public meeting or personal communication.

By contrast, in a large community, citizen-centered modes of decision-making and accountability are generally unavailing. Ordinary citizens are at pains to deliberate en masse and make decisions on every policy.

---

[7] Of course, differences exist across these concepts. However, considerable overlap is also found, justifying our broad-brush treatment.

Neither can they exert pressure on leaders without electoral mechanisms for doing so. We have shown various ways in which scale enhances electoral contestation (Chapter 8), along with features closely associated with the electoral model of democracy such as political parties (Chapter 6), professional politicians (Chapter 10), and institutionalized leadership succession (Chapter 9).

In this manner, scale imposes a trade-off across two enduring models of democracy. Indeed, one may credit the increasing size of polities in the modern era with the apparent victory of the competitive model of democracy over the participatory model of democracy. The former seems to be much more practical than the latter when applied to nation-states composed of millions of citizens.

Power: Individual vs. Collective

Scale affects the nature of democracy in another way, which some might regard as even more fundamental. Consider democracy as a form of *self-rule, self-determination,* or *autonomy* (Lakoff 1997). Now consider how the number of *selves* affects that ideal.

In a community of one, the individual is fully empowered over herself; she can make any and all decisions. Her preferences (which, let us say, are internally consistent) will govern policy. However, she can affect very little beyond her own actions.

By contrast, in a community of 1 billion, the individual citizen is considerably less powerful. As the size of a community increases, the ability of an individual to affect political outcomes attenuates. In an election, individual power attenuates with scale as a matter of definition, as the value of a vote declines in a linear fashion with the number of voters (Riker & Ordeshook 1968). The same attenuation of individual power probably also obtains in authoritarian settings, though perhaps not in a strictly linear fashion.[8]

Moreover, the diversity of preferences (including values, beliefs, issue-positions) should increase with the size of a community, as discussed in Chapter 3. For this reason, as well, the citizen's ideal point may not correspond very closely to the actual course of public policy in a large community.

However, as the size of a community increases, the collective power realized by that community also increases. Larger communities enjoy

---

[8] Although there are no competitive elections or other means for citizens to participate directly in politics, authoritarian leaders must fear popular reprisals, coups, and assassinations. And the power of an individual citizen to oppose the dictator is inversely related to the number of citizens in that society.

greater sovereignty, all other things being equal (Chapter 13). Consequently, they can undertake policies that would be unworkable for small communities. Taxation of investment or income, for example, is more difficult in very small communities because of the ease of capital migration and human migration ("brain drain") – both of which offer an escape from high taxes. Likewise, small communities may have difficulty restricting foreign trade, as they are more dependent upon external markets. And they will be at pains to control environmental degradation that spills over from neighboring communities.

In this fashion, scale introduces a trade-off between *individual* power and *collective* power. Individual power is a key element of the participatory model of democracy (see earlier in this chapter), so it may seem apodictic that a smaller polity is more democratic. However, collective power is also important. An individual who rules over herself is not living in a democracy, at least not in the usual sense of the term. Likewise, a commune of 200 individuals who rule over themselves is only partially democratic insofar as their sovereignty is likely to be extremely restricted. In the modern world, such a tiny community can scarcely insulate itself from global markets, global media, and global environmental changes. They can pass laws, but the laws will have little effect over many policies that citizens care about.

Arguably, democracy is fully achieved only when both individual and collective power is maximized. Yet scale effects suggest that they are irreconcilable. Dahl (1967: 960; quoted in Treisman 2007: 160) notes, "participation in very large units becomes minimal and in very small units it becomes trivial."[9]

Freedom

To be free, let us say, is to be able to pursue one's own projects and one's own vision of the good life – which may or may not conform to what others desire and what governments allow.[10]

In a large polity, the government is apt to be less intrusive, there are likely to be numerous subordinate units enjoying a degree of autonomy, and there will probably be a good deal of heterogeneity across these constituent units. Assuming citizens can move freely across those units, they enjoy a good deal more freedom than they would as members of a small polity. In the latter, the government is apt to be more intrusive and

[9] See also Saarimaa and Tukiainen (2014: 98)
[10] For an in-depth discussion of the concept see Gray (1990).

there are fewer places an unhappy citizen can remove to. Additionally, those places are likely to be less distinctive, offering less choice.

However, if individuals are mobile and can migrate from one polity to another the attraction of smaller scale becomes apparent, as there will be a larger and presumably more diverse menu of polities to choose from. The individual can escape laws she does not like and seek out a polity with laws more to her taste. There is, one might say, a marketplace of polities to choose from – each of which may operate under a different political philosophy and each of which will almost surely encompass a different culture, geography, and so forth.

The impact of scale on freedom thus hinges upon the question of physical mobility. Are individuals free to relocate or are they constrained – due to formal restrictions on cross-border migration or poverty – to live out their lives in the polity where they were born?

At the current moment in history the resolution of this question is troubling. Generalizing broadly, middle-class citizens of rich countries enjoy a high level of mobility. With some effort, they can emigrate to most countries of their choosing. Poor people in rich countries, however, along with almost everyone aside from the very rich people in poor countries, face much higher barriers to exit and entry. With much effort, they may be able to leave their country of origin, but they cannot choose where to live.

In this reality of closed borders – and therefore limited mobility – the implications of scale for freedom are ambivalent. For the rich, who enjoy mobility, a world comprised of small states would provide greater scope for personal freedom than a world comprised of very large states. They would have more choices about where to live and what sort of society they wish to live in. For the poor, however, most of whom are constrained to live out their lives within a single country, a world comprised of large states offers greater scope for the exercise of liberty. More variety is afforded within India than within the Maldives.

Summary of Trade-Offs

Some very important trade-offs occur as a product of scale. These trade-offs, summarized in Table 16.2, serve as leitmotifs of this book. Note that while most trade-offs are unconditional (meaning that they are expected to manifest themselves in virtually any setting), the impact of scale on freedom is conditional on options for mobility.

We acknowledge that highly abstract concepts such as these are amenable to varying interpretations. Consequently, there are different ways of cutting the cake, i.e., alternate ways of articulating trade-offs imposed by

Table 16.2 *Scale trade-offs*

	SMALL	LARGE
Efficiency	Preferences	Policies
Political relationships	Informal/Personal	Formal/Institutional
Systems of rule	Intensive	Extensive
Popular rule	Participatory	Competitive
Power	Individual	Collective
Freedom		
Mobility within polities	Constraint	Freedom
Mobility across polities	Freedom	Constraint

scale. Dahl and Tufte (1973) describe a trade-off between *citizen effectiveness* and *system capacity*, which is similar to what we have referred to as *individual versus collective power*. Economists often view scale as a trade-off between *heterogeneity* and *efficiency* (Alesina, Baqir, & Hoxby 2004; Alesina & Spolaore 1997, 2003; Bolton & Roland 1997; Ellingsen 1998), which is pretty close to what we have labeled *preference versus policy efficiency*.

Rather than try to reduce all scale trade-offs to a single binary contrast we have attempted to identify a range of trade-offs.[11] It follows that these trade-offs are to some extent overlapping. But they are not synonymous.

Of course, we cannot claim to have *proven* all of the trade-offs depicted in Table 16.2, which extend well beyond the empirical evidence presented in previous pages. Indeed, these concepts are so diffuse that they resist falsifiability. Nonetheless, we believe there is a strong theoretical rationale as well as substantial evidence to support these claims.

Which Is Best?

Having summarized a wide range of findings about scale effects (Table 16.1) and a smaller set of trade-offs (Table 16.2), let us grapple with what it all means for public policy and institutional design. Are larger political communities preferable to smaller communities? Or vice versa?

We shall take three cracks at this question. The first focuses on what one might call the *quality of governance*. The second explores options provided by *multilevel governance*. The third interrogates what we know about *citizen preferences*.

---

[11] For an even more disaggregated set of contrasts see Berreman (1978).

Quality of Governance

The quality of governance is a difficult question to wrap one's mind around as there are different understandings of what it means to be well governed (Nanda 2006).

Ignoring theory, one may take a barefoot empiricist approach to the question by identifying outcomes that most citizens presumably endorse, e.g., domestic peace, economic growth, non-corruption, and the provision of public services. With this set of measures one can then ask whether smaller or larger communities offer better governance.

Our examination of these questions reveals few conclusive findings. In Chapter 6, we found no discernible relationship between scale and corruption at national levels – perhaps because the latter is hard to measure in a way that avoids systematic bias. In Chapter 12, we showed that larger countries have smaller public sectors. However, it is unclear how we should regard small government – as a signal of enhanced efficiency or the under-provision of public goods. In Chapter 14, we showed that the relationship of scale to civil conflict is curvilinear – increasing up to about 10 million and decreasing thereafter. This might suggest to the reader that mid-sized states should be avoided. However, this solution hardly seems actionable; neither is a curvilinear relationship apparent with other outcomes under investigation. In Chapter 15, we reviewed extant studies showing that size has a modest impact, if any, on social inequality, economic development, and public services.

The inconclusiveness of these findings could be a product of the weakness of our research designs, as discussed in Chapter 2. Or it could be a product of causal heterogeneity. Increasing the scale of a political unit might enhance the quality of governance in some settings while diminishing the quality of governance in others, depending upon background conditions that we have not been able to identify. A third possibility is that the null result represents the truth of the matter: scale has no impact on the quality of governance, overall.

Perhaps clearer findings will emerge over time. For now, we can only conclude that the jury is out. We are unable to report that scale has positive or negative effects on the quality of governance *overall*, or that there is an identifiable size that is optimal for achieving good governance.

Multilevel Governance

If trade-offs are persistent and there is no overall solution to the problem of scale, perhaps we might contrive to delegate different functions to different levels of government so that each can do what it does best, taking advantage of the distinctive virtues of small and large communities. This solution draws on a distinguished tradition of work variously labeled *multilevel governance* (Marks 1992), *polycentric governance* (Ostrom, Tiebout, & Warren 1961), *federalism* (Mogi 1931), or *fiscal federalism* (Oates 1972).[12]

The reader will note that this book addresses scale effects, leaving aside the question of how differently scaled polities interact with one another and the structure that governs their interrelationship. Nonetheless, it seems worthwhile to explore the implications of multilevel governance for problems of institutional design even if that discussion is, perforce, highly abbreviated.

The case for multilevel governance may be briefly stated. Rather than attempting to find a single scale that achieves all objectives perhaps we should accept that different political objectives require different scales. If so, the diverging virtues associated with small and large scale might be achieved in the same polity if that polity is large and deconcentrated – allowing for a flexible approach to politics and policy. We have observed that as communities grow they tend to deconcentrate power (Chapter 11), so this solution is not at all fanciful.

In principle, dimensions of politics that benefit from small scale such as participation and representativeness could be facilitated by delegating power downward (to small, local-level units) and by offering multiple points of access where citizens can choose to engage. Dimensions of politics that benefit from a large scale could be handled at national – or even supranational – levels. Where policy preferences diverge across lower-level units, policy responsibilities could be decentralized. Where externalities arise, policy responsibilities could be centralized.

Multilevel governance offers the promise of improving both the quality of governance and the quality of democracy by adjusting the scale of politics and policymaking to suit the situation. Even so, there are reasons to doubt whether multilevel governance works as well in practice as it seems to work in theory (Lieberman 2011; O'Dwyer & Ziblatt 2006; Prud'homme 1995; Treisman 2007).

First, for a system of multilevel governance to function smoothly someone must decide which powers and responsibilities are to be centralized and which decentralized. While work on fiscal federalism provides suggestions for how to resolve this assignment problem, the various criteria outlined earlier in this book are often hard to operationalize and sometimes in conflict with one another. In many cases, there is no way to clearly and cleanly delineate functions across levels. In these situations,

---

[10] For an extensive set of references on these topics see Chapter 1.

the operative mode becomes one of "cooperation" – which is easy to prescribe but often hard to achieve, leading to our next topic.

Second, while constitutional designs exert an understandable attraction for scholars, one must ponder the realities of power. Politics is often refractory, and politicians have no incentive to follow precepts contained in ideal models of political economy. The history of multi-level governance is the history of jurisdictional fights across rival units, units that have different values and interests – where the interests of political leaders may diverge from the interests of their constituents and where the interests of subnational units may not be synchronized with the interests of the nation-state. As a result, it is difficult to reach consensus with respect to questions of constitutional design or public policy. The real world of federalism does not look very much like the ideal world of fiscal federalism (Bakvis, Baier, & Brown 2009; Banting & Simeon 1985; Rodden 2002; Rodden & Wibbels 2002; Scharpf 1988; Volden 2005; Wibbels 2006).

Third, a multilevel system of governance faces unenviable problems of legitimacy. Consider that a democratic politics demands that citizens identify themselves as members of a political community (Tussman 1974). This key element of identity underlies whatever demands – e.g., for participation, public service, military service, taxes, and loyalty – politics might make on citizens. However, in a multilevel system citizens must develop a sense of attachment to multiple political communities, e.g., local, regional, national, and supranational. This is a difficult trick. Recent threats to the health and survival of the European Union are testament to the strains introduced when disparate, overlapping communities fight with one another over the allegiance of the same citizens (Hurrelmann 2007).

Finally, some trade-offs imposed by scale are recalcitrant and unlikely to be solved through multilevel governance.

Consider the trade-off between individual power and collective power. There is no way to square this circle.

Consider a policy that evokes preference heterogeneity as well as externalities. On defense policy, there may be a great deal of disagreement over the correct level of spending – between "hawks" and "doves" – but it would be costly to decentralize policymaking power.

Consider the goal of political participation. In a large, deconcentrated community citizens may participate at many levels, enhancing the potential for participation. However, because there are many levels the structure of power is more complex, and this by itself is likely to serve as a barrier to participation. In all likelihood, citizens will focus their attention on those offices deemed most important, leaving others with reduced participation rates. More elective offices usually means lower turnout for each of them, as citizens' time and energy is limited.

Consider that while size reduces coordination problems across communities it enhances coordination problems *within* communities. A larger community embraces more people with a greater dispersion of interests and values. If deconcentrated, political power will also be fragmented, making it harder for citizens to monitor officeholders, assign blame, and hold appropriate politicians accountable. Electoral accountability is attenuated when lines of responsibility are blurred (J. Smith 2007). Any system of multilevel governance must struggle with this negative repercussion of complexity.

The success of multilevel governance depends upon addressing these problems, an issue that lies outside the scope of this book. We do not mean to imply that these problems cannot be mitigated, only to point out that they are formidable. There is no easy resolution to trade-offs imposed by scale. Multilevel governance may assist in this quest – indeed, it is probably inevitable. But it is no panacea.

Popular Preferences

Now, let us leave arguments and evidence aside so as to inquire about citizen preferences. What scale of government do people *prefer*?

At first glance, the evidence seems overwhelming. Citizens trust their neighbors and their local officials more than they trust distant authorities who rule over larger units, e.g., nations or confederations (Chapter 5). This perspective is embodied in political behavior: citizens are more likely to participate in smaller-scale political communities than in larger-scale communities (Chapter 7). In the business of government, smallness is perceived as a virtue and bigness as a vice.

Exceptions may be found in situations where a community faces an external threat. This might be geopolitical ("imperialism") or economic ("big business," "corporate capitalism," "globalization"). In a situation of vulnerability, questions of scale are viewed differently. Yet, even here, scale is not viewed as an intrinsic virtue but instead as a necessary vice. One must fight power with power.

So the question of attitudinal preferences seems settled. However, if we turn to behavioral measures of preferences ("revealed preferences"), things are more complicated. The same people who say they trust their local representatives more than their national or supranational representatives are not usually engaged in secessionist movements. The latter, though growing, are still rare.

Moreover, secessionist movements seem to be driven by grievances about how to define the national community and by perceived discrimination and exclusion. The optimal size of political communities does not seem to play a self-conscious role in the rhetoric of rebellion. Kurds who demand independence from Turkey, Iraq, Syria, and Iran are looking for self-determination. They do not have any special preferences over how large or small that state might be. Indeed, such a state would be sizeable if all Kurds in the Middle East were included.

Movements to decentralize power are perhaps easier to interpret as a preference for smaller scale. Even so, such movements often seem to be driven more by particular issues than by the principle itself. It is not hard to discern an element of forum-shopping in which citizens militate for greater decentralization of power on issues where they are unlikely to carry the day in national fora. Self-anointed "federalists" in US history were federalists only with respect to issues where they were (and are) a minority (Chapter 12). It is questionable whether there is a strong and informed opinion about centralization/decentralization among publics throughout the world.

In summary, it is difficult to answer the question of what political scale citizens prefer because answers to survey questions are ambiguous and citizen behavior equally so. In truth, it is a difficult question to wrap one's mind around – for all the reasons outlined in this book. But it is no less important, for all its complexity.

Appendix A   Interviews

Wouter Veenendaal conducted the following interviews during field visits to these states and territories.

Bonaire

Abraham, Clark (June 30, 2016, Kralendijk), commissioner in the Executive Council of Bonaire for the Bonaire Democratic Party (Partido Demokratiko Boneriano) (PDB).

Bernabela, Esther (July 8, 2016, Antriol), independent member of the Island Council of Bonaire.

Bijkerk, Michiel (July 2, 2016, Kralendijk), president of the Pro-Hustisia Union Party (Partido Hustisia i Union) (PHU).

Coffie, Desiree (June 28, 2016, Kralendijk), member of the Island Council of Bonaire for the Movement of Bonaire People (Movementu di Pueblo Boneriano) (MPB).

Den Heyer, Nina (July 4, 2016, Kralendijk), commissioner in the Executive Council of Bonaire for the MPB.

Gonzalez, Nereida (July 4, 2016, Kralendijk), general island secretary of Bonaire.

Janga, Marugia (July 7, 2016, Kralendijk), member of the Island Council of Bonaire for the PDB.

Oleana, Nolly (July 1, 2016, Kralendijk), senior civil servant for the Department of the Caribbean Netherlands (Rijksdienst Caribisch Nederland) (RCN).

Raphaela, Jeanoushka (July 5, 2016, Kralendijk), independent member of the Island Council of Bonaire.

Rijna, Edison (June 28, 2016, Kralendijk), island governor of Bonaire.

Silberie, Maritsa (July 4, 2016, Kralendijk), president of the Patriotic Union of Bonaire (Union Patriotiko Boneriano) (UPB); senior civil servant for the RCN.

Silberie, Milena (July 7, 2016, Kralendijk), member of the Island Council of Bonaire for the MPB.

Tjin Asjoe, Elvis (June 30, 2016, Kralendijk), party leader of the MPB.

Willem, Norwin (July 1, 2016, Kralendijk), president of the Good Governance Foundation (Fundashon Bon Gobernashon).

Liechtenstein

Amann-Marxer, Marlies (January 7, 2014, Vaduz), minister of infrastructure, environment, and sport for the Fatherland Union (Vaterländische Union) (VU).

Beck, Josef (January 14, 2014, Vaduz), president of the Liechtenstein Chamber of Commerce.

Büchel, Jakob (January 7, 2014, Vaduz), president of the VU.

Frick, Mario (January 13, 2014, Schaan), former head of government (1993–2001) for the VU; attorney-at-law.

Frick, Pepo (January 10, 2014, Schaan), president of the Free List (Freie Liste); member of parliament.

Fritz, Günther (January 8, 2014, Vaduz), chief editor of the *Liechtensteiner Vaterland* newspaper.

Hasler, Adrian (January 13, 2014, Vaduz), head of government of Liechtenstein for the Progressive Citizens' Party of Liechtenstein (Fortschrittliche Bürgerpartei Liechtenstein) (FBP).

Hasler, Martin (January 6, 2014, Vaduz), journalist for the *Volksblatt* newspaper.

Hilbe, Edith (January 8, 2014, Vaduz), chairwoman of the Liechtenstein Democracy Movement (Demokratiebewegung Liechtenstein).

Liechtenstein, Prince Hans-Adam II (January 16, 2014, Vaduz), reigning prince of Liechtenstein.

Pedrazzini, Mauro (January 9, 2014, Vaduz), minister of social affairs for the FBP.

Schürti, Pio (January 15, 2014, Schaan), member of parliament for The Independents (Die Unabhängigen) (DU).

Wohlwend, Sigvard (January 15, 2014, Schaan), journalist and democracy activist.

Malta

Abela, Carmelo (November 16, 2017, Valletta), minister of foreign affairs and trade promotion for the Labour Party.

Attard, Rachel (November 14, 2017, St. Julian's), news editor at *The Independent* daily newspaper.

Borg, Ian (November 6, 2017, Floriana), minister of transportation and infrastructure for the Labour Party.

Bugeja, Josef (November 3, 2017, Valletta), secretary-general of the General Workers' Union, Malta's largest trade union.

Bugeja, Ray (November 15, 2017, Mriehel), editor of the *Times of Malta* daily newspaper.

Busuttil, Simon (November 7, 2017, Valletta), former leader of the Nationalist Party; member of parliament; former member of the European Parliament (MEP).

Camilleri, Carla (November 2, 2017, Valletta), assistant director of the Aditus Foundation, a human rights advocacy nongovernmental organization (NGO).

Caruana, Justyne (November 22, 2017, Rabat, Gozo), minister of Gozo for the Labour Party.

Cassola, Arnold (November 13, 2017, Msida), leader of Democratic Alternative (Alternattiva Demokratika) (AD); associate professor of comparative literature at the University of Malta.

De Marco, Mario (November 15, 2017, Valletta), member of parliament for the Nationalist Party; former minister of tourism, the environment, and culture.

Delia, Manuel (November 20, 2017, Mqabba), blogger about Maltese politics.

Doublet, Nicholas (November 6, 2017, Floriana), diocesan archivist and historian at the Catholic Church in Malta.

Falzon, Michael (November 14, 2017, Valletta), minister of family and children's rights for the Labour Party.

Farrugia, Anglu (November 20, 2017, Valletta), speaker of the House of Representatives; former deputy leader of the Labour Party.

Farrugia, Joseph (November 6, 2017, Valletta), director general of the Malta Employers' Association.

Farrugia, Marlene (November 13, 2017, Qrendi), member of parliament for the Democratic Party; former member of parliament for the Labour Party and the Nationalist Party.

Farrugia, Michael (November 9, 2017, Valletta), minister of home affairs and national security for the Labour Party; former minister of family and social solidarity.

Gonzi, Lawrence (November 20, 2017, Valletta), former prime minister for the Nationalist Party (2004–13).

Mercieca, Ryan (November 22, 2017, Rabat, Gozo), president of the Gozo Youth Council; candidate for the Nationalist Party.

Muscat, Joseph (November 21, 2017, Valletta), prime minister of Malta for the Labour Party; former MEP.

Pullicino Orlando, Jeffrey (November 9, 2017, Kalkara), executive chairman of the Malta Council for Science and Technology; former member of parliament for the Nationalist Party.

Sant, Alfred (December 6, 2017, Brussels, Belgium), former prime minister for the Labour Party (1996–98); MEP.

Tabone, Anton (November 22, 2017, Rabat, Gozo), former Gozo minister for the Nationalist Party; former speaker of the House of Representatives.

Palau

Asanuma, Santy (July 5, 2011, Koror), former senator in the Palau National Congress (Olbiil Era Kelulau); guest editor of the *Tia Belau* newspaper.

Bedor, Roman, Ngirakebou (July 12, 2011, Meyungs), high chief of Ngchesar State; member of the Palau Council of Chiefs; attorney-at-law; former Palauan activist during the 1980s and 1990s Compact of Free Association (COFA) nego-tiations with the United States.

Chin, Hon. Elias Camsek (July 19, 2011, Ngerulmud), sena-tor in the Olbiil Era Kelulau; former vice president of Palau (2005–09); presidential candidate in the 2008 election.

Dengokl, Yukiwo P., Ngiraked (July 9, 2011, Koror), high chief (*ngiraked*) of Airai State; member of the Palau Council of Chiefs; attorney-at-law.

Gibbons, Jennifer K. (July 6, 2011, Koror, Palau), executive director of the Palau Chamber of Commerce.

Gibbons, Yutaka M., Ibedul (July 13, 2011, Koror), high chief of the Republic of Palau and Koror State; chairman of the Palau Council of Chiefs; chief executive officer (CEO) of Gibbons Enterprises; former presidential candidate.

Kesolei, Hon. Katherine (July 18, 2011, Ngerulmud), vice president of the Senate in the Olbiil Era Kelulau; member of Palau's women's association, the Mesechil Belau.

Kesolei, Ongerung Kambes (July 6, 2011, Koror), chairman of the Palau International Coral Reef Center; columnist at *Tia Belau*.

Mariur, Hon. Kerai (July 12, 2011, Ngerulmud), vice president of the Republic of Palau; former member of the House of Delegates in the Olbiil Era Kelulau (1992–2008).

Ngiraklsong, Mr. Arthur (July 5, 2011, Koror), chief justice of the Republic of Palau.

Pierantozzi, Sandra Sumang (July 11, 2011, Koror), former vice president of the Republic of Palau (2001–05); former minister of finance, health, and foreign affairs; former senator in the Olbiil Era Kelulau.

Rehuher-Marugg, Faustina K. (July 11, 2011, Koror), minister of community and cultural affairs of the Republic of Palau; former director of the Belau National Museum.

Shih-chang Huang, Bill (July 7, 2011, Koror), counselor at the Embassy of the Republic of China (Taiwan) in the Republic of Palau.

Tellei, Dr. Patrick U. (July 7, 2011, Koror), president of Palau Community College.

Toribiong, Hon. Johnson (July 14, 2011, Melekeok), president of the Republic of Palau; former *ngiraked* of Airai State.

Uludong, Moses Y. (July 6, 2011, Koror), chief editor and publisher of *Tia Belau*; former senator in the Olbiil Era Kelulau; former ombudsman of the Republic of Palau.

Saba

Buncamper, Carl (January 13, 2016, The Bottom), Island Council member for the Windwards Islands People's Movement (WIPM).

Janssens, Bastiaan (January 15, 2016, The Bottom), office manager of the Rijksdienst Caribisch Nederland (RCN).

Johnson, Chris (January 14, 2016, The Bottom), commissioner in the Executive Council of Saba for the WIPM.

Johnson, Jonathan (January 14, 2016, The Bottom), island governor of Saba.

Johnson, Will (January 11, 2016, Windwardside), president of the WIPM; former governor of Saba.

Levenstone, Akilah (January 13, 2016, The Bottom), island registrar of Saba.

Levenstone, Dave (January 12, 2016, The Bottom), head of the Department of Economic Affairs of Saba.

Wilson, Monique (January 12, 2016, The Bottom), Island Council member for the Saba Labour Party (SLP).

Wilson, Rolando (January 13, 2016, The Bottom), Island Council member for the WIPM.

Zagers, Bruce (January 14, 2016, The Bottom), commissioner in the Executive Council of Saba for the WIPM.

St. Eustatius

Berkel, Gerald (June 22, 2015, Oranjestad), island governor of St. Eustatius.

Brown, Franklin (June 18, 2015, Golden Rock), former Island Council member; journalist for FAB Radio; president of the St. Eustatius Empowerment Party (STEP).

Fortin, Ricardo (June 23, 2015, Oranjestad), journalist for CT Creativity Television.

Leerdam, Richeline (June 18, 2015, Oranjestad), Island Council member for the Progressive Labour Party (PLP).

Lijfrock-Marsdin, Millicent (June 22, 2015, Oranjestad), former Island Council member; president of the Statia Liberal Action Movement (SLAM).

McKenzie-Tatem, Astrid (June 24, 2015, Oranjestad), commissioner in the Executive Council of St. Eustatius for the PLP.

Merkman, Althea (June 28, 2015, Golden Rock), Journalist for the *Daily Herald.*

Schmidt, Glenville (June 19, 2015, Oranjestad), former commissioner of finances in the Executive Council of St. Eustatius.

Sneek, Koos (June 19, 2015, Golden Rock), party president and Island Council member for the Democratic Party (DP).

Spanner, Adelka (June 26, 2015, Oranjestad), Island Council member for the DP.

Van Putten, Clyde (June 24, 2015, Oranjestad), party president and Island Council member for the PLP.

St. Kitts and Nevis

Astaphan, Hon. G. A. Dwyer (January 10, 2011, Basseterre, St. Kitts), former minister of national security for St. Kitts and Nevis; resigned in 2008, a strong critic of the Labour government.

Brantley, Hon. Mark A. G. (January 19, 2011, Charlestown, Nevis), leader of the opposition in the National Assembly of St. Kitts and Nevis for the Concerned Citizens Movement (CCM).

Condor, Hon. Sam T. (January 28, 2011, Basseterre, St. Kitts), deputy prime minister and minister of foreign affairs for St. Kitts and Nevis.

Conway, Stanford (January 11, 2011, Basseterre, St. Kitts), editor in chief of the *St. Kitts and Nevis Vibes* (SKNVibes) online newspaper (www.sknvibes.com).

Grant, Hon. Lindsay F. P. (January 12, 2011, Basseterre, St. Kitts), leader of the People's Action Movement (PAM), the opposition party of St. Kitts.

Gumbs, Walford V. (January 17, 2011, Basseterre, St. Kitts), ombudsman of St. Kitts and Nevis; former speaker in the National Assembly of St. Kitts and Nevis for the Labour Party.

Harris, Hon. Timothy S., PhD (January 14, 2011, Basseterre, St. Kitts), minister of agriculture, lands, and housing for St. Kitts and Nevis for the Labour Party; author of several publications on Kittitian–Nevisian politics and history.

Inniss, Sir Probyn Ellsworth (January 17, 2011, Basseterre, St. Kitts), former governor-general of St. Kitts and Nevis (1975–81); author of several publications on Kittitian–Nevisian politics and history.

Richardson, Howard (January 18, 2011, Basseterre, St. Kitts), executive officer of the St. Kitts and Nevis Chamber of Commerce and Industry.

Seaton, S. W. Tapley, QC (January 12, 2011, Basseterre, St. Kitts), former attorney general of St. Kitts and Nevis; president of St. Christopher's National Trust; president of the Organization of Eastern Caribbean States (OECS) Bar Association.

Sebastian, Sir Cuthbert Montraville, GCMG, OBE (January 20, 2011, Basseterre, St. Kitts), governor-general of St. Kitts and Nevis (since 1995).

Warner, Dr. Asyll (January 12, 2011, Basseterre, St. Kitts), lecturer in political science at the University of the West Indies (UWI) Open Campus.

Williams, Kenneth (January 10, 2011, Charlestown, Nevis), editor in chief of the *St. Kitts and Nevis Observer*.

San Marino

Beccari, Marco (November 17, 2010, Domagnano), secretary-general of the Democratic Confederation of San Marino Workers (Confederazione Democratica Lavoratori Sammarinese) (CDLS) trade union.

Chiaruzzi, Giorgio (November 10, 2010, Città di San Marino), director of the San Marino Entrepreneurs' Organization (Organizzazione Sammarinese degli Imprenditori) (OSLA).

Ciavatta, Valeria (November 5, 2010, Città di San Marino), secretary of state for internal affairs; former captain regent; member of the Popular Alliance (Alleanza Popolare) (AP).

Felici, Claudio (November 10, 2010, Città di San Marino), leader of the Socialist–Democratic Party (Partito dei Socialisti e dei Democratici) (PSD) in the Great and General Council.

Ghiotti, Massimo (November 11, 2010, Fiorina di Domagnano), director general of the Chamber of Commerce of the Republic of San Marino (Camera di Commercio della Repubblica di San Marino).

Giorgetti, Roberto (November 12, 2010, Borgo Maggiore), party leader of the AP in the Great and General Council; former captain regent.

Michelotti, Francesca (November 10, 2010, Città di San Marino), *consigliere* (member of parliament) for United Left (Sinistra Unita) (SU) in the Great and General Council; member of the Council of Twelve (Consiglio dei Dodici); manager of the State Museums of San Marino.

Michelotti, Simona (November 11, 2010, Fiorina di Domagnano), managing director of the Transparent Packaging Printing Group (Gruppo Stampa Imballagi Trasparenti) (Gruppo SIT), one of the leading enterprises of San Marino; president of the Administrative Council of the Chamber of Commerce.

Morganti, Francesco (November 10, 2010, Città di San Marino), staff member of the OSLA.

Morganti, Giuseppe Maria (November 9, 2010, Città di San Marino), *consigliere* for the PSD in the Great and General Council; journalist for the *La Tribuna Sammarinese* daily newspaper; former captain regent.

Morri, Romeo (November 19, 2010, Città di San Marino), secretary of state for education, culture, and the university; former captain regent; former leader of the Sammarinese Christian Democratic Party (Partito Democratico Cristiano Sammarinese) (PDCS); now affiliated with the right-wing Union of Moderates (Unione dei Moderati).

Muccioli, Stiven (November 15, 2010, Città di San Marino), journalist for the *Notizie di San Marino – Libertas* online newspaper; author of several publications on Sammarinese politics and media.

Oddone, David (November 17, 2010, Borgo Maggiore), journalist for the *L'Informazione di San Marino* daily newspaper.

Rattini, Maurizio (November 16, 2010, Borgo Maggiore), party leader of the New Socialist Party (Nuovo Partito Socialista) (NPS) in the Great and General Council; former captain regent.

Rondelli, Paolo (November 4, 2010, Città di San Marino), Sammarinese ambassador to the United States; representative of San Marino at the Congress of Local and Regional Authorities of Europe (Congrès des Pouvoirs Locaux et Régionaux d'Europe) (CPLRE).

Rossi, Laura (November 18, 2010, Città di San Marino), professor of Sammarinese history; master of the state library.

Zani, Jeffrey (November 9, 2010, Città di San Marino), journalist for *La Tribuna Sammarinese*.

Zavoli, Luca (November 15, 2010, Città di San Marino), journalist for *Notizie di San Marino – Libertas*.

Seychelles

Adam, Hon. Jean-Paul (February 17, 2011, Mont-Fleuri), minister of foreign affairs for Seychelles for the People's Party (Parti Lepep).

Egonda-Ntende, Hon. Mr. Frederick M.S. (March 1, 2011, Victoria), chief justice of Seychelles, former chair of the Law Reporting Committee of Uganda.

Gay, Rita J. (March 2, 2011, Victoria), journalist at the *Seychelles Nation* newspaper.

Hollanda, Ivan N. (March 2, 2011, Victoria), journalist at the *Seychelles Nation*.

Lucas, Hon. Wilby, LLB (March 4, 2011, Île Perseverance), deputy speaker at the National Assembly of Seychelles; elected as a member of parliament for the Parti Lepep in the district of Baie Lazare.

Mondon, Hon. Macsuzy (February 18, 2011, Mont-Fleuri), minister of education, employment, and human resources for Seychelles for the Parti Lepep.

Morgan, Hon. Joel (February 17, 2011, Victoria), minister of home affairs, environment, and transport for Seychelles for the Parti Lepep.

Payet, Dr. Rolph, FRGS (March 4, 2011, Mont-Fleuri), president and vice-chancellor of the University of Seychelles; special advisor to the president of Seychelles.

Ramkalawan, Hon. Wavel (February 18, 2011, Mont-Fleuri), leader of the Seychelles National Party (SNP); former leader of the opposition in the National Assembly of Seychelles; former editor in chief of the *Regar* newspaper.

Sabino, Mr. Divino (March 1, 2011, Victoria), attorney-at-law; secretary of the Bar Association of Seychelles; part-time lecturer at the University of Seychelles; former state counsel at the Attorney-General's Chambers.

Sinon, Hon. Peter (March 1, 2011, Victoria), minister of investment, natural resources, and industry for Seychelles for the Parti Lepep.

Volcere, Ralph (February 22, 2011, Mont-Fleuri), leader and former presidential candidate for the New Democratic Party (NDP); editor in chief of *Le Nouveau Seychelles*.

Zatte, Dora (March 3, 2011, Mont-Fleuri), ombudsman of Seychelles; attorney-at-law and barrister-at-law; former advisor to the Seychelles People's Defense Forces; former board member of the Seychelles Broadcasting Corporation (SBC).

Suriname

Brave, Iwan (February 8, 2018, Paramaribo), chief editor of the *De Ware Tijd* newspaper.

Breeveld, Carl (February 7, 2018, Paramaribo), leader of the Democracy and Development in Unity Party (Democratie en Ontwikkeling in Eenheid) (DOE).

Breeveld, Hans (February 21, 2018, Paramaribo), political scientist at the Anton de Kom University of Suriname.

Del Castilho, Angelique (February 22, 2018, Paramaribo), leader of the Democratic Alternative '91 Party (Democratisch Alternatief '91) (DA'91).

Dikan, Edgar (February 20, 2018, Paramaribo), minister of regional development for the Brotherhood and Unity in Politics Party (Broederschap en Eenheid in de Politiek) (BEP).

Findlay, George (February 21, 2018, Paramaribo), chief editor of the *De West* daily newspaper.

Ganga, Sharda (February 8, 2018, Paramaribo), director of PROJEKTA, an NGO for governance, participation, and gender equality.

Misiekaba, André (February 23, 2018, Paramaribo), parliamentary leader of the National Democratic Party (Nationale Democratische Partij) (NDP).

Moestadja, Soewarto (February 16, 2018, Paramaribo), minister of labor for the NDP.

Neijhorst, Julian (February 12, 2018, Paramaribo), chief editor of *Parbode*, a monthly magazine focusing on Surinamese politics.

Neus, Maisha (February 7, 2018, Paramaribo), political activist and leader of the STREI! Party.

Polak, Cristien (February 7, 2018, Paramaribo), minister of social affairs and housing for the NDP.

Ramcharan, Nita (February 6, 2018, Paramaribo), chief editor of the *Starniews* online news platform.

Rusland, Gregory (February 16, 2018, Paramaribo), leader of the National Party of Suriname (Nationale Partij Suriname).

Santokhi, Chandrikapersad (February 24, 2018, Paramaribo), leader of the Progressive Reform Party (Vooruitstrevende Hervormingspartij).

Simons-Geerlings, Jennifer (February 19, 2018, Paramaribo), speaker of the National Assembly of Suriname.

Somohardjo, Paul (February 9, 2018, Paramaribo), leader of the Pertjajah Luhur Party.

Venetiaan, Ronald (February 20, 2018, Paramaribo), former president of Suriname (1991–96, 2000–10) for the National Party of Suriname.

Waterberg, Celsius (February 8, 2018, Paramaribo), leader of the BEP.

Welzijn, Ferdinand (February 12, 2018, Paramaribo), minister of trade, industry, and tourism for the NDP.

Wijdenbosch, Ruth (February 13, 2018, Paramaribo), former member and vice-speaker of parliament for the National Party of Suriname.

Vanuatu

Ligo, Godwin (November 29, 2018, Port Vila), senior journalist for the *Vanuatu Daily Post* newspaper.

Lini, Motarilavoa Hilda (November 27, 2018, Port Vila), chief of the Taruga Nation of Pentecost Island; former minister of health for the Our Land Party (Vanua'aku Pati); founder of the Vanuatu National Council of Women.

Loughman, Bob (November 28, 2018, Port Vila), deputy prime minister and minister of tourism, commerce, and trade for the Vanua'aku Pati.

Maoh, Alfred (November 28, 2018, Port Vila), minister of lands, geology, and mines for the Ground and Justice Party (Graon mo Jastis Pati).

Mataskelekele, Kalkot (December 7, 2018, Port Vila), former president of the Republic of Vanuatu (2004–09) for the National United Party.

McGarry, Dan (November 27, 2018, Port Vila), media director of the *Vanuatu Daily Post.*

Molgos, Alan Wai (November 23, 2018, Port Vila), acting ombudsman of Vanuatu.

Pakoa, Anne (November 26, 2018, Port Vila), founder and president of the Vanuatu Human Rights Coalition.

Plasua, Willy (November 21, 2018, Port Vila), chief from Meralava; president of the National Council of Chiefs (Malvatumauri).

Regenvanu, Ralph (November 26, 2018, Port Vila), minister of foreign affairs and leader of the Ground and Justice Party.

Regenvanu, Sethy (November 22, 2018, Port Vila), former deputy prime minister and minister of lands for the Vanua'aku Pati.

Rory, Eta (November 22, 2018, Port Vila), former member of parliament for the Vanuatu Republican Party.

Saimon, Esmon (December 3, 2018, Port Vila), speaker of parliament and former minister of infrastructure and public utilities (2013–15) for the Vanua'aku Pati.

Seremaiah Nawalu, Matai (November 26, 2018, Port Vila), member of parliament and former minister of agriculture for the Vanuatu Leaders' Party.

Sokomanu, Ati George (December 6, 2018, Mele), former president of the Republic of Vanuatu (1980–89) for the Vanua'aku Pati.

Sopé, Barak (December 6, 2018, Port Vila), former prime minister of Vanuatu (1999–2001) for the Melanesian Progressive Party.

Tom, Jean-Pierre (November 21, 2018, Port Vila), CEO of the Malvatumauri.

Vira, Alickson (December 3, 2018, Port Vila), member of parliament for the Natatok Indigenous Democratic Party.

Appendix B   Country-Level Data

Notes

- This Appendix includes variables employed in *country-level* analyses. Data employed for *within-country* analyses are discussed in the text and, in some cases, in other publications.
- For discussion of principal data sources – V-Dem, MLEA, GLP – see Chapter 2.
- For some variables whose coding is regarded as static through time, coding may be extended backward and forward in time to enhance coverage.

Table B1   *Variable definitions, sources (country-level)*

Age dependency ratio, old. Ratio of older people (64+) to the working-age population (ages 15–64). Proportion of dependents per 100 working-age population. *Source*: WDI (World Bank 2017). *Scale*: interval. *Agedependencyratiooldof*

Agricultural suitability. Geographic endowments favoring agricultural production including climate, soil, and terrain. *Source*: Agro-Ecological Zones (GAEZ) system, developed by the Food and Agriculture Organization (FAO) of the United Nations, downloaded (October 2017) from http://gaez.fao.org/Main.html#. *Scale*: logarithmic. *suita_GAEZ_ln*

Arable land. Arable land includes land defined by the FAO as land under temporary crops (double-cropped areas are counted once), temporary meadows for mowing or for pasture, land under market or kitchen gardens, and land temporarily fallow. Land abandoned as a result of shifting cultivation is excluded. *Source*: WDI 2017 (World Bank 2017). *Scale*: interval. *ArablelandoflandareaAG*

Battle deaths. Focusing on civil conflicts (e.g., insurrections, violent protests, and civil wars), we count the number of battlefield fatalities each year (if they surpass a threshold of twenty-five). For each conflict event, we accept the "best" estimate. Where unavailable, we arrive at a best estimate by averaging low and high estimates for an event. This is considered as a ratio of the total population (in thousands) to obtain a measure of battle deaths per 1,000 citizens. *Source*: Battle Deaths dataset (Lacina 2009). *Scale*: interval. *bdeadlow_sum_nomiss_per1000*

Bicameralism. The existence of two chambers in the national legislature and – if they exist – how closely matched their powers are, based on the coding of country experts. *Source*: V-Dem (Coppedge et al. 2017). *Scale*: ordinal. *Legbalance*

BMR. Summary measure of regime type. *Source*: Boix, Miller, and Rosato (2012). *Scale*: binary. *e_mibmr*

Table B1   *(cont.)*

Cabinet size. Statutory size of cabinet. *Sources*: GLP (Gerring, Oncel, et al. 2019) for 2018; Liu and Apfeld (2016) for previous years. *Scale*: logarithmic. *cabinet_size_2_ln*

Campaign spending. Total party income (by all major parties) per registered voter in (or around) 2011. *Source*: Poguntke, Scarrow, and Webb (2016: 664). *Scale*: logarithmic. *partyincome_pc_ln*

Capital city. Population of capital city as a share of total population. Calculated by authors. Sources for capital city population: UN (2014), supplemented by other sources. *Scale*: logarithmic. *capital_pop_share_ln*

Checks and balances. "The number of veto players in a political system, adjusting for whether these veto players are independent of each other, as determined by the level of electoral competitiveness in a system, their respective party affiliations, and the electoral rules." *Source*: DPI (Beck et al. 2001), where it is referred to as *Checks1*. *Scale*: logarithmic. *e_dpi_checks_ln*

Competitiveness. Calculated from the vote share of the largest party in national elections for the lower or unicameral chamber and the vote share of the largest vote-getter in presidential elections (if any). For each, we calculate 100 minus the vote share, and then take the average of all elections occurring in a given year (if there is more than one). A score of zero indicates a total absence of competitiveness (one party or candidate wins all the votes). A high score means that the largest party or candidate wins a minority of votes. *Source*: V-Dem (Coppedge et al. 2017). *Scale*: interval. *competitive_votes_lg_prezleg*

Compulsory voting. Compulsory voting: 0 = No. 1 = Yes, but there are no sanctions or sanctions are not enforced. 2 = Yes, sanctions exist and are enforced, but they impose minimal costs upon the offending voter. 3 = Yes, sanctions exist, they are enforced, and they impose considerable costs upon the offending voter. *Source*: V-Dem (Coppedge et al. 2017). *Scale*: ordinal. *v2elcomvot*

Cumulative elections. Number of lower-chamber or unicameral legislative elections (including the current election) held since 1900 – regardless of any constitutional or unconstitutional changes and interruptions that may have taken place. *Source*: V-Dem (Coppedge et al. 2017). *Scale*: logarithmic. *v2ellocumul_ln*

Democracy. See the *Lexical index of electoral democracy*, the default measure of democracy in this book.

Desert. Share of territory classified as desert. *Source*: Gerring, Tollefsen, et al. (2019). *Scale*: interval. *desert*

Education, mass (15+). Average years of education among citizens older than fifteen. *Source*: V-Dem (Coppedge et al. 2017), combining data from multiple sources. *Scale*: interval. *e_peaveduc*

Education, elite. The educational attainment of leaders – executives, members of parliament (lower or unicameral chamber), and the supreme (or constitutional) court. This is measured along a six-level ordinal scale registering (for each individual) the highest level of education completed: (a) primary, (b) secondary, (c) higher non-university education, (d) college or university, (e) postgraduate (anything except PhD degree), or (f) PhD. Data aggregated into a country-level mean for 2010–13. *Source*: GLP (Gerring, Oncel, et al. 2019). *Scale*: interval. *Edu_mean*

Election boycott. A deliberate and public refusal to participate in an election by a candidate or party who is eligible to participate. Responses: 0 = Total: all opposition

Table B1   *(cont.)*

parties and candidates boycotted the election. 1 = Significant: some but not all opposition parties or candidates boycotted but they constituted a major opposition force. 2 = Ambiguous: some but not all opposition parties or candidates boycotted but it is unclear whether they would have constituted a major electoral force. 3 = Minor: a few opposition parties or candidates boycotted and they were relatively insignificant ones. 4 = Nonexistent: no parties or candidates boycotted the elections. Transformed to an interval scale by the V-Dem measurement model. *Source*: V-Dem (Coppedge et al. 2017). *Scale*: interval. *v2elboycot*

Election type. Indicates the type or types of elections that occurred in a given year: (0) Legislative, lower, sole, or both chambers, first or only round. (1) Legislative, lower, sole, or both chambers, second round. (2) Legislative, upper chamber only, first or only round. (3) Legislative, upper chamber only, second round. (4) Constituent assembly, first or only round. (5) Constituent assembly, second round. (6) Presidential, first or only round. (7) Presidential, second round. *Source*: V-Dem (Coppedge et al. 2017). *Scale*: binary. *v2eltype_0 v2eltype_1 v2eltype_2 fv2eltype_3 v2eltype_4 v2eltype_5 v2eltype_6 v2eltype_7*

Electoral system. The electoral system used in an election for the lower or unicameral chamber of the legislature. 0 = Majoritarian. 1 = Proportional. 2 = Mixed. 3 = Other (e.g., single nontransferable voting, limited voting). *Source:* V-Dem (Coppedge et al. 2017). *Scale:* nominal. *v2elparlel*

Elevation. Mean elevation. *Source*: Gerring, Tollefsen, et al. (2019). *Scale*: interval. *eleva*

Elite positions. Total number of leadership positions within a country, as measured by the GLP. Leaders are classified into ten (sometimes overlapping) categories: (1) the apex, (2) the next ten, (3) the executive, (4) cabinet members, (5) executive staff, (6) party leaders, (7) assembly leaders, (8) supreme court justices, (9) members of parliament (MPs), and (10) unelected persons. (The vast majority are MPs.) *Source*: GLP (Gerring, Oncel, et al. 2019). *Scale*: logarithmic. *glp_ctotalelite_ln*

English colony. Current or former English colony. Source: La Porta et al. (1999), obtained from QoG (Teorell et al. 2013). *Scale*: binary. *English_legal_origin*

Ethnic fractionalization. Probability that two randomly chosen people are members of the same ethnic group. *Source*: Alesina et al. (2003). *Scale*: interval. *al_ethnic*

Ethnic misrepresentation index. To measure the representativeness of the elite class (R_B) we compare the representation of groups within the elite to their representation in the general population using a transformed version of the Rose Index of Proportionality: $R_B = \sum_{t-1}^{n} |G_{Pi} - G_{Bi}|$, where G_P is group i's share of the population, G_B is group i's share of a political body, and n is the number of groups in the population. A value of 0 describes a perfect correspondence between the body politic and a political body. Deviations from zero, i.e., misrepresentation, are potentially infinite, generating a long right tail. *Source*: GLP (Gerring, Oncel, et al. 2019). *Scale*: logarithmic. *C_E_R_all_ln*

Ethnolinguistic fractionalization. Probability that two randomly chosen people are members of the same ethnolinguistic group. *Source*: Fearon (2003). *Scale*: interval. *ef_fearon*

Federalism. An institutionalized division or sharing of responsibilities between a national authority and semiautonomous regional units, usually codified in a constitution. 0 = nonfederal (regional governments, if they exist, are granted minimal policymaking power). 1 = semi-federal (there are elective governments at the regional level but

Table B1   *(cont.)*

constitutional sovereignty is reserved to the national government). 2 = federal (elective regional governments plus constitutional recognition of subnational authority). *Source*: Gerring, Thacker (2008: 88). *Scale*: ordinal. *federalism_GT*

Foreign aid/GDP. Net development assistance and aid (Constant USD) as share of GDP. *Source*: WDI (World Bank 2018). *Scale*: interval. *wdi_aid_GDP*

Free and fair elections. A judgment, taking all aspects of the preelection period, election day, and the postelection process into account, about whether an election is free and fair. The only thing considered is the extent of suffrage (by law). Responses: 0 = No, not at all. The elections were fundamentally flawed and the official results had little if anything to do with the "will of the people" (i.e., who became president; or who won the legislative majority). 1 = Not really. While the elections allowed for some contestation, the irregularities in the end affected the outcome of the election (i.e., who became president, or who won the legislative majority). 2 = Ambiguous: there was substantial contestation and freedom of participation but there were also significant irregularities. It is hard to determine whether the irregularities affected the outcome (as defined earlier). 3 = Yes, somewhat: there were deficiencies and some degree of fraud and irregularities but these did not in the end affect the outcome (as defined earlier). 4 = Yes: there was some amount of human error and logistical restrictions but these were largely unintentional and without significant consequences. Transformed to an interval scale by the V-Dem measurement model. *Source*: V-Dem (Coppedge et al. 2017). *Scale*: interval. *v2elfrfair*

GDP. Gross domestic product in constant 1990 dollars. This is based on data from the Maddison Project (Bolt & Van Zanden 2014), supplemented by estimates from Bairoch (1976), Broadberry (2015), Broadberry and Klein (2012), Gleditsch (2002), and the WDI (World Bank 2016), which are combined in a dynamic, three-dimensional latent trait model. *Source*: Fariss et al. (2017). *Scale*: logarithmic. *Maddison_gdp_1990_estimate_ln*

GDP per capita. Gross domestic product per capita in constant 1990 dollars. This is based on data from the Maddison Project (Bolt & Van Zanden 2014), supplemented by estimates from Bairoch (1976), Broadberry (2015), Broadberry and Klein (2012), Gleditsch (2002), and the WDI (World Bank 2016), which are combined in a dynamic, three-dimensional latent trait model. *Source*: Fariss et al. (2017). *Scale*: logarithmic. *Maddison_gdppc_1990_estimate_ln*

GDP per capita growth. Annual change in per capita GDP. *Source*: V-Dem (Coppedge et al. 2017). *Scale*: interval. *e_migdpgro*

Gini index. The extent to which the distribution of income (or, in some cases, consumption expenditure) among individuals or households within an economy deviates from a perfectly equal distribution. A Lorenz curve plots the cumulative percentages of total income received against the cumulative number of recipients, starting with the poorest individual or household. The Gini index measures the area between the Lorenz curve and a hypothetical line of absolute equality, expressed as a percentage of the maximum area under the line. Thus a Gini index of 0 represents perfect equality, while an index of 100 implies perfect inequality. *Source*: WDI (World Bank 2017). *Scale*: interval. *wdi_gini*

Government consumption. General government final consumption expenditure (formerly general government consumption) as share (%) of GDP. Includes all government current expenditures for purchases of goods and services (including compensation of employees). It also includes most expenditures on national defense and security, but

Table B1   *(cont.)*

excludes government military expenditures that are part of government capital formation. *General government* usually refers to local, regional and central governments. *Source*: WDI (World Bank 2017). *Scale*: interval. *Generalgovernmentfinalconsump*

Government employee compensation. All payments in cash, as well as in kind (such as food and housing), to government employees in return for services rendered, and government contributions to social insurance schemes such as social security and pensions that provide benefits to employees. Calculated (by authors) as share of GDP. *Scale*: interval. *govemployeecompensation_gdp*

Government employees. Government employees as share (%) of total population. Employment data are provided by the International Labor Organization LABORSTA database for the years 2000–10 for "general government," "publicly owned enterprises," and the "public sector" (general government + state-owned enterprises). *Source*: Baddock, Lang, and Srivastava (2015). *Scale*: interval. *employ_pub*

Imports/GDP. Imports of goods and services as share (%) of GDP. *Source*: WDI (World Bank 2018). *Scale*: interval. *wdi_imp*

Independents. Number of independents as share (%) of the lower or unicameral chamber of the national legislature. Independents are defined as members who are not declared members of a political party. *Source*: V-Dem (Coppedge et al. 2017). *Scale*: interval. *v2elindss*

Institutionalized leadership succession. Attributes: (1) The previous executive leaves office in a regular fashion. (2) The former executive is at liberty, i.e., does not face imprisonment, harassment, exile, or death because of actions taken while in office. (3) The current executive is chosen through regular procedures, as laid out in a constitution or basic law. (4) The current executive has no family connection to any previously serving executive – a connection that we regard as prima facie evidence of nepotism. (5) The current executive has been in office for a decade or less. Aggregation: additive. *Source*: Gerring and Knutsen (2019). *Scale:* ordinal. *instit_add*

Iron and steel production. Production of pig iron (1816–99) and steel (1900–2012), calculated in thousands of tons. *Source*: Correlates of War (COW) dataset (Sarkees & Wayman 2010). *Scale*: logarithmic. *cow_irst_ln*

Island. Indicates whether a country is attached to a continental land mass. *Source*: authors. *Scale*: binary. *island*

Land area. Land area of country. *Source*: Agro-Ecological Zones (GAEZ) system, developed by the Food and Agriculture Organization (FAO) of the United Nations, downloaded (October 2017) from http://gaez.fao.org/Main.html#. Extra data are linearly imputed with data from WDI (World Bank 2016). *Scale*: logarithmic. *area_GAEZ_ln_imp*

Latitude. Distance from equator. *Source*: QoG (Teorell et al. 2016). *Scale*: logarithmic. *Latitude_ln*

Legislative professionalism. An index composed of three V-Dem indicators: *legislative resources* (In practice, does the legislature control the resources that finance its own internal operations and the perquisites of its members? [*v2lgfunds*]), *legislative committees* (Does the lower [or unicameral] chamber of the legislature have a functioning committee system? [*v2lgcomslow*]), and *legislative staff* (Does each member of the lower [or unicameral] chamber of the legislature have at least one staff member with policy expertise? [*v2lgstafflo*]). These are combined by addition into a composite index of legislative

Table B1   *(cont.)*

capacity. *Source*: authors, based on data from V-Dem (Coppedge et al. 2017). *Scale*: interval. *leg_instit*

Legislative fractionalization. Measures the probability that two randomly drawn representatives from the lower (or unicameral) chamber of the legislature will be from different parties. *Source*: PolCon (Henisz 2002). *Scale*: interval. *Legfralower*

Legislature size: lower or unicameral. The number of legislators in the lower or unicameral chamber of the national legislature. Data are drawn from three sources, in order of preference: IPU (www.ipu.org/), V-Dem (Coppedge et al. 2018), and CCP (Elkins, Ginsburg, & Melton 2009). These sources define the subject in slightly different ways, as discussed in Chapter 4. Once values are obtained from these three sources, we fill in missing values for each country by projecting past values forward so as to generate a country-year time series that is complete from the first observation to the present. We ignore interregnums, i.e., periods in which the legislature is displaced or dissolved. *Sources*: see earlier in this Appendix. *Scale*: logarithmic. *lower_unicam_chamber_N_ln*

Legislature size: lower and upper. The number of legislators in the lower and upper (if bicameral) chambers of the national legislature. *Source*: IPU (www.ipu.org/). *Scale*: logarithmic. *parl_lowerandupper_N_ln*

Legislature size: upper. The number of legislators in the upper chamber of the national legislature. *Source*: IPU (www.ipu.org/). *Scale*: logarithmic. *upper_chamber_N_ln*

Lexical index of electoral democracy. An ordinal index measuring the electoral components of democracy in a cumulative fashion. That is, to qualify for a given level (0–6) all previous conditions must be satisfied. 0 = No elections. (Elections are not held for any policymaking offices. This includes situations in which elections are postponed indefinitely or the constitutional timing of elections is violated in a more than marginal fashion.) 1 = Elections with no parties or with only one party. (There are regular elections but they are nonpartisan or only a single party or party grouping is allowed to participate.) 2 = Multiparty elections for legislature. (Opposition parties are allowed to participate in legislative elections and to take office.) 3 = Multiparty elections for executive. (The executive is chosen directly or indirectly – by an elected legislature – through elections. 4 = Minimally competitive elections for both executive and legislature. (The chief executive offices and the seats in the effective legislative body are – directly or indirectly – filled by elections characterized by uncertainty, meaning that the elections are, in principle, sufficiently free to enable the opposition to win government power.) 5 = Male or female suffrage. (Virtually all adult male *or* female citizens are allowed to vote in elections.) 6 = Universal suffrage. (Virtually all adult citizens are allowed to vote in elections.) *Source*: Skaaning, Gerring, and Bartusevičius (2015). *Scale*: ordinal. *lexical_index*

Linguistic fractionalization. Probability that two randomly chosen people are members of the same linguistic group. *Source*: Alesina et al. (2003). *Scale*: interval. *al_language*

Linguistic groups. Number of linguistic groups having more than 1,000 speakers. *Source*: Michalopoulos (2012), based on data from the World Language Mapping System (2006). *Scale*: logarithmic. *lnnmbrlang_percntry*

Manufacturing value added. *Manufacturing* refers to industries belonging to ISIC divisions 15–37. *Value added* is the net output of a sector after adding up all outputs and subtracting intermediate inputs. It is calculated without making deductions for depreciation of fabricated assets or depletion and degradation of natural resources. The origin of value added is determined by the International Standard Industrial Classification

Table B1   *(cont.)*

(ISIC), revision 3. Calculated as percent of GDP. *Source*: WDI 2015 (World Bank 2015), obtained from QoG 2016 (Teorell et al. 2013). *Scale*: interval. *wdi_manvagdp*

Meritocratic recruitment. Surveys ask experts to estimate what proportion of higher officials in the civil service enter via a formal examination system and, for those who enter through some other route, what proportion have university or postgraduate degrees. These variables are combined into an equal-weight index (assembled as part of the QoG dataset), intended to measure the extent of meritocratic recruitment in the civil service. *Source*: Evans and Rauch (1999), Rauch and Evans (2000), obtained from QoG (Teorell et al. 2016). *Scale*: interval. *er_merit*

Military expenditure. Total military budget, converted into a standard unit – British pounds sterling prior to 1914, US dollars thereafter – using the COW currency conversion dataset (which uses current exchange rates). Missing data are replaced by lowest values in the dataset (authors). *Source*: COW dataset (Singer, Bremer, & Stuckey 1972). *Scale*: logarithmic. *milper_ext_ln*

Military personnel. Number of military personnel (1000s). Missing data are replaced by lowest values in the dataset (authors). *Source*: COW dataset (Singer et al. 1972). *Scale*: logarithmic. *milper_ext_ln*

Mineral wealth. The aggregated real value of a country's petroleum, coal, natural gas, and metals production, as a share of total population. *Source*: Haber and Menaldo (2011). *Scale*: interval. *e_Total_Resources_Income_PC*

Minimum voting age. The minimum age at which citizens are allowed to vote in national elections. *Source*: V-Dem (Coppedge et al. 2017). *Scale*: interval. *v2elage*

Monarchy. A polity with an executive office that is (a) hereditary, (b) monopolized by a single individual or (occasionally) jointly by several members of the same family, (c) endowed with life tenure, and (d) of nontrivial importance. All criteria are necessary in order to qualify as monarchical. Hereditary succession may be either de jure (a clear statement of principle by someone in authority) or de facto (a well-established practice, as evidenced by family trees showing relationships among successive rulers). Life tenure is assumed if there is no constitutional method of removing a sitting ruler and if rulers typically die in office. Where a hereditary executive has no share in policymaking and is displaced by a fully democratic body we surmise that the king neither reigns nor rules; his or her power is trivial. Accordingly, present-day United Kingdom is not coded as monarchical. *Source*: Gerring, Wig, et al. (2019). *Scale*: binary. *monarchy_veenendaal*

MP Salary. Official annualized salary of members of the lower (or unicameral) chamber of parliament, converted to US dollars using purchasing power parity. *Source*: GLP (Gerring, Oncel, et al. 2019). *Scale*: interval. *MPSalaryUSAnnual*

Multiparty election. 0 = No: no party or a single party with no meaningful contestation (includes situations where a few parties are legal but they are all de facto controlled by the dominant party). 1 = Not really. No party or a single party (defined as earlier) but multiple candidates from the same party and/or independents contest legislative seats or the presidency. 2 = Constrained. At least one real opposition party is allowed to contest but contestation is highly constrained – legally or informally. 3 = Almost: elections are multiparty in principle but either one main opposition party is prevented (de jure or de facto) from contesting, or conditions such as civil unrest (excluding natural disasters) prevent contestation in a portion of the territory. 4 = Yes: elections are multiparty, even though a few marginal parties may not be permitted to contest (e.g., far-right/left

Table B1   *(cont.)*

extremist parties, antidemocratic religious or ethnic parties). Transformed to an interval scale by the V-Dem measurement model. *Source*: V-Dem (Coppedge et al. 2017). *Scale*: interval. *v2elmulpar*

Muslim. Share of population with Muslim heritage (%). *Source*: La Porta et al. (1999), obtained from QoG (Teorell et al. 2013). *Scale*: interval. *Muslim*

Naval tonnage. Weight (tons) of all naval ships. Missing data are replaced by lowest values in the dataset (authors). *Source*: Crisher and Souva (2014). *Scale*: logarithmic. *totton_ext_ln*

OPEC. Member of the Organization of the Petroleum Exporting Countries. *Source*: authors. *Scale*: binary. *OPEC*

Party institutionalization. Refers to the institutionalization of various attributes of political parties in a country, e.g., level and depth of organization, links to civil society, cadres of party activists, party supporters within the electorate, coherence of party platforms and ideologies, party-line voting among representatives within the legislature. A high score on these attributes generally indicates a more institutionalized party system. Considers the attributes of all parties with an emphasis on larger parties, i.e., those that may be said to dominate and define the party system. The index is formed by adding the indicators for party organizations (v2psorgs), party branches (v2psprbrch), party linkages (v2psprlnks), distinct party platforms (v2psplats), and legislative party cohesion (v2pscohesv), after standardization. *Source*: V-Dem (Coppedge et al. 2017). *Scale*: interval. *v2xps_party*

Patent applications. Patent applications are worldwide patent applications filed through the Patent Cooperation Treaty procedure or with a national patent office for exclusive rights for an invention – a product or process that provides a new way of doing something or offers a new technical solution to a problem. A patent provides protection for the invention to the owner of the patent for a limited period, generally twenty years. Resident patent applications are those for which the first-named applicant or assignee is a resident of the state or region concerned. *Source*: WDI (World Bank 2018). *Scale*: logarithmic. *Patent_apps_residents_ln*

Political rights. An index measuring the extent of political rights, reversed so that 0 is the least democratic and 6 is the most democratic. *Source*: Freedom House (2007). *Scale*: ordinal. *pol_rts_FH_reverse_scale*

Polity2. A weighted additive aggregation procedure across five subcomponents: competitiveness and openness of executive recruitment, competitiveness and regulation of political participation, and constraints on the chief executive. *Source*: Polity IV database (Marshall, Gurr, & Jaggers 2014). *Scale*: ordinal. *e_polity2*

Polyarchy. Electoral democracy index. *Source*: V-Dem (Coppedge et al. 2017; Teorell et al. 2019). *Scale*: interval. *v2x_polyarchy*

Population. Official population of a country, counting only those acknowledged as citizens. This is based on data from the Maddison Project (Bolt & Van Zanden 2014), supplemented by estimates from Broadberry and Klein (2012), Gleditsch (2002), Singer et al. (1972), and WDI (World Bank 2016), which are combined in a dynamic, three-dimensional latent trait model. *Source*: Fariss et al. (2017). *Scale*: logarithmic. *Maddison_pop_estimate_ln*

Protestant. Share of population with Protestant heritage (%). *Source*: La Porta et al. (1999), obtained from QoG (Teorell et al. 2013). *Scale*: interval. *lp_protmg80*

Table B1   *(cont.)*

Public education expenditure. General government expenditure on education (current, capital, and transfers) as a share (%)of GDP. Includes expenditure funded by transfers from international sources to government. *General government* usually refers to local, regional, and central governments. *Source*: WDI (World Bank 2017). *Scale*: interval. *educ_exp_GDP*

Public health expenditure Public expenditure on health as share (%) of GDP. *Source*: WDI (World Bank 2017). *Scale*: interval. *wdi_puhe*

Public trust in politicians. From a survey administered by the World Economic Forum to businesspeople around the world. Question: How would you rate the level of public trust in the ethical standards of politicians in your country? Responses registered on a Likert scale where 0 = very low and 7 = very high, subsequently aggregated to form a country mean. *Source*: The Global Competitiveness Report (Schwab & Sala-i-Martin 2015), obtained from QoG (Teorell et al. 2013). *Scale*: interval. *wef_ptp*

Regions. Comprising: Eastern Europe and Central Asia (including Mongolia), Latin America, the Middle East and North Africa, Sub-Saharan Africa, Western Europe and North America, East Asia, Southeast Asia, South Asia, the Pacific, and the Caribbean. *Source*: QoG (Teorell et al. 2013). *Scale*: nominal. *e_regionpol*

Revenue decentralization. Subnational revenue as share of total public revenue. *Source*: Enikolopov and Zhuravskaya (2007), compiled from Government Finance Statistics (IMF). *Scale*: interval. *Decentraliz_rev_EZ*

Separate powers. Measures the existence of separate powers, signaled by whether the dominant executive (either the head of state or head of government) is directly elected. *Source*: authors, calculated from V-Dem data (Coppedge et al. 2017). *Scale*: binary. *prez_JG2*

Small state. Indicates whether a country's population is less than 1 million. *Source*: authors, calculated from Population (earlier in this Appendix). *Scale*: binary. *small_state*

State history. History of statehood from AD 0 to 1950, recorded at fifty-year intervals and added together with a 1 percent depreciation rate. *Source*: Bockstette, Chanda, and Putterman (2002). *Scale*: interval. *Statehistn01*

Statistical capacity. An overview of the capacity of a country's national statistical system based on a diagnostic framework of twenty-five criteria assessing (a) methodology, (b) source data, and (c) periodicity/timeliness. *Source*: WDI 2016 (World Bank 2016). *Scale*: interval. *Overalllevelofstatisticalcap*

Subnational government layers. Comprised of two variables measuring whether local and regional governments exist, as coded by research assistants and regional experts. These are added together to form a three-level index: 0 = none, 1 = one level, or 2 = both levels. *Source*: authors, using data obtained from V-Dem (Coppedge et al. 2017). *Scale*: ordinal. *subnational_layers*

Suffrage. Share of adult citizens (as defined by statute) having the legal right to vote in national elections (%). Does not take into consideration restrictions based on age, residence, having been convicted for crime, or being legally incompetent. Covers legal (de jure) restrictions, not restrictions that may be operative in practice (de facto). The adult population (as defined by statute) is defined by citizens in the case of independent countries or the people living in the territorial entity in the case of colonies. Universal suffrage is coded as 100 percent. Universal male suffrage is coded as 50 percent. Years before electoral provisions are introduced are scored 0 percent. Scores do not reflect

Table B1   *(cont.)*

whether an electoral regime was interrupted. Only if new constitutions, electoral laws, or the like explicitly introduce new regulations of suffrage are the scores adjusted accordingly if the changes suggest doing so. If qualifying criteria other than gender apply (such as property, tax payments, income, literacy, region, race, ethnicity, religion, and/or "economic independence"), estimates have been calculated by combining information on the restrictions with different kinds of statistical information (on population size, age distribution, wealth distribution, literacy rates, size of ethnic groups, etc.), secondary country-specific sources, and – in the case of very poor information – the conditions in similar countries or colonies. The scores reflect de jure provisions of suffrage extension in a percentage of the adult population. If the suffrage law is revised in a way that affects the extension, the scores reflect this change as of the calendar year the law was enacted. *Source*: V-Dem (Coppedge et al. 2017). *Scale*: interval. *v2elsuffrage*

Tax revenue. Compulsory transfers to the central government for public purposes. Certain compulsory transfers such as fines, penalties, and most social security contributions are excluded. Refunds and corrections of erroneously collected tax revenue are treated as negative revenue. *Source*: WDI (World Bank 2017). *Scale*: interval. *TaxrevenueofGDPGCTAXT_2*

Temperature. Mean temperature. *Source*: Gerring, Tollefsen, et al. (2019). *Scale*: interval. *tmean*

Tenure. Number of years a leader has served continuously. *Source*: Archigos (Goemans, Gleditsch, & Chiozza 2009). *Scale*: interval. *e_tenure*

Tourism arrivals. International inbound tourists (overnight visitors) are the number of tourists who travel to a country other than that in which they have their usual residence, but outside their usual environment, for a period not exceeding twelve months and whose main purpose in visiting is other than an activity remunerated from within the country visited. When data on number of tourists are not available, the number of visitors, which includes tourists, same-day visitors, cruise passengers, and crew members, is shown instead. Sources and collection methods for arrivals differ across countries. In some cases data are from border statistics (police, immigration, and the like) and supplemented by border surveys. In other cases data are from tourism accommodation establishments. For some countries the number of arrivals is limited to arrivals by air and for others to arrivals staying in hotels. Some countries include arrivals of nationals residing abroad while others do not. Caution should thus be used in comparing arrivals across countries. The data on inbound tourists refer to the number of arrivals, not to the number of people traveling. Thus a person who makes several trips to a country during a given period is counted each time as a new arrival. *Source*: WDI (World Bank 2018). *Scale*: logarithmic. *tourism_arrivals_ln*

Turnout. Share of the adult voting-age population (VAP) that cast a vote according to official results (%). The VAP can reflect irregularities such as problems with the voters' register or registration system. The VAP numbers are estimates since they do not take into account legal or systemic barriers to the exercise of the franchise or account for non-eligible members of the population. Thus, it can occur that VAP values surpass 100, which is not an error but reflects such conditions. In cases where executive and legislative elections were held on the same day but there is a different turnout recorded for each election, turnout for this date is coded for the executive election only. *Source*: IDEA

Table B1 *(cont.)*

(Global Survey of Voter Turnout), obtained from V-Dem (Coppedge et al. 2017). *Scale*: interval. *v2elvaptrn*

Universities. Total number of universities. *Source*: authors. *Scale*: logarithmic. *cum_total_n_ln*

Urbanization. Share of population living in urban areas (%). *Source*: V-Dem (Coppedge et al. 2017). *Scale*: interval. *e_miurbani*

Vote-buying. Vote- or turnout-buying, i.e., the distribution of money or gifts to individuals, families, or small groups in order to influence their decision to vote/not vote or whom to vote for. Responses: 0 = Yes, there was systematic, widespread, and almost nationwide vote- or turnout-buying by almost all parties and candidates. 1 = Yes, some: there were nonsystematic but rather common vote-buying efforts, even if only in some parts of the country or by one or a few parties. 2 = Restricted: money and/or personal gifts were distributed by parties or candidates but these offerings were more about meeting an "entry-ticket" expectation and less about actual vote choice or turnout, even if a smaller number of individuals may also be persuaded. 3 = Almost none: there was limited use of money and personal gifts, or these attempts were limited to a few small areas of the country. In all, they probably affected less than a few percent of voters. 4 = None: there was no evidence of vote- or turnout-buying. Transformed to an interval scale by the V-Dem measurement model. *Source*: V-Dem (Coppedge et al. 2017). *Scale*: interval. *v2elvotbuy*

Years since independence. Years since a country became formally independent (i.e., recognized by the international community). *Source*: authors. *Scale*: logarithmic. *yrs_since_indep_ln*

Table B2 *Descriptive statistics (country-level)*

Variable name	Label	Obs.	Mean	SD	Min.	Max.
Age dependency ratio	Agedependencyratiooldof	10,534	10.07	6.02	0.87	43.91
Agricultural suitability (log)	suita_GAEZ_ln	20,943	2.96	1.21	0.00	4.38
Arable land	ArablelandoflandareaAG	9,372	13.92	13.57	0.04	73.39
Battle deaths	bdeadlow_sum_nomiss_per1000	12,081	0.007	0.08	0.00	5.40
Bicameralism	Legbalance	17,547	1.38	1.31	0.00	4.00
BMR	e_mibmr	11,838	0.39	0.49	0.00	1.00
Cabinet size (log)	cabinet_size_2_ln	434	2.82	0.44	1.10	3.85
Campaign spending (log)	partyincome_pc_ln	19	-0.30	0.73	-1.77	1.02
Capital city (log)	capital_pop_share_ln	20,110	-8.96	1.53	-15.40	-2.71
Checks and balances (log)	e_dpi_checks_ln	6,004	0.71	0.66	0.00	2.89
Competitiveness	competitive_votes_lg_prezleg	3,050	46.53	22.78	0.00	93.50
Compulsory voting	v2elcomvot	17,286	0.19	0.55	0.00	3.00
Cumulative elections (log)	v2ellocumul_ln	17,604	1.64	1.23	0.00	4.09
Desert	Desert	19,895	3.64	11.46	0.00	77.28
Education, mass	e_peaveduc	13,548	4.48	3.27	0.00	13.48
Education, elite	Edu_mean	160	3.18	1.27	0.00	5.00
Election boycott	v2elboycott	3,621	0.09	1.25	-4.79	1.85
Elevation	Eleva	19,895	577.73	528.20	33.82	2983.33
Elite positions	glp_crotalelite_ln	144	5.38	0.66	4.13	8.05
English colony	English_legal_origin	18,683	0.36	0.48	0.00	1.00
Ethnic fractionalization	al_ethnic	19,168	0.44	0.26	0.00	0.93
Ethnic misrepresentation index	C_E_R_all_ln	123	0.26	0.19	0.00	0.84
Ethnolinguistic fractionalization	ef_fearon	157	0.48	0.26	0.00	1.00
Federalism	federalism_GT	6,354	0.38	0.75	0.00	2.00

		N	Mean	SD	Min	Max
Foreign aid/GDP	wdi_aid_GDP	6,188	56.23	102.14	0.00	3370.00
Free and fair elections	v2elrfair	3,628	0.05	1.47	-3.26	2.95
GDP (log)	Maddison_gdp_1990_estimate_ln	17,437	7.84	1.19	3.87	14.40
GDP per capita (log)	Maddison_gdppc_1990_estimate_ln	17,437	7.84	1.19	3.87	14.40
GDP per capita growth	e_migdpgro	11,133	1.97	6.45	-61.49	86.95
Gini index	wdi_gini	819	42.67	10.09	20.96	74.33
Government consumption	Generalgovernmentfinalconsump	7,882	15.94	7.60	0.00	156.53
Government employee compensation	govemployeecompensation_gdp	3,540	0.07	0.05	0.00	0.84
Imports/GDP	wdi_imp	6,939	40.65	25.16	-17.14	219.07
Independents	v2elindss	3,108	9.97	25.94	0.00	100.00
Institutionalized leadership succession	instit_add	12,117	3.65	1.27	0.00	5.00
Government employees	employ_pub	708	8.05	4.39	0.42	25.43
Island	Island	22,509	0.23	0.42	0.00	1.00
Land area (log)	area_GAEZ_ln_imp	22,602	11.22	2.76	2.23	18.13
Latitude (log)	Latitude_ln	21,505	-1.60	0.95	-4.50	-0.34
Legislative capacity	leg_instit	12,874	0.33	3.10	-6.68	8.70
Legislative fractionalization	Legfralower	7,911	0.48	0.29	0.00	1.00
Legislature size: lower/unicameral	lower_unicam_chamber_N_ln	17,082	4.68	1.07	0	8.00
Legislature size: both chambers	parl_lowerandupper_N_ln	192	5.01	1.00	2.64	8.00
Legislature size: upper	upper_chamber_N_ln	79	4.11	0.83	2.40	6.67
Lexical index of electoral democracy	lexical_index	12,982	3.39	2.37	0.00	6.00
Linguistic fractionalization	al_language	19,129	0.39	0.28	0.00	0.92
Linguistic groups	lnnmbrlang_percntry	153	2.44	1.52	0.00	6.14
Manufacturing value added	wdi_manvagdp	5,677	14.19	7.55	0.00	45.67
Meritocratic recruitment	er_merit	2,118	0.57	0.25	0.04	1.00

Table B2 *(cont.)*

Variable name	Label	Obs.	Mean	SD	Min.	Max.
Military expenditure (log)	milex_ext_ln	39,593	3.14	5.40	0.00	20.36
Military personnel (log)	milper_ext_ln	37,352	1.04	1.91	0.00	9.43
Mineral wealth	e_Total_Resources_Income_PC	10,646	595.41	3228.97	0.00	81161.85
Minimum voting age	v2elage	3,009	19.06	2.11	3.00	30.00
Monarchy	monarchy_veenendaal	14,916	0.18	0.38	0.00	1.00
MP salaries	MPSalaryUSAnnual	145	52958.04	46895.85	0.00	187339.00
Multiparty election	v2elmulpar	3,628	0.11	1.41	-3.38	2.66
Muslim	Muslim	18,732	21.13	34.81	0.00	99.90
Naval tonnage (log)	totton_ext_ln	38,009	1.16	3.32	0.00	16.24
Party institutionalization	v2xps_party	13,085	0.50	0.29	0.00	1.00
Patent applications	Patent_apps_residents_ln	4,328	5.40	2.78	0.00	14.00
Political rights (reverse scale)	pol_rts_FH_reverse_scale	6,986	4.22	2.24	1.00	7.00
Polity2	e_polity2	11,894	0.44	7.31	-10.00	10.00
Polyarchy	v2x_polyarchy	17,036	0.32	0.28	0.01	0.95
Population (log)	Maddison_pop_estimate_ln	17,240	15.23	1.98	8.73	21.38
Protestant	lp_protmg80	22,849	14.11	21.63	0.00	97.80
Education expenditure	educ_exp_GDP	3,488	4.41	1.95	0.00	44.33
Public health expenditure	wdi_puhe	2,960	3.66	2.29	0.00	19.85
Public trust in politicians	wef_ptp	1,195	2.99	1.18	1.25	6.48
Revenue decentralization	Decentraliz_rev_EZ	1,398	15.97	13.55	0.13	56.25
Separate powers	prez_JG2	16,477	0.23	0.42	0.00	1.00
Small state	small_states	33,763	0.10	0.30	0.00	1.00
State history	Statehistn01	12,294	0.38	0.28	0.01	0.98
Statistical capacity	Overalllevelofstatisticalcap	1,839	65.49	16.83	16.67	98.89
Subnational government layers	subnational_layers	17,413	1.79	0.47	0.00	2.00
Suffrage	v2elsuffrage	17,309	64.80	43.47	0.00	100.00

Tax revenue	TaxrevenueofGDPGCTAXT_2	3,802	17.17	8.63	0.06	132.52
Temperature	Tmean	19,895	291.64	8.25	266.17	301.46
Tenure	e_tenure	12,132	7.19	8.13	1.00	68.00
Tourism arrivals (log)	tourism_arrivals_ln	4,207	13.52	2.08	6.55	18.25
Turnout	v2elvaptrn	1,936	63.99	19.76	2.14	223.70
Universities (log)	cum_total_n_ln	22,932	1.54	1.57	0.00	7.43
Urbanization	e_miurbani	20,764	0.35	0.25	0.01	1.00
Vote-buying	v2elvotbuy	3,628	0.14	1.37	-2.97	3.65
Years since independence (log)	yrs_since_indep_ln	21,965	2.43	2.34	0.00	7.57

Includes all country-level variables listed in Table B1 except nominal variables with more than two categories.

References

Abbott, Andrew (2014). *The System of Professions: An Essay on the Division of Expert Labor*. Chicago: University of Chicago Press.

Abdelal, Rawi, Yoshiko M. Herrera, Alastair I. Johnston, & Rose McDermott (2009). *Measuring Identity: A Guide for Social Scientists*. Cambridge: Cambridge University Press.

Abernethy, David B. (2000). *The Dynamics of Global Dominance: European Overseas Empires, 1415–1980*. New Haven, CT: Yale University Press.

Abramowitz, Alan I., Brad Alexander, & Matthew Gunning (2006). Incumbency, Redistricting, and the Decline of Competition in U.S. House Elections. *Journal of Politics*, 68(1), 75–88.

Abramowitz, Alan I. & Jeffrey A. Segal (1992). *Senate Elections*. Ann Arbor: University of Michigan Press.

Abramson, Scott F. (2017). The Economic Origins of the Territorial State. *International Organization*, 71(1), 97–130.

Acemoglu, Daron & James A. Robinson (2006) *Economic Origins of Dictatorship and Democracy*. Cambridge: Cambridge University Press.

Achen, Christopher H. (1978). Measuring Representation. *American Journal of Political Science*, 22(3), 475–510.

Adeney, Katharine (2007). *Federalism and Ethnic Conflict Regulation in India and Pakistan*. New York: Springer.

Ades, Alberto & Edward L. Glaeser (1995). Trade and Circuses: Explaining Urban Giants. *Quarterly Journal of Economics*, 110(1), 195–227.

Agrawal, Arun & Sanjeef Goyal (2001). Group Size and Collective Action: Third Party Monitoring in Common-Pool Resources. *Comparative Political Studies*, 34 (1), 63–93.

Ahlerup, Pelle & Ola Olsson (2012). The Roots of Ethnic Diversity. *Journal of Economic Growth*, 17(2), 71–102.

Aistrup, Joseph A. (2004). Constituency Diversity and Party Competition: A County and State Level Analysis. *Political Research Quarterly*, 57(2), 267–81.

Albanese, Robert & David D. van Fleet (1985). Rational Behavior in Groups: The Free-Riding Tendency. *Academy of Management Review*, 10(2), 244–55.

Alesina, Alberto (2003). The Size of Countries: Does It Matter? *Journal of the European Economic Association*, 1(2/3), 301–16.

Alesina, Alberto, Reza Baqir, & William Easterly (1999). Public Goods and Ethnic Divisions. *Quarterly Journal of Economics*, 114(4), 1214–84.

Alesina, Alberto, Reza Baqir, & Caroline Hoxby (2004). Political Jurisdictions in Heterogeneous Communities. *Journal of Political Economy*, 112(2), 348–96.

Alesina, Alberto, Arnaud Devleeschauwer, William Easterly, Sergio Kurlat, & Romain Wacziarg (2003). Fractionalization. *Journal of Economic Growth*, 8(2), 155–94.

Alesina, Alberto, William Easterly, & Janina Matuszeski (2011) Artificial States. *Journal of the European Economic Association*, 9(2), 246–77.

Alesina, Alberto & Edward L. Glaeser (2004). *Fighting Poverty in the US and Europe: A World of Difference*. Oxford: Oxford University Press.

Alesina, Alberto & Eliana La Ferrara (2000). Participation in Heterogeneous Communities. *Quarterly Journal of Economics*, 115(3), 847–904.

Alesina, Alberto & Roberto Perotti (1997). The Welfare State and Competitiveness. *American Economic Review*, 87(5), 921–39.

Alesina, Alberto, Roberto Perotti, & Enrico Spolaore (1995). Together or Separately? Issues on the Costs and Benefits of Political and Fiscal Unions. *European Economic Review*, 39(3/4), 751–58.

Alesina, Alberto & Enrico Spolaore (1997). On the Number and Size of Nations. *Quarterly Journal of Economics*, 112(4), 1027–56.

Alesina, Alberto & Enrico Spolaore (2003). *The Size of Nations*. Cambridge, MA: MIT Press.

Alesina, Alberto & Enrico Spolaore (2005) War, Peace, and the Size of Countries. *Journal of Public Economics*, 89(7), 1333–54.

Alesina, Alberto, Enrico Spolaore, & Romain Wacziarg (2000). Economic Integration and Political Disintegration. *American Economic Review*, 90(5), 1276–96.

Alesina, Alberto & Romain Wacziarg (1998). Openness, Country Size and Government. *Journal of Public Economics*, 69(3), 305–21.

Allers, Maarten A. & J. Bieuwe Geertsema (2016). The Effects of Local Government Amalgamation on Public Spending, Taxation, and Service Levels: Evidence from 15 Years of Municipal Consolidation. *Journal of Regional Science*, 56(4), 659–82.

Almond, Gabriel (1956). Comparative Political Systems. *Journal of Politics*, 18 (3), 391–409.

Alonso, William (1987). *Population in an Interacting World*. Cambridge, MA: Harvard University Press.

Altman, David (2010). *Direct Democracy Worldwide*. Cambridge: Cambridge University Press.

Alvarez, Michael, Jose A. Cheibub, Fernando Limongi, & Adam Przeworski (1996). Classifying Political Regimes. *Studies in Comparative International Development*, 31(2), 3–36.

Anckar, Carsten (2000). Size and Party System Fragmentation. *Party Politics*, 6 (3), 305–28.

Anckar, Carsten (2008). Size, Islandness, and Democracy: A Global Comparison. *International Political Science Review*, 29(4), 440–41.

Anckar, Dag (1997). Dominating Smallness: Big Parties in Lilliput Systems. *Party Politics*, 3(2), 243–63.

Anckar, Dag (1999). Homogeneity and Smallness: Dahl and Tufte Revisited. *Scandinavian Political Studies*, 22(1), 29–44.

Anckar, Dag (2002). Why Are Small Island States Democracies? *Round Table*, 91 (365), 375–90.

Anckar, Dag (2004). Direct Democracy in Microstates and Small Island States. *World Development*, 32(2), 379–90.

Anckar, Dag & Carsten Anckar (1995). Size, Insularity and Democracy. *Scandinavian Political Studies*, 18(4), 211–29.

Anckar, Dag & Carsten Anckar (2000). Democracies without Parties. *Comparative Political Studies*, 33(2), 225–47.

Anderson, Benedict (1983). *Imagined Communities: Reflections on the Origin and Spread of Nationalism*. London: Verso.

Andrews, Rhys & George A. Boyne (2009). Size, Structure and Administrative Overheads: An Empirical Analysis of English Local Authorities. *Urban Studies*, 46(4), 739–59.

Andrews, Rhys, George A. Boyne, Alex Chen, & Stephen James Martin (2006). Population Size and Local Authority Performance. Centre for Local and Regional Government Research, Cardiff University.

Angelopoulos, Konstantinos, Apostolis Philippopoulos, & Vanghelis Vassilatos (2009). The Social Cost of Rent Seeking in Europe. *European Journal of Political Economy*, 25(3), 280–99.

Ansolabehere, Stephen, James M. Snyder Jr., & Charles Stewart III (2001). Candidate Positioning in U.S. House Elections. *American Journal of Political Science*, 45(1), 136–59.

Anzia, Sarah F. & Terry M. Moe (2014). Public Sector Unions and the Costs of Government. *Journal of Politics*, 77(1), 114–27.

Arce, Moisés & Jorge Mangonnet (2013). Competitiveness, Partisanship, and Subnational Protest in Argentina. *Comparative Political Studies*, 46(8), 895–919.

Archer, Dane & Rosemary Gartner (1984). *Violence and Crime in Cross-Cultural Perspective*. New Haven, CT: Yale University Press.

Aristotle (1996). The Politics. In *The Politics and The Constitution of Athens*, ed. S. Everson. Cambridge: Cambridge University Press.

Armstrong, Harvey, R. Jouan de Kervenoael, Xiaming Li, & Robert Read (1998). A Comparison of the Economic Performance of Different Microstates and between Microstates and Larger Countries. *World Development*, 26(4), 639–56.

Arzaghi, Mohammad & Vernon Henderson (2005). Why Countries Are Fiscally Decentralizing. *Journal of Public Economics*, 89(7), 1157–89.

Ashraf, Quamrul & Oded Galor (2013). The "Out of Africa" Hypothesis, Human Genetic Diversity, and Comparative Economic Development. *American Economic Review*, 103(1), 1–46.

Aslanian, Sebouh David, Joyce E. Chaplin, Ann Mcgrath, & Kristin Mann (2013) How Size Matters: The Question of Scale in History. *American Historical Review*, 118(5), 1431–72.

Atlas, Cary M., Robert J. Hendershott, & Mark A. Zupan (1997). Optimal Effort Allocation by U.S. Senators: The Role of Constituency Size. *Public Choice*, 92 (3/4), 221–29.

Aubé, Caroline, Vincent Rousseau, & Sébastien Tremblay (2011). Team Size and Quality of Group Experience: The More the Merrier? *Group Dynamics: Theory, Research, and Practice*, 15(4), 357–75.

Auffhammer, Maximilian & Richard T. Carson (2009). Exploring the Number of First Order Political Subdivisions across Countries: Some Stylized Facts. *Journal of Regional Science*, 42(2), 243–61.

Auriol, Emmanuelle & Robert J. Gary-Bobo (2012). On the Optimal Number of Representatives. *Public Choice*, 153(3/4), 419–45.

Avellaneda, Claudia N. & Ricardo Corrêa Gomes (2015). Is Small Beautiful? Testing the Direct and Nonlinear Effects of Size on Municipal Performance. *Public Administration Review*, 75(1), 137–49.

Avineri, Shlomo & Avner de-Shalit (1992). *Communitarianism and Individualism*. Oxford: Oxford University Press.

Axtell, Robert L. (2001). Zipf Distribution of U.S. Firm Sizes. *Science*, 293 (5536), 1818–20.

Bache, Ian & Matthew Flinders (2004). Multi-level Governance and the Study of the British State. *Public Policy and Administration*, 19(1), 31–51.

Baddock, Emily, Peter Lang, & Vivek Srivastava (2015). *Size of the Public Sector: Government Wage Bill and Employment*. Washington, DC: World Bank.

Bagehot, Walter (1963)[1867]. *The English Constitution*. Ithaca, NY: Cornell University Press.

Bailey, Michael & David W. Brady (1998). Heterogeneity and Representation: The Senate and Free Trade. *American Journal of Political Science*, 42(2), 524–44.

Bairoch, Paul (1976). Europe's Gross National Product, 1800–1975. *Journal of European Economic History*, 5(2), 273–340.

Baker, Randall (1992). *Public Administration in Small and Island States*. Boulder, CO: Kumarian Press.

Bakvis, Herman, Gerald Baier, & Douglas Brown (2009). *Contested Federalism: Certainty and Ambiguity in the Canadian Federation*. Toronto: Oxford University Press.

Baldacchino, Godfrey (1993). Bursting the Bubble: The Pseudo-Development Strategies of Microstates. *Development and Change*, 24 (1), 29–52.

Baldacchino, Godfrey (2012). Islands and Despots. *Commonwealth and Comparative Politics*, 50(1), 103–20.

Baldacchino, Godfrey & Wouter Veenendaal (2018). Island Society and Community: The MITE Syndrome. In Godfrey Baldacchino, ed., *Handbook of Island Studies*. London: Routledge, pp. 339–52.

Baldassare, Mark (1985). Trust in Local Government. *Social Science Quarterly*, 66 (3), 704–12.

Baldersheim, Harald & Michael Keating (2015). *Small States in the Modern World: Vulnerabilities and Opportunities*. Cheltenham: Edward Elgar.

Baldwin, Nicholas (2013). *Legislatures of Small States: A Comparative Study*. London: Routledge.

Bales, Robert F. (1950). *Interaction Process Analysis: A Method for the Study of Small Groups*. Chicago: University of Chicago Press.

Banting, Keith G. & Richard Simeon (1985). *Redesigning the State: The Politics of Constitutional Change*. Toronto: University of Toronto Press.

Barber, Benjamin R. (2003). *Strong Democracy: Participatory Politics for a New Age*. Berkeley: University of California Press.

Bardhan, Pranab (2002). Decentralization of Governance and Development. *Journal of Economic Perspectives*, 16(4), 185–205.

Bardhan, Pranab & Dilip Mookherjee (2000). Capture and Governance at Local and National Levels. *American Economic Review*, 90(2), 135–39.

Bardhan, Pranab & Dilip Mookherjee (2006). *Decentralization and Local Governance in Developing Countries: A Comparative Perspective*. Cambridge, MA: MIT Press.

Bardhan, Pranab & Tsung-Tao Yang (2004). *Political Competition in Economic Perspective*. BREAD Working Paper No. 078, Bureau for Research in Economic Analysis of Development.

Barnes, Jeb & Thomas F. Burke (2015). *How Policy Shapes Politics*. Oxford: Oxford University Press.

Barnes, Samuel H., Klaus R. Allerbeck, Barbara G. Farah, Felix J. Heunks, Ronald F. Inglehart, M. Kent Jennings, Hans Dieter Klingemann, Alan Marsh, & Leopold Rosenmayr (1979). *Political Action: Mass Participation in Five Western Democracies*. London: Sage.

Barro, Robert J. (1973). The Control of Politicians: An Economic Model. *Public Choice*, 14(1), 19–42.

Barth, Fredrik (1969). *Ethnic Groups and Boundaries: The Social Organization of Culture Difference*. Oslo: Universitetsforlaget.

Barth, Fredrik (1978). *Scale and Social Organization*. Oslo: Universitetsforlaget.

Bartolini, Stefano (1999). Collusion, Competition and Democracy, Part I. *Journal of Theoretical Politics*, 11(4), 435–70.

Bartolini, Stefano (2000). Collusion, Competition and Democracy: Part II. *Journal of Theoretical Politics*, 12(1), 33–65.

Bates, Robert H. (2008). The Role of the State in Development. In Barry R. Weingast & Donald Wittman, eds., *The Oxford Handbook of Political Economy*. Oxford: Oxford University Press, pp. 708–23.

Batty, Michael (2006). Rank Clocks. *Nature*, 444(7119), 592.

Baum-Snow, Nathaniel, Matthew Freedman, & Ronni Pavan (2018). Why Has Urban Inequality Increased? *American Economic Journal: Applied Economics*, 10 (4), 1–42.

Baumer, Terry L. (1978). Research on Fear of Crime in the United States. *Victimology*, 3(3/4), 254–64.

Bavinck, Ben & Maithreyi Rajeshkumar (2011). *Of Tamils and Tigers: A Journey through Sri Lanka's War Years*. Colombo: Vijitha Yapa Publications.

Beck, Thorsten, George Clarke, Alberto Groff, Philip Keefer, & Patrick Walsh (2001). New Tools and New Tests in Comparative Political Economy: The Database of Political Institutions. *World Bank Economic Review*, 15(1), 165–76.

Becker, Gary S. (1958). Competition and Democracy. *Journal of Law and Economics*, 1, 105–09.

Bednar, Jenna (2008). *The Robust Federation*. New York: Cambridge University Press.

Beer, Caroline & Neil J. Mitchell (2004). Democracy and Human Rights in the Mexican States: Elections or Social Capital? *International Studies Quarterly*, 4 (8), 293–312.

Beine, Michel A. R., Frederic Docquier, & Maurice Schiff (2008). Brain Drain and Its Determinants: A Major Issue for Small States, IZA Discussion Papers, No. 3398.

Bel, Germà (2013). Local Government Size and Efficiency in Capital Intensive Services: What Evidence Is There of Economies of Scale, Density and Scope? In Santiago Lago-Peñas & Jorge Martinez-Vazquez, eds., *The Challenge of Local Government Size: Theoretical Perspectives, International Experience and Policy Reform*. Cheltenham: Elgar, pp. 148–70.

Bell, Roderick, David V. Edwards, & Robert Harrison Wagner (1969). *Political Power: A Reader in Theory and Research*. New York: Free Press.

Ben-Dor, Gabriel (1975). Institutionalization and Political Development: A Conceptual and Theoretical Analysis. *Comparative Studies in Society and History*, 17(3), 309–25.

Benedict, Burton (1967). *Problems of Smaller Territories*. London: Athlone Press.

Bennett, Stephen Earl & David Resnick (1990). Implications of Nonvoting for Democracy in the United States. *American Journal of Political Science*, 34(3), 771–803.

Bensel, Richard Franklin (1984). *Sectionalism and American Political Development, 1880–1980*. Madison: University of Wisconsin Press.

Benson, Lee (1955). *Merchants, Farmers, & Railroads: Railroad Regulations and New York Politics, 1850–1887*. Cambridge, MA: Harvard University Press.

Benz, Arthur & Jorg Broschek (2013). *Federal Dynamics: Continuity, Change, and the Varieties of Federalism*. Oxford: Oxford University Press.

Berezin, Mabel & Juan Diez-Medrano (2008). Distance Matters: Place, Political Legitimacy and Popular Support for European Integration. *Comparative European Politics*, 6(1), 1–32.

Berkowitz, Daniel & Karen B. Clay (2012). *The Evolution of a Nation: How Geography and Law Shaped the American States*. Princeton, NJ: Princeton University Press.

Berlin, Isaiah (1959). *Two Concepts of Liberty: An Inaugural Lecture Delivered before the University of Oxford on 31 October 1958*. Oxford: Clarendon Press.

Berman, Sheri (1997). Civil Society and the Collapse of the Weimar Republic. *World Politics*, 49(3), 401–29.

Berreman, Gerald D. (1978). Scale and Social Relations. *Current Anthropology*, 19 (2), 225–45.

Berry, William D., Evan J. Ringquist, Richard C. Fording, & Russell L. Hanson (1998). Measuring Citizen and Government Ideology in the American States, 1960–93. *American Journal of Political Science*, 42(1), 327–48.

Besley, Timothy & Stephen Coate (2003). Centralized versus Decentralized Provision of Local Public Goods: A Political Economy Approach. *Journal of Public Economics*, 87(12), 2611–37.

Besley, Timothy, Torsten Persson, & Daniel M. Sturm (2010). Political Competition and Economic Performance: Evidence from the United States. *Review of Economic Studies*, 77(3), 1329–52.

Besley, Timothy & Marta Reynal-Querol (2011). Do Democracies Select More Educated Leaders? *American Political Science Review*, 105(3), 552–66.

Besley, Timothy & Marta Reynal-Querol (2014). The Legacy of Historical Conflict: Evidence from Africa. *American Political Science Review*, 108(2), 319–36.

Bettencourt, Luis M. A. & Geoffrey West (2010). A Unified Theory of Urban Living. *Nature*, 467, 912–13.

Bettencourt, Luis M. A. & Geoffrey West (2011). Bigger Cities Do More with Less. *Scientific American*, 305(3), 52–53.

Bianco, William T. (1998). Uncertainty, Appraisal, and Common Interest: The Roots of Constituent Trust. In Valerie Braithwaite & Margaret Levi, eds., *Trust and Governance*. New York: Russell Sage Foundation, pp. 245–66.

Bidyut, Chakrabarthy & Rajat K. Kujur (2010). *Maoism in India: Reincarnation of Ultra-Left Wing Extremism in the Twenty-First Century*. New York: Routledge.

Bienen, Henry & Nicolas van de Walle (1991). *Of Time and Power: Leadership Duration in the Modern World*. Stanford, CA: Stanford University Press.

Binder, Sarah, Forrest Maltzman, & Lee Sigelman (1998). Senators' Home-State Reputations: Why Do Constituents Love a Bill Cohen So Much More Than an Al D'Amato? *Legislative Studies Quarterly*, 23(4), 545–60.

Bingle, Benjamin (2016). A Matter of Size: Examining Representation and Responsiveness in State Legislatures and City Councils. PhD thesis, Northern Illinois University.

Bishin, Benjamin G. (2003). Democracy, Heterogeneity and Representation: Explaining Representational Differences across States. *Legislative Studies Section Newsletter*, 26(1).

Bishin, Benjamin G., Jay K. Dow, & James Adams (2006). Does Democracy "Suffer" from Diversity? Issue Representation and Diversity in Senate Elections. *Public Choice*, 129(1/2), 201–15.

Bizzarro, Fernando, John Gerring, Allen Hicken, Carl Henrik Knutsen, Michael Bernhard, Svend-Erik Skaaning, Michael Coppedge, & Staffan I. Lindberg (2018). Party Strength and Economic Growth. *World Politics*, 70(2), 275–320.

Bizzarro, Fernando, Allen Hicken, & Darin Self (2017). *The V-Dem Party Institutionalization Index: A New Global Indicator (1900–2015)*. University of Gothenburg, Varieties of Democracy Institute: Working Paper No. 48.

Black, Gordon S. (1974). Conflict in the Community: A Theory of the Effects of Community Size. *American Political Science Review*, 68(3), 1245–61.

Blais, André (2000). *To Vote or Not to Vote? The Merits and Limits of Rational Choice*. Pittsburgh, PA: University of Pittsburgh Press.

Blais, André (2006) What Affects Voter Turnout? *Annual Review of Political Science*, 9, 111–25.

Blais, André & Kenneth Carty (1990). Does Proportional Representation Foster Voter Turnout? *European Journal of Political Research*, 18(2), 167–81.

Blais, André & Agnieszka Dobrzynska (1998). Turnout in Electoral Democracies. *European Journal of Political Research*, 33(2), 239–61.

Blais, André & Ignacio Lago (2009). A General Measure of District Competitiveness. *Electoral Studies*, 28(1), 94–100.

Blattman, Christopher & Edward Miguel (2010). Civil War. *Journal of Economic Literature*, (48)1, 3–57.

Blau, Peter M. (1970). A Formal Theory of Differentiation in Organizations. *American Sociological Review*, 35(2), 201–18.

Blau, Peter M. (1974). Presidential Address: Parameters of Social Structure. *American Sociological Review*, 39(5), 615–35.

Blesse, Sebastian & Thushyanthan Baskaran (2016). Do Municipal Mergers Reduce Costs? Evidence from a German Federal State. *Regional Science and Urban Economics*, 59(C), 54–74.

Blom-Hansen, Jens, Kurt Houlberg, & Søren Serritzlew (2014). Size, Democracy, and the Economic Costs of Running the Political System. *American Journal of Political Science*, 58(4), 790–803.

Blom-Hansen, Jens, Kurt Houlberg, Søren Serritzlew, & Daniel Treisman (2016). Jurisdiction Size and Local Government Policy Expenditure: Assessing the Effect of Municipal Amalgamation. *American Political Science Review*, 110(4), 812–31.

Blondel, Jean (2006). About Institutions, Mainly, but Not Exclusively, Political. In Roderick A. W. Rhodes, Sarah A. Binder, & Bert A. Rockman, eds., *Oxford Handbook of Political Institutions*. Oxford: Oxford University Press, pp. 716–30.

Bloom, David, David Canning, & Jaypee Sevilla (2003). *The Demographic Dividend: A New Perspective on the Economic Consequences of Population Change*. Santa Monica, CA: Rand Corporation.

Bloom, Nicholas, Raffaella Sadun, & John van Reenen (2012). The Organization of Firms across Countries. *Quarterly Journal of Economics*, 127(4), 1663–1705.

Boadway, Robin & Anwar Shah (2009). *Fiscal Federalism: Principles and Practice of Multiorder Governance*. Cambridge: Cambridge University Press.

Boatright, Robert G., Vincent G. Moscardelli, & Clifford Vickrey (2017). *Congressional Primary Elections Data*. Accessed 2018. https://wordpress.clarku.edu/primarytiming

Bockstette, Valerie, Areendam Chanda, & Louis Putterman (2002). States and Markets: The Advantage of an Early Start. *Journal of Economic Growth*, 7(4), 347–69.

Bodley, John H. (1999). Socioeconomic Growth, Culture Scale, and Household Well-Being: A Test of the Power-Elite Hypothesis. *Current Anthropology*, 40(5), 595–620.

Bodley, John H. (2013). *The Small Nation Solution*. Lanham, MD: AltaMira Press.

Boggs, Sarah L. (1971). Formal and Informal Crime Control: An Exploratory Study of Urban, Suburban and Rural Orientations. *Sociological Quarterly*, 12(3), 319–27.

Boix, Carles, Michael Miller, & Sebastian Rosato (2013). A Complete Data Set of Political Regimes, 1800–2007. *Comparative Political Studies*, 46(12), 1523–54.

Boix, Carles & Milan W. Svolik (2013). The Foundations of Limited Authoritarian Government: Institutions, Commitment, and Power-Sharing in Dictatorships. *Journal of Politics*, 75(2), 300–16.

Bollen, Kenneth & Rick H. Hoyle (1990). Perceived Cohesion: A Conceptual and Empirical Examination. *Social Forces*, 69(2), 479–504.

Bolt, Jutta & Jan Luiten van Zanden (2014). The Maddison Project: Collaborative Research on Historical National Accounts. *Economic History Review*, 67(3), 627–51.

Bolton, Patrick & Gerard Roland (1997). The Breakup of Nations: A Political Economy Analysis. *Quarterly Journal of Economics*, 112(4), 1057–90.

Bolton, Patrick, Gérard Roland, & Enrico Spolaore (1996). Economic Theories of the Break-Up and Integration of Nations. *European Economic Review* 40(3), 697–705.

Bonner, John Tyler (1988). *The Evolution of Complexity*. Princeton, NJ: Princeton University Press.

Bonner, John Tyler (2004). Perspective: The Size-Complexity Rule. *Evolution*, 58 (9), 1883–90.

Borchert, Jens & Jürgen Zeiss (2003). *The Political Class in Advanced Democracies: A Comparative Handbook*. Oxford: Oxford University Press.

Borck, Rainald (2002). Jurisdiction Size, Political Participation, and the Allocation of Resources. *Public Choice*, 113 (3–4), 251–63.

Borges, André (2008). State Government, Political Competition and Education Reform: Comparative Lessons from Brazil. *Bulletin of Latin American Research*, 27(2), 235–54.

Boserup, Ester (1965). *The Conditions of Agricultural Growth: The Economics of Agrarian Change under Population Pressure*. London: Allen & Unwin.

Bourgin, Frank (1989). *The Great Challenge: The Myth of Laissez-Faire in the Early Republic*. New York: George Braziller.

Bourguignon, François & Christian Morrisson (2002). Inequality among World Citizens: 1820–1992. *American Economic Review* 92(4), 727–44.

Bowen, Daniel Christopher (2010). District Characteristics and the Representational Relationship. PhD thesis, University of Iowa.

Bradbury, John C. & William M. Crain (2001). Legislative Organization and Government Spending: Cross-Country Evidence. *Journal of Public Economics*, 82(3), 309–25.

Brady, Henry E. & James E. McNulty (2011). Turning Out to Vote: The Costs of Finding and Getting to the Polling Place. *American Political Science Review*, 105 (1), 115–34.

Braithwaite, Valerie & Margaret Levi (1998). *Trust and Governance*. New York: Russell Sage Foundation.

Brancati, Dawn (2007). *Constituency-Level Elections (CLE) Dataset* [computer file]. New York: Constituency-Level Elections Dataset [distributor]. Accessed 2011. www.cle.wustl.edu

Brancati, Dawn (2008). The Origins and Strengths of Regional Parties. *British Journal of Political Science*, 38(1), 135–59.

Brantgärde, Lennart (1974). *Kommunerna och Kommunblocksbildningen*. Lund: Gleerup.

Bratton, Michael & Nicholas van de Walle (1997). *Democratic Experiments in Africa: Regime Transitions in Comparative Perspective*. Cambridge: Cambridge University Press.

Braungart, Margaret M., Richard G. Braungart, & William J. Hoyer (1980). Age, Sex, and Social Factors in Fear of Crime. *Sociological Focus*, 13(1), 55–66.

Bray, Mark (1991). *Making Small Practical: The Organisation and Management of Ministries of Education in Small States*. London: Commonwealth Secretariat.

Breton, Albert (1996). *Competitive Governments*. Cambridge: Cambridge University Press.

Breton, Albert & Anthony Scott (1978). *The Economic Constitution of Federal States*. Toronto: Toronto University Press.

Briguglio, Lino (1995). Small Island Developing States and Their Economic Vulnerabilities. *World Development*, 23(9), 1615–32.

Broadberry, Stephen (2015). *Accounting for the Great Divergence*. Accessed 2016. www.nuffield.ox.ac.uk/users/Broadberry/AccountingGreatDivergence6.pdf

Broadberry, Stephen & Alexander Klein (2012). Aggregate and per capita GDP in Europe, 1870–2000: Continental, Regional and National Data with Changing Boundaries. *Scandinavian Economic History Review*, 60(1), 79–107.

Brock, William Ranulf (1984). *Investigation and Responsibility: Public Responsibility in the United States, 1865–1900*. Cambridge: Cambridge University Press.

Brooks, Leah, Justin Phillips, & Maxim Sinitsyn (2011). The Cabals of a Few or the Confusion of a Multitude: The Institutional Trade-Off between Representation and Governance. *American Economic Journal: Economic Policy*, 3(1), 1–24.

Brown, J. Christopher & Mark Purcell (2005). There's Nothing Inherent about Scale: Political Ecology, the Local Trap, and the Politics of Development in the Brazilian Amazon. *Geoforum*, 36(5), 607–24.

Brückner, Markus (2010). Population Size and Civil Conflict Risk: Is There a Causal Link? *Economic Journal*, 120(544), 535–50.

Brunell, Thomas L. (2008). *Redistricting and Representation: Why Competitive Elections Are Bad for America*. New York: Routledge.

Brunell, Thomas L. & Justin Buchler (2009). Ideological Representation and Competitive Congressional Elections. *Electoral Studies*, 28(3), 448–57.

Brusco, Valeria, Marcelo Nazareno, & Susan Carol Stokes (2004). Vote Buying in Argentina. *Latin American Research Review*, 39(2), 66–88.

Bryan, Frank M. (2010). *Real Democracy: The New England Town Meeting and How It Works*. Chicago: University of Chicago Press.

Bryan, Frank & John McClaughry (1991). *The Vermont Papers: Recreating Democracy on a Human Scale*. Chelsea, VT: Chelsea Green Publishing.

Bryce, James (1908). *The American Commonwealth, Vol II*. 3rd ed. New York: Macmillan.

Bryce, James (1924). *Modern Democracies*. New York: Macmillan.

Buchanan, James M. (1995). Federalism As an Ideal Political Order and an Objective for Constitutional Reform. *Publius: The Journal of Federalism*, 25(2), 19–27.

Buchanan, James M. & Gordon Tullock (1962). *The Calculus of Consent: Logical Foundations of Constitutional Democracy*. Ann Arbor: University of Michigan Press.

Buchler, Justin (2005). Competition, Representation and Redistricting: The Case against Competitive Congressional Districts. *Journal of Theoretical Politics*, 17(4), 431–63.

Buchler, Justin (2011). The Proximity Paradox: The Legislative Agenda and the Electoral Success of Ideological Extremists. *Public Choice*, 148(1–2), 1–19.

Bueno de Mesquita, Bruce, James D. Morrow, & R. M. Siverson (2002). Political Institutions, Policy Choice and the Survival of Leaders. *British Journal of Political Science*, 32(4), 559–90.

Buhaug, Halvard (2010). Dude, Where's My Conflict? LSG, Relative Strength, and the Location of Civil War. *Conflict Management and Peace Science*, 27(2), 107–28.

Bull, Hedley (1977). *The Anarchical Society: A Study of Order in World Politics*. London: Macmillan.

Bull, Hedley (1987). Population and the Present World Structure. In William Alonso, ed., *Population in an Interacting World*. Cambridge, MA: Harvard University Press, pp. 74–94.

Bullock III, Charles S. (2010). *Redistricting: The Most Political Activity in America*. Lanham, MD: Rowman & Littlefield.

Bunce, Valerie (1981). *Do New Leaders Make a Difference? Executive Succession and Public Policy under Capitalism and Socialism*. Princeton, NJ: Princeton University Press.

Burbank, Jane & Frederick Cooper (2010). *Empires in World History: Power and the Politics of Difference*. Princeton, NJ: Princeton University Press.

Burke, Peter (1978). *Popular Culture in Early Modern Europe*. London: Temple Smith.

Burling, Robbins (1974). *The Passage of Power: Studies in Political Succession*. New York: Academic Press.

Burnside, Craig & David Dollar (2000). Aid, Policies, and Growth. *American Economic Review*, 90(4), 847–68.

Cadot, Olivier, Lars-Hendrik Röller, & Andreas Stephan (2006). Contribution to Productivity or Pork Barrel? The Two Faces of Infrastructure Investment. *Journal of Public Economics*, 90(6), 1133–53.

Cain, Bruce, John Ferejohn, & Morris Fiorina (1987). *The Personal Vote: Constituency Service and Electoral Independence*. Cambridge, MA: Harvard University Press.

Caldwell, John C., Graham E. Harrison, & Pat Quiggin (1980). The Demography of Micro-states. *World Development*, 8(12), 953–62.

Calvert, Peter (1987). *The Process of Political Succession*. London: Macmillan.

Cameron, David R. (1978). The Expansion of the Public Economy: A Comparative Analysis. *American Political Science Review*, 72(4), 1243–61.

Campbell, Andrea Louise (2011). Policy Feedbacks and the Impact of Policy Designs on Public Opinion. *Journal of Health Politics, Policy and Law*, 36(6), 961–73.

Campbell, Andrea Louise (2012). Policy Makes Mass Politics. *Annual Review of Political Science*, 15, 333–51.

Campbell, David E. (2013). Social Networks and Political Participation. *Annual Review of Political Science*, 16, 33–48.

Campbell, Frederick L. & Ronald L. Akers (1970). Organizational Size, Complexity, and the Administrative Component in Occupational Associations. *Sociological Quarterly*, 11(4), 435–51.

Campbell, Jeffrey R. & Hugo A. Hopenhayn (2005). Market Size Matters. *Journal of Industrial Economics*, 53(1), 1–25.

Cancela, Joao, & Benny Geys (2016). Explaining Voter Turnout: A Meta-analysis of National and Subnational Elections. *Electoral Studies*, 42, 264–75.

Canon, David T. (1989). The Institutionalization of Leadership in the U. S. Congress. *Legislative Studies Quarterly*, 14(3), 415–43.

Canovan, Margaret (1981). *Populism*. Boston: Houghton Mifflin Harcourt.

Caplow, Theodore (1957). Organizational Size. *Administrative Science Quarterly*, 1(4), 484–505.

Caren, Neal (2007). Big City, Big Turnout? Electoral Participation in American Cities. *Journal of Urban Affairs*, 29(1), 31–46.

Carey, John M. (2000). Parchment, Equilibria, and Institutions. *Comparative Political Studies*, 33(6/7), 735–61.

Carey, John M. & Matthew Soberg Shugart (1995). Incentives to Cultivate a Personal Vote: A Rank Ordering of Electoral Formulas. *Electoral Studies*, 14 (4), 417–39.

Carneiro, Robert L. (1967). On the Relationship between Size of Population and Complexity of Social Organization. *Southwestern Journal of Anthropology*, 23(3), 234–43.

Carpenter, Jeffrey P. (2007). Punishing Free-Riders: How Group Size Affects Mutual Monitoring and the Provision of Public Goods. *Games and Economic Behavior*, 60(1), 31–51.

Carr, Jered B. & Antonio Tavares (2014). City Size and Political Participation in Local Government: Reassessing the Contingent Effects of Residential Location Decisions within Urban Regions. *Urban Affairs Review*, 50(2), 269–302.

Carroll, Glenn R. & Michael T. Hannan (2000). *The Demography of Corporations and Industries*. Princeton, NJ: Princeton University Press.

Carsey, Thomas M., William D. Berry, Richard G. Niemi, Lynda W. Powell, & James M. Snyder (2007). *State Legislative Election Returns, 1967–2003* [Computer file]. Chapel Hill: University of North Carolina.

Casas-Zamora, Kevin (2005). *Paying for Democracy: Political Finance and State Funding for Parties*. Colchester: ECPR Press.

Castles, Francis G., Stephan Leibfried, Jane Lewis, Herbert Obinger, & Christopher Pierson (2012). *The Oxford Handbook of the Welfare State*. Oxford: Oxford University Press.

Cederman, Lars-Erik, Kristian Skrede Gleditsch, & Halvard Buhaug (2013). *Inequality, Grievances, and Civil War*. Cambridge: Cambridge University Press.

Chamberlain, Neil W. (1970). *Beyond Malthus: Population and Power*. New York: Basic Books.

Chamberlin, John R. (1974). Provision of Collective Goods As a Function of Group Size. *American Political Science Review*, 68(2), 707–16.

Chambers, Simone & Jeffrey Kopstein (2001). Bad Civil Society. *Political Theory*, 29(6) 837–65.

Chandler, Alfred D. (1962). *Strategy and Structure: Chapters in the History of the Industrial Enterprise*. Cambridge, MA: MIT Press.

Chandler, Alfred D. (1990). *Scale: The Dynamics of Industrial Capitalism*. Cambridge, MA: Harvard University Press.

Chaney, Thomas & Ralph Ossa (2013). Market Size, Division of Labor, and Firm Productivity. *Journal of International Economics*, 90(1), 177–80.

Charron, Nicholas, José Fernández-Albertos, & Victor Lapuente (2013). Small Is Different: Size, Political Representation and Governance. In Santiago Lago-Peñas & Jorge Martinez-Vazquez eds., *The Challenge of Local Government Size: Theoretical Perspectives, International Experience and Policy Reform*. Cheltenham: Elgar, pp. 189–220.

Chase-Dunn, Christopher, Yukio Kawano, & Benjamin D. Brewer (2000). Trade Globalization since 1795: Waves of Integration in the World-System. *American Sociological Review*, 65(1), 77–95.

Chattopadhyay, Raghabendra & Esther Duflo (2004). Women As Policy Makers: Evidence from a Randomized Policy Experiment in India. *Econometrica*, 72(5), 1409–43.

Chenoweth, Erica & Maria J. Stephan (2011). *Why Civil Resistance Works: The Strategic Logic of Nonviolent Conflict*. New York: Columbia University Press.

Childs, Geoff, Melvyn C. Goldstein, Ben Jiao, & Cynthia M. Beall (2005). Tibetan Fertility Transitions in China and South Asia. *Population and Development Review*, 31(2), 337–49.

Childs, Marquis (1936). *Sweden: The Middle Way*. New Haven, CT: Yale University Press.

Chittoo, Hemant B. (2011). Public Administration in "Small and Island Developing States": A Debate about Implications of Smallness. *Global Journal of Management and Business Research*, 11(9), 22–33.

Christenson, James A. & Don A. Dillman (1974). An Exploratory Analysis of Select Predictors of Law and Order. *Social Indicators Research*, 1(2), 217–28.

Christiane, Arndt & Charles Oman (2006). *Uses and Abuses of Governance Indicators*. Paris: OECD Publishing.

Chung, Jae Ho (2000). *Central Control and Local Discretion in China: Leadership and Implementation during Post-Mao Decollectivization*. Oxford: Oxford University Press.

Cincotta, Richard P. (2008). How Democracies Grow Up. *Foreign Policy*, 165, 80–82.

Cincotta, Richard P. (2008–09). Half a Chance: Youth Bulges and Transitions to Liberal Democracy. *Environmental Change and Security Project Report*, 13, 10–18.

Cincotta, Richard P. & John Doces (2012). The Age-Structural Maturity Thesis: the Impact of the Youth Bulge on the Advent and Stability of Liberal Democracy. In Jack A. Goldstone, Eric P. Kaufmann, & Monica Duffy Toft, eds., *Political Demography: How Population Changes Are Reshaping International Security and National Politics*. Oxford: Oxford University Press, pp. 98–116.

Clague, Christopher, Suzanne Gleason, & Stephen Knack (2001). Determinants of Lasting Democracy in Poor Countries: Culture, Development, and Institutions. *Annals of the American Academy of Political and Social Science*, 773, 16–41.

Clark, Gordon L., Alicia H. Munnell, & J. Michael Orszag (2006). *The Oxford Handbook of Pensions and Retirement Income*. Oxford: Oxford University Press.

Clark, Norman H. (1976). *Deliver Us from Evil: An Interpretation of American Prohibition*. New York: W. W. Norton.

Clark, Samuel (1995). *State and Status: The Rise of the State and Aristocratic Power in Western Europe*. Montreal: McGill-Queen's University Press.

Clark, Terry N. (1968). Community Structure, Decision-Making, Budget Expenditures, and Urban Renewal in 51 American Communities. *American Sociological Review*, 33(4), 576–93.

Clarke, Clifford J. (1987). The Durkheimian Relationship between the Division of Labor and Population: Cross-National Historical Evidence. *Sociological Focus*, 20(1), 13–31.

Clarke, Colin (2006). Politics, Violence and Drugs in Kingston, Jamaica. *Bulletin of Latin American Research*, 25(3), 420–40.

Clarke, Colin & Tony Payne (1987). *Politics, Security and Development in Small States*. London: Allen & Unwin.

Clarke, Harold D. & Alan C. Acock (1989). National Elections and Political Attitudes: The Case of Political Efficacy. *British Journal of Political Science*, 19 (4), 551–62.

Cleary, Matthew R. (2007). Electoral Competition, Participation, and Government Responsiveness in Mexico. *American Journal of Political Science*, 51(2), 283–99.

Clemente, Frank & Michael B. Kleiman (1977). Fear of Crime in the United States: A Multivariate Analysis. *Social Forces*, 52(2), 519–31.

Cohen, Frank (1997). Proportional versus Majoritarian Ethnic Conflict Management in Democracies. *Comparative Political Studies*, 30(5), 607–30.

Cole, Alistair (2010). France: Between Centralization and Fragmentation. In John Loughlin, Frank Hendriks, & Anders Lidstrom, eds., *The Oxford Handbook of Local and Regional Democracy in Europe*. Oxford: Oxford University Press, pp. 307–30.

Collier, Paul (1999). On the Economic Consequences of Civil War. *Oxford Economic Papers*, 51(1), 168–83.

Collier, Ruth Berins (1999). *Paths toward Democracy: The Working Class and Elites in Western Europe and South America*. Cambridge: Cambridge University Press.

Colomer, Josep Maria (2007). *Great Empires, Small Nations: The Uncertain Future of the Sovereign State*. London: Routledge.

Colyvas, Jeannette A. & Stefan Jonsson (2011). Ubiquity and Legitimacy: Disentangling Diffusion and Institutionalization. *Sociological Theory*, 29(1), 27–53.

Combes, Pierre-Philippe, Gilles Duranton, & Laurent Gobillon (2008). Spatial Wage Disparities: Sorting Matters! *Journal of Urban Economics*, 63(2), 723–42.

Congdon Fors, Heather (2014). Do Island States Have Better Institutions? *Journal of Comparative Economics*, 42(1), 34–60.

Coppedge, Michael (2012). *Approaching Democracy: Theory and Methods in Comparative Politics*. Cambridge: Cambridge University Press.

Coppedge, Michael, John Gerring, David Altman, Michael Bernhard, Steven Fish, Allen Hicken, & Matthew Kroenig (2011). Conceptualizing and Measuring Democracy: A New Approach. *Perspectives on Politics*, 9(2), 247–67.

Coppedge, Michael, John Gerring, Adam Glynn, Carl Henrik Knutsen, Staffan I. Lindberg, Daniel Pemstein, Brigitte Seim, Svend-Erik Skaaning, & Jan Teorell (2020). *Varieties of Democracy: Measuring a Century of Political Change*. Cambridge: Cambridge University Press.

Coppedge, Michael, John Gerring, Staffan I. Lindberg, Svend-Erik Skaaning, Jan Teorell, David Altman, Michael Bernhard, M. Steven Fish, Adam Glynn, Allen Hicken, Carl Henrik Knutsen, Kyle L. Marquardt, Kelly McMann, Valeriya Mechkova, Pamela Paxton, Daniel Pemstein, Laura Saxer, Brigitte Seim, Rachel Sigman, & Jeffrey Staton (2017). *V-Dem Codebook v7.1*. Varieties of Democracy (V-Dem) Project.

Corbett, Jack (2013). Politicians and Professionalization in the Pacific Islands: Revisiting Self-Regulation? *Politics & Policy*, 41(6), 852–76.

Corbett, Jack (2015a). *Being Political: Leadership and Democracy in the Pacific Islands*. Honolulu: University of Hawaii Press.

Corbett, Jack (2015b). "Everybody Knows Everybody": Practicing Politics in the Pacific Islands. *Democratization*, 22(1), 51–72.

Corbett, Jack & Wouter Veenendaal (2018). *Democracy in Small States: Persisting against All Odds*. Oxford: Oxford University Press.

Corbett, Jack, Wouter Veenendaal, & Lhawang Ugyel (2017). Why Monarchy Persists in Small States: The Cases of Tonga, Bhutan, and Liechtenstein. *Democratization*, 24(4), 689–706.

Coser, Lewis (1956). *The Functions of Social Conflict*. New York: Free Press.

Costa, Dora L. & Matthew E. Kahn (2003). Civic Engagement and Community Heterogeneity: An Economist's Perspective. *Perspectives on Politics*, 1(1), 103–11.

Cowell, Frank (2011). *Measuring Inequality*. Oxford: Oxford University Press.

Cox, Gary W. (1987). *The Efficient Secret: The Cabinet and the Development of Political Parties in Victorian England*. Cambridge: Cambridge University Press.

Cox, Gary W. & J. Morgan Kousser (1981). Turnout and Rural Corruption: New York As a Test Case. *American Journal of Political Science*, 25(4), 646–63.

Crémer, Jacques & Thomas R. Palfrey (1999). Political Confederation. *American Political Science Review*, 93(1), 69–83.

Crespin, Michael H. & Charles J. Finocchiaro (2013). Elections and the Politics of Pork in the US Senate. *Social Science Quarterly*, 94(2), 506–29.

Crisher, Brian & Mark Souva (2014). Power at Sea: A Naval Power Dataset, 1865–2011. *International Interactions*, 40(4), 602–29.

Croicu, Mihai & Ralph Sundberg (2015). UCDP Georeferenced Event Dataset Codebook Version 4.0. *Journal of Peace Research*, 50(4), 523–32.

Crowards, Tom (2002). Defining the Category of "'Small' States." *Journal of International Development*, 14(2), 143–79.

Daalder, Hans (1974). The Consociational Democracy Theme. *World Politics*, 26 (4), 604–21.

Dahl, Robert A. (1956). *A Preface to Democratic Theory*. Chicago: University of Chicago Press.

Dahl, Robert A. (1957). The Concept of Power. *Behavioral Science*, 2(3), 201–15.

Dahl, Robert A. (1967). The City in the Future of Democracy. *American Political Science Review*, 61(4), 953–70.

Dahl, Robert A. (1971). *Polyarchy: Participation and Opposition*. New Haven, CT: Yale University Press.

Dahl, Robert A. & Edward R. Tufte (1973). *Size and Democracy*. Stanford, CA: Stanford University Press.

Dalton, Russell J. & Martin P. Wattenberg (2000). *Parties without Partisans: Political Change in Advanced Industrial Democracies*. Oxford: Oxford University Press.

Darwin, Charles (1880). *On the Origin of Species by Means of Natural Selection: Or the Preservation of Favoured Races in the Struggle for Life*. London: John Murray.

Davis, Kingsley (1954). The Demographic Foundations of National Power. In Monroe Berger, Theodore Abel, & Charles H. Page, eds., *Freedom and Control in Modern Societies*. New York: Van Nostrand, pp. 206–42.

Davis, James & Diane Hart (2002). *Government of Palau*. Koror: Ministry of Education of Palau.

De Swaan, Abram (1990). *The Management of Normality: Critical Essays in Health and Welfare*. London: Routledge.

DeBardeleben, Joan & Achim Hurrelmann (2007). *Democratic Dilemmas of Multilevel Governance: Legitimacy, Representation and Accountability in the European Union*. New York: Springer.

Dennis, Christopher, Benjamin Bishin, & Politimy Nicolaou (2000). Constituent Diversity and Congress: The Case of NAFTA. *Journal of Socio-economics* 29(4), 349–60.

Denters, Bas (2002). Size and Political Trust: Evidence from Denmark, the Netherlands, Norway, and the United Kingdom. *Environment and Planning C: Government and Policy*, 20(6), 793–812.

Denters, Bas, Michael Goldsmith, Andreas Ladner, Poul Erik Mourtizen, & Lawrence E. Rose (2014). *Size and Local Democracy*. Cheltenham: Elgar.

Devlin, Patrick (1959). *The Enforcement of Morals*. Oxford: Oxford University Press.

Diamond, Jared M. (1998). *Guns, Germs and Steel: A Short History of Everybody for the Last 13,000 Years*. New York: Random House.

Diamond, Jared M. (2005). *Collapse: How Societies Choose to Fail or Succeed*. New York: Viking Press.

Diamond, Larry & Svetlana Tsalik (1999). Size and Democracy: The Case for Decentralization. In Larry Diamond, ed., *Developing Democracy: Towards Consolidation*. Baltimore, MD: Johns Hopkins University Press, pp. 117–60.

Dickovick, J. Tyler (2011). *Decentralization and Recentralization in the Developing World: Comparative Studies from Africa and Latin America*. University Park: Pennsylvania State University Press.

Diehl, Paul & Gary Goertz (1992). *Territorial Changes and International Conflict*. London: Routledge.

Dinopoulos, Elias & Peter Thompson (1998). Schumpeterian Growth without Scale Effects. *Journal of Economic Growth*, 3(4), 313–35.

Dometrius, Nelson C. & Joshua Ozymy (2006). Legislative Professionalism and Democratic Success: The Conditioning Effect of District Size. *State Politics & Policy Quarterly*, 6(1), 73–87.

Dommen, Edward (1980). Some Distinguishing Characteristics of Island States. *World Development*, 8(12), 931–43.

Dommen, Edward & Philippe Hein (1985). *States, Microstates and Islands*. London: Croom Helm.

Donzelot, Jacques (1979). *The Policing of Families: Welfare versus the State*. New York: Random House.

Douglas, Mary & Aaron Wildavsky (1983) *Risk and Culture: An Essay on the Selection of Technological and Environmental Dangers*. Berkeley: University of California Press.

Doumenge, François (1985). The Viability of Small Intertropical Islands. In Edward Dommen & Philippe Hein, eds., *States, Microstates, and Islands*. Dover, NH: Croom Helm, pp. 70–118.

Downes, Andrew S. (1988). On the Statistical Measurement of Smallness: A Principal Component Measure of Country Size. *Social and Economic Studies*, 37(3), 75–96.

Downs, Anthony (1957). An Economic Theory of Political Action in a Democracy. *Journal of Political Economy*, 65(2), 135–50.

Drew, Joseph, Michael A. Kortt, & Brian Dollery (2012). Economies of Scale and Local Government Expenditure: Evidence from Australia. *Administration & Society*, 46(6), 632–53.

Dubin, Michael J. (2007). *Party Affiliations in the State Legislatures: A Year by Year Summary, 1796–2006*. Jefferson, NC: McFarland.

Dubois, Hans F. W. & Giovanni Fattore (2009). Definitions and Typologies in Public Administration Research: The Case of Decentralization. *International Journal of Public Administration*, 32(8), 704–27.

Dunbar, Robin I. M. (1992). Neocortex Size As a Constraint on Group Size in Primates. *Journal of Human Evolution*, 22(6), 469–93.

Dunbar, Robin I. M. & Richard Sosis (2018). Optimising Human Community Sizes. *Evolution and Human Behavior* 39(1), 106–11.

Dunlavy, Colleen A. (1994). *Politics and Industrialization: Early Railroads in the United States and Prussia*. Princeton, NJ: Princeton University Press.

Durkheim, Emile (1964)[1893]. *The Division of Labor in Society*. New York: Free Press.

Durkheim, Emile (1976). *The Elementary Forms of the Religious Life*. London: Routledge.

Duursma, Jorri C. (1996). *Fragmentation and the International Relations of Microstates: Self-determination and Statehood*. Cambridge: Cambridge University Press.

Duverger, Maurice (1959). *Political Parties*. New York: Wiley.

Dyck, Joshua J. & James G. Gimpel (2005). Distance, Turnout, and the Convenience of Voting. *Social Science Quarterly*, 86(3), 531–48.

Dyson, Tim (2012). On Demographic and Democratic Transitions. *Population and Development Review*, 38, 83–102.

Easterly, William & Aart Kraay (2000). Small States, Small Problems? Income, Growth, and Volatility in Small States. *World Development*, 28(11), 2013–27.

Eaton, Kent J. (2004). *Politics beyond the Capital: The Design of Subnational Institutions in South America*. Stanford, CA: Stanford University Press.

Eaton, Kent J. & Tyler Dickovick (2004). The Politics of Re-centralization in Argentina and Brazil. *Latin American Research Review*, 39(1), 90–122.

Ebrey, Patricia (2006). Succession to High Office: The Chinese Case. In David R. Olson & Michael Cole, eds., *Technology, Literacy, and the Evolution of Society: Implications of the Work of Jack Goody*. Mahwah, NJ: Erlbaum, pp. 49–71.

Edelstein, J. David & Malcolm Warner (1975). *Comparative Union Democracy: Organization and Opposition in British and American Unions*. London: George Allen & Unwin.

Ehrenhalt, Alan (1992). *The United States of Ambition: Politicians, Power, and the Pursuit of Office*. New York: Three Rivers Press.

Ehrlich, Paul R. (1968). *The Population Bomb*. New York: Ballantine Books.

Eisenstadt, S. N. (1977). Soziologische Merkmale und Probleme kleiner Staaten. *Schweizerische Zeitschrift für Soziologie*, 3(1), 67–85.

Elazar, Daniel J. (1987). *Exploring Federalism*. Tuscaloosa: University of Alabama Press.

Elazar, Daniel J. (1995). From Statism to Federalism: A Paradigm Shift. *Publius: The Journal of Federalism*, 25(2), 5–18.

Elbahnasawy, Nasr G. & Charles F. Revier (2012). The Determinants of Corruption: Cross-Country Panel-Data Analysis. *Developing Economies*, 50(4), 311–33.

Elkins, Zachary, Tom Ginsburg, & James Melton (2009). *The Endurance of National Constitutions*. Cambridge: Cambridge University Press.

Ellingsen, Tore (1998). Externalities vs. Internalities: A Model of Political Integration. *Journal of Public Economics*, 68(2), 251–68.

Elman, Colin, John Gerring, & James Mahoney (2020). *The Production of Knowledge*. Cambridge: Cambridge University Press.

Ember, Melvin (1963). The Relationship between Economic and Political Development in Nonindustrialized Societies. *Ethnology*, 2(2), 228–48.

Endersby, James W. & Jonathan T. Krieckhaus (2008). Turnout around the Globe: The Influence of Electoral Institutions on National Voter Participation, 1972–2000. *Electoral Studies*, 27(4), 601–10.

Enikolopov, Ruben & Ekaterina Zhuravskaya (2007). Decentralization and Political Institutions. *Journal of Public Economics*, 91(11–12), 2261–90.

Ensser-Jedenastik, Laurenz & Wouter Veenendaal (2015). Population Size and Turnout: Evidence from a Quasi-Experiment. Prepared for presentation at the 5th Annual Conference of the European Political Science Association, Vienna, Austria.

Enos, Ryan D. (2017). *The Space between Us: Social Geography and Politics*. Cambridge: Cambridge University Press.

Ensley, Michael J., Michael W. Tofias, & Scott de Marchi (2009). District Complexity As an Advantage in Congressional Elections. *American Journal of Political Science*, 53(4), 990–1005.

Erdmann, Gero & Ulf Engel (2007). Neopatrimonialism Reconsidered: Critical Review and Elaboration of an Elusive Concept. *Commonwealth & Comparative Politics*, 45(1), 95–119.

Erikson, Kai (1966). *Wayward Puritans: A Study in the Sociology of Deviance*. Boston: Allyn & Bacon.

Esping-Andersen, Gosta (1990). *The Three Worlds of Welfare Capitalism*. Princeton, NJ: Princeton University Press.

Esteban, Joan & Debraj Ray (2001). Collective Action and the Group Size Paradox. *American Political Science Review*, 95(3), 663–72.

Evans, Peter & James E. Rauch (1999). Bureaucracy and Growth: A Cross-National Analysis of the Effects of "Weberian" State Structures on Economic Growth. *American Sociological Review*, 64(5), 748–65.

Ezrow, Natasha M. & Erica Frantz (2011). State Institutions and the Survival of Dictatorships. *Journal of International Affairs*, 65(1), 1–13.

Falleti, Tulia G. (2005). A Sequential Theory of Decentralization: Latin American Cases in Comparative Perspective. *American Political Science Review*, 99(3), 327–46.

Falleti, Tulia G. (2010). *Decentralization and Subnational Politics in Latin America*. New York: Cambridge University Press.

Farbman, Michael (1995). The Size Distribution of Family Income in U.S. SMSAs, 1959. *Review of Income and Wealth*, 21(2), 217–37.

Faris, Robert (1999). Unto Themselves: Insularity and Democracy. Unpublished MA thesis, University of North Carolina.

Fariss, Christopher J., Charles D. Crabtree, Therese Anders, Zachary M. Jones, Fridolin J. Linder, & Jonathan N. Markowitz (2017). Latent Estimation of GDP, GDP per capita, and Population from Historic and Contemporary Sources. Unpublished manuscript, University of Michigan.

Farrugia, Charles (1993). The Special Working Environment of Senior Administrators in Small States. *World Development*, 21(2), 221–26.

Faunce, William A. (1962). Size of Locals and Union Democracy. *American Journal of Sociology*, 68(3), 291–98.

Fearon, James D. (2003). Ethnic and Cultural Diversity by Country. *Journal of Economic Growth*, 8(2), 195–222.

Feinman, Gary M. (2011). Size, Complexity, and Organizational Variation: A Comparative Approach. *Cross-Cultural Research*, 45(1), 37–58.

Fenno, Richard F. (1982). *The United States Senate: A Bicameral Perspective*. Washington, DC: American Enterprise Institute.

Ferejohn, John A. (1974). *Pork Barrel Politics: Rivers and Harbors Legislation, 1947–1968*. Palo Alto, CA: Stanford University Press.

Farrington, David P. & Christopher P. Nuttall (1980). Prison Size, Overcrowding, Prison Violence, and Recidivism. *Journal of Criminal Justice*, 8(4), 221–31.

Festinger, Leon, Stanley Schachter, & Kurt Back (1950). *Social Pressures in Informal Groups: A Study of a Housing Project*. New York: Harper.

Fieldhouse, David Kenneth (1966). *The Colonial Empires: A Comparative Survey from the Eighteenth Century*. London: Weidenfeld and Nicolson.

Filippov Mikhail, Peter Ordeshook, & Olga Shvetsova (2004). *Designing Federalism: A Theory of Self-Sustainable Federal Institutions*. Cambridge: Cambridge University Press.

Fine, Gary Alan (2012). *Tiny Publics: A Theory of Group Action and Culture*. New York: Russell Sage Foundation.

Finer, Samuel Edward (1997). *The History of Government from the Earliest Times. 3 vols*. New York: Oxford University Press.

Finifter, Ada W. & Paul R. Abramson (1975). City Size and Feelings of Political Competence. *Public Opinion Quarterly*, 39(2), 189–98.

Fiorina, Morris P. (1973). Electoral Margins, Constituency Influence, and Policy Moderation: A Critical Assessment. *American Politics Quarterly*, 1(4), 479–98.

Fiorina, Morris P. (1974). *Representatives, Roll Calls, and Constituencies*. Lexington, MA: Lexington Books.

Fiorina, Morris P. (1999). Extreme Voices: A Dark Side of Civic Engagement. In Theda Skocpol & Morris P. Fiorina, eds., *Civic Engagement in American Democracy*. Washington, DC: Brookings Institution, pp. 405–13.

Firebaugh, Glenn (1983). Scale Economy or Scale Entropy? Country Size and Rate of Economic Growth, 1950–1977. *American Sociological Review*, 48(2), 257–69.

Fischer, Claude S. (1973). On Urban Alienations and Anomie: Powerlessness and Social Isolation. *American Sociological Review*, 38(3), 311–26.

Fischer, Paul H. (1953). An Analysis of the Primary Group. *Sociometry*, 16(3), 272–76.

Fisman, Raymond & Roberta Gatti (2002). Decentralization and Corruption: Evidence across Countries. *Journal of Public Economics*, 83(3), 325–45.

Foster, Kathryn A. (1993). Exploring the Links between Political Structure and Metropolitan Growth. *Political Geography*, 12, 523–47.

Fowler, Anthony (2015). Regular Voters, Marginal Voters and the Electoral Effects of Turnout. *Political Science Research and Methods*, 3(2), 205–19.

Fowler, James H. (2005). Turnout in a Small World. In Alan Zuckerman, ed., *The Social Logic of Politics*. Philadelphia, PA: Temple University Press, pp. 269–88.

Fraga, Bernard L. (2018). *The Turnout Gap: Race, Ethnicity, and Political Inequality in a Diversifying America*. Cambridge: Cambridge University Press.

Frandsen, Annie Gaardsted (2002). Size and Electoral Participation in Local Elections. *Environment and Planning C: Government and Policy*, 20(6), 853–69.

Franklin, Billy J. (1971). Urbanization and Party Competition: A Note on Shifting Conceptualization and a Report of Further Data. *Social Forces*, 49 (4), 544–49.

Franklin, Mark N. (2004). *Voter Turnout and the Dynamics of Electoral Competition in Established Democracies since 1945*. Cambridge: Cambridge University Press.

Franklin, Travis W., Cortney A. Franklin, & Noelle E. Fearn (2008). A Multilevel Analysis of the Vulnerability, Disorder, and Social Integration Models of Fear of Crime. *Social Justice Research*, 21(2), 204–27.

Frantz, Erica & Elizabeth A. Stein (2017). Countering Coups: Leadership Succession Rules in Dictatorships. *Comparative Political Studies*, 50(7), 935–62.

Frech, H. E. & Leland Burns (1971). Metropolitan Interpersonal Income Inequality. *Land Economics*, 45(1), 104–06.

Frederick, Brian (2008). Constituency Population and Representation in the US House. *American Politics Research*, 36(3), 358–81.

Frederick, Brian (2010). *Congressional Representation and Constituents: The Case for Increasing the U.S. House of Representatives*. New York: Routledge.

Freedom House (2007). *"Methodology," Freedom in the World 2007*. New York: Freedom House. Accessed 2017. www.freedomhouse.org/template.cfm? page=351&ana_page=333&year=2007

Freeman, Jo (1972–73). The Tyranny of Structurelessness. *Berkeley Journal of Sociology*, 17, 151–64.

Freese, Jeremy & David Peterson. 2020. Replication for Quantitative Research. In Colin Elman, John Gerring, & James Mahoney, eds., *The Production of Knowledge*. Cambridge: Cambridge University Press.

Freidson, Eliot (2001). *Professionalism, the Third Logic: On the Practice of Knowledge*. Chicago: University of Chicago Press.

Freudenburg, William R. (1986). The Density of Acquaintanceship: An Overlooked Variable in Community Research? *American Journal of Sociology*, 92(1), 27–63.

Frieden, Jeffry A. (2007). *Global Capitalism: Its Fall and Rise in the Twentieth Century*. New York: W. W. Norton.

Friedman, David (1977). A Theory of the Size and Shape of Nations. *Journal of Political Economy*, 85(1), 59–77.

Fung, Archon & Erik Olin Wright (2003). *Deepening Democracy: Institutional Innovations in Empowered Participatory Governance*. New York: Verso.

Gabaix, Xavier (1999). Zipf's Law for Cities: An Explanation. *Quarterly Journal of Economics*, 114(3), 739–67.

Gadenne, Lucie & Monica Singhal (2014). Decentralization in Developing Economies. *Annual Review of Economics*, 6, 581–604.

Gale (2010). *Encyclopedia of Associations: International Organizations. 49th ed.* Florence: Gale Cengage Learning.

Galiani, Sebastian & Sukkoo Kim (2011). Political Centralization and Urban Primacy: Evidence from National and Provincial Capitals in the Americas. In Dora L. Costa & Naomi R. Lamoreaux, eds., *Understanding Long-Run Economic Growth: Geography, Institutions, and the Knowledge Economy*. Chicago: University of Chicago Press, pp. 121–53.

Game, Chris & David Wilson (2011). *Local Government in the United Kingdom. 5th ed.* Basingstoke: Palgrave Macmillan.

Garfinkel, Irwin, Lee Rainwater, & Timothy Smeeding (2010). *Wealth and Welfare States: Is America a Laggard or Leader?* New York: Oxford University Press.

Garman, Christopher, Stephan Haggard, & Eliza Willis (2001). Fiscal Decentralization: A Political Theory with Latin American Cases. *World Politics*, 53(2), 205–36.

Garrett, Geoffrey & Jonathan Rodden (2003). Globalization and Fiscal Decentralization. In Miles Kahler & David Lake, eds., *Governance in a Global Economy: Political Authority in Transition*. Princeton, NJ: Princeton University Press, pp. 87–109.

Gastil, John (2010). *The Group in Society*. Thousand Oaks, CA: Sage.

Gastil, John (2014). *Democracy in Small Groups: Participation, Decision Making, and Communication*. Gabriola Island: New Society.

Gat, Azar (2008). *War in Human Civilization*. Oxford: Oxford University Press.

Geddes, Barbara (1994). *Politician's Dilemma: Building State Capacity in Latin America*. Berkeley: University of California Press.

Geiger, Roger L. (2014). *The History of American Higher Education: Learning and Culture from the Founding to World War II*. Princeton, NJ: Princeton University Press.

Gerber, Alan S., Donald P. Green, & Edward H. Kaplan (2014). The Illusion of Learning from Observational Research. In Dawn Langan Teele, ed., *Field Experiments and Their Critics: Essays on the Uses and Abuses of Experimentation in the Social Sciences*. New Haven, CT: Yale University Press, pp. 9–32.

Gerber, Alan S., Donald P. Green, & Christopher W. Larimer (2008). Social Pressure and Voter Turnout: Evidence from a Large-Scale Field Experiment. *American Political Science Review*, 102(1), 33–48.

Gerber, Elisabeth R. & Jeffrey B. Lewis (2004). Beyond the Median: Voter Preferences, District Heterogeneity, and Political Representation. *Journal of Political Economy*, 112(6), 1364–83.

Gerring, John (1997). Ideology: A Definitional Analysis. *Political Research Quarterly*, 50(4), 957–94.

Gerring, John (1998). *Party Ideologies in America, 1828–1996*. Cambridge: Cambridge University Press.

Gerring, John (2010). Causal Mechanisms: Yes, But … *Comparative Political Studies*, 43(11), 1499–1526.

Gerring, John (2012). *Social Science Methodology: A Unified Framework*. 2nd ed. Cambridge: Cambridge University Press.

Gerring, John (2017). *Case Study Research: Principles and Practices*. 2nd ed. Cambridge: Cambridge University Press.

Gerring, John, Allen Hicken, Daniel Weitzel, & Lee Cojocaru (2018). *Electoral Contestation: Country-Level Data and Analysis*. Unpublished manuscript, University of Texas at Austin.

Gerring, John & Carl Henrik Knutsen (2019). Polity Size and the Institutionalization of Leadership Succession. *Studies in Comparative International Development* 54:4 (December) 451–72.

Gerring, John, Matthew Maguire, & Jillian Jaeger (2018). A General Theory of Power Concentration: Demographic Influences on Political Organization. *European Political Science Review*, 10(4) (November), 491–513.

Gerring, John, Erzen Oncel, Kevin Morrison, & Daniel Pemstein (2019). Who Rules the World? A Portrait of the Global Leadership Class. *Perspectives on Politics*, 17(4).

Gerring, John, Maxwell Palmer, Jan Teorell, & Dominic Zarecki (2015). Demography and Democracy: A Global, District-Level Analysis of Electoral Contestation. *American Political Science Review*, 109(3), 574–91.

Gerring, John & Strom C. Thacker (2008). *A Centripetal Theory of Democratic Governance*. Cambridge: Cambridge University Press.

Gerring, John, Andreas Forø Tollefsen, Tore Wig, & Brendan Apfeld (2019). Harbors and Democracy. Unpublished paper, Department of Government, University of Texas at Austin.

Gerring, John, Tore Wig, Wouter Veenendaal, Daniel Weitzel, Jan Teorell, & Kyosuke Kikuta (2019). Why Monarchy? The Rise and Demise of a Regime Type. Unpublished manuscript, University of Texas at Austin.

Gerring, John, Daniel Ziblatt, Johan van Gorp, & Julian Arevalo (2011). An Institutional Theory of Direct and Indirect Rule. *World Politics*, 63(3), 377–433.

Gerstle, Gary (2009). The Resilient Power of the States across the Long Nineteenth Century. In Lawrence Jacobs & Desmond King, eds., *The Unsustainable American State*. New York: Oxford University Press, pp. 61–87.

Gerstle, Gary (2015). *Liberty and Coercion: The Paradox of American Government from the Founding to the Present*. Princeton, NJ: Princeton University Press.

Gibler, Douglas M. (2010). Outside-In: The Effects of External Threat on State Centralization. *Journal of Conflict Resolution*, 54(4), 519–42.

Gibson, Clark C., Elinor Ostrom, & Toh-Kyeong Ahn (2000). The Concept of Scale and the Human Dimensions of Global Change: A Survey. *Ecological Economics*, 32(2), 217–39.

Giddens, Anthony (1985). *The Nation-State and Violence*. Berkeley: University of California Press.

Gingerich, Daniel W. & Luis Fernando Medina (2013). The Endurance and Eclipse of the Controlled Vote: A Formal Model of Vote Brokerage under the Secret Ballot. *Economics and Politics*, 25(3), 453–80.

Glaeser, Edward L. & Bruce Sacerdote (1999). Why Is There More Crime in Cities? *Journal of Political Economy*, 107(S6), S225–S258.

Glassman, Ronald M. (2017). *The Origins of Democracy in Tribes, City-States and Nation-States*. New York: Springer.

Gleditsch, Kristian S. (2002). Expanded Trade and GDP Data. *Journal of Conflict Resolution*, 46(5), 712–24.

Gleditsch, Nils Petter, Peter Wallensteen, Mikael Eriksson, Margareta Sollenberg, & Håvard Strand (2002). Armed Conflict 1946–2001: A New Dataset. *Journal of Peace Research*, 39(5), 615–37.

Globerman, Steven & Daniel Shapiro (2002). Global Foreign Direct Investment Flows: The Role of Governance Infrastructure. *World Development*, 30(11), 1899–1919.

Go, Sun & Peter Lindert (2010). The Uneven Rise of American Public Schools to 1850. *Journal of Economic History*, 70(1), 1–26.

Goemans, Hein E., Kristian Skrede Gleditsch, & Giacomo Chiozza (2009). Introducing Archigos: A Dataset of Political Leaders. *Journal of Peace Research*, 46(2), 269–83.

Goemans, Hein E., Kristian Skrede Gleditsch & Giacomo Chiozza (2016). *ARCHIGOS A Data Set on Leaders 1875–2015, Version 4.1*. Accessed 2016. www.essex.ac.uk/~ksg/papers/Archigos-27-Feb-2016.pdf

Goetschel, Laurent (2013). *Small States Inside and Outside the European Union: Interests and Policies*. New York: Springer.

Goffman, Erving (1963). *Behavior in Public Places*. New York: Free Press.

Golden, Miriam A. (2003). Electoral Connections: The Effects of the Personal Vote on Political Patronage, Bureaucracy and Legislation in Postwar Italy. *British Journal of Political Science*, 33(2), 189–212.

Golden, Miriam A. & Lucio Picci (2008). Pork-Barrel Politics in Postwar Italy, 1953–94. *American Journal of Political Science*, 52(2), 268–89.

Goldin, Claudia & Lawrence F. Katz (1997). *Why the United States Led in Education: Lessons from Secondary School Expansion, 1910 to 1940*. No. 6144. National Bureau of Economic Research.

Goldstone, Jack A. (1991). *Revolution and Rebellion in the Early Modern World.* Berkeley: University of California Press.

Goldstone, Jack A. (2002). Population and Security: How Demographic Change Can Lead to Violent Conflict. *Journal of International Affairs,* 56(1), 3–21.

Goldstone, Jack A., Eric P. Kaufmann, & Monica Duffy Toft (2012). *Political Demography: How Population Changes Are Reshaping International Security and National Politics.* Oxford: Oxford University Press.

Gomez-Reino, Juan Luiz & Jorge Martinez-Vazquez. (2013). An International Perspective on the Determinants of Local Government Fragmentation. In Santiago Lago-Peñas & Jorge Martinez-Vazquez, eds., *The Challenge of Local Government Size: Theoretical Perspectives, International Experience and Policy Reform.* Cheltenham: Elgar, pp. 8–54.

Goodrich, Carter (1960). *Government Promotion of American Canals and Railroads, 1800–1890.* New York: Columbia University Press.

Goody, Jack (1966). *Succession to High Office.* Cambridge: Cambridge University Press.

Gordon, Sanford C. & Gregory A. Huber (2007). The Effect of Electoral Competitiveness on Incumbent Behavior. *Quarterly Journal of Political Science,* 2(2), 107–38.

Gordon, Scott (1999). *Controlling the State: Constitutionalism from Ancient Athens to Today.* Cambridge, MA: Harvard University Press.

Graebner, William (1977). Federalism in the Progressive Era: A Structural Interpretation of Reform. *Journal of American History,* 64(2), 331–57.

Granovetter, Mark S. (1973). The Strength of Weak Ties. *American Journal of Sociology,* 78(6), 1360–80.

Gray, Tim (1990). *Freedom.* New York: Springer.

Green, Elliott (2010). Patronage, District Creation, and Reform in Uganda. *Studies in Comparative International Development,* 45(1), 83–103.

Green, Elliott (2012). On the Size and Shape of African States. *International Studies Quarterly,* 56(2), 229–44.

Greene, Jack P. (1981). Legislative Turnover in British America, 1696 to 1775: A Quantitative Analysis. *William and Mary Quarterly,* 38(3), 442–63.

Griffin, John D. (2006). Electoral Competition and Democratic Responsiveness: A Defense of the Marginality Hypothesis. *Journal of Politics,* 68(4), 911–21.

Gronke, Paul (2000). *The Electorate, the Campaign, and the Office: A Unified Approach to Senate and House Elections.* Ann Arbor: University of Michigan Press.

Gross, Neil & William E. Martin (1952). On Group Cohesiveness. *American Journal of Sociology,* 57, 546–54.

Grossman, Guy & Janet I. Lewis (2014). Administrative Unit Proliferation. *American Political Science Review,* 108(1), 196–217.

Grossman, Guy, Jan H. Pierskalla, & Emma Boswell Dean (2017). Government Fragmentation and Public Goods Provision. *Journal of Politics,* 79(3), 823–40.

Grusky, Oscar (1961). Corporate Size, Bureaucratization, and Managerial Succession. *American Journal of Sociology,* 67(3), 261–69.

Grzymala-Busse, Anna (2007). *Rebuilding Leviathan: Party Competition and State Exploitation in Post-Communist Democracies*. Cambridge: Cambridge University Press.

Gulati, Girish J. (2004). Revisiting the Link between Electoral Competition and Policy Extremism in the U.S. Congress. *American Politics Research*, 32(5), 495–520.

Guldi, Jo & David Armitage (2014). *The History Manifesto*. Cambridge: Cambridge University Press.

Gunnemark, Erik V. (1991). *Countries, Peoples, and Their Languages: The Linguistic Handbook*. Gothenburg: Lanstryckeriet.

Gusfield, Joseph R. (1963). *Symbolic Crusade: Status Politics and the American Temperance Movement*. Champaign: University of Illinois Press.

Haber, Stephen & Victor Menaldo (2011). Do Natural Resources Fuel Authoritarianism? A Reappraisal of the Resource Curse. *American Political Science Review*, 105(1), 1–26.

Hadenius, Axel (1992). *Democracy and Development*. Cambridge: Cambridge University Press.

Hajnal, Zoltan L., Paul G. Lewis, & Hugh Louch (2002). *Municipal Elections in California: Turnout, Timing, and Competition*. San Francisco: Public Policy Institute of California.

Hall, Richard H., Norman J. Johnson, & J. Eugene Haas (1967). Organizational Size, Complexity, and Formalization. *American Sociological Review*, 32(6), 903–12.

Hamburger, Henry, Melvin Guyer, & John Fox (1975). Group Size and Cooperation. *Journal of Conflict Resolution*, 19(3), 503–31.

Hamilton, Alexander, James Madison, & John Jay (2008)[1787]. *The Federalist Papers*, ed. Lawrence Goldman. Oxford: Oxford University Press.

Hamilton, William D. (1964). The Genetical Evolution of Social Behaviour. *Journal of Theoretical Biology*, 7, 1–52.

Hammond, George W. & Mehmet Tosun (2011). The Impact of Local Decentralization on Economic Growth: Evidence from U.S. Counties. *Journal of Regional Science*, 51(1), 47–64.

Handlin, Oscar & Mary Flug Handlin (1969). *Commonwealth: A Study of the Role of Government in the American Economy: Massachusetts, 1774–1861*. Cambridge, MA: Belknap Press.

Hanes, Niklas (2015). Amalgamation Impacts on Local Public Expenditures in Sweden. *Local Government Studies*, 41(1), 63–77.

Hankinson, Michael (2018). When Do Renters Behave Like Homeowners? High Rent, Price Anxiety, and NIMBYism. *American Political Science Review*, 112(3), 483–93.

Hansen, Henrik & Derek Headey (2010). The Short-Run Macroeconomic Impact of Foreign Aid to Small States: An Agnostic Time Series Analysis. *Journal of Development Studies*, 46(5), 877–96.

Hansen, Mogens Herman & Thomas Heine Nielsen (2004). *An Inventory of Archaic and Classical Poleis*. Oxford: Oxford University Press.

Hansen, Stephen, Thomas R. Palfrey, & Howard Rosenthal (1987). The Downsian Model of Electoral Participation: Formal Theory and Empirical Analysis of the Constituency Size Effect. *Public Choice*, 52(1), 15–33.

Hansen, Sune Welling (2011). *Towards Genesis or the Grave. Financial Effects of Local Government Mergers*. Odense: University Press of Southern Denmark.

Hansen, Sune Welling (2013). Polity Size and Local Political Trust: A Quasi-experiment Using Municipal Mergers in Denmark. *Scandinavian Political Studies*, 36(1), 43–66.

Hansen, Sune Welling (2015). The Democratic Costs of Size: How Increasing Size Affects Citizen Satisfaction with Local Government. *Political Studies*, 63 (2), 373–89.

Hansen, Sune Welling, Kurt Houlberg, & Lene Holm Pedersen (2014). Do Municipal Mergers Improve Fiscal Outcomes? *Scandinavian Political Studies*, 37(2), 196–214.

Hanson, Jonathan K. & Rachel Sigman (2013). Leviathan's Latent Dimensions: Measuring State Capacity for Comparative Political Research. Unpublished manuscript, Gerald R. Ford School of Public Policy University of Michigan.

Harden, Jeffrey J. & Thomas M. Carsey (2012). Balancing Constituency Representation and Party Responsiveness in the US Senate: The Conditioning Effect of State Ideological Heterogeneity. *Public Choice*, 150(1), 137–54.

Harden, Sheila (1985). *Small Is Dangerous: Micro States in a Macro World*. London: Frances Pinter.

Harrington, Brooke & Gary Alan Fine (2006). Where the Action Is: Small Groups and Recent Developments in Sociological Theory. *Small Group Research*, 37 (1), 4–19.

Harrison, J. Richard, David L. Torres, & Sal Kukalis (1988). The Changing of the Guard: Turnover and Structural Change in the Top-Management Positions. *Administrative Science Quarterly*, 33, 211–32.

Hartz, Louis (1948). *Economic Policy and Democratic Thought: Pennsylvania, 1776–1860*. Cambridge, MA: Harvard University Press.

Hartz, Louis (1955). *The Liberal Tradition in America*. San Diego, CA: Harcourt Brace.

Harvey, Anna L. (1998). *Votes without Leverage: Women in American Electoral Politics, 1920–1970*. Cambridge: Cambridge University Press.

Hassan, Mai (2016). A State of Change: District Creation in Kenya after the Beginning of Multi-party Elections. *Political Research Quarterly*, 69(3), 510–21.

Heclo, Hugh & Henrik Madsen (1987). *Policy and Politics in Sweden: Principled Pragmatism*. Philadelphia, PA: Temple University Press.

Heilig, Peggy & Robert Mundt (1984). *Your Voice at City Hall: The Politics, Procedures and Policies of District Representation*. Albany: State University of New York Press.

Held, David. 2006. *Models of Democracy*. Palo Alto, CA: Stanford University Press.

Hellebrandt, Tomas & Paolo Mauro (2015). The Future of Worldwide Income Distribution. Peterson Institute for International Economics Working Paper No. 15–7.

Heller, William B., Andreas P. Kyriacou, & Oriol Roca-Sagalés (2011). Party Competition and Government Quality: The Politics of Turning a Blind Eye to

Poor Governance. Presented at the annual meetings of the Midwest Political Science Association, Chicago, IL.

Helmke, Gretchen & Steven Levitsky (2004). Informal Institutions and Comparative Politics: A Research Agenda. *Perspectives on Politics*, 2(4), 725–40.

Hendershot, Gerry E. (1973). Population Size, Military Power, and Antinatal Policy. *Demography*, 10(4), 517–24.

Henderson, Conway W. (1993). Population Pressures and Political Repression. *Social Science Quarterly*, 74(2), 322–33.

Henderson, Vernon (2003). The Urbanization Process and Economic Growth: The So–What Question. *Journal of Economic Growth*, 8(1), 47–71.

Hendrix, Cullen S. (2010). Measuring State Capacity: Theoretical and Empirical Implications for the Study of Civil Conflict. *Journal of Peace Research*, 47(3), 273–85.

Henisz, Witold J. (2002). The Institutional Environment for Infrastructure Investment. *Industrial and Corporate Change*, 11(2), 355–89.

Hesketh, Therese, Li Lu, & Zhu Wei Xing (2005). The Effect of China's One-Child Family Policy after 25 Years. *New England Journal of Medicine*, 353(11), 1171–76.

Hess, Stephen (1991). *Live from Capitol Hill: Studies of Congress and the Media.* Washington, DC: Brookings Institution.

Hewitt de Alcántara, Cynthia (1998). Uses and Abuses of the Concept of Governance. *International Social Science Journal*, 50(155), 105–13.

Hey, Jeanne A. K. (2003). *Small States in World Politics: Explaining Foreign Policy Behavior.* Boulder, CO: Lynne Rienner.

Hibbing, John R. & John R. Alford (1990). Constituency Population and Representation in the U.S. Senate. *Legislative Studies Quarterly*, 15(4), 581–98.

Hibbing, John R. & Sara L. Brandes (1983). State Population and the Electoral Success of U.S. Senators. *American Journal of Political Science*, 27(4), 808–19.

Hibbing, John R. & Elizabeth Theiss-Morse (2002). *Stealth Democracy: Americans' Beliefs about How Government Should Work.* Cambridge: Cambridge University Press.

Hibbs, Douglas A., Jr. (1973). *Mass Political Violence.* New York: Wiley.

Hicken, Allen (2011). Clientelism. *Annual Review of Political Science*, 14, 289–310.

Hicken, Allen & Erik Martinez Kuhonta (2015). *Party System Institutionalization in Asia: Democracies, Autocracies, and the Shadows of the Past.* Cambridge: Cambridge University Press.

Hicks, Alexander M. & Duane H. Swank (1992). Politics, Institutions, and Welfare Spending in Industrialized Democracies, 1960–82. *American Political Science Review*, 86(3), 658–74.

Higgs, Robert (1989). *Crisis and Leviathan: Critical Episodes in the Growth of American Government.* New York: Oxford University Press.

Hill, Kim Quaile & Jan E. Leighley (1992). The Policy Consequences of Class Bias in State Electorates. *American Journal of Political Science*, 36(2), 351–65.

Hintjens, Helen M. & Malen D. Newitt (1992). *Political Economy of Small Tropical Islands: The Importance of Being Small.* Exeter: University of Exeter Press.

Hirczy, Wolfgang (1995). Explaining Near-Universal Turnout: The Case of Malta. *European Journal of Political Research*, 27(2), 255–72.

Hirschman, Albert O (1970). *Exit, Voice, Loyalty: Responses to Decline in Firms, Organizations, and States.* Cambridge, MA: Harvard University Press.

Hiscox, Michael J. & David A. Lake (2001). Democracy and the Size of States. Unpublished manuscript, Harvard University.

Hoch, Irving (1976). City Size Effects, Trends, and Policies. *Science*, 193(4256), 856–63.

Hogan, Robert E. (2003). Sources of Competition in State Legislative Primary Elections. *Legislative Studies Quarterly*, 28(1), 103–26.

Holbrook, Thomas M., & Aaron C. Weinschenk (2014). Campaigns, Mobilization, and Turnout in Mayoral Elections. *Political Research Quarterly*, 67(1), 42–55.

Holcombe, Randall G. & DeEdgra W. Williams (2009). Are There Economies of Scale in Municipal Government Expenditures? *Public Finance and Management*, 9(3), 416.

Holland, Paul W. (1986). Statistics and Causal Inference. *Journal of the American Statistical Association*, 81(396), 945–60.

Holzer, Marc, John Fry, Etienne Charbonneau, Gregg van Ryzin, Tiankai Wang, & Eileen Burnash (2009). *Literature Review and Analysis Related to Optimal Municipal Size and Efficiency.* Report prepared for the Local Unit Alignment, Reorganization, and Consolidation Commission. Accessed 2018. www.nj.gov /dca/affiliates/luarcc/pdf/final_optimal_municipal_size_&_efficiency.pdf

Homans, George (1950). *The Human Group.* New York: Harcourt Brace.

Homans, George (1974). *Social Behavior: Its Elementary Forms.* 2nd ed. New York: Harcourt, Brace & Jovanovich.

Hooghe, Liesbet & Gary Marks (2012). Beyond Federalism: Estimating and Explaining the Territorial Structure of Government. *Publius: The Journal of Federalism*, 43(2), 179–204.

Hooghe, Liesbet & Gary Marks (2016). *Community, Scale, and Regional Governance: A Postfunctionalist Theory of Governance.* Vol. 2. Oxford: Oxford University Press.

Hooghe, Liesbet, Gary Marks, & Arjan Schakel (2010). *The Rise of Regional Authority: A Comparative Study of 42 Democracies.* New York: Routledge.

Horowitz, Donald L. (1985). *Ethnic Groups in Conflict.* Berkeley: University of California Press.

Howe, Neil & Richard Jackson (2012). Demography and Geopolitics: Understanding Today's Debate in Its Historical and Intellectual Context. In Jack A. Goldstone, Eric P. Kaufmann, & Monica Duffy Toft, eds., *Political Demography: How Population Changes Are Reshaping International Security and National Politics.* Oxford: Oxford University Press, pp. 31–48.

Hu, Anning (2017). Radius of Trust: Gradient-Based Conceptualization and Measurement. *Social Science Research*, 68, 147–62.

Huang, Jing (2008). Institutionalization of Political Succession in China: Progress and Implications. In Li Cheng, ed., *China's Changing Political Landscape: Prospects for Democracy.* Washington, DC: Brookings Institution, pp. 80–97.

Hueglin, Thomas O. & Alan Fenna (2015). *Comparative Federalism: A Systematic Inquiry*. Toronto: University of Toronto Press.

Hunt, Alan (1996). *Governance of Consuming Passions: A History of Sumptuary Law*. London: Macmillan.

Hunt, Alan (1999). *Governing Morals: A Social History of Moral Regulation*. Cambridge: Cambridge University Press.

Hunt, Morton (1997). *How Science Takes Stock: The Story of Meta-analysis*. New York: Russell Sage Foundation.

Huntington, Samuel P. (1968). *Political Order in Changing Societies*. New Haven, CT: Yale University Press.

Hurrelmann, Achim (2007). Multilevel Legitimacy: Conceptualizing Legitimacy Relationships between the EU and National Democracies. In Joan DeBardeleben & Achim Hurrelmann, eds., *Democratic Dilemmas of Multilevel Governance*. London: Palgrave Macmillan, pp. 17–37.

Hurst, James Willard (1956). *Law and the Conditions of Freedom in the Nineteenth-Century United States*. Madison: University of Wisconsin Press.

Hwang, Sean-Shong & Steve H. Murdock (1988). Residential Segregation and Ethnic Identification among Hispanics in Texas. *Urban Affairs Quarterly*, 23(3), 329–45.

Hayek, Friedrich (1944). *The Road to Serfdom*. London: Routledge Press.

IDEA. [2002] *Global Survey of Voter Turnout*. Accessed 2018. www.idea.int/pub lications/catalogue/voter-turnout-1945-global-report

Ijiri, Yuji & Herbert A. Simon (1977). *Skew Distributions and the Sizes of Business Firms*. New York: North-Holland.

Ikenberry, G. John (2011). *Liberal Leviathan: The Origins, Crisis, and Transformation of the American World Order*. Princeton, NJ: Princeton University Press.

Imai, Kosuke, Luke Keele, Dustin Tingley, & Teppei Yamamoto (2011). Unpacking the Black Box of Causality: Learning about Causal Mechanisms from Experimental and Observational Studies. *American Political Science Review*, 105(4), 765–89.

Ingebritsen, Christine, Iver Neumann, Sieglinde Gstohl, & Jessica Beyer (2012). *Small States in International Relations*. Seattle: University of Washington Press.

Ingham, Geoffrey K. (1970). *Size of Industrial Organisation and Worker Behaviour*. Cambridge: Cambridge University Press.

Inglehart, Ronald & Pippa Norris (2000). The Developmental Theory of the Gender Gap: Women's and Men's Voting Behavior in Global Perspective. *International Political Science Review*, 21(4), 441–63.

Inman, Robert P. & Daniel L. Rubinfeld (1997). Rethinking Federalism. *Journal of Economic Perspectives*, 11(4), 43–64.

Irvin, Renee A. & John Stansbury (2004). Citizen Participation in Decision Making: Is It Worth the Effort? *Public Administration Review*, 64(1), 55–65.

Isaac, R. Mark, James M. Walker, & Arlington W. Williams (1994). Group Size and the Voluntary Provision of Public Goods: Experimental Evidence Utilizing Large Groups. *Journal of Public Economics*, 54(1), 1–36.

Isenman, Paul (1976). Biases in Aid Allocations against Poorer and Larger Countries. *World Development*, 4(8), 631–41.

Ivarsson, Tore (1992). *Kommunernas Släktträd: Sveriges Kommuner 1863–1992.* Älvsjö: Kommentus.

Iversen, Torben & Thomas R. Cusack (2000). The Causes of Welfare State Expansion: Deindustrialization or Globalization? *World Politics,* 52(3), 313–49.

Jackson, Robert H. & Carl Gustav Rosberg (1982a). *Personal Rule in Black Africa: Prince, Autocrat, Prophet, Tyrant.* Berkeley: University of California Press.

Jackson, Robert H. & Carl Gustav Rosberg (1982b). Why Africa's Weak States Persist. *World Politics,* 35(1), 1–24.

Jacobson, Gary C. & Samuel Kernell (1983). *Strategy and Choice in Congressional Elections.* 2nd. ed. New Haven, CT: Yale University Press.

Jalan, Bimal (1982). *Problems and Policies in Small Economies.* New York: St. Martin's Press.

Jasper, James M. (1990). *Nuclear Politics: Energy and the State in the United States, Sweden, and France.* Princeton, NJ: Princeton University Press.

Jeanson, Raphaël, Jennifer H. Fewell, Root Gorelick, & Susan M. Bertram (2007). Emergence of Increased Division of Labor As a Function of Group Size. *Behavioral Ecology and Sociobiology,* 62(2), 289–98.

Jervis, Robert (1997). *System Effects.* Princeton, NJ: Princeton University Press.

John, Richard R. (2009). *Spreading the News: The American Postal System from Franklin to Morse.* Cambridge, MA: Harvard University Press.

Johnson, Allen W. & Timothy Earle (2000). *The Evolution of Human Societies: From Foraging Group to Agrarian State.* Palo Alto, CA: Stanford University Press.

Johnson, Gregory A. (1982). Organizational Structure and Scalar Stress. In Colin A. Renfrew, Michael J. Rowlands, & Barbara A. Segraves, eds., *Theory and Explanation in Archaeology,* 389–421.

Jones, Benjamin F. & Benjamin A. Olken (2009). Hit or Miss? The Effect of Assassinations on Institutions and War. *American Economic Journal: Macroeconomics,* 1(2), 55–87.

Jones, Charles I. (1999). Growth: With or without Scale Effects? *American Economic Review,* 89(2), 139–44.

Jones, Mark P. & Scott Mainwaring (2003). The Nationalization of Parties and Party Systems: An Empirical Measure and an Application to the Americas. *Party Politics,* 9(2), 139–66.

Jones, Philip Edward (2013). The Effect of Political Competition on Democratic Accountability. *Political Behavior,* 35(3), 481–515.

Judd, Charles M., David A. Kenny, & Gary H. McClelland (2001). Estimating and Testing Mediation and Moderation in Within-Subject Designs. *Psychological Methods,* 6(2), 115–34.

Jugl, Marlene (2018). Finding the Golden Mean: Country Size and the Performance of National Bureaucracies. *Journal of Public Administration Research and Theory,* 29(1), 118–32.

Jung, Chan Su (2013). Navigating a Rough Terrain of Public Management: Examining the Relationship between Organizational Size and Effectiveness. *Journal of Public Administration Research and Theory,* 23(3), 663–86.

Kagan, Robert (2001). *Adversarial Legalism: The American Way of Law.* Cambridge, MA: Harvard University Press.

Kameda, Tatsuya, Mark F. Stasson, James H. Davis, Craig D. Parks, & Suzi K. Zimmerman (1992). Social Dilemmas, Subgroups, and Motivation Loss in Task-Oriented Groups: In Search of an "Optimal" Team Size in Division of Work. *Social Psychology Quarterly*, 55(1), 47–56.

Kaminarides, John, Lino Briguglio, & Henk N. Hoogendonk (1989). *The Economic Development of Small Countries Problems Strategies and Policies*. Delft: Eburon.

Kang, Seonjou, & James Meernik (2005). Civil War Destruction and the Prospects for Economic Growth. *Journal of Politics*, 67(1), 88–109.

Kanter, Rosabeth Moss (1972). *Commitment and Community: Communes and Utopias in Sociological Perspective*. Cambridge, MA: Harvard University Press.

Kasarda, John D. (1974). The Structural Implications of Social System Size: A Three-Level Analysis. *American Sociological Review*, 39(1), 19–28.

Kasarda, John D. & Morris Janowitz (1974). Community Attachment in Mass Society. *American Sociological Review*, 39(3), 328–39.

Katz, Nancy, David Lazer, Holly Arrow, & Noshir Contractor (2004). Network Theory and Small Groups. *Small Group Research*, 35(3), 307–32.

Katz, Richard S. & Peter Mair (1995). Changing Models of Party Organization and Party Democracy: The Emergence of the Cartel Party. *Party Politics*, 1(1), 5–28.

Katzenstein, Peter J. (1985). *Small States in World Markets: Industrial Policy in Europe*. Ithaca, NY: Cornell University Press.

Kaufmann, Daniel, Aart Kraay, & Massimo Mastruzzi (2011). The Worldwide Governance Indicators: Methodology and Analytical Issues. *Hague Journal on the Rule of Law*, 3(2), 220–46.

Kautsky, John H. (1982). *The Politics of Aristocratic Empires*. Chapel Hill: University of North Carolina Press.

Keefer, Philip E., Ambar Narayan, & Tara Vishwanath (2006). Decentralization in Pakistan: Are Local Governments Likely to Be More Accountable Than Central Governments? In Pranab Bardhan & Dilip Mookherjee, eds., *Decentralization and Local Governance in Developing Countries: A Comparative Perspective*. Cambridge, MA: MIT Press, pp. 285–303.

Keena, James Alexander (2016). *The Electoral Consequences of Size in American Politics*. PhD Dissertation, University of California at Irvine.

Kelleher, Christine A. & David Lowery (2004). Political Participation and Metropolitan Institutional Contexts. *Urban Affairs Review*, 39(6), 720–57.

Kelleher, Christine A. & David Lowery (2008). Central City Size, Metropolitan Institutions and Political Participation. *British Journal of Political Science*, 39(1), 59–92.

Keller, Morton (1981). The Pluralist State: American Economic Regulation in Comparative Perspective, 1900–1930. In Thomas K. McCraw ed., *Regulation in Perspective: Historical Essays*. Cambridge, MA: Harvard University Press, pp. 56–94.

Keller, Morton (1990). *Regulating a New Economy: Public Policy and Economic Change in America, 1900–1933*. Cambridge, MA: Harvard University Press.

Kelman, Steven (1981). *Regulating America, Regulating Sweden: A Comparative Study of Occupational Safety and Health Policy*. Cambridge. MA: MIT Press.

Kenig, Ofer, Gideon Rahat, & Or Tuttnauer (2015). Competitiveness of Party Leadership Selection Processes. In William Paul Cross & Jean-Benoît Pilet, eds., *The Politics of Party Leadership: A Cross-National Perspective*. Oxford: Oxford University Press, pp. 50–73.

Kennedy, Paul (2010). *The Rise and Fall of the Great Powers*. New York: Vintage.

Kenyon, Cecelia M. (1955). Men of Little Faith: The Anti-Federalists on the Nature of Representative Government. *William and Mary Quarterly*, 12(1), 4–43.

Keohane, Robert O. (1969). Lilliputians' Dilemmas: Small States in International Politics. *International Organization*, 23(2), 291–310.

Kersting, Norbert & Angelika Vetter (2003). *Reforming Local Government in Europe: Closing the Gap between Democracy and Efficiency*. Opladen: Leske + Budrich.

Khalaf, Nadim G. (1976). Country Size and Economic Instability. *Journal of Development Studies*, 12(4), 423–28.

Khalaf, Nadim G. (1979). Country Size and Economic Growth and Development. *Journal of Development Studies*, 16(1), 67–72.

Kimberly, John R. (1976). Organizational Size and the Structuralist Perspective: A Review, Critique, and Proposal. *Administrative Science Quarterly*, 21(4), 571–97.

Kincaid, Harold (1990). Defending Laws in the Social Sciences. *Philosophy of the Social Sciences*, 20(1), 56–83.

Kincaid, Harold (2004). Are There Laws in the Social Sciences? In Christopher Hitchcock, ed., *Contemporary Debates in Philosophy Of Science*. Malden, MA: Blackwell, pp. 168–85.

King, James D. (2000). Changes in Professionalism in US State Legislatures. *Legislative Studies Quarterly*, 25, 327–43.

King, James D., & Jeffrey E. Cohen (2005). What Determines a Governor's Popularity? *State Politics & Policy Quarterly*, 5(3), 225–47.

Kisanga, Eliawony J. & Sarah Jane Danchie (2007). *Commonwealth Small States: Issues and Prospects*. London: Commonwealth Secretariat.

Kitamura, Shuhei & Nils-Petter Lagerlöf (2015). *Natural Borders*. IIES Seminar Paper. No. 773.

Kitschelt, Herbert (2000). Linkages between Citizens and Politicians in Democratic Polities. *Comparative Political Studies*, 33(6/7), 845–79.

Kittel, Bernhard (2006). A Crazy Methodology? On the Limits of Macro-quantitative Social Science Research. *International Sociology*, 21(5), 647–77.

Kjaer, Ulrik & Jorgen Elklit (2014). The Impact of Assembly Size on Representativeness. *Journal of Legislative Studies*, 20(2), 156–73.

Klofstad, Casey A. (2011). *Civic Talk: Peers, Politics, and the Future of Democracy*. Philadelphia, PA: Temple University Press.

Knack, Stephen & Omar Azfar (2003). Trade Intensity, Country Size and Corruption. *Economics of Governance*, 4(1), 1–18.

Knoke, David (1990). Networks of Political Action: Toward Theory Construction. *Social Forces*, 68(4), 1041–63.

Koetzle, William (1998). The Impact of Constituency Diversity upon the Competitiveness of U.S. House Elections, 1962–96. *Legislative Studies Quarterly*, 2(3), 561–73.

Kohli, Atul (2004). *State-Directed Development: Political Power and Industrialization in the Global Periphery.* Cambridge: Cambridge University Press.

Kohr, Leopold (1978). *The Breakdown of Nations.* New York: E. P. Dutton.

Kokkonen, Andrej & Anders Sundell (2014). ADDIN EN.REFLIST Delivering Stability: Primogeniture and Autocratic Survival in European Monarchies 1000–1800. *American Political Science Review*, 108(2), 438–53.

Kollman, Ken (2013). *Perils of Centralization: Lessons from Church, State, and Corporation.* Cambridge: Cambridge University Press.

Kollman, Ken, Allen Hicken, Daniele Caramani, & David Backer (2011). *Constituency-Level Elections Archive* [dataset]. Ann Arbor: University of Michigan.

Kondo, Naoki, Rob van Dam, Grace Sembajwe, S. V. Subramanian, Ichiro Kawachi, & Zentaro Yamagata (2012). Income Inequality and Health: The Role of Population Size, Inequality Threshold, Period Effects and Lag Effects. *Journal of Epidemiology and Community Health*, 66(6), e11–e11.

Konisky, David M. & Michiko Ueda (2011). The Effects of Uncontested Elections on Legislator Performance. *Legislative Studies Quarterly*, 36(2), 199–229.

Konrad, Kai A. & Benny Geys (2010). Federalism and Optimal Allocation across Levels of Governance. In Henrik Enderlein, Sonja Walti, & Michael Zurn, eds., *Handbook on Multilevel Governance.* Cheltenham: Elgar, pp. 32–46.

Kosse, Krisztina (1990). Group Size and Societal Complexity: Thresholds in the Long-Term Memory. *Journal of Anthropological Archaeology*, 9(3), 275–303.

Kosse, Krisztina (1994). The Evolution of Large, Complex Groups: A Hypothesis. *Journal of Anthropological Archaeology*, 13(1), 35–50.

Kosse, Krisztina (2000). Some Regularities in Human Group Formation and the Evolution of Societal Complexity. *Complexity*, 6(1), 60–64.

Kostelka, Filip (2017). Does Democratic Consolidation Lead to a Decline in Voter Turnout? Global Evidence since 1939. *American Political Science Review*, 111(4), 653–67.

Kraditor, Aileen S. (1981). *The Radical Persuasion, 1890–1917: Aspects of the Intellectual History and the Historiography of Three American Radical Organizations.* Baton Rouge: Louisiana State University Press.

Kraaykamp, Gerbert, Marcel van Dam, & Theo Toonen (2001). Institutional Change and Political Participation: The Effect of Municipal Amalgamation on Local Electoral Turnout in the Netherlands. *Acta Politica*, 36(4), 402–18.

Kranton, Rachel E. (1996). Reciprocal Exchange: a Self-Sustaining System. *American Economic Review*, 86(4), 830–51.

Krasno, Jonathan S. (1994). *Challengers, Competition, and Reelection.* New Haven, CT: Yale University Press.

Krebs, Ronald R., & Jack S. Levy (2001). Demographic Change and the Sources of International Conflict. In Myron Weiner & Sharon Stanton Russell, eds., *Demography and National Security.* New York: Berghahn Books, pp. 62–105.

Kremer, Michael (1993). Population Growth and Technological Change: 1,000,000 B.C. to 1990. *Quarterly Journal of Economics*, 108(3), 681–716.

Kriesberg, Louis (1962). Careers, Organization Size, and Succession. *American Journal of Sociology*, 68(3), 355–59.

Krugman, Paul (1991). Increasing Returns and Economic Geography. *Journal of Political Economy*, 99(3), 483–99.

Kuklinski, James H. (1977). District Competitiveness and Legislative Roll-Call Behavior: A Reassessment of the Marginality Hypothesis. *American Journal of Political Science*, 21(3), 627–38.

Kurrild-Klitgaard, Peter (2000). The Constitutional Economics of Autocratic Succession. *Public Choice*, 103(1), 63–84.

Kuznets, Simon (1963). Economic Growth of Small Nations. In E. A. G. Robinson, ed., *Economic Consequences of the Size of Nations*. London: Macmillan, pp. 14–34.

La Porta, Rafael, Florencio Lopez-de-Silanes, Andrei Shleifer, & Robert W. Vishny (1999). The Quality of Government. *Journal of Economics, Law and Organization*, 15(1), 222–79.

La Raja, Raymond J. (2008). *Small Change: Money, Political Parties, and Campaign Finance Reform*. Ann Arbor: University of Michigan Press.

Lachat, Romain (2011). Electoral Competitiveness and Issue Voting. *Political Behavior*, 33(4), 645–63.

Lacina, Bethany (2006). Explaining the Severity of Civil Wars. *Journal of Conflict Resolution*, 50(2), 276–89.

Lacina, Bethany (2009). *Battle Deaths Dataset 1946–2008: Codebook for Version 3.0*. Oslo: Centre for the Study of Civil War (CSCW), International Peace Research Institute.

Ladner, Andreas (2002). Size and Direct Democracy at the Local Level: The Case of Switzerland. *Environment and Planning C: Government and Policy*, 20 (6), 813–28.

Lago-Peñas, Santiago & Jorge Martinez-Vazquez, eds., (2013). *The Challenge of Local Government Size: Theoretical Perspectives, International Experience and Policy Reform*. Cheltenham: Elgar.

Laitin, David D. & Rajesh Ramachandran (2015). Linguistic Diversity, Official Language Choice and Nation Building: Theory and Evidence. Unpublished Manuscript, Stanford University.

Lake, David A. (2009). *Hierarchy in International Relations*. Ithaca, NY: Cornell University Press.

Lake, David A. & Angela O'Mahony (2004). The Incredible Shrinking State: Explaining Change in the Territorial Size of Countries. *Journal of Conflict Resolution*, 48(5), 699–722.

Lake, Ronald La Due & Robert Huckfeldt (1998). Social Capital, Social Networks, and Political Participation. *Political Psychology*, 19(3), 567–84.

Lakoff, Sanford A. (1997). *Democracy: History, Theory, Practice*. Boulder, CO: Westview Press.

Lambsdorff, Johann Graf (1999). The Transparency International Corruption Perceptions Index 1999 – Framework Document. Transparency International, Berlin.

Langbein, Laura & Stephen Knack (2010). The Worldwide Governance Indicators: Six, One, or None? *Journal of Development Studies*, 46(2), 350–70.

Lange, Matthew (2009). *Lineages of Despotism and Development: British Colonialism and State Power.* Cambridge: Cambridge University Press.

Larsen, Christian Albrekt (2002). Municipal Size and Democracy: A Critical Analysis of the Argument of Proximity Based on the Case of Denmark. *Scandinavian Political Studies*, 25(4), 317–32.

Larsen, Stein Ugelvik (2005). *Theory and Methods in Political Science.* New York: Columbia University Press.

Lascher, Edward L., Jr. (2005). Constituency Size and Incumbent Safety: A Reexamination. *Political Research Quarterly*, 58(2), 269–78.

Laslett, Peter (1956). *Philosophy, Politics and Society.* Oxford: Backwell.

Lassen, David Dreyer & Søren Serritzlew (2011). Jurisdiction Size and Local Democracy: Evidence on Internal Political Efficacy from Large-Scale Municipal Reform. *American Political Science Review*, 105(2), 238–58.

Latane, Bibb (1981). The Psychology of Social Impact. *American Psychologist*, 36 (4), 343–56.

Lauth, Hans-Joachim (2000). Informal Institutions and Democracy. *Democratization*, 7(4), 21–50.

Law, Gwillim (1999). *Administrative Subdivisions of Countries: A Comprehensive World Reference, 1900 through 1998.* Jefferson, NC: McFarland.

Lawrence, Thomas B., Monika I. Winn, & P. Devereaux Jennings (2001). The Temporal Dynamics of Institutionalization. *Academy of Management Review*, 26(4), 624–44.

Le Bon, Gustave (1896). *The Crowd.* London: T. Fischer Unwin.

Leamer, Edward E. (1983). Let's Take the Con Out of Econometrics. *American Economic Review*, 73(1), 31–43.

Lebowitz, Barry D. (1975). Age and Fearfulness: Personal and Situational Factors. *Journal of Gerontology*, 30(6), 696–700.

Lee, Frances E. (1998). Representation and Public Policy: The Consequences of Senate Apportionment for the Geographic Distribution of Federal Funds. *Journal of Politics*, 60(1), 34–62.

Lee, Frances E. (2000). Senate Representation and Coalition Building in Distributive Politics. *American Political Science Review*, 94(1), 59–72.

Lee, Frances E. (2004). Bicameralism and Geographic Politics: Allocating Funds in the House and Senate. *Legislative Studies Quarterly* 29(2), 185–213.

Lee, Frances E. & Bruce I. Oppenheimer (1999). *Sizing up the Senate: The Unequal Consequences of Equal Representation.* Chicago: University of Chicago Press.

Leighley, Jan E. (1990). Social Interaction and Contextual Influences on Political Participation. *American Politics Quarterly*, 18(4), 459–75.

Leighley, Jan E. (1995). Attitudes, Opportunities and Incentives: A Field Essay on Political Participation. *Political Research Quarterly*, 48(1), 181–209.

Lenski, Gerhard E. (1966). *Power and Privilege.* New York: McGraw Hill.

Leroy, Marcel (1978). *Population and World Politics: The Interrelationships between Demographic Factors and International Relations.* Leiden: Martinius Nijhoff.

Letelier, Leonardo S. (2005). Explaining Fiscal Decentralization. *Public Finance Review*, 33(2), 155–83.

Levendusky, Matthew S. & Jeremy C. Pope (2010). Measuring Aggregate-Level Ideological Heterogeneity. *Legislative Studies Quarterly*, 35(2), 259–82.

Levi, Margaret & Laura Stoker (2000). Political Trust and Trustworthiness. *Annual Review of Political Science*, 3(1), 475–507.

Levine, John M. & Richard L. Moreland (1990). Progress in Small Group Research. *Annual Review of Psychology*, 41(1), 585–634.

Levine, Mark & Simon Crowther (2008). The Responsive Bystander: How Social Group Membership and Group Size Can Encourage as Well as Inhibit Bystander Intervention. *Journal of Personality and Social Psychology*, 95(6), 1429–39.

Levine, Stephen (2016). *Pacific Ways: Government and Politics in the Pacific Islands*. 2nd ed. Wellington: Victoria University Press.

Levitsky, Steven (1998). Institutionalization and Peronism: The Concept, the Case and the Case for Unpacking the Concept. *Party Politics*, 4(1), 77–92.

Levy, Jack S. & William R. Thompson (2005). Hegemonic Threats and Great-Power Balancing in Europe, 1495–1999. *Security Studies*, 14(1), 1–33.

Lewis, Paul G. (2011). Size and Local Democracy: Scale Effects in City Politics. *PS: Political Science and Politics*, 44(1), 107–09.

Li, Lianjiang & Kevin O'Brien (1996). Villagers and Popular Resistance in Contemporary China. *Modern China*, 22(1), 28–61.

Lieberman, Evan S. (2005). Nested Analysis As a Mixed-Method Strategy for Comparative Research. *American Political Science Review*, 99(3), 435–52.

Lieberman, Evan S. (2009). *Boundaries of Contagion: How Ethnic Politics Have Shaped Government Responses to AIDS*. Princeton, NJ: Princeton University Press.

Lieberman, Evan S. (2011). The Perils of Polycentric Governance of Infectious Disease in South Africa. *Social Science & Medicine*, 73(5), 676–84.

Lieberthal, Kenneth (2004). *Governing China: From Revolution through Reform*. 2nd ed. New York: W. W. Norton.

Liebman, Robert C., John R. Sutton, & Robert Wuthnow (1988). Exploring the Social Sources of Denominationalism: Schisms in American Protestant Denominations, 1890–1980. *American Sociological Review*, 53(3), 343–52.

Lijphart, Arend (1977). *Democracy in Plural Societies*. New Haven, CT: Yale University Press.

Lijphart, Arend (1997). Unequal Participation: Democracy's Unresolved Dilemma, Presidential Address, American Political Science Association, 1996. *American Political Science Review*, 91(1), 1–14.

Lijphart, Arend (1999). *Patterns of Democracy: Government Forms and Performance in Thirty-Six Countries*. New Haven, CT: Yale University Press.

Lima, Ricardo Carvalho de Andrade & Raul da Mota Silveira Neto (2017). Secession of Municipalities and Economies of Scale: Evidence from Brazil. *Journal of Regional Science*, 58(1), 1–22.

Linder, Wolf (2010). *Swiss Democracy*. Basingstoke: Palgrave Macmillan.

Lindert, Peter H. (2004). *Growing Public: Volume 1, The Story: Social Spending and Economic Growth since the Eighteenth Century*. Cambridge: Cambridge University Press.

Linebarger, Christopher & Andrew Enterline (2016). Third Party Intervention and the Duration and Outcomes of Civil Wars. In T. David Mason & Sara McLaughlin Mitchell, eds., *What Do We Know about Civil Wars?* Lanham, MD: Rowman & Littlefield, pp. 93–108.

Lipset, Seymour Martin (1996). *American Exceptionalism.* New York: W. W. Norton.

Lipset, Seymour Martin & Gary Marks (2001). *It Didn't Happen Here: Why Socialism Failed in the United States.* New York: W. W. Norton.

Lipset, Seymour Martin, Martin A. Trow, & James Samuel Coleman (1956). *Union Democracy: The Internal Politics of the International Typographical Union.* New York: Free Press.

Listhaug, Ola (1995). The Dynamics of Trust in Politicians. In Hans-Dieter Klingemann & Dieter Fuchs, eds., *Citizens and the State.* New York: Oxford University Press, pp. 261–97.

Liu, Amy H. & Brendan Apfeld (2016). *Education Prioritization and Language Standardization.* Paper presented at IPSA World Congress (July 23–28), Poznan.

Lively, Jack (1975). *Democracy.* New York: St. Martin's.

Lockhart, Douglas G., David Drakakis-Smith, & John Schembri (1993). *The Development Process in Small Island States.* London: Routledge.

Long, James, David Rasmussen, & Charles Haworth (1977). Income Inequality and City Size. *Review of Economics and Statistics,* 59(2), 244–46.

Lorwin, Val (1971). Segmented Pluralism: Ideological Cleavages and Political Cohesion in the Smaller European Democracies. *Comparative Politics,* 3(2), 141–75.

Loughlin, John (2001). *Subnational Democracy in the European Union.* Oxford: Oxford University Press.

Loughlin, John (2007). *Subnational Government: The French Experience.* Basingstoke: Palgrave.

Lowenthal, David (1987). *Social Features.* In Colin Clarke & Tony Payne, eds., *Politics, Security and Development in Small States.* London: Allen & Unwin, pp. 26–49.

Lublin, David (2013). *Election Passport.* American University. Accessed 2013. www.electionpassport.com

Luca, Dara Lee, Emily Owens, & Gunjan Sharma (2015). Can Alcohol Prohibition Reduce Violence against Women? *American Economic Review,* 105 (5), 625–29.

Lucas, Robert E., Jr. (1978). On the Size Distribution of Business Firms. *Bell Journal of Economics,* 9(2), 508–23.

Luchinger, Simon & Alois Stutzer (2002). Skalenerträge in der öffentlichen Kernverwaltung: Eine empirische Analyse anhand von Gemeindefusionen. *Swiss Political Science Review,* 8(1), 27–50.

Lukes, Steven (1986). *Power.* New York: New York University Press.

Maass, Matthias (2017). *Small States in World Politics: The Story of Small State Survival 1648–2016.* Manchester: Manchester University Press.

MacSweeney, Naoíse (2004). Social Complexity and Population: A Study in the Early Bronze Age Aegean. *Papers from the Institute of Archaeology,* 15, 52–65.

Maddison, Angus (2010). *Statistics on World Population, GDP and per capita GDP, 1–2008 AD*. Accessed 2016. www.ggdc.net/maddison/oriindex.htm

Mainwaring, Scott & Timothy Scully (1995). *Building Democratic Institutions: Party Systems in Latin America*. Stanford, CA: Stanford University Press.

Mair, Peter & Ingrid van Biezen (2001). Party Membership in Twenty European Democracies, 1980–2000. *Party Politics*, 7(1), 5–21.

Malesky, Edmund (2009). Gerrymandering – Vietnamese Style: Escaping the Partial Reform Equilibrium in a Nondemocratic Regime. *Journal of Politics*, 71 (1), 132–59.

Malik, Iffat (2002). *Kashmir: Ethnic Conflict, International Dispute*. Oxford: Oxford University Press.

Malthus, Thomas (1798). *An Essay on the Principle of Population*. London: J. Johnson, in St. Paul's Church-Yard.

Mann, Michael (1986). *The Sources of Social Power, Vol. 1*. Cambridge: Cambridge University Press.

Mann, Thomas & Raymond Wolfinger (1980). Candidates and Parties in Congressional Elections. *American Political Science Review*, 74(3), 617–32.

Manor, James (1999). *The Political Economy of Democratic Decentralization*. Washington, DC: World Bank.

Mansbridge, Jane J. (1983). *Beyond Adversary Democracy*. Chicago: University of Chicago Press.

Mansbridge, Jane J. (1999). Should Blacks Represent Blacks and Women Represent Women? A Contingent "Yes." *Journal of Politics*, 61(3), 628–57.

Marks, Gary (1992). Structural Policy in the European Community. In Alberta Sbragia, ed., *Europolitics: Institutions and Policymaking in the "New" European Community*. Washington, DC: Brookings Institution, pp. 191–224.

Marshall, Monty, Ted Gurr, & Keith Jaggers (2014). *Polity IV Project: Dataset Users' Manual*. Accessed 2014. www.systemicpeace.org/inscr/p4manualv2013.pdf

Masala, Carlo (2004). Schwimmende Politeia? Demokratische Mikroinseln im Südpazifik und in der Karibik. *Politische Vierteljahresschrift*, 45(2), 237–58.

Matsubayashi, Tetsuya (2007). Population Size, Local Autonomy, and Support for the Political System. *Social Science Quarterly*, 88(3), 830–49.

Matsusaka, John G. (2015). "Responsiveness" As a Measure of Representation. Unpublished paper, University of South Carolina.

Mauro, Paolo (1995). Corruption and Growth. *Quarterly Journal of Economics*, 110(3), 681–712.

Mauss, Marcel (1954). *The Gift: The Form and Functions of Exchange in Archaic Societies*. New York: Free Press.

Mawdsley, Emma (2002). Redrawing the Body Politic: Federalism, Regionalism and the Creation of New States in India. *Commonwealth & Comparative Politics*, 40(3), 34–54.

Mayhew, Bruce H. (1973). System Size and Ruling Elites. *American Sociological Review*, 38(4), 468–75.

Mayhew, Bruce H. (1980). Structuralism versus Individualism: Part 1, Shadowboxing in the Dark. *Social Forces*, 59(2), 335–75.

Mayhew, Bruce H. (1981). Structuralism versus Individualism: Part II, Ideological and Other Obfuscations. *Social Forces*, 59(3), 627–48.

Mayhew, Bruce H. & Roger L. Levinger (1976a). On the Emergence of Oligarchy in Human Interaction. *American Journal of Sociology*, 81(5), 1017–49.

Mayhew, Bruce H. & Roger L. Levinger (1976b). Size and the Density of Interaction in Human Aggregates. *American Journal of Sociology*, 82(1), 86–110.

Mayhew, Bruce H., Roger L. Levinger, J. Miller McPherson, & Thomas F. James (1972). System Size and Structural Differentiation in Formal Organizations: A Baseline Generator for Two Major Theoretical Propositions. *American Sociological Review*, 37(5), 629–33.

Mayhew, Bruce H. & Paul T. Schollaert (1980). The Concentration of Wealth: A Sociological Model. *Sociological Focus*, 13(1), 1–35.

McCauley, John F. & Daniel N. Posner (2015). African Borders As Sources of Natural Experiments Promise and Pitfalls. *Political Science Research and Methods*, 3(2), 409–18.

McCauley, Martin & Stephen Carter (1986). *Leadership and Succession in the Soviet Union, Eastern Europe, and China*. Palgrave: Macmillan.

McClurg, Scott (2003). Social Networks and Political Participation: The Role of Social Interaction in Explaining Political Participation. *Political Research Quarterly*, 56(4), 449–64.

McMann, Kelly M., Daniel Pemstein, Brigitte Seim, Jan Teorell, & Staffan I. Lindberg (2016). *Strategies of Validation: Assessing the Varieties of Democracy Corruption Data*. Varieties of Democracy Working Paper SERIES 2016:23.

McNeill, William Hardy (1990). *Population and Politics since 1750*. Charlottesville: University Press of Virginia.

McNicoll, Geoffrey (1999). Population Weights in the International Order. *Population and Development Review*, 25(3), 411–42.

Mearsheimer, John (2001). *The Tragedy of Great Power Politics*. London: Norton.

Medina, Luis Fernando & Susan Stokes (2007). Monopoly and Monitoring: An Approach to Political Clientelism. In Herbert Kitschelt & Steven I. Wilkinson, eds., *Patrons, Clients and Policies: Patterns of Democratic Accountability and Political Competition*. New York: Cambridge University Press, pp. 150–82.

Meyer, Marshall W. (1972a). *Bureaucratic Structure and Authority: Coordination and Control in 254 Government Agencies*. New York: Harper & Row.

Meyer, Marshall W. (1972b). Size and the Structure of Organizations: A Causal Analysis. *American Sociological Review*, 37(4), 434–40.

Michalopoulos, Stelios (2012). The Origins of Ethnolinguistic Diversity. *American Economic Review*, 102(4), 1508–39.

Michels, Robert (1962). *Political Parties*. New York: Free Press.

Milgram, Stanley (1970). The Experience of Living in Cities. *Science*, 167(3924), 1461–68.

Millar, John (1806). *The Origin of the Distinction of Ranks*. 4th ed. Edinburgh: William Blackwood.

Miller, Arthur H. & Ola Listhaug (1990). Political Parties and Confidence in Government: A Comparison of Norway, Sweden and the United States. *British Journal of Political Science*, 20(3), 357–86.

Miller, Gary & Norman Schofield (2003). Activists and Partisan Realignment in the United States. *American Political Science Review*, 97(2), 245–60.

Miller, Michael K. (2012). Economic Development, Violent Leader Removal, and Democratization. *American Journal of Political Science*, 56(4), 1002–20.

Miller, Warren E. & Donald E. Stokes (1963). Constituency Influence in Congress. *American Political Science Review*, 57(1), 45–56.

Mills, C. Wright (1967). *The Power Elite*. Oxford: Oxford University Press.

Milner, Chris & Tony Westaway (1993). Country Size and the Medium-Term Growth Process: Some Cross-Country Evidence. *World Development*, 21(2), 203–11.

Mogi, S. (1931). *The Problem of Federalism: A Study in the History of Political Theory*. 2 vols. London: Allen & Unwin.

Moisio, Antti & Roope Uusitalo (2013). The Impact of Municipality Mergers on Local Public Expenditures in Finland. *Public Finance and Management*, 13(3), 148–66.

Montero, Alfred P. & David J. Samuels (2004). *Decentralization and Democracy in Latin America*. Notre Dame, IN: University of Notre Dame Press.

Montesquieu, Charles Louis Secondat de (1748). *De l'Esprit des loix*. Tome I. Genève: Barrillot et fils.

Montesquieu, Charles Louis Secondat de (1949)[1748]. *De l'Esprit des Lois*, ed. Thomas Nugent. New York: Hafner Press.

Montesquieu, Charles Louis Secondat de (1989)[1748]. *The Spirit of the Laws*. Cambridge: Cambridge University Press.

Montinola, Gabriella, Yingyi Qian, & Barry R. Weingast (1995). Federalism, Chinese Style: The Political Basis for Economic Success in China. *World Politics*, 48(1), 50–81.

Moody, James & Douglas R. White (2003). Structural Cohesion and Embeddedness: A Hierarchical Concept of Social Groups. *American Sociological Review*, 68(1), 103–27.

Mookherjee, Dilip (2006). Decentralization, Hierarchies, and Incentives: A Mechanism Design Perspective. *Journal of Economic Literature*, 44(2), 367–90.

Mooney, Christopher Z. (1995). Citizens, Structures, and Sister States: Influences on State Legislative Professionalism. *Legislative Studies Quarterly*, 20(1), 47–67.

Moore, Mick (2004). Revenues, State Formation, and the Quality of Governance in Developing Countries. *International Political Science Review*, 25(3), 297–319.

Moreno, Luis (2013). *The Federalization of Spain*. London: Routledge.

Morgan, Stephen L. & Christopher Winship (2015). *Counterfactuals and Causal Inference: Methods and Principles for Social Research*. Cambridge: Cambridge University Press.

Morgenthau, Hans (1993)[1948]. *Politics among Nations*. New York: McGraw Hill.

Moriss, Peter (1987). *Power: A Philosophical Investigation*. Manchester: Manchester University Press.

Morris, Henry (1972). Native Courts: A Cornerstone of Indirect Rule. In H. F. Morris & James S. Read, eds., *Indirect Rule and the Search for Justice: Essays in E. African Legal History*. Oxford: Clarendon Press.

Mosca, Gaetano (1939). *The Ruling Class*. New York: McGraw-Hill.

Mumford, Lewis (1961). *The City in History: Its Origins, Its Transformations, and Its Prospects*. New York: Houghton Mifflin Harcourt.

Munck, Gerardo L. & Richard Snyder (2007). *Passion, Craft, and Method in Comparative Politics*. Baltimore, MD: Johns Hopkins University Press.

Murillo, Maria Victoria & Cecilia Martinez-Gallardo (2007). Political Competition and Policy Adoption: Market Reforms in Latin American Public Utilities. *American Journal of Political Science*, 51(1), 120–39.

Murray, B. (1969). Metropolitan Interpersonal Income Inequality. *Land Economics*, 45(1), 121–25.

Musgrave, Richard Abel (1959). *Theory of Public Finance*. New York: McGraw-Hill.

Musthaq, Fathima (2014). Tumult in the Maldives. *Journal of Democracy*, 25(2), 164–70.

Mutz, Diana (2002). The Consequences of Cross-Cutting Networks for Political Participation. *American Journal of Political Science*, 46(4), 838–55.

Muzzio, Douglas & Tim Tompkins (1989). On the Size of the City Council: Finding the Mean. *Proceedings of the Academy of Political Science*, 37(3), 83–96.

Nanda, Ved P. (2006). The "Good Governance" Concept Revisited. *Annals of the American Academy of Political and Social Science*, 603(1), 269–83.

Naroll, Raoul (1956). A Preliminary Index of Social Development. *American Anthropologist*, 58(4), 687–715.

Nelson, Arthur C. & Kathryn A. Foster (1999). Metropolitan Governance Structure and Income Growth. Journal of Urban Affairs, 21(3), 309–24.

Nelson, Nici & Susan Wright (1995). *Power and Participatory Development: Theory and Practice*. London: Intermediate Technology Publications.

Newbury, Colin (2003). *Patrons, Clients, and Empire: Chieftaincy and Over-rule in Asia, Africa, and the Pacific*. Oxford: Oxford University Press.

Nichter, Simeon (2008). Vote Buying or Turnout Buying? Machine Politics and the Secret Ballot. *American Political Science Review*, 102(1), 19–31.

New York Times Editorial Board (2018). America Needs a Bigger House. *New York Times*. Accessed 2018. www.nytimes.com/interactive/2018/11/09/o pinion/expanded-house-representatives-size.html

Nielsen, Hans Jorgen (1981). Size and Evaluation of Government: Danish Attitudes towards Politics at Multiple Levels of Government. *European Journal of Political Research*, 9(1), 47–60.

Noell, James J. (1974). On the Administrative Sector of Social Systems: An Analysis of the Size and Complexity of Government Bureaucracies in the American States. *Social Forces*, 52(4), 549–58.

Nolan, Patrick D. (1979). Size and Administrative Intensity in Nations. *American Sociological Review*, 44(1), 110–25.

Nord, Stephen (1980a). An Empirical Analysis of Income Inequality and City Size. *Southern Economic Journal*, 46(3), 863–72.

Nord, Stephen (1980b). Income Inequality and City Size: An Examination of Alternative Hypotheses for Large and Small Cities. *Review of Economics and Statistics*, 62(4), 502–08.

Norris, Pippa & Andrea Abel van Es (2016). *Checkbook Elections? Political Finance in Comparative Perspective*. Oxford: Oxford University Press.

North, Douglass & Barry Weingast (1989). Constitutions and Commitment: The Evolution of Institutions Governing Public Choice in Seventeenth-Century England. *Journal of Economic History*, 49(4), 803–32.

Novak, William J. (1996). *The People's Welfare: Law and Regulation in Nineteenth-Century America*. Chapel Hill: University of North Carolina Press.

Nozick, Robert (1974). *Anarchy, State, and Utopia*. New York: Basic Books.

Nye, Joseph S., Jr. (2005). *Soft Power: The Means to Success in World Politics*. New York: Public Affairs.

Oates, Wallace E. (1972). *Fiscal Federalism*. New York: Harcourt Brace Jovanovich.

Oates, Wallace E. (1999). An Essay on Fiscal Federalism. *Journal of Economic Literature*, 37(3), 1120–49.

Oates, Wallace E. (2005). Toward a Second-Generation Theory of Fiscal Federalism. *International Tax and Public Finance*, 12(4), 349–74.

O'Dwyer, Conor & Daniel Ziblatt (2006). Does Decentralisation Make Government More Efficient and Effective? *Commonwealth & Comparative Politics*, 44(3), 326–43.

Ogburn, William F. & Otis Dudley Duncan (1964). City Size As a Sociological Variable. In Ernest W. Burgess & Donald J. Bogue, eds., *Contributions to Urban Sociology*. Chicago: University of Chicago Press, pp. 129–47.

O'Gorman, Frank (2001). Patronage and the Reform of the State in England, 1700–1860. In Simona Piattoni, eds., *Clientelism, Interests, and Democratic Representation: The European Experience in Historical and Comparative Perspective*. Cambridge: Cambridge University Press, pp. 54–76.

Oldfield, Adrian (1990). *Citizenship and Community: Civic Republicanism and the Modern World*. London: Routledge.

O'Leary, Cornelius (1962). *The Elimination of Corrupt Practices in British Elections, 1868–1911*. Oxford: Oxford University Press.

Oliver, J. Eric (2000). City Size and Civic Involvement in Metropolitan America. *American Political Science Review*, 94(2), 361–73.

Oliver, J. Eric, with Shang E. Ha & Zachary Callen (2012). *Local Elections and the Politics of Small-Scale Democracy*. Princeton, NJ: Princeton University Press.

Olken, Benjamin A. (2007). Monitoring Corruption: Evidence from a Field Experiment in Indonesia. *Journal of Political Economy*, 115(2), 200–49.

Olken, Benjamin A. & Monica Singhal (2011). Informal Taxation. *American Economic Journal: Applied Economics*, 3(4), 1–28.

Olsen, Johan P. (2009). Change and Continuity: An Institutional Approach to Institutions of Democratic Government. *European Political Science Review*, 1 (1), 3–32.

Olson, Mancur (1965). *The Logic of Collective Action: Public Goods and the Theory of Groups*. Cambridge, MA: Harvard University Press.

Olson, Mancur (1982). *The Rise and Decline of Nations: Economic Growth, Stagflation, and Social Rigidities*. New Haven, CT: Yale University Press.

Olsson, Andreas, Jeffrey P. Ebert, Mahzarin R. Banaji, & Elizabeth A. Phelps (2005). The Role of Social Groups in the Persistence of Learned Fear. *Science*, 309(5735), 785–87.

Olsson, Ola (2009). On the Democratic Legacy of Colonialism. *Journal of Comparative Economics*, 37(4), 534–51.

Olsson, Ola & Gustav Hansson (2011). Country Size and the Rule of Law: Resuscitating Montesquieu. *European Economic Review*, 55(5), 613–29.

O'Neill, Kathleen (2005). *Decentralizing the State: Elections, Parties, and Local Power in the Andes*. Cambridge: Cambridge University Press.

O'Neill, Michael (2000). Great Britain: From Dicey to Devolution. *Parliamentary Affairs*, 53(1), 69–95.

Openshaw, Stan (1984). Ecological Fallacies and the Analysis of Areal Census Data. *Environment and Planning A*, 16(1), 17–31.

Oppenheimer, Bruce I. (1996). The Representational Experience: The Effect of State Population on Senator–Constituency Linkages. *American Journal of Political Science*, 40(4), 1280–99.

Organski, Abramo Fimo Kenneth (1958). *World Politics*. New York: Knopf.

Organski, Katherine & Abramo Fimo Kenneth Organski (1961). *Population and World Power*. New York: Knopf.

O'Rourke, Kevin H. & Jeffrey G. Williamson (2002). When Did Globalisation Begin? *European Review of Economic History*, 6(1), 23–50.

Ostrom, Elinor (1972). Metropolitan Reform: Propositions Derived from Two Traditions. *Social Science Quarterly*, 53(3), 474–93.

Ostrom, Elinor (1990). *Governing the Commons: The Evolution of Institutions for Collective Action*. Cambridge: Cambridge University Press.

Ostrom, Elinor (2010). A Long Polycentric Journey. *Annual Review of Political Science*, 13, 1–23.

Ostrom, Vincent (1971). *The Political Theory of a Compound Republic: Designing the American Experiment*. Lanham, MD: Lexington Books.

Ostrom, Vincent, Charles M. Tiebout, & Robert Warren (1961). The Organization of Government in Metropolitan Areas: A Theoretical Inquiry. *American Political Science Review*, 55(4), 831–42.

Ott, Dana (2000). *Small Is Democratic: An Examination of State Size and Democratic Development*. New York: Garland.

Oxhorn, Philip, Joseph S. Tulchin, & Andrew Selee (2004). *Decentralization, Democratic Governance, and Civil Society in Comparative Perspective: Africa, Asia, and Latin America*. Washington, DC: Woodrow Wilson Center Press.

Padovano, Fabio & Roberto Ricciuti (2009). Political Competition and Economic Performance: Evidence from the Italian Regions. *Public Choice* 138 (3/4), 263–77.

Palanza, Valeria, Carlos Scartascini, & Mariano Tommasi (2016). Congressional Institutionalization: A Cross-National Comparison. *Legislative Studies Quarterly*, 41(1), 7–34.

Panebianco, Angelo (1988). *Political Parties: Organization and Power*. Cambridge: Cambridge University Press.

Panizza, Ugo (1999). On the Determinants of Fiscal Centralization: Theory, and Evidence. *Journal of Public Economics*, 74(1), 97–139.

Pareto, Vilfredo (1909). *Manuel d'economie politique*. Paris: Giard et Briere.

Parker, Glenn R. (1986). *Homeward Bound: Explaining Changes in Congressional Behavior*. Pittsburgh, PA: University of Pittsburgh Press.

Parsons, Talcott (1951). *The Social System*. Glencoe, IL: Free Press.

Patapan, Haig, John Wanna, & Patrick Moray Weller (2005). *Westminster Legacies: Democracy and Responsible Government in Asia and the Pacific*. Kensington: University of New South Wales Press.

Pateman, Carole (1970). *Participation and Democratic Theory*. Cambridge: Cambridge University Press.

Patterson, Samuel C. & Gregory A. Caldeira (1984). The Etiology of Partisan Competition. *American Political Science Review*, 78(3), 691–707.

Pavkovic, Aleksandar & Peter Radan (2013). *Creating New States: Theory and Practice of Secession*. Farnham: Ashgate.

Peacock, Alan & Alex Scott (2000). The Curious Attraction of Wagner's Law. *Public Choice*, 102(1/2), 1–17.

Pecorino, Paul (1999). The Effect of Group Size on Public Good Provision in a Repeated Game Setting. *Journal of Public Economics*, 72(1), 121–34.

Pegram, Thomas R. (1998). *Battling Demon Rum: The Struggle for a Dry America, 1800–1933*. Chicago: Ivan R. Dee.

Pemstein, Daniel, Kyle L. Marquardt, Eitan Tzelgov, Yi-ting Wang, Joshua Krusell, & Farhad Miri (2017). *The V-Dem Measurement Model: Latent Variable Analysis for Cross-National and Cross-Temporal Expert-Coded Data*. University of Gothenburg, Varieties of Democracy Institute: Working Paper No. 21, 2nd edition.

Penrose, Edith Tilton (1959). *The Theory of the Growth of the Firm*. New York: Wiley.

Peretto, Pietro & Sjak Smulders (2002). Technological Distance, Growth and Scale Effects. *Economic Journal*, 112(481), 603–24.

Perkins, Dwight H. & Moshe Syrquin (1989). Large Countries: The Influence of Size. In Hollis Chenery & Thirukodikaval N. Srinivasan, eds., *Handbook of Development Economics. Vol. 2*. Amsterdam: Elsevier, pp. 1691–1753.

Peters, Donald C. (1992). *The Democratic System in the Eastern Caribbean*. New York: Greenwood.

Pettersson-Lidbom, Per (2012). Does the Size of the Legislature Affect the Size of Government? Evidence from Two Natural Experiments. *Journal of Public Economics*, 96(3/4), 269–78.

Pfeffer, Jeffrey & William L. Moore (1980). Average Tenure of Academic Department Heads: The Effects of Paradigm, Size, and Departmental Demography. *Administrative Science Quarterly*, 25, 387–406.

Phillips, Anne (1995). *The Politics of Presence*. Oxford: Oxford University Press.

Pierson, Paul (2004). *Politics in Time: History, Institutions, and Social Analysis*. Princeton, NJ: Princeton University Press.

Pitkin, Hanna Fenichel (1967). *The Concept of Representation*. Berkeley: University of California Press.

Pitkin, Hanna Fenichel & Sara M. Shumer (2001). On Participation. In Ricardo Blaug & John Schwarzmantel, eds., *Democracy: A Reader*. New York: Columbia University Press, pp. 452–57.

Plato (1960). The Laws. In A. E. Taylor ed., *The Laws*. London: Dent.

Poguntke, Thomas, Susan E. Scarrow, & Paul D. Webb (2016). Party Rules, Party Resources and the Politics of Parliamentary Democracies: How Parties Organize in the 21st Century. *Party Politics*, 22(6), 661–78.

Polsby, Nelson W. (1968). The Institutionalization of the House of Representatives. *American Political Science Review*, 62(1), 144–68.

Polsby, Nelson W. (1983). *Consequences of Party Reform*. New York: Oxford University Press.

Pontusson, Jonas (2005). *Inequality and Prosperity: Social Europe vs. Liberal America*. Ithaca, NY: Cornell University Press.

Poole, Marshall Scott & Andrea B. Hollingshead (2005). *Theories of Small Groups: Interdisciplinary Perspectives*. Thousand Oaks, CA: Sage.

Popper, Karl (1959). *The Logic of Scientific Discovery*. London: Hutchinson.

Posner, Daniel N. (2004). The Political Salience of Cultural Difference: Why Chewas and Tumbukas Are Allies in Zambia and Adversaries in Malawi. *American Political Science Review*, 98(4), 529–45.

Powell, G. Bingham (1982). *Contemporary Democracies: Participation, Stability, and Violence*. Cambridge, MA: Harvard University Press.

Powell, G Bingham, Jr. (1986). American Voter Turnout in Comparative Perspective. *American Political Science Review*, 80(1), 17–43.

Powell, G. Bingham, Jr. (2000). *Elections As Instruments of Democracy: Majoritarian and Proportional Visions*. New Haven, CT: Yale University Press.

Preuhs, Robert R. (2007). Descriptive Representation As a Mechanism to Mitigate Policy Backlash: Latino Incorporation and Welfare Policy in the American States. *Political Research Quarterly*, 60(2), 277–92.

Prewitt, Kenneth (1969). From the Many Are Chosen the Few. *American Behavioral Scientist*, 13(2), 169–87.

Prud'homme, Remy (1995). The Dangers of Decentralization. *World Bank Research Observer*, 10(2), 201–20.

Przeworski, Adam (1991). *Democracy and the Market: Political and Economic Reforms in Eastern Europe and Latin America*. Cambridge, MA: Cambridge University Press.

Przeworski, Adam (2013). *Political Institutions and Political Events (PIPE)* [dataset]. New York University.

Pumain, Denise (2006). *Hierarchy in Natural and Social Sciences*. Dordrecht: Springer.

Putnam, Robert D. (2000). *Bowling Alone*. New York: Simon and Schuster.

Putnam, Robert D. (2007). E Pluribus Unum: Diversity and Community in the Twenty-First Century. The 2006 Johan Skytte Prize Lecture. *Scandinavian Political Studies*, 30(2), 137–74.

Putterman, Louis & David N. Weil (2010). Post-1500 Population Flows and the Long-Run Determinants of Economic Growth and Inequality. *Quarterly Journal of Economics*, 125(4), 1627–82.

Querubin, Pablo (2016). Family and Politics: Dynastic Persistence in the Philippines. *Quarterly Journal of Political Science*, 11(2), 151–81.

Quintelier, Ellen, Dietlind Stolle, & Allison Harell (2012). Politics in Peer Groups: Exploring the Causal Relationship between Network Diversity and Political Participation. *Political Research Quarterly*, 65(4), 868–81.

Rahn, Wendy M. & Thomas J. Rudolph (2005). A Tale of Political Trust in American Cities. *Public Opinion Quarterly*, 69(4), 530–60.

Rainnie, Al (2016). *Industrial Relations in Small Firms: Small Isn't Beautiful.* London: Routledge.

Rakove, Jack N. (1997). *Original Meanings: Politics and Ideas in the Making of the Constitution.* New York: Vintage.

Raleigh, Clionadh & Håvard Hegre (2009). Population Size, Concentration, and Civil War. A Geographically Disaggregated Analysis. *Political Geography*, 28 (4), 224–38.

Rallings, Colin S. & Michael Thrasher (1997). *Local Elections in Britain.* London: Routledge.

Rallings, Colin S., Michael Thrasher & L. Ware (2006). *British Local Election Database, 1889–2003.* Plymouth: University of Plymouth.

Rao, Nirmala & Ken Young (1997). *Local Government since 1945.* Hoboken, NJ: Wiley-Blackwell.

Rauch, James E. & Peter B. Evans (2000). Bureaucratic Structure and Bureaucratic Performance in Less Developed Countries. *Journal of Public Economics*, 75(1), 49–71.

Rawls, John (1971). *A Theory of Justice.* Cambridge, MA: Harvard University Press.

Rehfeld, Andrew (2006). Towards a General Theory of Political Representation. *Journal of Politics*, 68(1), 1–21.

Reilly, Benjamin (2002). Social Choice in the South Seas: Electoral Innovation and the Borda Count in the Pacific Island Countries. *International Political Science Review*, 23(4), 355–72.

Reingewertz, Yaniv (2012). Do Municipal Amalgamations Work? Evidence from Municipalities in Israel. *Journal of Urban Economics*, 72(2/3), 240–51.

Reinhard, Wolfgang (1996). *Power Elites and State Building.* Oxford: Oxford University Press.

Remmer, Karen L. (2010a). Political Scale and Electoral Turnout: Evidence from the Less Industrialized World. *Comparative Political Studies*, 43(3), 275–303.

Remmer, Karen L. (2010b). Why Do Small States Have Big Governments? *European Political Science Review*, 2(1), 49–71

Reynolds, Andrew (2011). *Designing Democracy in a Dangerous World.* Oxford: Oxford University Press.

Rhodes, Rod A. W. & Paul 't Hart (2014). *The Oxford Handbook of Political Leadership.* Oxford: Oxford University Press.

Rich, Roland, Luke Hambly, & Michael G. Morgan (2006). *Political Parties in the Pacific Islands.* Canberra: Australian National University Press.

Richards, Janet & Mary van Buren (2001). *Order, Legitimacy and Wealth in Ancient States.* Cambridge: Cambridge University Press.

Richards, Jeffrey (1982). Politics in Small Independent Communities: Conflict or Consensus? *Journal of Commonwealth & Comparative Politics*, 20(2), 155–71.

Riker, William (1964). *Federalism: Origin, Operation, Significance.* Boston: Little, Brown.

Riker, William & Peter C. Ordeshook (1968). A Theory of the Calculus of Voting. *American Political Science Review,* 62(1), 25–42.

Robinson, Edward A. G. (1963). *Economic Consequences of the Size of Nations.* London: Macmillan.

Robinson, Ronald (1972). Non-European Foundations of European Imperialism: Sketch for a Theory of Collaboration. In Roger Owen & Bob Sutcliffe, eds., *Studies in the Theory of Imperialism.* London: Longman, pp. 118–40.

Rodden, Jonathan (2002). The Dilemma of Fiscal Federalism: Grants and Fiscal Performance around the World. *American Journal of Political Science,* 46(3), 670–87.

Rodden, Jonathan (2005). *Hamilton's Paradox: The Promise and Peril of Fiscal Federalism.* Cambridge: Cambridge University Press.

Rodden, Jonathan & Erik Wibbels (2002). Beyond the Fiction of Federalism: Macroeconomic Management in Multitiered Systems. *World Politics,* 54(4), 494–531.

Rodden, Jonathan & Erik Wibbels (2019). *Decentralized Governance and Accountability: Academic Research and the Future of Donor Programming.* Cambridge: Cambridge University Press.

Rodrik, Dani (1998). Why Do More Open Economies Have Bigger Governments? *Journal of Political Economy,* 106(5), 997–1032.

Rogowski, Ronald (1987). Trade and the Variety of Democratic Institutions. *International Organization,* 41(2), 202–23.

Rosanvallon, Pierre (2008). *Counter-Democracy. Politics in an Age of Mistrust.* Cambridge: Cambridge University Press.

Rose, Andrew K. (2006). Size Really Doesn't Matter: In Search of a National Scale Effect. *Journal of Japanese and International Economies,* 20(4), 482–507.

Ross, Michael L. (2001). Does Oil Hinder Democracy? *World Politics,* 53(3), 325–61.

Rotberg, Robert I. (2010). *When States Fail: Causes and Consequences.* Princeton, NJ: Princeton University Press.

Rotolo, Thomas & Charles R. Tittle (2006). Population Size, Change, and Crime in US Cities. *Journal of Quantitative Criminology,* 22(4), 341–67.

Rousseau, Jean-Jacques (1994)[1762]. *Discourse on Political Economy and The Social Contract.* Oxford: Oxford University Press.

Rousseau, Jean-Jacques (1995)[1762]. Du Contrat Social ou Princepes du Droit Politicque. In S. van den Braak ed., *Het maatschappelijk verdrag of Beginselen der Staatsinrichting.* Amsterdam: Boom.

Rousseau, Jean-Jacques (1762). *Du Contract social.* Amsterdam: Marc M. Rey.

Royle, Stephen A. (2001). *A Geography of Islands: Small Island Insularity.* London: Routledge.

Royuela, Vicente, Paolo Veneri, & Raul Ramos (2018). The Short-Run Relationship between Inequality and Growth: Evidence from OECD Regions during the Great Recession. *Regional Studies,* 1–13.

Rubin, Donald B. (2005). Causal Inference Using Potential Outcomes: Design, Modeling, Decisions. *Journal of the American Statistical Association*, 100(469), 322–31.

Rubinchik-Pessach, Anna (2005). Can Decentralization Be Beneficial? *Journal of Public Economy*, 89(7), 1231–49.

Rudra, Nita (2002). Globalization and the Decline of the Welfare State in Less-Developed Countries. *International Organization*, 56(2), 411–45.

Rueda, Miguel R. (2017). Small Aggregates, Big Manipulation: Vote Buying Enforcement and Collective Monitoring. *American Journal of Political Science*, 61(1), 163–77.

Rueschemeyer, Dietrich (2009). *Usable Theory: Analytic Tools for Social and Political Research*. Princeton, NJ: Princeton University Press.

Rusk, David (2013). *Cities without Suburbs: A Census 2010 Perspective*. Washington, DC: Woodrow Wilson Center Press.

Russett, Bruce M. (1968). Is There a Long-Run Trend toward Concentration in the International System? *Comparative Political Studies*, 1(1), 103–22.

Saarimaa, Tuukka & Janne Tukiainen (2014). I Don't Care to Belong to Any Club That Will Have Me as a Member: Empirical Analysis of Municipal Mergers. *Political Science Research and Methods*, 2(1), 97–117.

Sacco, Vincent (1985). City Size and Perceptions of Crime. *Canadian Journal of Sociology/Cahiers canadiens de sociologie*, 10(3), 277–93.

Sadalla, Edward K. (1978). Population Size, Structural Differentiation, and Human Behavior. *Environment and Behavior*, 10(2), 271–91.

Saideman, Stephen M., David J. Lanoue, Michael Campenni, & Samuel Stanton (2002). Democratization, Political Institutions, and Ethnic Conflict: A Pooled Time-Series Analysis, 1985–1998. *Comparative Political Studies*, 35(1), 103–29.

Saks, Michael J. (1977). *Jury Verdicts: The Role of Group Size and Social Decision Rule*. Lexington, MA: D. C. Heath.

Sale, Kirkpatrick (2017). *Human Scale Revisited: A New Look at the Classic Case for a Decentralist Future*. Chelsea: Chelsea Green Publishing.

Salvatore, Dominick, Marjan Svetlicic, & Joze B. Damijan (2001). *Small Countries in a Global Economy: New Challenges and Opportunities*. New York: Springer.

Samuels, David J. (1999). Incentives to Cultivate a Party Vote in Candidate-centric Electoral Systems. *Comparative Political Studies*, 32(4), 487–518.

Sandel, Michael J. (1982). *Liberalism and the Limits of Justice*. Cambridge: Cambridge University Press.

Sarkees, Meredith & Frank Wayman (2010). *Resort to War: 1816–2007*. Washington, DC: Congressional Quarterly Press.

Sartori, Giovanni (1976). *Parties and Party Systems*. Cambridge: Cambridge University Press.

Sawyer, Malcolm C. (1991). *The Economics of Industries and Firms: Theories, Evidence and Policy*. London: Routledge.

Scarrow, Susan E. (2002). Parties without Members? Party Organization in a Changing Electoral Environment. In R. J. Dalton & Martin P. Wattenberg, eds., *Parties without Partisans: Political Change in Advanced Industrial Democracies*. Oxford: Oxford University Press, pp. 79–101.

Scarrow, Susan E. (2007). Political Finance in Comparative Perspective. *Annual Review of Political Science*, 10, 193–210.

Schaffer, Frederic Charles, ed. (2007). *Elections for Sale: The Causes and Consequences of Vote Buying*. Boulder, CO: Lynne Rienner.

Schaffer, Frederic Charles (2008). *The Hidden Costs of Clean Election Reform*. Ithaca, NY: Cornell University Press.

Schaffer, Stephen (1982). Policy Differences between Voters and Non-voters in American Elections. *Western Political Quarterly*, 35, 496–510.

Scharpf, Fritz W. (1988). The Joint-Decision Trap: Lessons from German Federalism and European Integration. *Public Administration*, 66(3), 239–78.

Schattschneider, Elmer E. (1942). *Party Government*. New York: Rinehart.

Scheiber, Harry N. (1969). *Ohio Canal Era*. Athens: Ohio University Press.

Scheiber, Harry N. (1972). Government and the Economy: Studies of the "Commonwealth" Policy in Nineteenth-Century America. *Journal of Interdisciplinary History*, 3(1), 135–51.

Schlesinger, Joseph A. (1966). *Ambition and Politics: Political Careers in the United States*. Chicago: Rand McNally.

Schlozman, Kay Lehman & John T. Tierney (1986). *Organized Interests and American Democracy*. New York: Harper & Row.

Schmidt, Steffen W. (1977). *Friends, Followers, and Factions: A Reader in Political Clientelism*. Berkeley: University of California Press.

Schofer, Evan & Wesley Longhofer (2011). The Structural Sources of Association. *American Journal of Sociology*, 117(2), 539–85.

Schraufnagel, Scot & Benjamin S. Bingle (2015). Legislature Size and Non-elite Populations: Theory and Corroborating Evidence. *Journal of Politics & Law*, 8 (4), 242–53.

Schudson, Michael (1998). *The Good Citizen*. New York: Free Press.

Schumacher, Ernst F. (1973). *Small Is Beautiful: Economics As if People Mattered*. London: Blond & Briggs.

Schumacher, Gijs & Nathalie Giger (2017). Who Leads the Party? On Membership Size, Selectorates and Party Oligarchy. *Political Studies* 65(1) suppl., 162–81.

Schumpeter, Joseph A. (1950)[1942]. *Capitalism, Socialism and Democracy*. New York: Harper.

Schwab, Klaus & Xavier Sala-i-Martin. (2015). *The Global Competitiveness Report 2014–2015*. World Economic Forum.

Schwartzman, Felipe (2017). Inequality across and within US Cities around the Turn of the Twenty-First Century. *Economic Quarterly*, 103(1/4), 1–35.

Sciubba, Jennifer Dabbs (2010). *The Future Faces of War: Population and National Security: Population and National Security*. Santa Barbara, CA: ABC-CLIO.

Scott, James C. (1998). *Seeing Like a State: How Certain Schemes to Improve the Human Condition Have Failed*. New Haven, CT: Yale University Press.

Seawright, Jason (2010). Regression-Based Inference: A Case Study in Failed Causal Assessment. In Henry E. Brady & David Collier, eds., *Rethinking Social*

Inquiry: Diverse Tools, Shared Standards. 2nd ed. Lanham, MD: Rowman & Littlefield, pp. 247–71.

Sellers, Jefferey M., Daniel Kübler, Melanie Walter-Rogg, & R. Alan Walks (2013). *The Political Ecology of the Metropolis: Metropolitan Sources of Electoral Behaviour in Eleven Countries*. Colchester: ECPR Press.

Serhan, Yasmeen (2017). Emmanuel Macron's State of the Union. *The Atlantic*.

Shaheed, Ahmed & Jonathan Upton (2008). Maldives: Reform Deferred? Challenges and Lost Opportunities for Democratic Transition. Center for the Study of Islam and Democracy.

Shelton, Cameron A. (2007). The Size and Composition of Government Expenditure. *Journal of Public Economics*, 91(11), 2230–60.

Shepsle, Kenneth A. & Barry R. Weingast (1981). Political Preferences for the Pork Barrel: A Generalization. *American Journal of Political Science*, 25(1), 96–111.

Shirk, Susan L. (2018). The Return to Personalistic Rule. *Journal of Democracy*, 29(2), 22–36.

Shleifer, Andrei (1998). State versus Private Ownership. *Journal of Economic Perspectives*, 12(4), 133–50.

Shleifer, Andrei & Robert W. Vishny (1993). Corruption. *Quarterly Journal of Economics*, 108(3), 599–617.

Shleifer, Andrei & Robert W. Vishny (2002). *The Grabbing Hand: Government Pathologies and Their Cures*. Cambridge, MA: Harvard University Press.

Shugart, Matthew Soberg & Martin P. Wattenberg (2003). *Mixed-Member Electoral Systems: The Best of Both Worlds?* Oxford: Oxford University Press.

Sikk, Allan & Rein Taagepera (2014). How Population Size Affects Party Systems and Cabinet Duration. *Party Politics*, 20(4), 591–603.

Simmel, Georg (1902a). The Number of Members As Determining the Sociological Form of the Group (I). *American Journal of Sociology*, 8(1), 1–46.

Simmel, Georg (1902b). The Number of Members As Determining the Sociological Form of the Group (II). *American Journal of Sociology*, 8(2), 158–96.

Simmel, Georg (1950). *The Sociology of Georg Simmel*. New York: Free Press.

Simmons, Beth (2019). Border Rules. *International Studies Review*, 21(2), 256–83.

Simpser, Alberto (2012). Does Electoral Manipulation Discourage Voter Turnout? Evidence from Mexico. *Journal of Politics*, 74(3), 782–95.

Sinclair, Robert K. (1991). *Democracy and Participation in Athens*. Cambridge: Cambridge University Press.

Singer, J. David, Stuart Bremer, & John Stuckey (1972). Capability Distribution, Uncertainty, and Major Power War, 1820–1965. In Bruce Russett ed., *Peace, War, and Numbers*. Beverly Hills, CA: Sage, pp. 19–48.

Skaaning, Svend-Erik, John Gerring, & Henrikas Bartusevičius (2015). A Lexical Index of Electoral Democracy. *Comparative Political Studies*, 48(12), 1491–1525.

Skocpol, Theda (1992). *Protecting Soldiers and Mothers*. Cambridge, MA: Harvard University Press.

Skocpol, Theda & John Ikenberry (1983). The Political Formation of the American Welfare State in Historical and Comparative Perspective. *Comparative Social Research*, 6, 87–148.

Skowronek, Stephen (1982). *Building a New American State: The Expansion of National Administrative Capacities, 1877–1920*. Cambridge: Cambridge University Press.

Skrentny, John D. (2006). Law and the American State. *Annual Review of Sociology*, 32, 213–44.

Smith, Adam (1776). *An Inquiry into the Nature and Causes of the Wealth of Nations. Vol.* 1. London: Strahan & Cadell.

Smith, Daniel Jordan (2010). *A Culture of Corruption: Everyday Deception and Popular Discontent in Nigeria*. Princeton, NJ: Princeton University Press.

Smith, Jennifer (2007). Federalism and Democratic Accountability. In Joan DeBardeleben & Achim Hurrelmann, eds., *Democratic Dilemmas of Multilevel Governance*. London: Palgrave Macmillan, pp. 38–58.

Snyder, James M. (1993). The Market for Campaign Contributions: Evidence for the US Senate 1980–1986. *Economics & Politics*, 5(3), 219–40.

Soboroff, Shane (2012). Group Size and the Trust, Cohesion, and Commitment of Group Members. PhD thesis, University of Iowa.

Sokolow, Alvin D. (1989). Legislators without Ambition: Why Small-Town Citizens Seek Public Office. *State and Local Government Review*, 21(1), 23–30.

Solijonov, Abdurashid (2016). *Voter Turnout Trends around the World*. Stockholm: International Idea.

Somit, Albert, Rudolf Wildenmann, Bernhard Boll, & Andrea Rommele (1994). *The Victorious Incumbent: A Threat to Democracy?* Aldershot: Dartmouth.

Spencer, Herbert (1882). *Principles of Sociology. Vol 2, Part V*. New York: Appleton.

Spencer, Herbert (1898). *Principles of Sociology. Vol 1*. New York: Appleton.

Spiro, Melford E. (1970). *Kibbutz: Venture in Utopia*. Cambridge, MA: Harvard University Press.

Spolaore, Enrico & Romain Wacziarg (2005). Borders and Growth. *Journal of Economic Growth*, 10(4), 331–86.

Squire, Peverill (1992). The Theory of Legislative Institutionalization and the California Assembly. *Journal of Politics*, 54(4), 1026–54.

Squire, Peverill (1993). Professionalization and Public Opinion of State Legislatures. *Journal of Politics*, 55(2), 479–91.

Squire, Peverill (2006). Historical Evolution of Legislatures in the United States. *Annual Review of Political Science*, 9, 19–44.

Squire, Peverill (2017). *The Rise of the Representative: Lawmakers and Constituents in Colonial America*. Ann Arbor: University of Michigan Press.

Srebrnik, Henry (2004). Small Island Nations and Democratic Values. *World Development*, 32(2), 329–41.

Srinivasan, Thirukodikaval N. (1986). The Costs and Benefits of Being a Small, Remote, Island, Landlocked, or Mini-state Economy. *World Bank Research Observer*, 1(2), 205–18.

Stanley, Michael H. R., Luis A. N. Amaral, Sergey V. Buldyrev, Shlomo Havlin, Heiko Leschhorn, Philipp Maass, Michael A. Salinger, & H. Eugene Stanley

(1996). Scaling Behavior in the Growth of Companies. *Nature*, 379(6568), 804–06.

Stasavage, David (2010). When Distance Mattered: Geographic Scale and the Development of European Representative Assemblies. *American Political Science Review*, 104(4), 625–43.

Stein, Barry (1974). *Size, Efficiency, and Community Enterprise*. Piscataway, NJ: Transaction.

Stein, Robert M. & Gavin Dillingham (2004). *Political Participation in an Urbanized Society*. Paper Presented at the Annual Meeting of the American Political Science Association, Chicago, IL, September 2–6.

Steinmetz, George (1993). *Regulating the Social: The Welfare State and Local Politics in Imperial Germany*. Princeton. NJ: Princeton University Press.

Steinmo, Sven (1996). *Taxation and Democracy: Swedish, British, and American Approaches to Financing the Modern State*. New Haven, CT: Yale University Press.

Stepan, Alfred C. (2001). *Arguing Comparative Politics*. Oxford: Oxford University Press.

Stepan, Alfred C. & Cindy Skach (1993). Constitutional Frameworks and Democratic Consolidation: Parliamentarism versus Presidentialism. *World Politics*, 46(1), 1–22.

Stigler, George J. (1958). The Economies of Scale. *Journal of Law and Economics*, 1, 54–71.

Stigler, George J. (1972). Economic Competition and Political Competition. *Public Choice*, 13, 91–106.

Stigler, George J. (1976). The Sizes of Legislatures. *Journal of Legal Studies*, 5(1), 17–34.

Stokes, Susan C. (2005). Perverse Accountability: A Formal Model of Machine Politics with Evidence from Argentina. *American Political Science Review*, 99(3), 315–25.

Stokes, Susan C., Thad Dunning, Marcelo Nazareno, & Valeria Brusco (2013). *Brokers, Voters, and Clientelism: The Puzzle of Distributive Politics*. New York: Cambridge University Press.

Streeten, Paul (1993). The Special Problems of Small Countries. *World Development*, 21(2), 197–202.

Strøm, Kaare W. (1989). Inter-party Competition in Advanced Democracies. *Journal of Theoretical Politics*, 1(3), 277–300.

Strøm, Kaare W. (1992). Democracy As Competition. *American Behavioral Scientist*, 35(4/5), 375–96.

Strøm, Kaare W. & Benjamin A. T. Graham (2014). Variations in Federalism: Explaining Subnational Policy Authority. Unpublished manuscript, University of California.

Subasic, Emina & Katherine J. Reynolds (2011). Power Consolidation in Leadership Change Contexts: A Social Identity Perspective. In Paul 't Hart & John Uhr, eds., *How Power Changes Hands: Transition and Succession in Government*. Basingstoke: Palgrave Macmillan, pp. 174–90.

Sullivan, John L. (1973). Political Correlates of Social, Economic and Religious Diversity in the American States. *Journal of Politics*, 35(1), 70–84.

Summers, Lawrence H. (1991). The Scientific Illusion in Empirical Macroeconomics. *Scandinavian Journal of Economics*, 93(2), 129–48.

Sundberg, Ralph, Kristine Eck, & Joakim Kreutz (2012). Introducing the UCDP Non-state Conflict Dataset. *Journal of Peace Research*, 49(2), 351–62.

Sutton, Paul (1987). Political Aspects. In Colin Clarke & Anthony Payne, eds., *Politics, Security and Development in Small States*. London: Allen & Unwin.

Sutton, Paul (1999). Democracy in the Commonwealth Caribbean. *Democratization*, 6(1), 67–86.

Sutton, Paul (2007). Democracy and Good Governance in Small States. In Eliawany Kisanga & Sarah J. Danchie, eds., *Commonwealth Small States: Issues and Prospects*. London: Commonwealth Secretariat, pp. 201–17.

Sutton, Paul & Anthony Payne (1993). Lilliput under Threat: The Security Problems of Small Island and Enclave Developing States. *Political Studies*, 41(4), 579–93.

Svolik, Milan W. (2012). *The Politics of Authoritarian Rule*. Cambridge: Cambridge University Press.

Svorny, Shirley (2000). Licensing, Market Entry Regulation. *Encyclopedia of Law and Economics*, 3, 296–328.

Svorny, Shirley (2003). The Economics and Politics of City Size. Unpublished manuscript, California State University.

Swamy, Arun R. (1996). Sense, Sentiment and Populist Coalitions: The Strange Career of Cultural Nationalism in Tamil Nadu. In Subrata Mitra, ed., *Subnational Movements in South Asia*. Boulder, CO: Westview Press, pp. 191–236.

Swamy, Arun R. (1998). Parties, Political Identities and the Absence of Mass Political Violence in South India. In Atul Kohli & Amrita Basu, eds., *Community Conflicts and the State in India*. Oxford: Oxford University Press, pp. 108–48.

Swenson, Peter (2002). *Capitalists against Markets: The Making of Labor Markets and Welfare States in the United States and Sweden*. Oxford: Oxford University Press.

Swers, Michele L. (1998). Are Women More Likely to Vote for Women's Issue Bills than Their Male Colleagues? *Legislative Studies Quarterly*, 23(3), 435–48.

Swers, Michele L. (2002). *The Difference Women Make: The Policy Impact of Women in Congress*. Chicago: University of Chicago Press.

Swers, Michele L. (2005). Connecting Descriptive and Substantive Representation: An Analysis of Sex Differences in Cosponsorship Activity. *Legislative Studies Quarterly*, 30(3), 407–33.

Taagepera, Rein (1972). The Size of National Assemblies. *Social Science Research*, 1(4), 385–401.

Taagepera, Rein (1978). Size and Duration of Empires: Systematics of Size. *Social Science Research*, 7(2), 108–27.

Taagepera, Rein (2008). *Making Social Sciences More Scientific: The Need for Predictive Models*. Oxford: Oxford University Press.

Taagepera, Rein & Steven P. Recchia (2002). The Size of Second Chambers and European Assemblies. *European Journal of Political Research*, 41(2), 165–85.

Tambiah, Stanley Jeyaraja (1986). *Sri Lanka: Ethnic Fratricide and the Dismantling of Democracy*. Chicago: University of Chicago Press.

Tambiah, Stanley Jeyaraja (1992). *Buddhism Betrayed? Religion, Politics, and Violence in Sri Lanka*. Chicago: University of Chicago Press.

Tan, Alexander C. (1998). The Impacts of Party Membership Size: A Cross-National Analysis. *Journal of Politics*, 60(1), 188–98.

Tan, Alexander C. (2000). *Members, Organization and Performance: An Empirical Analysis of the Impact of Party Membership Size*. Farnham: Ashgate.

Tanzi, Vito & L. Schuknecht (2000). *Public Spending in the 20th Century*. Cambridge: Cambridge University Press.

Tarrow, Sidney & Charles Tilly (2015). *Contentious Politics*. Oxford: Oxford University Press.

Tavares, António F. & Jered B. Carr (2013). So Close, Yet So Far Away? The Effects of City Size, Density and Growth on Local Civic Participation. *Journal of Urban Affairs*, 35(3), 283–302.

Taylor, Charles (1969). Statistical Typology of Micro-States and Territories. *Social Science Information*, 8(3), 101–17.

Taylor, Charles Lewis & Michael C. Hudson (1972). *World Handbook of Political and Social Indicators*. New Haven, CT: Yale University Press.

Teaford, Jon C. (1984). *The Unheralded Triumph: City Government in America, 1870–1900*. Baltimore, MD: Johns Hopkins University Press.

Teaford, Jon C. (2002). *The Rise of the States: Evolution of American State Government*. Baltimore, MD: Johns Hopkins University Press.

Teorell, Jan (2006). Political Participation and Three Theories of Democracy: A Research Inventory and Agenda. *European Journal of Political Research*, 45(5), 787–810.

Teorell, Jan (2010). *Determinants of Democratization: Explaining Regime Change in the World, 1972–2006*. Cambridge: Cambridge University Press.

Teorell, Jan, Michael Coppedge, Staffan Lindberg, & Svend-Erik Skaaning (2019). Measuring Polyarchy across the Globe, 1900–2017. *Studies in Comparative International Development*, 54(1), 71–95.

Teorell, Jan, Nicholas Charron, Stefan Dahlberg, Sören Holmberg, Bo Rothstein, Petrus Sundin, & Richard Svensson (2013). *The Quality of Government Dataset, version 15* [dataset]. University of Gothenburg: The Quality of Government Institute. Accessed 2018. www.qog.pol.gu.se

't Hart, Paul & John Uhr (2011). *How Power Changes Hands: Transition and Succession in Government*. Basingstoke: Palgrave Macmillan.

Thomas, Edwin J. & Clinton F. Fink (1963). Effects of Group Size. *Psychological Bulletin*, 60(4), 371–84.

Thomas, Reuben J. & Noah P. Mark (2013). Population Size, Network Density, and the Emergence of Inherited Inequality. *Social Forces*, 92(2), 521–44.

Tiebout, Charles M. (1956). A Pure Theory of Local Government Expenditure. *Journal of Political Economy*, 64(5), 416–24.

Ting, Michael M., James M. Snyder Jr., Shigeo Hirano, & Olle Folke (2013). Elections and Reform: The Adoption of Civil Service Systems in the U.S. States. *Journal of Theoretical Politics*, 25(3), 363–87.

Tolbert, Pamela S. & Richard H. Hall (2009). *Organizations: Structures, Processes and Outcomes*. 10th ed. London: Pearson.

Tönnies, Ferdinand (2011)[1887]. *Community and Society*. Mineola, NY: Dover.

Treisman, Daniel S. (2006). Explaining Fiscal Decentralization: Geography, Colonial History, Economic Development, and Political Institutions. *Journal of Commonwealth and Comparative Politics*, 44(3), 289–325.

Treisman, Daniel S. (2007). *The Architecture of Government: Rethinking Political Decentralization*. Cambridge: Cambridge University Press.

Treisman, Daniel S. (2015). Income, Democracy, and Leader Turnover. *American Journal of Political Science*, 59(4), 927–42.

Trounstine, Jessica (2008). *Political Monopolies in American Cities: The Rise and Fall of Bosses and Reformers*. Chicago: University of Chicago Press.

Trounstine, Jessica. (2012). Turnout and Incumbency in Local Elections. *Urban Affairs Review*, 49(2), 167–89.

Truman, David Bicknell (1951). *The Governmental Process*. New York: Alfred A. Knopf.

Tsebelis, George (2000). Veto Players in Institutional Analysis. *Governance*, 13 (4), 441–74.

Tsebelis, George (2002). *Veto Players*. Princeton, NJ: Princeton University Press.

Tsebelis, George & Jeannette Money (1997). *Bicameralism*. Cambridge: Cambridge University Press.

Tullock, Gordon (1969). Social Cost and Government Action. *American Economic Review*, 59(2), 189–97.

Turner, John C. & S. Alexander Haslam (2001). Social Identity, Organizations and Leadership. In Marlene E. Turner ed., *Groups at Work: Theory and Research*. Mahwah, NJ: Erlbaum, pp. 25–65.

Turner, Mark, Sonam Chuki, & Jit Tshering (2011). Democracy by Decree: The Case of Bhutan. *Democratization*, 18(1), 184–210.

Tussman, Joseph (1974). *Obligation and the Body Politic*. Oxford: Oxford University Press.

US Census (2014). *Population Estimates: Incorporated Places* [dataset]. Accessed 2016. www.census.gov/popest/data/cities/totals/2014/SUB-EST2014-3.html

United Nations (2014). *World Urbanization Prospects: The 2014 Revision, CD-ROM Edition*. Department of Economic and Social Affairs, Population Division, United Nations.

Urdal, Henrik (2006). A Clash of Generations? Youth Bulges and Political Violence. *International Studies Quarterly*, 50(3), 607–29.

Uslaner, Eric M. (1981). The Case of the Vanishing Liberal Senators: The House Did It. *British Journal of Political Science*, 11(1), 105–13.

Van Biezen, Ingrid, Peter Mair, & Thomas Poguntke (2012). Going, Going, . . . Gone? The Decline of Party Membership in Contemporary Europe. *European Journal of Political Research*, 51(1), 24–56.

Van de Kaa, Dirk J. (2006). Temporarily New: On Low Fertility and the Prospect of Pro-natal Policies. *Vienna Yearbook of Population Research*, 4, 193–211.

Van Dunk, Emily (1997). Challenger Quality in State Legislative Elections. *Political Research Quarterly*, 50(4), 793–807.

Van Houwelingen, Pepijn (2017). Political Participation and Municipal Population Size: A Meta-study. *Local Government Studies*, 43(3), 408–28.

Vanhanen, Tatu (2000). A New Dataset for Measuring Democracy, 1810–1998. *Journal of Peace Research*, 37(2), 251–65.

Veenendaal, Wouter P. (2013). Political Representation in Microstates: St. Kitts and Nevis, Seychelles, and Palau. *Comparative Politics*, 45(4), 437–56.

Veenendaal, Wouter P. (2014). A Big Prince in a Tiny Realm: Smallness, Monarchy, and Political Legitimacy in the Principality of Liechtenstein. *Swiss Political Science Review*, 21(2), 333–49.

Veenendaal, Wouter P. (2015). *Politics and Democracy in Microstates*. London: Routledge.

Veenendaal, Wouter P. (2017). Analyzing the Foreign Policy of Microstates: The Relevance of the International Patron-Client Model. *Foreign Policy Analysis*, 13, 561–77.

Veenendaal, Wouter P. (2018). Islands of Democracy. *Area* (forthcoming, published online).

Veenendaal, Wouter P. & Jack Corbett (2015). Why Small States Offer Important Answers to Large Questions. *Comparative Political Studies*, 48(4), 527–49.

Veliz, Claudio (1980). *The Centralist Tradition of Latin America*. Princeton, NJ: Princeton University Press.

Verba, Sidney (1961). *Small Groups and Political Behavior: A Study of Leadership*. Princeton, NJ: Princeton University Press.

Verba, Sidney & Norman H. Nie (1972). *Participation in America: Political Democracy and Social Equality*. Chicago: University of Chicago Press.

Verba, Sidney, Kay Lehman Schlozman, & Henry E. Brady (1995). *Voice and Equality: Voluntarism in American Politics*. Cambridge, MA: Harvard University Press.

Verba, Sidney, Kay Lehman Schlozman, Henry E. Brady, & Norman H. Nie (1993). Citizen Activity: Who Participates? What Do They Say? *American Political Science Review*, 87(2), 303–18.

Vicente, Pedro C. (2014). Is Vote Buying Effective? Evidence from a Field Experiment in West Africa. *Economic Journal*, 124(574), F356–F387.

Vile, M. J. C. (1998)[1967]. *Constitutionalism and the Separation of Powers*. Indianapolis, IN: Liberty Fund.

Vital, David (1967). *The Inequality of States: A Study of the Small Power in International Relations*. Wotton-under-Edge: Clarendon Press.

Volden, Craig (2005). Intergovernmental Political Competition in American Federalism. *American Journal of Political Science*, 49(2), 327–42.

von Rueden, Christopher & Mark van Vugt (2015). Leadership in Small-Scale Societies: Some Implications for Theory, Research, and Practice. *Leadership Quarterly*, 26(6), 978–90.

Waldron, Jeremy (2002). One Law for All? The Logic of Cultural Accommodation. *Washington & Lee Law Review*, 59(1), 3–34.

Wallin, Gunnar (1973). Småkommuner på avskrivning. In Gunnar Wallin, Hans G. Andersson, & Nils Andrén, eds., *Kommunerna i förvandling*. Stockholm: Almqvist & Wiksell, pp. 9–35.

476   References

Wallis, John Joseph & Wallace E. Oates (1988). Decentralization in the Public Sector: An Empirical Study of State and Local Government. In Harvey Rosen, ed., *Fiscal Federalism: Quantitative Studies*. Chicago: University of Chicago Press, pp. 5–32.

Walter, Barbara F. (2009). Bargaining Failures and Civil War. *Annual Review of Political Science*, 12, 243–61.

Waltz, Kenneth N. (1979). *Theory of International Politics*. Reading, MA: Addison-Wesley.

Walzer, Michael (1983). *Spheres of Justice: A Defense of Pluralism and Equality*. New York: Basic Books.

Wångmar, Erik (2006). *Samlingsstyre – blockstyre – mångstyre: Kommmunalpolitiska styrelseformer 1952–2002*. Stockholm: Stads- och kommunhistoriska institutet.

Waschkuhn, Arno (1990). Strukturbedingungen und Entwicklungsprobleme des Kleinstaates. *Schweizerisches Jahrbuch für Politische Wissenschaft*, 30, 137–55.

Wasserman, Ira M. (1982). Size of Place in Relation to Community Attachment and Satisfaction with Community Services. *Social Indicators Research*, 11(4), 421–36.

Watts, Ronald L. (1998). Federalism, Federal Political Systems, and Federations. *Annual Review of Political Science*, 1, 117–37.

Weber, Hannes (2013). Demography and Democracy: The Impact of Youth Cohort Size on Democratic Stability in the World. *Democratization*, 20(2), 335–57.

Weber, Max (1961). *From Max Weber: Essays in Sociology*, ed. Hans Gerth & C. Wright Mills. London: Routledge & Paul.

Weidmann, Nils B., Doreen Kuse, & Kristian Skrede Gleditsch (2010). The Geography of the International System: The CShapes Dataset. *International Interactions*, 36(1), 86–106.

Weiher, Gregory R. (1991). *The Fractured Metropolis: Political Fragmentation and Metropolitan Segregation*. Albany: State University of New York Press.

Weiner, Myron (1971). Political Demography: An Inquiry into the Political Consequences of Population Change. In National Academy of Science, ed., *Rapid Population Growth: Consequences and Policy Implications*. Baltimore, MD: Johns Hopkins University Press, pp. 567–617.

Weiner, Myron & Sharon Stanton Russell (2001). *Demography and National Security*. New York: Berghahn Books.

Weiner, Myron & Michael S. Teitelbaum (2001). *Political Demography, Demographic Engineering*. New York: Berghahn Books.

Weingast, Barry R. (1994). Reflections on Distributive Politics and Universalism. *Political Research Quarterly*, 47(2), 319–27.

Weingast, Barry R. (1995). The Economic Role of Political Institutions: Market-Preserving Federalism and Economic Development. *Journal of Law, Economics, and Organization*, 11(1), 1–31.

Weingast, Barry R., Kenneth A. Shepsle, & Christopher Johnsen (1981). The Political Economy of Benefits and Costs: A Neoclassical Approach to Distributive Politics. *Journal of Political Economy*, 89(4), 642–64.

Weitz-Shapiro, Rebecca (2012). What Wins Votes: Why Some Politicians Opt Out of Clientelism. *American Journal of Political Science*, 56(3), 568–83.

Weitz-Shapiro, Rebecca (2014). *Curbing Clientelism in Argentina: Politics, Poverty, and Social Policy*. Cambridge: Cambridge University Press.

Weldon, Steven (2006). Downsize My Polity? The Impact of Size on Party Membership and Member Activism. *Party Politics*, 12(4), 467–81.

Wellhofer, E. Spencer & Timothy M. Hennessey (1974). Political Party Development: Institutionalization, Leadership Recruitment, and Behavior. *American Journal of Political Science*, 18(1), 135–65.

West, Geoffrey (2017). *Scale: The Universal Laws of Growth, Innovation, Sustainability, and the Pace of Life in Organisms, Cities, Economies, and Companies*. New York: Penguin.

Western, Bruce (1991). A Comparative Study of Corporatist Development. *American Sociological Review*, 56(3), 283–94.

Wettenhall, R. (2001). Machinery of Government in Small States: Issues, Challenges and Innovatory Capacity. *Public Organisation Review*, 1(1), 167–92.

Wheelan, Susan A. (2009). Group Size, Group Development, and Group Productivity. *Small Group Research*, 40(2), 247–62.

Whiteley, Paul & Patrick Seyd (2002). *High-Intensity Participation: The Dynamics of Party Activism in Britain*. Ann Arbor: University of Michigan Press.

Wibbels, Erik (2005). Decentralized Governance, Constitution Formation, and Redistribution. *Constitutional Political Economy*, 16(2), 161–88.

Wibbels, Erik (2006). Madison in Baghdad? Decentralization and Federalism in Comparative Politics. *Annual Review of Political Science*, 9, 165–88.

Wilensky, Harold L. (1975). *The Welfare State and Equality: Structural and Ideological Roots of Public Expenditures*. Berkeley: University of California Press.

Wilensky, Harold L. (2002). *Rich Democracies: Political Economy, Public Policy, and Performance*. Berkeley: University of California Press.

Williams, Andrew & Abu Siddique (2008). The Use (and Abuse) of Governance Indicators in Economics: A Review. *Economics of Governance*, 9(2), 131–75.

Williamson, Jeffrey G. (1965). Regional Inequality and the Process of National Development: A Description of the Patterns. *Economic Development and Cultural Change*, 13(4), 1–84.

Willis, Eliza, Christopher da C. B. Garman, & Stephan Haggard (1999). The Politics of Decentralization in Latin America. *Latin American Research Review*, 34(1), 7–56.

Wilson, Georjeanna & Mark Baldassare (1996). Overall "Sense of Community" in a Suburban Region: The Effects of Localism, Privacy, and Urbanization. *Environment and Behavior*, 28(1), 27–43.

Wilson, James Q. (1962). *The Amateur Democrat: Club Politics in Three Cities*. Chicago: University of Chicago Press.

Wilson, James Q. (1989). *Bureaucracy: What Government Agencies Do and Why They Do It*. New York: Basic Books.

Wilson, Thomas C. (1986). Community Population Size and Social Heterogeneity: An Empirical Test. *American Journal of Sociology*, 91(5), 1154–69.

Wirth, Louis (1938). Urbanism As a Way of Life. *American Journal of Sociology*, 44 (1), 1–24.

Wittman, Donald (1989). Why Democracies Produce Efficient Results. *Journal of Political Economy*, 97(6), 1395–1424.

Wittman, Donald (1991). Nations and States: Mergers and Acquisitions, Dissolution and Divorce. *American Economic Review*, 81(2), 126–29.

Wittman, Donald (2000). The Wealth and Size of Nations. *Journal of Conflict Resolution*, 44(6), 868–84.

Wlezien, Christopher (2017). Public Opinion and Policy Representation: On Conceptualization, Measurement, and Interpretation. *Policy Studies Journal*, 45(4), 561–82.

Wlezien, Christopher & Stuart Soroka (2007). The Relationship between Public Opinion and Policy. In Russell J. Dalton & Hans-Dieter Klingemann, eds., *The Oxford Handbook of Political Behavior*. Oxford: Oxford University Press, pp. 800–17.

Wolf, Sebastian (2016). *State Size Matters: Politik und Recht im Kontext von Kleinstaatlichkeit und Monarchie*. Berlin: Springer.

Wolfinger, Raymond E. & Steven J. Rosenstone (1980). *Who Votes?* New Haven, CT: Yale University Press.

Wolford, Scott (2016). Wars of Succession. *International Interactions*, 44(1), 173–87.

Wong, Cara J. (2010). *Boundaries of Obligation in American Politics: Geographic, National, and Racial Communities*. Cambridge: Cambridge University Press.

Woo-Cumings, Meredith, ed. (1986). *The Developmental State*. Ithaca, NY: Cornell University Press.

Wood, Donald P. J. (1967). The Smaller Territories: Some Considerations. In Burton Benedict, ed., *Problems of Smaller Territories*. London: Athlone Press, pp. 23–34.

World Bank (2005). *World Development Indicators 2005*. Washington, DC: World Bank.

World Bank (2007). *World Development Indicators 2007*. Washington, DC: World Bank.

World Bank (2011). *World Development Report 2011*. Washington, DC: World Bank.

World Bank (2012). *World Development Indicators 2012*. Washington, DC: World Bank.

World Bank (2015). *World Development Indicators 2015*. Washington, DC: World Bank.

World Bank (2016). *World Development Indicators 2016*. Washington, DC: World Bank.

World Bank (2017). *World Development Indicators 2017*. Washington, DC: World Bank.

World Bank (2018). *World Development Indicators 2018*. Washington, DC: World Bank.

World Health Organization (2004). *Global Status Report: Alcohol Policy*. World Health Organization, Substance Abuse Department.

World Language Mapping System (WLMS) (2006). *World Language Mapping System, Version 3.2.* Accessed 2018. www.gmi.org/wlms/

World Values Survey 1981–2014: Longitudinal Aggregate v.20150418. World Values Survey Association. Aggregate File Producer: JDSystems, Madrid SPAIN.

Wren, Anne (2008). Comparative Perspectives on the Role of the State in the Economy. In Barry R. Weingast & Donald Wittman, eds., *The Oxford Handbook of Political Economy.* Oxford: Oxford University Press, pp. 642–55.

Xie, Danyang, Heng-Fu Zhou, & Hamid Davoodi (1999). Fiscal Decentralization and Economic Growth in the United States. *Journal of Urban Economics,* 4(2), 228–39.

Xin, Xiaohui & Thomas K. Rudel (2004). The Context for Political Corruption: A Cross-National Analysis. *Social Science Quarterly,* 85(2), 294–309.

Xu, Chenggang (2011). The Fundamental Institutions of China's Reforms and Development. *Journal of Economic Literature,* 49(4), 1076–151.

Young, Alwyn (1998). Growth without Scale Effects. *Journal of Political Economy,* 106(1), 41–63.

Young, Alwyn (2013). Inequality, the Urban–Rural Gap, and Migration. *Quarterly Journal of Economics,* 128(4), 1727–85.

Young, Alwyn (2017). *Consistency without Inference: Instrumental Variables in Practical Application.* Working Paper, London School of Economics.

Zacher, Mark W. (2001). The Territorial Integrity Norm: International Boundaries and the Use of Force. *International Organization,* 55(2), 215–50.

Zax, Jeffrey S. (1989). Is There a Leviathan in Your Neighborhood? *American Economic Review,* 79(3), 560–67.

Ziblatt, Daniel (2006). *Structuring the State: The Formation of Italy and Germany and the Puzzle of Federalism.* Princeton, NJ: Princeton University Press.

Zipf, George Kingsley (1949). *Human Behavior and the Principle of Least Effort: An Introduction to Human Ecology.* Cambridge, MA: Addison-Wesley.

Zittel, Thomas, & Dieter Fuchs (2006). *Participatory Democracy and Political Participation: Can Participatory Engineering Bring Citizens Back In?* London: Routledge.

Zmora, Hillay (2000). *Monarchy, Aristocracy and State in Europe 1300–1800.* London: Routledge.

Index